RETIREMENT LIVING COMMUNITIES

A National Directory to over 400 communities, listed state by state, that offer high-quality independent living and a full range of health care services

DEBORAH FREUNDLICH

Macmillan • USA

To my parents, Harriet and William Fine, who, by taking charge of their retirement years and future health care needs by moving into The Forest at Duke, have given my brothers and me one of the greatest gifts parents can give their children—peace of mind.

MACMILLAN
A Simon & Schuster Macmillan Company
1633 Broadway
New York, NY 10019-6785

Library of Congress Cataloging-in-Publication Data

Freundlich, Deborah Fine.
Retirement living communities : a national directory / Deborah Fine Freundlich.
p. cm.
Includes index.
ISBN 0-02-050991-X
1. Retirement communities—United States—Directories. 2. Life care communities—United States—Directories. I. Title.
HQ1063.2.U6F74 1995
646.7'9'02573—dc20 95-18571
CIP

Manufactured in the United States of America
10 9 8 7 6 5 4 3 2 1

Cover photograph: Kendal at Hanover, New Hampshire, a member of the Kendal family of not-for-profit Continuing Care retirement communities reflecting basic Quaker principles. Courtesy of the Kendal Corporation.

Contents

Acknowledgments

I am indebted to my mother and father for getting me involved in their search for a Continuing Care community and for beginning my education on this vast subject. Their interest in these communities sparked my own and resulted in the creation of this directory.

Thanks to all the listed communities that took the time to share their information with us and to check our copy to make sure the information listed was correct and current.

Thanks to Dr. James A. Crapo, Michael Gilfix, Esquire, and Steven Hays for lending their medical, legal, and financial expertise to the directory.

Special thanks to my associate, Jonathan Weidlinger, and my assistants Paul Kaup and Stephanie Lutz, who were in constant touch with the retirement communities, gathering and clarifying information and checking facts.

Special thanks to Emily and Don Eldridge, Gerald Entringer, my parents Harriet and William Fine, Luana and Bill Hammett, Lib and Russ Horner, Marilyn Jones, Barbara King, June and Dr. Frances Mackey, Ruth Meyers, Carmen and Admiral Mumma, Jean and Bob O'Boyle, Mary Alice and Max Roby, Ella Shaap, Camille Shinn, Jean Taplinger, and Mary and Sam Weigle, who talked with me at length about how and why they decided to move into a retirement living community, and to Janet Alsteen, Pat Lutz, and Peter Tenbeau for sharing how they helped their parents make the decision. It is a very complicated and difficult decision to reach and I hope their stories will help you as you begin to make your own decision.

Special thanks to Emily Heckman, my editor, and Natalie Chapman, my publisher, for their interest and support throughout the publishing process.

A very special thank you to Rosemarie Morse, my first editor, whose enthusiasm for this project showed no bound. Rosie loved the idea from its inception and thoughtfully guided this directory through its initial phases.

And warm thanks and hugs to my own family—my husband, Larry, and our sons, Bart and Oliver—who, like my myself and our wonderful housekeeper, Velma Holiday, have lived with this project for several years, stepping around and over mounds of paper as the task of compiling this directory took on a life of its own.

I

INTRODUCTION

The Creation of This Directory

In 1990, when my parents began their search for a retirement community with full health care services, I was unaware that such communities existed; the term "retirement community" simply conjured up an image of a warm climate with condominiums surrounding a golf course.

My parents were looking for a Continuing Care retirement community, one that offered Independent Living with a full range of health care services for life, including long-term nursing care, should one or both of them ever need it. They didn't want my brothers and me to worry about caring for them as they got older, and they didn't want to become financially dependent on us. Plus, they wanted to make their *own* decision about where they would live—not leave it to us to make under pressure when a medical crisis occured. They wanted to move into a community while they were physically fit and active so that they could become involved, make friends, and establish a home.

My parents did a great deal of research. They talked to friends, read ads, reviewed brochures, and visited numerous communities in California, Colorado, Oklahoma, Pennsylvania, New Jersey, Maryland, and North Carolina.

As they shared their search with me and my brothers, I became more and more interested in the different types of retirement living communities in existence and under development. And although we came across a few directories, they were limited to either a specific state (California) or a specific type of community (e.g., nonprofit Continuing Care). Most communities were recommended by friends or friends of friends, and we began to realize that the best information on retirement living communities traveled by word of mouth, by people who knew of someone who had done the research themselves and had finally found an appropriate community. The more information we gathered in our search, the more it seemed like a good idea to share it with others—and hence this directory was born.

To create this directory, we developed a written profile for each community based on the information listed in that community's brochure. We then sent this standard profile to each community to be corrected and revised.

This book is similar to *Barron's College Guide*, which offers basic information and full descriptions, but it is not a critique. We wanted to include retirement living communities across the country that offer Independent Living and some form of health care (i.e., Assisted Living, personal care, respite care, and various types of Continuing Care Contracts).

Our hope is that this directory will serve as the primary resource for people who are searching for a retirement living community—whether they be prospective residents or their children, relatives, or friends.

The more than four hundred communities profiled in this directory were compiled by a vast and complex network of friends, associations (such as the Continuing Care Accreditation Commission), relatives, and the communities themselves. This is by no means a complete list of every retirement community in existence in the U.S. As mentioned before, we included only those communities that provide some form of health care for every resident. Also, it has been virtually impossible to keep abreast of all of the communities currently under development: It is estimated that in the next decade, the number of retirement living communities in the United States (of which there are currently nearly 700) will double. And because of the obvious need for and explosive growth in the development of retirement living communities, we intend to update this directory on a regular basis.

We Are All Living Longer

Did you know that?

- The fastest growing segment of the U.S. population is over 65 years old?
- In the year 2000, for the first time in U.S. history, ther will be more Americans over 65 than teenagers? There will be more than 35 million Americans over 65. That's more than 25.5 million more retirement-age citizens than in 1980.
- In the next ten years, one out of every five people will be over the age of 65?
- The number of Americans aged 75 to 84 will increase 40% by the year 2000? And that during this same short time the number of Americans 85 and older will increase by 82%? (U.S. Census Bureau)
- That Americans can expect to spend 20–25% of their lives retired?

What Is a Retirement Living Community?

The retirement living communities featured in this directory function as any normal residence would with the added benefits of: 1) health care (with around-the-clock, on-call staff) available on the premises; 2) 24-hour security services; 3) the assumption of the burdens of property management and upkeep; 4) meal services; and 5) a community of peers. There are no restrictions imposed on resident lifestyles. Community residents are free to come and go as they please and are encouraged to become actively involved in the local culture and community of the town or city in which the retirement community is located. Within the communities themselves, residents are encouraged to become involved in community governance through residents' boards, councils, and various committees.

Some of the communities listed offer a full range of health care services, up to and including long-term nursing care. These are categorized as Continuing Care communities. There are two types of Continuing Care contracts: all-inclusive and modified. With an all-inclusive contract, all health care and nursing costs (with the possible exception of additional meals) are included in the resident's monthly fee. With a modified contract, health care and nursing costs are billed as they are incurred. Other communities simply offer assistance with daily living, such as aid with dressing, bathing, medication, and other routine activities. These are referred to as "Assisted Living" or "personal care" communities. All of the communities listed, however, regardless of the level of advanced health care available, offer Wellness programs and 24-hour access to emergency care. To help clarify these distinctions, we've included a list of relevant terms for easy reference.

Not only do all of the communities listed offer some form of health care, they also have a full range of services that simplify resident life. These may include meal plans, transportation, housekeeping, beauty and barbershops, guest accommodations, and parking. They also feature excellent recreational facilities, open to all residents, which may include art and craft studios, woodworking shops, libraries, game rooms, exercise and fitness centers, and swimming pools. All of the communities listed offer planned, supervised activities for residents, which may include creative arts, gardening, reading groups, concerts, theatrical performances, films, continuing education classes (often in conjunction with local colleges and universities), bingo and card games, and off-site trips and outings. Of course, residents choose the activities in which they wish to participate.

Some communities are sponsored by and affiliated with nonprofit religious groups such as the Presbyterians, Episcopalians, Baptists, Methodists, Lutherans, or Quakers. Others are owned and managed for profit by large corporations such as Marriott Senior Living Services, Classic Residences by Hyatt, or Life Care Services, Inc.

The design, size, and location of each community varies, as do the type of resident dwellings available. Some are high-rise apartment buildings in the hearts of major cities while others are made up of apartments, condominiums, and/or townhouses set on landscaped campuses in suburban areas. Many communities are adjacent to and affiliated with major colleges and universities, providing residents with opportunities in continuing education, study groups, and other educational involvement.

The communities offer various financial plans, including the option to buy your dwelling (with or without entrance and maintenance fees) or the option to rent (on a monthly basis or a longer term lease). Every community director, marketing manager, or salesperson we spoke with was fully knowledgeable about the financial plans offered by the community he or she represented and was more than willing to provide additional information on the community's fiscal health and structure. We encountered no resistance to our often probing financial queries. In fact, we were impressed by how the communities, while very interested in "selling" their assets, never engaged in a hard-sell with us. It is clear that the last thing any of the communities want is for a prospective resident to move in and become unhappy. One unhappy resident can alter a pleasant atmosphere and disrupt the entire community. And the continual success of retirement living communities depends on satisfied, happy residents

Moving into a retirement living community is a major life decision: The community you select will probably be your home for the rest of your life. You will need to ask yourself many important questions before you make a final decision, such as, "Will I be able to live as freely and actively here as I want to?" "Does this community provide all of the amenities I need to make my retirement years as productive and stress-free as I wish?" "Does the community offer a full array of health services, including eventual long-term care?" "Is the community located in an area that is accessible to my family? Friends?" "Do the financial plans offered by the community meet my needs?" To help you keep track of the myriad considerations involved in making such a decision, we've included a checklist of questions you should ask yourself, as well as a cost comparison worksheet in the appendix that will help you compare your current expenses to those you will incur as a resident of a retirement living community.

To give you insight into how and why others have chosen retirement living communities, we talked with a number of residents (both singles and couples) around the country and have included their stories about how they finally reached a decision and how they like community life.

My parents moved into The Forest at Duke in Durham, North Carolina, a not-for-profit Continuing Care community that opened in the fall of 1992 and has affiliations with Duke University and the Duke

Health Care Issues for People over Sixty-five

- Sixty-nine percent of Senior citizens say their main concern with aging is the possibility of failing health. (AARP)
- Nearly half of all Americans who turned 65 years old in 1990 will spend some time in a nursing home. And the longer they live, the more likely that a nursing home is in their future. (*The New York Times*, February 28, 1991)
- Americans over 65 years account for 44% of all days spent in hospitals and 33% of the nation's health care expenditures. (*The New York Times*, May 31, 1991)
- Twenty-two percent of those age 85 are now in nursing homes, where the average cost for their care is roughly $30,000 per year. (Seniors Insurance Group)

The risk of needing nursing home care increases geometrically after age 75. As we become older, our need for assistance with such things as housekeeping, transportation, meal preparation, shopping, and getting adequate health care increases at roughly the following rates:

- Twelve percent of Americans over age 65 need assistance with one or more of these activities.
- Thirty-seven percent of Americans over age 75 need assistance with one or more of these activities.
- Seventy percent of Americans over age 85 need assistance with one or more of these activities.

(Percentages figured by the Ohio Presbyterian Homes Association)

University Medical Center. They have settled in happily and are participating in many community activities. They've made terrific new friends and are always on the go—attending lectures given by Duke professors, going to concerts and films, volunteering on various committees, giving tours, visiting with health care residents, and entertaining in their cottage. They have had many overnight visitors—friends and family who have come to experience and enjoy community life themselves. My father has even become a docent at Duke's Primate Center and my mother is an active member of The Forest's food service committee. I know that they are enjoying life at The Forest because they are rarely in their cottage and often my only contact with them is by answering machine.

I know that moving into The Forest at Duke was one of the great decisions in my parents' lives. Knowing that they are living in a caring community—where, should they ever need it, they will receive great health care—gives me great solace and peace of mind. I hope this directory will help you, your parents, or your friends and relatives make a similarly wise and wonderful decision.

A Brief History of Retirement Living Communities in the United States

Long before pension plans, Social Security, or Medicare, older members of religious and fraternal organizations donated their savings and property and in return were provided with care for life. For many years, the typical not-for-profit retirement community accepted a lump sum payment—often the remainder of the resident's estate—upon entry. This payment was never to be refunded.

Beginning in the late 1800s, large family homes were donated to the church or organization and were converted into retirement communities. These early accommodations were often limited, offering only small, single hotel-like rooms, a communal dining room, and sometimes nursing care.

Over the years, communities have evolved to offer many different financial plans and options for housing and services. No community listed in this directory requires residents to turn over all of their personal assets. A variety of payment plans reflect the many needs of retirement living community residents. There are refundable entrance fee programs, monthly rental options, and even equity investment options.

Just as the financial plans have become more sophisticated and flexible, so too have the housing options. Whereas studio apartments were popular 30 years ago, today's retirement community residents want more spacious and private accommodations. As a consequence, more two- and three-bedroom units are being built and, in some cases, studios are being renovated and combined to form larger apartments. Some communities have private cottages, townhouses, or villas, and a few offer freestanding homes.

Each state has its own laws governing retirement living communities that provide health care. For example, until recently, the state of New York did not allow the prepayment of health care and, therefore, did not permit Continuing Care communities to operate in the state. In 1991, this changed: the New York State legislature passed a bill that allows the prepayment of health care (usually in the form of an entrance fee) and since then several Continuing Care communities have opened, with more in development.

It is interesting to note that in Europe retirement homes with Assisted Living benefits outnumber nursing homes three to one. This is based on the belief that most elderly people are not unhealthy but simply need a little help performing life's daily activities. It is heartening to realize that this attitude is finally beginning to take hold here in the United States, too, and is best reflected in retirement living communities.

The Features of the Directory

Basic Financial, Legal, and Medical Considerations

A qualified physician, an accountant, and an attorney, all of whom specialize in areas particular to retirement-age citizens, have provided brief statements outlining the major financial, legal, and medical questions one should address before committing to a retirement living community.

Some Important Questions to Ask

This section poses the most essential questions prospective residents need answered before they can make a final decision.

A List of Terms to Know

A list of retirement living community terminology precedes the community profiles to help you understand what services and lifestyle choices are available at each community.

The Community Profiles

The vast body of this directory is made up of a listing of over 400 retirement living communities that offer some form of health care. Listed alphabetically by state, then city, then by community name, the directory was designed and organized to afford maximum ease in finding and gathering the crucial information needed to make this important decision. Each profile contains the following information: community name, address, telephone number, and contact person; type of community; a brief description; financial plans available; ownership and management; year opened; age requirements; number of residents; number of housing units (including a breakdown of the number of Independent and Assisted Living units); dining plan; services included in the fee; services available at additional cost; activities; availability; health care services; and comments from the community itself.

An Index

Designed and included for easy reference, the index lists each community alphabetically by name.

> Residents living in Continuing Care retirement communities in the 1980s lived significantly longer (15%) than the overall U.S. population. The explanation? Better nutrition, healthy and active companionship, access to superior health care and nursing care, increased safety and personal security, and the reduction of the stress of daily task and management concerns. (Continuing Care Retirement Community Mortality Study conducted by Stan Roberts of Milliman & Robertson)

Appendixes

These include lists of communities that provide Alzheimer's care and respite care, a list of accredited communities, and a cost-comparison worksheet.

Making the Decision

"When you're ready, it's too late."

This sign used to hang over the desk of Roz Hernandez, the retired director of admissions for Pennswood, in Newtown Square, Pennsylvania. Another community representative I spoke with revised this quotation to say, "When you *think* you're ready, it's too late."

These are important words of advice. Ms. Hernandez was one of the first directors of admission I talked to when I started the research for this directory. She and her counterparts throughout the country believe that careful planning is key to finding the community that is best for you. If you wait too long to begin the search, you may discover that the community you like cannot immediately accommodate you. Most communities have a waiting list period ranging from six months to ten years.

Moving into a retirement living community is a major decision. To be admitted to most communities, residents must be in reasonably good health and able to maintain a fairly high level of independence. If you are married, it is advisable to move in while you are both still active and healthy, so that you and your spouse can enjoy the full benefits of community life.

Statistics show that the average age of a resident moving into a Continuing Care community is 79, with the average age of residents in general being in the early 80s. This means that if the community you are most interested in has a waiting list of many years and you wish to move in by the time you are 75, you will need to complete your research, make your decision, and be placed on that waiting list by the time you're in your mid to late 60s. In short, it is never too early to begin to plan for your retirement years. Our hope is that this directory will help anyone who is approaching retirement age begin to plan ahead, and also help adult children of retirement-age people aid in the search.

Choosing the Retirement Living Community That Is Right for You

Every community in this directory has a brochure that describes the community in words, photographs (and/or maps and drawings), and floor plans. A few offer video tours of the community and these are available for the asking. Simply call the community and ask for any and all promotional material and application material.

Call the admissions departments of those communities that interest you and arrange for a tour. You should try to arrange an overnight stay so that you can see the community in action. The majority of communities included in the directory have guest accommodations available at a reasonable rate, and some even offer prospective residents a complimentary overnight stay. All of them encourage such visits and want prospective residents to learn as much as possible about their communities. Once you're there, ask questions. Talk to residents and staff members. Walk the grounds. Eat in the dining room. Check out the health care facilities. Try to get a feel for what it would be like to make your home there.

Many communities publish newsletters several times a year, often with the help of residents. These offer an "insider's" view of life in the community and provide excellent information to keep you abreast of the changes and growth of the community while you are making your decision or are on a waiting list. Communities are more than happy to add you to their mailing list, and once you're on a waiting list, you'll receive relevant community publications automatically.

Above all, ask lots of questions and carefully compare the costs of your prospective retirement living community with your current expenses. Give yourself plenty of time to make your final decision. Once you've found the community that is right for you, stay actively in touch: stop by from time to time and say hello to the director of admissions or visit with residents you've gotten to know. Remember that choosing to move and choosing the place that's right for you is as important a decision as choosing a mate or career. Once you've gathered as much factual information as possible, the decision will be one of intuition and faith. Be not afraid. And do not hesitate.

Important Questions to Ask

Here are some important questions to ask when you've begun to research a community:

Management and Finances

1. Is the community for profit or is it not-for-profit? (If it is not-for-profit, is there a for-profit corporation or organization that manages the community and its facilities?)
2. Who owns and who manages the community?
3. How long has the community been owned and managed by the present company?
4. Does the community have a board of directors?
5. Do residents serve on the board?
6. How is the community financed?
7. Is a copy of the community's financial statement available?
8. What are the payment options?
9. Do residents own or lease their dwellings?
10. What are the refund policies?
11. How often is the monthly fee increased? What have the past increases been? What are the projected increases for the future? Have there ever been any unplanned or unforeseeable increases?
12. Does a resident have to sign over all of his or her assets?
13. What happens if a resident runs out of money?
14. What happens if the community runs into financial difficulty?
15. What is the occupancy rate?
16. What are the state and local taxes for residents?

Accommodations

1. What types of housing units are available?
2. What standard furnishings (carpeting, drapes, etc.) are included in the fees?
3. What alterations are you allowed to make to basic floor plans?
4. What type of home security is provided?
5. Who pays for and takes care of home maintenance?

Services and Amenities

1. Within the terms of the community dining plan, is credit given for missed meals? Is it possible to buy additional meals?
2. If you become ill or housebound, is meal delivery available?

3. Is personal assistance or the services of a home attendant included in the basic fee?
4. Is housekeeping included in the basic fee? If not, can housekeeping services be purchased for an additional fee?
5. What are the fees for services such as the beauty or barbershops? Laundry and dry cleaning? Transportation? Or guest accomodations?
6. Are there any fees for community activities and outings?

Health Care

1. Who is in charge of the health center?
2. Does the community have its own medical staff or do they employ an outside agency?
3. Can a resident retain his or her own doctor?
4. Is the staff fully trained in geriatric medicine?
5. What is the ratio of medical staff to residents?
6. Is 24-hour-a-day health care available?
7. What accommodations are available in the health center? Are there private rooms?
8. Is a resident ever asked to leave the health center?
9. What happens if a health center bed is not available?
10. What are the criteria for transferring patients to the Skilled Nursing facility? Does the patient and his or her family participate in this decision? Who does?
11. What happens to a resident's dwelling in the event that he or she is moved into the Skilled Nursing facility?
12. Can residents receive care in their apartments?
13. Is there a clinic available for those residents who do not need admission to the health center?
14. Is there dental service?
15. Are there rehabilitation and therapy services?
16. Are Alzheimer's patients cared for?
17. Is short term/respite care available?
18. Are residents required to carry private health insurance policies? Does the community specify which ones?
19. Are the costs of health care included in the monthly fee? Are there ever any exceptions?
20. Are living wills honored?
21. What happens if a prospective resident is on the priority waiting list and has a change in health status? Does this affect his or her admission?

Admission

1. What are the criteria for admission?
2. Who approves the application?
3. How long does it take for the application to be approved?
4. What is the waiting list policy?

Miscellaneous

1. Are pets allowed?
2. Can the community accommodate your car?
3. Are grandchildren or young children allowed to stay? How long?

4. What happens in the event of a divorce or remarriage?
5. Is your investment protected in the event the community runs into financial difficulty?
6. Can a resident ever be asked to leave the community?
7. What happens in the event that you decide to leave the community?

A Word about Accreditation

Which Agency Provides Accreditation?

The Continuing Care Accreditation Commission (CCAC) is the national accrediting agency sponsored by the American Association of Homes and Services for the Aging (AAHSA). The 16-member commission, formed in 1985, administers the only national, voluntary accreditation program for Continuing Care retirement communities. Members of the commission include 11 provider members (executive directors, presidents, and the administrators of Continuing Care communities) and five private members. (In 1994 these five private members were representatives from AARP, the Middle States Commission on Higher Education, Hospice Care, Widener University, and the Retired Senior Volunteer Program.)

CCAC accredits communities meeting stringent criteria relating to the facility's finances, administration, quality of resident life, and health care. Communities must be 90% occupied for at least one year before they may apply for accreditation. Once they've received accreditation, it is valid for five years. At the end of that period, the community is reevaluated by the CCAC.

As of 1995, 176 communities had received accreditation.

How Does a Continuing Care Community Apply for Accreditation?

The community voluntarily applies for CCAC accreditation and engages in an extensive self-study based on its own mission and the established CCAC standards. The community's self-study is analyzed and verified during an on-site visit by a review team of trained volunteer evaluators dispatched by the CCAC. The self-study and the report of the review team are submitted to the CCAC for the final determination of accredited status.

If the community reviewed by the CCAC is judged to be effective in achieving its stated mission and meets all CCAC standards, it is granted CCAC accreditation status for a five-year period. The accredited community then agrees to act upon recommendations made by the CCAC regarding areas of marginal compliance.

Only a few communities seeking accreditation have been denied, usually for financial reasons. No accreditation has ever been revoked. Even though accreditation is a verification of excellence, there are many fine communities in existence that have not yet received accreditation simply because they are new and not yet at 90% occupancy.

The Fourteen Standards of Accreditation

1. A statement of mission submitted by the community that outlines the community's philosophy of service and the allocation of resources.
2. Evidence of an effective planning process and procedure to review the community's goals, growth, and plans for the future.
3. A governing board that oversees the development and implementation of community policy and procedure and monitors the quality of service provided.
4. A written constitution or set of bylaws that clearly describes the structure and responsibilities of the facility's organization and management.
5. A qualified administration that is adequate in both numbers and expertise.

6. A physical plant that meets the objective goals of the community and meets the needs of the residents.
7. A high-quality standard of life that meets the physical and psychological needs of the residents while enhancing residents' rights, independence, and self-determination.
8. Promotional materials that are accurate, clear, and fairly represent the community.
9. A marketing plan that indicates the community is moving toward achieving and maintaining full occupancy.
10. A copy of the resident contract that establishes the legal rights of the resident and the facility and their obligations to each other.
11. Evidence of the financial resources needed to meet current and projected needs as stated in the resident contract.
12. Evidence of sound management capable of determining, controlling, and managing the financial operations of the community.
13. Copies of disclosure statements that are available for applicants, residents, and other appropriate parties.
14. A health care philosophy that is effectively implemented and integrated into the health care services provided by the community.

(Based on the 14 standards of accreditation used by the CCAC)

Basic Financial Considerations

By Steve Hays, partner and chairman of Long-Term Care Network for Ernst & Young LLP, Cleveland, Ohio.

There are many financial issues to consider when evaluating retirement communities. Because it is crucial that you understand the financial background and current financial position of the community you will be living in, you should ask your personal accountant or hire a financial analyst to help you evaluate the community's financial information.

Assessing the community's financial health

In most states, retirement living communities are required to provide disclosure statements to prospective residents before the facility is allowed to accept a deposit or before a resident moves in. These statements contain specific information about the facility: who comprises the organization, the most recent audited financial statement, a copy of the complete residency agreement, and other relevant information. Approximately 37 states regulate retirement communities that require the payment of an entrance fee and/or offer health care as part of a residency agreement. If no disclosure statement is available, ask to see the audited financial statements of the community.

The occupancy of a successful operation varies by facility but should average 85% or greater. This rate will tell you not only how popular the community is but whether people have accepted the community's financial structure and management. Check to see that the community has adequate reserves and is not carrying too much debt. Generally, a lower level of cash reserves (15–20%) to debt can be acceptable if little or no health or nursing home care is included as part of the residency agreement. Conversely, a higher level of cash reserves (30–40%) to debt should be expected with an extensive health or nursing care provision. Since each retirement community's debt and payment structure differs, be careful to evaluate financial soundness on a facility-by-facility basis.

Review the type of financing the community has and determine if the annual debt service and maturities are consistent with reserves on hand and/or cash flow from the operation. In more concise terms, can the community pay for its obligations when they are owed?

Monthly service fees

The monthly service fees are just that: fees you are paying for the services you receive. Accordingly, as the cost of services (i.e., salaries, food, utilities, etc.) increases, the monthly service fees go up. However, look at the history of monthly service fee increases. Do these increases parallel basic standard of living increases? Have there been any aberrant years? If so, why? Remember, this is a check you will have to write every month, so make sure you understand how frequent rate increases can occur and how they will affect your lifestyle.

Refund provisions

Some communities have a choice of refundable and nonrefundable entrance fees. There is always a "premium" paid for the benefit of receiving a refund on the entrance fee. Because of this additional cost, the total payment made for the refundable entrance fee is significantly higher than the payment for a nonrefundable entrance fee for the same unit type and the same services. For example, at The Forest at Duke the 50% refund entrance fee for the 2-bedroom cottage is approximately 27% higher than the amortized entrance fee.

When deciding what entrance fee payment plan is best for you, consider your overall health, age, and how long you expect to live in the community. Depending on your circumstances, it may clearly be to your distinct advantage to select one plan over the other. You may be better off selecting a nonrefundable entrance fee, keeping the difference between the nonrefundable entrance fee and the amortized/standard entrance fee and managing your own money. As always, it is critical that an informed professional helps you decide which option is right for you, based on your circumstances.

What are the tax consequences of moving into a community where you purchase a contract for care (Assisted Living or Continuing Care)?

Most people moving into retirement communities are using money from the sale of their home. If you are 55 or over, the IRS (Sec. 121) grants you a one-time capital gains exclusion of $125,000. You must have owned and used the residence as your principal residence for an aggregate time of at least three years during the five-year period ending on the date of the sale of the residence. If you are a nursing home resident, you need only have lived in the residence one of the preceding five years. *Note:* This rule is narrowly interpreted and aggressively enforced by the IRS. There is one $125,000 capital gains exclusion per couple and the owner of the property must meet all requirements. Check with your accountant to see if you qualify.

Any unprotected gain can avoid the capital gains tax if a replacement residence is purchased. When you are purchasing a Continuing Care contract and will not have equity in the community, traditionally you cannot roll over the proceeds of the sale of your home.

Tax implications of a refundable entrance fee

According to the Internal Revenue Code (IRC), if the entrance fee is refundable you may have to pay tax on the amount of "imputed interest income" annually of the part of the refundable entrance fee paid over an inflation-indexed exclusion. In 1995, the exclusion is $124,300. Again, a refundable entrance fee can be viewed as a loan to the community by the IRS, so be sure to ask about it.

Can proceeds from the sale of your home be rolled over?

Some of the more recently opened communities offer the resident an option to purchase an interest in a cooperative or other form of equity that qualifies for the IRC Sec. 1034 rollover of proceeds of sales of the prospective resident's home. However, the structure of governance and management is different and should be checked very carefully.

What health care costs can you deduct?

Check with the IRS regarding current provisions made for the deduction of health care costs. Each community must obtain a private-letter-ruling regarding the amount residents may deduct on their federal income tax return for the entrance fee and the monthly service fee as prepayment of health care. A Continuing Care community, in which residents receive unlimited nursing care, offers a higher deduction than a community where residents are limited to a certain number of free days of health care annually. Generally, the more days of health care that are prepaid or provided for, the higher the deduction. Since these are based on the provisions made in each community's residency agreement, the amount of the entrance fee and monthly service fee that can be deducted varies by community.

Trial residencies

Most communities have an implied or required trial residency period. This varies by community policy and/or by state regulation. Generally, a period of 30 to 90 days is allowed. There is no financial penalty if the resident decides to move out within that period. Ask about the community's policy and the state regulations on trial residency periods.

Rental versus entrance fee communities

A community offering a rental plan usually does not require more than a year's commitment from the resident and some communities even offer month-to-month plans. The monthly fee of a rental community is usually higher—significantly at times—than the monthly fee of an entrance fee community. Be aware that many of the monthly rentals do not have the range of services and amenities (i.e., Skilled Nursing, Alzheimer's care, and others) that the entrance fee communities may have. You need to carefully weigh the service and financial implications before signing a residency agreement and selecting a payment option or community type.

The importance of equity ownership

There are very few equity ownership retirement communities in existence, and most of those are on the East and West Coasts. One of the primary benefits is the one-time capital gains benefit you receive when you are over age 55 and selling your home. Another positive aspect of an equity community is the fact that some people like the feeling of actual ownership. However, along with ownership comes certain responsibilities, such as maintenance. It is particularly important to analyze the performance of the management company before making such an investment.

Note: There has been a tremendous increase in the value of homes, especially in certain West Coast areas. This may lead to higher capital gains tax when the home is sold. It is essential for prospective retirement community residents to seek financial advice before selling their home.

What only your eyes can tell you

Not only should you look carefully at the financial health and structure of a community, but be sure to walk around and carefully assess its physical attributes. Are the grounds and dwellings well maintained? Are the common areas kept as clean and maintained as you would have your home? Are items in disrepair? Are the carpets clean? A simple but complete walk and thorough look around the community and into various units can be as revealing and critical as an examination of the community's financial statements.

Obviously, needs differ based on one's age, financial situation, and health status. Fortunately, there are myriad choices available to fit any financial and lifestyle requirements. However, as with any big decision in life, it is crucial to gather information and obtain informed and professional assistance before making a commitment to a retirement living community.

Basic Legal Considerations

By Michael Gilfix, Esq., principal with the law firm of Gilfix Associates in Palo Alto, California, who specialize in estate and tax planning and asset preservation. Mr. Gilfix is a Fellow of the National Academy of Elder Law Attorneys and is a certified specialist in estate planning, trust, and probate law.

Everyone who moves into a retirement community should create a durable power of attorney. The execution of this document can literally save thousands of dollars for the resident and his or her family. A durable power of attorney is critical because it legally empowers someone to be the resident's advocate, someone who will carry out the resident's wishes if he or she should become incapacitated.

Once you've narrowed down your options and begin to look closely at contracts, there are some specific questions you need to ask:

What is the track record of the community?

Familiarize yourself with the management and ownership of the community. Find out about the community's reputation for management and finances. Does the community maintain a cash reserve? Determine if the various levels of health care services are regulated by state and/or federal authorities. Ask about the number of people on staff and the ratio of staff to residents. Is staff turnover high?

What are the rights and obligations of the resident and the community?

Inquire about residents' rights to a financial accounting by the operator and owner. Ask what health insurance coverage you are required to carry. What happens in the event of divorce or marriage? What happens if the community declares bankruptsy or closes? Also, you should never sign a waiver or document that limits your legal rights if you are subjected to medical malpractice or any form of neglect. It is important to find out what financial and legal protection you have in the event the community fails to meet its contractual obligation to you.

What are the circumstances under which the contract may be terminated?

Although it is rare that either the resident or the community requests that a contract be terminated, it is wise to know if there is an adjustment period during which there is no penalty to the resident for withdrawing. You should also ask under what circumstances the community may ask a resident to leave. You should also know what rights a widowed spouse will retain—especially if he or she is under the minimum age requirement—when his or her spouse dies.

Who decides when a resident should move to a higher level of care?

One of the issues that a lot of people gloss over when reviewing Continuing Care contracts is who is in charge of making the final decision that a resident must receive more care and, consequently, move from Independent Living to Assisted Living or Skilled Nursing. When prospective residents are examining these contracts, they are usually healthy and living independently. The fact that Assisted Living and Skilled Nursing are available on-site satisfies most prospective residents. However, it is very important that you clearly understand who has the authority to make this decision and what criteria are used. Most contracts say the final decision is to be made by the facility's medical director, in consultation with the resident. Ideally, you or your family or the person named in your durable power of attorney should make the decision with professional input from your personal physician.

WHAT IS THE AVAILABILITY OF NURSING BEDS?

Obviously, the ideal situation is that a nursing bed will be waiting for you should you become ill. From the point of view of resident couples, an important selling feature of a Continuing Care contract is the ability to visit one's spouse easily and frequently on premises.

Ask about the proportion of nursing beds to residents. The fact that a community has nursing beds and that your contract states you will have access to them doesn't necessarily mean that when the time comes, a bed will be available.

Although communities hope this will never happen, it is conceivable that at the time a resident needs Skilled Nursing all beds may be occupied. If on-site beds are full and you need this level of care, it is entirely possible that you will be moved to a nursing home that is miles from the community. (With rare exceptions, Continuing Care facilities have relationships with nursing homes in their area should their Skilled Nursing units be full when a resident needs a bed.)

In the case of new communities with a population that is healthy, a certain number of beds may even be made available to the people outside the community in order to cover nursing overhead. This can further limit on-site availability and increase the likelihood that a bed will not be available when you need it.

WHO PAYS FOR NURSING CARE OFF PREMISES?

Read your contract carefully. If the resident has to be moved off premises it is important to find out who pays for these services. Is there a limit on the amount the community will pay and is there additional financial exposure to the resident? And how will this affect your resident status, especially if you are moved off-site for a long period of time?

The best advice I can give about selecting a retirement community is to plan ahead so you have time to examine all of your options carefully and wisely. Ask questions, scrutinize the agreement you are asked to sign, and, when appropriate, seek and use professional, legal, and accounting counsel.

Basic Medical Considerations

By James A. Crapo, professor of medicine & pathology and chief of allergy, critical care, and respiratory medicine, Duke University; president, The Forest at Duke retirement community.

It is important that a retirement living community enable residents to live a high quality, active life in spite of any restrictions that occur due to age or illness. The community's physical plant should enable residents to function independently as normal aging occurs.

Most people tend to underestimate their life span. With the average age of residents moving into a retirement community being 76 years old, their average expected life span will be another 14 years. Thus, prospective residents should not underestimate their future needs. To be accepted for admission, most communities require prospective residents to function independently—to be able to move about on their own and to care for themselves.

Prospective residents should examine a retirement community in terms of possible future physical impairments rather than any present ones. Decreased mobility and a loss of visual acuity are common occurrences with age, and it is particularly important to examine the facility in terms of these two aspects.

Common Areas and Individual Living Units

Mobility: Check to see that the community is well laid out. For example, residents should be able to move throughout the community without having to use stairs. Inclines should be gradual so that walking is easy and motorized carts can travel safely. Handrails should be present. Seating should be available on long hallways or walking paths. Well-planned communities will have apartment hallways with "way-finding cues." Lots of windows and distinctive artwork assist persons with memory loss to identify their surroundings. Ask about wheelchair accessibility—i.e., if a resident needs to use a wheelchair, can he or she continue to live in his or her apartment?

Handicap accessibility: As a result of the Americans with Disabilities Act, facilities built during or after 1992 must conform to stricter codes that mandate greater accessiblity for the handicapped in both individual units and the common community facilities. Are doorways wide enough (at least 36 inches) for full-sized wheelchairs? Are bathroom and kitchen facilities accessible by wheelchair? Take note that living units that are fully handicap-accessible may be less optimal for nonhandicapped residents and have a more institutional appearance. A good compromise is to look for a community that has a designated portion of the living units fully handicap-accessible with the remainder of the campus designed to be flexible in accommodating changing population needs.

Sight: Areas should be well lit during the day and at night. The design should feature lighting that aids depth-perception. This requires a combination of ambient lighting and appropriately-placed task lighting.

Safety features: Be aware of safety features and plans. There should be fire alarms, smoke alarms, a sprinkler system, proper exits, and an overall emergency evacuation plan. Ask what type of construction materials were used; multistory wood construction carries increased risk from fire and smoke. What type of emergency call system is in place? How does it work? Can you carry this call system on your person? Can you carry the emergency signaling device throughout the community and still expect this call system to work? Ask if there is a system in place for checking on people who live alone, so that everybody is accounted for every day.

User-friendly features: Many small design features can make life easier for residents, particularly those with arthritis. Doorknobs can be replaced with levers, cabinets can have pulls, controls can be on the front instead of the back of stoves, electrical plugs can be located higher on the walls for easy access, and light switches lowered to accommodate shorter residents.

Medical Care and Facilities

Routine health care: Ask about the community's Wellness program. Is there a clinic on site? Who operates it? If there are physicians on the premises, what are their hours and how are their services charged? Is there a pharmacy on site or nearby access to a pharmacy, and is there a bulk-buying program for pharmaceuticals, which passes along lower costs to residents? Are specialties such as podiatry and dentistry offered and how are they charged? When a physician is not on the premises, who is in charge? Is there a nurse on duty 24 hours a day? How are medical emergencies handled? Serious emergencies are almost all routed directly by ambulance to the nearest emergency room. Can less serious emergencies be handled by a nurse and/or physician on call? Is a resident allowed to receive help in his or her living unit if he or she does not need to move to the next level of care?

Social services: Social services should be available for residents. Any time a person exhibits a medical dysfunction or is behaving abnormally, it is this staff that is often alerted. Ask what social services are offered and what resources the staff has. Is there, for example, a companion service for a resident who might need help getting to and from meals? Issues relating to the changing health care needs of a resident should be brought to the attention of the community's health care committee by the social services staff. Beware of situations where life issues such as transfer from Independent Living to Assisted Living or Skilled Nursing are handled by one person. All resident health care needs should be addressed by a team of professionals that should include the medical director, director of nursing, nursing home administrator and social services staff.

Assisted Living: The challenge with Assisted Living is to offer a comfortable living environment for those residents with mild limitations so that they can remain active. Ask about the services provided, accommodations, activities, and any restrictions placed on residents. Assisted Living should be home-like and comfortable. Residents should be afforded access to events and activity programs available to Independent Living residents. Check to see that the dining service program for Assisted Living residents is not too institutionalized.

Skilled Nursing: Most nursing facilities are highly regulated by the government, resulting in great standardization. But the physical plant can vary a great deal. Be sure to tour the health center and nursing area. What fraction of the nursing rooms are private? Are residents receiving long-term care allowed to bring their own furniture and belongings? Are physical, occupational, and speech therapies available? Who delivers these services and how are they charged? Investigate what happens if one member of a couple has to be admitted to skilled nursing—how is the resident's monthly fee altered in such a case? Who participates in the decision to move a resident into the nursing facility? How are Alzheimer's patients cared for and how does the facility accommodate the needs of the wanderer?

Health care billing: Will the community help residents with insurance forms and billing? How do the costs of living in Assisted Living or Skilled Nursing compare to the cost of being in an Independent Living unit? Do residents have any need for long-term care insurance? In a true "life care" retirement community there would be no substantial increase in monthly charges for a single person who moves from an Independent Living unit to Assisted Living or Nursing Care. Since most people don't think they will ever be in a nursing home, they often fail to carefully examine the potential costs. This can be an additional several thousand dollars per month in a Continuing Care community that features a modified rather than all-inclusive contract. The annual cost of a Skilled Nursing bed versus an Independent Living unit over the course of a year should be calculated and compared. This issue becomes much more complex when a couple occupies an Independent Living unit and one or both must move to the health care center. This situation occurs not uncommonly and, irrespective of community type, the additional costs can be substantial.

Important Terms to Know

Accreditation: Retirement living communities offering Independent Living and health care services (including nursing) may apply for accreditation from the American Association of Homes and Services for the Aging Continuing Care Accreditation Commission. If a community has been accredited, this should add positively to your assessment of that community since this is the industry's "seal of approval." However, many new communities have not yet reached the minimum occupancy required to be reviewed for accreditation, and many of these still merit your full examination. Consider the fact that a community is accredited as a bonus but don't exclude newly opened communities from your search.

Admissions: All communities listed in this directory admit residents without regard to race, creed, color, national origin, or sex. Some communities owned and managed by religious groups have a higher proportion of that religious affiliation as residents; where this is true, it has been noted.

American Association of Homes and Services for the Aging: A national organization, founded in 1961, which represents not-for-profit nursing homes, independent housing facilities, community service agencies, and Continuing Care retirement communities. AAHSA facilities are sponsored by religious, fraternal, labor, private, and government organizations committed to providing quality services for their residents and for elderly persons in the community at large. AAHSA has over 800 associate members, including attorneys, professionals, and students interested in long-term care and housing for the elderly. Thirty-seven affiliated state associations are also members. AAHSA sponsors a national accreditation program for Continuing Care retirement communities and national conferences for directors and staff.

Assisted Living: Residents are assisted with the activities of daily living, including monitoring of medication and assistance with grooming, bathing, and eating. Some communities have separate Assisted Living residences; some offer services to residents in their apartments. Three meals a day are included in the monthly fee for Assisted Living residents.

Continuing Care: Continuing Care retirement communities provide a comprehensive array of services tailored to the individual resident's needs. Typical services and amenities include: nursing and other health care services, meals and special diets, housekeeping, scheduled transportation, emergency help, personal assistance, recreational and educational activities. Most Continuing Care communities have a Skilled Nursing facility on premises; those that do not usually have arrangements with nursing facilities nearby. Some Continuing Care communities have endowments that assist residents should they live long enough to deplete their financial resources.

There are two types of Continuing Care contract: With **all-inclusive contracts,** the cost of health care and nursing are included in the resident's monthly fee. If the resident moves into the health care center permanently, he or she continues to pay the same monthly fee he or she was paying in Independent Living. With **modified contracts**, health care and nursing are billed on an as-needed basis with residents paying only for services used. The health care center monthly fees are considerably more than the Independent Living fees.

Financial plans: Many communities offer a choice of two basic financial plans for residents.

Plan 1: Entrance fee and monthly fee

Entrance fee and monthly fee: Residents pay an entrance fee or lump-sum payment, plus a monthly fee for services (which usually includes some utilities; one, two, or three meals a day; scheduled transportation; and weekly housekeeping). Fees for health care services (Assisted Living, Intermediate and Skilled Nursing, and/or clinics) vary by community. Sometimes they are covered by the resident's entrance fee and monthly fee, meaning that should the resident move to the nursing center permanently, he or she will continue to pay only the basic monthly fee (Continuing Care, all-inclusive contract). Other communities charge residents for these services on a fee-for-service basis (Continuing Care, modified contract, Assisted Living). Within this category there are three popular refund plans currently being offered.

Nonrefundable entrance fee: Entrance fee is a one-time payment and becomes the property of the community immediately upon payment.

Amortized entrance fee: The entrance fee is "earned out" by the community over a period of years. The longer the resident lives in the community the smaller his or her potential refund becomes. With most amortized entrance fee plans, refunds decrease to zero within 50 months of establishing residence.

Partially refundable entrance fee: A portion of this entrance fee is refundable. An example is the entrance fee plan at The Forest at Duke in Durham, North Carolina. Their 50% refund plan is amortized at a rate of 2% over 25 months, after which the refund remains 50%. The entrance fee for the 50% refund plan is approximately 27% higher than the amortized entrance fee.

Entrance fee with equity: A resident's entrance fee payment actually buys equity in the community, often in the form of ownership of a condominium. At Villa Marin in San Rafael, California, owners are free to sell or trade their condominiums or bequeath ownership. The only restriction is that the new owner must be approved by the admissions committee. Some communities, such as The Forum Pueblo Norte in Scottsdale, Arizona, offer a choice of financial plans, including an equity plan, a traditional nonrefundable plan, and a 12-month lease program.

Plan 2: A monthly rental fee with no entrance fee

Monthly rental fee only: Residents pay a monthly rental fee for accommodations and standard services (usually includes utilities; one, two, or three meals a day; scheduled transportation; and weekly housekeeping; with access to health care services at an additional charge). Often a security deposit of one month's rent is required. One variation on this plan is offered by The Classic Residence by Hyatt in Teaneck, New Jersey. In addition to the monthly rental fee, a "one-time reservation fee" of $1,500 is required.

Westminster Village in Bloomington, Illinois, offers both a monthly rental fee only plan and the traditional entrance fee/monthly fee plan. The monthly rental fee only, depending on the size of the unit, can cost between $150 and $900 more per month than a monthly fee paid in conjunction with an entrance fee.

Independent Living: Requires that residents be capable of living and managing themselves in an apartment without assistance from another person. Residents must be physically able to get to meals and services in the main building, manage their own personal care needs (such as bathing), make reasonable and rational decisions, and have an intact memory so that they can follow instructions related to safety, medical care, and basic community policies. A variety of accommodations are available depending upon the community, including apartments (studio, 1-bedroom, 2-bedroom, 3-bedroom), cottages, duplexes, garden apartments, townhouses, and sometimes private homes. Meal plans vary by community. Most communities listed in this directory require prospective residents to be active and independent of assistance, though some will allow direct admission to the health center, space permitting.

Life care: You may hear the term "life care" during your search. For a long time "life care" was synonymous with the strictest definition of Continuing Care—the all-inclusive contract, i.e., a community where residents pay a one-time entrance fee for the life care contract and a monthly fee in exchange for accommodations and services for the rest of their lives. However, industry experts agree that this term is being misused. For the sake of consistency and credibility we are not defining communities as "life care" in this directory.

Multiple ownerships: Many communities are part of a group of communities owned and managed by the same organization—whether it be a for-profit company such as Life Care Services or Marriott Senior Living Services, or not-for-profit religious groups such as the Northern California Presbyterian Homes, Inc., or The Kendal Corporation, which is governed by a board of directors composed of members of the Religious Society of Friends (Quakers).

Respite care: Short-term nursing care available for residents who have had surgery or been hospitalized and need supervision before returning to their own community dwelling. Some communities offer respite care to nonresidents for a day, week, or month, depending on availability.

Waiting list: Most communities have waiting lists varying anywhere from six months to ten years, depending on the type of accommodation desired. At most communities, when an apartment becomes available, prospective residents have a choice of moving in immediately or asking to be kept on the waiting list if they are not yet ready to move in. Usually they will have several opportunities to decline acceptance without losing their place on the waiting list.

Priority waiting list: When communities reach full occupancy, a priority waiting list is established.

Applicants wishing to reserve a place pay a refundable fee and are placed on the priority waiting list until the unit of their choice becomes available. Depending on the community and the popularity of the type of residence, this can take anywhere from several months to several years.

Future waiting list: This is a waiting list for those not ready to move in at the moment, but who will be ready in five to ten years. Often future residents can partake in activities and dine at the community while they are on the priority or future wait list. At Shenandoah Valley Westminster-Canterbury in Winchester, Virginia, for example, future residents are entitled to the guest-meal rate in the community's dining room and are invited to participate in community activities. Prior to taking residence, future residents have priority access to the health care center and its services should a change in health status make this necessary.

Wellness program: Provides basic health care information/services for all residents, including basic physical exams, blood pressure checks, dispensing of medication, injections, eye exams, etc. All of the communities listed offer some type of Wellness program.

Now that you have a basic understanding of the terminology of retirement living communities and a sense of the many questions you must ask and answer before you make your decision, you are ready to use this directory to find the community that is right for you. We've designed and organized the directory so that it is easy to read and provides you with the maximum amount of information at a glance. Most importantly, we've given you the information you need to contact each community directly. And sprinkled throughout the community profiles are statements from community residents who have graciously shared their experiences with us. We hope these will give you added insight into community life and enhance the profiles of those communities represented by these actual residents.

It is important to note that the costs listed here are always subject to change, including regular fee increases established by each community. Also, personnel and contacts at the communities may change, but you should be able to get any new information about rates and services simply by contacting the community directly. We feel confident that the majority of this information is up-to-date enough to give you a great start in finding the right retirement living community, and we will revise the directory on a regular basis to keep the information as accurate and current as possible.

Above all, it is our hope that this directory will help you make a wonderful choice about where to spend your retirement years.

II

PROFILES OF THE COMMUNITIES

ALABAMA

GALLERIA WOODS

3850 Galleria Woods Drive
Birmingham, AL 35244
(205) 985-7537
Bob Porter, marketing director

Type of community: Nonprofit Continuing Care, modified contract.

Located in grassy woodlands on a 20-acre site in suburban Birmingham, Galleria Woods offers apartment and garden home Independent Living units, as well as Assisted Living suites and a Skilled Nursing facility. Trails and flower-bordered walkways surround buildings of classic Georgian architecture featuring bay windows and porches. Clubhouse has rooms for seminars, arts and crafts, and games. Nearby are restaurants, churches, Riverchase Galleria, banks, cinemas, Hoover Metropolitan stadium, golf courses, and tennis courts.

Financial plan: Entrance fee plus monthly fee. Two plans: **1)** 100% refundable. **2)** Refundable entrance fee, amortized over 36 months.

Ownership and management: Affiliated with the Baptist Health Systems of Birmingham, Alabama. Opened in 1991.

Minimum age: 55 years (average age 82 years).

Population: 200 residents; 66% women, 34% men, 46% couples. From 16 states.

Number of units: 129 Independent Living apartments and 25 garden homes; 24 Assisted Living suites, 30-bed Skilled Nursing facility.

Dining plan: One main meal (lunch or dinner) included. Private dining room with catering available.

INDEPENDENT LIVING HOUSING

Type/size of apartment	*Entrance fee 1/2*	*Monthly fee 1/2**
1-Bedroom, 658–671 sq. ft.	$77,500/50,000	$1,037/982
2-Bedroom, 987 sq. ft.	$110,000/70,000	$1,038/1,327
2-Bedroom, 1,038 sq. ft.	$140,000/85,000	$1,558/1,497
Garden homes	*Entrance fee*	*Monthly fee*
2-Bedroom/deck, 1,450 sq. ft.	$155,000/25,000	$1,640/2,195

**For double occupancy add $461 to apartments and $329 to garden homes monthly fee. All utilities except telephone and cable included. All-electric kitchen, individually controlled heating and air-conditioning, 24-hour emergency call system, porch, patio or bay window.* Note: *Garden homes residents may choose to not have housekeeping, one meal, or laundry service and deductions will be made to monthly fee.*

Services: *Included in the monthly fee:* Weekly housekeeping, flat-linen service, scheduled transportation, long-term care insurance, storage areas on each floor, subscription to *Senior Choice* magazine (part of Baptist Health Systems, covers travel, VIP health care, etc.).

At additional cost: Beauty/barbershop, branch banking, convenience store, reserved/covered parking.

Activities: Arts and crafts, shuffleboard, horseshoes, croquet, exercise programs, putting green, heated pool, woodworking shop, measured walking trails, nature paths, therapeutic whirlpool, seminars, birdwatching, gazebos, fishing, nondenominational chapel, library and reading rooms.

Availability: Waiting list for one-bedroom apartments.

Health services and rates: Residents receive two years in Assisted Living or Skilled Nursing at no additional cost after they have resided at Galleria Woods for 100 days. Regularly scheduled on-site physician consultations. Full range of pharmaceutical services, physical therapy, assistance in completing insurance forms. Priority admission and VIP checkout at Baptist Medical Center hospitals.

- 24 Assisted Living units
  Suite with private bath $70.35/day
- 30 Skilled Nursing
  Private rooms $110.25/day

"Our long-term care policy sets us apart from other communities in the area. Combining independence with attentive services, Galleria Woods offers an invigorating approach to life in a warm and gracious setting. The spaciousness of the outdoors has been brought to both community areas and residences."

KIRKWOOD BY THE RIVER

3605 Ratliff Road
Birmingham, AL 35210
(205) 956-2184
Eileen B. Bostick, director of marketing

Type of community: Nonprofit Continuing Care, modified contract

Three mid-rise and low-rise apartment buildings—Mountainview, Rearview, and Skyview—are located on a hilly 120-acre wooded campus within minutes of Eastwood Mall, Brookwood Mall, and the Galleria. The Cahaba River winds through the campus.

Financial plan: Entrance fee plus monthly fee. Two plans: **1)** Five-year prorated refund of entrance fee after six months of occupancy. **2)** 95%-100% refund, depending upon circumstances of departure. Plan 2 has two options: higher entrance fee and lower monthly fee or lower entrance fee and higher monthly fee. Also $100 nonrefundable deposit.

INDEPENDENT LIVING HOUSING

Type/size of unit	*Entrance fee 1/2*	*Monthly fee single/double*
Studio, 325 sq. ft.	$21,750/33,700	$746/1,196
Efficiency, 380 sq. ft.	$24,300/37,700	$662/1,046
1-Bedroom, 600–642 sq. ft.	$50,000/77,500	$835–883/1,219–1,266
2-Bedroom, 800–1,002 sq. ft.	$70,300/108,965	$1,124–1,197/1,508–1,582
3-Bedroom, 1,285 sq. ft.	$90,059/139,578	$1,518/1,902

A second version of Plan 2 is available, offering a lower entrance fee and higher monthly fee. All utilities except telephone included. Fully equipped kitchen, individually controlled heat and air-conditioning, 24-hour emergency call systems, balcony or patio, wall-to-wall carpeting, draperies.

Ownership and management: Owned by the Presbyterian Homes of Birmingham, Inc. Managed by board of directors. Opened in 1980.

Minimum age: 62 years.

Population: 160 residents.

Number of units: 79 Independent Living apartments; 44 Assisted Living, 51 Skilled Nursing beds.

Dining plan: One meal per day included. Private dining room available.

Services: *Included in the monthly fee:* Weekly housekeeping, flat-linen service, scheduled transportation, parking.

At additional cost: Beauty/barbershop, guest rooms.

Activities: Full-time activities director. Swimming pool, three activity rooms, billiards room, exercise room, arts and crafts room, library, interdenominational religious services, nature trails, game field and walking course, resident's association, bingo, planned excursions, trips to the theater, travelogues, music club, birdwatching, Bible study.

Availability: Limited.

Health services and rates: Emergency nursing service is included in the monthly fee.

- 44 Assisted Living units

Type of unit	*Entrance fee 1/2*	*Monthly rental single/double*
Studio	$21,750/33,700	$1,809/2,897
Efficiency	$24,300/37,700	$2,028/3,283

A 100% refund option is available, offering a lower entrance fee and higher monthly fee.

- 51 Nursing beds

	Nonresident monthly fee
Triple	$2,464
Semiprivate	$3,072–3,589
Private	$3,802

WESTMINSTER VILLAGE

500 Spanish Fort Boulevard
Spanish Fort, AL 36537
(205) 626-2900
Susan Keslar

Type of Community: Nonprofit Continuing Care, all-inclusive contract

This Alabama Golf Coast community is nestled on 53 acres in a wooded area of the eastern shore of Mobile Bay. Independent Living garden apartments are located near a contemporary main building. The main building houses Independent apartments and large gracious areas, including a three-story fireside lounge, a main dining room, a library, and multipurpose rooms. Ten minutes away is metropolitan Mobile for opera, symphony, theater, and sporting events. Lovely beaches and boating and fishing areas are nearby, as are shopping centers, churches and hospitals, golf courses, tennis courts, and restaurants. Assisted Living, Intermediate and Skilled Nursing are available.

Financial Plan: Entrance fee plus monthly fee. Two plans: **1)** Nonrefundable entrance fee. **2)** 90% refundable entrance fee.

Ownership and management: Owned by the Presbyterian Retirement Corporation, a nonprofit corporation not affiliated with any church or denomination. Managed by Life Care Services Corporation, which has built and managed more than 50 life care communities in 18 states and the District of Columbia. Opened in 1983.

Minimum age: 62 years.

Population: 237 residents; 74% women, 26% men, 22% couples.

Number of units: 191 Independent Living apartments and 100 garden apartments; 14 Assisted Living beds, 60-bed nursing facility.

Dining plan: One meal per day selected by the resident is included. Additional meals, special diets, and delivery service available. Private dining rooms. Licensed dietitian is available for consultation.

Services: *Included in the monthly fee:* Biweekly housekeeping and weekly flat-linen services (laundry facilities are available on each floor and hookups in garden apartments), scheduled transportation.

At additional cost: Full-service bank, beauty/barbershop, village store, pharmacy.

Activities: Full-time social director organizes lectures, guest speakers, cultural, music, and drama programs, scheduled trips to social events. Jacuzzi and indoor heated swimming pool, water exercise classes, arts and crafts, gardening, woodworking shop, library, billiards room, shuffleboard, nature trails, exercise room, golf driving range all on-site.

Availability: A short waiting list for two-bedroom garden apartments. All other apartments are available.

Health services and rates: Residents receive 15 days (noncumulative) per year in the health center at half price. Residents who move into the health center permanently receive a lifetime monthly credit that is equivalent to 1/60th of the entrance fee. Health center provides laboratory work; physical, speech, and occupational therapy; and rehabilitation and preventive medicine.

- 14 Assisted Living units $65/day
- 60-Bed Skilled Nursing facility
  - Semiprivate $70/day
  - Private $80/day

"The facility offers a 100% Resident-Satisfaction Guarantee: If any resident is not completely satisfied at Westminster Village during the first year of residency, the entire entrance fee is refunded."

INDEPENDENT LIVING HOUSING

Main building apts./size	*Entrance fee 1/2*	*Monthly fee**
Studio, 300 sq. ft.	$36,000/62,900	$800
1-Bedroom, 528–618 sq. ft.	$48,900–56,500/72,900–84,900	$854–934
2-Bedroom, 792 sq. ft.	$73,800/110,400–136,000	$1,011
Garden apartments		
1-Bedroom, 708–892 sq. ft.	$56,500–64,000/84,900–96,400	$940–1,004
2-Bedroom, 982–1,178 sq. ft.	$82,400–90,600/123,900–136,000	$1,135–1,197

**For double occupancy add $397 to the monthly fee. All utilities except telephone included. All-electric kitchen, wall-to-wall carpeting, individually controlled heating and air-conditioning, cable TV, 24-hour emergency call system, private patio or balcony, variety of floor plans.*

ARIZONA

CHANDLER VILLAS

101 South Yucca Street
Chandler, AZ 85224
(602) 899-7650
Virginia Sheele, assistant administrator

Type of community: Independent Living with Assisted Care

There are 29 one-story and nine two-story Independent Living apartment buildings set on an eight-acre parklike campus with a small pond in grassy courtyard and tree-lined paths. Assisted Living services are available. The facility is close to shopping, banks, churches, medical facilities, the Chandler Theater, a golf course, cultural events, and recreational facilities in the greater Phoenix area.

Financial plan: Monthly rental fee; 12-month lease.

Ownership and management: Owned and managed by American Retirement Villas, owner and manager of 26 retirement communities in California, with 20 years of experience. Opened in 1985.

Minimum age: 55 years.

Population: 173 residents; 85% women, 15% men, 16% couples.

Number of units: 164 Independent Living apartments.

Dining plan: No meals included in the monthly fee. Three meals served daily. Breakfast: $65/month. Lunch: $125/month. Dinner: $75/month. Special diets accommodated. Occasional meals served in room due to illness. Private dining room available.

Services: *Included in the monthly fee:* Bimonthly housekeeping, flat-linen service, scheduled transportation, garages.

At additional cost: Laundry, beauty/barbershop, general store.

Activities: Full-time activities director. Movies, card games, parties, trips, arts and crafts, exercise classes, adult education classes, library, billiards room, pool, spa, hobby room, bingo, concerts, dominoes, Trivial Pursuit, Bible study, bridge club, sing-alongs, painting, happy hours with bands, ice-cream socials, ceramics, shuffleboard, Las Vegas Nights, barbecues,

INDEPENDENT LIVING HOUSING

Type/size of apartment	*Monthly fee**
1-Bedroom, 450–717 sq. ft.	$582–771
2-Bedroom, 830–900 sq. ft.	$824–897

**For double occupancy add $50 to the monthly fee. Individually controlled heating and air-conditioning, 24-hour emergency call system, fully equipped kitchens, cable TV. Many apartments with washer/dryer; some furnished.*

theater excursions, dinner and luncheon outings, walking club, water exercise.

Availability: Waiting list ($250 deposit) approximately six months

Health services and rates: Assisted Living services (bathing, dressing, grooming, scheduled monitoring, personal companionship and escort service) available in the resident's apartment.

- $300/Month added to rent

"Chandler Villas offers a friendly, secure community. Trial stays are available to prospective residents."

THE FORUM AT DESERT HARBOR

13840 North Desert Harbor Drive
Peoria, AZ 85345
(602) 972-0995
Joyce Abbott, marketing director

Type of Community: Continuing Care, modified contract

Designed to blend harmoniously with the southwestern architecture of the area, The Forum has a distinctive, residential character. The three-story Independent Living apartment building has a Spanish mission-style exterior of beige stucco and clay tile features striking turquoise-colored accent tiles. A three-story interior atrium is framed by stately freestanding columns. Generous windows provide panoramic waterfront views of the mountains in the distance and the lake at Desert Harbor. Assisted Living and Skilled Nursing are available in the on-site health care center. New River runs along the east side of the community, located in northwestern Phoenix.

Financial plan: Monthly rental plan; $500 deposit; one-year lease.

Ownership and management: The Forum Group, Inc., which owns and manages over 27 retirement communities across the U.S. and has over 25 years experience in the industry. Opened in 1990.

Minimum age: 60 years.

Population: 176 residents; 75% women, 25% men, 20% couples.

Number of units: 129 Independent Living apartments; 25 Ambassador suites, 30 Assisted Living units, 61-bed health center.

Dining plan: One meal per day and continental breakfast included. Private dining room available.

Services: *Included in the monthly fee:* Weekly housekeeping, flat-linen service, laundry facilities, scheduled transportation.

At additional cost: Personal transportation outside 10-mile radius, beauty/barbershop, guest accommodations.

Activities: Full-time program director. Lectures, movies, exercise classes, travel tours, swimming pool, spa, billiards room, arts and crafts room, library, boating, fishing, bridge, trips to area cultural events, bocce, Scrabble, backgammon, bingo, parlor games,

INDEPENDENT LIVING HOUSING

Type/size of apartment	*Monthly rental**
1-Bedroom, 635–855 sq. ft.	$1,450–2,100
2-Bedroom, 922–1,377 sq. ft.	$1,875–3,225

**For double occupancy add $310 to the monthly rental. All utilities except telephone included. Individually controlled heating and air-conditioning, fully equipped electric kitchen, wall-to-wall carpeting, 24-hour emergency call system, additional storage areas, walk-in closets, cable TV, choice of balcony, patio, or bay window.*

talent shows, social hours, putting green, shuffleboard.

Availability: Waiting list for some Independent Living apartments and Assisted Living units.

Health services and rates: Residents receive 15 free days in the health care center per year, with a lifetime total of 60 days. Medical director, list of attending physicians and therapists always available. Activities program promoting self-esteem, psychological well-being, and physical rehabilitation. Physical, occupational, and speech therapy available.

- 31 Ambassador suites (assistance with medication only) $2,295–2,995/month
- 30 Assisted Living units
  Suite, 288–410 sq. ft., starting at $1,300/month
- 57-Bed health center with Intermediate and Skilled Nursing

	Intermediate Nursing	*Skilled Nursing*
Semiprivate	$92/day	$101/day
Private	$120/day	$129/day

"The Forum at Desert Harbor offers residents worry-free lifestyle with a friendly and professional staff providing fine services. As a community offering a Continuum of Care, the staff is dedicated to meeting the needs of all residents as well as any health care concerns that may arise."

ORANGEWOOD

7550 North 16th Street
Phoenix, AZ 85020
(602) 944-4455
Susan Kitchens, director of marketing

Type of Community: Nonprofit Continuing Care, modified contract

Accreditation: Continuing Care Accreditation Commission

The community consists of 25 one-level apartment buildings on a 20-acre garden campus near the base of Squaw Peak and across from the Pointe Resort. Long, covered walkways bridge landscaped grounds, connecting Independent Living residences, Assisted Living, and Skilled Nursing facilities. It is located in a semi-residential neighborhood with easy access to Squaw Peak Parkway and major city transit route and minutes from Scottsdale, downtown Phoenix cultural events, and Valley of the Sun attractions.

Financial plan: Entrance fee plus monthly fee or monthly rental. Entrance fee plan includes care, services, and amenities even if a resident's finances become exhausted. Monthly rental plan involves extra charge for services and amenities, no life care guarantee, no financial safety net.

INDEPENDENT LIVING HOUSING

Type/size of apartment	*Entrance fee 1**	*Monthly fee 1**	*Monthly rental*
Studio, 288–348 sq. ft.	$21,300–25,300	$703–771	$665
1-Bedroom, 475–540 sq. ft	$44,200–52,400	$875–900	$747–1,014
2-Bedroom, 660 sq. ft.	$63,400–67,400	$922–963	N/A
2-Bedroom, 1,050–1,190 sq. ft.	$89,900	$1,455	N/A

**For double occupancy add 10% to the entrance fee and $300 to the monthly fee or add $200 to the monthly rent. All utilities except telephone included. 24-hour emergency call system, wall-to-wall carpeting. 1- and 2-bedrooms have fully equipped kitchens. Patios optional.*

Ownership and management: Owned by American Baptist Estates. Managed by American Baptist Homes of the West, manager of 17 retirement communities in California. Opened in 1963.

Minimum age: 62 years (if couple, spouse may be younger).

Population: 230 residents; 83% women, 17% men, 22% couples.

Number of units: 218 Independent Living apartments; 20 Assisted Living suites, 64-bed nursing facility.

Dining plan: One meal per day included in the entrance fee plan. Two extra meals available for $220/month.

Services: *Included in the monthly fee:* Biweekly housekeeping and weekly flat-linen services for those on entrance fee plan, laundry facilities.

At additional cost: Covered parking, transportation, beauty/barbershop, guest accommodations. Rental residents may purchase services such as housekeeping, laundry.

Activities: Members of the residents' council work with the director of resident services to develop programs. Arts and crafts center, exercise room with billiards table and exercise bikes, chapel, library, social center with big-screen TV and VCR, woodworking/lapidary shop, year-round swimming pool with spa, horseshoe pit, lighted shuffleboard courts and croquet lawn.

Availability: Waiting list with $250 application fee ($400 for couple). All but $50 of fee is refundable after two years if type of unit applied for is not available.

Health services and rates: Outpatient nurse available 24 hours to residents in Independent Living. Physician at wellness clinic every Tuesday and Thursday morning. Prepaid medical option plan available to those who pay entrance fee; $30/month will pay $225/month toward Intermediate Nursing, $275/month toward Skilled Nursing. Decisions on option must be made in first six months of residency.

- 20 Assisted Living studios

Entrance Fee	*Monthly Fee*	*Monthly Rent*
$10,650	$1,325	$1,531

- 64-Bed nursing center

Intermediate Care	$56/day or $1,700/month
Skilled Care	$91/day or $2,766/month

"The aim of Orangewood's Continuing Care Contract is to contribute to the 'psychic hygiene' of our society and to help seniors to enjoy retirement by providing a wise choice for living one's last years. Orangewood offers a few days or weekend complimentary guest visit."

THE FORUM, PUEBLO NORTE

7090 East Mescal Street
Scottsdale, AZ 85254
(602) 948-3990
Joy Ricci, marketing director

Type of community: Continuing Care, modified contract

Situated on 20 landscaped acres, The Forum has Independent Living apartments and villas, plus a health center offering personal care and Intermediate and Skilled Nursing. The apartments and villas are two-story stucco, tile-roofed buildings. The Forum is close to downtown Scottsdale and shopping centers and eight miles from Scottsdale Mayo Clinic.

Financial plan: Entrance fee and monthly fee. Two plans: **1)** life care Estate, 90% refundable, reduced by 1.5 percent per month of residency. **2)** Nonrefundable Entrance Fee (call for details).

Ownership and management: Forum Lifecare, a wholly owned subsidiary of The Forum Group, Inc., which has been involved in developing and managing over 27 retirement communities in the U.S. Opened in 1984.

INDEPENDENT LIVING HOUSING

Type/size of apartment	*Entrance plan 1*	*Monthly fee**
Studio, 400 sq. ft.	$43,775	$942
1-Bedroom, 668 sq. ft.	$68,560	$1,115
2-Bedroom, 875 sq. ft.	$87,035	$1,264
Deluxe, 1,336 sq. ft.	$147,625	$1,437
Villas		
1-Bedroom, 692 sq. ft.	$73,377	$1,149
2-Bedroom, 962 sq. ft.	$111,705	$1,298
Deluxe, 1,228 sq. ft.	$134,106	$1,437

**For double occupancy add $577 to the monthly fee. All utilities included. All-electric kitchen, individually controlled heating and air-conditioning, washer/dryer hookups, plush carpeting, 24-hour emergency call system, balcony or patio.*

Minimum age: 62 years.

Population: 270 residents; 75% women, 25% men, 20% couples. Residents are from all parts of the United States.

Number of units: 169 Independent Living apartments and villas; 128-bed health care center.

Dining plan: One meal per day included. Private dining room.

Services: *Included in the monthly fee:* Weekly housekeeping services, personal laundry facilities, scheduled transportation.

At additional cost: Beauty/barbershop, ice-cream parlor, guest accommodations.

Activities: Heated swimming pool, Jacuzzi, fitness programs, movies, library, game room, craft room, putting green, lawn bowling court, shuffleboard court, trips to cultural and other area events. Full range of activities.

Availability: At present, limited; priority wait list.

Health services and rates: Wellness programs. If long-term care in the on-site facility is required, the monthly fee will not exceed that of the lowest priced one-bedroom apartment, adjusted for three meals a day.

- 128-Bed health care center
  Admission is available directly to the health care center, and rates vary depending upon level of care ($68 to $136 per day)

"Our community offers a broad range of services and amenities that enables our residents to maintain their lifestyle—with an important difference. They enjoy a new sense of freedom, enabling them to experience life to its fullest—free from the worries or chores of home ownership. The most frequently heard comment is: 'What took me so long to make up my mind!' "

FRIENDSHIP VILLAGE OF TEMPE

2645 East Southern Avenue
Tempe, AZ 85282
(602) 831-5000
Suzanne Gammage, marketing director

Type of community: Nonprofit Continuing Care, all-inclusive contract

The complex consists of a three-story beige Southwestern-style, Independent Living apartment building

as well as duplex and fourplex garden homes with red tile roofs. It is located on a 45-acre campus that is half desert landscaped and half parklike. Apartments provide a view of the Superstition Mountain range. Assisted Living and Skilled Nursing are available on campus. Desert Samaritan Hospital, Arizona State University, Sky Harbor Airport, shopping centers, various arts, sports, and entertainment are all nearby, as is the Phoenix area.

Financial plan: Entrance fee plus monthly fee. Two plans: **1)** Standard entrance fee, which is refundable less 1% per month of residency. **2)** Return-of-capital plan, where 90% of the entrance fee is refundable at any time. If within one year a resident becomes dissatisfied, 100% of the entrance fee will be returned.

Ownership and management: Nonprofit organization managed by a local board of directors who employ Life Care Services of Des Moines, Iowa, as management company. Life Care Services manages over 50 life care retirement communities throughout the U.S. Residents' council. Opened in 1980.

Minimum age: 62 years.

Population: 700+ residents; 68% women, 32% men, 28% couples. Residents come from all parts of the U.S.

Number of units: 211 Independent Living apartments and 292 garden homes; 120-bed health center

Dining plan: Choice of one meal per day included. Special diets and tray service available.

Services: *Included in the monthly fee:* Twice weekly housekeeping, weekly flat-linen service, scheduled transportation, tram service within village.

At additional cost: Beauty/barbershop, guest accommodations.

Activities: Full-time social director and recreation center. Movies, crafts room, woodworking shop, card room, library, swimming pool, Jacuzzi, painting, weaving, ceramics, exercise classes, lapidary, photography, dancing, billiards, pottery, golf, concerts, chapel, volunteering, shuffleboard, aerobics, chess and checkers, cooking classes, Spanish classes, drama club, various other clubs, happy hours, weekly intergenerational gatherings.

Availability: No waiting list at present.

Health services and rates: Residents receive 90 free days of Assisted Living services, after which there is

INDEPENDENT LIVING HOUSING

Type/size of apartment	*Entrance fee 1/2**	*Monthly fee**
Studio, 308 sq. ft.	$34,750/60,825	$824
Studio/alcove, 440 sq. ft.	$47,250/82,700	$921
1-Bedroom, 576–748 sq. ft.	$59,750–74,700/104,575–130,725	$1,013–1,068
2-Bedroom, 792–1,060 sq. ft.	$78,300–99,500/ 137,025–174,125	$1,107–1,218
3-Bedroom, 1,152 sq. ft.	$109,200/191,100	$1,297
Garden homes		
1-Bedroom, 675–840 sq. ft.	$65,000–78,800/119,875–137,900	$1,107–1,162
2-Bedroom, 950–1,538 sq. ft.	$95,300–148,750/166,775–260,325	$1,192–1,740

**For double occupancy add $3,000 to the entrance fee for apartments, $3,500 for garden homes; $539 to the monthly fee. All utilities except telephone included. Fully equipped electric kitchen, individually controlled heat and air-conditioning, satellite dish TV reception, 24-hour emergency call system. Garden homes have washer/dryer, covered parking.*

a nominal fee calculated by services required. Nursing fees are included in resident's basic monthly payment with the exception of the addition of two extra meals. Recuperative and long-term care available.

- Assisted Living services offered in residents' apartments
- 120-Bed nursing facility

"Friendship Village is a vital community, full of energy and responsive to new ideas but respectful of traditional ways."

CAMPANA DEL RIO

1550 East River Road
Tucson, AZ 85718
(602) 299-1941
Pauline Zwick, marketing director

Type of community: Independent and Assisted Living

Set on five acres in the Catalina Mountain foothills, the facility features Spanish-style architecture with red-tiled roofs and soft desert colors accenting the community buildings. The Independent Living apartments overlook either a courtyard with lush landscaping, flower beds, and a sparkling pool, or the desert landscape, with plants native to the Southwest. The campus offers a shady ramada with outdoor furniture, landscaped walking trail adjacent to the apartments, and a private courtyard. There also are Assisted Living apartments. The community is located near Arizona's largest shopping mall, major grocery chains, two major hospitals, churches, synagogues, and cultural activities.

Financial plan: Monthly rental fee; $350 initial deposit of $350; one year lease required.

Ownership and management: Owned and managed by The Hillhaven Corporation, owner and manager of communities in California and Arizona with over 40 years of experience. Opened in 1988.

Minimum age: 55 years.

Population: 220 residents; 75% women, 25% men, 11% couples.

Number of units: 190 Independent Living apartments/villas; 24 Assisted Living apartments.

Dining plan: Two meals per day included. Private dining room and tray service available.

Services: *Included in the monthly fee:* Weekly housekeeping and flat-linen services, free use of washers/dryers, scheduled transportation, open parking, one hour of consultation with an interior decorator.

INDEPENDENT LIVING HOUSING

Type/size of apartment	*Monthly fee**
Alcove, 430–515 sq. ft.	$940–1,055
1-Bedroom, 540–647 sq. ft.	$1,087–1,276
2-Bedroom, 658–796 sq. ft.	$1,286–1,528
Villas	
2-Bedroom, 792–1,015 sq. ft.	$1,580–1,980

**For double occupancy add $250 to the monthly fee. All utilities except telephone and cable TV included. Fully equipped kitchen, individually controlled heat and air-conditioning, 24-hour emergency call system, wall-to-wall carpeting, private balconies and patios, cable TV setup, miniblinds on all windows.*

At additional cost: Beauty/barbershop, personal laundry service, covered parking spaces.

Activities: Activities director. Trips, speakers, community projects, crafts, special events, theme dinners, dances, heated swimming pool, two well-stocked libraries, regulation-size billiards table, exercise rooms, activity rooms, chapel.

Availability: 30 persons on waiting list at present. Waiting list varies according to accommodations desired.

Health services and rates: Assisted living apartments offer daily assistance.

- 24 Assisted Living apartments

Alcove, 430 sq. ft.	$1,600/month
1-Bedroom, 540 sq. ft.	$1,843/month

THE FORUM AT TUCSON

2500 North Rosemont Boulevard
Tucson, AZ 85712
(602) 325-4800
Carolyn Davis or Sue Molenda, leasing counselors

Type of community: Continuing Care, modified contract

Four-story Independent Living apartment community with red-tiled roofs and striking southwestern-style architecture. Stunning Santa Catalina Mountain views frame the community, which is located on a 14 acre desert landscaped campus with a cactus-lined courtyard. An elegant atmosphere is reflected in the common areas. Tucson Medical Center, doctors offices, shopping malls, theaters, and banking services are located nearby. Assisted Living and Intermediate and Skilled Nursing are available in the on-site health care center.

Financial plan: Monthly rental fee.

Ownership and management: Owned and managed by The Forum Group, Inc., which owns and manages over 27 retirement communities in the U.S. and has over 25 years experience in the retirement living industry. Opened in 1989.

Minimum age: 60 years.

Population: 165 residents; 75% women, 25% men, 20% couples.

Number of units: 150 Independent Living apartments; 30 Assisted Living units, 67-bed health center.

Dining plan: One meal per day and continental breakfast included. Private dining room available.

Services: *Included in the monthly fee:* Weekly housekeeping, flat-linen service, laundry facilities, scheduled transportation, covered parking.

At additional cost: Transportation outside five-mile radius of the Forum, gift shop, beauty/barbershop, overnight guest apartment.

Activities: Full-time program director. Billiards, heated swimming pool, spa, movies, lectures, exercise classes, travel tours, scheduled transportation

INDEPENDENT LIVING HOUSING

Type/size of apartment	*Monthly rental fee**
1-Bedroom, 650–800 sq. ft.	$1,255–1,595
2-Bedroom, 903–1,247 sq. ft.	$1,895–3,750

**For double occupancy add $295 to the monthly rental fee. All utilities except telephone included. Fully equipped electric kitchen, wall-to-wall carpeting, individually controlled heating and air-conditioning, 24-hour emergency call system, walk-in closets, balcony, patio or bay window, cable TV, storage lockers.*

to cultural and sporting events, library, arts and crafts, bridge, happy hours, walking club, picnics, game room, multipurpose auditorium, nondenominational services, bookmobile, yoga classes.

Availability: Limited.

Health services and rates: Residents receive 10 free days per year in health care center, up to a lifetime total of 40 days. Short- and long-term care available. Medical director, list of attending physicians and therapists always available. Activities program promotes self-esteem, psychological well-being, and physical rehabilitation. Western Rehab Services provides physical, occupational, and speech therapy.

- 30 Assisted Living units, starting at $1,595/month
- 67-Bed health center

	Intermediate Nursing	*Skilled Nursing*
Semiprivate	$75/day	$90/day
Private	$110/day	$110/day

"The Forum at Tucson offers residents a worry-free lifestyle with a friendly and professional staff providing fine service. As a community offering a continuum of care, the staff is dedicated to meeting the needs of all residents including any health care concerns that may arise."

VILLA CAMPANA

6653 East Carondelet Drive
Tucson, AZ 85710
(602) 886-3600
Judith Brooks, executive director

Type of community: Continuing Care, modified contract

A Mediterranean-style mansion built in the 20s is the focal point of the community, with hand-painted Mexican and Italian tiles, imported woods, and fireplaces. Independent Living, Assisted Living, and Skilled Nursing residences are located in modern buildings surrounding the mansion. Situated on the highest point of a 14-acre campus, the community offers a panoramic view of several mountain ranges. It is near shopping malls, restaurants, theaters, medical offices, clinics, and hospitals.

Financial plan: Monthly rental fee; fully refundable deposit of one month's rent and $350 nonrefundable administrative fee upon admission; standard one-year lease.

Ownership and management: Owned and managed by the Hillhaven Corporation, with over 40 years experience in serving seniors. Opened in 1984.

Minimum age: 55 years.

Population: 147 residents; 83% women, 17% men, 10% couples.

INDEPENDENT LIVING HOUSING

Type/size of apartment	*Monthly rental**
1-Bedroom, 607–712 sq. ft.	$1,250–1,800
Deluxe 1-bedroom, 789–865 sq. ft.	$1,850–2,400
2-Bedroom, 961–1,066 sq. ft.	$2,300–2,850
Deluxe 2-bedroom, 1,130–1,472 sq. ft.	$2,650–3,450

**For double occupancy add $375 to the monthly rental. All utilities except telephone and cable TV included. Private patio or balcony, fully equipped kitchens, individually controlled heat and air-conditioning, 24-hour emergency call system, walk-in closets, central TV antenna, wall-to-wall carpeting, window coverings. Small pets allowed.*

Number of units: 140 Independent Living apartments; 120-bed health center.

Dining plan: One meal per day (lunch or dinner) included. Private dining room, tray service, and special diets available.

Services: *Included in the monthly fee:* Biweekly housekeeping, laundry facilities, scheduled transportation, open parking.

At additional cost: Beauty/barbershop.

Activities: Full-time activity director. Formal dances, costume parties, classical concerts, sing-alongs, lectures, card games, Jacuzzi, excursions within Tucson and southeastern Arizona, travelogues, exercise groups, swimming pool, spa and cabana, game room with billiards table, library, exercise room, yoga and aerobics classes, residents' lounge with big-screen TV, meeting rooms, movies, bingo.

Availability: Waiting list varies according to accommodations desired.

Health services and rates: Long-term and temporary rehabilitative care available. A fully licensed facility including nursing, therapists, dietitians, social services, activity experts, and specially trained nursing assistants.

- 120-Bed Health Center

	Intermediate Nursing	*Skilled Nursing*
Semiprivate	$94/day	$112/day
Private	$114/day	$124/day

"Villa Campana also offers the convenience of Vacation Care to family members who are full-time caregivers. This program provides accommodations, nutritious meals and snacks, and a stimulating environment while the caregiver takes a break. Short or long stays can be arranged."

Gerald, 88 years

The Moorings, Arlington Heights, Illinois

"Now I don't have to worry that Dad is safe and being cared for."

"About four years ago Dad had a bad reaction to some medication following surgery and became very ill," explains Janet, Gerald's daughter. "He came to my house to get well and at that point I went to the Jewish Community Center and borrowed a book from them that recommended Continuing Care communities." Janet then visited communities with her father, keeping in mind his paramount objective of finding a community with a high percentage of residents who were professional people. At this point, she said her father saw one too many people in walkers and headed back to Florida, feeling he wasn't ready to move yet.

In November of 1991, Gerald began looking for a Continuing Care community in the Ft. Myers area. His wife had died in 1982, and he had fewer and fewer social contacts. "I almost signed up down there, but I wanted to be able to see my children more frequently than I could if they had to fly to Florida," he says. "So I decided to move near my daughter in the Chicago area, figuring Chicago was an easy place for my son to fly to from New Jersey."

Gerald, who is 88 and a retired cosmetic manufacturing company executive, has a two-bedroom apartment at The Moorings. He uses one of the bedrooms as his office/computer room. "Physically, I'm not able to get around much anymore, and The Moorings is serving my purpose about as well as it might be served," he explains. "I am not able to walk a great deal or travel, but have no disabilities otherwise—my heart is just getting old."

Gerald's daughter reports that her dad has made friends and goes to dinner nightly with people from his floor. "He realized when he moved back to

Florida that he wasn't going to have good social contacts living alone in his house," she says. "The Moorings is great for me, too, because my home is not designed for someone in Dad's condition. I would have had to rearrange it completely. This way, with him at The Moorings, I don't have to worry that he is safe and being cared for. And, I can visit him often. He likes it so much that he's been trying to convince his sisters to move in," Janet says.

ARKANSAS

BUTTERFIELD TRAIL VILLAGE

1923 East Joyce Street
Fayetteville, AR 72703
(501) 442-7220 or (800) 441-9996
Linda Priest, marketing consultant

Type of community: Nonprofit Continuing Care, all-inclusive contract

The 25-acre campus is surrounded by the Ozark Mountains with a health care center on site. Buildings are constructed of native stone with cedar shake roofs. A horticulturist works on the grounds to keep them in condition. Three area golf courses, stores, restaurants, and churches are all just minutes away. The University of Arkansas and 22 city parks are located in Fayetteville.

Financial plan: Entrance fee plus monthly fee. Two plans: **1)** Standard entrance fee: refundable less initial 10% and 1.5% per month of residency. **2)** 94% return policy: resident shall receive 94% refund of entrance fee, less any incurred expenses, regardless of length of stay.

Ownership and management: Arkansas nonprofit corporation. Its corporate membership is elected by the following Fayetteville churches: First Presbyterian Church, First Christian Church, Central United Methodist Church, St. Paul's Episcopal Church, and First Baptist Church. Opened in 1986.

Minimum age: 62 years.

Population: 336 residents; 74% women, 26% men, 38% couples.

Number of units: 248 Independent Living apartments and cottages; 44-bed health center.

Dining plan: One meal per day included. Private dining room, tray service, and special diets available.

Services: *Included in the monthly fee:* Biweekly housekeeping, weekly flat-linen service, scheduled transportation, parking for residents and guests.

INDEPENDENT LIVING HOUSING

Type/size of unit	*Entrance fee*	*Monthly fee*
Studio, 196 sq. ft.	$51,500	$921
1-Bedroom, 380 sq. ft.	$75,000	$1,153
2-Bedroom, 485–650 sq. ft.	$99,500	$1,346
2-Bedroom cottage, 575 sq. ft.	$125,600	$1,612
Fourplex, 1,150 sq. ft.	$125,600	$1,612

For double occupancy add $613 to the monthly fee. All utilities except telephone and cable TV included. Emergency call system, wall-to-wall carpeting, individually controlled heat and air-conditioning, fully equipped kitchen, cable TV (optional).

At additional cost: Beauty/barbershop, coin-operated laundry facilities.

Activities: Indoor swimming pool, putting green, aerobics classes, library, residents' association, musical performances, spelling bees, outings to areas of interest, ice-cream socials, Bible study, vespers services, bowling, exercise classes, bingo, reading groups, picnics, movies, gardening, croquet, BTV theater group, bridge, glee club, pinochle.

Availability: Waiting list of approximately one year.

Health services and rates: Health care is included in the monthly fee except for personal physician, extra meals, dental care, physical therapist, special nurses, drugs and medicine, ancillary items, and all medical, therapeutic, and nonmedical extras; 24-hour nursing services available for emergencies. Private rooms available to residents if space permits, but an additional charge is levied. State-of-the-art medical facilities nearby include two major hospitals, rehabilitation center, and radiation therapy institute.

- 53-Bed health center

"Fayetteville has been consistently ranked in the top 10 cities nationwide for retirement living. Butterfield is a top life care community. Approximately 60% of the community residents are retired educators from around the country."

PARKWAY VILLAGE

14300 Chenal Parkway
Little Rock, AR 72211-9989
(501) 227-1626
Carolyn Neal

Type of community: Not-for-profit Continuing Care, modified contract

The facility is surrounded by 87 acres of pines and oaks, with walking trails, open spaces, and three stocked lakes. Three three-story apartment buildings are connected to each other and community facilities with covered walkways. Duplex, triplex, fourplex, and fiveplex cottages also house Independent Living residences. Personal care plus Intermediate and Skilled Nursing are offered at the health center.

Financial plan: Entrance fee plus monthly fee. A refund of between 70% and 85% of the entrance fee is returned to the resident or resident's estate after the unit is vacated and reoccupied. The refund is available to the resident for long-term nursing care, if needed.

Ownership and management: Sponsored by Baptist Medical System, health care provider for 75 years. Opened in 1985.

Minimum age: 60 years.

Population: 315 residents; 73% women, 27% men, 37% couples.

Number of units: 148 Independent Living apartments and 125 cottages (10 additional cottages under construction); 35 Assisted Living apartments; 75-bed Skilled and Intermediate Nursing facility.

Dining plan: Two meals are served daily. One meal daily is included in apartment residents' monthly fee and 20 meals per month in Cottage residents' fee. Meals can be delivered if requested by medical staff.

Services: *Included in the monthly fee:* Scheduled transportation to area shopping and medical appointments. Weekly housekeeping, bed/bath linens are included for apartments (optional for cottages), maintenance for all interior and exterior and grounds.

At additional cost: Beauty/barbershop, convenience store, guest accommodations.

Activities: Heated indoor swimming pool, water aerobics and water volleyball, exercise room/gym equipment, whirlpool, arts and crafts shop, concerts, movies, parties, woodworking shop, big-screen TV, library, chapel, guest speakers, seminars, cultural events, lighted walking and exercise trails, cards/games, chapel.

INDEPENDENT LIVING HOUSING

*Apartment units/size**	*Entrance fee**	*Monthly fee**
Studio, 475–515 sq. ft.	$40,000–44,500	$701–741
1-Bedroom, 650 sq. ft.	$57,000	$1,024
2-Bedroom, 930 sq. ft.	$80,000	$1,300
*Cottage units**		
1-Bedroom, 930 sq. ft.	$82,550	$1,071
2-Bedroom, 1,170–1,180 sq. ft.	$98,500–110,500	$1,295
2-Bedroom/sunroom, 1,550 sq. ft.	$129,500	$1,488
2-Bedroom/sunroom, 1,800 sq. ft.	$162,000	$1,786

**For double occupancy add $7500 to the entrance fee; $150 to the monthly fee. All utilities except telephone and cable TV are included. Central antenna outlet, fully equipped kitchens, individually controlled heating and air-conditioning, 24-hour emergency call system, wall-to-wall carpeting. Additional costs vary for Lakefront Cottages. New cottages are to be built as reserved. All 2-bedroom apartments and cottages have two baths.*

Availability: Waiting list and occasional availability. Average occupancy is 97%.

Health services and rates: Residents receive one prepaid day in the health care center for each month of Parkway Village residency; up to 60 days per resident for short- or long-term nursing care. Payment for continuing long-term health care (beyond accrued prepaid days) can be provided through the refund policy. Health center opened in May 1989.

- 35 Assisted Living apartments starting at $1,500/month
  75-Bed nursing facility
-

Type of room	*Intermediate Nursing*	*Skilled Nursing*
Semiprivate	$2,313/month	$2,472/month
Private	$2,786/month	$2,940/month

"Our goal at Parkway Village is to help residents make the most of their retirement years. We strive to extend their independent years by relieving them of many of life's hassles and by seeking to expand their opportunities and friendships."

WOODLAND HEIGHTS

8700 Riley Drive
Little Rock, AR 72205
(501) 224-4242
Frank Bizzell, marketing director

Type of community: Continuing Care, modified contact

This is a modern six-story apartment building with two wings of Independent Living units connected by a main section. It is situated on the crest of a wooded hill overlooking Rock Creek and Kanis Park, visible from the dining room. A two-story atrium in the main unit houses a landscaped garden and fountain. The adjacent health center offers Assisted Living and Nursing services. Shopping areas and medical facilities are nearby. The facility is located minutes from downtown Little Rock and the airport.

Financial plan: Entrance fee plus monthly fee. Two plans: **1)** Refundable entrance fee. 85% refund of entrance fee if resident decides to leave within first year; 5% per year amortization of this fee up to three years thereafter. After four years of residency the resident is guaranteed a 70% refund, regardless of length of stay. **2)** Refundable entrance fee that is lower with higher monthly payment.

Ownership and management: Owned and operated by Riley's, Inc. Opened in 1985.

Minimum age: 62 years.

Population: 81 residents; 73% women, 27% men, 53% couples.

Number of units: 82 Independent Living apartments; 40 Assisted Living rooms in the 224-bed health center.

Dining plan: Dinner and continental breakfast included. Private dining room and tray service available; catering; tray service during illness.

Services: *Included in the monthly fee:* Weekly housecleaning, flat-linen service, scheduled transportation, laundry facilities.

At additional cost: Beauty/barbershop.

Activities: Social director and certified fitness instructor. Library, card room, heated swimming pool, billiards, chapel, gym, arts and crafts center with kiln and painting studio, woodworking shop, aerobics classes, movies, ice-cream socials, bingo, whirlpool, aquatics program, Tai Chi programs approved by Arthritis Foundation and trips to theater, ballet, symphony, sporting and civic events, art galleries and museums.

Availability: Waiting list ($1,000 refundable application fee) for some accommodations.

Health services and rates: Medicare-certified physical therapy department. First 24 hours of health care are included.

- 40 Assisted Living units
  Studio $1,965/month
- 224-Bed health center

	Intermediate Nursing	*Skilled Nursing*
Semiprivate	$72/day	$77/day
Private	$88/day	$96/day

"Residents are free to set their own pace, develop new interests and pursue old hobbies, to come and go as they please. Woodland Heights is designed to provide gracious, secure, active living at surprisingly affordable rates."

INDEPENDENT LIVING HOUSING

Type/size of apartment	*Entrance fee 1/2*	*Monthly fee 1/2*
Studio, 413 sq. ft.	$41,900/41,900	$707/707
1-Bedroom, 601 sq. ft.	$59,700/55,700	$967/831
1-Bedroom, 653 sq. ft.	$60,700/56,700	$967/865
2-Bedroom, 901 sq. ft.	$89,500/80,000	$1,228/1,031
2-Bedroom, 958 sq. ft.	$95,400/88,900	$1,228/1,065
1-Bedroom, 1,072 sq. ft.	$116,800/108,900	$1,567/1,398
2-Bedroom, 1,254 sq. ft.	$126,500/118,300	$1,652/1,512
2-Bedroom, 1,660 sq. ft.	$176,700/165,000	$2,029/1,779

**For double occupancy add $210 to the monthly fee. All utilities except telephone included. Individually controlled heating and air-conditioning, 24-hour emergency call system, fully equipped kitchen, balcony, wallpaper, carpeting. Custom-designed and three-bedroom apartments available by combining two apartments.*

CALIFORNIA

ROSEWOOD

1301 New Stine Road
Bakersfield, CA 93309-3515
(805) 834-0620
J. Carolyn Gilliland, retirement counselor

Type of community: Nonprofit Continuing Care, modified contract

Accreditation: Continuing Care Accreditation Commission

Rosewood is centrally located on a beautifully landscaped 11-acre campus. Independent Living apartments are available in a nine-story high-rise or in two-story garden apartments. Assisted Living apartments are located on the second floor of the high-rise, and a 79-bed Skilled Nursing facility is adjacent. The grounds contain several rose gardens with lighted walkways. The facility is centrally located in Bakersfield with major medical facilities, shopping centers, churches, golf course, park nearby.

Financial plan: Entrance fee plus monthly fee. Entrance fee is refundable under certain conditions. Monthly fees for those moving in after age 85 will be slightly higher.

Ownership and management: Owned and managed by American Baptist Homes of the West, owner and manager of 17 retirement communities in Arizona, California, and Washington. Opened in 1974.

Minimum age: 62 years.

Population: 167 residents; 80% women, 20% men, 23 couples.

Number of units: 135 Independent Living apartments and 18 garden apartments; 17 Assisted Living apartments, 79 Skilled Nursing beds.

Dining plan: One meal per day included; other meals optional. Private dining room. Meals can be delivered to apartment in case of illness.

Services: *Included in the monthly fee:* Twice monthly housekeeping.

At additional cost: Extra housekeeping, laundry services, transportation, beauty/barbershop.

Activities: Full-time activities director. Game night, planned trips, movies, and dinner.

INDEPENDENT LIVING HOUSING

Type/size of unit	*Entrance fee**	*Monthly fee single/double*
Studio, 332–408 sq. ft.	$25,900–33,400	$1,153–1,207/NA
1-Bedroom, 634–740 sq. ft.	$60,900–63,000	$1,366–1,475/1,980–2,089
2-Bedroom, 1,065–1,150 sq. ft.	$92,000–94,900	$1,610–1,678/2,224–2,292

**For double occupancy in studio and 1-bedroom add 10% to the entrance fee. Wall-to-wall carpeting, fully equipped kitchen, individual temperature control, 24-hour emergency call system. High-rise apartments have balconies, garden apartments have patios.*

Availability: Waiting List. Studios have short wait; for one- and two-bedrooms there is a longer wait.

Health services and rates: Residents receive ten days per year in the health center free of charge. Long-term nursing-care insurance, emergency medical services, outpatient clinic, and payment of Medicare deductibles included in the monthly fee.

- 17 Assisted Living units
  Entrance fee — *Monthly fee*
  $27,900 — $2,137–2,111
- 79-Bed Skilled Nursing center
  $3,265–4,540/month

"At Rosewood, a family-like atmosphere is created by a staff that is caring and dedicated to the overall wellness of the residents."

RETIREMENT INN OF BURLINGAME

250 Myrtle Road
Burlingame, CA 94010
(415) 343-2747
Shakina Lea, administrator

Type of community: Independent Living with personal care services

Located near the San Francisco International Airport and 15 miles south of downtown San Francisco. This facility offers Independent Living, with personal care services available. Most residences in the four-story traditional-style building have a patio or balcony. Each floor has lounges and there is a terrace deck in front affords residents outdoor seating with a view of tree-lined streets of the suburban, residential neighborhood. The facility is within walking distance of shopping and across the street from the Burlingame Senior Center in Washington Park. Health care and hospital facilities are nearby.

Financial plan: Monthly rental fee (guaranteed for one year). No lease, no security deposit.

Ownership and management: American Retirement Villas, owner and manager of 26 retirement communities in California and one in Arizona. Opened in 1977.

Minimum age: None. SSI recipients accepted.

Population: 70 residents; 80% women, 20% men.

Number of units: 68 Independent Living apartments

Dining plan: Three meals a day, plus snacks, included. Tray service available. Special diets can be provided. Private dining room for entertaining.

Services: *Included in the monthly fee:* Personal laundry and flat-linen service, housekeeping, scheduled transportation.

At additional cost: Guest accommodations, beauty/barbershop, general store. Prospective residents are offered one-week stays on trial basis for small fee. Residents may join residents of other Retirement Inn communities for trips and to attend large events.

INDEPENDENT LIVING HOUSING

Type/size of apartment	*Monthly fee*
Standard studio, 204 sq. ft.	$1,375–1,975
Large studio, 240 sq. ft.	$1,475–2,075
1-Bedroom with kitchenette, 408 sq. ft.	$1,875–2,475

All utilities except telephone included. Individually controlled heating and air-conditioning, 24-hour emergency call system, basic cable. Many apartments have balconies or patios. Furnishings available at additional cost.

Activities: Activities program director. Exercise classes, films, bridge, sing-alongs, arts and crafts, scenic drives, field trips, bingo, billiards, dominos, reading club, poker, world culture, happy hour, live entertainment, current events, and many more.

Availability: Limited.

Health services and rates: Personal care program offers assistance with bathing, dressing and personal grooming, medication monitoring, escort service to meals. Respite care available. Rates vary with services provided.

"The Retirement Inn of Burlingame offers a warm, secure, and caring environment. It shows with our responsive staff of professionals, the design and planning of each residence, and in food, social activities, and extensive recreational amenities."

RETIREMENT INN OF CAMPBELL

290 North San Tomas Aquino Road
Campbell, CA 95008
(408) 378-2535
Mina Hassanzadeh, administrator

Type of community: Independent Living and Assisted Living

This is a two-story ranch-style building with semiprivate and private rooms, most with secluded patios or balconies. Common areas include a barbecue terrace, open outdoor courtyard, lounges, and television areas. Advantages include nearby city conveniences plus the serenity of a quiet residential neighborhood minutes away from churches, shops, service businesses, banks, and full medical and hospital facilities.

Financial plan: Monthly rental with rate guaranteed for one year. No lease.

Ownership and management: American Retirement Villas, owner and manager of 26 retirement communities in California and one in Arizona, with 20 years of experience. Opened in 1977.

Minimum age: 62 years.

Population: 90 residents; 70% women, 30% men.

Number of units: 72 Independent Living units.

Dining plan: Three meals per day plus snacks included. Private dining room. Occasional meals delivered if resident isn't feeling well.

Services: *Included in the monthly fee:* Housekeeping, personal laundry and flat-linen service, scheduled transportation.

At additional cost: Beauty/barbershop, general store.

Activities: Exercise, movies, continuing education classes, concerts, library, bookmobile, arts and crafts workshop, shuffleboard, poker party, cooking lessons, bingo, bridge, excursions, Bible study, sing-alongs.

INDEPENDENT LIVING HOUSING

Type/size of apartment	*Monthly fee single/double*
Studio, 187 sq. ft.	$1,335–1,375/1,700
Large room, 220 sq. ft.	$1,350–1,375/1,700
Semiprivate	N/A / $775–850

All utilities except telephone included. Furnishings are available. Individually controlled heating and air-conditioning, 24-hour emergency call system, carpeting, draperies, private baths, cable TV.

Availability: Limited.

Health services and rates: Two levels of personal care services (assistance with bathing, dressing, grooming, scheduled monitoring, personal companionship and escort service, etc.) available in resident's apartment. Respite care available for short periods of time, prorated on monthly fee.

- Level 1 (medication monitoring only) $1,625–1,675/month
  Level 2 (medication monitoring, plus care) $1,925–1,975/month

"If you're not sure if you're ready for a retirement residence, the Retirement Inn of Campbell offers one- and two-week trial stays: $100 for one week; $250 for two weeks, including our regular services."

CARMEL VALLEY MANOR

8545 Carmel Valley Road
Carmel, CA 93923
(408) 624-1281
Betty Welge, director of admissions

Type of community: Continuing Care, all-inclusive contract

Award-winning Mediterranean-style architecture in garden setting is surrounded by the rolling hills of the Monterey Peninsula. Located on 26 landscaped acres, the campus community is five miles from Carmel, famous for its artists, galleries, music, and literary life. Most buildings are single story, several are two story. Carmel has a year-round moderate climate.

Financial plan: Entrance fee plus monthly fee. On application a $1,000 refundable deposit is made, plus a $150 nonrefundable processing fee. If residents leave during the first three months, the entrance fee will be refunded in full, less the daily cost of care during the period of occupancy.

Ownership and management: Developed by Northern California Congregational Retirement Homes, Inc. Governed by board of directors responsible for hiring the executive director. Opened in 1962.

Minimum age: 65 years (if couple, spouse may be younger).

Population: 240 residents; 25% men; 75% women; 33% couples.

INDEPENDENT LIVING HOUSING

Type/size of apartment	*Entrance fee**	*Monthly fee**
Studio, 405 sq. ft.	$68,500	$1,445
Modified studio, 450 sq. ft.	$86,500	$1,499
1-Bedroom, 575 sq. ft.	$132,500 and up*	$1,552
Double studio, 810 sq. ft.	$178,500 and up*	$1,805
2-Bedroom/1-bath, 825 sq. ft.	$162,500 and up*	$2,177
2-Bedroom/2-bath, 875 sq. ft.	$251,500 and up	$2,956
2-Bedroom conversion, 1,120 sq. ft.	$353,000	$3,193
Cottage, 1,035 sq. ft.	$280,000–343,000 and up	$3,090–3,215

**For double occupancy in the double studio and 1-bedrooms add $30,000 to the entrance fee and $727–$1,085 to the monthly fee. All utilities except long-distance calls and cable TV included. Wall-to-wall carpeting, draperies and casement curtains, cable connection, fully equipped kitchen, private patios or lanai-balconies, individually controlled heating. Cottages have carports.*

Number of units: 161 Independent Living apartments and cottages; 24 Personal Care beds, 29 Skilled Nursing beds.

Dining plan: Three meals per day included. Private dining room and parlor for private parties. Catering for personal parties.

Services: *Included in the monthly fee:* Weekly housecleaning and flat-linen services, limousine transportation to Carmel and Monterey, porter service, self-service laundries.

At additional cost: Laundry and dry cleaning pickup and delivery, beauty/barbershop, daily newspaper delivery, guest accommodations, group rates for personal property insurance, carports, shopping corner operated by residents.

Activities: Swimming pool, spa, game and recreation areas, craft rooms, library, gardening, card and billiards room, group travel trips arranged for special events and scenic excursions, golf, shuffleboard, croquet, lawn bowling.

Availability: Waiting list, except for studios.

Health services and rates: No additional charges for home health care or Skilled Nursing. Should residents transfer to Personal Care or Skilled Nursing permanently they will give up their apartment, but continue to pay the same monthly fee. Therapy treatment provided. Acute care hospitalization and surgery. Four levels of health care: home health care for short-term minor illness, personal care, Skilled Nursing, and Community Hospital with which the facility has a transfer policy for the acutely ill.

- 24-Bed personal care facility
- 29-Bed Skilled Nursing facility

"The mission of Carmel Valley Manor is to provide comprehensive support and an environment that enhances residents' well-being and peace of mind."

ESKATON VILLAGE

3839 Walnut Avenue
Carmichael, CA 95608
(916) 974-2000
Myrna Smith, membership services director

Type of community: Continuing Care, modified contract

Award-winning three-story California stucco apartment building and separate cottages stand on 37-acre campus with walking paths throughout landscaped grounds and rose and vegetable gardens maintained by residents. American River Hospital is nearby. It is in a central location in a quiet residential neighborhood with a small lake and lies two hours from mountains, San Francisco, and ocean.

Financial plan: Entrance fee plus monthly fee. Entrance fee 90% refundable at any time as well as 50% of the appreciation value of the unit; 20% deposit refundable, less $500.

Ownership and management: Managed by Eskaton. Opened in 1992.

Minimum age: 62 years.

Population: 340 residents; 50% women, 50% men, 50% couples.

Number of units: 283 Independent Living apartments; 36 Assisted Living units, 30 Skilled Nursing beds.

Dining plan: Three meals per day included. Private dining rooms available for special occasions.

Services: *Included in the monthly fee:* Weekly housecleaning and flat-linen service, scheduled transportation.

At additional cost: Beauty/barbershop, ice cream and soda shop, reserved transportation.

INDEPENDENT LIVING HOUSING

Type/size of apartments	*Entrance fee*	*Monthly fee**
1-Bedroom, 700 sq. ft.	$87,000–102,000	$1,350–1,450
2-Bedroom, 1,024 sq. ft.	$120,000–218,000	$1,550–1,950
2-Bedroom/den, 1,500 sq. ft.	$240,500	$2,585
Cottages		
1-Bedroom, 1,038 sq. ft.	$150,000–155,000	$1,700
2-Bedroom, 1,282 sq. ft.	$159,000–172,000	$1,850
3-bedroom, 1,569 sq. ft.	$251,000–265,000	$2,000

**For double occupancy add $450 to the monthly fee. All utilities, except telephone, included. Fully equipped kitchens, French doors and windows, patio or balcony, individually controlled heating and air-conditioning, 24-hour emergency call system.*

Activities: Full-time activities coordinator. Multipurpose room for special events and meetings, swimming pool, spa, putting green, lawn bowling court, croquet, walking paths, tennis, golf, shuffleboard, card and billiards rooms, music room with grand piano, several exercise studios, business center, library, painting and craft studios, club rooms, media room with big-screen TV, woodworking shop, dances, live entertainment, educational classes, travel excursions.

Availability: Limited; $2,500 places you on waiting list and is applicable toward entrance fee ($2,000 is refundable should you elect not to move in).

Health services and rates: Home health care and Assisted Living offered. Village health office offers rooms for visiting physicians. Prospective Resident Coverage covers one for nursing home stays prior to becoming a resident.

- 36 Assisted Living suites
  - Studio — $1,950/month
  - 1-Bedroom — $2,300/month
- 30-Bed health center
  - Semiprivate — $113/day
  - Private — $145/day

"The primary mission of Eskaton, whose name is derived from the Greek word meaning 'the beginning of a new age' is to enhance the quality of life of seniors through innovative health, housing, and social services."

THE FORUM AT RANCHO SAN ANTONIO

23500 Cristo Rey Drive
Cupertino, CA 95104
(415) 969-0600
Linda Purucker, director of marketing

Type of community: Nonprofit Continuing Care with equity, all-inclusive contract

California Mission-inspired architecture marks the five stucco and red-tiled residential buildings terraced into the contours of the 55-acre site. Spectacular views of the surrounding mountain ridges are available from the buildings, which are linked with covered arcades. Sixty 2-bedroom villas are spread around the perimeter of the community, as are hundreds of acres of parkland and nature preserve. Assisted Living and Intermediate and Skilled Nursing are available. Cupertino is 40 miles from San Francisco.

Financial plan: Membership fee plus monthly fee. The membership fee, which provides equity in the community, is fully refundable; $500 application fee. Should long-term health care become necessary, The Forum at Rancho San Antonio will assist in the sale of resident's membership and provide health care for as long needed at a fee not exceeding the fee for the least expensive one-bedroom. Upon sale, resident receives 100% of the equity and 50% of the appreciation value.

Ownership and management: Solely owned by residents. Managed by The Forum Group, Inc., owner and manager of 27 retirement communities in the United States. Opened in 1991.

Minimum age: 62 years.

Population: 400 residents.

Number of units: 259 Independent Living apartments and 60 villas; 34 Assisted Living units, 48 Skilled Nursing beds.

Dining plan: Thirty meals a month per person included. Private dining room available at no charge.

Services: *Included in the monthly fee:* Weekly housekeeping and flat-linen services, transportation, parking.

At additional cost: Transportation to private appointments or airport, Forum Ambassador Service for assistance with packages or errands, country store.

Activities: Full-time program director. Swimming pool, sauna, Jacuzzi, library, arts and crafts rooms, woodworking room, multipurpose room. Health and fitness classes, exercise room, guest lectures, movies, bridge and other games, trips to area cultural and sporting events and group tours, college-level adult studies programs.

Availability: Limited.

Health services and rates: Unlimited Assisted Living and Skilled Nursing are included in the monthly fee. Residents receive emergency call button (weighing less than one ounce) which can be worn and carried throughout the community.

- 34 Assisted Living units arranged around central landscaped courtyard with dining room and activity rooms.
- 48-Bed Skilled Nursing facility

"Life care plan with equity enables active retirees to ensure unlimited long-term nursing care and preserve their assets. The Forum at Rancho San Antonio is the only cooperative organization in the state offering this type of plan."

INDEPENDENT LIVING HOUSING

Type/size of apartment	*Membership fee*	*Monthly fee**
1-Bedroom, 720–800 sq. ft.	$199,000–295,000	$1,287–1,390
1-Bedroom, den, 950 sq. ft.	$355,500–380,000	$1,593
2-Bedroom, 1,020–1,260 sq. ft.	$388,000–520,500	$1,787–2,102
2-Bedroom villa, 1,280 sq. ft.	$555,000–595,000	$2,102
2-Bedroom deluxe villa, 1,404 sq. ft.	$640,000	$2,612

**For double occupancy add $529 to the monthly fee. All utilities except telephone included. Fully equipped, all-electric kitchens, microwave ovens, washer/dryer, plush carpeting, individual temperature control. All villas and most top floor apartments have fireplaces, high ceilings, and electric garage door openers.*

DIABLO LODGE

950 Diablo Road
Danville, CA 94526
(510) 838-8300
Carolyn Rosenbusch, marketing manager

Type of community: Independent Living with Assisted Care

Private apartments are located in the wooded foothills of Mount Diablo with Green Valley Creek running in back and a horse ranch lined with oak trees across the way. Award-winning architecture and interior design feature a landscaped walkway around the perimeter and a fountain with benches. Some apartments have a garden view and patio. Outdoor fountain provides view of Mount Diablo. Danville, Alamo, San Ramon, Contra Costa County are all nearby.

Financial plan: Monthly fee.

Ownership and management: Family-owned-and-operated management company. Resident councils have input into many aspects of the community life. Opened in 1990.

Minimum age: 62 years.

Population: 100 residents; 65% women, 35% men, 8% couples.

Number of units: 118 Independent Living apartments.

Dining plan: Three meals daily included. Private dining room.

Services: *Included in the monthly fee:* Weekly housecleaning, flat-linen service, laundry, scheduled transportation, parking.

At additional cost: Beauty/barbershop, gift shop, general store.

Activities: Full-time social director. Day trips, educational courses, arts and crafts, gardening, exercise room, discussion groups, reading courses, ballroom dancing, evening entertainment, shopping trips, card games, men's club.

Availability: Waiting list for some apartments.

Health services and rates: Three levels of care available to residents in their apartments on daily or monthly rate.

- Level 1 : basic assistance in personal and nursing care on occasional basis, along with monitoring of medications if needed. $8.35/day; $250/month
- Level 2 : designed to meet the needs of residents needing a higher level of care or closer supervision. $13.35/day; $400/month
- Level 3 : daily personal care services needed due to recovery from an illness, increasing frailty, confusion, anxiety, or depression. $26.67/day; $800/month

"Diablo Lodge is a place where seniors can feel independent and preserve their dignity, a place to be part of a lively community and still receive personal assistance."

INDEPENDENT LIVING HOUSING

Type/size of unit	*Monthly fee**
Studio, 385 sq. ft.	$1,595–1,945
1-Bedroom, 580 sq. ft.	$1,895–2,195
2-Bedroom, 700 sq. ft.	$2,595–2,795

For double occupancy add $385 to the monthly fee. All utilities included. Patios or deck, greenhouse window, wall-to-wall carpeting, 24-hour emergency call system, individual heating and air-conditioning, cable TV, kitchenettes. Rental furniture available.

ROYAL OAKS MANOR

1763 Royal Oaks Drive
Duarte, CA 91010
(818) 359-9371
Shirley Douglas, marketing director

Type of community: Nonprofit Continuing Care, modified contract

Accreditation: Continuing Care Accreditation Commission

Located in a secluded setting at the foot of the San Gabriel Mountains, once the site of the historic Bradbury Estate, the community is set on 18.5 acres and reflects its early California heritage. Grounds include walking trails that lead through acres of majestic oaks, a private pond, and an enclosed courtyard with birdbaths and comfortable seating areas. Royal Oaks Manor is ten miles from Pasadena, close to cultural events, professional services, and shopping areas. Independent Living, Assisted Living, and Skilled Nursing are available on campus.

Financial plan: Entrance fee plus monthly fee.

Ownership and management: Southern California Presbyterian Homes, owner/manager of 13 retirement communities in Southern California, with 35 years experience. Opened in 1959.

Minimum age: 62 years.

Population: 176 residents; 80% women, 20% men, 30% couples.

Number of units: 166 Independent Living apartments; 24 personal care rooms, five-bed short-term stay infirmary, 48-bed Skilled Nursing facility.

Dining plan: Three meals per day included in the monthly fee.

Services: *Included in the monthly fee:* Biweekly housekeeping, transportation, use of laundry facilities.

At additional cost: Beauty/barbershop, sundries store, limousine service, personal laundry service.

Activities: Guest lectures, concerts, arts and crafts, exercise groups, croquet court, billiards room, woodworking shop, lapidary, weaving, ceramics, gardening, trips, darkroom, library, greenhouse.

Availability: Some apartments available.

Health services and rates: A new state-of-the-art, two-story health center opened in Fall 1991.

- 5-Bed infirmary for short-term care
  Private room $40/day

INDEPENDENT LIVING HOUSING

Type/size of unit	*Entrance fee*	*Monthly fee*
Single, 333 sq. ft.	$39,000–45,000	$935
Alcove, 378 sq. ft.	$44,000–51,500	$1,120
1-Bedroom, 565 sq. ft.	$52,000–66,700	$1,560*
2 Alcoves comb., 756 sq. ft.	$91,500–103,500	$1,915*
1-Bedroom/studio comb., 898 sq. ft.	$105,000–115,000	$1,915*
2-Bedroom, 1,040 sq. ft.	$109,500–132,000	$2,170*
2-Bedroom cottage, 1,040 sq. ft.	$156,000–185,000	$2,170*

**For double occupancy add $310 to the monthly fee. All utilities except telephone included. Wall-to-wall carpeting, draperies, individually controlled heating and air-conditioning, 24-hour emergency call system. Many apartments have balconies or patios and some have individual gardens.*

- 24 Assisted Living rooms
  Private room and bath $1,960/month
- 48 Skilled Nursing beds
  Semiprivate $64/day
  Private $135/day

"Royal Oaks Manor is a community of people from different backgrounds with various skills and interests who have chosen a way of life that allows them freedom and independence while providing them with security and many amenities."

REDWOOD TERRACE

710 West Thirteenth Avenue
Escondido, CA 92025-5599
(619) 747-7751 or (800) 842-6775
Susan Strassburger, director of marketing

Type of communtiy: Not-for-profit Continuing Care, modified contract

Accreditation: Continuing Care Accreditation Commission

The facility consists of single-level cottages and a two-story Independent Living building surrounded by pines and lawns in a residential setting. There are walking paths and grounds for strolling. Residential, Assisted Living, and Skilled Nursing are available on campus, which is 30 minutes north of San Diego. North County Fair Shopping Center, The Wild Animal Park, Lawrence Welk Resort Village performances, restaurants, medical facilities, and supermarkets are all nearby.

Financial plan: Entrance fee plus monthly fee. Monthly rental option for Assisted Living.

Ownership and management: Owned by the Redwood Terrace Lutheran Home. Managed by a 15-member board of directors made up of volunteers. Affiliated with Redwood Senior Services. Opened in 1978.

Minimum age: 60 years.

Population: 202 residents; 75% women, 25% men, 16% couples.

Number of units: 30 Independent Living cottages and 94 apartments; 34 Assisted Living apartments, 59 Skilled Nursing beds.

Dining plan: Resident's choice of one meal per day included. Tray service when approved by nursing staff.

Services: *Included in the monthly fee:* Weekly housekeeping and flat-linen services, personal laundry facilities, scheduled transportation, garage parking.

At additional cost: Beauty/barbershop.

Activities: Full-time resident activity director and social director. Discussion classes, card games,

INDEPENDENT LIVING HOUSING

Type/size of unit	*Entrance fee**	*Monthly fee**
Studio, 326–336 sq. ft.	$38,000–42,000	$867–978
1-Bedroom, 416–600 sq. ft.	$47,000–69,000	$1,004–1,146
1-Bedroom, 784 sq. ft.	$85,000	$1,303
2-Bedroom, 1,079–1,176 sq. ft.	$111,000–116,000	$1,576
2-Bedroom deluxe, 1,445 sq. ft.	$142,000	$2,217

**For double occupancy add $15,000 to the entrance fee and $440 to the monthly fee. All utilities except telephone and cable TV included. Patio or balcony, 24-hour emergency call system, wall-to-wall carpeting, cable TV, individually controlled heating and air-conditioning, fully equipped kitchen.*

library, hydrotherapy spa, craft room, workshop center, exercise room, billiards, various outings, kiln, bridge room, chapel.

Availability: Limited, depending on type of unit preferred.

Health services and rates: Social service director, resident/family council, pastoral program, and full-time chaplain all available. Physical and occupational therapy facilities. Primary nurse makes an initial assessment and develops an individualized care plan based upon the resident's medical diagnosis and prescribed regime of care.

- 24 Assisted Living apartments

	*Monthly fee (nonresidents)**
Studio, 300 sq. ft.	$1,908
Alcove, 486 sq. ft.	$2,279
2-Room suite, 600–612 sq. ft.	$2,650

**For double occupancy add $505 to the monthly fee.*

- 59 Skilled Nursing beds: $60/day

"Redwood Terrace operates on the theme of caring for all its residents in a Christian environment (although not associated with any denomination). Its mission is to provide quality retirement housing and health care to people 60 years of age and older in a secure, caring, and aesthetic environment."

SAN JOAQUIN GARDENS

5555 North Fresno Street
Fresno, CA 93710
(209) 439-4770
Robin Bushell, marketing director

Type of community: Not-for-profit Continuing Care, modified contract

Accreditation: Continuing Care Accreditation Commission

This 26-acre park-like campus in northern part of Fresno with gardens throughout and wide well-lit walkways offers Independent Living apartments, Assisted Living and Skilled Nursing facilities. Most buildings are one-story, garden-style apartments designed in California-ranch architecture style. Two-story Orchard apartments have elevators. The facility is conveniently situated near major medical facilities, shopping centers, churches, and other services.

Financial plan: Entrance fee plus monthly fee. Entrance fee is fully refundable if resident chooses to leave during the first 90 days. After 90 days, the fee amortizes at 1.5% per month.

Ownership and management: Owned and managed by American Baptist Homes of the West, owner/manager of 17 retirement communities in California, Washington, and Arizona. Opened in 1966.

Minimum age: 62 years.

INDEPENDENT LIVING HOUSING

Type/size of apartment	*Entrance fee*	*Monthly fee**
Evergreen, 500–912 sq. ft.	$53,295–93,705	$963–1,700
1-Bedroom, 562–913 sq. ft.	$60,741–96,255	$1,052–1,721
The Orchard, 727–1,007 sq. ft.	$71,100–102,022	$1,081–1,817
Amber/Myrtle, 710–1,250 sq. ft.	$79,902–115,403	$1,082–1,950
2-Bedroom, 765–1,258 sq. ft.	$81,957–115,403	$1,165–1,950

**Prices reflect smallest apartment for one person to largest apartment for two. All utilities except telephone and cable TV included in the monthly fee. Individually controlled heating and air-conditioning, 24-hour emergency call system, wall-to-wall carpeting, fully equipped kitchens.*

Population: 360 residents; 80% women, 20% men, 20% couples.

Number of units: 200 Independent Living apartments; 55 Assisted Living units, 88-bed health center.

Dining plan: One meal per day included in the monthly fee. Tray service available upon request.

Services: *Included in the monthly fee:* Scheduled transportation, monthly housekeeping.

At additional cost: Weekly housekeeping, carports, beauty/barbershop, guest accommodations.

Activities: Gardening, exercise classes, bingo, plays, concerts, day and longer trips, exercise classes, bridge, special programs, guest speakers.

Availability: Limited.

Health services and rates: Residents receive 10 days of health care per year at no cost. Physical, occupational, speech therapies.

- 55 Assisted Living units — $1,395–3,139/month
- 88-Bed health center
  - Semiprivate — $3,632/month
  - Private — $4,259/month

"San Joaquin Gardens is the only Continuing Care retirement community in the Fresno area. Residents tell us it feels more like home, with room for their own gardens as well as the lovely landscaping. After 27 years we have built a reputation for providing quality, professional, personal care to our residents and their families."

MORNINGSIDE OF FULLERTON

800 East Bastanchury Road
Fullerton, CA 92635
(714) 529-2952 in state or (800) 499-6010
Bill Wilmoth, assistant marketing director

Type of community: Continuing Care, all-inclusive contract

Three-, four-, and five-story Mediterranean-style Independent Living apartment buildings and separate one-level villas are located on a 41-acre park-like campus with rose garden, small lake, and walkways and bike trail. St. Jude's Hospital is next door. Personal care and Skilled Nursing facilities are on site. Fullerton Arboretum (26-acre park), Heritage House Museum, Fullerton Civic Light Opera, 41 churches, and four colleges and universities are all nearby. Anaheim Stadium, Crystal Cathedral (Garden Grove), Disneyland, Knott's Berry Farm, and Orange County Performing Arts Center are within a 15-minute drive. Orange County, Los Angeles, and Long Beach airports are within hour's drive. Fullerton has 46 parks.

Financial plan: Entrance fee plus monthly fee. Entrance fee refundable up to 100% and no less than 75% (5% per year amortization up to five years).

Ownership and management: Joint venture owned by CoreCare, a group of local residents and physicians, and Spieker Partners, a real estate company. Managed by Life Care Services, manager of 50 retirement communities across the United States. Opened in 1991.

Minimum age: 62 years.

Population: 340 residents; 65% women, 35% men, 50% couples.

Number of units: 330 Independent Living apartments and villas; 54 units for personal care, 99-bed Skilled Nursing facility.

Dining plan: One meal per day included in the monthly fee. Special diets available. Private dining room. Cocktail lounge.

Services and amenities: *Included in the monthly fee:* Biweekly housekeeping, weekly flat-linen service, scheduled transportation.

At additional cost: Beauty/barbershop, guest accommodations.

INDEPENDENT LIVING HOUSING

Type/size of unit	*Entrance fee*	*Monthly fee**
Studio, 410 sq. ft.	$97,950	$1,226
1-Bedroom, 620–870 sq. ft.	$142,950–204,950	$1,408–1,721
2-Bedroom, 963–1,340 sq. ft.	$216,950–292,950	$1,747–2,070
3-Bedroom, 1,643 sq. ft.	$348,950	$2,346
Villas		
2-Bedroom, 1,576 sq. ft.	$301,950	$2,268
3-Bedroom, 1,831 sq. ft.	$342,950–372,950	$2,450

**For double occupancy add $700 to the monthly fee. All utilities except telephone included. Fully equipped kitchens, 24-hour emergency call system, wall-to-wall carpeting, cable TV (optional), individually controlled heating and air-conditioning.*

Activities: Full-time activities director. Library, arts and crafts, 260-seat auditorium, concerts, parties, lectures, guest speakers, Morningside cable TV channel, gardening, bike trail, game room, health club with weight room, exercise classes, hot whirlpool spa, swimming pool, putting green, croquet court, horseshoe area, Continuing Learning Experience and Distinguished Lecture series at California State University, Friends of Music Sunday concert series, outdoor theater at Muckenthaler Cultural Center, summer concert series at Hunt branch library.

Availability: No waiting list at present.

Health services and rates: Unlimited health care, Assisted Living, and Skilled Nursing included in the resident's monthly fee. The only additional charge is for the two extra meals. Private wing of health center devoted to care of those with Alzheimer's disease.

- 54-Unit Assisted Living
- 99-Bed Skilled Nursing facility with 24 Alzheimer's beds

"Carefully designed for privacy and comfort, Morningside's Continuing Care program is the choice of those who want a luxurious lifestyle as well as protection for their health and finances."

THE TAMALPAIS

501 Via Casitas
Greenbrae, CA 94904
(415) 461-2300
Nancy E. Martin, director of admissions

Type of community: Not-for-profit Continuing Care, all-inclusive contract

Accreditation: Continuing Care Accreditation Commission

Offering some of the prettiest views in the San Francisco Bay Area, this high-rise life care community is located on the crest of a six-acre wooded knoll in the heart of Marin County. Panoramic vistas show Mt. Tamalpais and the nearby San Francisco Bay. Outside walkways feature gardens and decks. Full range of health care services offered. Within one-half mile are a full-service shopping center, the College of Marin, Marin General Hospital, and extensive hiking/biking trails.

Financial plan: Entrance fee plus monthly fee. $1,200 waiting list deposit per person is refundable or applicable to entrance fee. $300 per person nonrefundable processing fee.

Ownership and management: Northern California Presbyterian Homes, Inc., owner and manager of three other life care communities in the Bay Area. Opened in 1969.

INDEPENDENT LIVING HOUSING

Type/size of apartment	*Entrance fee*	*Monthly fee*
Studio, 425–525 sq. ft.	$43,000–69,300	$1,263–1,347
Alcove, 645 sq. ft.	$90,000–108,000	$1,443–1,460
1-Bedroom, 700–780 sq. ft.	$101,600–139,300*	$1,508–1,587*
2-Bedroom, 1,100–1,300 sq. ft.	$231,800–262,900**	$2,483–2,785**

**For double occupancy add $20,000 to the entrance fee and $896 to the monthly fee. **Fees listed are for double occupancy. All utilities except telephone included. Carpeting, drapes, 24-hour emergency call system, individually controlled heating and air-conditioning, fully equipped kitchens, balcony or deck.*

Minimum age: 65 years. Applicants must apply for residency by age of 80 for studio, alcove, and one-bedroom apartments; by age 76 for waiting list application for two-bedroom apartments.

Population: 338 residents; 76% women, 24% men, 33% couples.

Number of units: 276 Independent Living apartments; 11 Assisted Living apartments, 52 Skilled Nursing beds.

Dining plan: Three meals per day are included in the monthly fee. Circular dining room has floor-to-ceiling windows. Buffet options for breakfast and lunch. Modified menu plans for those with special dietary considerations. Catering service for private parties.

Services: *Included in the monthly fee:* Housekeeping and flat-linen service, van service.

At additional cost: Two beauty shops, gift shop, valet parking.

Activities: New indoor/outdoor swimming pool, college courses from nearby College of Marin's Emeritus Program offered on-site, gardening, woodworking shop, exercise room, billiards, weaving, croquet, shuffleboard, miniature putting green, badminton, table tennis, aerobics, Tai Chi classes.

Availability: Waiting list depends on size of apartment.

Health services and rates: Residents receive lifetime access to nursing care when necessary, including temporary and home health care, Assisted Care, Skilled Nursing, and hospitalization at no additional cost. Registered nurses on duty 24 hours a day.

- 11 Assisted Care apartments
- 52-Bed Skilled Nursing facility

"The Tamalpais is Marin's only accredited Continuing Care community. Each Northern California Presbyterian Home retirement community maintains high standards of living and is continually enhanced and modernized to accommodate changing requirements. All are administered by caring professionals who see to it that every resident feels a complete sense of independence, security, and belonging."

THE VILLAGE

2200 West Acacia
Hemet, CA 92343
(909) 658-3369
Janet Adams, director of marketing

Type of community: Continuing Care, modified contract

Accreditation: Continuing Care Accreditation Commission

Set on 14 acres, this resort-like community features a separate health center, mountain views, lush gardens and landscaping, and a central four-story building designed to meet the most recent earthquake standards. Mt. San Jacinto Community College is nearby and shopping is within walking distance.

Financial plan: Entrance payment plus monthly fee. Two plans: **1)** 50% refundable. **2)** If you pay 150% of entrance fee, 100% of entrance fee is refundable. Low monthly rates are guaranteed and can only be raised with the approval of the state of California. All entrance payments are placed in an escrow account and transferred to a master trust agreement. The trust will use these entrance fees to pay off the construction loan and will hold the deed on the community. Each resident is a member of the trust.

Ownership and management: Owned by Freedom Properties. Operated by Freedom Group, operators of five other continuing care communities in Florida, California, Arizona, and Michigan. Opened in 1974.

Minimum age: 60 years.

Population: 330 residents; 23% couples.

Number of Units: 276 Independent Living apartments; 52 Assisted Living units, 54 Skilled Nursing beds.

Dining plan: One main meal included. Coffee shop. Private dining room.

Services: *Included in the monthly fee:* Weekly maid and flat-linen service, covered parking space, scheduled transportation.

At additional cost: Bank, beauty/barbershop, guest accommodations.

Activities: Activities director. Arts and crafts, book reviews, dancing, horseshoes, croquet, shuffleboard, exercise, yoga, water therapy, swimming pool, sing-alongs, birdwatching, travel club, films, cards, billiards, gardening, spa.

Availability: Waiting list.

Health services and rates: Residents receive 360 free nonconsecutive days of nursing care during their stay; 22 days a year. If these days are exceeded, residents pay fees listed below.

- Assisted Living units

Private room	$1,860/month
Suite	$2,250/month

For double occupancy add $450 to the monthly fee.

- Skilled Nursing beds

Semiprivate room	$79/day

"The Village has no long-term mortgage debt to service or be concerned about because of how entrance fees are handled."

INDEPENDENT LIVING HOUSING

Type/size of apartment	*Entrance fee*	*Monthly fee single/double*
Studio	$45,000–51,500	$730
1-Bedroom	$74,500–83,500	$919/1,265
2-Bedroom	$80,500–108,500	$1,024/1,370
Deluxe 2-bedroom	$105,000–118,000	$1,097/1,444

All utilities except telephone included. Fully equipped kitchen, carpeting, draperies, individually controlled heating and air-conditioning, 24-hour emergency call system. Decorator package: choice of carpeting color and wallpaper in kitchen and baths.

REGENTS POINT

19191 Harvard Avenue
Irvine, CA 92715
(714) 854-9500
Jeannette Baker, director of marketing

Type of community: Nonprofit Continuing Care, modified contract

Accreditation: Continuing Care Accreditation Commission

This resort-style community set on 15 acres has four-story Independent Living apartments with balconies and villas with patios on landscaped grounds overlooking a park and lake, plus the San Joaquin hills. Assisted Living units and Skilled Nursing beds on campus. Newport Beach Marina is minutes away.

Financial plan: Entrance fee plus monthly fee; $1,000 application fee.

Ownership and management: Southern California Presbyterian Homes, with 38 years experience, is owner and manager of 13 other communities in Southern California. Opened in 1982.

Minimum age: 62 years.

Population: 395 residents; 72 couples.

Number of units: 250 Independent Living apartments; 60 Assisted Living units, 59-bed Skilled Nursing facility.

Dining plan: One meal is included in the monthly fee. Additional meals available at cost. Special luncheon and dinner parties. Catering services available. For private parties lounges can be reserved.

Services: *Included in the monthly fee:* Twice-monthly housekeeping, scheduled transportation, launderettes.

At additional cost: Beauty/barbershop, sidewalk café, guest accommodations.

INDEPENDENT LIVING HOUSING

Type/size of apartment	*Entrance fee*	*Monthly fee single/double*
Semisuite, 462 sq. ft.	$40,900–58,800	$1,015
1-Bedroom, 557 sq. ft.	$82,400–106,000	$1,140/1,650
2-Bedroom, 848 sq. ft.	$176,400–211,600	$1,800/1,930
Combination apartments and villas		
1-Bedroom villa, 584 sq. ft.	$94,000–111,800	$1,180/1,690
2 Semisuites, 924 sq. ft.	$135,400–183,700	$1,800/1,930
Large 1-bedroom villa, 743 sq. ft.	$135,400–141,700	$1,280/1,790
Semisuite/1-bedroom, 1,019 sq. ft.	$176,400–205,800	$1,810/1,940
2 1-Bedroom apartments, 1,114 sq. ft.	$205,800–231,000	$1,820/1,950
2-Bedroom villa, 966 sq. ft.	$229,400–309,700	$1,810/1,940
2 1-Bedroom villas, 1,168 sq. ft.	$258,000–278,200	$2,120/2,250

All utilities except telephone included in the monthly fee. Individually controlled thermostats, 24-hour emergency call system, cable TV hookup, fully equipped kitchens.

Activities: Exercise classes, swimming pool, lawn bowling, putting green, card games, hobbies, local plays and concerts.

Availability: Limited.

Health services and rates: On-site infirmary and emergency care clinic. Independent Living residents are given five free days of care per year in the Skilled Nursing facility (accumulated up to a maximum of 15). On-site dental, X-ray services, laboratory, physician facilities, rehabilitation program (occupational, physical, speech therapies), ophthalmology, century tub and whirlpool. Full-time program coordinator. Activities room. Wheelchair-equipped van.

- 60 Assisted Living rooms with patios and gardens.

Small room*	$2,155/month
Medium room	$2,480/month
Large room	$2,525/month

**Nonresidents can be admitted to small Assisted Living rooms for $3,080 per month. Medium and large rooms are reserved for residents.*

- 59-Bed Skilled Nursing facility (winner of the Robert Thornblad Long-Term Care Facility of the Year Award in 1989).

Semiprivate*	$103/day
Private	$152/day

**Nonresidents can be admitted to semiprivate Skilled Nursing rooms for $131 per day. Private rooms are reserved for residents.*

"Residents of Regents Point are interesting people who want to continue living interesting, independent lives. The atmosphere is exceptional, from the tasteful apartments and villas on our landscaped grounds to the view of the lake next door. Within our resort-style community, it's easy to find the niche that best suits you."

MARRIOTT VILLA VALENCIA

24552 Paseo de Valencia
Laguna Hills, CA 92653
(714) 837-2200
Nancy Hudson, director of marketing

Type of community: Continuing Care, modified contract

The seven-story modern building with two wings off of central lobby and dining rooms is surrounded by landscaped grounds, walkways, and a rose garden, providing garden and mountain views. It is located a short walk from the Laguna Hills mall, 10 miles to John Wayne Airport, 15 minutes from the ocean, 15 miles to Orange County Performing Arts Center and South Coast Plaza.

Financial plan: Monthly rental.

Ownership and management: Owned and managed by Marriott Senior Living Services, a wholly owned subsidiary of Marriott Corporation, which owns and operates 13 retirement communities in Arizona, California, Florida, Illinois, Indiana, Maryland, New York, Pennsylvania, Texas, and Virginia. Opened in 1975.

Minimum age: 65 years (if couple, spouse may be younger).

Population: 375+ residents.

Number of units: 245 Independent Living apartments; 99 Assisted Living apartments, 50 Skilled Nursing beds.

Dining plan: Two meals included in the monthly fee. Private dining room. Party-planning assistance.

INDEPENDENT LIVING HOUSING

Type/size of apartment	*Monthly fee*
Studio, 432 sq. ft.	$1,470
1-Bedroom, 864–899 sq. ft.	$2,225*
1-Bedroom/den, 950 sq. ft.	$2,700*
2-Bedroom, 1,296 sq. ft.	$3,400*

**For double occupancy add $350 to the monthly fee. All utilities except telephone included. Sliding glass doors, full-length drapes, color-coordinated wall-to-wall carpeting, large closets, individually controlled zone heating and air-conditioning, 24-hour emergency call system and intercom, satellite television, telephone jacks. Kitchenettes optional.*

Services: *Included in the monthly fee:* Weekly housekeeping, all linens, private bus transportation, parking.

At additional cost: Beauty/barbershop, guest accommodations.

Activities: Swimming pool, putting green, bingo/game/card room, table tennis, exercise facilities, line dancing, shuffleboard, theater and seminar room, weekly movies and special events. Nearby Saddleback College provides selection of specially prepared classes.

Availability: Limited.

Health services and rates: Recreational program provided by professional therapists (physical, respiratory, occupational). Social services also available for residents and their families. Respite care (postoperative) and vacation stays provided if rooms are available.

- 99 Assisted Living apartments
  Studio, 432 sq. ft. $1,995/month
  1-Bedroom, 864–899 sq. ft. $2,995*/month

  **For double occupancy add $500 to monthly fee.*

- 59-Bed Skilled Nursing facility
  Semiprivate $142/day
  Private $160/day

"At Villa Valencia, residents enjoy all the benefits of living in and contributing to a caring community, fostering a life of the mind with a sense of purpose. Service is more than just a business philosophy, it's been a Marriott tradition for over 60 years. And all that we've learned is applied to satisfy the needs of older adults living in our retirement communities."

THE WHITE SANDS OF LA JOLLA

7450 Olivetas Avenue
La Jolla, CA 92037
(619) 454-4201 or (800) 892-7817
Sandra Lesar, director of marketing

Type of Community: Nonprofit Continuing Care, modified contract

Accreditation: Continuing Care Accreditation Commission

This three-story Pacific oceanfront community is located within walking distance of La Jolla Village and offers direct access to the beach. It is close to cultural events, professional and community services, educational opportunities, and shopping. Offered are Independent Living, personal care, and Skilled Nursing.

Financial plan: Entrance fee plus monthly fee. Refundable $1,000 deposit required for waiting list.

INDEPENDENT LIVING HOUSING

Type/size of apartment	*Entrance fee*	*Monthly fee**
Single, 378 sq. ft.	$35,900–85,000	$1,100
Semisuite, 756 sq. ft.	$85,000–116,500	$1,380
Suite, 640 sq. ft.	$81,500–145,000	$1,930
Double, 770 sq. ft.	$79,000–170,000	$1,985–2,040
2-Bedroom	$125,500–500,000	$2,150–2,205

**For double occupancy add $475 to the monthly fee. All utilities except telephone included. Individually controlled heating, 24-hour emergency call system, color-coordinated decor with carpeting, painting, draperies.*

Ownership and management: Southern California Presbyterian Homes, owner/manager of three other accredited Continuing Care communities in Irvine, Duarte, and Glendale. Opened in 1956.

Minimum age: 62 years.

Population: 250 residents.

Number of units: 170 Independent Living apartments; 18 personal care rooms, 50-bed Skilled Nursing facility.

Dining plan: Three meals per day with menu selection included. Tray service and special diets are available.

Services: *Included in the monthly fee:* Local transportation, laundry facilities on each floor, biweekly housekeeping, parking.

At additional cost: Beauty/barbershop, guest accommodations, limousine and bus service, personal laundry service, garages.

Activities: Computer classes, heated swimming pool and spa, shuffleboard, lawn bowling, cactus garden, book and current events discussion groups, gardening, special speakers, trips to nearby musical and theatrical performances, library, hobby and sewing rooms, deck and direct access to beach, exercise/fitness room, educational/social/recreational programs, volunteer opportunities.

Availability: Waiting list.

Health services and rates: Clinic care. Physical, occupational, and speech therapies available.

- 18 Private personal care rooms: $76/day
- 50-Bed Skilled Nursing facility: $52/day

"Overlooking a prime stretch of ocean beach, White Sands sets a high standard of quality with its warm, experienced staff. All religious denominations are welcome. White Sands can assure quality of life with over 35 years of experience and the assurance of on-site continuing levels of care."

BIXBY KNOLLS TOWERS

3737 Atlantic Avenue
Long Beach, CA 90807
(310) 426-6123
Ted Stulz, administrator

Type of community: Nonprofit Continuing Care, modified contract

This beautiful 14-story apartment building with an adjacent six-story health care building is located in a well-established neighborhood. Long Beach is an excellent urban retirement locale, with an average temperature of 82° in the summer and 65° in the winter. Easily accessible are southern California's sunny beaches, the San Gabriel mountains, the desert, and Los Angeles. Churches, public library, shopping, banking, and other services are all within a short walking distance.

INDEPENDENT LIVING HOUSING

Type/size of apartment	*Monthly fee**
Studio, 365 or 465 sq. ft.	$1,245–1,445
1-Bedroom, 545 or 615 sq. ft.	$1,630–1,790
2-Bedroom, 700 or 915 sq. ft.	$1,780–2,260

**For double occupancy add $500 to the monthly fee. All utilities included except telephone. Central heating and air-conditioning, wall-to-wall carpeting, draperies, fully equipped kitchens, 24-hour emergency call system, cable TV.*

Financial plan: Month-to-month lease. Nonrefundable organization fee of $500. $1,000 refundable security deposit.

Ownership and management: Owned and managed by Retirement Housing Foundation, a nonprofit organization affiliated with the Council for Health and Human Services Ministries of the United Church of Christ. Retirement Housing Foundation is the largest nonprofit provider of housing in the country, with more than 115 facilities in 26 states serving over 14,000 residents. Opened in 1965.

Minimum age: 60 years.

Population: 140 residents; 75% women, 25% men, 7% couples.

Number of units: 168 Independent Living apartments; 60 Assisted Living units, 99-bed Nursing facility.

Dining plan: Three meals a day included in the monthly fee. One meal a day is required, and meal credits are available for up to two meals per day. Tray service for nominal charge. Private dining room.

Services: *Included in the monthly fee:* Weekly housekeeping and flat-linen service, scheduled transportation.

At additional cost: Beauty/barbershop, laundry facilities, underground parking, guest accommodations (rollaway bed or vacant apartment), personal laundry.

Activities: Billiards room, woodworking shop, pottery shop, library, concerts, Bible study and Sunday worship with facility chaplain, movies, card and other games, sing-alongs.

Availability: Apartments are available.

Health services and rates: Residents receive five free days per year in a respite care room in Assisted Living facility. Three studios are set aside for this purpose. Physical, occupational, speech, and respiratory therapy available at additional cost. Catered Living services offered Independent Living residents à la carte (bathing, dressing, etc.) with the hopes of helping them stay in Independent Living longer.

- 60 Assisted Living apartments
  - Studio $1,700/month
  - 1-Bedroom $2,055/month
- 99-Bed Skilled Nursing facility
  - Triple $85/day
  - Double $90/day
  - Private $150/day

"The Towers is more than just a place to live. It is a place where residents can expand their horizons by making special new friends and getting involved in fulfilling and rewarding activities, educational opportunities, and planned social events."

FREEDOM VILLAGE

23442 El Toro Road
Lake Forest, CA 92630
(714) 472-4700
Georgia Byrne, director of marketing

Type of community: Continuing Care, modified contract

A three-story complex containing Independent Living, Assisted Living, and Skilled Nursing accommodations is set on eight acres. Three wings face courtyards, one with a swimming pool, one with a garden and putting green, and the third facing the Activity Pavilion. The facility, located midway between San Diego and Los Angeles, is adjacent to a park and public golf course, and nearby are major shopping malls, movies, restaurants, and Laguna Beach.

Financial plan: Entrance fee plus monthly fee. Two plans: **1)** 50% refundable forever. **2)** 50% refundable after two years.

Ownership and management: Owned and managed by Freedom Management Company, which also manages The Village in Hemet, California. Opened in 1987.

Minimum age: 62 years.

Population: 320 residents; 77% women, 23% men, 15% couples.

Number of units: 282 Independent Living units; 60 Assisted Living apartments, 52 Skilled Nursing beds.

Dining plan: One meal (lunch or dinner) included. Additional meals available at nominal cost. Private dining room, catering.

Services: *Included in the monthly fee:* Weekly housekeeping and flat-linen service, scheduled transportation, cable TV with in-house cable channel, parking, washers/dryers.

At additional cost: Guest accommodations, coffee shop, beauty/barbershop.

Activities: Activities director. Exercise, table tennis, duplicate bridge, swimnastics, heated pool and spa, dominos, bingo, Scrabble, needlework.

Availability: Limited. Waiting list for two bedrooms.

Health services and rates: Residents are entitled to 360 days of nursing care in the health center at no additional cost. Of these, 22 may be used by residents each quarter.

- 60 Assisted Living units: $80/day
- 52 Skilled Nursing beds: $121/day

"Freedom Village is close to the beach, fine shopping centers, and the gated community of Leisure World, from which over 75% of the residents come. We have a reputation as a preferred retirement center in this part of the country."

INDEPENDENT LIVING HOUSING

Type/size of apartment	*Entrance fee*	*Monthly fee single/double*
Studio, 450 sq. ft.	$50,000–71,000	$1,050
1-Bedroom, 650 sq. ft.	$70,500–100,500	$1,265/1,715
2-Bedroom, 950 sq. ft.	$123,900–177,000	$1,425/1,875
2-Bedroom/dining room, 1,250 sq. ft.	$134,400–192,000	$1,580–2,030

All utilities except telephone included. Fully equipped kitchen, carpeting, draperies, 24-hour emergency call system, individually controlled heating and air-conditioning, patio or balcony.

PILGRIM HAVEN

373 Pine Lane
Los Altos, CA 94022
(415) 948-8291
Marilyn Sell, director of retirement counseling

Type of community: Nonprofit Continuing Care, modified contract

Accreditation: Continuing Care Accreditation Commission

This campus community, nestled in the quiet residential community of Los Altos, offers colorful gardens filled with 100 varieties of roses. Independent Living residences and Assisted Living and Skilled Nursing facilities are available. Located on the peninsula between San Francisco and San Jose, Los Altos' superb climate (average summer temperature 65°; winter temperature 52°) invites participation in a variety of outdoor activities.

Financial plan: Entrance fee plus monthly fee. If resident leaves during the 90-day probationary period, 100% of the entrance fee is refunded. Application processing fee: $250 per person or $450 per couple.

Ownership and management: American Baptist Homes of the West, owner and manager of 17 retirement communities. Opened in 1949.

Minimum age: 62 years (if couple, spouse may be younger).

Population: 90+ residents; 67% women, 33% men, 40% couples.

Number of units: 94 Independent Living apartments; 12 Assisted Living rooms, 66 Skilled Nursing beds.

Dining plan: One meal a day included in the monthly fee. Tray service is available for temporary illness. Private dining room and catering services.

Services: *Included in the monthly fee:* Monthly housekeeping (weekly for studios), flat-linen service for some apartments, scheduled transportation.

At additional cost: Beauty/barbershop, guest accommodations, residents' store.

Activities: Activities director. Swimming pool, events at Stanford University and Foothill/DeAnza

INDEPENDENT LIVING HOUSING

Type/size of apartment	*Entrance fee**	*Monthly fee**
Studio, 292–345 sq. ft.	$19,500–34,300	$1,122
1-Bedroom, 460 sq. ft.	$38,800–68,600	$1,252–1,355
2-Bedroom, 730 sq. ft.	$60,000–64,700	$1,416
Willow Apartments		
2-Bedroom, 950–970 sq. ft.	$170,000–172,000	$2,021
Birch Apartments		
1-Bedroom, 650 sq. ft.	$110,000–112,000	$1,880
2-Bedroom, 924–940 sq. ft.	$170,000–172,000	$2,021

**For double occupancy of studios and 1-bedrooms there is an additional entrance fee charge of 10% with a $1,500 minimum. For double occupancy for all apartments add $380 to the monthly fee. All utilities except telephone included. Full kitchens, wall-to-wall carpet, draperies, individually controlled heating and air-conditioning, 24-hour emergency call system.*

Colleges (Flint Center for the Performing Arts), opera, symphony, ballet, theater, celebrity lecture series, concerts, gardening classes. Golf, tennis, hiking nearby.

Availability: Long waiting list.

Health services and rates: Resident's monthly fee includes long-term nursing care insurance, which pays a specific amount for as long as health care is required. Those 85 years or older have an additional insurance fee of $78 per month. Each resident is entitled to ten days per year in the health center at no additional cost. Direct admission to health center on space-available basis with payment of entrance fee.

- 20 Residential care rooms

	Entrance fee/Monthly fee
Studio	$14,600–16,500/1,088–1,304

- 12 Assisted Living rooms

	Entrance fee/Monthly fee
Private room	$15,600/1,549

- 66-Bed Skilled Nursing facility

4-Bed room	$2,872/month
Semiprivate	$3,126–3,215/month
Private	$3,691–3,952/month

"Pilgrim Haven has a wonderful location. The community is in an upscale residential quiet neighborhood on seven beautifully landscaped acres. This the flagship community of American Baptist Homes of the West."

LOS GATOS MEADOWS

110 Wood Road
Los Gatos, CA 95030
(408) 354-0211
Patricia M. Welch, admissions adviser

Type of community: Nonprofit Continuing Care, all-inclusive contract

Located on an 11-acre campus once part of the historic Rancho Rinconcada de Los Gatos, Los Gatos Meadows offers Independent Living garden apartments and cottages. Assisted Living and Skilled Nursing facilities also are on site. The community is one hour from San Francisco; two blocks from downtown Los Gatos. Buildings are connected by covered walkways. Pacific Ocean beaches, the Santa Cruz Mountains, and the Monterey Peninsula are within easy driving distance. Shops, theaters, churches of many denominations, a museum, a library, banks, investment houses, and adult education facilities are within walking distance.

Financial plan: Entrance fee plus monthly fee. Entrance fee refunded less $1^2/_3$% per month of residency.

Ownership and management: Owned and managed by the Episcopal Homes Foundation, owner and operator of St. Paul's Towers in Oakland, Canterbury Woods in Pacific Grove, Spring Lake Village in Santa Rosa, Oak Center Towers in Oakland and Presidio Gate Apartments in San Francisco. Opened in 1971.

Minimum age: 65 years.

Population: 200 residents; 65% women, 35% men, 15% couples.

Number of units: 173 Independent Living garden apartments and cottages; 39-bed Skilled Nursing facility.

Dining plan: Three meals per day included in the monthly fee. Private dining rooms available.

Services: *Included in the monthly fee:* Weekly housekeeping and flat-linen service, scheduled transportation.

At additional cost: Beauty/barbershop, parking.

INDEPENDENT LIVING HOUSING

Type/size of unit	*Entrance fee*	*Monthly fee*
Studio, 417 sq. ft.	$46,000–58,800	$1,224–1,283
Alcove, 680 sq. ft.	$67,600–85,900	$1,405
1-Bedroom, 753 sq. ft.	$109,200–151,700*	$1,554–1,627*
2-Bedroom, 1,282 sq. ft.	$202,100–227,200	$3,061 (couples only)
2-Bedroom cottage, 1,110 sq. ft.	$211,900–226,300	$3,061 (couples only)

**For double occupancy in 1-bedroom add $12,000 to the entrance fee and $902 to the monthly fee. All utilities except telephone included. Individually controlled heating and air-conditioning, wall-to-wall carpeting, kitchenette, balcony or patio, 24-hour emergency call system. Some cottages have carports and fireplaces.*

Activities: Concerts, films, lectures, worship services, theater, outings to countryside and seashore, library, exercise room, movies, residents' council, music programs, exercise classes, cultural programs.

Availability: Limited. Waiting list for two-bedroom apartments and cottages.

Health services and rates: Assisted Living and Skilled Nursing, including physicians' and surgeons' fees as well as hospitalization and convalescent care, are included in the monthly fee. Residents are covered whether they receive treatment at Los Gatos Meadows or an outside hospital. Physical, occupational, speech, and massage therapy offered.

- Assisted Living services offered in residents' apartments
- 39-Bed Skilled Nursing facility

"One of the prime benefits of life at Los Gatos Meadows is associating with men and women in the same position in life. You'll find that many of them share your ideas and opinions and that they like doing the things you like. Los Gatos Meadows' full life care concept frees you from tedious chores and concerns, leaving more time for your newfound friends."

THE TERRACES OF LOS GATOS

800 Blossom Hill Road
Los Gatos, CA 95032
(408) 356-1006
Jane Walker, marketing director

Type of community: Nonprofit Continuing Care, modified contract

The Terraces of Los Gatos offers spacious patio homes and apartments for Independent Living. The community is located on nine acres of meticulously tended grounds and gardens in a suburban residential neighborhood nestled in the foothills of the Santa Cruz Mountains. Next door is a shopping center, beautiful park with lighted tennis courts, and a church. Vasona Park and Reservoir provide miles of trails for walkers and cyclists. The community is located near Los Gatos' downtown, churches, and shopping areas.

Financial plan: Entrance fee plus monthly fee.

Ownership and management: American Baptist Homes of the West (ABHOW), owner and manager of 17 retirement communities in Arizona, California, and Washington. ABHOW was established in 1949. Opened in December 1992.

Minimum age: 62 years.

Population: 148 residents; 70% women, 30% men, 50% couples.

INDEPENDENT LIVING HOUSING

Type/size of apartment	*Entrance fee*	*Monthly fee single/double*
Alcove, 623 sq. ft.	$84,000	$1,400
1-Bedroom, 788 sq. ft.	$147,000	$1,650/2,130
2-Bedroom, 1,070 sq. ft.	$258,000	$2,255/2,735
Patio homes		
1-Bedroom, 1,312 sq. ft.	$310,000	$2,315/2,835

All utilities except telephone included. Carpeting, drapes, 24-hour emergency call system, fully equipped kitchen.

Number of units: 165 Independent Living apartments and 10 patio homes; 33 Assisted Living units, 59 Skilled Nursing beds.

Dining plan: Resident's choice of one main meal daily included in the monthly fee. Additional meals available.

Services: *Included in the monthly fee:* Bimonthly housekeeping, flat-linen service, scheduled transportation.

At additional cost: Coffee shop, beauty/barbershop, guest accommodations, parking, two hospitality suites.

Activities: Library, lap pool, spa, assembly hall, arts and crafts, woodworking, resident business center, art studios, game room.

Availability: Some availability.

Health Services and rates: Wellness center and comprehensive health program that covers basic health, diet, and exercise. Physical, occupational, and speech therapy available.

- 33 Assisted Living rooms: $2,800/month
- 59-Bed Skilled Nursing facility
  - Semiprivate $118/day
  - Private $180/day

"Location, location, location. The Terraces at Los Gatos are located next to shopping mall, churches, schools, and single-family homes. Because of our well-managed system of operations, we enjoy a great reputation for service and financial stability."

BETHEL RETIREMENT COMMUNITY

2345 Scenic Drive
Modesto, CA 95355
(209) 577-1901
Kathy Linn, marketing director

Type of community: Independent Living with Assisted Living

Located in a quiet residential district, Bethel's three-story modern apartment complex consists of two facilities, one for Independent Living and one for Assisted Living. The complex surrounds a beautiful patio and outdoor swimming pool area. Within walking distance is a shopping center. Nearby state and junior colleges offer plays and courses.

Financial plan: Monthly rental. $250 deposit.

Ownership and management: Owned by a limited partnership and managed by Post Management, Inc., who also manages People's Retirement Community, Tacoma, Washington. Opened in 1989.

Minimum age: 62 years.

Population: 148 residents; ratio of women to men, 8:1; 12 couples in Independent Living.

INDEPENDENT LIVING HOUSING

Type/size of apartment	*Monthly rent**
1-Bedroom, 564 sq. ft.	$1,095–1,280
2-Bedroom, 834 sq. ft.	$1,595

**For double occupancy add $300 to the monthly fee. All utilities except telephone and cable TV included. Wall-to-wall carpeting, draperies, fully equipped kitchen, 24-hour emergency call system. Some apartments have balconies.*

Number of units: 129 Independent Living Apartments; 90-bed Assisted Living facility.

Dining plan: Three meals a day included in the monthly rent. Private dining room. Coffee bar.

Services: *Included in the monthly fee:* Transportation, laundry facilities, weekly housekeeping, individual storage area, covered parking.

At additional cost: Beauty/barbershop.

Activities: Outdoor pool, equipped exercise room, billiards, game areas, grand piano, television/video recorder, library, crafts room, Bible study, conference room.

Availability: Limited.

Health services and rates:

- 90-Bed Assisted Living facility

Semiprivate	$950/month
Private suite, 300 sq. ft.	$1,400/month
Parlor suite, 420 sq. ft.	$2,000*/month

**For double occupancy add $600 to the monthly rent.*

"Bethel is a Christian community committed to a fulfilling lifestyle for each resident and dedicated to the premise that a caring and compassionate environment can do much to mitigate some consequences of declining mobility. The feeling of family is appreciated by all residents who enjoy the casual, low-key atmosphere and really consider Bethel to be their home."

CASA DORINDA

300 Hot Springs Road
Montecito, CA 93108
(805) 969-8011
Bill Krebaum, admissions director

Type of community: Nonprofit Continuing Care, all-inclusive contract

Accreditation: Continuing Care Accreditation Commission

Located on 48 acres of oak woodland, Casa Dorinda was once a famous estate owned by the Bliss family. The mountains offer the perfect backdrop to the one- and two-story stucco, red-tiled roof buildings with Spanish-style architecture. The historic mansion houses the oak-paneled library, game and music rooms, and dining room. Beautiful walkways lead through the lushly landscaped grounds. The community is located five minutes from downtown Montecito, ten minutes from Santa Barbara, one mile from the Pacific Ocean, and 100 miles north of Los Angeles.

Financial plan: Entrance fee plus monthly fee. Entrance fee based on age and apartment size. Nonrefundable administrative processing fee of $200 per person is required with all applications. $1,000 per person waiting list deposit, which is refundable or applicable to the entrance fee upon acceptance for occupancy. Holding fee is a one-time charge per month prorated daily when applicant accepts an apartment until signing the Lifetime Residence and Services Plan Agreement. Prospective resident has 60 days from date of holding agreement to sign care agreement.

INDEPENDENT LIVING HOUSING

Type/size of apartment	*Entrance fee**	*Monthly fee*	*Holding fee*
Studio, 410 sq. ft.	$50,500	$1,781	$460
1-Bedroom, single, 580 sq. ft.	$75,500	$1,979	$640
1-Bedroom, std., 675 sq. ft.	$99,500	$2,136	$795
1-Bedroom, large, 780 sq. ft.	$119,500	$2,129	$825
2-Bedroom, std., 1,050 sq. ft.	$195,000	$3,943	$1,210
2-Bedroom, large, 1,320 sq. ft.	$245,000	$4,022	$1,250

**Entrance fees vary by age of applicant. The fees listed above are based on entry at age 75. 1-Bedroom standard and large are listed at single rate. For double occupancy add $55,500 to the entrance fee and $1,552 to the monthly fee. 2-Bedrooms are listed at double occupancy rate. All utilities except long-distance telephone included. Wall-to-wall carpeting, draperies, 24-hour emergency call system, individually controlled heating, cable TV hookup.*

Ownership and management: Owned and managed by the Montecito Retirement Association, a non-profit corporation. Opened in 1975.

Minimum age: 62 years (if couple, spouse may be younger).

Population: 300 residents, 80% women, 20% men, 40% couples.

Number of units: 240 Independent Living apartments; 22 Assisted Living units, 46-bed Skilled Nursing facility.

Dining plan: Three meals a day included in the monthly fee. Dining room alcoves available for parties.

Services: *Included in the monthly fee:* Scheduled transportation, weekly housekeeping and flat-linen services.

At additional cost: Beauty/barbershop, parking, guest accommodations.

Activities: Heated outdoor swimming pool with deck, Jacuzzi, resident gardens, lawn bowling, numerous trips to cultural events, stage shows, concerts, and festive holiday celebrations. Frequent programs and speakers held in auditorium. Outstanding musical ensembles and lectures can be heard at nearby Music Academy of the West and the University of California at Santa Barbara.

Availability: Waiting list six months. No waiting time for smaller units.

Health services and rates: Residents receive unlimited care in the medical center or personal care unit. In the event a husband or wife of a couple is temporarily hospitalized or permanently transferred to the medical center or personal care unit, no charges are added to the monthly fee. Casa Dorinda covers virtually all costs related to hospitalization. Acute hospital care is provided at any of the three hospitals in Santa Barbara and all physician services rendered during an acute hospital stay are covered. Outpatient clinic provides temporary nursing care for resident in his or her apartment while recovering from illness as well as daily personal care as needed.

- 22-Room Assisted Living annex
  Assisted Living has its own dining room, but residents may also dine in the main dining room. All rooms are private and have balconies overlooking landscaped lawns and gardens.
- 46-Bed Skilled Nursing facility. Plans are being developed for a new facility.

"Casa Dorinda has earned a national reputation for its exquisite charm, high-quality service, caring staff and residents. The mission is to operate a Continuing Care program with a standard of excellence in the quantity and quality of its services so that its residents can continue to live their lives with dignity, security and as independently and fully as they are able."

THE PARK LANE, A CLASSIC HYATT RESIDENCE

200 Glenwood Circle
Monterey, CA 93940
(408) 373-6126 or (800) 782-5730
Sandra Bryan, director of sales

Type of community: Independent Living with a Continuum of Care

Located between San Francisco and Los Angeles in one of California's most fascinating coastal communities, The Park Lane is made up of seven two-story chalet buildings and a seven-story main tower that overlooks the Monterey Bay and Del Monte Forest. Independent and Assisted Living units are offered. The community is near Community Hospital, Monterey Peninsula Airport, country clubs, and golf courses—including world-famous Pebble Beach—and three miles from the heart of Carmel.

Financial plan: Monthly fee. Fully refundable security deposit of one month's rent.

Ownership and management: Jointly owned by Matteson Investment Corp. of Menlo Park, California, and Classic Residence by Hyatt, an affiliate of the Hyatt Corporation, which owns/operates Classic Residences in Texas, Maryland, Nevada, New Jersey, and Connecticut. Opened in mid-1960s; completely renovated in 1990.

Minimum age: 55 years.

Population: 250 residents; 71% women, 29% men, 21% couples.

Number of units: 205 Independent Living apartments and 48 chalets; 32 Assisted Living apartments.

Dining plan: Continental breakfast daily, plus choice of lunch or dinner included in the monthly fee. Classically Caring Cuisine menu selections low in sodium, fat, and cholesterol are available at every meal. Room service available for short-term illness.

Services: *Included in the monthly fee:* 24-hour concierge, scheduled transportation, biweekly housekeeping, weekly flat-linen service, additional storage, well-lit/reserved covered parking. Classic Club Membership: long-term care insurance underwritten by Lloyd's of London, membership in airline club and discount buying service, complimentary overnight accommodations at Classic Residences, exclusive travel opportunities.

INDEPENDENT LIVING HOUSING

Type/size of apartment	*Monthly fee**
Studio, 415 sq. ft.	$1,275–1,650
1-Bedroom, 580 sq. ft.	$2,250–2,450
Deluxe 1-bedroom, 830 sq. ft.	$2,350–2,650
Luxury 1-bedroom, 830 sq. ft.	$2,550–2,850
2-Bedroom, 825 sq. ft.	$2,350–2,800
2-Bedroom chalet, 1,085 sq. ft.	$2,350–2,550

**For double occupancy add $500 to the monthly fee. All utilities except telephone included. All apartments have balconies or patios, fully equipped kitchens, individually controlled heating, 24-hour emergency call system, wall-to-wall carpeting, window treatments, spacious closets, basic cable TV. Chalets are freestanding.*

At additional cost: Bank courier service, postage, facsimile and copy service. Beauty/barbershop, guest apartments, dry cleaning pick-up and delivery, prescription drug and delivery service.

Activities: Personalized computer lifestyle profile provides full-time resident relations/programming staff with opportunity to individually tailor variety of educational, cultural, social, and recreational programs to residents' interests. Classes, lectures, movies, concerts, dances, and other indoor/outdoor activities, crafts/hobby rooms, art studio, walking paths, putting green, shuffleboard courts, billiards room, bocce ball court.

Availability: Waiting list for certain apartment styles.

Health services and rates: All residents who relocate to the Assisted Living Center from within Classic Residence remain eligible to receive benefits of long-term insurance underwritten by Lloyd's of London, should long-term care become necessary.

- 32 Assisted Living apartments

Studio, 415 sq. ft.	$2,550/month
1-Bedroom, 580–830 sq. ft.	$3,025/month
2-Bedroom, 825 sq. ft.	$3,590/month

**For double occupancy with one person needing care add $500 to the monthly fee; with both occupants needing care, add $800. All apartments have kitchens and are available furnished or unfurnished.*

Respite care in a furnished studio is available at $90/day.

"A distinguished leader in the hospitality industry for more than three decades, Hyatt has set the standard for high-quality accommodations and attentive service. Classic Residence has built upon Hyatt's expertise, bringing innovative cuisine, striking interior design, and personalized supportive services to the senior living industry."

GRAND LAKE GARDENS

401 Santa Clara Avenue
Oakland, CA 94610
(510) 893-8897
Teri Moore, director of retirement counseling

Type of community: Nonprofit Continuing Care, modified contract

Accreditation: Continuing Care Accreditation Commission

This modern six-story structure is centrally located in a residential area of Oakland and surrounded by three gardens. Quiet, parklike settings for informal entertaining or private garden plots for residents are offered. Grand Lake Gardens is within walking distance of historic Lake Merritt and its surrounding park area. Assisted Living and Skilled Nursing are available at sister community, Piedmont Gardens, one mile away. Medical facilities, major shopping areas, arts and recreation centers are all nearby. One block away is the shopping district of Grand and Lake Shore avenues in which banking, postal services, restaurants, grocery stores, specialty shops, and the historic Grand Lake Theater are located. Public transportation to downtown Oakland, Berkeley, and San Francisco is readily available.

Financial plan: Entrance fee plus monthly fee. Full refund of entrance fee within the first 90 days of residency. After 90 days, entrance fee amortizes at 1.5% per month of residency for period of 5½ years.

Ownership and management: Owned and operated by American Baptist Homes of the West, which has 17 retirement communities in California, Washington, and Arizona and has provided retirement housing and health care services for over 40 years. Opened in 1967.

Minimum age: 62 years (if couple, spouse may be younger).

Population: 110 residents; 85% women, 15% men, 8% couples.

INDEPENDENT LIVING HOUSING

Type/size of unit	*Entrance fee**	*Monthly fee single/double*
Studio, 390 sq. ft.	$39,000–47,200	$935/N/A
1-Bedroom, 522 sq. ft.	$58,600–69,800	$1,180/1,751
2-Bedroom, 643 sq. ft.	$79,100–90,600	$1,356/1,927
3-Bedroom	Prices available upon request	

**For double occupancy in 1-bedroom apartment add 10% of entrance fee; 2-bedroom already includes double occupancy. All utilities except telephone included in the monthly fee. Fully equipped all-electric kitchen, wall-to-wall carpeting, individually controlled heating and air-conditioning, 24-hour emergency call system, cable TV, walk-in closets. Balcony or patio in 1- and 2-bedroom apartments.*

Number of units: 102 Independent Living apartments; 72 Assisted Living rooms and 94-bed health care center at sister facility, Piedmont Gardens.

Dining plan: One meal per day included in the monthly fee. Lunch available Monday through Friday at additional charge. Tray service for temporary illness.

Services: *Included in the monthly fee:* Monthly housekeeping, laundry facilities, transportation to medical appointments and shopping.

At additional cost: Beauty/barbershop, covered parking in security garage.

Activities: Gardening, shuffleboard, movies, van and bus tours, library, exercise bikes, billiards, game room, vespers, holiday parties, guest speakers, art classes, piano and organ.

Availability: Limited. Studios and one-bedrooms generally available. One-year wait for two-bedrooms. Nonrefundable application fee of $250 for singles; $450 for couples for waiting list.

Health services and rates: Health center at Piedmont Gardens, Grand Lake Gardens' sister facility, offers Intermediate and Skilled Nursing as well as Assisted Living. Piedmont Gardens is one mile from Grand Lake Gardens. Nurse visits Grand Lake Gardens once a week. Residents receive ten days per year at no charge in the health center. Long-term health insurance included in the monthly fee (for residents over 85 there is an additional $85 per month).

- 72 Assisted Living at Piedmont Gardens, private rooms

	Entrance fee	*Monthly fee**
Nonambulatory/ Private	$30,900	$1,938
Ambulatory	$34,500	$2,432

**For double occupancy add $525 to the monthly fee.*

- 94-Bed health center

4-Bed room	$3,070/month
2-Bed room	$3,407/month
Private room	$4,537/month

"This is an invigorating community for friendly people with a wide variety of interests. Conveniently located near shopping areas as well as the excitement of San Francisco, Grand Lake Gardens provides residents with an active and independent lifestyle to fit their individual personalities."

LAKE PARK

1850 Alice Street
Oakland, CA 94612
(510) 835-5511
Paul Basting, marketing director

Type of community: Continuing Care, all-inclusive contract

Lake Park is housed in 23-year old contemporary twin towers overlooking Lake Merritt. Downtown

INDEPENDENT LIVING HOUSING

Type of apartment	*Entrance fee*	*Monthly fee single/double*
Studio	$27,800–40,600	$1,191
Alcove	$44,100	$1,429/2,152
Junior 1-bedroom	$56,900–86,200	$1,549/2,272
1-Bedroom	$82,300–111,700	$1,670/2,393
1-Bedroom/2-bath	$92,000–121,300	$1,910/2,633
2-Bedroom	$130,100–159,500	$2,860

All utilities except telephone included in the monthly fee. Fully equipped kitchen, wall-to-wall carpeting, draperies, 24-hour emergency call system, individually controlled heating and air-conditioning.

Oakland's shopping district and historic Paramount theater, home of the Oakland symphony and showcase for the performing arts, are within easy walking distance. Bay Area Rapid Transit takes 12 minutes to San Francisco. World-famous vineyards are a short drive away.

Financial plan: Entrance fee plus monthly fee. $1,000 deposit required.

Ownership and management: California-Nevada Methodist Homes. Opened in 1965.

Minimum age: 62 years.

Population: 247 residents.

Number of units: 150 Independent Living apartments; 50 Assisted Living units, 23 Skilled Nursing beds.

Dining plan: Three meals per day included in the monthly fee. Two-meal-per-day plan also available.

Services: *Included in the monthly fee:* Weekly housekeeping and flat-linen services, scheduled transportation, reserved parking.

At additional cost: Beauty/barbershop, coffee shop, convenience store.

Activities: Rooftop solarium and gardens, library, lounges, activities and crafts room, artist studio, exercise room, auditorium, square dancing, holiday parties, musical recitals, chartered bus trips, weekly interdenominational chaplain service.

Availability: No waiting list.

Health services and rates: Unlimited nursing care included in the monthly fee. 24-hour licensed nursing staff. Long-term care available on-site or at Prathe Methodist Memorial Home ten minutes away in Alameda.

- 50 Assisted Living units
- 23 Skilled Nursing beds

"Total physical and financial security is offered by Lake Park's life care agreement. Bright, spacious apartments overlook beautiful Lake Merritt in the heart of Oakland, renowned for its Mediterranean climate and ambiance. Everything's under one roof: great food, health care, bridge groups . . . and *on* the roof there's a garden with views forever!"

PIEDMONT GARDENS

110 41st Street
Oakland, CA 94611
(510) 654-7172
Ann-Marie Meehan, director of community relations

Type of community: Nonprofit Continuing Care, modified contract

Accreditation: Continuing Care Accreditation Commission

Three high-rise buildings—11-story Oakmont, 16-story Crestmont, and three-story Garden Terrace—are surrounded by a garden area and connected by enclosed walkways. Residents of sister community, Grand Lake Gardens, one mile away, use Piedmont Gardens' Assisted Living and Skilled Nursing facilities. Piedmont Gardens is centrally located in an urban setting just minutes from downtown Oakland and within a few blocks of freeway access to Berkeley, San Francisco, the peninsula, and Contra Costa County. University of California, theaters, museums, churches, and department stores are all nearby.

Financial plan: Entrance fee plus monthly fee. Entrance fee is refundable in the first three months should resident desire to leave. By the fourth month, entrance fee amortizes at a rate of 1 1/2% per month for 5 1/2 years.

Ownership and management: Owned and managed by American Baptist Homes of the West, which has 17 communities in California, Washington, and Arizona and has provided retirement housing and health care services for over 40 years. Opened in 1969.

Minimum age: 62 years.

Population: 450 residents; 75% women, 25% men, 8% couples.

Number of units: 229 Independent Living apartments; 72 Assisted Living rooms, 94-bed health care center.

Dining plan: One meal per day included in the monthly fee, except studio residents who receive three.

Services: *Included in the monthly fee:* Monthly housekeeping, flat-linen service, scheduled transportation.

At additional cost: Beauty/barbershop, parking.

Activities: Adult education classes, sewing, exercise classes, painting, sketching, ceramics, Bible study, chapel services, bus tours, special outings, movies, slide shows, plays, readings, operettas, book reviews, recitals, dance groups, teas, picnics, ice-cream socials, bridge, billiards, chess, jigsaw puzzles, dominoes, shuffleboard, library, woodworking shop, rooftop jogging, and walking areas.

Availability: Most apartments and studios are available. One- and two-bedrooms sometimes have a short wait. Nonrefundable application fee: $250 single, $450 for couple.

Health services and rates: Long- and short-term care. Choice of two health plans. **1)** Basic medical care plan, resident receives 10 free days per year in health center. **2)** Nursing home insurance plan offers Independent Living resident unlimited health care upon qualifying.

INDEPENDENT LIVING HOUSING

Type/size of apartment	*Entrance fee**	*Monthly fee**
Studio, 270–360 sq. ft.	$24,000–49,500	$1,018–1,239
Alcove, 375 sq. ft.	$54,500–67,500	$1,068
1-Bedroom, 560–610 sq. ft.	$70,500–91,500	$1,181
2-Bedroom, 740–760 sq. ft.	$104,500–115,500	$1,414

**For double occupancy add 10% of entrance fee and $425 to the monthly fee (2-bedroom apartments already include second person entrance fee). All utilities except telephone included. Wall-to-wall carpeting, individually controlled heating and air-conditioning, fully equipped all-electric kitchen, 24-hour emergency call system.*

- 72 Assisted Living Rooms

	Entrance fee/ nonresidents	Monthly fee*
Nonambulatory/ Private	$30,900	$1,938
Ambulatory/ Private	$34,500	$2,432

**For double occupancy add $525 to the monthly fee.*

- 94-Bed nursing facility

4-Bed room	$3,070 month
2-Bed room	$3,407/month
Private room	$4,537/month

"American Baptist Homes of the West, as an expression of Christian mission, seeks to enhance the independence, well-being, and security of older people through the provision of housing, health care, and supportive services."

ST. PAUL'S TOWERS

100 Bay Place
Oakland, CA 94610
(510) 835-4700
David F. Armstrong, director of sales/marketing

Type of community: Nonprofit Continuing Care, all-inclusive contract

This contemporary brick and steel 22-story high-rise apartment building overlooks Lake Merritt near Oakland's downtown district. Museums, theaters, art galleries, the opera, the symphony, libraries, and internationally known restaurants are all nearby. The community offers easy access to San Francisco and surrounding Bay Area; public transportation is within walking distance.

Financial plan: Entrance fee plus monthly fee. Entrance fee is 100% refundable within 90 days. Within five years, refund is prorated.

Ownership and management: Owned and operated by Episcopal Homes Foundation, which also owns and operates five retirement communities in Northern California. Opened in 1966.

Minimum age: 65 years.

Population: 227 residents; 85% women, 15% men, 25% couples.

Number of units: 261 Independent Living apartments; 11 Assisted Living units, 43-bed health care center.

INDEPENDENT LIVING HOUSING

Type/size of unit	*Entrance fee**	*Monthly fee**
Studio, 440 sq. ft.	$26,875–40,450	$1,497
Alcove, 500 sq. ft.	$44,950–63,400	$1,697
1-Bedroom, 500–650 sq. ft.	$59,425–100,175	$1,788–1,941
$1^1/_2$-Bedroom, 675 sq. ft.	$105,400–114,400	$2,061
2-Bedroom, 850–925 sq. ft.	$113,100–140,275	$2,130–2,196

**For double occupancy add $12,000 to the entrance fee; $1,055 to the monthly fee. All utilities, except telephone, included. Kitchenettes, private balconies, 24-hour emergency call system, wall-to-wall carpeting, individually controlled heating and air-conditioning.*

Dining plan: Three meals per day included in the monthly fee. Private banquet room available. Special diets and dietitian consultants available.

Services: *Included in the monthly fee:* Weekly housekeeping and flat-linen services, use of laundry rooms, transportation.

At additional cost: Beauty/barbershop, parking, guest accommodations.

Activities: Planned social events and cultural programs, exercise classes, chaplain services, TV and music lounge, solariums, residents' association, arts and crafts rooms, library, dominoes, bingo, card games, films, afternoon socials.

Availability: Waiting list varies from six months to two years, depending on type of apartment desired. Nonrefundable application fee and refundable reservation deposit place you on waiting list.

Health services and rates: Comprehensive medical, surgical, nursing, convalescent, and hospital care program as well as Assisted Living included in resident's monthly fee. If resident needs a specialist not represented on the health center staff, one will be called in at no extra charge. Physician's visits are unlimited. Hospitalization within local county is covered under life care contract. If hospitalized outside the county, St. Paul's will pay up to the amount of resident's monthly fee. Psychiatric services are not included in the life care program. Occupational, physical, and massage therapy services available.

- 11 Assisted Living units
- 43-Bed health center

"St. Paul's Towers is dedicated to enhancing the residents' emotional, spiritual, and physical well-being in an atmosphere of motivation and encouragement to maintain and build their independence and self-worth."

CHANNING HOUSE

850 Webster Street
Palo Alto, CA 94301
(415) 327-0950
Ruth Barnes, resident coordinator

Type of community: Nonprofit Continuing Care, all-inclusive contract

An 11-story modern apartment building, Channing House is located 32 miles south of San Francisco in a tree-shaded quiet residential section of Palo Alto. The 11th floor houses a penthouse lounge built around a large circular fireplace, with open and protected decks that grant spectacular views of San Francisco Bay and distant foothills. Independent Living, Assisted Living, and Skilled Nursing are on-site. Stanford University is nearby; Palo Alto's downtown is three blocks away.

Financial plan: Entrance fee plus monthly fee. $300 nonrefundable processing fee.

Ownership and management: Nonprofit corporation run by elected trustees. Opened in 1964.

INDEPENDENT LIVING HOUSING

Type/size of apartment	*Entrance fee**	*Monthly fee single/double*
Studio, 431–465 sq. ft.	$54,000–74,000	$1,015–1,169
Alcove, 575 sq. ft.	$91,700–97,700	$1,288
1-Bedroom, 745–1,000 sq. ft.	$107,400–193,100	$1,452–1,852/ 2,238–2,638
2-Bedroom, 1,126 sq. ft.	$210,000–220,000	$2,012–2,802

**For double occupancy add $12,000 to the entrance fee. All utilities except telephone included. Small kitchenette, carpets, draperies, 24-hour emergency call system, air-conditioning.*

Minimum age: 62 years (individuals must move in before their 80th birthday).

Population: 280 residents; 85% women, 15% men, 10% couples.

Number of units: 240 Independent Living apartments; 48 Assisted Living beds, 21 Skilled Nursing beds.

Dining plan: Three meals per day included in the monthly fee. Small private dining rooms with complete kitchen facilities, adjoining beautifully appointed lounges, are available to residents for private parties.

Services: *Included in the monthly fee:* Weekly housekeeping and flat-linen service, scheduled transportation.

At additional cost: Beauty/barbershop, guest accommodations.

Activities: Library, large auditorium, movies, lectures, arts/crafts, golf nearby, hobby shop.

Availability: Waiting list: Studios one to two years; one-bedrooms six to eight years; two-bedrooms 10 to 12 years.

Health services and rates: Comprehensive medical, surgical, and hospital care in conjunction with Medicare is covered in resident's basic monthly fee. Palo Alto Medical Foundations, a local group practice representing all medical specialties, offers services. Post-hospital care and appropriate care for other illness is provided.

- 33 Assisted Living rooms
- 21 Skilled Nursing beds

"Channing House is a very special place for people who want to be relieved of day-to-day responsibilities and who desire the ultimate in gracious and independent living."

PALO ALTO COMMONS

4075 El Camino Way
Palo Alto, CA 94306
(415) 494-0760
Mary Claire Meijer, marketing director

Type of community: Independent and Assisted Living

Located 35 miles south of San Francisco, this three-story facility, which offers Independent and Assisted Living, has been thoughtfully designed and decorated to be residential—not institutional—in character. The art and appointments have been carefully selected. Secure walking paths are located throughout the lovely gardens, gazebo, sun porches, barbecue area, and inner courtyard. A two-story solarium adjacent to the lobby has couches, tables, and chairs. The City of Palo Alto enjoys outstanding community services including 30 parks, a cultural center, community theater, five libraries, and a very active senior center. Nearby Stanford University offers a wide range of cultural events.

INDEPENDENT LIVING HOUSING

Type/size of apartment	*Monthly fee**
Studio, 370 sq. ft.	$1,850–2,250
1-Bedroom, 470 sq. ft.	$2,150–2,500

**For double occupancy add $500 to the monthly fee. All utilities except telephone and cable TV included. Kitchenette with microwave and full refrigerator, wall-to-wall carpeting, draperies, individually controlled heating and air-conditioning, 24-hour emergency call system. Most apartments have sliding glass doors that provide easy access to balconies and patios. Furniture is available upon request.*

Financial plan: Monthly fee. Security deposit equal to one month's rent. No leases. Present policy, subject to change, provides rental rates do not change for 12-month period.

Ownership and management: Owned by Palo Alto Commons, a California Limited Partnership. Managed by The Hillsdale Group, a corporation that manages other senior facilities including congregate care, Assisted Living, and convalescent care. Opened in 1990.

Minimum age: 62 years.

Population: 104 residents.

Number of units: 37 studios and 84 one-bedroom Independent Living apartments.

Dining plan: Three meals per day included in the monthly fee. Snacks available in the afternoon. Catering available.

Services: *Included in the monthly fee:* Housekeeping and flat-linen service, laundry facilities, scheduled transportation, personal care assistance with bathing, grooming, medication reminders, assistance with daily chores.

At additional cost: Beauty/barbershop.

Activities: Area trips, group tours, special gardening area, crafts classes, exercise program, cultural, educational, and social events, lounge with piano, library with fireplace, hobby and crafts rooms.

Availability: Limited.

Health services and rates: Registered nurse is director of Assisted Living. Outstanding medical facilities such as Palo Alto Medical Clinic, Stanford Medical Center, and El Camino Hospital are nearby.

- Assisted Living services in resident's apartment. Five levels of care are offered.

"Palo Alto Commons is owned by a family that has lived in the community for over 30 years and is committed to the welfare of senior citizens. We offer an approach to Assisted Living that is committed to service and responsive to individual needs in an environment that promotes independence and vitality."

WEBSTER HOUSE

401 Webster Street
Palo Alto, CA 94301
(415) 325-9094
Julie Gutierrez, marketing director

Type of community: Not-for-profit Continuing Care, all-inclusive contract

This spacious five-level brick apartment building in downtown Palo Alto offers a fifth-level skyline terrace and landscaped dining room. Lap pool, fourth-level laundry facilities, and card room also are provided. First level contains handsomely decorated living room and television area. Webster House is within walking distance of all community services, shopping, banking, and groceries in Palo Alto. Independent Living is

INDEPENDENT LIVING HOUSING

Type/size of unit	*Entrance fee*	*Monthly fee*
1–2-Bedroom, 656–1,300 sq. ft.	$395,000–795,000	$1,310

All utilities except telephone included in the monthly fee. Wall-to-wall carpeting, 24-hour emergency call system, individually controlled heating and air-conditioning, fully equipped kitchens.

available at Webster House; Assisted Living and Skilled Nursing are guaranteed for life at nearby facilities.

Financial plan: Entrance fee plus monthly fee. $25,000 deposit reserves unit. Full refund of deposit before residency begins if prospective resident fails to pass medical exam. After residency begins, resident must give 120-day notice before withdrawal. The monthly fees for this 120-day period are to be paid by the resident as well as any other fees incurred, at which point the remaining portion of the entrance fee will be refunded. 30% of entrance fee is returned to resident's estate for an individual; 15% for couple.

Ownership and management: Managed by board of directors of the Palo Alto Medical Foundation and community. Webster House is a not-for-profit corporation. Opened in 1985.

Minimum age: 65 years.

Population: 47 residents; 81% women, 19% men, 12% couples.

Number of units: 37 Independent Living apartments; Assisted Living and Skilled Nursing off premises.

Dining plan: Meals are optional. Menus are distributed monthly. Meals are billed from $6.95 to $11.95, depending on entrée of the day. Weekly buffet lunch is $9. Room service is available, as is private dining room.

Services: *Included in the monthly fee:* Weekly housekeeping and flat-linen service, van use for medical appointments, grocery shopping, and resident-planned excursions, parking garage.

At additional cost: Extra housekeeping, personal van use.

Activities: Card room, TV room, heated lap pool, residents' council, hospitality community, decorating committee, excursions.

Availability: Waiting list for larger two-bedroom units. $300 nonrefundable processing fee for waiting list.

Health services and rates: Lifetime health care contractually guaranteed at no additional cost, including physicians' services and other outpatient ancillary services, hospitalization, nursing and convalescent care in licensed facility, therapy, prescription drugs, prosthetic and orthopedic devices, ambulance services, and psychiatric care. Managed and physician and outpatient services provided by the Palo Alto Medical Foundation. Covers:

- Assisted Living and Skilled Nursing available off premises. Hospital services provided by Stanford University Hospital under supervision of resident's Foundation physician. Home health care provided by contracted home health care agency, including physical and occupational therapists, home aids, or social workers. Intermittent personal and home health care available.

"Our residents are independent and active in civic and volunteer work. The residents' council ensures control of their lifestyle. At the same time, the security and warmth of Webster House is a much-needed support as aging occurs. Independence is the keynote for life at Webster House."

VILLA GARDENS

842 East Villa Street
Pasadena, CA 91101-1259
(818) 796-8162
Louise Plomgren Myers, director of admissions

Type of community: Continuing Care, modified contract

Villa Gardens is housed in a five-story, contemporary design apartment building with balconies.

Independent Living, plus Assisted Living services and Skilled Nursing, are on-site. The community is within walking distance of churches, banks, and markets.

Financial plan: Entrance fee plus monthly fee. A deposit of 10% of entrance fee is required at time of accepting a unit.

Ownership and management: Managed by Foundation to Assist California Teachers (FACT). Opened in 1933 (started by group of southern California teachers); new facility built in 1987.

Minimum age: 62 years.

Population: 210 residents; 81% women, 19% men, 25 couples.

Number of units: 186 Independent Living apartments; 54-bed health care center.

Dining plan: One meal per day included in the monthly fee. Optional meal plans. Two meals per day add $115/month; three meals per day add $275. Catering services available.

Services: *Included in the monthly fee:* Weekly flat-linen service, housekeeping, scheduled transportation, lighted parking.

At additional cost: General store, beauty/barbershop.

Activities: Library, classes, bridge, exercise facilities, memory enhancement, play reading, swimming pool, musical programs, tours, concerts, theater, picnic gazebo, yoga, lipreading, travelogues, chime choir, painting, flower committee, men's club, volunteering (almost 50% of the residents volunteer).

Availability: Waiting list of six months to two years, depending upon size of apartment.

Health services and rates: If Independent Living residents move into Skilled Nursing, they continue to pay the same monthly fee. Supervision by experienced gerontologists, creation of individualized treatment plan. Full range of therapies administered by registered professionals. Full-time licensed social worker. Therapy spa.

- Assisted Living services offered in resident's apartment
  $15/Hour, broken into 15 minute increments; if ongoing the charge is $40/month in addition to the monthly fee
- 54-Bed health center
  Semiprivate $119/day (nonresidents)

"Villa Gardens offers residents unparalleled peace of mind by eliminating any surprise regarding future health care needs. They can enjoy a rich, independent lifestyle secure in the knowledge that around-the-clock nursing care is available whenever needed. There is no extra charge for nursing service and no limit on the length of stay."

INDEPENDENT LIVING HOUSING

Type/size of apartment	*Entrance fee**	*Monthly fee**
Studio, 415 sq. ft.	$71,430	$940
1-Bedroom, 615 sq. ft.	$107,558	$1,151
Deluxe 1-bedroom	$127,720	$1,233
2-Bedroom, 915 sq. ft.	$147,290	$1,360
Deluxe 2-bedroom, 1,015 sq. ft.	$161,710	$1,498

**For double occupancy add $15,000 to the entrance fee and $589 to the monthly fee. All utilities except telephone included. Wall-to-wall carpeting, 24-hour emergency call system, fully equipped kitchens, draperies, garbage disposals.*

BRADFORD SQUARE

1180 North Bradford Avenue
Placentia, CA 92670
(714) 996-9292
Ms. G. G. Brashear, administrator

Type of community: Independent Living with personal care services

This charming two-story, Cape Cod–style building situated on 2.5 acres of parklike grounds is located on peaceful, secluded Bradford Avenue. Surrounded by landscaped gardens, the facility's central courtyard has a bubbling fountain and rose garden, gazebo, and wandering garden paths. Bradford Square's neighborhood setting in the heart of Orange County is close to shopping, entertainment, banks, houses of worship, and complete medical facilities.

Financial plan: Monthly rent. Rental rate is guaranteed for one year.

Ownership and management: Owned and managed by American Retirement Villas, owner and manager of over 26 retirement communities located in California and Arizona. Opened in 1987.

Minimum age: 62 years (exceptions can be made).

Population: 110 residents; 18% men, 72% women, 2 couples.

Number of units: 92 Independent Living apartments.

Dining plan: Three meals and snacks per day included in the monthly fee. Outdoor and indoor dining areas. Private dining room.

Services: *Included in the monthly fee:* Weekly housekeeping and linen service, scheduled transportation, parking, personal laundry.

At additional cost: Beauty/barbershop, laundry service, banking.

Activities: Activities and special events, arts and crafts, exercise programs, educational programs, library, continuing education classes, picnics, card and other games, billiards, shuffleboard, cooking lessons, movies, scenic country rides, lectures, gardening.

Availability: Most rooms available.

Health services and rates: Personal care services (bathing, dressing, medication reminders) available as required for an additional cost of $300, $600, or $1,000 (total care) per month.

"We're dedicated to providing the very best in carefree retirement living. When you live in an American Retirement Villas residence you get something special—a truly caring attitude. Our friendly staff of responsive professionals is dedicated to making your life easier and more enjoyable."

INDEPENDENT LIVING HOUSING

Type/size of apartment	*Monthly rent*
Semiprivate*, 288 sq. ft.	$850–950
Private room, 504 sq. ft.	$1,200–1,850

**Only a few semiprivates are available. All utilities except long-distance telephone are included in the monthly rent. Individually controlled heating and air-conditioning, 24-hour emergency response system, wall-to-wall carpeting, draperies, cable TV hookup.*

MT. SAN ANTONIO GARDENS

900 East Harrison Avenue
Pomona, CA 91767
(909) 624-5061
Ruth Davis, vice president of marketing

Type of community: Nonprofit Continuing Care, all-inclusive contract

Seven Independent Living apartment buildings and cottages are located on a 27-acre campus, which is half in Claremont and half in Pomona. Patios, balconies, hanging plants, ferns, shrubs, trees, and flowers fill the parklike campus where outdoor living is popular. Assisted Living and Skilled Nursing facility is on-site. Near are Mt. Baldy, Laguna Beach, and Palm Springs. Claremont is home to many colleges. Pomona offers large shopping resources, civic center, public library, Community Hospital, parks and recreational facilities, and is home of the Los Angeles County Fair. Numerous attractions are within a day's drive.

Financial plan: Entrance fee plus monthly fee. $250 nonrefundable application fee for single person; $350 for couple. $1,000 refundable deposit. Entrance fee is fully refundable within first 90 days. After 90 days entrance fee is refunded on a 5-year prorated basis. Homeship Fund is available for those who might be unable to afford the entrance or monthly fees.

Ownership and management: Owned by Congregational Homes, Inc. Managed by a board of directors. Residents are represented on every committee. Opened in 1961.

Minimum age: 62 years.

Population: 450 residents; 77% women, 23% men, 18% couples.

Number of units: 294 Independent Living apartments and cottages; 60 Assisted Living units, 66-bed health center.

Dining plan: Three meals per day included in the monthly fee. Tray service when ill. Private dining room.

INDEPENDENT LIVING HOUSING

Type/size of apartment	*Entrance fee*	*Monthly fee*
Semisuite, 375–470 sq. ft.	$32,118–59,737	$1,358
Circle semisuite, 400 sq. ft.	$59,737	$1,358
Efficiency, 470 sq. ft.	$72,012	$1,358
1-Bedroom, 650–830 sq. ft.	$87,356–111,906	$1,358/2,037
Full suite, 775 sq. ft.	$65,000–69,421	$2,037
Garden suite, 800 sq. ft.	$66,842–69,421	$2,037
Cottages		
1-Bedroom, 759–836 sq. ft.	$149,959	$1,358/2,037
2-Bedroom, 1,000–1,250 sq. ft.	$240,000	$2,716

Several houses with 3–4 bedrooms are also part of the campus .

**Entrance fee depends on age when entering. Semisuites and efficiency apartments are singles; 1-bedrooms can be for single or double; 2-bedrooms are doubles. All utilities except telephone included. Fully equipped kitchens (except semisuite and circle semisuite), patio, wall-to-wall carpeting, individually controlled heating and air-conditioning, 24-hour emergency call system.*

Services: *Included in the monthly fee:* Parking, biweekly housekeeping, weekly flat-linen service.

At additional cost: Guest accommodations.

Activities: Painting, gardening, jewelry making, card games, lipreading, calligraphy, woodworking, needlepoint, handicrafts, exercise classes, billiards, swimming pool, whirlpool spa, golfing at nearby courses, discussion groups, creative writing groups, book reviews, committee work, monthly newsletter production, local volunteering, movies, library.

Availability: Waiting list for larger accommodations.

Health services and rates: Unlimited stays at health center and Assisted Living Care are included in entrance and monthly fees. Temporary help in own residence is available. Director of health care services. Physical therapy, exercise classes, professional social services, educational programs on nutrition and health, preventive medicine measures, and daily checking and reporting system that assures the medical staff that each resident is well.

- 60 Private Assisted Living rooms
- 66-Bed Skilled Nursing facility

"Residents are represented on every committee of the board of directors, and six residents are full voting members. In addition, all residents belong to the Gardens Club, from which representatives are elected to serve as members of the Gardens Club Council. Working closely together, the board of directors, the Gardens Club Council, and the executive director and administrative staff carry out the management of the Gardens."

THE SEQUOIAS–PORTOLA VALLEY

501 Portola Road
Portola Valley, CA 94028
(415) 851-1501
Connie Loughary, marketing/admissions director

Type of community: Nonprofit Continuing Care, all-inclusive contract

Accreditation: Continuing Care Accreditation Commission

This beautiful pastoral setting includes 42 beautifully landscaped acres. Located in the residential hill estates of Portola Valley near Palo Alto, this resort-like community is composed of California ranch-style patio units and villas for Independent Living, Assisted Living, and Skilled Nursing. Each apartment opens onto meticulously landscaped courtyards and common areas. Patios offer private vistas. Stanford University is nearby; San Francisco is a one-hour drive.

Financial plan: Entrance fee plus monthly fee. $300 nonrefundable processing fee with application.

INDEPENDENT LIVING HOUSING

Type of apartment	*Entrance fee*	*Monthly fee single/double*
Studio, 340 sq. ft.	$41,000	$1,418
Large studio, 430 sq. ft.	$58,000	$1,547
1-Bedroom, 560–584 sq. ft.	$136,000–147,000	$1,733/2,664
Combination units, 770–990 sq. ft.	$204,000	$2,965
2-Bedroom, 860 sq. ft.	$251,000–261,000	$3,094
Villas, 1,389 sq. ft.	$350,000–370,000	3,421
Homes, 1,445 sq. ft.	Information on request	

All utilities except telephone included. Fully equipped kitchens, fully carpeted, 24-hour emergency call system, individually controlled heating and air-conditioning, patio. Note: *double occupancy only for 2-bedrooms, villas, and homes.*

Ownership and management: Owned by Northern California Presbyterian Homes, Inc., owner of three other life care communities in the San Francisco Bay Area. Opened in 1963.

Minimum age: 62 years (prospective residents must apply before 76th birthday).

Population: 235 residents; 40% couples.

Number of units: 222 Independent Living apartments, 15 villas and 2 homes; 20 Assisted Living units, 48 Skilled Nursing beds.

Dining plan: Three meals per day are included in the monthly fee. Buffet option for breakfast and lunch. Catering service for private parties. Modified menu for those with special dietary considerations. Private dining room.

Services: *Included in the monthly fee:* Weekly housekeeping and flat-linen service, scheduled transportation, parking.

At additional cost: Guest accommodations, beauty/barbershop.

Activities: Activities director. Covered lap pool and spa, lawn bowling, woodworking shop, crafts classes, flower and vegetable gardening, library. Shopping, golf, libraries, Stanford University nearby.

Availability: Long waiting list. $1,200 deposit per person for waiting list, which is applied to entrance fee upon acceptance. $300 per-person nonrefundable processing fee.

Health services and rates: Lifetime health care included in resident's monthly fee. Registered nurses on duty 24 hours a day. Temporary home health care.

- 20 Assisted Living units
- 48 Skilled Nursing beds

"The Sequoias–Portola Valley has a spectacular location, featuring 42 landscaped acres that border on 2,000 acres of public parklands. Three levels of care are covered by the resident's entrance fee and monthly fee. Should the resident require nursing care there are no increases in the monthly fee. Thiry-three percent of the entrance fee can be used as a one-time tax deduction and $7,000 + annually can be deducted. The Tomorrow's Fund protects residents whose funds become depleted."

PLYMOUTH VILLAGE

900 Salem Drive
Redlands, CA 92373
(909) 792-5329
Glen Belka, marketing director

Type of community: Not-for-profit Continuing Care, modified contract

Accreditation: Continuing Care Accreditation Commission

Located on 37 acres of landscaped campus in the heart of Redlands' mature residential area, Plymouth Village consists of Independent Living apartments and single-family homes, a health center, Assisted Living and Village Center. All apartments are on ground level and many offer views of mountain range in the distance. Historic Kendall Place serves as a center for social events in the community. The community is close to shopping, churches, medical facilities, and the business district.

Financial plan: Entrance fee plus monthly fee. Entrance fee amortized at rate of 1.5% per month of residency and is fully refundable within the first 90 days of residency.

Ownership and management: Owned and managed by American Baptist Homes of the West, which has 17 retirement communities in California, Washington, and Arizona. Opened in 1962.

INDEPENDENT LIVING HOUSING

Type/size of unit	*Entrance fee*	*Monthly fee**
Studio, 365 sq. ft.	$50,000–54,000	$1,020
1-Bedroom, 500–726 sq. ft.	$53,000–64,000	$1,072
2-Bedroom, 675–1,010 sq. ft.	$60,000–81,000	$1,110
2-Bedroom, 900–1,188 sq. ft.	$73,700–95,500	$1,177
3-Bedroom, 1,210–1,399 sq. ft.	$94,600–104,500	$1,175
Homes		
2-, 3-Bedroom, 900–2,000 sq. ft.	$80,850–179,000	$1,212–1,379

**For double occupancy add $528 to the monthly fee. Wall-to-wall carpeting, fully equipped kitchens, carport, garage or parking space, 24-hour emergency call system, individually controlled heating and air-conditioning.*

Minimum age: 60 years (if couple, spouse may be younger).

Population: 280 residents; 75% women, 25% men, 18% couples.

Number of units: 193 Independent Living apartments and homes; 30 Assisted Living units, 48-bed health center.

Dining plan: One meal per day included in the monthly fee. Extra meals are available by the meal or by a meal contract.

Services: *Included in the monthly fee:* Monthly housekeeping, scheduled transportation.

At additional cost: Village store, Old Curiosity Shop, guest cottage, extra housekeeping, beauty/barbershop services.

Activities: Swimming pool, tours, special workshops and classes, residents' association, weekly vespers, Bible study, prayer group, festivals, lectures, concerts, book reviews, painting, photography, square dancing, putting green, lawn bowling, shuffleboard, arts and crafts, volunteer projects.

Availability: Immediate availability.

Health services and rates: Residents receive ten free days per year in health center. Physical, speech, and occupational therapy, respiratory care, hospice care, social services, activities, medical and nursing services available. A long-term nursing-care policy is provided to residents who qualify in Independent Living, which reduces Skilled Nursing fees.

Admission directly to Assisted Living on space-available basis.

- 30 Assisted Living Units

	Entrance fee single/double	*Monthly fee single/double*
Ambulatory	$18,700/ 20,600	$1,980/ 3,056
Nonambulatory	$22,600/ 24,860	$2,080/ 3,156

- 48-Bed health center

	Private room	$113/day

"Plymouth Village is a premier retirement living option in the Inland Empire. Plymouth Village offers a unique residential setting and provides residents with more independence, security, and peace of mind than is possible in a traditional residence. Our dedicated staff, comprehensive services, and the guarantee of lifetime care will satisfy the present and future needs of the people who live here."

THE CANTERBURY

5801 West Crestridge Road
Rancho Palos Verdes, CA 90274
(310) 541-2410
Donnie Wilcox, director of marketing

Type of community: Nonprofit Continuing Care, modified contract

Nestled in Rancho Palos Verdes, The Canterbury is a modern, three-story, five-building complex joined by covered walkways, set in a beautiful hillside neighborhood with dramatic views. The exterior complements the attractive Palos Verdes area and is accented with brightly colored flowers and greenery. A large outdoor garden patio, lovely living room and recreation room, outdoor lap-swimming pool, indoor spa, and library are all provided. Independent Living, home health services, and Skilled Nursing are available. The complex of 5.2 acres is located close to a regional shopping center, the Norris Theatre, colleges, and California beaches.

Financial plan: Entrance fee plus monthly fee or monthly rental. Entrance fee plus monthly fee. Entrance fee is amortized over ten years. If the agreement is canceled at any time during the first ten years of occupancy, the unamortized portion will be refunded. It is prorated over 120 months. Entrance fee may be financed with 10% down and a ten-year promissory note with an interest rate on the unpaid balance equal to 1.5% plus the prime rate. A $750 nonrefundable processing fee is required. For monthly rental only a $750 nonrefundable processing and a $1,300 refundable cleaning deposit are required.

Ownership and management: Owned and managed by a nonprofit corporation sponsored by The Episcopal Home, Alhambra, California. Opened in 1983.

Minimum age: 60 years.

Population: 130 residents; 20% men, 80% women, 15% couples. (Admission is not limited to Episcopalians.)

Number of units: 127 Independent Living apartments; 28-bed Skilled Nursing facility.

Dining plan: Dinner daily included in the monthly fee. Lunch is available at an extra charge as is tray delivery for evening meal. Library and living room may be booked for private parties.

Services: *Included in the monthly fee:* Regular housecleaning, weekly flat-linen service, scheduled transportation, outdoor parking.

At additional cost: Country store, beauty/barbershop, coin-operated laundry facilities, garage parking, guest accommodations.

Activities: Group excursions, movies, billiards, library, outdoor swimming pool, indoor Jacuzzi spa, exercise room, music appreciation, card/game room, happy hours, picnics, ceramics, book discussions.

Availability: Limited.

Health services and rates: Health clinic offers medical services and therapy.

- Home health services (personal assistance

INDEPENDENT LIVING HOUSING

Type/size of apartment	*Entrance fee/Monthly fee**	*Monthly rental*
1-Bedroom, 560 sq. ft.	$75,000–80,000/1,097	$2,214–2,732
2-Bedroom, 852 sq. ft.	$115,000–125,000/1,297	$2,732–2,788

**For double occupancy with entrance fee/monthly fee add $610 per month to 1-bedroom and $656 per month to 2-bedroom. For double occupancy with monthly rental add $533 per month to 1-bedroom and $518 per month to 2-bedroom. All utilities except telephone are included. All-electric kitchenettes, private garden patios, 24-hour emergency call system, cable TV, wall-to-wall carpeting, draperies, storage closets, balcony or patio.*

including bathing, dressing, supervision of medication, plus personal companionship, light housekeeping/light meal preparation) available at an hourly rate from 8 a.m. to 6 p.m. To use home health services, the resident must be able to function independently during the nighttime hours.

- 28-Bed Skilled Nursing facility

Regular semiprivate	$100/day
Large semiprivate	$110/day
Extra-large semiprivate	$125/day
Private	$139/day

"The Canterbury is special because of its location on the famous Palos Verdes Peninsula in the rural area near the city of Los Angeles, close to the LAX Airport. Its caring staff, fine cuisine, landscaped grounds, fellowship and friendship among the residents make residents feel special and very much at home."

THE REMINGTON CLUB

16916 Hierba Drive
San Diego, CA 92128
(619) 673-6323
Cindy Nye, leasing counselor

Type of community: Continuing Care, modified contract

The Mediterranean-style architecture, reflected in the red-tiled roofs, is surrounded by lush, tropical landscaping. The Remington Club offers a two-story foyer and spacious living room furnished with an eclectic blend of contemporary and traditional styles. The setting provides beautiful mountain and garden views. Independent Living, Assisted Living, and nursing care are available on-site.

Financial plan: Monthly rental plan.

Ownership and management: Managed by The Forum Group, Inc., owner/manager of 27 retirement communities in the U.S. The original building opened in 1987 and within 12 months had reached full occupancy. An addition was completed in 1990.

Minimum age: 62 years.

Population: 405 residents; 70% women, 30% men, 20% couples.

Number of units: 246 Independent Living apartments; 100 Assisted Living suites, 59-bed health care center.

Dining plan: Resident's meal of choice each day is included in the monthly fee. Private dining room.

Services: *Included in the monthly fee:* Weekly housekeeping and flat-linen services, scheduled transportation.

At additional cost: Beauty/barbershop, professional drivers, lighted parking.

INDEPENDENT LIVING HOUSING

Type/size of apartment	*Monthly rental fee**
1-Bedroom, 677–826 sq. ft.	$2,150
2-Bedroom, 1,013–1,303 sq. ft.	$2,650
2-Bedroom/den, 1,404 sq. ft.	$3,500

**For double occupancy add $500 to the monthly fee. All utilities except telephone included. Fully equipped, all-electric kitchen, washer/dryer, carpeting, sheer draperies, additional storage areas, individual temperature control, 24-hour emergency call system. Balcony, patio, or bay window.*

Activities: Full-time activities director. Swimming pool, spa, exercise room, guest lectures, movies, classes and meetings, travel tours, library, arts and crafts, special cultural and sporting events.

Availability: Limited. Waiting list for some apartment styles.

Health services and rates: Residents receive 15 days of free care per year (60 days lifetime) in either the on-site health care center or in Assisted Living. Speech, physical, and occupational therapy offered. Full-time activity therapist. Many doctors in the area make calls at the health care center.

- 100 Assisted Living units*
  Suites, 268–395 sq. ft. $2,250–3,250/month

  **Four floor plans, some with balconies. Rental furniture available.*

- 59-Bed nursing facility
  Semiprivate $95/day
  Private $115/day

"An attitude of caring is evident in the dedicated and energetic staff of The Remington Club. Each staff member is trained to provide the friendly, personalized service that has become our hallmark."

RANCHO PARK VILLA

1500 West Cypress
San Dimas, CA 91773
(909) 592-9662
Caroline Chipman, administrator

Type of community: Independent Living with personal care services

Rancho Park Villa is located in a neighborhood setting on 17 acres. A distinctive seven-storybuilding houses suites as well as private and semiprivate rooms for Independent Living, each with either a private balcony or patio offering panoramic views of the San Gabriel Mountains or the valley below. A two-story common area is attached by walkway. Personal care services are available in residents' apartments. Nearby service facilities include a major hospital, several medical centers with physicians and dentists, churches, shopping center, restaurants, and banks. Rancho Park Villa is 30 miles east of Los Angeles.

Financial plan: Monthly rental. Rental rate guaranteed for one year. No lease.

Ownership and management: American Retirement Villas, owner and manager of 26 retirement communities in California and one in Arizona. Twenty years of experience. Opened in 1987.

Minimum age: 62 years.

Population: 159 residents; 124 women, 34 men, 3 couples.

Number of units: 163 Independent Living units; 23 rooms for residents who are nonambulatory.

Dining plan: Three meals plus snacks per day included in the monthly fee. Private dining room. Occasional meals delivered if resident isn't feeling well.

INDEPENDENT LIVING HOUSING

Type/size of apartment	*Monthly fee**
Studio, 208 sq. ft.	$1,300
Suite, 2 rooms, 416 sq. ft.	$2,400

**For double occupancy add $300 to the monthly fee. All utilities except telephone included. Furnishings are available. Individually controlled heating and air-conditioning, 24-hour emergency call system, carpeting, draperies, private baths, cable TV.*

Services: *Included in the monthly fee:* Housekeeping, personal laundry and flat-linen service, scheduled transportation.

At additional cost: Beauty/barbershop, gift shop.

Activities: Exercise, movies, continuing education classes, concerts, library, arts and crafts workshop, shuffleboard, poker party, cooking lessons, bingo, bridge, excursions, Bible study, sing-alongs.

Availability: Limited.

Health services and rates: Two levels of personal care service (assistance with bathing, dressing, grooming, scheduled monitoring, personal companionship and escort service, etc.) available in resident's apartment. Respite care offered for short-term stays, prorated on monthly fee.

- Personal care services

  Level 1 $300/in addition to monthly fee
  Level 2 $600/in addition to monthly fee

"Rancho Park Villa offers one- and two-week trial stays: $100 for one week; $250 for two weeks. Fee includes three meals per day plus snacks, scheduled activities, completely furnished room with TV, local transportation, laundry and linen service, personal attention to individual needs."

THE CARLISLE

1450 Post Street
San Francisco, CA 94109
(415) 929-0200
Oliver Spencer, marketing manager

Type of community: Nonprofit Continuing Care, modified contract

Located on beautiful Cathedral Hill, with a stunning view of San Francisco's skyline, the Carlisle contains 121 condominium residences in a 12-story, new, modern building. The Carlisle offers a dramatic entry lobby with parlor, lounge with grand piano, terrace, outdoor gardens and walking paths. St. Mary's Hospital, which offers Skilled Nursing, is next door. Assisted Living services are offered in resident's condominium.

Financial plan: Condominium purchase fee plus monthly fee.

Ownership and management: Jointly managed by St. Mary's Hospital and Medical Center and Senior Living Communities. Managers of The Breaks in Long Beach and the Rossmore Regency in Laguna Hills. Opened in 1992.

INDEPENDENT LIVING HOUSING

Type/size of apartment	*Purchase fee*	*Monthly fee**
Studio, 400 sq. ft.	$145,000–170,000	$1,455
Junior 1-bedroom, 550 sq. ft.	$190,000–265,000	$1,575
1-Bedroom, 690 sq. ft.	$286,000–300,000	$1,635
1-Bedroom, 825 sq. ft.	$335,000–435,000	$1,675
1-Bedroom, den, 970 sq. ft.	$410,000–450,000	$1,775
1-Bedroom, den, 1,100 sq. ft.	$490,000–550,000	$1,955
2-Bedroom, 1,225 sq. ft.	$525,000–580,000	$2,255

Purchase price is higher for top floor and corners.

**For double occupancy add $655 to the monthly fee. All utilities except telephone included. Wide choice of carpeting and window treatments, individually controlled thermostats, convenient kitchenettes, 24-hour emergency call system. Many condominiums have balconies with city views.*

Minimum age: 62 years.

Population: 150 residents; 73% women, 27% men, 50% couples.

Number of units: 121 Independent Living condominiums.

Dining plan: Continental breakfast plus choice of lunch or dinner daily included in the monthly fee. Champagne brunch on Sunday. Private dining room.

Services: *Included in the monthly fee:* Weekly housekeeping and flat-linen service, scheduled transportation, garage parking, valet parking.

At additional cost: Beauty/barbershop, guest accommodations.

Activities: Daily social, cultural, or recreational events, theater outings, concerts, lectures, arts and crafts. TV, game, and card rooms, library, continuing education classes, excursions and tours.

Availability: Limited.

Health services and rates: Registered nurse practitioner on-site. Each condominium is licensed to receive Assisted Living services. Skilled Nursing is off-site at nearby St. Mary's Hospital.

"Basic long-term care insurance program included in the monthly fee covers basic costs beyond limited hospital stay, covering up to $500 a month in Assisted Living services and up to $1,000 per month for Skilled Nursing care. The Premier Long-Term Care Plan is available for an additional $190 per month and has no minimum, covers all Assisted Living and Skilled Nursing expenses.

"The Carlisle's premium location and views, luxurious amenities, first-rate services, and the advantages of condominium ownership set it apart."

THE SEQUOIAS–SAN FRANCISCO

1400 Geary Boulevard
San Francisco, CA 94109
(415) 922-9700
Nadine Naughton, director marketing/admissions

Type of community: Nonprofit Continuing Care, all-inclusive contract

Accreditation: Continuing Care Accreditation Commission

This 25-story high-rise contemporary apartment building atop San Francisco's Cathedral Hill offers breathtaking views of the city and the Golden Gate Bridge and is perfectly suited for those who enjoy a cosmopolitan setting. The building's elegant Garden Court area features skylights rivaling those of many fine hotels, and open corridors overlook the atrium. The main level also includes a gift shop, library, chapel, a woodworking shop, and several meetings rooms. The complex has great roof walking and viewing areas. Independent Living, Assisted Living, and Skilled Nursing are located on premises. The facility is less than two blocks from Japantown, theaters, and shopping, and eight blocks from Davies Symphony Hall and Civic Center.

Financial plan: Entrance fee plus monthly fee. Residents are entitled to a refund of a portion of the entrance fee under certain circumstances set forth in the Continuing Care Agreement, which each resident signs. $1,500 waiting list deposit per person, partially refundable.

Ownership and management: Northern California Presbyterian Homes, Inc., owner of three other life care communities in the Bay Area. Opened in 1969.

Minimum age: 65 years; must apply before 79th birthday (if couple, spouse may be younger).

Population: 381 residents.

Number of units: 300 Independent Living apartments; 11 Assisted Living apartments, 49 Skilled Nursing beds.

INDEPENDENT LIVING HOUSING

Type/size of apartment	*Entrance fee*	*Monthly fee*
Studio, 371 sq. ft.	$40,000–46,000	$1,175–1,221
Large studio, 458 sq. ft.	$48,600–85,000	$1,311–1,325
1-Bedroom, 583 sq. ft. single	$95,200–150,000	$1,423–1,444
1-Bedroom, 583 sq. ft. double	$115,200–170,000	$2,233–2,253
2-Bedroom, 1,045 sq. ft. double	$175,000–269,000	$2,549–2,802

All utilities except telephone included. Newly decorated with wall-to-wall carpeting, new paint, draperies, blinds in selected apartments, updated kitchenettes and bathrooms, 24-hour emergency call system.

Dining plan: Three meals a day included in the monthly fee. Buffet option for breakfast and lunch. Catering service for private parties. Modified menu plans for those with special dietary considerations. Private dining room.

Services: *Included in the monthly fee:* Weekly housekeeping and flat-linen services.

At additional cost: Guest accommodations, parking, beauty/barbershop, faxing/copying/notarization.

Activities: Access to enclosed swimming pool, convenient access to downtown San Francisco and its enormous array of cultural events. At least 35 committees plan a variety of activities, including concerts, seminars, bridge lessons, Tai Chi practice, exercise, films, religious services, dominos, white elephant sales.

Availability: Some apartments are reserved, others are available for immediate occupancy.

Health services and rates: Temporary home health care, Assisted Living, Skilled Nursing fees covered with the resident's monthly fee. Registered nurses are on duty 24 hours a day. Physical therapy on-site.

- 11 Assisted Living units
- 49 Skilled Nursing beds

"Independence and a sense of permanence come with living at The Sequoias, where residents are free to come and go as they please, worship and entertain as they choose, and participate as much or as little as they like in an active and varied social life among friends and neighbors. Residents at The Sequoias also enjoy the peace of mind that comes with knowing that they have a permanent home, even if life should take them beyond the limits of their financial resources."

THE INN AT WILLOW GLEN

1185 Pedro Street
San Jose, CA 95125
(408) 275-9040
Jeanie Lalor, administrator

Type of community: Independent and Assisted Living

This two-story Mediterranean-style building with landscaped interior courtyard is located in a residential neighborhood. Shops, banks, churches, and full medical and hospital services are nearby.

Financial plan: Monthly rental fee.

Ownership and management: American Retirement Villas has financed, developed, and managed retirement residences for the past 20 years, housing over 3,000 residents. Opened in 1970. (Owned by American Retirement Villas since 1989.)

INDEPENDENT LIVING HOUSING

Type/size of apartment	*Monthly rental fee*
Studio, 187–200 sq. ft.	$1,250–2,400
1-Bedroom, 374–440 sq. ft.	$1,600–2,600

Monthly fees vary depending on size, location, and services required. All utilities except telephone included in the monthly rental fee. Individually controlled heating and air-conditioning, 24-hour emergency call system.

Minimum age: 65 years.

Population: 100 residents; 75% women, 25% men, 10% couples.

Number of units: 84 Independent Living units.

Dining plan: Three meals per day and snacks included in the monthly fee. Tray service is available when residents are not feeling well.

Services: *Included in the monthly fee:* Weekly house cleaning, personal laundry, flat-linen service, scheduled transportation.

At additional cost: Beauty/barbershop, general store, in-room telephone.

Activities: Full-time social director. Exercise classes, picnics and barbecues, piano concerts, movies, and other in-house entertainment. Game gatherings such as bridge club, weekly bingo, poker parties, billiards tournaments. Bible study, arts and crafts workshops, including painting and ceramics. Happy hours, lectures on health and travel.

Availability: Limited.

Health services and rates: Three levels of Assisted Living services are available to residents who need a little extra assistance to remain as independent as possible. Services offered in resident's apartment for an additional charge.

- Level 1 $300/month
- Level 2 $600/month
- Level 3 $1,000/month

"It is our staff and homelike atmosphere that makes The Inn at Willow Glen a wonderful place for seniors to call home. The Inn offers a warm, secure, and caring environment. Our philosophy is to encourage independence by providing the extra services and assistance needed so that seniors can do what they most enjoy."

VILLA FONTANA

5555 Prospect Road
San Jose, CA 95129
(408) 255-5555
June Fox, sales director

Type of community: Continuing Care, modified contract

Located in the Santa Clara Valley, this community is made up of three buildings on a small, self-contained campus that houses Independent Living, Assisted Living, and Skilled Nursing. Villa Fontana is a two-story stucco, Mediterranean-style building. Westgate Convalescent Center is a one-story building with several garden courtyards. Each building has a garden courtyard and patio. The facility is near major roadways, shopping areas, banks, and restaurants.

Financial plan: Monthly rental fee.

Ownership and management: Beverly Enterprises, a financially strong corporation, owner/manager of 12 retirement communities. Opened in 1974.

Minimum age: None.

Population: 395 residents; 80% women, 20% men, 10% couples.

INDEPENDENT LIVING HOUSING

Type/size of apartment	*Monthly rental fee**
Studio, 450 sq. ft.	$1,775
Alcove, 550 sq. ft.	$1,995
1-Bedroom, 700 sq. ft.	$2,400

**For double occupancy add $300 to the monthly fee. All utilities except telephone included. Wall-to-wall carpeting, draperies, 24-hour emergency call system, kitchenette (refrigerator, sink, countertop).*

Number of units: 85 Independent Living apartments; 31 Assisted Living studios, 265 Skilled Nursing beds.

Dining plan: Three meals included in the monthly fee. Private dining room. Room service available.

Services: *Included in the monthly fee:* Weekly housekeeping and flat-linen service, scheduled transportation, ice-cream parlor, check cashing service.

At additional cost: Beauty/barbershop, postal service.

Activities: Gardening, library, bridge club, poker nights, scenic drives, indoor walking, culture club, road runners travel club, armchair travel, golf, films, reading programs, games, bowling, bingo, trips to cultural and entertainment events.

Availability: Limited; three- to six-month waiting list for some type of units.

Health services and rates:

- 31 Assisted Living studios
  Semiprivate $1,975/month
  Private $2,495/month*

**For double occupancy add $300 to the monthly fee.*

- 265 Skilled Nursing beds
  2- or 3-Bedrooms $90–$145/day

"The Continuum of Care available on a rental basis is unique in the San Jose area. Celebrating 20 years of service to area senior citizens, Villa Fontana has an outstanding record of success and stability. Our emphasis is on individual and personalized service, from seven-day transportation to the select menu and tableside service in our dining room."

THE PENINSULA REGENT

One Baldwin Avenue
San Mateo, CA 94401
(415) 579-5500
Janet Meiselman, marketing director

Type of community: Continuing Care, modified contract

The Peninsula Regent offers elegant condominium living with all the amenities of a fine resort, the equity preservation of home ownership, and the security and peace of mind of a comprehensive health care program. An 11-story building of Mediterranean design houses Independent and Assisted Living. The community is within walking distance to downtown San Mateo, surrounded by four award-winning landscaped courtyards, including a covered swimming pool and spa, lily pond and fountain court, potting shed, croquet lawn and putting green.

Financial plan: Purchase price plus monthly fee. Transfer fee is 10% of the original price of the unit and 75% of any appreciated value.

Ownership and management: Bay Area Senior Services, a nonprofit, for-public-benefit subsidiary of Bridge Housing Corporation in San Francisco. Owned by developers Gerson Bakar, Peter Applegate, and Thomas Callinan (BAC Associates). Opened in 1988.

INDEPENDENT LIVING HOUSING

Type/size of unit	*Purchase price*	*Monthly fee**
1-Bedroom, 850–1,150 sq. ft.	$275,000–430,000	$1,800–2,200
2-Bedroom, 1,150–1,350 sq. ft.	$450,000–575,000	$2,300–2,500

**For double occupancy add $1,132 to the monthly fee. Fully equipped kitchens, 24-hour emergency call system, wall-to-wall carpeting, cable TV, individually controlled heating and air-conditioning, balcony, washer/dryer.*

Minimum age: 60 years.

Population: 260 residents; 70% women, 30% men, 20% couples.

Number of units: 207 Independent Living apartments; 20 Assisted Living suites; Skilled Nursing provided off-site.

Dining plan: One meal per day included in the monthly fee. Private dining area available.

Services: *Included in the monthly fee:* Weekly housecleaning and flat-linen services, scheduled transportation.

At additional cost: Guest accommodations on penthouse level, beauty/barbershop.

Activities: Social director. Library, card and club rooms, arts and crafts studio, exercise room, covered swimming pool and spa, gardening, lawn croquet, exercise classes, water aerobics, shopping excursions, watercolor classes, penthouse meeting room, movies, lectures.

Availability: Limited.

Health services and rates: Comprehensive health care plan that includes a medical supplement and a long-term care insurance program. Wellness program individually tailors health programs for each resident. On-site nursing and on-call medical teams. Nearby Mills Peninsula Hospital provides Skilled Nursing and acute care.

- 20 Assisted Living suites $2,277/month
- Skilled Nursing off-site (at Mills Hospital) $2,277/month

"The Peninsula Regent is an innovative Continuing Care community offering its residents luxury living combined with a comprehensive health care program and the preservation of equity. A true feeling of warmth and community has evolved here, which contributes to The Peninsula Regent's appeal. The location and design truly complement and enhance residents' lifestyles."

THE STRATFORD

601 Laurel Avenue
San Mateo, CA 94401
(415) 342-4106
Ann L. Murray, marketing director

Type of community: Continuing Care, modified contract

Ideally situated across from San Mateo's beautiful Central Park, The Stratford is an elegant, new ten-story building with European-style balconies. There is a light, spacious feeling throughout the building including the large, elegant common living room with wood-burning marble fireplace and library with bird's-eye maple molding and finishes. A dining terrace is located outside the dining room. Independent Living and Assisted Living are on-site, and Skilled Nursing is included in the long-term care plan. The Stratford is just a short walk away from downtown's many restaurants, shops, and services.

Financial plan: Condominium purchase plus monthly fee.

INDEPENDENT LIVING HOUSING

Type of residence	*Purchase price*	*Monthly fee single/double*
1-Bedroom, 880 sq. ft.	$430,000–450,000	$2,250
2-Bedroom, 1,155–1,630 sq. ft.	$560,000–845,000	$2,250/3,400
3-Bedroom/dining room, 2,930 sq. ft.	$1,590,000	$3,870/4,400

Residents pay for their own utilities. Fully carpeted, draped, full kitchen, washer/dryer, marble fireplace, wet bar, 24-hour emergency call system, individually controlled heating and air-conditioning. Pets allowed.

Ownership and management: Privately owned. Developer-occupied and -managed. Opened in August 1992.

Minimum age: 62 years.

Population: 85 residents.

Number of units: 65 Independent Living condominiums; 9 Assisted Living units, Skilled Nursing off-site.

Dining plan: One meal per day included in the monthly fee. The classically trained chef uses natural ingredients and locally grown produce. Afternoon tea is offered daily in the living room. Two private dining rooms and catering services are available.

Services: *Included in the monthly fee:* Weekly housekeeping and flat-linen services, scheduled transportation, concierge desk, valet parking.

At additional cost: Beauty/barbershop, guest accommodations.

Activities: Swimming pool, bridge room, library, garden room, woodworking area, whirlpool and sauna, fitness center, tennis courts, walking paths in park across the street, golf nearby.

Availability: Limited.

Health services and rates: Comprehensive long-term care plan included in the resident's monthly fee. All health insurance forms and claims are administered by Stratford personnel. Therapy room and health spa in main building. Medical director supervises on-site RN and around-the-clock staff.

The resident's monthly fee remains the same should the resident move into Assisted Living or Skilled Nursing.

- 9 Assisted Living units
- Skilled Nursing off-site

"The Stratford combines the best features of a small European hotel with complete medical and financial security for retirement. And with a staff-to-resident ratio of 1 to 1.5, every service is merely an inquiry away. The Stratford also welcomes pets and is perfectly situated across from 16 acres of Central Park."

ALDERSLY

326 Mission Avenue
San Rafael, CA 94901
(415) 453-7425
Hayley Severe, director of marketing

Type of community: Nonprofit Continuing Care, modified contract

Aldersly, a carefully designed complex of individual redwood, brick, and glass Independent Living apartments, is nestled in the hillside on three acres in the heart of Marin County. The community offers beautiful garden paths and a magnificent view of Mt. Tamalpais. The Danish heritage is reflected in the names of its buildings, the celebration of the Danish traditional holidays, and a white milestone near the

INDEPENDENT LIVING HOUSING

Type/size of apartment	*Entrance fee**	*Monthly fee**
Studio, 390 sq. ft.	$25,000–46,150	$1,120–1,468
Alcove, 392 sq. ft.	$43,120–47,500	$1,170–1,445
1-Bedroom, 450–700 sq. ft	$40,800–93,000	$1,120–2,200

**For double occupancy add $10,000 to the entrance fee and $615 to the monthly fee. All utilities except telephone included. Apartments may be furnished by the resident or by the facility. Individually controlled heating and air-conditioning, 24-hour emergency call system.*

entrance reads "7,174 miles to Denmark." Aldersly provides easy access to buses providing transportation throughout Marin County and the San Francisco Bay Area. Business and professional offices as well as shops, restaurants, and theaters are within walking distance. An airport bus is available connecting with San Francisco Airport. Assisted Living apartments and Skilled Nursing are on-site.

Financial plan: Entrance fee plus monthly fee.

Ownership and management: Nonprofit corporation. Opened in 1921.

Minimum age: 62 years.

Population: 100 residents (40% Danish); 69% women, 31% men.

Number of units: 69 Independent Living apartments; 17 Assisted Living units, 20-bed Skilled Nursing facility.

Dining plan: Three meals per day are included in the monthly fee.

Services: *Included in the monthly fee:* Biweekly housekeeping, flat-linen service.

At additional cost: Beauty/barbershop, personal laundry, sundries.

Activities: Activities scheduled daily, including entertainment, outings, current events, health/fitness classes, art classes, games, crafts, seasonal events.

Availability: Waiting lists vary from several months to ten years, depending on the type of accommodation desired.

Health services and rates: Assistance with daily living in resident's apartment is offered free of charge, including help with dressing and bathing.

- 17 Assisted Living units $67/day
- 20 Skilled Nursing beds $115/day

"Aldersly is a special place for special people. Visiting Aldersly is discovering a small village of apartment-style housing tucked away in a beautiful garden setting. It is a world set apart from the hustle and bustle of everyday existence and yet it is within walking distance to services and shops. In the 72 years of its existence, Aldersly continues to move forward to meet the needs of its residents. The most recent addition is a new health care and community center. Historically, Aldersly continues to be a significant part of Marin County's rich past."

DRAKE TERRACE AT NORTHGATE

275 Los Ranchitos Road
San Rafael, CA 94903
(415) 491-1935
Susan Edwards, manager

Type of community: Independent and Assisted Living

This three-story apartment complex lies in an urban, residential, tree-lined setting. Independent Living and Assisted Living apartments are under one roof.

INDEPENDENT LIVING HOUSING

Type/size of apartment	*Monthly fee**
1-Bedroom, 475–600 sq. ft.	$1,195–1,795
2-Bedroom, 650–900 sq. ft.	$1,795–2,495

**For double occupancy add $400 to the monthly fee. All utilities, except telephone, included. Kitchenettes, wall-to-wall carpeting, 24-hour emergency call system. Individually controlled heating and air-conditioning. Small pets are allowed on first-floor apartments with patios.*

Vegetable garden and patio garden are provided. The Mall at Northgate, the largest mall in Marin County, with over 100 shops, 13 restaurants, and theaters, is one block away. Marin County Civic Center and Kaiser Hospital are nearby. Easy access to San Francisco is also provided.

Financial plan: Monthly rental fee. Month-to-month lease. Rental fee is guaranteed for the first 12 months.

Ownership and management: Owned by Transamerica Retirement Corporation. Managed by Transamerica Retirement Management, which has more than 20 years experience in the management of retirement communities. Opened in 1989.

Minimum age: 65 years.

Population: 130 residents; 84% women, 16% men, 7% couples.

Number of units: 93 Independent Living apartments; 30 Assisted Living studios.

Dining plan: Three meals per day included in the monthly fee. Tray service available. Private dining room. Meal credits available when residents are on vacation.

Services: *Included in the monthly fee:* Weekly housekeeping, personal laundry, transportation, parking, laundry facilities.

At additional cost: Beauty/barbershop, gift shop.

Activities: Social director. Community and individual gardening areas, library, two lounges with game tables and big-screen TV, arts and crafts, sing-alongs, happy hours.

Availability: Waiting list. Two years for one-bedroom; two to six months for two-bedroom. $100 fee for waiting list.

Health services and rates: Home care services are available to residents in their apartments, i.e., monitoring of prescribed medications, assistance with personal activities, therapeutic diets.

- 30 Assisted Living units
  Studio $1695–2,595/month
  (furnished studios available)

"TRM believes that resident participation ensures good, responsive management. They also believe that the management must not only be willing to listen but also eager to act on issues of importance to its residents. By combing this genuine concern with years of experience in operational strategy, TRM creates an atmosphere at Drake Terrace in which care and respect are part of every management decision."

SMITH RANCH HOMES

100 Deer Valley Road
San Rafael, CA 94903
(415) 491-4918 or (800) 772-6264
Connie L. Kirwin

Type of community: Independent Living with long-term care insurance

The luxury condominiums that make up Smith Ranch Homes are situated on 37 spacious, secluded acres of

meticulously landscaped grounds in Marin County, north of San Francisco. The centrally located clubhouse is the focal point of all services and amenities. An expansive terrace overlooks the pool and surrounding hills. Landscaped walking paths, streams, raised gardening areas, and a putting green are all on campus, while nearby McInnis Park offers a nine-hole golf course, driving range, clubhouse, soccer and baseball fields, canoeing, fishing, and picnicking—all only 30 minutes from downtown San Francisco.

Financial plan: Condominium purchase fee plus monthly fee.

Ownership and management: Owned by residents. Smith Ranch Homes was developed by Tishman Speyer Partnership. Once all units are sold homeowners will take over management. Opened in 1990.

Minimum age: 55 years.

Population: 230 residents; 64% women, 36% men.

Number of units: 226 Independent Living residences.

Dining plan: Twenty meals per month included in the monthly fee. Continental breakfast served weekdays. Two restaurants, cocktail lounge. Full wine and cocktail service available during lunch and dinner. Private dining in each residence and catered receptions are available. If residents are away for an extended time, a credit of up to 50% may be issued toward the dining portion of the monthly fee.

Services: *Included in the monthly fee:* Weekly housekeeping, concierge and valet service, regularly scheduled transportation.

At additional cost: General store, beauty salon, guest accommodations.

Activities: Fitness center, heated lap pool, aerobics, hiking along miles of the area's hills and valleys, day and weekend trips, croquet, horseshoes, lawn bowling, bocci ball, table tennis, bridge, poker, dominoes, Scrabble, bingo, gardening, library. Marin Civic Center offers lecture and music series. Intercommunity television network lists activities.

Availability: Some units available.

Health services and rates: Long-term care insurance (for those who qualify) included in residents' monthly fee covers residents for one year to life, depending on plan chosen. Residents select from health care providers in the local community. In-home care, Assisted Living, and Skilled Nursing are available. Marin General Hospital Health Services has a branch office on campus and offers home care services and an educational program. The Guardian Foundation runs Guardian at Smith Ranch, which has 80 Assisted Living and Skilled Nursing beds.

"It is the distinctive level of quality, the thoughtful attention to detail and the abundance of

INDEPENDENT LIVING HOUSING

Type/size of home	*Purchase price*	*Monthly fee**
1-Bedroom, 753–882 sq. ft.	$195,000–250,000	$1,620–1,675
1-Bedroom/den, 948–1,099 sq. ft.	$280,000–360,000	$1,705–1,770
2-Bedroom, 1,261–2,209 sq. ft.	$350,000–600,000	$1,840–1,895

**For double occupancy add approximately $600 to the monthly fee. Electricity charges and telephone not included. Gas-lighted fireplace, 24-hour emergency call system, fully equipped kitchen, washer/dryer, individually controlled heating and air-conditioning, wood trim, terrace access from master bedroom.*

services and amenities that make Smith Ranch Homes such a truly exceptional value. Smith Ranch Homes offers unrivaled beauty and discerning design; country living with city amenities close by."

VILLA MARIN

100 Thorndale Drive
San Rafael, CA 94903
(415) 492-2408
Suzanne McGuinn, marketing director

Type of community: Continuing Care, all-inclusive contract

Crowning a six-acre ridgetop 17 miles north of San Francisco's Golden Gate Bridge, Villa Marin is surrounded by more than 20 acres of protected open space. On Quail Hill in San Rafael, Villa Marin's four-story modern complex of Independent Living apartments have expansive views of rolling hills and a promenade deck. Four levels of health care are offered including Assisted Living and Skilled Nursing. Shopping centers, movie theaters, golf courses, hiking and bicycle trails, Muir Woods, Marin Civic Center and Memorial Theater, and California wine country are all nearby.

Financial plan: Purchase fee plus monthly fee. Condominiums are purchased by the residents. Owners are free to sell or trade their condominiums or bequeath ownership. The only restriction is that the new owner must be approved by the admissions committee, meeting the prescribed medical, physical, and financial standards.

Ownership and management: Owned by residents who elect a board of directors. The board hires a manager. Opened in 1985.

Minimum age: 62 years.

Population: 275 residents; 80% women, 20% men, 25% couples.

Number of units: 224 Independent Living condominium apartments; 14 Assisted Living rooms, 31 Skilled Nursing beds

Dining plan: Choice of one meal included in the monthly fee. Additional meals available at reasonable cost. Private dining room. Catering services.

Services: *Included in the monthly fee:* Weekly housekeeping and flat-linen services, courtesy transportation, indoor parking.

At additional cost: Beauty/barbershop, gift shop, guest accommodations. Maintenance staff available to provide services at a reasonable fee.

Activities: Activities director. Crafts, indoor swimming, paddle tennis, shuffleboard, gardening, woodworking, library, expertly organized excursions, concerts, lectures, films, card room, auditorium, parties, gym.

INDEPENDENT LIVING HOUSING

Type/size of apartment	*Purchase price*	*Monthly fee**
1-Bedroom, 660–790 sq. ft.	$210,000–290,000	$1,052–1,136/1,669
1-Bedroom/den, 1,000/1,096 sq. ft.	$375,000–425,000	$1,271–1,333/1,804–1,866
2-Bedroom, 1,234 sq. ft.	$500,000–550,000	$1,421/1,954
3-Bedroom, 1,400–3,000 sq. ft.	$650,000–750,000	$1,796–2,235/1,846–3,000

**For double occupancy add $648 to the monthly fee. Full kitchen, generous closets, balcony, 29 variations of floor plans, 24-hour emergency call system, individually controlled heating and air-conditioning.*

Availability: Priority waiting list varies depending on specific floor plan.

Health services and rates: Comprehensive medical care is covered with purchase of condominium and monthly fee. Four levels of health care. Clinic care. Hospital care for acute illnesses is nearby. Physical therapy and outpatient clinic with physicians.

- 14 Assisted Living rooms
- 31 Skilled Nursing units

"Villa Marin offers the best of two worlds: the independence of individual home ownership and the security of a safe environment, assured medical care, and warmly supportive associates. Villa Marin's residents are well traveled, sophisticated, and accomplished people who have a high level of independence and are involved in activities and decision-making of the community."

Harriet and Bill, 75 and 79 years

The Forest at Duke, Durham, North Carolina

"WHAT? . . . A retirement community?"

This is how some of Harriet and Bill's friends reacted when they were told about their plan to move into The Forest at Duke, a life care retirement community in Durham, North Carolina. "People thought we were going into a nursing home," says Harriet. "There's a misconception among many people that a nursing home and a retirement community are one and the same."

Harriet and Bill are healthy and active and are making their life at The Forest rich and fulfilling. As Harriet explains, "We wanted to move into a retirement community while we were still able to be active in the community and take advantage of all that it offers." Bill adds, "It is also a base from which we can travel." Because they are still active, traveling is one activity that they want to do more of; and in their new North Carolina location, they are two hours away from the ocean to the east and the mountains to the west. Harriet and Bill participate in Duke University's continuing education program, as well as all the community activities.

Harriet and Bill visited the community several times before they moved in. They had a chance to taste the food and to meet a few of the residents; in the end, they were confident in their decision to move from their home in Denver, where they had lived for the preceding four years.

Although they left friends behind, Harriet points out that they have made plenty of new friends at The Forest at Duke. Bill's former position as vice-president of sales for a heavy machinery company had required his family to relocate many times throughout his career, so the move to Durham, in itself, did not bother Bill; but the realization "that this is really the last move" did. "Once you move in, although you could get out, the financial burden would be pretty heavy."

They chose a financial plan with an entrance fee that is amortized over five years. They could have paid a higher, refundable entrance fee, and if they had gone into the retirement community at the age of 85, that plan might have been more appropriate. Bill points out, "Harriet and I expect to be able to invest the money we save with the lower entrance fee better than The Forest at Duke would be able to. You also have to consider, with the cost of living increasing 5% per year, what the monthly cost of living will be ten years from now."

The Forest at Duke opened in September 1992. Because it is a new community, about 62% of the occupants are couples. This is a relatively high percentage of couples and one reason that The Forest at Duke appeals to Harriet and Bill.

Another reason Harriet and Bill chose The Forest at Duke is the impression they received while visiting. "The management and staff are great people," says Bill. "They were interested in us and friendly and knew their business. In some of the other places we visited, we asked a few questions and the answers were, 'Well, I don't really know the answer to that question yet.'" Harriet and Bill also like the fact that both Duke University and the University of North Carolina at Chapel Hill are just around the corner. Other pluses they point out are the moderate climate and The Forest's strong financial record, which they had an accountant examine for them.

"This is our gift to our children," Harriet says. "We wanted to be in a location that wasn't too near or too far from any of our three children, and we did not want to become a burden to our children if we became ill. If our children had to put us in a nursing home, besides the heavy financial burden (upwards of $30,000 a year) they would have to be on the scene, checking regularly to see that things were getting done. When you are in an establishment like The Forest at Duke, you can count on everything being taken care of for you."

THE SAMARKAND

2550 Treasure Drive
Santa Barbara, CA 93105-4148
(805) 687-0701
Pam Bigelow, marketing representative

Type of community: Not-for-profit Continuing Care, modified contract

Accreditation: Continuing Care Accreditation Commission

Six two-story Independent Living apartment buildings and cottages, a 59-bed health center, and two Assisted Living Centers—Brandel Hall and Heritage Court—are set amid 16 landscaped acres with views of surrounding mountains, Santa Barbara Mission, and the Pacific Ocean. The campus includes a center courtyard with pond and an outdoor swimming pool. Santa Barbara offers fine museums, theater, symphonies, the Presidio, as well as botanical gardens, beaches, sailing and fishing, public golf courses, and lawn-bowling green. The Samarkand is within an hour and a half drive to Los Angeles. Cottage Hospital, an acute care hospital, is three blocks away.

Financial plan: Entrance fee plus monthly fee. Entrance fee amortizes at 2% per month.

Ownership and management: Owned/managed by the Evangelical Covenant Church/Covenant Retirement Communities that owns/manages 12 retirement communities in California, Connecticut, Florida, Illinois, Minnesota, and Washington. Covenant Retirement Communities was founded in 1886. Opened in 1966.

Minimum age: 62 years.

Population: 380 residents; 74% women, 26% men, 26% couples.

INDEPENDENT LIVING HOUSING

Type/size of unit	*Entrance fee**	*Monthly fee**
Studio, 271 sq. ft.	$41,000–49,500	$1,015
1-Bedroom, 562 sq. ft.	$69,500–112,000	$1,585
2-Bedroom, 689 sq. ft.	$117,000–175,000	$1,750

**For double occupancy add 10% to the entrance fee and $375 to the monthly fee. All utilities except telephone and cable TV included. Fully equipped kitchen or kitchenette, wall-to-wall carpeting, individually controlled heating, 24-hour emergency call system.*

Number of units: 200 Independent Living apartments; 68 Assisted Living units, 59-bed Skilled Nursing facility.

Dining plan: Three meals per day included in the monthly fee. Special diets and dietitian consultants, private banquet room, and tray service available.

Services: *Included in the monthly fee:* Weekly housekeeping and flat-linen services, scheduled transportation, free use of laundry facilities.

At additional cost: Beauty/barbershop, personal transportation.

Activities: Heated swimming pool, Jacuzzi, shuffleboard, putting green, library, chapel and vespers services, Bible study, exercise room, auditorium, TV and music lounge, billiards room, woodworking shop, arts and crafts rooms, various trips.

Availability: Limited. A couple of studios available; one-bedroom one to two year waiting list; two-bedroom three to five years; custom units five years or more.

Health services and rates: Independent Living residents receive 60 days free health care in the health center.

Geriatric nurse practitioner/walk-in clinic and physical therapy department. Residents select their own physicians.

- 68 Assisted Living units

Entrance fee	*Monthly fee*
$31,000	$1,680 or 2,200*

**Nonambulatory care.*

- 59-Bed health center

Semiprivate	$122.50/day

"The mission of Covenant Retirement Communities is to provide a balance, through facilities and programs, between security and independence for the resident, assisting in the achievement of the resident's maximum physical, mental, emotional, and spiritual capabilities and enjoyment."

VALLE VERDE

900 Calle de los Amigos
Santa Barbara, CA 93105
(805) 687-1571
Dereth Godar, retirement counselor

Type of community: Nonprofit Continuing Care, modified contract

Accreditation: Continuing Care Accreditation Commission

Single-story garden apartments of Spanish design are set among beautiful lawns, trees, and flowering gardens. The community is located on 56 acres nestled in the valley between the ocean and the Santa Barbara foothills. Valle Verde is one mile from the ocean and in close proximity to shopping center, services, and public transportation. The community adjoins a park, golf course, and residential district. Rolling hills covered with native shrub and oak trees surround the area. Valle Verde offers four levels of accommodations and care, ranging from Independent Living apartments to Skilled Nursing care.

Financial plan: Entrance fee plus monthly fee. The entrance fee is amortized at a rate of 1.5% per month. There is a 90-day trial period during which the entire entrance fee is refundable. Nonrefundable application fee of $250 ($450 for couples).

Ownership and management: American Baptist Homes of the West, a nonprofit corporation providing retirement housing and health care services for over 40 years. Owner/manager of 17 continuing care communities in Arizona, California, and Washington. Opened in 1957.

Minimum age: 62 years.

Population: 400 residents; 70% women, 30% men, 30% couples.

INDEPENDENT LIVING HOUSING

Type/size of apartment	*Entrance fee**	*Monthly fee**
Studio, 340 sq. ft.	$35,000	$1,250
1-Bedroom, 530–774 sq. ft.	$60,000–85,000	$1,250–1,470
2-Bedroom, 900–1,127 sq. ft.	$100,000–145,000	$1,470–1,785

**For double occupancy add $5,000 to the entrance fee and $510 to the monthly fee. All utilities except telephone included. Individually controlled heating and air-conditioning, wall-to-wall carpeting, drapes, kitchen appliances, cable TV, 24-hour emergency call system.*

Number of units: 242 Independent Living apartments; 52 Assisted Living suites, 80-bed Skilled Nursing center.

Dining plan: One meal per day included in the monthly fee, except the studio, which includes three meals per day. Tray service and special diets available when ordered by a physician. Catered parties can be arranged.

Services: *Included in the monthly fee:* Scheduled transportation, weekly flat-linen service, bimonthly housekeeping, parking.

At additional cost: Beauty/barbershop, resident's shop, guest accommodations, personal coin-operated laundry facilities.

Activities: Birdwatching, woodworking shop, print shop, arts and crafts, billiards room, putting green, swimming pool, art studio, music corner, drama group, folk dancing, exercise classes, adult education, game nights, concerts, trips and tours, religious services, Jacuzzi, fireside lounge, prayer chapel, library, outings.

Availability: Some one-bedroom apartments available; two-bedroom apartments have a four to six-year waiting list.

Health services and rates: Residents are covered by the basic medical and nursing home insurance plan included in their monthly fee. There is no age or time limitation to the benefit of this plan, and it provides a $1,000 per month benefit toward care when transferring to the health center or Skilled Nursing. Weekly clinics operated by physicians who also serve on call for emergencies. Physical therapy. Resident services home care program provides occasional personal care to Independent Living residents.

- 52 Assisted Living rooms
  - Single suite $2,070/month
  - Deluxe suite $2,600/month
- 80-Bed Skilled Nursing facility
  - 3- and 4-Bed rooms $105/112 day
  - Semiprivate $128/day
  - Private $185/day

"When residents come to Valle Verde, they change their address, not their lifestyle. They may come and go as they please, remaining actively involved in their special organizations and interests. Residents participate in the activities and programs as they wish, enjoying the freedom to live an active lifestyle at their own pace."

MARIA DEL SOL

1405 East Main Street
Santa Maria, CA 93454
(805) 925-8713
Margarita Perry, assistant administrator, community relations

Type of community: Independent Living and Assisted Living

Located on 3.8 acres in northern Santa Barbara County, approximately 170 miles north of Los Angeles and 270 miles south of San Francisco, Maria Del Sol

INDEPENDENT LIVING HOUSING

Type/size of unit	*Monthly fee*
Studio, 285 sq. ft.	$975–1,200
2-Room suites, 570 sq. ft.	$1,600–1,850

All utilities except telephone included in the monthly fee. Apartments may be furnished by the resident, or resident may select furnished apartment. Individually controlled heating and air-conditioning, 24-hour emergency call system.

consists of a modern four-story Independent Living residence (52,000 square feet) connected to a facilities building via an enclosed hallway. The facility maintains beautifully manicured courtyards with flower gardens, grass, and walking paths. Maria Del Sol is located in a quiet neighborhood in the vicinity of major hospitals, several medical centers with physicians and dentists, a regional shopping center, restaurants, banks, and churches. Assisted Living services are available.

Financial plan: Monthly rental. Rental rates are guaranteed for one year. No security or down payment.

Ownership and management: American Retirement Villas, which owns and manages 26 retirement facilities in California. Opened in 1988.

Minimum age: 62 years.

Population: 100 residents; 83% women, 17% men.

Number of units: 125 private and semiprivate Independent Living rooms and suites.

Dining plan: Monthly fee includes three meals per day. Meals can be delivered in case of temporary illness.

Services: *Included in the monthly fee:* Housekeeping, free washers and dryers, scheduled transportation.

At additional cost: Beauty/barbershop, country store.

Activities: A full-time social director organizes various activities each week. Exercise classes, picnics and barbecues, piano concerts, movies, and other in-house entertainment. Games such as bridge, weekly bingo, poker parties, and billiards tournaments. Bible study, library, arts and crafts workshops, including jewelry making, painting, and ceramics. Happy hours, lectures on health and travel.

Availability: Limited.

Health services and rates: Assisted Living is offered in resident's apartment at an additional fee of $300 to $600 per month, depending on the amount of assistance a resident requires.

"The American Retirement Villas management team is dedicated to meeting the needs of today's active retiree. This group of skilled professionals has financed, developed, and managed retirement residences of excellence and distinction for the past 15 years. More than 1,000 seniors now call American Retirement Villas their home."

SPRING LAKE VILLAGE

5555 Montgomery Drive
Santa Rosa, CA 95409
(707) 538-8400
Jim Valinoti, marketing director

Type of community: Nonprofit Continuing Care, all-inclusive contract

This campus-style complex lies on a 26-acre site at the east end of Santa Rosa. Spring Lake Village is adjacent to Spring Lake Park on one side and Santa Rosa Creek on the other and surrounded by redwoods and hills. Vine-covered walkways and informal gardens blend into the natural terrain. Independent Living apartments and cottages, Assisted Living, and Skilled Nursing are all available. Santa Rosa is a lovely small city of 110,000 and growing rapidly. The Village is within an hour's drive of the Golden Gate Bridge and San Francisco.

Financial plan: Entrance fee plus monthly fee. The entrance fee is fully refundable up to the first 90 days of residency. After 90 days, the entrance fee is refundable, less $1^{1}/_{2}$% per month. If residents exhaust their finances, they will continue to be cared for at no charge.

Ownership and management: Developed and managed by the Episcopal Homes Foundation, owner/manager of three retirement communities in California. Resident input is sought through an elected independent council. Opened in 1986.

Minimum age: 65 years (maximum age for application is 79).

Population: 425 residents; 67% women, 23% men, 35% couples.

Number of units: 300 Independent Living apartments and cottages; 10-bed Assisted Living unit, 50 Skilled Nursing beds.

Dining plan: Three meals per day included in the monthly fee. Special diets and dietitian consultants available. Tray service on approval by staff physician. Three private banquet rooms.

Services: *Included in the monthly fee:* Weekly maid and flat-linen services, laundry rooms, resident locker and storage rooms, scheduled transportation.

At additional cost: Beauty/barbershop, gift shop, parking, sidewalk café.

Activities: Exercise room, indoor swimming pool and whirlpool, library, auditorium, chapel, billiards room, arts and crafts rooms.

Availability: Waiting list for two-bedroom. Other apartments have limited availability.

Health services and rates: Fees for physicians and surgeons are covered in the resident's monthly fee, as well as the cost of hospitalization at one of two acute care hospitals and convalescent care center. No deductibles or time limitations. Physicians and specialists on staff. Specialists not represented on the staff will be called in at no additional cost.

- 10-Bed personal care unit
- 50-Bed Skilled Nursing facility

"Residents in our life care program know that our medical care and services continue regardless of what happens to them financially. Should they be unable to meet their obligations, this care would continue without any change in accommodations or reduction in services."

INDEPENDENT LIVING HOUSING

Type/size of apartment	*Entrance fee**	*Monthly fee**
Studio, 490 sq. ft.	$61,600–75,000	$1,242
Alcove, 530 sq. ft.	$82,200–99,800	$1,289
1-Bedroom, 580–750 sq. ft.	$106,700–167,300	$1,353–1,540
2-Bedroom, 1,020 sq. ft.	$197,800–236,800	$1,905
Cottages		
1-Bedroom, 750 sq. ft.	$164,400–192,800	$1,566
2-Bedroom, 1,050 sq. ft.	$240,900–282,600	$1,943

**For double occupancy add $12,000 to the entrance fee and $956 to the monthly fee. All utilities including local telephone service included. Wall-to-wall carpeting, draperies, and kitchenettes, individually controlled heating and air-conditioning, individual patio or deck, 24-hour emergency call system.*

MOUNT MIGUEL COVENANT VILLAGE

325 Kempton Street
Spring Valley, CA 91977-5899
(619) 479-4790
Debbie Delinger, marketing director

Type of community: Not-for-profit Continuing Care, modified contract

Accreditation: Continuing Care Accreditation Commission

Set amid 28 parklike acres overlooking Sweetwater Lake, the Village's center building serves as the center of activity for the community. Gardens, sheltered walkways, and a 50-by-100-foot oval pond with three fountains are all on-site. The community is close to the recreational and cultural resources of San Diego, including the San Diego Zoo, Scripps Institute of Oceanology, and Sea World. Easy access is available to beaches, parks, theaters, shops, museums, galleries, and restaurants.

Financial plan: Entrance fee plus monthly fee. Full refund of entrance fee within the first 90 days of residency upon move out. If move out occurs after 90 days, the entrance fee is refunded at a prorated rate over a period of 50 months.

Ownership and management: Owned/managed by the Evangelical Covenant Church/Covenant Retirement Communities, which owns/manages 12 retirement communities in California, Connecticut, Florida, Illinois, Minnesota, and Washington. Covenant Retirement Communities was founded in 1886. Opened in 1965.

Minimum age: 62 years.

Population: 475 residents; 64% women, 36% men, 33% couples.

Number of units: 231 Independent Living apartments; 48 Assisted Living rooms, 99-bed Skilled Nursing facility.

Dining plan: Two meals per day included in the monthly fee. One meal per day option available.

Services: *Included in the monthly fee:* Weekly housekeeping and flat-linen services, scheduled transportation, parking, laundry rooms.

At additional cost: Beauty/barbershop, medical transportation.

Activities: Activities director. Swimming pool, spa, pitch-and-putt golf course, Bible study, arts and crafts, field trips, sports, nearby 18-hole golf course, game room, fitness center, library, craft and hobby rooms, gardening areas, lounges, woodworking shop, day trips to the ocean or mountains, weekly chapel services, tennis court, choir.

Availability: 8- to 12-month waiting list for smaller apartments, 7- to 8-year wait for larger apartments. $1,350 places you on waiting list.

INDEPENDENT LIVING HOUSING

Type/size of apartment	*Entrance fee single/double*	*Monthly fee**
Studio, 456 sq. ft.	$44,000–47,000/N/A	$736/N/A
1-Bedroom, 526 sq. ft.	$61,000–66,000/67,100–72,600	$918
2-Bedroom, 841 sq. ft.	$84,000–90,000/92,400–99,000	$1,098
Deluxe 2-bedroom, 1,021 sq. ft.	$94,000–101,000/103,400–111,100	$1,246/1,571

**For double occupancy add $325 to the monthly fee. All utilities except telephone included. Wall-to-wall carpeting, fully equipped kitchen, balcony or patio, individually controlled heating and air-conditioning, 24-hour emergency call system, cable TV.*

Health services and rates: Residents receive 60 days of nursing care at no extra charge. After 60 days, residents must pay 90% of the prevailing daily charge for such services. Respite program, physical therapy, and rehabilitative services.

- 48 Assisted Living units

Type of unit	*Entrance fee single/double*	*Monthly fee single/double*
Single suite	$33,500/ 43,500	$1,690/ 2,535
Connecting suites	N/A/$67,000	N/A/$3,380

- 99-Bed Skilled Nursing facility
  Semiprivate $110/day

"The mission of Covenant Retirement Communities is to provide a balance, through facilities and programs, between security and independence for the resident, assisting in the achievement of the resident's maximum physical, mental, emotional, and spiritual capabilities and enjoyment."

QUAKER GARDENS

12151 Dale Street
Stanton, CA 90680
(714) 530-9100
Barbara Williamson, director of admissions

Type of community: Nonprofit Continuing Care, all-inclusive contract

Quaker Gardens is located in Orange County, southern California, approximately 40 miles southeast of Los Angeles on seven acres of landscaped gardens. Three low-rise brick buildings and 16 houses adjacent to the campus house Independent Living residences. All campus units are linked with each other, the health center, and community buildings by covered walkways. Nearby attractions are Disneyland, Knott's Berry Farm, Universal Studios, and the Queen Mary.

Financial plan: Entrance fee plus monthly fee.

Ownership and management: Founded by a group of dedicated members of the Friends Southwest Yearly Meeting. The Yearly Meeting acts as sponsor

INDEPENDENT LIVING HOUSING

Type of apartment	*Entrance fee*	*Monthly fee single/double*
Single	$59,000	$1,195/2,390
Single/sunroom	$77,000	$1,195/2,390
Deluxe single	$71,000	$1,195/2,390
Deluxe suite	$89,000–97,000	$1,855/2,120
Homes		
1-Bedroom/garage	$98,000	$2,091/2,390
2-Bedroom	$95,000	$2,300/2,629
2-Bedroom/garage	$128,000–150,000	$2,300/2,629
3-Bedroom	$155,000–200,000	$2,300/2,629
4-Bedroom	$200,000	$2,300/2,629

All utilities except long-distance telephone included. Individually controlled heating and air-conditioning, 24-hour emergency call system, new wall-to-wall carpeting, draperies. Houses have fully equipped kitchens, laundry facilities, private patio and yard. 2-, 3-, and 4-bedroom houses have deluxe kitchen and wood-burning fireplace. Small pets allowed in houses. Apartment residents may have microwave ovens and small refrigerators.

to the Gardens, which is operated by a nonprofit corporation. The policies of Quaker Gardens are established by the board of trustees. Opened in 1965.

Minimum age: 62 years (if couple, spouse may be younger).

Population: 275 residents; 82% women, 18% men, 12% couples.

Number of units: 123 Independent Living apartments and 16 homes; 34 Assisted Living units, 58-bed Skilled Nursing facility, 50-bed Secured Living center.

Dining plan: Three meals per day included in the monthly fee. If desired by house residents, credits for two or three meals can be applied to monthly fee by special arrangement. Tray service and special diets, when approved by administration for medical reasons. Coffee and tea service, fresh fruit in lounge.

Services: *Included in the monthly fee:* Scheduled transportation, personal laundry facilities, weekly flat-linen service and housekeeping.

At additional cost: Beauty/barbershop, postal services, UPS package delivery and shipping, guest accommodations, carports.

Activities: Gardening, shuffleboard, library, art classes, Bible study, musical groups, woodworking, big-screen TV and video movies, trips, cultural programs. Opportunities for volunteer service.

Availability: Waiting list for some apartments.

Health services and rates: Assisted Living and Skilled Nursing covered in resident's monthly fee. The medical director is a practicing internist and geriatrician available by appointment in the outpatient clinic and on emergency 24-hour call. Hospital acute care is provided by University of California, Irvine (20 minute drive). Surgical expenses, general medical supplies, prescriptions, ambulance available at no additional cost (if not a preexisting condition). Physical, occupational and hydro therapy. Full-time activities director in Skilled Nursing. Podiatry and audiology extra.

- 34 Assisted Living units
- 58-Bed Skilled Nursing facility
- 50-Bed Secured Living center for Alzheimer's and dementia patients

"Quaker Gardens is unique because it is authorized by the state of California to offer Life Care contracts. This means that our facility includes a promise to residents to provide all levels of care (including some physician's and acute care service) for the duration of their life with no additional increase to the resident's monthly fee.

"Quaker Gardens is sponsored by the Friends Church but is open to members of any denomination, race, color, or national origin."

RETIREMENT INN OF SUNNYVALE

175 East Remington Drive
Sunnyvale, CA 94087
(408) 738-3410
Sarah Birnbaum, community relations

Type of community: Independent Living with Personal Care Services

This community is located eight miles northwest of San Jose in a residential neighborhood. The two-story Mediterranean-style buildings, most with private balcony or patio, are located on 2.1 acres. A landscaped interior courtyard provides an ideal place for socializing. Personal care services are available to Independent Living residents. The community is minutes away from churches, shops, banks, community park, medical facilities, and hospitals.

Financial plan: Monthly fee guaranteed for one year. No lease. Nonrefundable $350 processing fee per person or $500 per couple.

INDEPENDENT LIVING HOUSING

Type/size of apartment	*Monthly fee**
Studio, 220–287 sq. ft.	$1,275
1-Bedroom with kitchenette, 440–574 sq. ft.	$1,700

**For double occupancy add $300 to the monthly fee. All utilities except telephone included. Individually controlled heating and air-conditioning, 24-hour emergency call system. Most apartments have balcony or patio.*

Ownership and management: American Retirement Villas, owner of 26 retirement communities throughout California, with one in Arizona. Opened in 1978.

Minimum age: None. SSI recipients accepted.

Population: 131 residents; 80% women, 20% men, 3% couples.

Number of units: 126 Independent Living apartments

Dining plan: Three meals daily, plus snacks, included in the monthly fee. Private dining room. Meals can be delivered if resident is not feeling well.

Services: *Included in the monthly fee:* Housekeeping, personal laundry service, scheduled transportation.

At additional cost: Beauty/barbershop, general store. Residents may join residents of other Retirement Inn communities for trips and to attend large events. One-week stays offered to prospective residents.

Activities: Recreation and activities director. Hobby room, library, shuffleboard courts, bingo, bridge, travel lectures, sing-alongs, arts and crafts studio, exercise, continuing education classes.

Availability: Waiting list for one-bedroom. Short wait (one month) for studio.

Health services and rates: Personal care services are offered in residents' apartments at additional cost (dispensing medication, assistance with bathing, grooming, etc.). Hourly, daily, monthly rates vary with services provided.

"American Retirement Villas offer something special: a warm, secure, and caring environment. It shows in the sensitive, responsive professionals working on our staff. It shows in the careful design and planning of each residence. It shows in the fine food, social activities, and extensive recreational amenities."

COVENANT VILLAGE

2125 North Olive Avenue
Turlock, CA 95380
(209) 632-9976
Jim D'Avis, marketing director

Type of community: Not-for-profit Continuing Care, modified contract

Accreditation: Continuing Care Accreditation Commission

Four single-story apartment buildings house four wings of Independent Living and Assisted Living apartments, a central activities center, and Brandel Medical Center (Skilled Nursing), located on 17-acre campus. Covenant Village is adjacent to Emanuel Hospital, which offers short-term care. Covered walkways connect all buildings. California State University and areas for walking or biking are nearby. The facility is within two hours' travel to the Bay Area, Yosemite, and Sacramento and centrally located between the mountains and beaches.

Financial plan: Entrance fee plus monthly fee. Full refund of entrance fee within first 90 days. After 90 days, 2% amortization up to 50 months. $1,350 deposit is due upon application; $1,000 is refundable.

Ownership and management: Owned/managed by the Evangelical Covenant Church/Covenant Retirement Communities, owner/manager of 12 retirement communities in California, Connecticut, Florida, Illinois, Minnesota, and Washington. Covenant Retirement Communities was founded in 1886. Opened in 1977.

Minimum age: 62 years.

Population: 295 residents; 70% women, 30% men, 25% couples.

Number of units: 147 Independent Living apartments; 34 Assisted Living rooms, 145-bed health center.

Dining plan: Two meals per day included in the monthly fee. Private dining room available.

Services: *Included in the monthly fee:* Housekeeping, flat-linen service, local transportation.

At additional cost: Transportation to airport or train station, extra cleaning, minimarket, carports, beauty/barbershop.

Activities: Recreational director. Game room, exercise facilities, shop and activity room, chapel services, community concerts, trips to scenic and vacation areas, heated swimming pool, various educational classes, Bible classes, whirlpool, ceramics, weaving, painting, sewing, billiards, library, shuffleboard, gardening.

Availability: Waiting list.

Health services and rates: Therapeutic and rehabilitative therapy offered at Brandel Manor Health Care facility. 145-bed Emanuel Medical Center Hospital is adjacent to campus and available for short-term care. Each resident receives 60 days of free care at Brandel Manor or Sequoia Personal Care Residence. After 60 days, resident must pay regular rate less 10%.

- 34 Assisted Living rooms

	Resident	*Nonresident*
Adjoining	$1,166/month	$1,296/month
Semiprivate	$1,574/month	$1,749/month
Private	$2,956/month	$3,284/month

- 145 Skilled Nursing beds

Semiprivate	$124/day
Private	$164/day

"The Covenant Village tradition allows for independence and privacy while encouraging Christian fellowship, giving residents the opportunity to continue their spiritual growth through their retirement years. Respect for the Christian faith and spiritual concerns of the Evangelical Covenant Church is expected."

INDEPENDENT LIVING HOUSING

Type/size of unit	*Entrance fee**	*Monthly fee**
Studio, 470 sq. ft.	$48,000	$786
1-Bedroom, 570 sq. ft.	$64,000	$948
2-Bedroom, 815–865 sq. ft.	$79,500–108,000	$1,121–1,418
Custom 2-bedroom, 1,032–1,330 sq. ft.	$125,000–145,000	$1,668–1,776
Elm Terrace patio homes, 1,272 sq. ft.	$146,900	$799

**For double occupancy add 10% to the entrance fee and $390 to the monthly fee. All utilities except telephone included. Patios, 24-hour emergency call system, kitchenettes, wall-to-wall carpeting, cable TV, individually controlled heating and air-conditioning.*

KENSINGTON PLACE

1580 Geary Road
Walnut Creek, CA 94596
(510) 943-6705
Barb McNair, resident services coordinator;
Lois Truelson, administrator

Type of community: Independent and Assisted Living

Built around two inner courtyards, Kensington Place is a two-story building set on five acres. Rose gardens and a pond with a bridge are part of the landscape. The facility is 45 minutes from downtown San Francisco.

Financial plan: Monthly rental fee.

Ownership and management: Owned by partnership. Managed by Parkford Management. Opened in 1988.

Minimum age: 60 years.

Population: 187 residents; 66% women, 34% men, 20% couples.

Number of units: 177 Independent Living apartments; 44 Assisted Living apartments.

Dining plan: Three meals per day included in the monthly fee. Private dining room. Community kitchen.

Services: *Included in the monthly fee:* Weekly housekeeping and flat-linen services, covered parking, scheduled transportation.

At additional cost: Ice-cream parlor and sundries shop, beauty/barbershop, gift shop, dry cleaning service.

Activities: Bingo, Scrabble, bridge, exercise classes, sightseeing, theater, day trips, current events, adult education classes, concerts, movies, sing-alongs, bowling, arts and crafts, Spanish class, travelogue.

Availability: Waiting list.

Health services and rates: Therapeutic tub. Blood pressure readings. Massage therapy. Podiatrist and hearing specialists make visits.

- 44 Assisted Living apartments, services are offered in resident's apartment
  $500/month in addition to resident's regular monthly fee

"Kensington Place offers an unconditional guarantee for the first 90 days with a total refund if the resident is dissatisfied. Our community has a warm, elegant atmosphere in which residents have as much freedom and independence or as much companionship as they desire."

INDEPENDENT LIVING HOUSING

Type/size of apartment	*Monthly fee**
1-Bedroom, 570 sq. ft.	$1,595–2,795
2-Bedroom, 800 sq. ft.	$2,495–2,700

**For double occupancy add $400 to the monthly fee. All utilities except telephone included. Kitchenette, wall-to-wall carpeting, window covering, 24-hour emergency call system.*

VALLEY VIEW LODGE AT ROSSMOOR

1228 Rossmoor Parkway
Walnut Creek, CA 94595
(510) 937-7300, fax 415-937-0109
Lily Trethric, community relations

Type of community: Independent and Assisted Living

Forty-four Independent Living apartments and 81 Assisted Living units are housed in a two-story stucco and wood building located on a five-acre campus in a country environment with several attractively landscaped courtyards. Apartments are accessed through exceptionally wide, lighted hallways. Lounges have scenic views and are scattered throughout the apartments. The community is within walking distance to medical facilities, shopping, entertainment, and churches.

Financial plan: Monthly rental. $350 deposit. No lease required.

Ownership and management: Owned and operated by American Retirement Villas. Opened in 1975.

Minimum age: 60 years.

Population: 122 residents; 75% women, 25% men, 2% couples.

Number of units: 44 Independent Living apartments; 81 Assisted Living units.

Dining plan: Three meals per day included in the monthly fee. Private dining room. Tray service available.

Services: *Included in the monthly fee:* Housekeeping, flat-linen services, local transportation, parking, rollaway beds for guests.

At additional cost: Beauty/barbershop.

Activities: Hobby room, library, movies, bingo, exercise classes, lectures, dominoes, bridge, Bible study, sing-alongs, scenic rides, painting, residents' council, dining out, happy hours, ice-cream socials, poker parties, weekly live entertainment, excursions, scenic drives, garden club.

Availability: Waiting list varies according to accommodations desired.

Health services and rates: Daily assistance with bathing, grooming, dressing, medication supervision. Skilled Nursing care is available at facility next door.

- 81 Assisted Living units

Studio, 362 sq. ft.	$1,700–2,050/month
Alcove, 500 sq. ft.	$2,000–2,325/month
1-Bedroom, 550 sq. ft.	$2,225–2,550/month

**For double occupancy add $700 to the monthly rent ($400 if only one person needs assistance).*

"Valley View is set way back from the street, so there's no traffic. Some apartments look out on mature, landscaped grounds; others look across open space to hills and valleys."

INDEPENDENT LIVING HOUSING

Type/size of unit	*Monthly rental**
Studio, 362 sq. ft.	$1,450
Alcove, 500 sq. ft.	$1,700–1,725
1-Bedroom, 550 sq. ft.	$1,925–1,950

**For double occupancy add $400 to the monthly rent. All utilities except telephone included. Cable TV, 24-hour emergency call system, individually controlled heating and air-conditioning, wall-to-wall carpeting, kitchenettes.*

COLORADO

THE ARVADA MERIDIAN

555 West 59th Avenue
Arvada, CO 80004
(303) 425-1900
Tracy Unger, marketing

Type of community: Independent and Assisted Living

This three-story modern apartment complex is located on 4.5 parklike acres. The Arvada Meridian's fully landscaped campus lies in a residential setting with landscaped patios and walking paths throughout. Ralston Cove Park, with six miles of Greenway trails for walking, lies directly to the north and adjacent to the campus; views of the Rocky Mountain foothills are to the west. The Arvada Meridian is close to local banks, shopping and restaurants and only 15 to18 miles from downtown Denver.

Financial plan: Entrance fee plus monthly fee or monthly rental. Entrance fee Trust Deposit Program allows residents to reduce their monthly charge by maintaining a Trust Deposit Account at a designated bank. The account is solely in the resident's name and insured by the FDIC. The account is a non-interest-bearing account. The Meridian receives a monthly fee from the bank for having the resident establish the account. Benefits of the Trust Deposit Program include lower monthly fee, cap on increases, and smaller increases.

Ownership and management: Owned and managed by LeGan, Inc., of Denver, Colorado, which owns and operates five other Meridians in Colorado and one in Texas. Opened in 1988.

Minimum age: 62 years.

Population: 147 residents; 80% women, 20% men, 22% couples.

Number of units: 124 Independent Living apartments; 16 Assisted Living apartments.

Dining plan: 180 meals per year included in monthly fee for Independent apartments. Private dining room available.

Services: *Included in the monthly fee:* Housekeeping, weekly flat-linen service, scheduled transportation.

At additional cost: Beauty/barbershop, covered parking, guest apartment.

INDEPENDENT LIVING HOUSING

Type/size of unit	*Entrance fee/Monthly fee**	*Monthly rental**
1-Bedroom, 650–788 sq. ft.	$80,000–90,000/1,100–1,360	$1,400
2-Bedroom, 900 sq. ft.	$99,900/1,450	$1,785

**For double occupancy add $250 to the monthly fee and rental. All utilities except telephone included. Wall-to-wall carpeting, 24-hour emergency call system, balconies or patios, walk-in closets, individually controlled heat and air-conditioning, cable TV.*

Activities: Full-time activities director. Educational and cultural events, social events, library, card room, crafts room, exercise room, meeting rooms, exercise classes, swimming, painting, music recitals, sing-alongs, knitting, Bible study, movie trips, game night, bingo, various day trips; social hours, residents' council.

Availability: $4,000 fee for waiting list ($2,000 membership fee and $2,000 refundable security deposit).

Health services and rates: Assisted Living offers assistance with ambulation, dressing, personal hygiene, personal support, and supervision and monitoring medication. Resident receives ten free health care days upon occupancy and accumulates one additional day per month with a maximum of 30 days.

- 16 Assisted Living Apartments

Type/size of unit	*Entrance fee/ Monthly fee**	*Monthly rental**
1-Bedroom	$90,000–110,000 $1,830–1,985	$2,195–2,350
2-Bedroom	$120,000/2,050	$2,450

**For double occupancy add $795 to the monthly fee. Three meals per day included in Assisted Living.*

"The Arvada Meridian Retirement Community encompasses three levels of living: Independent Living, Special Services, and Assisted Living. The programs are flexible and support independence. The Arvada Meridian encourages residents to take control of their lives and remain in control."

THE BOULDER MERIDIAN

801 Gillaspie Drive
Boulder, CO 80303
(303) 494-3900
Lori Stang, retirement counselor

Type of community: Independent and Assisted Living

The Boulder Meridian is a two-story, wood-sided apartment building on a ten-acre campus in a residential neighborhood of northeastern Boulder. Outdoor patios, fountains, and ponds are located throughout the campus. Many apartments feature a Rocky Mountains view. Grocery, retail, and other shopping lies directly across the street.

Financial plan: Entrance fee plus monthly fee or monthly rent. Entrance fee Trust Deposit Program allows residents to decrease their monthly fee, place a cap on increases, and have smaller increases overall by depositing money in a designated bank. The money is FDIC-insured, and the interest to the amount deposited (approximately 4.50%) will be deducted from the regular monthly fee. Monthly charge, membership fee, and security deposit are fully refundable if after the first 90 days the resident decides to leave.

Ownership and management: Owned and operated by LeGan, Inc., of Denver, which owns and operates five other Meridians in Colorado and one in Texas. Opened in 1985.

Minimum age: 62 years.

INDEPENDENT LIVING HOUSING

Type/size of unit	*Monthly rent**
1-Bedroom, 620–800 sq. ft.	$1,450
2-Bedroom, 983–1,200 sq. ft.	$1,700–2,000

**For double occupancy add $250 to the monthly fee. Fully equipped kitchen, storage space, wall-to-wall carpeting, individual heating and air-conditioning, 24-hour emergency call system, cable TV, walk-in closets, and balconies or patios.*

Population: 125 residents; 70% women, 30% men, 16% couples.

Number of units: 96 Independent Living apartments; 10 Assisted Living units.

Dining plan: 180 meals per year included in the monthly fee. Private dining room available.

Services: *Included in the monthly fee:* Local transportation, biweekly housekeeping, flat-linen service, parking.

At additional cost: Beauty/barbershop, garages, guest suite.

Activities: Full-time activities director. Library, arts and crafts center, big-screen TV theater, indoor therapeutic hot pools, hobby rooms, volunteering, various classes, walking group, bridge, poker, cribbage, sing-alongs, musical performances, movies, canasta, card and billiards room, exercise room, whirlpool, sundeck, theater.

Availability: Six- to nine-month waiting list.

Health services and rates: On-site nursing staff. Health aides provide health services for long- or short-term basis. Physical and massage therapists available.

- 10 Assisted Living units
  Studio $2,100–2,495/month

"The friendly outgoing residents and the skilled staff are outstanding. The optional meal plan and the social activities give residents choices."

MEDALION/MEDALION WEST

1719 East Bijou Street
Colorado Springs, Colorado 80909
(719) 471-9812
Louise Spear, retirement counselor

Type of community: Not-for-profit Continuing Care, all-inclusive contract

Medalion is a ten-story apartment building of poured concrete one mile east of downtown Colorado Springs. Medalion West is a 12-story building of red brick and concrete on the eastern edge of downtown. Both buildings offer views of Pike's Peak and the front range of the Rocky Mountains. Medalion has a second-floor outside deck with a small swimming pool. Medalion West has a first-floor patio off the dining room for outdoor activities. The Colorado Springs Municipal Airport is 15 minutes to the east. Churches, medical and cultural centers are within a few minutes of the communities, as are the Rocky Mountains.

Financial plan: Entrance fee plus monthly fee or monthly rent. Three plans: **1)** Estate refund plan: 80% refund of entrance fee when resident leaves community regardless of the length of stay. **2)** Standard: Lower entrance fee and higher monthly fee. **3)** Preferred: Higher entrance fee and lower monthly fee.

Ownership and management: Medalion and Medalion West are owned by a Colorado

INDEPENDENT LIVING HOUSING

Type/size of apartment	*Entrance fee 2/3*	*Monthly fee 2/3**
Studio, 425–516 sq. ft.	$32,412–45,081/52,991–73,703	$857–1,576/591–1,149
1-Bedroom, 550–748 sq. ft.	$39,692–64,947/64,893–106,184	$1,022–1,654/705–1,141
2-Bedroom, 788–1,046 sq. ft.	$54,488–81,201/89,084–132,757	$1,246–1,939/859–1,337

**Monthly rent available ranging from $529–1,521 for studios; $681–1,755 for 1-bedrooms; and $982–2,101 for 2-bedrooms. All utilities except telephone and cable TV included. 24-hour emergency call system, fully equipped kitchens, wall-to-wall carpeting, cable TV hookup, individually controlled heating. Air-conditioning in Medalion only.*

not-for-profit corporation: members of the Sisters of Charity Health Care Systems, Inc., of Cincinnati, Ohio. The board of directors is made up of four residents, members of the Sisters of Charity Health Care Systems, and area professionals. The board makes decisions for all four Sunny Acres of Colorado communities. The Sisters of Charity Health Care Systems is composed of 20 hospitals located in five states, and four long-term care facilities and four life care retirement communities in Colorado. Medalion opened in 1969; Medalion West opened in 1972.

Minimum age: 55 years.

Population: 230 residents; 81% women, 19% men, 16% couples.

Number of units: 180 Independent Living apartments; 40 Assisted Living units, 32-bed health care center.

Dining plan: One meal per day included in the monthly rental program. No meals included in the entrance fee/monthly fee program. Meals are available with options of occasional or one, two, and three meals per day programs. Special diets available.

Services: *Included in the monthly fee:* Biweekly housekeeping, biweekly flat-linen service, scheduled transportation, open parking.

At additional cost: Personalized transportation, beauty/barbershops, guest rooms.

Activities: Activities coordinator. Chapel services, various outings, classes, study groups, libraries, exercise room with equipment, outdoor swimming pool at Medalion, billiards tables.

Availability: Waiting list at Medalion; some availability at Medalion West. 10% deposit for waiting list.

Health services and rates: Several levels of care available: Home Health Care, Assisted Living, Intermediate and Skilled Nursing Care. Unlimited health care included for those residents choosing entrance fee and monthly fee program. Monthly rental residents pay fees listed below. Physical, occupational, and speech therapies available.

- 40 Assisted Living rooms
  Single rooms and suites $35–40/day
- 32-Bed health center
  Semiprivate $85/day

"Medalion and Medalion West are two of the four communities of Sunny Acres of Colorado, the only unlimited life care communities in the state of Colorado."

VILLA PUEBLO TOWERS

1111 Bonforte Boulevard
Colorado Springs, CO 80909
(719) 545-5911
Joe Fox, retirement counselor

Type of community: Not-for-profit Continuing Care, all-inclusive contract

This community is housed in a 15-story apartment building connected to a 90-bed health center in the Belmont section of Pueblo, a city of approximately 100,000 people. Buildings are constructed of concrete and red brick. Pueblo is located along the Arkansas River in the plains just east of the Rocky Mountains. Churches, medical services, and cultural centers are within a few minutes of the community, as are the Rocky Mountains.

Financial plan: Entrance fee and monthly fee or monthly rent. Three choices for entrance fee: **1)** Estate refund plan: 80% refund of entrance fee when resident leaves regardless of length of stay. **2)** Standard Program: Lower entrance fee and higher monthly fee. **3)** Preferred Program: Higher entrance fee and lower monthly fee.

Ownership and management: Colorado not-for-profit corporation. Member of the Sisters of Charity Health Care Systems, Inc., of Cincinnati, Ohio. The board of directors is made up of four residents, members of the Sisters of Charity Health Care Systems and area professionals. The board makes decisions for all four Sunny Acres of Colorado communities. The Sisters of Charity Health Care Systems is composed of 20 hospitals located in five states, and four long-term care facilities and four life care retirement communities in Colorado. Opened in 1971.

Minimum age: 55 years.

Population: 229 residents; 83% women, 17% men, 12% couples.

Number of units: 146 Independent Living apartments; 30 Assisted Living units, 90-bed health center.

Dining plan: No meals included in the monthly fee. One, two, or three meals per day programs available. Special diets available.

Services: *Included in the monthly fee:* Biweekly housekeeping, biweekly flat-linen service, scheduled transportation, open parking.

At additional cost: Personalized transportation, laundry facilities, beauty/barbershops, guest apartments.

Activities: Activities coordinator. Chapel services, various outings, classes, study groups, library, exercise room with equipment, whirlpool, billiards tables, crafts room, carpentry shop.

Availability: Waiting list for 1-bedrooms. Some Studios and 2-bedrooms available. 10% deposit for waiting list.

Health services and rates: Several levels of care available: Home Health Care, Assisted Living, Intermediate and Skilled Nursing Care. Health Care included in the fees for residents who pay entrance fees; monthly renters pay fees listed below. Physical, speech, and occupational therapies available.

- 30 Assisted Living units
  Private rooms (no kitchens) $47.50/day
- 90-Bed health center
  Semiprivate $75.50–91.50/day
  Private $88.50–99.50/day

"Our mission is to provide the most appropriate level of care to our residents in the least restrictive setting. We provide home health care in residents' apartments to help them to continue living independently; but we also have Assisted Living and Skilled Nursing on-site for those who need a greater level of care. We also provide supportive services such as transportation and housekeeping, as well as activities and volunteer opportunities, to help keep residents as active as they want to be. Colorado is a semi-arid region that boasts over 300 days of sunshine a year—more hours of annual sunshine than San Diego or Miami Beach. Villa Pueblo is one of four communities owned by Sunny Acres of Colorado, the only unlimited life care communities in Colorado."

INDEPENDENT LIVING HOUSING

Type/size of unit	*Entrance fee 2/3*	*Monthly fee 2/3*
Studio, 476 sq. ft.	$34,700–41,650/56,750–68,100	$951–1,398/656–965
1-Bedroom, 616–809 sq. ft.	$44,800–65,600/73,230–107,250	$1,088–1,713/750–1,182
2-Bedroom, 891–1042 sq. ft.	$62,600–85,000/102,300–139,000	$1,348–1,988/930–1,371

Monthly rental is also available—studios, $862–1,116; 1-bedroom, $1,010–1,315; 2-bedroom, $1,295–1,810. Estate refund entrance fee plan also available. All utilities except telephone included in the monthly fee. Fully equipped kitchens, wall-to-wall carpeting, 24-hour emergency call system, cable TV, custom drapes.

HERITAGE CLUB

2020 South Monroe Street
Denver, CO 80210
(303) 756-0025
Lesa Ragains, marketing director

Type of community: Independent Living and Assisted Living

This elegant eight-story contemporary apartment building is located on 4.5 acres in a beautiful residential neighborhood. In the vicinity of shopping centers, golf courses, and hospitals, Heritage Club offers spectacular views of the Colorado Rockies and beautiful floral landscaping and wooded courtyards. Independent Living and Assisted Living apartments are available.

Financial plan: Monthly rental fee.

Ownership and management: National Retirement Company, owner and manager of 23 retirement communities in Arizona, Florida, and Texas. Headquartered in Brentwood, Tennessee. Opened in 1988.

Minimum age: 62 years.

Population: 250 residents; 72% women, 18% men, 14% couples.

Number of units: 198 Independent Living apartments; 35 Assisted Living apartments.

Dining plan: 25 meals per month included in the monthly fee. Additional meal programs are available. Catering services available for private parties.

Services: *Included in the monthly fee:* Weekly housekeeping, scheduled transportation, storage lockers on each floor.

At additional cost: Beauty/barbershop, ice-cream parlor, covered parking, special personal transportation.

Activities: Full-time social director. Exercise classes, the Happy Hoofers walking club, Jacuzzi group, painting class, musical entertainment (barbershop quartet, piano). Bingo, bridge, and canasta clubs. Movies, lectures, trips to the theater and other cultural entertainment, library, indoor whirlpool and spa, shuffleboard, putting greens, and horseshoes.

Availability: Four- to eight-month wait for two-bedroom apartments; two-month wait for Assisted Living.

Health services and rates:

- 35 Assisted Living apartments*

1-Bedroom	$2,195/month
2-Bedroom	$2,445–2,590/month

**For double occupancy add $525 to the monthly fee.*

"From our elegant dining room to our residents' luxurious apartments, club-style living at Heritage Club offers every comfort and convenience residents can imagine in one place for only a monthly rental fee. Unlike many other retirement communities, there are no entry or endowment fees. Resident satisfaction is the highest priority of Heritage Club's professional, courteous staff."

INDEPENDENT LIVING HOUSING

Type/size of apartment	*Monthly fee**
1-Bedroom, 646 sq. ft.	$1,510–1,750
2-Bedroom, 969–1,300 sq. ft.	$1,760–3,600

**For double occupancy add $350 to the monthly fee. All utilities except telephone included. Balcony or bay window, fully equipped all-electric kitchen, washer/dryer, master antenna system and cable hookups, wall-to-wall carpeting, individually controlled heating and air-conditioning, 24-hour emergency call system.*

PARKPLACE

111 Emerson Street
Denver, CO 80218
(303) 744-0400
Evelyn Brown, director of marketing

Type of community: Independent and Assisted Living

This facility is housed in an 18-story luxury brick-and-tile building at the intersection of Speer and Emerson. A glass-enclosed 18th-floor Skyline Room offers stunning panoramic views of the Denver skyline and the snowcapped mountain peaks of the Rockies. Wood trim accents every room including the windows, and wood-encased glass doors lead to the balconies. Outside, residents enjoy beautifully manicured lawns, rose gardens, and walking paths. Parkplace is situated in the midst of established neighborhoods, medical facilities, and cultural attractions and adjacent to a lovely, well-lit city park. Nearby Cherry Creek boutiques and the new Cherry Creek Mall provide marvelous shopping opportunities. Less than a block away, access to the Cherry Creek bicycle and walking paths allows residents to venture as far as Larimer Square (less than two miles) without crossing a street.

Financial plan: Monthly rental fee.

Ownership and management: Parkplace is owned by the Living Environments for an Aging America Fund (LEAAF), a closed-end investment fund for pension fund investors. JMB Realty serves as acquisition and management advisors for LEAAF. Opened in 1988.

Minimum age: 62 years.

Population: 246 residents; 78% women, 22% men, 10% couples.

Number of units: 223 Independent Living apartments; 53 Assisted Living suites.

Dining plan: One meal a day included in the monthly rental fee, with optional plans for additional meals available.

Services: *Included in the monthly fee:* Weekly apartment cleaning, scheduled transportation in a limousine or 24-passenger coach, private parking spaces, laundry facilities on every floor.

At additional cost: Convenience store, beauty/barbershop, covered parking.

Activities: Health spa with an indoor swimming pool, whirlpool, and exercise room. Exercise classes both in and out of the pool are held three times per week. In the lounge are a big-screen television, billiards, and cocktail hour. Crafts room where painting and sewing classes are held. Worship services, barbecues, mystery trips, lectures, dance groups, and trips to the theater.

Availability: Limited.

Health services and rates: Parkplace provides space for physicians to use for examination and on-site treatment. Resident's personal physician is welcome to use these facilities. A nurse is on duty 24 hours a day.

INDEPENDENT LIVING HOUSING

Type/size of apartment	*Monthly rental fee*
1-Bedroom, 625–632 sq. ft.	$1,425–1,750
2-Bedroom, 950–970 sq. ft.	$1,725–2,025

All utilities except telephone included in the monthly fee. Fully equipped kitchen with traditional wood cabinets, deluxe dishwasher, refrigerator with ice maker, range and microwave oven. Ceramic-tiled bathroom floors, individually controlled heating and air-conditioning, 24-hour emergency call system, cable and master television antenna.

- 53 Assisted Living units
  Suites $1,825/month

"Beyond the brick and mortar of the physical plant of Parkplace is the most important aspect of our community: the special care and attention that is given to each resident."

THE VILLAS AT SUNNY ACRES

2501 East 104th Avenue
Denver, CO 80233
(303) 452-4181 or (800) 447-2092
Steve Rigsby/Fred Smith, retirement counselors

Type of community: Not-for-profit Continuing Care, all-inclusive contract

Three apartment buildings (three-story Villa, four-story Villager, and five-story Ambassador), 31 cottages, and 118-bed health center are located on 64-acres of landscaped grounds with two fishing lakes. The blond brick buildings are spread over the grounds, which boast 1,000 trees and numerous walking paths. Thirty-four apartment floor plans are offered. Views of downtown Denver and the Rocky Mountains are available from most apartments. Denver International Airport, churches, and medical and cultural centers are all within convenient distance of the community, which is 15 minutes from downtown Denver.

Financial plan: Entrance fee plus monthly fee or monthly rent. Three entrance fee plans: **1)** Estate refund plan: 80% refund of entrance fee when resident leaves community regardless of the length of stay. **2)** Standard: Lower entrance fee and higher monthly fee. **3)** Preferred: Higher entrance fee and lower monthly fee.

Ownership and management: A Colorado not-for-profit corporation. Member of the Sisters of Charity Health Care Systems, Inc., of Cincinnati, Ohio. Owner of the Medalion and Medalion West in Colorado Springs. The board of directors is made up of four residents, members of the Sisters of Charity Health Care Systems, and area professionals. The board makes decisions for all four Sunny Acres of Colorado communities. The Sisters of Charity Health Care Systems is made up of 20 hospitals located in five states, and four long-term care facilities and four life care retirement communities in Colorado. Opened in 1969.

Minimum age: 55 years.

Population: 440 residents; 77% women, 23% men, 16% couples.

Number of units: 322 Independent Living residences; 34 Assisted Living units, 118-bed health center.

Dining plan: No meals are required but an option of a one, two, or three meals per day program is available. Special diets available. Private dining room.

Services: *Included in the monthly fee:* Biweekly housekeeping, weekly flat-linen service, scheduled transportation, open parking.

INDEPENDENT LIVING HOUSING

Type/size of unit	*Entrance fee 2/3**	*Monthly fee 2/3**
Studio, 380–450 sq. ft.	$33,100–39,700/54,100–64,900	$857–1,576/591–1,149
1-Bedroom, 440–900 sq. ft.	$39,900–68,050/65,350–111,200	$916–2,002/632–1,443
2-Bedroom, 720–1,040 sq. ft.	$58,800–76,850/96,100–128,100	$1,184–1,934/817–1,334

Monthly rental also available: studio, $762–1,009; 1-bedroom, $782–1,477; 2-bedroom, $1,221–1,618.

**Double occupancy increases entrance and monthly fees. All utilities except telephone included in monthly fee. Fully equipped kitchens, wall-to-wall carpeting, 24-hour emergency call system, cable TV.*

At additional cost: Garages, personalized transportation, beauty/barbershops, guest apartments.

Activities: Activities coordinator. Chapel services, various outings, classes, study groups, libraries, fitness center with exercise room and equipment, whirlpool, billiards tables, fishing, gardening, arts and crafts rooms, woodworking and carpentry shop.

Availability: Waiting list for cottages and some apartments. 10% deposit required for waiting list.

Health services and rates: Several levels of care available: home health care, extended care, Assisted Living, Intermediate Nursing care, Skilled Nursing care. All health care services included in monthly fee for those residents who have paid an entrance fee. Residents on the monthly rental plan pay fees listed below. Speech, physical, and occupational therapies available.

- 34 Assisted Living units
  Single rooms and suites $47–61/day
- 118-Bed health center
  Semiprivate $84/day

"The Villas at Sunny Acres is one of the four communities of Sunny Acres of Colorado, the only unlimited life care communities in Colorado. It is the largest full-service retirement community in the state and one of only a few with its variety of building types, cottages, and grounds."

THE ENGLEWOOD MERIDIAN

3455 South Corona
Englewood, CO 80110
(303) 761-0300
Anita Shelffo, marketing director

Type of community: Continuing Care, modified contract

Located in a residential section of suburban Denver, the eight-story brick building has four wings with Independent Living apartments, Assisted Living units, and a health care center.

Financial plan: Monthly fee.

Ownership and management: LeGan, Inc., owner and manager of six communities, five in Colorado and one in Texas. Opened in 1990.

Minimum age: 62 years.

Population: 300 residents; 67% women, 32% men, 46% couples.

Number of units: 181 Independent Living apartments; 24 Assisted Living apartments, 72 Skilled Nursing beds.

Dining plan: 180 meals included annually in the monthly fee. Flexible meal programs. Breakfast, lunch, and dinner served. Private dining room, hospitality snack bar, monthly theme dinners, Sunday brunch, monthly candlelit dinner.

Services: *Included in the monthly fee:* Move-in assistance, housekeeping and flat-linen service, scheduled transportation, storage facilities, laundry facilities, appliance maintenance.

INDEPENDENT LIVING HOUSING

Type/size of apartment	*Monthly fee**
1-Bedroom, 715–945 sq. ft.	$1,520–1,900
2-Bedroom, 1,030–1,720 sq. ft.	$1,980–3,400

**For double occupancy add $250 to the monthly fee. All utilities except telephone included. Wall-to-wall carpeting, full-size appliances, individually controlled heat and air-conditioning, 24-hour emergency alert system. Cable TV, balconies, patios, and bay windows available.*

At additional cost: Postal services, beauty salon, guest accommodations, convenience shop, banking services, underground parking garage.

Activities: Card and billiards room, crafts room, woodworking shop, extensive library, planned trips, educational and cultural events, residents' special interest events, card clubs, exercise programs, art classes, theater, exercise facilities.

Availability: Apartments available.

Health services and rates: Independence Plus services include short-term care aimed at getting the resident back to independent living: assistance with dressing, hygiene, domestic chores, dietary supervision. Resident Centered Care emphasizes the personalized relationship between a resident and a specific staff member, who is that resident's primary caregiver. As such, the primary caregiver knows the resident's interests, needs, abilities, and potential, and so is able to interact with the resident with greater understanding and sensitivity as the partnership and friendship grows on a continuous basis.

- 24 Assisted Living apartments

1-Bedroom	$2,470/month
2-Bedroom	$2,890/month

- 72-Bed Skilled Nursing facility

Semiprivate	$98–110/day
Private	$135–165/day

"The Englewood Meridian is a commmunity offering the ultimate in quality service, safe environment, caring staff, wonderful new friendships, and opportunities to participate in teaching and other stimulating activities as well as receiving new experiences. We create an environment in which one may find peace and harmony, joy and laughter."

Jean, 83 years

Applewood Estates, Freehold, New Jersey

"I didn't want to wait any longer."

Three years ago, when he was 80, Jean decided it was time to move into a life care community. "I had a friend who needed to move and had helped her family look for a place, and I became interested," explains Jean. "I looked at 17 or 18 communities in New Jersey and Pennsylvania and found one I really liked in Moorstown, but it was under construction and wouldn't be opening for two years." Jean was ready to move in 1993 and didn't want to wait. He was concerned about paying high premiums on his long-term health care insurance.

"Of all the places I went to, Applewood Estates was the best," says Jean. "It was only four years old when I came in. I like the people here—they're friendly. I like the comparatively reasonable price, and it was very important that Applewood offered life care. Also, the campus is not too spread out, and there are not too many people using appliances [walkers, wheelchairs, etc.] here."

Jean reports that the average age at Applewood Estates is 75. He loves the activities, particularly the dramatic group that he helped found. The fact that he never needs to go outside if he doesn't want to and doesn't need a car is also important.

"I wanted to make the decision to move myself. I didn't want it to be a last-minute thing when I got sick one day, involving my family; because you don't have as many choices at that point, and other people are making the final decision. Once you're in a place like this, you're taken care of for life; that's great security." Prior to Applewood Estates, Jean lived by himself in Concordia for eight years, taking care of a house and yard.

Jean's advice: As a resident, be sure to keep involved to the greatest possible extent in the governing of your community.

THE LAKEWOOD MERIDIAN

1805 South Balsam
Lakewood, CO 80232
(303) 980-5500
Karen Sailor, marketing director

Type of community: Continuing Care, modified contract

The two- and three-story brick buildings with wood trim are located in a residential neighborhood in the western part of Lakewood. The site is well landscaped with walking paths, a pond, gazebo, and putting green. Many apartments have a wonderful view of the Rocky Mountains. Grocery stores and various shops and community services are located within blocks of the property. Independent Living apartments and Assisted Living and Skilled Nursing services are available.

Financial plan: Entrance fee plus monthly fee or monthly fee only. Entrance fee Trust Deposit Program allows residents to reduce their monthly fee by maintaining a trust deposit account at a designated bank. This account is solely in the resident's name and is insured by the FDIC. The account is a non-interest-bearing account. The Meridian receives a monthly fee from the bank for having the resident establish the account, and in exchange the resident's monthly fee is reduced. Benefits of the Trust Deposit Program include lower monthly fee, cap on increases, and smaller increases. A reservation deposit is required with the execution of a residency agreement ($2,000 membership fee and $2,000 refundable security deposit).

Ownership and management: LeGan, Inc., owner and manager of six communities, five in Colorado and one in Texas. Opened in 1987.

Minimum age: 62 years.

Population: 187 residents; 80% women, 20% men, 25% couples.

Number of units: 101 Independent Living apartments; 13 Assisted Living apartments, 60-bed Nursing facility.

Dining plan: 15 meals per month included in the monthly fee. Special diets, tray service. Credit for unused meals. Private dining room.

Services: *Included in the monthly fee:* Complete move-in service arranged by the staff, housekeeping and flat-linen services, scheduled transportation, parking, laundry facilities, hospitality snack bar. If housekeeping and flat-linen service are not desired, they can be deducted from the monthly fee or rent.

At additional cost: Convenience shop, beauty/barbershop, postal services.

Activities: Full-time activities director. Exercise class, billiards, book hour, painting class, crafts class, Bible study, cards/bridge, movies in a theater with a big-screen TV, lectures, outings, library, whirlpool, woodworking shop.

Availability: Waiting list.

INDEPENDENT LIVING HOUSING

Type/size of apartment	*Entrance fee/Monthly fee**	*Monthly rental**
1-Bedroom, 620–764 sq. ft.	$84,000–100,000/1,035–1,220	$1,420–1,675
2-Bedroom, 895–1,132 sq. ft.	$100,000–150,000/1,270–1,465	$1,725–2,150

**For double occupancy add $250 to the monthly fee and the monthly rental. All utilities except telephone included. Wall-to-wall carpeting, full-size appliances, individually controlled heating and air-conditioning, and 24-hour emergency call system. Some apartments have balconies, patios, and/or fireplaces.*

Health services and rates: Working cooperatively with each resident's individually selected physician, the Meridian Caregiver Team consists of staff members with a variety of skills and knowledge. This team meets regularly to exchange ideas both formally, at resident care conferences attended by the resident and his or her family, and less formally, through caregiver meetings where individual resident goals and successes are shared.

- 13 Assisted Living Units

Type/size of unit	*Entrance fee/ Monthly fee**	*Monthly rent**
1-Bedroom	$99,600/1,595	$2,050
2-Bedroom	$150,000/1,810	$2,495

**For double occupancy add $795 to the monthly fee for special services.*

- 60-Bed Skilled Nursing center

Semiprivate	$80–95/day
Private	$115–130/day

"Resident Centered Care distinguishes Meridian by assisting our residents to maximize their potential for independence and enhance their sense of well-being. We help them maintain control of the physical as well as the emotional and social aspects of their lives. Respect for each resident's individuality is at the heart of Meridian's unique approach to caregiving."

CONNECTICUT

DUNCASTER

40 Loeffler Road
Bloomfield, CT 06002
(203) 726-2000
Annika Thomson, marketing director

Type of community: Not-for-profit Continuing Care, modified contract

Located on a 72-acre site with woodlands and gently rolling open fields, Duncaster is set up like a small New England village with three distinct, interconnected "neighborhoods" clustered around a traditional village green. Assisted Living, plus Intermediate and Skilled Nursing, are available on campus. Talcott Mountain and the historic towns of the Farmington Valley lie to the west, and downtown Hartford with cultural attractions is just six miles south. The area is midway between Boston and New York City. Bradley International Airport is only a few minutes' drive to the north.

Financial plan: Entrance fee plus monthly fee. Full refund of the entrance fee is made if the resident elects to leave for whatever reason within the first three months of occupancy. The refund will be paid, after the apartment has been resubscribed. After this three month period, Duncaster retains 20% of the entrance fee plus 2% for each month or portion of a month of occupancy. *Note:* Monthly rental plan also available.

Ownership and management: Independent corporation run by the board of directors. Opened in 1984.

Minimum age: 65 years.

Population: 242 residents; 62% women, 38% men.

Number of units: 216 Independent Living apartments; 10 Assisted Living apartments, 7 Intermediate Care beds, 53 Skilled Nursing beds.

Dining plan: One meal a day included in the monthly fee. Additional meals for residents or for guests available at a modest cost. During short-term illness, meals are brought to resident's apartment. Private dining room.

INDEPENDENT LIVING HOUSING

Type/size of apartment	*Entrance fee single/double*	*Monthly fee single/double*
Studio, 514 sq. ft.	$81,246	$2,146
1-Bedroom, 657 sq. ft.	$105,621/117,709	$2,468/3,541
1-Bedroom, 822 sq. ft.	$134,020/147,480	$2,787/3,861
2-Bedroom, 986 sq. ft.	$161,684/177,913	$3,110/4,184
2-Bedroom, 1,126 sq. ft.	$186,860/205,626	$3,433/4,506

All utilities included except telephone and cable TV. Full kitchens, wall-to-wall carpeting, draperies, central air-conditioning, generous storage space, and private balconies or patios.

Services: *Included in the monthly fee:* Weekly maid service, twice-a-year heavy cleaning, flat-linen service, transportation.

At additional cost: Small gift shop, post office, bank, beauty/barbershop. Additional storage space and covered parking.

Activities: Auditorium, library, exercise programs, arts and crafts, small group gatherings, woodworking shop, greenhouse, vegetable and flower gardens, sports events, plays, concerts.

Availability: Limited.

Health services and rates: Caleb Hitchcock Health Center has an outpatient clinic, dental clinic, and rehabilitation department. Residents receive unlimited health care. Should a resident move into the Caleb Hitchcock Health Center permanently, the monthly fee remains the same.

- 10 Assisted Living apartments
- 30 Intermediate Care beds
- 30 Skilled Nursing beds

"Duncaster's founders believed that a Continuing Care retirement community for people 65 and older allows its residents to avoid much of the loneliness, anxiety, and feeling of uncertainty that all too often diminish the zest and flavor of life."

3030 PARK

3030 Park Avenue
Bridgeport, CT 06604
(203) 374-5611
Anne D. Gallo, director of retirement planning

Type of community: Nonprofit Continuing Care, modified contract

Accreditation: Continuing Care Accreditation Commission

3030 Park is a ten-story contemporary apartment building overlooking Long Island Sound and located on 15 acres of parklike land. The building features an elegant main lobby with high ceilings and fountain surrounded by flowers and plants. Personal gardens are available to residents as well as a lawn bowling and putting green. Independent Living apartments plus Intermediate and Skilled Nursing services are available. The facility is minutes away from sailing, yacht clubs, and beautiful beaches. The Performing Arts Center at Fairfield University offers theater and music opportunities. Sacred Heart University provides a variety of cultural, sports, and entertainment opportunities.

Financial plan: Entrance fee plus monthly fee. Entrance fee is 90% refundable within the first 90 days, after which the refund depreciates monthly according to the age of the resident and actuarial tables. Application fee for waiting list is $1,500 for couples; $1,100 for singles. Application fee less $200 will be applied against entrance fee or refunded.

INDEPENDENT LIVING HOUSING

Type/size of apartment	*Entrance fee*	*Monthly fee single/double*
Studio, 242 sq. ft.	$36,000	$1,003
Alcove, 374 sq. ft.	$55,000	$1,140
1-Bedroom, 624 sq. ft.	$80,000	$1,277/1,952
Large 1-bedroom, 745 sq. ft.	$115,000	$1,401/2,100
2-Bedroom, 910 sq. ft.	$146,000	$1,541/2,222

All utilities except telephone included in the monthly fee. Individually controlled heating and air-conditioning, kitchenette, wall-to-wall carpeting, custom blinds, draperies, 24-hour emergency call system, choice of paint color.

Ownership and management: Founded under the sponsorship of the Council of Churches of Greater Bridgeport. Board of directors comprised of community leaders of the Greater Bridgeport Area. The feelings and opinions of every resident are given voice through the residents' association, which works closely with the management. Opened in 1968.

Minimum age: 62 years (if couple, spouse may be younger).

Population: 340 independent Living residents and 240 residents in the health center; 79% women, 21% men. 3030 Park is an academic community with a large percentage of college graduates.

Number of units: 310 Independent Living apartments; 111 Intermediate Nursing beds, 133-bed Skilled Nursing beds.

Dining plan: Lunch and dinner included in the monthly fee. Breakfast is optional.

Services: *Included in the monthly fee:* Weekly cleaning and flat-linen services.

At additional cost: Beauty/barbershop, gift shop, parking, laundress, transportation, guest accommodations.

Activities: Exercise classes, music room, shuffleboard, billiards room, lawn bowling, putting green, nonsectarian chapel, gardening, cultural events planned by a social director.

Availability: One-year waiting list for most apartments. Waiting list applicants may use guest rooms and dining room by making reservations in advance.

Health services and rates: Residents can choose own doctors and specialists. State-of-the-art clinics are located within 3030 Park to provide medical, nursing, podiatry, ophthalmology, dentistry, and rehabilitative services to all residents. Newly acquired 144-bed health center two minutes away.

- 100-Bed health care center

	Intermediate Nursing	*Skilled Nursing*
Semiprivate	$142/day	$160/day
Private	$140/day	$170/day

"Many residents serve as volunteers in local community groups. Interaction between 3030 Park and the community is a long-standing and valued tradition. 3030 Park is now enjoying second-generation residents—those who had family living here in the early years."

CHESTER VILLAGE WEST

317 West Main Street
Chester, CT 06412
(203) 526-6800
Jennifer H. Rannstad, executive director

Type of community: Not-for-profit Continuing Care, modified contract

Chester Village is located in the Connecticut River Valley on 31 wooded acres with a living pond and gazebo. The community consists of 90 Independent Living units and a 60-bed Skilled Nursing facility. Situated in the heart of the cultural center of Connecticut, Chester Village is within easy driving distance of Hartford and New Haven.

Financial plan: Entrance fee plus monthly fee. 94% of the Entrance fee is refundable.

Ownership and management: Managed by AdvantageHEALTH Management Corporation, manager of eight retirement facilities in Connecticut, Florida, and New York. Opened in September 1992.

Minimum age: 62 years.

Population: 190 to 200 resident capacity.

Number of units: 90 Independent Living apartments; 60 Skilled Nursing beds.

INDEPENDENT LIVING HOUSING

Type/size of apartment	*Entrance fee*	*Monthly fee**
1-Bedroom, 850 sq. ft.	$207,752	$1,330
1-Bedroom/den, 1,105 sq. ft.	$230,836	$1,480
2-Bedroom, 1,190 sq. ft.	$293,848	$1,830
Deluxe 2-bedroom, 1,209 sq. ft.	$324,100	$2,220
Custom 2-bedroom, 1,337 sq. ft.	$386,837	$2,220
Custom deluxe 2-bedroom, 1,468 sq. ft.	$396,199	$2,540

**For double occupancy add $750 to the monthly fee. All utilities except telephone and cable TV included. Fully equipped kitchen, individually controlled heating and air-conditioning, 24-hour emergency call system.*

Dining plan: One meal per day (dinner Monday–Saturday and brunch on Sunday) is included in monthly fee. Lunches are available at cost. Private dining room for small parties. Pub.

Services: *Included in the monthly fee:* Weekly housekeeping and flat-linen services, scheduled transportation, parking.

At additional cost: Convenience store, guest accommodations.

Activities: Swimming pool, Jacuzzi, exercise room, library, auditorium, several activity areas.

Availability: Limited.

Health services and rates: A health and wellness nurse is available on premises 40 hours a week and on call at other times. Full lifetime nursing care is covered with entrance fee and monthly fee. Only additional charges are for private room and additional meals.

- 60 Skilled Nursing beds
  Private $25/day
  (in addition to resident's monthly fee)

"Chester Village West is situated in a lovely small town known as a culinary and cultural resource for the state."

COVENANT VILLAGE OF CROMWELL AND PILGRIM MANOR

Missionary Road
Cromwell, CT 06416
(203) 635-2690
Marv Burgoyne, marketing representative

Type of community: Not-for-profit Continuing Care, modified contract

Accreditation: Continuing Care Accreditation Commission

This community offers rural New England living with all the attractions of Hartford and New Haven less than 20 minutes away. Located on 31 beautifully landscaped acres, Covenant Village at Cromwell features New England–style, gray clapboard two-, three-, and four-story apartment buildings that house interconnecting Independent Living residences and 30 cottages. Assisted Living and nursing care are available on campus at Pilgrim Manor. Nearby are historic seaports and landmarks, colonial inns, and abundant recreational facilities.

Financial plan: Entrance fee plus monthly fee. $1,350 deposit, of which $1,000 is refundable. Entrance fee is refundable on a prorated basis over 50 months.

Ownership and management: Owned and managed by the Evangelical Covenant Church/Covenant Retirement Communities, owner and manager of

INDEPENDENT LIVING HOUSING

Type/size of apartment	*Entrance fee**	*Monthly fee**
Studio, 480–520 sq. ft.	$55,500	$734.80
1-Bedroom, 650–675 sq. ft.	$73,800	$922.60
2-Bedroom, 900 sq. ft.	$92,500–105,500	$1,110.40–1,130.40
Cottages		
Studio, 505 sq. ft.	$56,900	$827.60
1-Bedroom, 760–775 sq. ft.	$76,800	$1,023.20
2-Bedroom, 910 sq. ft.	$105,500	$1,238.81

**For double occupancy add 10% to the entrance fee and $255 to the monthly fee. All utilities except telephone included. Balcony or patio, 24-hour emergency call system, wall-to-wall carpeting (selection of color), draperies selected by resident, individually controlled electric heating, full kitchen.*

12 retirement communities in California, Connecticut, Florida, Illinois, Minnesota, and Washington. Covenant Retirement Communities was founded in 1886. Covenant Village opened in 1976.

Minimum age: 62 years.

Population: 343 residents; 75% women, 25% men, 42% couples.

Number of units: 194 Independent Living apartments and 30 cottages; 51 Assisted Living units, 30 Intermediate Nursing beds, 30-bed Skilled Nursing facility.

Dining plan: Daily main meal included in monthly fee. Catering for special events available. During long absences, an adjustment in monthly fee will be made to reflect meal savings.

Services: *Included in the monthly fee:* Housekeeping, weekly flat-linen service, parking, scheduled transportation.

At additional cost: Beauty/barbershop, additional housekeeping services, transportation to medical appointments and connecting travel services, laundry facilities, village store, gift nook.

Activities: Library, craft and hobby rooms, workshop, picnic areas, nearby health club available without cost (swimming pool, jogging/walking track), weekly Chapel service, Bible study, bridge, cribbage.

Availability: Waiting list.

Health services and rates: Pilgrim Manor Health Care Center has trained staff of nurses, therapists, and dietitians. Nonresidents may enter Assisted Living directly by paying entrance fee.

- 51 Assisted Living units

	Entrance fee	*Daily fee*
Private room	$13,500	$93
Suite	$17,000	$113/$166 (double)

- 60-Bed nursing facility

	Intermediate Nursing	*Skilled Nursing*
Semiprivate	$144/day	$180/day
Private	$175/day	$217/day

"The mission of Covenant Retirement Communities is to provide a balance, through facilities and programs, between security and independence. We assist the resident in achieving maximum physical, mental, emotional, and spiritual capabilities and enjoyment within a Christian environment."

ESSEX MEADOWS

30 Bokum Road
Essex, CT 06426
(203) 767-7201
Elaine M. Bristol, marketing director

Type of community: Continuing Care, all-inclusive contract

Over 100 acres of woodlands, wetlands, and meadows surrounds this life care community within the picturesque community of Essex. Designed around knolls with trees and rocks, the Northeast Colonial buildings reflect typical architecture of Essex, which was first settled in 1648. Independent Living apartments and Skilled Nursing center are available.

Financial plan: Entrance fee plus monthly fee. Return of Capital plan: A percentage, up to 90%, of the entrance fee is refundable. The percentage varies according to the apartment type.

Ownership and management: Owned by the Weitz Corporation, which owns the management company Life Care Services Corporation, a recognized leader in development and management of life care retirement communities in the United States. Opened in 1988.

Minimum age: 62 years.

Population: 260 residents; 65% women, 35% men, 30% couples.

Number of units: 189 Independent Living apartments; 45 Skilled Nursing beds.

Dining plan: Daily meal is included in the monthly fee. Three meals per day are available at additional cost. Professional dietitian. Private dining room.

Services: *Included in the monthly fee:* Weekly housekeeping, flat-linen service, regularly scheduled transportation.

At additional cost: Guest accommodations, garages, beauty/barbershop, sundries shop.

Activities: Full-time social director. Musical entertainment, lectures, movies, cards, games, and billiards room, woodworking shop, arts and crafts room, nature paths, gardening areas for flowers and vegetables, nine-hole executive golf course and putting green, aquatic center with swimming pool, whirlpool, and exercise area, library, auditorium, lounges, reception lobby, scenic seating areas.

Availability: Waiting list usually of at least one year. Length of time depends on size of apartment.

Health services and rates: Short-term recuperative and long-term Skilled Nursing care. A resident may receive Skilled Nursing care in the health care center for as long as needed for virtually the same cost as living in an apartment.

- 45-Bed health care center

"Why Essex Meadows? The people, the location, the service, the apartments, the pool, the golf course,

INDEPENDENT LIVING HOUSING

Type/size of apartment	*Entrance fee*	*Monthly fee*
Studio, 450 sq. ft.	$98,000	$1,164
1-Bedroom, 600–800 sq. ft.	$146,000–200,500*	$1,263–1,432*
2-Bedroom, 900–1,050 sq. ft.	$224,500–276,000*	$1,495–1,596*
2-Bedroom/den, 1,300 sq. ft.	$311,600–322,000*	$1,726*

**For double occupancy add $12,000 to the entrance fee; $704 to the monthly fee. All utilities except telephone included. All kitchens come equipped with refrigerator, range, dishwasher, and garbage disposal; 24-hour emergency call system, basic cable TV hookup. Most apartments have balconies or patios. Small pets allowed.*

the health care center, the meadows, the fund, the security, the independence—retirement living for the non-retiring! Consider joining those already on our waiting list who are responsibly and excitedly planning for their futures."

THE GABLES AT GUILFORD

201 Granite Road
Guilford, CT 06437
(203) 458-3337
Connor Jefcoat, Lynn Jefcoat, managers

Type of community: Independent Living and Assisted Living

The Gables at Guilford is nestled on 50 wooded acres overlooking a tranquil pond and adjoining the Westwood hiking trails system. Three-story buildings house Independent Living and Assisted Living apartments. Minutes away are an excellent shopping center, fine restaurants, many cultural opportunities for which New Haven is famous, and two renowned hospitals. Guilford itself is a charming shoreline community. Nearby is Jacobs Beach on Long Island Sound, Lake Quonnipaug, tennis courts, and a golf course.

Financial plan: Monthly rental fee.

Ownership and management: Holiday Retirement Corporation, which owns over 130 communities across the United States and Canada. Opened in 1990.

Minimum age: 55 years.

Population: 90 residents; 75% women, 25% men, 20% couples.

Number of units: 101 Independent Living apartments; 28 Assisted Living apartments.

Dining plan: Three meals per day included in the monthly fee for Independent Living residents. Tray services available for residents in case of illness.

Services: *Included in the monthly fee:* Weekly housekeeping and flat-linen services, scheduled transportation, laundry facilities.

At additional cost: Beauty/barbershop, convenience store.

Activities: Full-time activities director. Indoor and outdoor recreational areas and walking paths, gardening, social/cultural clubs and activities, arts and crafts room, library.

Availability: Limited.

Health services and rates: Full-time director of health services, who is a registered nurse with geriatric experience. Health and wellness program. Assisted Living program on site. Couples may continue to live together in the same apartment when one spouse has special care needs and the other is well and independent. Should the need arise, special assistance in securing nursing home placement is available.

INDEPENDENT LIVING HOUSING

Type/size of apartment	*Monthly rental fee**
1-Bedroom, 600–889 sq. ft.	$1,795–2,495
2-Bedroom, 900–1,000 sq. ft.	$2,795–2,995

**For double occupancy add $300 to the monthly fee. All utilities except telephone and cable TV included. Individually controlled heating and air-conditioning, wall-to-wall carpeting, draperies, 24-hour emergency call system, fully equipped kitchens. Garages available for additional $75 per month. Special accommodations for residents with pets.*

- Assisted Living services offered to those in Independent Living apartments for an additional $1,195 per month.
- Catered Living services are available on a fee-for-specific-service basis.

"At The Gables, residents enjoy the privacy of their own spacious rental apartment, enhanced with security, services, and friends that make life a carefree pleasure. Should a resident's health care needs change, our Assisted Living program provides the services needed for the resident to live independently in his or her apartment. Because we are a rental community, there is no entrance or endowment fee. A team of four managers resides at the residence and is available for assistance any time residents may require it."

WHITNEY CENTER

200 Leeder Hill Drive
Hamden CT 06517
(203) 281-6745
Bill Warne, sales manager

Type of community: Nonprofit Continuing Care, all-inclusive contract

Whitney Center is housed in a six-story, S-shaped red brick building situated on 10.5 wooded acres near Lake Whitney. The grounds are landscaped with flowering trees and vegetable and flower gardens. Many apartments have exceptional views. Independent Living apartments and a nursing facility are available. Assisted Living services offered in resident's apartment. Whitney Center is located near New Haven, which offers fine concert halls, museums, theaters, and restaurants. It is minutes away from shopping centers and the Yale/New Haven medical facilities.

Financial plan: Entrance fee plus monthly fee. Entrance fees may be partially refundable.

Ownership and management: Nonprofit corporation. Lisa Giller, president since 1991, has more than 15 years of health care management experience. Under the guidance of 15 volunteer trustees from the local business and medical community. Opened in 1979.

Minimum age: 62 years.

Population: 204 residents; 80% women, 20% men, 10% couples.

Number of units: 199 Independent Living apartments; 59-bed nursing facility.

Dining plan: One meal per day is included in the monthly fee. All three meals are offered daily.

INDEPENDENT LIVING HOUSING

Type/size of apartment	*Entrance fee*	*Monthly fee**
Studio, 296 sq. ft.	$49,000	$955
Alcove, 460 sq. ft.	$76,650	$1,077
1-Bedroom, 592 sq. ft.	$117,600	$1,197
Custom 1-bedroom, 700 sq. ft.	$136,050	$1,320
2-Bedroom, 829 sq. ft.	$156,800	$1,439
Custom 2-bedroom, 883 sq. ft.	$169,900	$1,494
Deluxe 2-bedroom, 987 sq. ft.	$184,150	$1,559

**For double occupancy add $575 to the monthly fee. All utilities included. Individual heating and air-conditioning controls, fully equipped kitchens, 24-hour emergency call system. Some apartments have wonderful views of Lake Whitney and the grounds.*

Registered dietitian, special diets, and tray service when needed.

Services: *Included in the monthly fee:* Bimonthly house cleaning service, weekly flat-linen service, personal laundry facilities, household chores, regularly scheduled transportation.

At additional cost: Beauty/barbershop.

Activities: Trips to concerts, the museum, and New Haven's many theaters. Tours, lectures, Yale University events, library, ecumenical chaplain, personal garden areas.

Availability: Apartments are available immediately.

Health services and rates: Unlimited emergency, recuperative, and long-term care and complete therapy services at no additional cost. Assisted care is available at a per-service rate in resident's apartment. Admission can be made directly to health center if space is available.

- 59-Bed on-site health center

Semiprivate	$160/day nonresident
Private	$180/day nonresident

"At Whitney Center, residents are buying a lifestyle, not real estate, and thus we are committed to ensuring that the return on each resident's investment is a fulfilling and rewarding retirement. The staff and residents are a remarkable collection of people. Many staff members have been with us since our doors opened in 1979, and they take an active interest in getting to know residents on a personal level and are extremely responsive to each resident's particular needs."

EVERGREEN WOODS

88 Notch Hill Road
North Branford, CT 06471
(203) 488-8000
John Propst, marketing director

Type of community: Continuing Care, all-inclusive contract

Evergreen Woods is located on 20 acres of land and surrounded by an additional 68 acres of natural woodland. Three-story buildings are connected by covered walkways to a beautiful red brick community center. Independent Living and Skilled Nursing care available. Assistance with daily living is offered in the resident's apartment. Evergreen Woods is five miles from the shore and a short drive from the city of New Haven, which offers historical and cultural attractions, Yale University, world-renowned hospitals, airport and train station.

Financial plan: Entrance fee plus monthly fee. The entrance fee is 90% refundable.

Ownership and management: Managed by the Life Care Services Corporation of Des Moines, Iowa, developer and manager of more than 50 communities in the United States. Opened in 1991.

Minimum age: 62 years.

Population: 149 residents; 54% women, 46% men, 48% couples.

INDEPENDENT LIVING HOUSING

Type/size of apartment	*Entrance fee*	*Monthly fee**
1-Bedroom, 500–950 sq. ft.	$150,000–215,000	$1,000–1,365
2-Bedroom, 985–1,600 sq. ft.	$225,000–295,000	$1,420–1,530

**For double occupancy add $640 to the monthly fee. All utilities except telephone included. Fully equipped kitchen, individually controlled heating and air-conditioning, 24-hour emergency call system.*

Number of units: 176 Independent Living apartments; 40-bed Skilled Nursing facility.

Dining plan: One meal per day (lunch or dinner) included in the monthly fee. Meals may be distributed, so long as the number of meals per month does not exceed the number of days in the month. Private dining room. Tray service.

Services: *Included in the monthly fee:* Weekly housekeeping service, weekly flat-linen service, scheduled transportation.

At additional cost: Beauty/barbershop.

Activities: Library, arts and crafts room, heated indoor swimming pool, Jacuzzi, walking trails, exercise room, billiards room, woodworking shop, private gardening plots.

Availability: Limited.

Health services and rates: The health center's nursing services are available to all residents at no additional cost except for the price of two additional meals per day. Medication can be dispensed on a temporary basis at no additional cost. Assisted Living services are available to residents in their apartments and charged per service.

- 40-Bed Skilled Nursing facility

"Evergreen Village has New England history and charm, combined with big-city convenience and excitement."

EAST HILL WOODS

611 East Hill Road
Southbury, CT 06488
(203) 262-6161
Margaret Warner, marketing director

Type of community: Nonprofit Continuing Care, all-inclusive contract

Located in the rolling hills of the Pomperaug River Valley on 55 acres, East Hill Woods offers one- and two-bedroom Independent Living residences, Assisted Living, and comprehensive health care facilities. Apartment buildings are connected to each other, the health center, and the community center by enclosed walkways.

Financial plan: Entrance fee plus monthly fee. Entrance fee is 94% refundable. Deposit equal to 5% of entrance fee is due at time of application.

Ownership and management: East Hill Woods, Inc., a nonprofit corporation. Managed by CRSA, Inc. Opened in 1991.

Minimum age: 62 years (if spouse is under 62, the entrance fee is higher).

INDEPENDENT LIVING HOUSING

Type/size of apartment	*Entrance fee*	*Monthly fee**
1-Bedroom, 576 sq. ft.	$127,750	$1,385
Deluxe 1-bedroom, 768 sq. ft.	$163,250	$1,620
2-Bedroom, 896 sq. ft.	$193,750	$1,685
Deluxe 2-bedroom, 1,216 sq. ft.	$247,750	$1,920
2-Bedroom comb., 1,536 sq. ft.	$311,500	$2,335

**For double occupancy add $915 to the monthly fee. All utilities except telephone included. Fully equipped kitchen, individually controlled heating and air-conditioning, wall-to-wall carpeting, 24-hour emergency call system, balcony or patio. Small pets allowed in ground-level apartments.*

Population: 190 residents.

Number of units: 173 Independent Living apartments; 21 Assisted Living suites, 30-bed Skilled Nursing facility.

Dining plan: One meal per day included in monthly fee; others available at cost. Private dining room and catering services available. Tray service when approved for medical reasons.

Services: *Included in the monthly fee:* Biweekly housekeeping, weekly flat-linen service, scheduled transportation.

At additional cost: Beauty/barbershop, country store, guest accommodations.

Activities: Library, fitness center, whirlpool, crafts room, lectures, travelogues, programs, game room, gardening and picnic areas, gazebo, walking trails, trips to popular area destinations.

Availability: Limited.

Health services and rates: Residents are entitled to an unlimited number of days in either Assisted Living or the on-site health care center with no increase in monthly fee except for two additional meals. The cost of dental care, physical therapist, special nurses, and personal physicians are borne by the resident.

- 21 Assisted Living suites
- 30-Bed Skilled Nursing facility

"East Hill Woods is already home to many people who share a zest for life. People who have the freedom and independence to relax and enjoy themselves. People who have traded responsibility for services and amenities that simplify life."

POMPERAUG WOODS

80 Heritage Road
Southbury, CT 06488
(203) 262-6555
Terry Hobart, marketing director

Type of community: Nonprofit Continuing Care, all-inclusive contract

On a campus of 22 acres, Pomperaug Woods offers one- and two-story New England-style buildings surrounded by woodlands in historic Southbury. Several apartment plans are available for Independent Living. Assisted Living services are available in apartments in addition to a 30-bed nursing facility. Twenty-seven holes of golf are nearby. This community is less than one hour from Hartford and New Haven and 1½ hours from New York City.

Financial plan: Entrance fee plus monthly fee. With Return-of-Capital plan, up to 90% of the entrance fee is refundable.

Ownership and management: Pomperaug Woods is a nonprofit corporation, managed by Life Care Services Corporation (LCS). LCS has been involved with the development and management of more than 50 retirement communities over the past 20 years. Opened in 1988.

INDEPENDENT LIVING HOUSING

Type/size of apartment	*Entrance fee*	*Monthly fee**
1-Bedroom, 461–640 sq. ft.	$99,100–140,000	$1,292–1,433
Deluxe 1-bedroom, 722–922 sq. ft.	$165,900–200,500	$1,532–1,602
2-Bedroom, 922–1,156 sq. ft.	$206,700–243,900	$1,658–1,786

**For double occupancy add $826 to the monthly fee. All utilities including basic telephone and basic cable TV included. Fully equipped kitchen, wall-to-wall carpeting, individual heating and air-conditioning, 24-hour emergency call system.*

Minimum age: 65 years.

Population: 160 residents; 85% women, 15% men, 22% couples.

Number of units: 146 Independent Living apartments; 30 Nursing beds.

Dining plan: Monthly fee includes one meal per day. Three meals a day are offered. Dietitian consultant and tray service are available.

Services: *Included in the monthly fee:* Weekly house cleaning and flat-linen services, washers and dryers, scheduled transportation.

At additional cost: Beauty/barbershop, carports (when available).

Activities: Full-time activities director. Monthly trips to some of the best theaters in Hartford, New Haven, and the surrounding area. Movies, concerts in the auditorium, exercise classes, woodworking and other arts and crafts, library, billiards room.

Availability: 3- to 12-month waiting list, depending on the type of apartment selected.

Health services and rates: Licensed staff on duty 24 hours a day. Nursing care in a semiprivate room is covered in resident's monthly fee; additional charge for two extra meals per day. Private rooms available at additional cost. Emergency care, recuperative care, long-term care, and therapy services available. For 15 minutes, 10 times a month, residents may receive help in dressing, bathing, etc., at no additional charge. Residents who need daily assistance may hire private nursing aides.

- 30-Bed nursing facility

"Retiring in historic Southbury gives residents the opportunity for a wide range of cultural, educational, and shopping experiences, in addition to the convenience of a travel center with interstate bus service and limousine service to the regional airports."

ASHLAR VILLAGE

Cheshire Road, P.O. Box 70
Wallingford, CT 06492
(203) 949-4400
Paul Gradwell, director of marketing

Type of community: Nonprofit Continuing Care, modified contract

Accreditation: Continuing Care Accreditation Commission

Situated on 168 acres, half developed, half woodland, Ashlar Village's hilltop campus has open lawns with groves of trees and a large eight-acre pond where residents fish, boat, and stroll around the perimeter on a walking trail. The Village is stair-free and made up of small cottages and a main building that houses Independent Living apartments, a spacious fireplace lounge, and the main dining room. Assisted Living services, Intermediate Nursing, and Skilled Nursing are available. Ashlar Village is located near Mystic Seaport, where 19th-century whalers are docked and quaint shops and seafood restaurants run up and down Main Street.

Financial plan: Entrance fee plus monthly fee.

Ownership and management: Sponsored by the Masonic Charity Foundation of Connecticut, which has been in existence for over 100 years. Built in two phases: Phase I opened in 1984, Phase II in 1991.

Minimum age: 62 years (if couple, spouse may be younger).

Population: 228 residents; 66% women, 34% men, 21% couples.

INDEPENDENT LIVING HOUSING

Phase II apartments	*Entrance fee single/double*	*Monthly fee single/double*
1-Bedroom, 739 sq. ft.	$105,400/125,000	$1,240/1,490
2-Bedroom, 967 sq. ft.	$146,900/166,900	$1,490/1,740
Cottages		
Traditional, 966 sq. ft.	$167,400/187,400	$1,270/1,380
Contemporary, 1,110 sq. ft.	$177,400/197,400	$1,400/1,520

All utilities except telephone included in the monthly fee. Kitchens come equipped with modern electric appliances: counter cooktop and wall oven and refrigerator. A double sink, garbage disposal, thermopane windows, master antenna television system, 24-hour emergency call system.

Phase I apartments and cottages (opened in 1984) are also available at somewhat lower entrance and monthly fees.

Number of units: 172 Independent Living apartments and 72 cottages; 234 Intermediate and Skilled Nursing beds.

Dining plan: Apartment residents receive one meal per day included in monthly fee. Cottage residents have the option of utilizing the dining room on a reservation basis. Private dining room is available for special occasions.

Services: *Included in the monthly fee:* Bimonthly housekeeping, transportation to grocery stores and the local shopping mall, laundry facilities, individual storage space.

At additional cost: Store, bank, snack shop, beauty/barbershop, guest accommodations.

Activities: Full-time professional activities staff. Exercise classes, wellness programs, walking club, trips and tours, parties, educational series, religious services, music programs, arts and crafts room, woodworking shop, library.

Availability: Waiting list.

Health services and rates: Guaranteed access to the Masonic Charity Foundation's Continuum Health Care. Residents receive ten days in the health center per year, noncumulative, at no additional cost. Five full-time doctors and a staff of RNs, LPNs, and physical therapists.

- Assisted Living services are available in resident's apartment and charged per service.
- 234 Intermediate Nursing beds and 58 Skilled Nursing beds

	Intermediate Nursing	*Skilled Nursing*
Semiprivate	$145/day	$185–221/day
Private	N/A	$219–255/day

"At first glance, the immediate appeal of Ashlar Village is its magnificent setting, spacious cottages and apartments, numerous amenities, and outstanding medical care. But most impressive is the feeling of stability and security because Ashlar Village is sponsored by the Masonic Charity Foundation, an organization that has been providing superior services and care to older adults for over 100 years. The sense of tradition, community, and friends helping friends at Ashlar Village creates a wonderful atmosphere. We are accredited by the national Continuing Care Accreditation Commission and committed to upholding the highest standards of retirement living."

WESTFIELD COURT

77 Third Street
Stamford, CT 06905
(203) 327-4551
Julie Forester, administrator

Type of community: Independent Living with Assistance

This 15-story contemporary high-rise building houses Independent Living apartments. Rooftop garden and skyroom with cozy fireplace and summer room offer magnificent views of the Long Island Sound, the Connecticut countryside, and the Manhattan skyline. Westfield Court is located 45 minutes from New York City and an hour from New Haven; the Long Island Sound shore is a few minutes away. Cultural opportunities include music, theater, and dance at the Stamford Center for Arts, the Connecticut Grand Opera, Stamford Symphony, the New England Lyric Operetta Company, and local colleges and museums.

Financial plan: Monthly rental fee or yearly lease.

Ownership and management: Owned by B&G Associates, a partnership of the Benson Family of the Stamford area, which has real-estate holdings in 37 states; and Abraham Gosman, chairman and CEO of Mediplex, a national health care company based in Boston. Mediplex, a publicly held company, owns and operates rehabilitation hospitals, nursing homes, and retirement care facilities. A subsidiary of Mediplex oversees the management of Westfield Court. Opened in 1975.

Minimum age: 62 years.

Population: 164 residents; 85% women, 15% men, 10% couples.

Number of units: 168 Independent Living apartments.

Dining plan: Three meals a day included in the monthly fee.

Services: *Included in the monthly fee:* Weekly maid and flat-linen services, additional towel and bathroom cleaning twice a week, indoor parking, laundry facilities, scheduled transportation.

At additional cost: Beauty/barbershop, ice-cream shop and convenience store, guest suites.

Activities: Book reviews, seminars, performing arts series, bridge, painting, traveling gourmet club, 2,500 volume library, supervised exercise program and equipped fitness center, indoor swimming pool, religious services.

Availability: Limited. Waiting list for some types of apartments.

Health services and rates: A health counselor RN is on duty 24 hours a day. Additional services to assist with activities of daily living available. Residents have priority access to Mediplex Continuing Care facilities, including Mediplex of Stamford, located less than two miles from Westfield Court.

INDEPENDENT LIVING HOUSING

Type/size of apartment	*Monthly fee**
Studio, 356 sq. ft.	$2,440–2,540
Alcove, 376 sq. ft.	$2,705–2,910
1-Bedroom, 500+ sq. ft.	$3,145–3,585
2-Bedroom/2 bath, 725 sq. ft.	$3,940–4,040
Deluxe 1-bedroom, 752 sq. ft.	$4,280–4,380

**For double occupancy add $795 to the monthly fee. All utilities except telephone included. 24-hour emergency call system, wall-to-wall carpeting, draperies, food center with refrigerator and sink, individually controlled heating and air-conditioning. Many apartments have balconies.*

"Westfield Court is known for its fine dining experience, exceptional among retirement communities. In addition to restaurant-style service and a wide selection of food choices, a selection of excellent wines is available at dinner. Monthly tastings inform residents and their guests about wines and give them a chance to vote for the wines they prefer. The other distinguishing feature at Westfield Court is its varied activity program. In addition to up to ten programs each day, a fitness program based on the latest research from Tufts' Center for the Study on Aging is offered. After completing an assessment, personal trainers work with residents (a service included in the monthly fee) three times a week on aerobic and strength-training equipment. Residents are reassessed periodically and eventually go on a maintenance schedule."

THE McAULEY

275 Steele Road
West Hartford, CT 06117
(203) 236-6300
Terry Blau

Type of community: Not-for-profit Continuing Care, modified contract

Located on the Mercy Campus, a 125-acre site in West Hartford, The McAuley consists of a commons building containing service and administrative areas and two five-story residential apartment buildings joined by a heated and air-conditioned link. The Mercy Grounds, shared by Saint Joseph College, Connor Chapel, Saint Mary Home, and MercyKnoll offer jogging and walking trails and shaded lawns. Nearby are acute care medical facilities, shopping centers, and the Hartford Golf Club. Downtown Hartford is five minutes away.

Financial plan: Entrance fee plus monthly fee. The entrance fee is refundable in an amount that decreases 2% per month for the first 12 months. Thereafter, 2/3 of the entrance fee is always refundable when your participation in the McAuley program terminates and a like living unit is occupied. The McAuley also offers unique customized pricing options.

Ownership and management: Sponsored by the Sisters of Mercy of Connecticut and managed by Classic Residence by Hyatt. A voluntary, nondenominational board of trustees oversees the business affairs and property. Opened in 1988.

Minimum age: 62 years.

Population: 270 residents; 21% men, 79% women, 18% couples.

Number of units: 227 Independent Living apartments; 40 Intermediate Nursing beds, 177 Skilled Nursing beds in Saint Mary Home.

Dining plan: Choice of lunch or dinner included in monthly fee. Extra meals are charged separately to the resident's account. Catering is available for

INDEPENDENT LIVING HOUSING

Type/size of apartment	*Entrance fee*	*Monthly fee*
Studio, 592 sq. ft.	From $92,000	$1,750
Deluxe 1-bedroom, 818 sq. ft.	From $133,000*	$2,100*
2-Bedroom, 1,118 sq. ft.	From $178,000*	$2,600*

**For double occupancy add 10% to the entrance fee and $950 to the monthly fee. All utilities included except telephone. Wall-to-wall carpeting and sheer draperies in living room and bedrooms, all-electric kitchens with dishwasher and garbage disposal, 24-hour emergency call system, prewiring for telephone, master TV antenna and cable TV, individually controlled heating and air-conditioning.*

private parties at a reasonable charge. Coffee shop featuring lighter fare at lunch.

Services: *Included in the monthly fee:* Housekeeping, weekly flat-linen service, scheduled car and van transportation, washers and dryers.

At additional cost: Beauty/barbershop, convenience store, guest accommodations.

Activities: Crafts, golf (putting green), shuffleboard, tennis, community garden, greenhouse, exercise programs, jogging/walking trails, library, concerts, lectures, plays, trips, educational/ cultural opportunities at Saint Joseph College. Residents are active on numerous committees. Access to the O'Connell Center with Olympic-size swimming pool and exercise room.

Availability: Limited.

Health services and rates: Nurse available 24 hours a day for emergency response and nursing intervention. The nurse focuses on teaching management of chronic conditions, diet, and medication; assessment of symptoms and communication with resident's private physician. Personal care assistance is also available to provide support services enabling residents to remain functional and at home. If and when an extended care facility is needed either temporarily or permanently, The McAuley program covers the per diem cost in a semiprivate room.

DELAWARE

STONEGATES

4031 Kennett Pike
Greenville, DE 19807
(302) 658-6200
Eileen Mallouk, director of marketing

Type of community: Continuing Care, modified contract

Stonegates is located three miles from downtown Wilmington on 37 acres adjacent to the village of Greenville and two acre–zoned residential communities. Clusters of cottages and apartment buildings house Independent Living. Buildings are connected by an art gallery corridor with changing exhibits. An unusually large number of common rooms are furnished with antiques and fine decorations. The campus has flowering trees, bulbs, and shrubs and a wildflower garden beside a stream that flows by the rear of the campus. Exclusive shops, a post office, and a bank are within walking distance. Many cultural landmarks are close by including Winterthur, Delaware Art Museum, Longwood Gardens, University of Delaware. Stonegates is within an hour of Philadelphia and Baltimore; two hours from Washington D.C., New York City, and Atlantic City.

INDEPENDENT LIVING HOUSING

Westfield House apartments	*Purchase fee*	*Monthly fee**
Efficiency, 500 sq. ft.	$78,225	$1,522
1-Bedroom, 850 sq. ft.	$135,500	$1,750
2-Bedroom, 1,200 sq. ft.	$163,500	$1,621
Manor House apartments		
1-Bedroom, 940 sq. ft.	$132,500	$1,489
1-Bedroom/den, 1,078 sq. ft.	$163,500	$1,557
Deluxe 2-bedroom, 1,211 sq. ft.	$172,500	$1,621
Cottages		
2-Bedroom, 1,290 sq. ft.	$175,000	$1,689
Deluxe 2-bedroom, 1,480 sq. ft.	$205,275	$1,758
3-Bedroom, 1,720 sq. ft.	$246,500	$2,027
Deluxe 3-bedroom, 1,890 sq. ft.	$286,500	$2,748

**For double occupancy add $441 to the monthly fee. All utilities except telephone included in apartment monthly fee. Cottage residents receive an annual utility allowance of $1,200 per calendar year for 2-bedroom and $1,500 for 3-bedroom accommodations. Wall-to-wall carpeting, 24-hour emergency call system, individual heating and air-conditioning controls, fully equipped kitchens. Cottages have attics, patios, porches, or sunrooms and are equipped for laundry appliances. Additional fee for garages.*

Financial plan: Condominium purchase plus monthly fee. Residents own a deed to a cottage or apartment and pay the New Castle county property tax. Stonegates will buy the unit back if the resident leaves or enters the health center on a permanent basis. Cottages and apartments depreciate 7% the first year and 4% a year thereafter for ten or more years. The maximum depreciation is 47%.

Ownership and management: Stonegates Retirement Community, Limited Partnership. Managed by The Forum Group, Inc., developer and manager of more than 27 retirement communities in the U. S., six of which are located in the Wilmington area. Opened in 1984.

Minimum age: 55 years.

Population: 200 residents; 63% women, 37% men, 26% couples. Resident demographics span 22 states.

Number of units: 88 Independent Living cottages and 74 apartments; 39-bed Skilled Nursing facility.

Dining plan: Choice of lunch or dinner daily included in the monthly fee. Under an optional meal plan, residents can choose to eat in the dining room for 13 meals per month. Private dining room.

Services: *Included in the monthly fee:* Transportation to scheduled social activities, housekeeping and flat-linen services, parking. Laundry facilities on every floor in apartments. Cottage residents are driven to and from dinner.

At additional cost: Transportation to outside appointments, beauty/barbershop, personal laundry services, newspaper delivery.

Activities: Concerts, cocktail parties, aerobics, tennis, putting green, shuffleboard, museum visits, local theater and symphony performances, library, billiards room.

Availability: Some availability. Waiting list for specific accommodations.

Health services and rates: Residents are entitled to 60 lifetime free days in the health care center and are given a discounted rate on semiprivate accommodations. Medical director works with the director of nursing, registered nurses, practical nurses, licensed aides, dietary specialists, and social director to create an individual care plan for each patient. Physical, occupational, and speech therapy are available at additional cost.

- 39 Skilled Nursing beds

Semiprivate	$114–115/day
Private	$117–128/day
Private suite	$138/day

"Care and individual attention are the most important at Stonegates. The dining services, for example, are overseen by our Executive Chef de Cuisine, John J. Gangloff, who brings personal expertise achieved from his years of training, culminating at Cornell University. His talented staff of chefs, some Johnson and Wales culinary school graduates, prepare meals to order. Individual reservations and seating policies ensure that from the minute you walk into the dining room lobby each evening, you will receive the personal attention for which Stonegates is noted."

COKESBURY VILLAGE

726 Loveville Road
Hockessin, DE 19707-1519
(302) 239-2371
Carol Powell, marketing manager

Type of community: Not-for-profit Continuing Care, modified contract

Accreditation: Continuing Care Accreditation Commission

Clusters of cottages and a contemporary main building house Independent Living residents. Located on 52 acres of rolling countryside partly surrounded by woods, Cokesbury Village boasts flower gardens, walking trails, and two ponds where Canadian geese come to raise

their young in the springtime. Assisted Living, Skilled Nursing, and Alzheimer's unit are available. Minutes away are the Delaware Symphony, Delaware Theater Company, the Playhouse, and the Grand Opera House. Philadelphia is 45 minutes away.

Financial plan: Entrance fee plus monthly fee. Entrance fee is refundable less 2% per month for the first 50 months of occupancy.

Ownership and management: Peninsula United Methodist Homes Inc. (PUMH), an affiliate of the Peninsula Annual Conference of the United Methodist Church. PUMH, Inc., owns and manages three continuing care facilities in Delaware and one in Maryland and has been providing this service since 1960. An advisory Resident Council represents residents' views. Opened in 1978.

Minimum age: 60 years (if couple, spouse may be younger).

Population: 427 residents; 62% couples.

Number of units: 282 Independent Living apartments and cottages; 30 Assisted Living apartments, 114-bed nursing facility, 18 Alzheimer's beds.

Dining plan: Three meals a day are included in the monthly fee; however, residents with cooking facilities may choose credit for all meals. Registered dietitian. Residents who are away from Cokesbury for an extended period, 30 days or more, will receive credit for meals not taken.

Services: *Included in the monthly fee:* Weekly housekeeping and flat-linen service for apartment residents; however, they may choose credit for these services. Scheduled transportation and a shuttle service that runs from the cottages to the main building.

At additional cost: Housekeeping and flat-linen services for cottage residents, gift shop, country store, beauty/barbershop, post office.

Activities: More than 20 active residents' committees are available—from horticulture to music, and lapidary, film, and lectures. Crafts room, painting, needlework, ceramics, weaving. Fully equipped workshop, stretchercise sessions, speakers and concert performances, dances, bridge parties, library, Sunday worship services.

Availability: A few apartment styles are available immediately.

Health services and rates: Health center offers physical therapy and therapeutic recreational programs to stimulate creativity and the joy of accomplishment. Village physician is on call around the clock; frequent screenings, regular physicals. The facility is staffed with a resident nurse and assistant who can help with temporary minor illness, administer medication, have meals delivered on trays. A dietitian helps residents with nutritional counseling. Consulting specialist in psychiatry, podiatry, dentistry, and communication therapy.

INDEPENDENT LIVING HOUSING

Type/size of unit	*Entrance fee**	*Monthly fee**
Studio, 378 sq. ft.	$38,900	$1,365
Efficiency, 557 sq. ft.	$55,150–56,400	$1,522
1-Bedroom, 759–782 sq. ft.	$89,250–91,800	$2,050–2,124
2-Bedroom, 1,035–1,058 sq. ft.	$108,450–114,800	$2,531
2-Bedroom cottage, 1,277–1,361 sq. ft.	$118,650–136,450	$2,555

**For double occupancy add $10,000 to the entrance fee and $418–524 to the monthly fee. All utilities included. Fully equipped kitchen except in studio apartment. Wall-to-wall carpeting, draperies, 24-hour emergency call system, individually controlled heating and air-conditioning. Cottages have a dishwasher, washer/dryer. Some cottages have a garage.*

Monthly fees for Assisted Living, Alzheimer's unit, and nursing are $1,446.

- 30 Assisted Living rooms
- 18-Bed Alzheimer's wing
- 114-Bed nursing facility

"Cokesbury Village is one of only three accredited retirement communities in Delaware, each owned and operated by PUMH, Inc. Our goal is provide an exceptional lifestyle and the highest quality of care for older adults."

MILLCROFT

255 Possum Park Road
Newark, DE 19711
(302) 366-0160
Kristie Augenblick, leasing counselor

Type of community: Continuing Care, modified contract

This contemporary Georgian-style residence located on eight acres offers screened-in porches and open patios. Independent Living and Intermediate and Skilled Nursing are available. Located near the heart of a progressive business and college community, Millcroft's country setting features rolling green acres, courtyards with flower gardens, woods, and a pond. Within a few miles are hospitals, shopping centers, theaters, golf courses, museums, and restaurants. New York City, Philadelphia, Atlantic City, Baltimore, and Washington, D.C., are all within a two hours' drive. Renowned attractions nearby include Winterthur, Hagley Museum, Longwood Gardens, University of Delaware, Brandywine River Museum, and historic churches.

Financial plan: Monthly rental fee. One month's rent nonrefundable security deposit.

Ownership and management: Managed by The Forum Group, which has more than 25 years of experience in managing retirement communities and 27 communities across the nation—six of which are in the Wilmington area. Opened in 1982.

Minimum age: 60 years.

Population: 160 residents; 70% women, 30% men, 25% couples.

Number of units: 62 Independent Living Apartments; 100 Intermediate and Skilled Nursing beds.

Dining plan: Continental breakfast, lunch, and dinner are included in the monthly rental fee.

Services: *Included in the monthly fee:* Weekly housekeeping and flat-linen services, regularly scheduled transportation, laundry facilities.

At additional cost: Beauty/barbershop, gift shop, personal laundry service, dry cleaning pick-up and delivery, newspaper delivery, guest accommodations.

INDEPENDENT LIVING HOUSING

Type/size of apartment	*Monthly rental fee**
Efficiency, 340–390 sq. ft.	$1,500
1-Bedroom, 495–576 sq. ft.	$1,675–1,795
1-Bedroom/balcony, 570 sq. ft.	$1,825
2-Bedroom, 760–1,060 sq. ft.	$2,000
2-Bedroom/balcony, 876 sq. ft.	$2,100

**For double occupancy add $450 to the monthly rental fee. All utilities except telephone and cable TV included. Kitchenette, wall-to-wall carpeting, draperies, individual temperature controls, and 24-hour emergency call system.*

Activities: Exercise classes, arts and crafts classes, sing-alongs, lectures, bridge, bingo, trips to the local cultural entertainment, cocktail hour, movies, table games, musical programs.

Availability: Some apartments are available immediately.

Health services and rates: House physician available or personal physician may be used if resident prefers. Physical, occupational, and speech therapy are provided at additional cost. Long- and short-term Skilled Nursing care.

- 100-Bed health center

Semiprivate	$87/day
Private	$101/day

"Millcroft offers its residents security, comfort, and hospitality in a warm and gracious environment. Residents enjoy the conveniences of home within a community setting. The Millcroft health care center has been recognized by the state of Delaware, Division of Licenses, as 'Deficiency-Free.'"

METHODIST MANOR HOUSE

1001 Middleford Road
Seaford, DE 19973
(302) 629-4593
Karen K. Records, residency counselor

Type of community: Nonprofit Continuing Care, modified contract

Accreditation: Continuing Care Accreditation Commission

Methodist Manor House is made up of a three-story contemporary Independent Living apartment building and cottages built in clusters of four located on 33 partially wooded acres adjacent to the Nanticoke River. A boardwalk runs along the river where residents can walk and fish. Walking and biking paths run throughout the campus. Assisted Living, Skilled Nursing, and a facility for residents with memory disorders are available. The Nanticoke Wildlife Area brings an annual migration of Canada geese, mallards, and wood ducks. The Chesapeake Bay is minutes away; stores and specialty shops are just around the corner from the Manor, including a local farmer's market. Seaford offers theaters and restaurants. The Manor is within a few hours of Washington, D.C., Baltimore, Philadelphia, and Wilmington. Four colleges and two universities are nearby.

Financial plan: Entrance fee plus monthly fee. Entrance fee is partially refundable at a rate of 2% less per month within the first 50 months of residency.

Ownership and management: Peninsula United Methodist Homes, Inc. (PUMH), in existence

INDEPENDENT LIVING HOUSING

Type/size of apartment	*Entrance fee**	*Monthly fee*
1-Bedroom, 500–750 sq. ft.	$55,200–71,700	$768–969*
2-Bedroom, 750–1,000 sq. ft.	$71,700–121,500	$969–1,181*
Cottages		
1-Bedroom, 800 sq. ft.	$82,700	$688
2-Bedroom, 1,008–1,355 sq. ft.	$93,700–126,800	$741–768

**For double occupancy add $5,000 to the entrance fee for both apartments and cottages and $275 to the monthly fee in apartments. All utilities except telephone included. Fully equipped kitchen, wall-to-wall carpeting, individually controlled heating and air-conditioning, 24-hour emergency call system, laundry facilities. Cottages have garages, patios, or decks; some have fireplaces.*

since 1960. Affiliated with the Peninsula Annual Conference of the United Methodist Church. Resident Council represents residents' views. Opened in 1966.

Minimum age: 60 years (if couple, spouse may be younger).

Population: 250 residents; 86% women, 14% men, 32% couples.

Number of units: 186 Independent Living apartments; 29 Assisted Living units, 78-bed nursing facility, 17-bed unit for residents with memory disorders.

Dining plan: Apartment residents have evening meal included in the monthly fee. Meals are optional for cottage residents. Additional meals are available at the following monthly fees: breakfast, $26; lunch, $53; dinner, $106.

Services: *Included in the monthly fee:* Scheduled transportation, biweekly housekeeping.

At additional cost: Flat-linen, beauty/barbershop, housekeeping, guest accommodations, gift shop, bank.

Activities: Concerts, crab feasts, harvest festivals, croquet, billiards room, bingo, horseshoes, organized outings to plays, concerts, and scenic spots; various musicians perform at the community, fitness classes, gardening, ceramics, painting, stenciling, arts and crafts, library, woodworking, Bible study, chapel, volunteering, game room, walking club.

Availability: Depending on the accommodation, waiting lists vary from none to one year.

Health services and rates: Apartment and cottage residents receive $10/day discount for personal or health care stay, up to total discount of $5,000. Solarium within health center, pharmacy services included in monthly fee. An annual checkup by the health center medical director is available at no additional cost. Physical therapy is available at an additional fee.

- 29 Assisted Living units
  Studios $70/day
- 78-Bed Skilled Nursing facility
  Semiprivate $90/day
  Private $100/day
- 17-Bed facility for patients with memory disorders
  Private $110/day

"The whole idea of Methodist Manor House is to make residents always feel right at home. You'll find that you have the same comfort, privacy and independence that you have in your present home, and you'll add the wonderful sense of security and companionship that comes with living in a fine Continuing Care retirement community."

FORWOOD MANOR

1912 Marsh Road
Wilmington, DE 19810
(302) 529-1600
Bonnie Baggett, marketing director

Type of community: Continuing Care, modified contract

Forwood Manor is an elegant, contemporary Georgian-style mansion on 13 acres. Trees, grassy areas, flower gardens, a greenhouse, and walking paths are on the grounds. The community is located in the tranquil tree-lined suburban setting of Brandywine Hundred, in a secure and established residential neighborhood just northeast of Wilmington. Independent Living, Assisted Living, and Intermediate and Skilled Nursing are all available. Forwood Manor is close to Branmar shopping center and the Concord Mall and less than 30 minutes from Philadelphia International Airport.

Financial plan: Monthly rental fee. One year lease with 60-day cancellation clause. One month fully refundable security deposit/damage deposit.

INDEPENDENT LIVING HOUSING

Type/size of apartment	*Monthly rental fee**
1-Bedroom, 661–793 sq. ft.	$1,850–2,450
2-Bedroom, 896–1,140 sq. ft.	$2,450–3,050

**For double occupancy add $490 to the monthly rental fee. All utilities except telephone are included. Fully equipped all-electric kitchen, carpeting, individual temperature control, 24-hour emergency call system.*

Ownership and management: Owned by The Forum Retirement Community and managed by The Forum Group, Inc., which owns and manages 27 retirement communities in the United States. Opened in 1988.

Minimum age: 60 years (if couple, spouse may be younger).

Population: 220 residents; 82% women, 18% men, 16% couples.

Number of units: 119 Independent Living apartments; 30 Assisted Living suites, 60-bed nursing facility.

Dining plan: 30 meals per month (choice of lunch or dinner) and a continental breakfast on weekdays are included in the monthly rental fee. Unused meals may be used by guests.

Services: *Included in the monthly fee:* Weekly housekeeping and flat-linen service, scheduled transportation, private transportation within a five-mile radius, laundry facilities.

At additional cost: Beauty/barbershop, country store, private transportation beyond a five-mile radius, personal laundry service, dry cleaning pick-up and delivery, newspaper and mail delivery.

Activities: Exercise classes, arts and crafts club, sing-alongs, lectures, Bible study, card groups, bingo, trips to the local cultural entertainment, happy hour, and in-house entertainment.

Availability: Some apartments are available immediately.

Health services and rates: Residents receive 15 free days in the health center or Assisted Living per year, up to 60 days total. Physical, occupational, and speech therapy, plus dentist, are available at additional cost. Regular blood pressure checks.

- 30 Assisted Living suites
  $400 in addition to resident's monthly rental fee or $103/day for nonresidents*

  **For double occupancy add $125 to the monthly fee.*

- 60-Bed Skilled Nursing facility

Semiprivate	$105/day
Private	$122/day

"Forwood Manor is unique because of its four levels of lifestyle: fully independent Ambassador Suites with personal aid nearby; Assisted Living with 24-hour services; and Intermediate and Skilled Nursing with on-site therapy—all in elegant surroundings. Forwood Manor received a five-star rating and was the number one retirement community in the nation in The Forum Group survey."

FOULK MANOR NORTH

1212 Foulk Road
Wilmington DE 19803
(302) 478-4296
Lucille B. Yeatman, leasing counselor

Type of community: Continuing Care, modified contract

Foulk Manor North consists of a Georgian-style manor house and cottages located on ten acres of landscaped lawns and beautiful creekside woods in a suburban residential area. Independent Living, Assisted Living, Intermediate and Skilled Nursing are available. Some cultural landmarks close by include Winterthur, Hagley Museum, Delaware Art Museum, Longwood Gardens, University of Delaware, Rockwood, Grand Opera House, Brandywine River Museum, and Delaware Museum of Natural History. This community is within an hour of Philadelphia and Baltimore, and two hours from Washington, D.C., New York City, and Atlantic City.

Financial plan: Monthly rental fee.

Ownership and management: Managed by Forum Group, Inc., owner and manager of 27 retirement communities in the United States. Opened in 1974.

Minimum age: None.

Population: 123 residents; 77% women, 23% men, 13% couples.

Number of units: 37 Independent Living apartments, 20 cottages; 11 Assisted Living units, 46-bed Skilled Nursing facility.

Dining plan: Two meals a day for apartment residents and one meal a day for cottage residents are included in the monthly fee. Three meals for resident in single room.

Services: *Included in the monthly fee:* Weekly housekeeping and flat-linen services, scheduled as well as special transportation.

At additional cost: Personal laundry, professional dry cleaning, beauty/barbershop, guest accommodations.

Activities: Full-time program director. Arts and crafts, library, exercise classes, religious services, wellness programs, films, games, picnics, and lectures. Golf is available at nearby courses.

Availability: Apartments and cottages are available.

Health services and rates: Apartment residents receive ten credit days per year in the health center, up to a maximum of 30 credit days. Residents can apply these credit days toward a short-term stay or a long-term stay in the nursing center. Alzheimer's and related disorders unit on-site.

- 11-Unit Assisted Living center*
  - Regular private $85/day
  - Large private $90/day
  - Suite $125/day

  **For double occupancy add $20 to the daily fee.*

- 46-Bed Skilled Nursing center
  - Semiprivate $98/day
  - Large semiprivate $102/day
  - Private $117/day

INDEPENDENT LIVING HOUSING

Manor house	*Monthly rental fee**
Single room	$1,150
Efficiency	$1,400–1,600
1-Bedroom	$1,780–1,900
Cottages	
1-Bedroom	$1,875
2-Bedroom	$1,995

**For double occupancy add $350 to the monthly fee. All utilities except telephone and cable TV included. Wall-to-wall carpeting, individually controlled heating and air-conditioning, 24-hour emergency call system. Cottages have living room opening onto a terrace, washer/dryer area.*

"Residents who have lived in Forum communities for ten years feel even better about the staff than they did when they moved in. The staff at every Forum community is carefully selected and trained to provide professional, courteous service that is the finest available in any retirement community. As one of our executive directors said, 'People who work at The Forum communities have a need to give and to care. After time, the residents consider the staff to be almost one of the family—they grow to care deeply about one another.'"

Lib and Russ, 80 and 82 years

Willow Valley Manor, Willow Street, Lancaster, Pennsylvania

"It's so easy for us when we travel. We simply lock up and leave."

Now in their eighties, Lib and Russ have been residents of Willow Valley Manor for seven years. Russ worked all his life for the Pennsylvania Railroad in Harrisburg, Philadelphia, and, for most of his career, Wilmington, Delaware, where he was president of the Mutual Benefit Association. When he retired in 1975, he and his first wife moved to Naples, Florida, where they bought a house and then later built a new one. Russ's wife and Lib's husband died within a year of each other, and as the couples had been lifelong friends in Wilmington—even the children knew one another well—Lib and Russ married in 1977, continuing to live in Naples.

Nine years ago, Lib and Russ paid a visit to some friends living in Willow Valley, and they couldn't stop talking about the community on their way back to Florida. By the time they reached home, Russ says they had pretty much decided to sell their house and move to Lancaster. "We loved the beautiful countryside surrounding Willow Valley. The fact that Willow Valley offered life care was the real selling point for us," they say. "We also wanted to be close to our children who live in Wilmington and Columbus." The children, by the way, are delighted with Lib and Russ's decision and come to visit frequently.

Another selling point for Lib and Russ was that their heirs will receive 33$^1/_3$% of the selling price of their apartment, which, in their case, also includes its appreciated value. (New residents to Willow Valley now receive 33$^1/_3$% of the entrance fee, with no appreciation included.)

"We looked around Florida, and nothing we saw in the same price range was as nice and convenient as Willow Valley," says Russ.

Lib and Russ have a two-bedroom, two-bath apartment with a living room, balcony, heated garage and fully equipped kitchen, where Lib says she still does a lot of cooking. "At Willow Valley, men are required to wear jackets and ties for dinner," she explains, "and sometimes we just don't feel like getting dressed up."

Lib and Russ are very active and in excellent physical condition. She likes to bowl (there are teams at Willow Valley), and he likes to play golf and bowl. They both like to play cards and read, but their passion is travel. Last spring they took a trip from Cardiff, Wales, to Capetown, South Africa. "It's so easy for us when we travel. We simply lock up and leave. And the community takes care of everything while we're gone," comments Russ.

METHODIST COUNTRY HOUSE

4830 Kennett Pike
Wilmington, DE 19807-1899
(302) 654-5101
Ginny Leagans, residency counselor

Type of community: Nonprofit Continuing Care, all-inclusive contract

Accreditation: Continuing Care Accreditation Commission

Designed in the classical Georgian architecture style, the Country House stands on 43 acres of beautifully manicured grounds featuring colorful flower gardens and shrubbery (originally part of du Pont Winterthur estate). Independent Living apartments and nursing facility available. Within a few miles' radius are hospitals, shopping centers, theaters, golf courses, museums, and restaurants. The Country House is within one and two hours from New York City, Philadelphia, Atlantic City, Baltimore, and Washington, D.C. Renowned attractions nearby included Hagley Museum, Longwood Gardens, University of Delaware, and Brandywine River Museum.

Financial plan: Entrance plus monthly fee. Entrance fee is refundable less 2% per month during the first 50 months of residency.

Ownership and management: Peninsula United Methodist Homes, Inc. (PUMH), an affiliate of the Annual Conference of the United Methodist Church. A residency council advises the administration. Opened in 1960.

Minimum age: 60 years.

Population: 170 residents; 75% women, 25% men, 15% couples.

Number of units: 132 Independent Living studios and 101 apartments; 18 personal care units, 59 nursing beds.

Dining plan: Three meals a day included in the monthly fee. Registered dietitian. Residents who live in apartments may also choose a one meal/day plan and receive credit for the two extra meals.

Services: *Included in the monthly fee:* Community van provides door-to-door service, weekly housekeeping and flat-linen services, laundry facilities, parking.

At additional cost: Gift shop with a snack and soda bar, beauty/barbershop, mailing service.

Activities: Library, chapel/auditorium, fine arts, woodworking, gardening, exercise groups, musical events, men's chorus, sing-alongs, annual talent show. Trips to the symphony, Opera Delaware, theater, Winterthur (home of the Henry Francis du Pont renowned collection of majestic trees and opulent architecture), the Delaware Art Museum, other cultural events. Interdenominational services are

INDEPENDENT LIVING HOUSING

Type/size of unit	*Entrance fee**	*Monthly fee**
Studio, 250–305 sq. ft.	$21,500–62,650	$1,337–2,190
1-Bedroom, 485–670 sq. ft.	$48,000–64,900	$2,050–2,190
Deluxe 1-bedroom, 705–959 sq. ft.	$62,650–95,900	$2,190–2,500
2-Bedroom, 1,050–1,075 sq. ft.	$105,000–108,000	$2,600

**For double occupancy add $10,000 to the entrance fee and $500 to the monthly fee. All utilities except long-distance telephone included. Fully equipped kitchens, 24-hour emergency call system, wall-to-wall carpeting, draperies, individually controlled heating and air-conditioning, cable TV, local telephone. Some apartments come with washer/dryer, garbage disposal, and dishwasher.*

held weekly in the chapel. Private visits with the chaplain and Bible study groups.

Availability: Some one-bedroom apartments are available immediately.

Health services and rates: Physician's care, personal care, Skilled Nursing, and physical therapy are included in monthly fee. RNs, LPNs, and nursing assistants are on staff around the clock, and a medical director is always on call. Physical therapy and recreational programs provided. Specialized care for residents with Alzheimer's disease or related disorders available.

- 18 Personal care beds
- 79-Bed nursing facility

"The Methodist Country House provides residents with gracious country living in a convenient location and offers the security of full-service health care."

SHIPLEY MANOR

2723 Shipley Road
Wilmington, DE 19810
(302) 479-0111
Jane Burslem, leasing counselor

Type of community: Continuing Care, modified contract

A former elementary school with a warm country-like decor, Shipley Manor is surrounded by ten acres of northern Delaware rolling hills in the heart of a progressive business and college community. Independent Living and Intermediate and Skilled Nursing are available. Within a radius of a few miles are hospitals, shopping centers, theaters, golf courses, museums, and restaurants. Within one or two hours are New York City, Philadelphia, Atlantic City, Baltimore, and Washington, D.C. Renowned attractions nearby include Winterthur, Hagley Museum, Longwood Gardens, University of Delaware, Brandywine River Museum, and Old Swedes Church.

Financial plan: Monthly rental fee. Refundable security deposit.

Ownership and management: Forum Group, Inc., owner/manager of over 27 communities in the United States, six in Delaware. Opened in 1985.

Minimum age: 60 years.

Population: 71 residents; 67% women, 33% men, 21% couples.

INDEPENDENT LIVING HOUSING

Type/size of apartment	*Monthly rental fee**
Efficiency, 415 sq. ft.	$1,350
1-Bedroom, 640 sq. ft.	$1,600–2,100
2-Bedroom, 980 sq. ft.	$2,100–2,275
Cottage	
1-Bedroom, 874 sq. ft.	$1,700
2-Bedroom, 1,142 sq. ft.	$2,100

**For double occupancy add $450 to the monthly rental fee. All utilities except telephone included. Private telephones are optional. Kitchenette, wall-to-wall carpeting, sheer draperies, cable TV, individual temperature control, 24-hour emergency call system.*

Number of units: 51 Independent Living apartments and 10 cottages; 82 Intermediate and Skilled Nursing beds.

Dining plan: Lunch and dinner are included in the monthly rental fee.

Services: *Included in the monthly fee:* Weekly housekeeping and flat-linen services, regularly scheduled transportation, personal laundry centers.

At additional cost: Beauty/barbershop, country store, private transportation, dry cleaning pick-up and delivery, newspaper delivery.

Activities: Full-time program director. Exercise classes, cooking classes, arts and crafts club, sing-alongs, lectures, Bible study, bridge club, bingo, trips to he local cultural entertainment, happy hour with entertainment, movies.

Availability: Some apartments are available immediately.

Health services and rates: Residents receive ten free days in the health care center per year up to 30 days total, after which time residents pay the rates listed below. A $50 one-time fee is required upon first entry into the health center. Intermediate and Skilled Nursing available. Physical, occupational, and speech therapy are provided at additional cost. Shipley Manor has a transfer agreement with local hospitals in the event hospitalization is required.

- 82-Bed health center

Semiprivate	$98/day
Private	$118/day

"Shipley Manor is designed to provide a pleasant and worry-free atmosphere for residents used to independent living. We are a community committed to consistent quality services; resident satisfaction is our number one goal."

FLORIDA

EDGEWATER POINTE ESTATES

23315 Blue Water Circle
Boca Raton, FL 33433
(407) 391-3114
Jay Hibbard, marketing representative

Type of community: Nonprofit Continuing Care, all-inclusive contract

This community is housed in three five-story white apartment buildings with red-tiled roofs on a 30-acre parklike campus surrounded by small body of water. Grassy fields and tree-lined walkways are throughout the campus. Buildings are interconnected by covered walkways for convenience of residents. The community is close to all services and shopping areas in the Boca Raton area.

Financial plan: Entrance fee plus monthly fee. Entrance fee is refundable less 1% per month (depreciation charge).

Ownership and management: Owned and managed by Adult Communities Total Services, Inc. (ACTS), operator of 15 communities in Florida, North Carolina, and Pennsylvania. Opened in 1983.

Minimum age: 60 years.

Population: 600 residents; 65% women, 35% men, 35% couples.

Number of units: 360 Independent Living apartments; 44 Assisted Living units, 60-bed nursing facility, 60-bed special care center for Alzheimer's patients.

Dining plan: Two meals per day included in the monthly fee. Private dining room available.

INDEPENDENT LIVING HOUSING

Type/size of unit	*Entrance fee*	*Monthly fee single/double*
Studio, 641 sq. ft.	$63,800	$904
1-Bedroom, 726 sq. ft.	$84,800	$967/1,666
2-Bedroom, 1,036 sq. ft.	$116,800	$1,133/1,801
3-Bedroom, 1,346 sq. ft.	$146,800	$1,268/1,940

Prices reflect units on first three floors. Add $1,000 for a fourth-floor unit, $2,000 for a fifth-floor unit. All utilities except telephone included in the monthly fee.

Fully equipped kitchens, individually controlled heating and air-conditioning, 24-hour emergency call system, wall-to-wall carpeting, patio or balcony. (1-, 2-, and 3-bedroom apartments have walk-in closets). Pets are allowed.

Services: *Included in the monthly fee:* Weekly flat-linen service and housekeeping, free laundry room on each floor, transportation, parking.

At additional cost: Beauty/barbershop, maid service, guest accommodations.

Activities: Full-time activity director. Central recreation/activity center, swimming pools, theater-style auditorium, library, billiards, woodworking shop, crafts room, card room, gardening, walking paths, biking, croquet, shuffleboard.

Availability: Waiting list of six months. $1,000 deposit places you on waiting list. The deposit is credited toward the entrance fee.

Health services and rates: Assisted Living and nursing care are included in resident's entrance and monthly fees. Special care section for Alzheimer's patients.

- 44 Assisted Living units
- 60-Bed nursing facility
- 60-Bed special care center for Alzheimer's patients

"Edgewater Pointe offers independent apartment living in Boca Raton's best neighborhood. A full lifetime health care plan is provided for all residents to use in the event of a future medical problem. A full spectrum of health care is available on campus at no additional cost. An active social life and real friendship is experienced by 600 residents every day."

ST. ANDREWS ESTATES NORTH/ SOUTH

6152 North Verde Trail
Boca Raton, FL 33433
(407) 487-5500 or (800) 850-2287
Cindy Brown, marketing representative

Type of community: Nonprofit Continuing Care, all-inclusive contract

Six three-story residential apartment buildings are designed in Spanish-Mediterranean style with beige exteriors and red-tiled roofs. Landscaped courtyards abound. Independent Living, Assisted Living, an activity center, and a 120-bed health center are offered on the 60-acre wooded campus that has four small lakes and walking paths throughout. Enclosed walkways connect all buildings. The community is surrounded by a residential environment offering dining and shopping in the Town Center Mall; various plazas and restaurants are all within walking distance.

Financial plan: Entrance fee plus monthly fee. Entrance fee refundable less 1% per month of residency.

Ownership and management: Owned by Adult Communities Total Services, Inc. (ACTS), which operates 15 communities in Florida, North Carolina, and Pennsylvania with more than 6,000 residents. Managed by Total Care Systems, Inc. Opened in 1978.

Minimum age: 60 years.

INDEPENDENT LIVING HOUSING

Type/size of apartment	*Entrance fee*	*Monthly fee single/double*
Studio, 484 sq. ft.	$49,800–52,800	$904
1-Bedroom, 662 sq. ft.	$79,800–82,800	$967/1,666
2-Bedroom, 956 sq. ft.	$104,800–109,800	$1,113/1,801
3-Bedroom, 1,255 sq. ft.	$137,800–142,800	$1,268/1,940

**For double occupancy add $5,000 to the entrance fee. All utilities except telephone included in the monthly fee. Wall-to-wall carpeting, individually controlled heating and air-conditioning, fully equipped kitchens, patio or balcony, cable TV, 24-hour emergency call system. Pets are allowed.*

Population: 800 residents; 60% men, 40% women, 40% couples.

Number of units: 604 Independent Living apartments; 44 private suite Assisted Living wing, 120-bed health center.

Dining plan: Two meals per day included in the monthly fee. Private dining room.

Services: *Included in the monthly fee:* Weekly flat-linen service, housekeeping, open parking, scheduled transportation, washers and dryers on each floor.

At additional cost: Beauty/barbershop, covered parking, maid service, guest accommodations.

Activities: Full-time activities director and residents' association. Auditorium, craft rooms, exercise room, library, billiards room, swimming pool, woodworking shop, fully equipped card room, garden plots, walking paths, biking, shuffleboard, day trips, films, concerts, lectures, parties, tours, volunteering.

Availability: Waiting list for certain accommodations. Limited immediate occupancy.

Health services and rates: Resident's health care costs are covered under monthly fee. Three meals a day in Assisted Living and health center included at no additional charge. Therapeutic activities for patients, personal care rooms for those who require Assisted Living and specialized health care services. Resident nurse's office apart from the nursing facility.

- Four levels of care are offered:
  Level 1: Registered nurses are dispatched to private residences for at-home services.
  Level 2: Short-term care for residents at the community medical center.
  Level 3: Assisted Living in private suites.
  Level 4: 24-hour-a-day Skilled Nursing care at the community's private medical center.

"The ACTS full life care plan offers seniors spacious apartment living, an independent/active lifestyle, and, most important, a complete spectrum of health care services on campus whenever needed for however long with no increase in fees."

FREEDOM VILLAGE

6501 17th West
Bradenton FL, 34209
(813) 798-8122
J. Allan Dolman, Jr., marketing director

Type of community: Continuing Care, modified contract

The campus-like environment at Freedom Village features three residential apartment buildings in which approximately 600 active residents live. The campus of 36-acres incorporates walking paths, shuffleboard courts, gardening areas, and two lakes. The Landings is the "main street" of the community and includes a 140-seat auditorium, indoor pool, full-service bank, doctor's clinic, convenience center, two restaurants, library, health club, and "Artists in Residence" gallery. The community is located near Blake Hospital and within minutes of three golf courses, two tennis facilities, the Gulf of Mexico, and several shopping centers.

Financial plan: Entrance fee plus monthly fee. Entrance fee refundable up to 96% and no less than 50%.

Ownership and management: Locally owned and managed by Southern Management Services. Opened in 1984.

Minimum age: 60 years.

Population: 600 residents; 65% women, 35% men, 30% couples.

Number of units: 483 Independent Living apartments and 32 villas; two Skilled Nursing centers with a total of 360 beds plus 140-bed dementia-specific Alzheimer's unit.

Dining plan: One meal per day included in the monthly fee. Meal plans may be customized to suit resident's needs.

INDEPENDENT LIVING HOUSING

Type/size of apartment	*Entrance fee*	*Monthly fee**
Studio, 528 sq. ft.	$39,900	$885
1-Bedroom, 728–1,050 sq. ft.	$63,500–101,000	$1,100–1,320
2-Bedroom, 1,256–1,376 sq. ft.	$110,500–149,000	$1,435–1,480
Villas		
1-Bedroom, 1,030 sq. ft.	$102,000	$1,480
2-Bedroom, 1,425 sq. ft.	$145,500	$1,560
Colonial Building		
1-Bedroom, 878–1,132 sq. ft.	$79,000–110,000	$1,075–1,325
2-Bedroom, 1,286–1,422 sq. ft.	$127,500–149,000	$1,400–1,500
3-Bedroom, 1,296–1,910 sq. ft.	$136,500–190,000	$1,450–1,875

**For double occupancy add $495 to the monthly fee. All utilities except telephone included. Fully equipped kitchen, wall-to-wall carpeting, 24-hour emergency call system, individually controlled heating and air-conditioning, cable TV.*

Services: *Included in the monthly fee:* Weekly housekeeping, flat-linen service, parking, scheduled transportation.

At additional cost: Beauty/barbershop, convenience center.

Activities: Activities coordinator. Pool, crafts classes, billiards, library, fitness center, entertainment two to three evenings/week, woodworking.

Availability: Waiting list for some models. One-bedroom and some two-bedroom plans generally available.

Health services and rates: Three health care centers located on campus. Each facility is open to the community as well as Freedom Village residents. Two Skilled Nursing centers plus an Assisted Living facility.provide multiple levels of professional care. An activity-intensive individualized Harmony Program for dementia-specific/Alzheimer's residents is offered. Blake Hospital is nearby.

- 140 Assisted Living suites
  Depending on size of unit and level of care: $1,140–3,180/month
- 360 Skilled Nursing beds
  Semiprivate $99.50–101.50/day
  Private $123.50–126.50/day

"Freedom Village is well known for the exciting Continuing Care living offered to its residents. Nestled in the residential greenery of lovely Bradenton, Freedom Village presents a new way to enjoy resort-style retirement living. Opportunity and choice are the key words in describing the lifestyle at Freedom Village."

WESTMINSTER ASBURY: THE TOWERS; THE MANOR

1533 4th Avenue West; 1700 21st Avenue
West Bradenton, FL 34205
The Towers: (813) 747-1881; The Manor: (813) 748-4161
Lois Seabert, marketing director, The Towers
Esther Concett, marketing director, The Manor

Type of community: Not-for-profit Continuing Care, modified contract

Accreditation: Continuing Care Accreditation Commission

Westminster Asbury is made up of two apartment buildings, The Manor and The Towers, separate garden

INDEPENDENT LIVING HOUSING

Manor apartments	*Entrance fee*	*Monthly fee**
Studio	$22,900–29,000	$809–864
1-Bedroom	$37,150–53,000	$1,269–1,428
Tower apartments		
Studio	$22,900–31,600	$809–978
1-Bedroom	$40,150–55,000	$1,319–1,552
Garden apartments		
Studio, 458 sq. ft.	$36,000	$647
1-Bedroom, 602 sq. ft.	$49,000	$966
2-Bedroom, 916 sq. ft.	$68,000	$1,105
Villas	$71,000	$1,105

50% guaranteed refund entrance fee also available; entrance fee less than 90% guaranteed plan.

** For double occupancy, add to entrance fee: Traditional—$10,000; 90% guaranteed refund option—$14,000; 50% guaranteed refund option—$11,000. Add to monthly fee: Manor and Towers—$350; garden apartments and villas—$195.*

All utilities included for Manor and Tower apartments. Individual climate control, 24-hour emergency call system, wall-to-wall carpeting, kitchens (on request).

apartments and villas, and a 93-bed health center located in downtown Bradenton. The Manor overlooks Wares Creek, and The Towers community overlooks an inlet to the ocean and the banks of the Manatee River. The five-story masonry buildings are surrounded by beautiful gardens and paved walks. The Gulf of Mexico and beautiful beaches are nearby. The community offers easy access to shopping, banks, restaurants, and other points of interest such as the Gamble Plantation, Ringling Museum, and a community theater.

Financial plan: Entrance fee plus monthly fee. Three plans: **1)** Traditional: refundable less 4% for processing and 2% for each month of residency. **2)** 90% guaranteed refund option. **3)** 50% guaranteed refund option. $1,000 fully refundable deposit upon application. Rental and financing programs available.

Ownership and management: Owned by Presbyterian Retirement Communities, Inc. Managed by a board of directors. Opened in 1960.

Minimum age: 62 years.

Population: 345 residents; 75% women, 25% men, 4% couples.

Number of units: Independent Living: 120 Manor apartments, 96 Tower apartments, 8 villas, 25 garden apartments; 48 Assisted Living units, 59-bed Manor health center, 34-bed Towers health center.

Dining plan: Three meals per day included in the monthly fee for Manor and Tower apartments. One meal per day for garden apartments and villas. Special diet preparations are available. Private dining room available.

Services: *Included in the monthly fee:* Parking, scheduled transportation, housekeeping, laundry facilities, bicycle shelter, flat-linen service for Manor and Towers, cable TV.

At additional cost: Beauty/barbershop, convenience store, thrift shop, unscheduled transportation, covered parking, guest accommodations.

Activities: Arts and crafts room, shuffleboard courts, sewing and weaving room, chapel, library, putting green, lawn bowling court.

Availability: Waiting list. Apartments available intermittently.

Health services and rates: No charge for first 15 days of care for those in Manor and Towers; $8/day for those in garden apartments and villas, after which residents pay rates listed below. 24-hour licensed nursing supervision and certified nursing assistants. Limited clinical care included in monthly fee. Physical, occupational, and recreational therapy offered. Direct admission on space-available basis.

- 48 Assisted Living units

	Entrance fee	*Daily fee*
Studio	$22,900	$50.75

- 93-Bed health center

  $58.50/day for 16–90 days or $73.50/day for permanent care

(During the first 90 days, if it is decided that resident needs permanent care the rate is $73.50/day and 90-day period of nominal fee does not apply.)

"Westminster Asbury Towers and Manor is currently the only accredited Continuing Care retirement community in this county. We have a superior (top) rating in the state for our Skilled Nursing facility."

GULF COAST VILLAGE

1333 Santa Barbara Boulevard
Cape Coral, FL 33991
(813) 772-1333
Merlyn Moore, retirement counselor

Type of community: Not-for-profit Continuing Care, modified contract

A six-story community building with Independent Living apartments and health care center is surrounded by a 20-acre wooded campus where eagles nest. Assisted Living suites are located in the Village Manor, adjacent to the community building. A swimming pool and outdoor patio are the focal points of the community, which has a small lake to the east. A half-mile walking path lies around the perimeter of the campus. The community is minutes from beautiful beaches, shelling, fishing, and golfing and close to area shopping.

Financial plan: Entrance fee plus monthly fee. Entrance fee is 90% refundable.

Ownership and management: Owned by Gulf Care, Inc., and managed by Greystone Communities, Inc., Dallas, Texas. Board of trustees consists of prominent community leaders. Opened in 1989.

Minimum age: 60 years.

Population: 181 residents; 85% women, 15% men, 30% couples.

Number of units: 173 Independent Living apartments; 51 Assisted Living units, 60-bed nursing facility.

Dining plan: One meal per day included in the monthly fee. Private dining room available. Dietary manager on-site.

Services: *Included in the monthly fee:* Biweekly housekeeping, scheduled transportation five days a week.

At additional cost: Beauty/barbershop, covered parking, guest suites, sundry shop.

Activities: Full-time social director. Reception room, multipurpose room, library, sewing room, arts and crafts room, woodworking shop, swimming pool, courtyard lounge, exercise room with whirlpool, shuffleboard courts, chapel, billiards room, big-screen TV theater, volunteering, health spa, game room.

Availability: Waiting list for certain apartments.

INDEPENDENT LIVING HOUSING

Type of unit	*Entrance fee*	*Monthly fee**
Studio	$57,000	$826
1-Bedroom	$79,000–105,000	$955–1,193
2-Bedroom	$109,000–139,000	$1,279–1,549

**For double occupancy add $433 to the monthly fee. All utilities except telephone included. Patio or balcony, fully equipped kitchen, walk-in closet, wall-to-wall carpeting, 24-hour emergency call system, individually controlled heating and air conditioning, cable TV. Laundry and ironing room on each floor.*

Health services and rates: Residents receive priority access to health center and Assisted Living area plus a 15% discount on expenses. Long-term care insurance, with optional additional coverage, available. Rehabilitative and restorative care programs available. Specialized programs for speech, hearing, physical, occupational, and respiratory therapy. Medical director on-site. Dental and podiatrist consultant services, Alzheimer's day care center on-site.

- 51 Assisted Living units

1-Room		$1,550/month
2-Room (single)		$2,650/month
2-Room (double)		$3,000/month

- 60-Bed health center

Semiprivate	$95/day	$2,850/month
Private	$105/day	$3,150/month

"Gulf Coast Village has added a new program: Adult Day Stay. This is a day program aimed at giving primary caregivers help. The program is a full day ($30) or half day ($15), and includes one meal and two snacks, activities, and transportation."

THE OAKS AT CLEARWATER

420 Bay Avenue
Clearwater, FL 34616
(813) 445-4700
Betty Jones, marketing representative

Type of community: Not-for-profit Continuing Care, modified contract

Offering a spectacular view from every apartment window, The Oaks is situated on the Intracoastal Waterway, overlooking the Gulf of Mexico and the skylines of Clearwater and St. Petersburg. The Oaks consists of one 15-story building and two-story garden apartments/villas. A waterfront sundeck and outdoor garden patio are provided. Three levels of care are offered. The Oaks is located within walking distance of churches, banks, restaurants, and the downtown shopping area. Clearwater Beach is minutes away.

Financial plan: Monthly rental. $500 security deposit.

Ownership and management: Oaks of Clearwater. Opened in 1975.

Minimum age: 62 years.

Population: 200 residents; 80% women, 20% men, 20% couples.

Number of units: 295 Independent Living apartments; 60-bed Intermediate and Skilled Nursing facility.

Dining plan: Choice of one of three meals daily included in the monthly fee. Additional meals available at extra cost.

Services: *Included in the monthly fee:* Weekly housekeeping and flat-linen service, delivery service, scheduled transportation.

At additional cost: Beauty/barbershop.

INDEPENDENT LIVING HOUSING

Type/size of apartment	*Monthly fee*
Efficiency, 410 sq. ft.	$935*
1-Bedroom, 492 sq. ft.	$1,095*
Deluxe 1-bedroom, 697 sq. ft.	$1,375*
2-Bedroom, 820 sq. ft.	$1,645*
Garden Apartments	
1-Bedroom (large, sq. ft. N/A)	$935
2-Bedroom (large, sq. ft. N/A)	$1,100

**For double occupancy add $300 to the monthly fee. All utilities except telephone included. Fully equipped kitchenette, individually controlled heating and air-conditioning, 24-hour emergency call system.*

Activities: Library, waterfront sundeck, outdoor garden patio, billiards and crafts room, shuffleboard, cards, excursions, exercise room.

Availability: Units available. Priority waiting list.

Health services and rates:

- Assisted Care Program available in high-rise apartments

Efficiency	$1,749/month
1-Bedroom	$1,925/month
Deluxe 1-bedroom	$1,980/month
2-Bedroom	$2,321/month

For double occupancy (both requiring personal care) add $550 to the monthly fee.

- 60-Bed nursing facility

4-Bed ward	$74.50/day
3-Bed ward	$77.50/day
Semiprivate	$85/day
Private	$104/day

"At The Oaks, we realize that retirement doesn't mean a sudden loss of independence. We understand that your needs are as individual as you are, and it shapes our outlook in everything we do."

THE PARK SUMMIT OF CORAL SPRINGS

8500 Royal Palm Boulevard
Coral Springs, FL 33065
(305) 752-9500
Margie Harr, director of marketing

Type of community: Continuing Care, modified contract

Ideally situated in the model city of Coral Springs, this well-planned and maintained community is located in a tranquil, country-like setting on 7.5 landscaped acres. Six buildings (seven, six, and five stories) are built in a slight curve and connected by walkways. Five apartments are in each corridor. Independent Living apartments, Assisted Living, and a health care center are available. Coral Springs offers numerous leisure opportunities, convenient shops and services, country clubs, sports and cultural facilities.

Financial plan: Monthly rental fee.

Ownership and management: Owned and managed by The Forum Group, Inc., owner/manager of 27 retirement communities throughout the United States. Opened in 1986.

Minimum age: 62 years.

Population: 225 residents; 62% women, 38% men, 58% couples.

INDEPENDENT LIVING HOUSING

Type/size of apartment	*Monthly fee**
Studio, 572 sq. ft.	$1,565–1,595
1-Bedroom, 722–1,023 sq. ft.	$1,665–1,935
2-Bedroom, 1,023–1,948 sq. ft.	$1,735–2,295
3-Bedroom, 2,016 sq. ft.	$3,070

**For double occupancy add $375 to the monthly fee. All utilities included. All-electric kitchen, individually controlled heating and air-conditioning, window treatments, washer/dryer hookups, plush carpeting, 24-hour emergency call system, balcony or terrace.*

Number of units: 200 Independent Living apartments; 21 Assisted Living apartments, 35-bed health care center.

Dining plan: Complimentary continental breakfast and one meal per day included in the monthly fee. Private dining room.

Services: *Included in the monthly fee:* Weekly housekeeping services, personal laundry facilities, parking, scheduled transportation.

At additional cost: Beauty/barbershop, card and gift shop.

Activities: Heated outdoor swimming pool and Jacuzzi, exercise facilities, billiards and game room, arts and crafts, card room, covered shuffleboard courts.

Availability: Units available. Priority waiting list.

Health services and rates: Residents receive 15 free days in health care center (30 days maximum). Admission may be made directly to the health center when space is available.

- 24 Assisted Living apartments

Small studio, 400 sq. ft.	$1,595/month
Deluxe studio, 500 sq. ft.	$1,675/month
Small 1-bedroom, 723 sq. ft.	$2,095/month
1-Bedroom, 850 sq. ft.	$2,295/month
2-Bedroom, 1,000–1,920 sq. ft.	$2,400/month

**For double occupancy add $450 to the monthly fee.*

- 35-Bed health care center

Semiprivate	$115/day
Private	$136/day

"To be America's leading retirement community is our main goal. We have a long-term, corporate-wide commitment to quality and excellence. Attention to detail and quality is everywhere you look."

THE FORUM AT DEER CREEK

3001 Deer Creek Country Club Boulevard
Deerfield Beach, FL 33442
(305) 698-6269
Loise Renaldo, marketing director

Type of community: Continuing Care, modified contract

Located on a five-acre landscaped campus within the Deer Creek Country Club, The Forum at Deer Creek has two seven-story residential apartment buildings surrounded by an expansive courtyard area and connected by a community building designed in the style of a Spanish mission. A 60-bed health center is adjacent to the residential buildings. Lakes and golf courses surround the community on all sides. The community is close to the Atlantic Ocean and Boca Raton, with easy access to shopping, banks, and medical facilities.

Financial plan: Monthly rental.

INDEPENDENT LIVING HOUSING

Type/size of apartment	*Monthly fee**
1-Bedroom, 631–789 sq. ft.	$1,750–2,025
2-Bedroom, 875–1328 sq. ft.	$1,850–2,895

**For double occupancy add $375 to the monthly fee. All utilities included. Fully equipped all-electric kitchens, wall-to-wall carpeting, individually controlled heating and air-conditioning, washer and dryer, 24-hour emergency call system, walk-in closets, cable TV, balconies, bay windows, and sunrooms available.*

Ownership and management: Owned and operated by The Forum Group, Inc., headquartered in Indianapolis, Indiana, and having more than 25 years experience in the retirement living industry. Owners and operators of 27 communities around the United States. Opened in 1990.

Minimum age: 62 years.

Population: 160 residents; 70% women, 30% men, 13% couples.

Number of units: 164 Independent Living units; 30 Assisted Living units, 60-bed health center.

Dining plan: 30 meals per month and continental breakfast included in the monthly fee. Private dining room available. Tray service available.

Services: *Included in the monthly fee:* Weekly housekeeping, weekly flat-linen service, scheduled transportation within a five-mile radius of The Forum.

At additional cost: Covered parking, beauty/barbershop, transportation outside five-mile radius of The Forum.

Activities: Full-time activities director. Swimming pool, billiards room, spa, guest lectures, movies, exercise programs, travel tours, library, crafts room, arts and crafts, bridge, golfing, walking club, creative writing class, bingo, garden club, Scrabble tournaments, theater outings, concerts, ceramics, canasta, shopping excursions, painting class.

Health services and rates: Residents receive free health care 15 days per year; a total of 30 days per lifetime.

- 30 Assisted Living units
  - Studios $70–75/day
  - Ambassador suites $2,395–2,995/month
- 60 Skilled Nursing beds
  - Semiprivate $117/day
  - Private $130/day

"The Forum is set amid the country club community of Deer Creek, and is built on the philosophy that the beauty of the building and its surroundings is nothing without the caring staff that makes The Forum home. The Forum is a full-service rental retirement community."

MARRIOTT HORIZON CLUB

1208 South Military Trail
Deerfield Beach, FL 33442
(305) 481-2304 or (800) 223-9624
Lee Myers, retirement counselor

Type of community: Independent and Assisted Living

The Horizon Club is located on 18 acres of grounds featuring four buildings, tropical courtyards, a waterfall and fishpond, outdoor areas for entertaining, a lavishly landscaped garden atrium courtyard, lake, fishing pier, and gazebo. Buildings housing Independent Living and Assisted Living are connected by outdoor breezeways. Conveniently located on Military Trail near Interstate 95, the Florida Turnpike, and Sawgrass Expressway, the community is situated between Palm

INDEPENDENT LIVING HOUSING

Type/size of apartment	*Monthly fee**
Studio, 420 sq. ft.	$1,480–1,600
1-Bedroom, 575 sq. ft.	$1,650–1,850
2-Bedroom, 1 bath, 850 sq. ft.	$1,825–1,925
2-Bedroom, 2 bath, 875 sq. ft.	$1,900–2,300

**For double occupancy add $400 to the monthly fee. All utilities included except telephone and electricity. Fully equipped kitchen, washer/dryer, individually controlled heating and air-conditioning, 24-hour emergency call system, large closets and storage room, basic cable TV hookup, wall-to-wall carpeting, vertical window blinds, screened-in terraces or balconies. Some apartments have lakefront view.*

Beach and Miami and within walking distance to shopping.

Financial plan: Monthly rental. Deposit equals one month's rent.

Ownership and Management: Owned and managed by Marriott Senior Living Services, a wholly owned subsidiary of Marriott Corporation. Marriott owns and manages 13 retirement communities in Arizona, California, Florida, Illinois, Indiana, Maryland, New Jersey, Pennsylvania, Texas, and Virginia. Opened in 1986.

Minimum age: 65 years (if couple, spouse may be younger).

Population: 242 residents; 80% women, 20% men, 10% couples.

Number of units: 228 Independent Living apartments; 60 Assisted Living apartments.

Dining plan: Continental breakfast Monday through Saturday, plus choice of one meal daily included in the monthly fee. Extra meals available for an additional fee. Private dining room.

Services: *Included in the monthly fee:* Weekly housekeeping and flat-linen services, reserved parking space, move-in coordination, scheduled transportation.

At additional cost: Personal laundry, assistance with bill paying and insurance forms, beauty and barbershop, convenience store and ice-cream parlor, cocktail lounge, full-service bank, covered parking, laundry/dry cleaning, additional (non-scheduled) housekeeping services.

Activities: Heated swimming pool and whirlpool, game/billiards/exercise rooms, large auditorium with stage, shuffleboard courts and horseshoe area, putting green and lawn croquet, chapel, library, walking club, arts and crafts room, current events discussions, creative writing, movie outings, concerts, foreign language lessons.

Availability: Limited availability, depending on floor plan.

Health services and rates: Physical, occupational, and speech therapy and clinic services available.

- 34 Assisted Living apartments
  Studio, 420 sq. ft. $1,860/month
  1-Bedroom, 575 sq. ft. $2,250/month
  26 Assisted Living suites $2,100/month

"Although the Horizon Club respects the individual's need for privacy, residents will enjoy all the qualitative benefits of living in and contributing to a caring community, fostering life of the mind with a sense of purpose. Excellent service is more than just a business philosophy, it's been a Marriott family tradition for over 60 years. And all that we've learned as a leader in the service and hospitality industry is applied to satisfy the needs of older adults living in our retirement communities."

ABBEY DELRAY

2000 Lowson Boulevard
Delray Beach, FL 33445
(407) 278-3249
Diane Church, marketing director

Type of community: Not-for-profit Continuing Care, all-inclusive contract

Five three-story apartment buildings, 28 villa units, activity center, and health care center are located on a 27-acre campus. The architecture is Mediterranean style. The community offers a heated patio pool surrounded by open green lawns and palm tree–lined covered walkways. Bank and drugstore are on premises, and the community is close to shopping, the Atlantic Ocean, and cultural activities. Golf course is located across the street.

Financial plan: Entrance fee plus monthly fee. Refund of entrance fee less 2% per month of residency.

Ownership and management: Owned by Life Care Retirement Communities, Inc., current owner and operator of eight life care communities across the United States. Managed by Life Care Services Corporation, of Des Moines, Iowa, managers of more than 50 retirement communities over the past 30 years. Opened in 1979.

Minimum age: 62 years.

Population: 425 residents; approximately 82% women, 18% men, 23% couples.

Number of units: 360 Independent Living apartments; 100-bed nursing facility.

Dining plan: One meal per day included in the monthly fee. Special diets and tray service available. Dietitian on-site. Three meals prepared daily. Private dining room.

Services: *Included in the monthly fee:* Weekly housecleaning, flat-linen service, personal laundry facilities, scheduled transportation, parking.

At additional cost: Beauty/barbershop, guest accommodations.

Activities: Activities director, chaplain, interdenominational chapel services. Heated swimming pool, shuffleboard courts, billiards tables, meeting rooms, arts and crafts rooms, whirlpool, exercise room, lectures, films, holiday festivities, group outings, library, day trips, volunteering, chapel, bingo, vespers, singalongs, sewing, Ping-Pong, guest speakers, aqua aerobics, music concerts, card games, resident meetings, exercise classes.

Availability: Approximately 95% occupied at present time; one- to two-year wait for specific units.

Health services and rates: No additional charge for services in the health center (except extra meals, personal medications, and certain nursing supplies). Assisted Living program offers minimal assistance to residents in their apartments (i.e., assistance with dressing, bathing, medications, meal deliveries, escorts to dining room and other areas within the community). Physical, speech, and occupational therapy available.

- 100 Skilled Nursing beds (mostly semiprivate). Nonresidents are accommodated on a space-available basis at $118/day.

INDEPENDENT LIVING HOUSING

Type/size of unit	*Entrance fee*	*Monthly fee**
Alcove, 450 sq. ft.	$49,700–53,200	$773
1-Bedroom, 625 sq. ft.	$68,300–73,100	$999
2-Bedroom, 925 sq. ft.	$95,100	$1,168–1,273
Villa, 1,200 sq. ft.	$112,250–114,500	$1,273

**For double occupancy add $605 to the monthly fee. All utilities except long-distance telephone included. Fully equipped kitchens, wall-to-wall carpeting, individually controlled heating and air-conditioning, 24-hour emergency call system, patios and Florida Rooms.*

"Abbey Delray is known for its warm, homey environment, immaculate grounds and buildings and friendly neighborhood atmosphere. We have a high rate of longevity among staff."

HARBOUR'S EDGE

401 East Linton Boulevard
Delray Beach, FL 33483
(407) 272-7979
Pat Cordie, marketing director

Type of community: Continuing Care, all-inclusive contract

Located on the Intracoastal Waterway with 20 acres of lush landscaping, Harbour's Edge is one block from the Atlantic Ocean and beaches. The community consists of contemporary six-floor apartment buildings with water views. A Waterway dining room, cocktail lounge with nightly entertainment, and Harbor Light Theater are offered. The guardhouse checks incoming and outgoing traffic. Skilled Nursing available with all private rooms on-site.

Financial plan: Membership (entrance) fee plus monthly fee. Substantial portion of membership fee is refundable. 250 different membership fees available, which vary by type of apartment and care desired.

Ownership and management: Life Care Services (LCS). Since 1961, LCS has been involved in the planning, development, and management of over 50 retirement communities in the United States. Opened in 1987.

Minimum age: 62 years.

Population: 348 residents; 66% women, 39% men, 33% couples.

Number of units: 276 Independent Living apartments; 54 Skilled Nursing beds.

Dining plan: One meal per day included in the monthly fee. Tray service and special diets, when approved by administration for medical reasons. Private dining room. Cocktail lounge. Dockside dining. Theme dinners.

Services: *Included in the monthly fee:* Concierge, valet, scheduled transportation, housekeeping.

At additional cost: Beauty/barbershop, guest rooms, banking services.

Activities: Harbour Light Theater, heated swimming pool, indoor and outdoor whirlpools, sauna, steam room, exercise and locker rooms, library, gardening club, dance club, resident council, card clubs, shuffleboard, theme nights, outings, Bible study, men's breakfast club, movies, couples dance club, walking club, lecture series.

Availability: Limited availability. Some apartments have waiting list.

Health services and rates: Residents receive unlimited health care as part of the membership fee and monthly fee. Assisted Living services available in resident's apartment. Speech, occupational, and physical therapy offered at additional charge.

INDEPENDENT LIVING HOUSING

Type/size of unit	*Entrance fee**	*Monthly fee**
1-Bedroom, 1,000–1,100 sq. ft.	$212,000	$1,668
2-Bedroom, 1,430–2,000 sq. ft.	$665,000	$1,844–1,958

**For double occupancy add $615 to the entrance fee and $165 to the monthly fee.*

All utilities except telephone included. Individually controlled heating and air-conditioning, basic cable TV, fully equipped kitchen, washer/dryer, 24-hour emergency call system, balconies.

- 54-Bed Skilled Nursing facility, private rooms

"Harbour's Edge has a wonderful resort-like setting. The membership plan at Harbour's Edge provides for the return of a substantial portion of the entrance fee to the resident or the resident's estate. The purpose is to provide true life care living without permanent disruption of a resident's estate capital."

MEASE MANOR

700 Mease Plaza
Dunedin, FL 34698
(813) 733-1161
Maria Siemons, marketing director

Type of community: Not-for-profit Continuing Care, modified contract

Mease Manor is a nine-story high-rise apartment building located on 36 acres of wooded campus in a residential neighborhood. The two-story Mease Continuing Care and Skilled Nursing center is located adjacent to the Manor and is physically connected via an indoor concourse. Assisted Living accommodations are located on the second floor of Mease Manor. Mease Hospital and Clinic are next door. The city of Dunedin is located where the Gulf of Mexico joins St. Joseph's Sound and the Intracoastal Waterway.

Financial plan: Entrance fee plus monthly fee or yearly lease paid monthly. $750 processing fee.

Ownership and management: Founded by Dr. John Mease. Managed by Mease Manor board of trustees and president and CEO, Richard E. Lewis. Opened in 1964.

Minimum age: 62 years (if couple, spouse may be younger).

Population: 324 residents; 80% women, 20% men, 15% couples.

Number of units: 400 Independent Living apartments; 66 Assisted Living units, 90-bed Skilled Nursing facility.

Dining plan: Evening meal included in the monthly fee. Optional meal plans available. Private dining room.

Services: *Included in the monthly fee:* Weekly housekeeping and flat-linen services, scheduled transportation.

At additional cost: Beauty/barbershop, convenience store, guest accommodations.

Activities: Auditorium with stage, library (updated monthly), card room, woodworking shop, private fishing pond, arts and crafts classes, dance and exercise classes, entertainment.

Availability: Limited availability depending upon unit desired. Priority waiting list.

INDEPENDENT LIVING HOUSING

Type/size of apartment	*Entrance fee/Monthly fee*	*Monthly fee only*
Studio, 280 sq. ft.	$15,500/695	$935
Efficiency, 410 sq. ft.	$23,000/895*	$1,240*
1-Bedroom, 540 sq. ft.	$32,000/1,030*	$1,445*
2-Bedroom, 820–840 sq. ft.	$45,000/1,240*	$1,965*

**For double occupancy add $8,000 to the entrance fee and approximately $400 to the monthly fee. All utilities included. Individually controlled heating and air-conditioning, wall-to-wall carpeting, vertical blinds, private screened balconies, fully equipped kitchen (except studio), master TV antenna and cable TV hookup, 24-hour emergency call system.*

Health services and rates: Licensed nurse is on duty 24 hours to provide emergency medical aid or to arrange transportation to resident's physician or medical facilities. Residents receive a 10% discount of fees listed below.

- 66 Assisted Living units

Studio, 280 sq. ft.	$1,490/month
Efficiency, 410 sq. ft.	$1,785/month
1-Bedroom, 540 sq. ft.	$2,035/month

**For double occupancy add $425 to the monthly fee.*

- 90-Bed Skilled Nursing facility

Semiprivate	$92/day
Private	$117/day

"At Mease Manor, an independent, carefree lifestyle prevails amidst a warm, friendly environment. Residents' independence is maintained and supportive aid is always available. Unobtrusive security ensures residents' protection. The people, the lifestyle, and the facilities create elegance in independent living."

MARRIOTT CALUSA HARBOUR

2525 East First Street
Fort Myers, FL 33901
(813) 332-3333
James L. Mott, general manager

Type of community: Continuing Care, modified contract

This 20-story high-rise building with Independent Living apartments overlooks the Caloosahatchee River. Yacht harbor visible from screened-in lanai. Adjacent four-story building houses Assisted Living apartments. Health care center is on site. The community is conveniently located on the Intracoastal Waterway, off Interstate 75 in historic downtown Fort Myers and within walking distance of the Burroughs Museum, Harborside Convention Center, Centennial Park, and shopping.

Financial plan: Monthly rent. $250 interest-bearing refundable deposit.

Ownership and management: Owned and managed by Marriott Senior Living Services, a wholly owned subsidiary of Marriott Corporation. Marriott owns and manages 20 retirement communities in Arizona, California, Florida, Illinois, Maryland, Pennsylvania, Texas, and Virginia. Marriott manages communities in New Jersey. Opened in 1981.

Minimum age: 55 years (if couple, spouse may be younger).

Population: 460 residents; 60% women, 40% men, 20% couples.

Number of units: 224 Independent Living apartments; 147 Assisted Living apartments, 100 Skilled Nursing beds.

Dining plan: One meal per day, plus light continental breakfast) included in the monthly fee. Private dining room.

Services: *Included in the monthly fee:* Weekly housekeeping and flat-linen services, scheduled transportation, conveniently located laundry rooms.

INDEPENDENT LIVING HOUSING

Type/size of apartment	*Monthly fee**
Studio, 384–524 sq. ft.	$835–1,330
1-Bedroom, 412–576 sq. ft.	$1,035–1,630
2-Bedroom, 960–1,100 sq. ft.	$1,780–2,270

**For double occupancy add $295 to the monthly fee. All utilities included except telephone and cable TV. Wall-to-wall carpeting, window treatment, individually controlled heating and air-conditioning, 24-hour emergency call system. Kitchenettes in most apartments.*

At additional cost: Beauty/barbershop, country store.

Activities: Screened-in heated swimming pool, lounge with big-screen TV and VCR, game room, arts and crafts room, exercise room, library, ballroom dance floor, stage.

Availability: Limited.

Health services and rates: Speech, physical, and occupational therapy available for additional cost.

- 147 Assisted Living apartments

Studio, 280–460 sq. ft.	$1,150–1,460/month
1-Bedroom, 560 sq. ft.	$1,465–1,775/month
2-Bedroom, 790–872 sq. ft.	$2,095–2,400/month

For double occupancy add $295 to the monthly fee. Additional fee if more assistance required.

- 100-Bed Skilled Nursing facility

4 Beds per room	$89/day
Semiprivate	$95/day
Private	$131/day

"Although Calusa Harbour respects the individual's need for privacy, residents will enjoy all the qualitative benefits of living in and contributing to a caring community, fostering life of the mind with a sense of purpose. Excellent service is more than just a business philosophy, it's been a Marriott family tradition for over 60 years. And all that we've learned as a leader in the service and hospitality industry is applied to satisfy the needs of older adults living in our retirement communities."

SHELL POINT VILLAGE

15000 Shell Point Boulevard
Fort Myers, FL 33908
(813) 466-1131 or (800) 780-1131
David Moreland, vice president, marketing and sales

Type of community: Nonprofit Continuing Care, all-inclusive contraact

Shell Point Village is located on a 75-acre island on the Caloosahatchee River on Florida's Gulf Coast. This idyllic setting offers tropical promenades, palm trees, and courtyards of blooming hibiscus, allamanda, and

INDEPENDENT LIVING HOUSING

Low-rise	*Founders fee*	*Monthly fee*
Studio, 470 sq. ft.	$44,000	$629
1-Bedroom, 704 sq. ft.	$67,000	$735
2-Bedroom, 938–1,056 sq. ft.	$87,000	$878–1,186
Scenic mid-rise		
1-Bedroom, 759–815 sq. ft.	$96,000	$787
2-Bedroom, 1,000–1,232 sq. ft.	$102,000	$969–1,325
Harbor Court		
2-Bedroom, 1,400–1,625 sq. ft.	$167,000+	$1,535
3-Bedroom, 2,000–2,300 sq. ft.	$213,000+	$1,880

All utilities except telephone included. Individually controlled heating and air-conditioning, attached patio or balcony, carpeting and draperies, fully equipped kitchen, 24-hour emergency call system.

gardenia. The community boasts miles of scenic lighted walkways, a bridged lagoon, fountains, lakes, and canals. Apartments have magnificent views of the waterways or of the professionally landscaped gardens. Shell Point Village includes Independent Living apartments, Assisted Living apartments, a Skilled Nursing facility, and expansive, elegant common areas.

Financial plan: Entrance (founders) fee plus monthly fee.

Ownership and management: Owned and managed by the Christian and Missionary Alliance Foundation, Inc. Opened in 1968.

Minimum age: 60 years.

Population: 1,200 residents; 66% women, 34% men, 42% couples.

Number of units: 714 Independent Living apartments; 120 Assisted Living apartments, 180 Skilled Nursing beds.

Dining plan: Meals can be purchased individually or monthly at discounted rates. Private dining room.

Services: *Included in the monthly fee:* Weekly housekeeping and flat-linen services, laundry facilities, scheduled transportation, 24-hour emergency maintenance serviced, satellite TV system.

At additional cost: Beauty/barbershop, ice-cream parlor, deli, minimart, home-delivered pharmacy services, full-service bank, automobile service/repair, guest accommodations.

Activities: Health spa, 2 heated pools, 2 Jacuzzis, exercise classes, steam room, sauna, library, tennis courts, 18-hole putter golf course, boat dockage, shuffleboard, woodworking shop, model railroad exhibit, art studio, classes, lectures, civic/cultural/sports events, garden plots, greenhouse, pottery shop.

Availability: Very limited. Priority waiting list.

Health services and rates: Residents enjoy unlimited access to medical staff at no additional cost. Should residents move into Assisted Living or Skilled Nursing permanently, they continue to pay their monthly fee. If one member of a couple needs permanent care and the second person is healthy, they continue to pay the monthly fee (no additional charges for nursing). Three full-time physicians, dental and rehabilitation services, X ray on site.

- 120 Assisted Living apartments
- 180-Bed Skilled Nursing facility

"If there is one word that describes Shell Point, it is independence. That's because we know one of the greatest concerns about retirement is retaining one's freedom. Shell Point is founded on the principle that each resident should enjoy the highest level of independence that his or her health allows."

THE WATERFORD

601 South U.S. Highway 1
Juno Beach, FL 33408
(407) 627-3800
Sharon Bross, director of marketing

Type of community: Not-for-profit Continuing Care, all-inclusive contract

The Waterford is located on 15 acres along U.S. Highway 1, opposite the prestigious Seminole Golf and Country Club in the heart of Juno Beach. Tower apartments, villas, and garden apartments offer 15 different floor plans, each with spacious a balcony or patio. Independent Living, Assisted Living services, and Intermediate and Skilled Nursing are available. Community overlooks its own private lagoon.

Financial plan: Entrance fee plus monthly fee. A deposit equal to 10% of the entrance fee is required to reserve a residence.

Ownership and management: Planned and developed by Life Care Services Corporation, Des Moines, Iowa, planner and developer of more than 50 life care communities in the United States, ten

INDEPENDENT LIVING HOUSING

Type of apartment/villa	*Entrance fee*	*Monthly fee**
Studio	$40,000	$879
Alcove	$50,000	$994
1-Bedroom	$76,500–93,500	$1,110–1,228
2-Bedroom villa	$120,500–149,500	$1,347–1,622
3-Bedroom	$159,500–168,500	$1,643–1,720
Penthouse	$231,500	$1,870

**For double occupancy add $579 to the monthly fee. All utilities included. Fully equipped electric kitchen, individually controlled heating and air-conditioning, 24-hour emergency call system.*

in Florida. Owned, sponsored by Life Care Retirement Communities, Inc., Des Moines. Opened in 1982.

Minimum age: 62 years.

Population: 360 residents.

Number of units: 294 Independent Living tower apartments, garden apartments, and villas; 60 Intermediate and Skilled Nursing beds.

Dining plan: One meal per day included in the monthly fee. Additional meals at extra cost. Tray service available in the event of illness. Private dining room.

Services: *Included in the monthly fee:* Weekly housekeeping, flat-linen service, scheduled transportation.

At additional cost: Beauty/barbershop, guest accommodations, covered parking.

Activities: Heated swimming pool, outdoor Jacuzzi, library, woodworking shop, billiards, fitness center.

Availability: Units available. Priority waiting list.

Health services and rates: Resident's monthly fee includes health center services. Only additional charges are for medication, therapy, and two additional meals per day.

- Limited Assisted Living services offered to residents in apartments at additional cost, depending upon services required
- 60 Intermediate and Skilled Nursing beds

"Life care at The Waterford offers financial security amidst an active, independent, and luxurious lifestyle. An abundance of personal services and amenities usually associated with resort living are offered in addition to the security of professional health care should it be needed. Life Care Services Corporation has a proven track record of successful management and is known as the leader in the life care retirement field, having a recognized commitment to excellence."

FLORIDA UNITED PRESBYTERIAN HOMES

16 Lake Hunter Drive
Lakeland, FL 33803
(813) 688-5521
Brigitte Goodmon, marketing coordinator

Type of community: Nonprofit Continuing Care, modified contract

Located on scenic Lake Hunter, the Lake Hunter Homes are surrounded by beautiful oaks, lush gardens, and exotic Florida flora on 12 rolling acres. Independent

INDEPENDENT LIVING HOUSING

Terrace Gardens	*Entrance fee*	*Monthly fee single/double*
Efficiency, 576 sq. ft.	$26,750	$205/231
1-Bedroom, 810–910 sq. ft.	$40,000–45,000	$235/263
2-Bedroom, 1,052–2,700 sq. ft.	$48,500–94,750	$251/278
Lakeside Heights		
1-Bedroom, 755 sq. ft.	$46,750	$252/279
2-Bedroom, 1,033 sq. ft.	$62,750–88,500	$268/296
3-Bedroom home, 2,330–2,709 sq. ft.	$66,750–113,500	$421/448
Congregate apartments		
Efficiency, 333–387 sq. ft.	$16,000–22,500	$580/626
1-Bedroom, 682 sq. ft.	$38,500–44,000	$642/898
2-Bedroom, 803 sq. ft.	$44,750–66,750	$735/1,014

Fully equipped kitchens, carpeting, blinds, 24-hour emergency call system. Some Terrace Gardens and Lakeside Heights have patios or enclosed porches and carports or garages.

Living is available in Terrace Garden and Lakeside Heights apartments as well as freestanding homes. The community also includes two congregate living buildings and three Assisted Living buildings with private rooms. The Florida architecture features a low, rambling type of construction. The community's health center has 185 beds and is located nearby at 1919 Lakeland Hills Avenue. Residents can easily make day trips to all of Central Florida's main attractions (Walt Disney World, Epcot, MGM studios).

Financial plan: Entrance fee plus monthly fee. $100 nonrefundable processing fee and $1,000 refundable deposit.

Ownership and management: Sponsored by the South Atlantic Presbyterian Churches, USA, sponsor of five other retirement communities in Florida: The Manor and The Towers, Bradenton; Jacksonville Regency House, Jacksonville; Westminster Towers, Orlando; Westminster Oaks and Village, Tallahassee; Winter Park Towers and Village, Winter Park. Opened in 1956.

Minimum age: 55 years for application; 65 years for admission (if couple, spouse must be at least 62).

Population: 237 residents; 68% women, 32% men, 26% couples. (Many residents are retired professionals, church officers, ministers, and teachers.)

Number of units: 74 Independent Living houses and duplexes, some lakefront; 64 congregate living apartments; 31 Assisted Living apartments, 185-bed Skilled Nursing facility.

Dining plan: One meal per day included in the monthly fee for congregate apartment residents. Terrace Gardens and Lakeside Heights residents have one meal per week included in monthly fee. More comprehensive meal program is available for additional fee.

Services: *Included in the monthly fee:* Weekly housekeeping for apartment residents, scheduled transportation, laundry facilities.

At additional cost: Beauty/barbershop, personal shopping by driver, gift shop.

Activities: Musical programs, crafts, cooking classes, pet therapy, cookouts, shopping trips, large screened-in swimming pool, shuffleboard courts, ceramics, well-stocked library, fishing and boating on Lake Hunter, handbell choir, choral groups, volunteer groups.

Availability: Waiting list depends on unit desired.

Health services and rates: Home care services available. Full-time physical therapist. Occupational and speech therapists available when needed.

- 185 Intermediate and Skilled Nursing beds
  - Semiprivate $89/day
  - (Residents allowed $10/day credit)
  - Private $115/day
  - (Residents allowed $15/day credit)
- 31 Assisted Living rooms

	Monthly fee single/double
Small single	$1,407
Large single/double	$1,647/2,277
1-Bedroom/kitchenette	$1,524/2,165

(Nonresidents may enter Assisted Living directly by paying an entrance fee ranging from $16,000–42,500, depending on size of unit.)

"The mission of Florida United Presbyterian Homes is to establish and maintain facilities and programs in which older adults can experience a Christian environment and receive quality care in accordance with their individual needs."

MERIDIAN

3061 Donnelly Drive
Lantana, FL 33462
(407) 965-7200
Ilene Oxenhandler, marketing director

Type of community: Independent and Assisted Living

Meridian's three-story apartment buildings are distinctively accented with arched dormer windows, gabled roofs, brick-and-cedar clapboard siding, and latticework trellises and are located on a landscaped campus in the heart of Florida's Gold Coast. The community features a spacious lobby with a baby grand piano and stone fireplace and is minutes away from Palm Beach's Worth Avenue, Lake Worth, Boynton Beach Mall, many houses of worship, and the Atlantic Ocean. Boca Raton and Delray Beach are immediately to the south. John F. Kennedy Hospital is less than one mile from Meridian. The community offers easy access to Interstate 95 and the Florida Turnpike.

Financial plan: Monthly rent. Security deposit of one month's rent.

Ownership and management: Owned and operated by The Hillhaven Corporation, which has more than 30 years experience in serving seniors. Opened in 1986.

Minimum age: 60 years.

Population: 198 residents; 75% women, 25% men, 7% couples.

INDEPENDENT LIVING HOUSING

Type/size of unit	*Monthly fee**
Studio, 250 sq. ft.	1,495–1,545
1-Bedroom, 322 sq. ft	$1,545–1,595
2-Bedroom, 410 sq. ft.	$1,845–2,195

**For double occupancy add $395 to the monthly fee. All utilities except telephone included in monthly fee. Emergency call system, wall-to-wall carpeting, draperies, private balcony, kitchenette, individually controlled heating and air-conditioning, cable TV. Laundry rooms are located on each floor.*

Number of units: 172 Independent Living apartments; 33 Assisted Living units.

Dining plan: Choice of one, two, or three meals per day included in monthly rent. Tray service available. Private dining room and special diets available.

Services: *Included in the monthly fee:* Weekly housekeeping and flat-linen services, scheduled transportation, cable TV.

At additional cost: Beauty/barbershop, private transportation, banking, minimart.

Activities: Heated swimming pool, large Jacuzzi, shuffleboard, billiards, exercise room, card and game rooms, arts and crafts center, movies, educational programs, sporting and scenic trips, library, gardening, happy hours, book reviews, yoga, Trivial Pursuit matches, various group outings, bingo, dance classes, darts, poetry, music appreciation.

Availability: Waiting list, usually not too long.

Health services and rates: Home health care agency cares for resident in apartment when necessary. Assisted Living center on-site. Some additional nursing services are available.

- 33 Assisted Living units

Studio	$2,295/month
1-Bedroom	$2,495/month

**For double occupancy add $495 to the monthly fee if no services are required, $795 if Assisted Living services are required.*

"Good neighbors and beautiful surroundings with your own comfortable belongings—these are the things that Meridian offers residents. Lush lawns, heated pool, quiet courtyard, and bright sunlit parlors welcome you each time you come in the door. Meridian offers a full-service rental retirement community under one roof, including Assisted Living."

VILLAGE ON THE GREEN

500 Village Place
Longwood, FL 32779
(407) 788-2300 or (800) 432-8833
Peggy D. Clem, marketing director

Type of community: Not-for-profit Continuing Care, all-inclusive contract

Village on the Green is made up of mid-rise brick-and-stucco buildings with tile roofs located on 29 acres in a country club–like setting. Bordering on five holes and five water features of the Sabal Point Golf Course, this community offers outdoor and indoor lounges, walking paths, and covered walkways throughout. 2,000 acres of surrounding woodland have been set aside as a nature and wildlife preserve. Independent Living apartments, villas, and a health care center are offered. The community is located 15 minutes north of

INDEPENDENT LIVING HOUSING

Type/size of unit	*Entrance fee*	*Monthly fee**
1-Bedroom, 850–1,000 sq. ft.	$112,500–153,000	$1,217–1,262
2-Bedroom, 1,200–1,850 sq. ft.	$170,500–292,000	$1,312–1,433
Villa, 1,750 sq. ft.	$277,500–297,500	$1,433

**For double occupancy add $519 to the monthly fee. All utilities except long-distance telephone included. Wall-to-wall carpeting, washer and dryer, fully equipped kitchens, 24-hour emergency call system, cable TV, walk-in closets, enclosed Florida rooms. Villas include a garage and patio.*

downtown Orlando. Shopping, hospitals, Winter Park, Orlando Museum of Art, Civic Theater, Orlando Science Center, Leu Botanical Gardens, Mark Two Dinner Theater, Bob Carr Auditorium (Symphony, Southern Ballet, Broadway Series, Orlando Opera), Orlando Arena, Expo Center, Orlando Stadium, Orange County Convention Center, and Orlando International Airport are all nearby. Walt Disney World Resort and the Kennedy Space Center are within a one-hour drive.

Financial plan: Entrance fee plus monthly fee. A substantial portion of entrance fee may be refunded to resident or resident's estate.

Ownership and management: Owned and managed by Life Care Services Corporation of Des Moines, Iowa, which is involved in the development or management of more than 50 life care communities throughout the United States. Sponsored by Life Care Retirement Communities, a national not-for-profit company that sponsors or owns nine life care retirement communities and is incorporated in the state of Iowa. Opened in 1986.

Minimum age: 55 years.

Population: 330 residents; 50% couples.

Number of units: 203 Independent Living apartments and 38 villas; 60-bed health center.

Dining plan: One meal per day included in the monthly fee. Continuous dining available from 8 a.m. to 7:30 p.m. Private dining room and cocktail lounge available. Special diets accommodated.

Services: *Included in the monthly fee:* Weekly housekeeping and flat-linen services, scheduled transportation, reserved covered parking.

At additional cost: Beauty/barbershop, social activities, guest accommodations.

Activities: Full-time social director. Library, game room, arts and crafts studio, woodworking shop, cocktail lounge, swimming pool, whirlpool, exercise facilities, auditorium, walking paths, seminar programs, billiards room, full array of social cultural and recreational activities.

Availability: Three to six month waiting list.

Health services and rates: Health center on-site. Nursing staff has a broad educational background with experience in geriatrics, rehabilitation, and restorative care. Therapeutic recreation offered. 90 days of health care included in the monthly fee. Additional days of health care at reduced rate. Assisted Living at additional cost based on needs.

- Assisted Living services are offered in resident's apartment for $2.75 for every 15 minutes
- 60-Bed health center

Semiprivate	$1,142/month
Private	$1,142/month plus $63 per day

"The things that distinguish Village on the Green from other communities are its proven track record and the joint commitment of Life Care Services, the owner and manager, and Life Care Retirement Communities, the not-for-profit sponsor, to efficiently manage and operate the community. Our corporate attention ensures the highest level of service and fiscally sound management. Our location provides easy and quick access to hospital and major medical centers, cultural and recreational activities, local attractions, the beach, and Orlando International Airport. The country club atmosphere within the community is enhanced by the surrounding 18-hole championship Sabal Point Golf Course. And, of course, the climate is wonderful."

EAST RIDGE RETIREMENT VILLAGE

19301 South West 87th Avenue
Miami, FL 33157
(305) 238-2623
Dick Mulfinger, administrator

Type of community: Not-for-profit Continuing Care, all-inclusive contract

Ground-floor Independent Living apartments and villas and a 60-bed health center are located on a 76-acre parklike campus. An oasis of grass and trees, the campus features a lily pond and wide walkways that lead across the lawns to the buildings. Public library, many shopping centers, churches and other houses of worship are nearby.

Financial plan: Entrance fee plus monthly fee. Two plans: **1)** Traditional plan: refund of entrance fee less 2% per month of residency. **2)** Return-of-capital plan: 90% refund of entrance fee regardless of length of stay.

Ownership and management: Wholly owned by the residents and operated by a board of directors elected by the residents. Managed by Life Care Services Corporation, which has assisted in the development and management of more than 50 retirement communities throughout the United States. Opened in 1962.

Minimum age: 62 years.

Population: 400 residents; 85% women, 15% men, 15% couples.

Number of units: 312 Independent Living units (apartments and villas); 60 Assisted Living apartments, 60-bed health center.

Dining plan: One meal per day included in the monthly fee. Special diets available. Dining room serves three meals a day. Resident may choose any meal and change daily if they so desire.

Services: *Included in the monthly fee:* Weekly housekeeping and flat-linen services, parking.

At additional cost: Beauty/barbershop, bus to area stores.

Activities: Full-time activities director and activities center. Crafts and library rooms, heated swimming pool, chapel services, three lighted shuffleboard courts, auditorium, workshop, billiards, pottery wheels and kilns, sewing, oil painting, tours, lectures, films, holiday festivities, group outings.

Availability: Waiting list varies in length according to accommodations desired. Six months for smaller units; up to two years for larger units.

Health services and rates: Unlimited use of health center and Assisted Living included in entrance and monthly fees. Emergency, recuperative, and long-term care available. Therapy services available.

- 60 Assisted Living apartments
- 60-Bed health care center

"East Ridge is a life care community located on 76 acres, comprised of cottages and villas, in addition to a 60-bed nursing home for the highest quality nursing care. Activities are varied and include a heated pool, shuffleboard, pottery, painting, sewing, library, lectures, films, and outings. A nondenominational chapel is available for spiritual needs."

INDEPENDENT LIVING HOUSING

Type/size of apartment	*Entrance fee 1/2**	*Monthly fee**
1-Bedroom, 675 sq. ft.	$46,350–56,750/81,100–99,300	$1,046–1,249
2-Bedroom, 1,055 sq. ft.	$69,200–91,350/121,100–159,900	$1,413–1,568
Villas		
1-Bedroom, 970 sq. ft.	$76,200/133,350	$1,422
2-Bedroom, 1,170 sq. ft.	$97,850/171,200	$1,610

**For double occupancy add $4,650 to Plan 1, $8,150 to Plan 2, and $382 to the monthly fee. All utilities except telephone. Wall-to-wall carpeting, 24-hour emergency call system, cable TV, fully equipped kitchen, patio, individually controlled heating and air-conditioning.*

THE GLENVIEW AT PELICAN BAY

100 Glenview Place
Naples, FL 33963
(813) 591-0011
David Pavlik, marketing director

Type of community: Continuing Care with Equity, all-inclusive contract

The Glenview at Pelican Bay is a 12-story high-rise situated one-quarter mile from the Gulf of Mexico in the beautiful resort town of Naples, Florida. The Glenview consists of 119 one-, two-, and three-bedroom apartments ranging from 786 to 3,189 square feet. Contiguous to the Independent Living apartments is the health care facility, Premiere Place, which offers Assisted Living and Skilled Nursing. Bordered to the north by the five-star Ritz-Carlton Hotel and on the south by the four-diamond Registry Resort, Pelican Bay offers Gulf-side living at its finest. An elevated boardwalk leads to a three-mile private beach. A 27-hole golf course, shopping complex with Saks Fifth Avenue and Jacobson's, and the Philharmonic Center for the Arts are all nearby.

Financial plan: Purchase fee plus monthly fee. Residents purchase their apartments and, at the time of sale, their purchase price is fully recoverable. There is also an opportunity to share in the apartment's appreciation.

Ownership and management: Developed and managed by Freedom Group, Inc., of Bradenton, Florida. Set up as a cooperative structure with the residents exercising ownership through a board of directors. Opened in 1992.

Minimum age: 62 years.

Population: 172 residents; 63% women, 37% men, 65% couples.

Number of units: 119 Independent Living apartments; 35-bed health center (half Assisted Living and half Skilled Nursing).

Dining plan: One meal per day included in the monthly fee. Flexible meal plan allows choice of 30-, 25-, or 20-meal plans. Main dining room seats 125 people; grillroom seats 40 people. Private dining room seats 12. Private catering available.

Services: *Included in the monthly fee:* Weekly housekeeping and flat-linen services, scheduled transportation, valet parking and package service, underground gated parking.

At additional cost: Beauty/barbershop, room service, branch banking services.

Activities: Full-time activities director. Heated swimming pool, spa, library, arts and crafts room, fitness classes, multipurpose room, bar and lounge, walking club, boardwalk to three-mile private beach, two Pelican Bay beach restaurants, ten-acre Commons Park area with ten tennis courts and community

INDEPENDENT LIVING HOUSING

Type/size of apartment	*Purchase fee*	*Monthly fee*
1-Bedroom, 786 sq. ft.	$198,000–310,000	$1,150–1,623
2-Bedroom, 1,073–1,554 sq. ft.	$330,000–600,000	$1,460–2,620
3-Bedroom, 2,146–2,646 sq. ft.	$715,000–840,000	$2,610–3,612
Penthouses		
3-Bedroom, 2,069–3,189 sq. ft.	$850,000–1,200,000	$2,589–3,927

All utilities except telephone included in the monthly fee. Fully equipped all-electric kitchen, wall-to-wall carpeting, individually controlled heating and air-conditioning, 24-hour emergency call system and monitored smoke detectors, sprinkler system, cable TV, walk-in closets, washer and dryer, 1 or 2 balconies.

center, lectures, movies, card room, regularly scheduled trips to shopping center five blocks away featuring Saks Fifth Avenue and Jacobson's and the Naples Philharmonic Center for the Arts, four blocks away.

Availability: Length of waiting list depends on accommodations desired.

Health services and rates: All health care is included in resident's monthly fee and contractually guaranteed for life. Assisted Living and Skilled Nursing offered. Special Skilled Nursing section features a limited-memory wing with selectively trained personnel to assist those with memory difficulties. Rehabilitative programs. Health center is available to nonresidents on a private-pay basis.

- 35-Bed health care center

Assisted Living	$170/day for nonresidents
Skilled Nursing	$185/day for nonresidents

"The Glenview at Pelican Bay provides splendid homes on the Gulf of Mexico in a setting that rivals a world-class resort. Beyond the beauty of the buildings is the security of a health care center that assures lifelong care and a financial plan that allows families to retain their investment and even improve upon it. 'It is our challenge to provide the inspiration, support, and encouragement so that residents may have the opportunity to grow, to set and achieve new goals, dream new dreams, learn, play, laugh, and share in the joy of living.' —Robert Roskamp, CEO, The Freedom Group."

MOORINGS PARK

120 Moorings Park Drive
Naples, FL 33942
(813) 261-1616
Janet Kennedy, director of marketing

Type of community: Not-for-profit Continuing Care, all-inclusive contract

Located on 53 landscaped acres dotted with ponds, Moorings Park consists of Independent Living apartments in two eight-story towers and low-rise garden apartments, in addition to Assisted Living and a health care center. Paths meander through the property for walking, bicycling, and golf carts. A flower garden is bordered by an expansive patio where residents enjoy subtropical surroundings and two 18-hole putting greens. A shade house is provided for orchids and other fragile plant life. Centrally situated within minutes of shopping, hospitals, and beaches, Moorings Park is 35 minutes from the Naples Airport.

INDEPENDENT LIVING HOUSING

Tower apartments	*Entrance fee*	*Monthly fee**
1-Bedroom, 882 sq. ft.	$95,000	$1,301
2-Bedroom, 1,304–1,768 sq. ft.	$162,000–191,000	$1,519–1,646
2-Bedroom, 1,824 sq. ft.	$234,000	$1,820
3-Bedroom, 1,853 sq. ft.	$246,000	$2,038
Garden apartments		
1-Bedroom, 1,202 sq. ft.	$142,000	$1,386
2-Bedroom, 1,452–1,853 sq. ft.	$179,000–231,000	$1,693–1,865
3-Bedroom, 1,720–2,006 sq. ft.	$279,000	$2,087

**For double occupancy (except studio) add $519 to the monthly fee. All utilities included. Individually controlled heating and air-conditioning, humidifier, cable TV, 24-hour emergency call system.*

Financial plan: Entrance fee plus monthly fee.

Ownership and management: Owned by The Moorings, Inc. Managed by Life Care Services Corporation of Des Moines, Iowa, owner, developer, and manager of 50 retirement communities throughout the United States. Opened in 1981.

Minimum age: 62 years.

Population: 386 residents.

Number of units: 281 Independent Living apartments; 30 Assisted Living apartments, 76 Skilled Nursing beds.

Dining plan: One meal per day included in the monthly fee. Extra meals available at additional cost. Private dining room.

Services: *Included in the monthly fee:* Weekly housekeeping and flat-linen services, scheduled transportation, parking.

At additional cost: Two beauty parlors, barbershop, bank branch, guest accommodations.

Activities: Heat swimming pool, Jacuzzi, two 18-hole putting greens, individual garden areas, exercise facilities, lectures, films, music and entertainment programs.

Availability: Units available. Priority waiting list.

Health services and rates: Resident's monthly fee covers unlimited services of health care center with the exception of two extra meals. Home health services available.

- 30 Assisted Living apartments
  Single $105/day for nonresidents
- 76-Bed health center offers emergency care, recuperative care, long-term care, and therapy services
  Semiprivate $105/day for nonresidents
  Private $130/day for nonresidents

"Moorings Park is not-for-profit, which means all the fees are put back into the community. We pride ourselves on our friendliness and family-type feeling, and our food is comparable to the food of many fine restaurants."

WESTMINSTER TOWERS

70 West Lucerne Circle
Orlando, FL 32081
(407) 841-1310
Carol Jenkins, marketing representative

Type of community: Not-for-profit Continuing Care, modified contract

Accreditation: Continuing Care Accreditation Commission

INDEPENDENT LIVING HOUSING

Type/size of unit	*Entrance fee 1/2**	*Monthly fee**	*Monthly rental**
Studio, 475 sq. ft.	$34,000/57,800	$790	$1,680
1-Bedroom, 712–950 sq. ft	$55,000/60,000	$1,034	$2,168
1-Bedroom, 950 sq. ft.	$93,508/102,000	$1,417	$3,180
2-Bedroom, 1,187 sq. ft.	$83,000/141,100	$1,619	$3,338

**For double occupancy add $9,000 to the entrance fee; between $200–325 to the monthly fee; $620 to the monthly rental for studio and 1-bedroom. For double occupancy in 2-bedroom add $370 to the monthly rental and no increase to the entrance fee. All utilities included. Fully equipped kitchens, 24-hour emergency call system, individually controlled heating and air-conditioning, cable TV.*

This 19-story brick apartment building is located on Lake Lucerne in a convenient downtown location with rose gardens and new park recreation areas. Easy access is available to banks, restaurants, churches, shopping, doctor's and attorney's offices, hospitals and dental clinics, arts, theater, civic center, and library. Lake Lucerne has been newly landscaped to include a pedestrian bridge, fountains, and palm trees to designate it as the Southern Gateway to the City of Orlando.

Financial plan: Entrance fee plus monthly fee. Two plans for entrance fee: **1)** Traditional: amortization of 2% per month of residency plus 4% processing fee. **2)** Guaranteed refund option: Guaranteed refund of 90% or 4% plus 2% per month of residency, whichever is the most favorable to the resident. **3)** Monthly rental fee only.

Ownership and management: Owned and managed by Presbyterian Retirement Communities, owner and manager of three other retirement communities in Florida: Westminster Asbury in Bradenton, Westminster Oaks in Tallahassee, and Winter Park Towers in Winter Park. Opened in 1975.

Minimum age: 62 years.

Population: 440 residents; 80% women, 20% men, 10% couples.

Number of units: 233 Independent Living apartments; 50 Assisted Living units, 120-bed health center.

Dining plan: One meal per day included in the monthly fee. Special diets available. Private dining room and tray service available.

Services: *Included in the monthly fee:* Biweekly housekeeping (not included in the monthly rental option), scheduled transportation, parking (not included in the monthly rental option), clinic service, and wellness program.

At additional cost: Beauty/barbershop, guest accommodations.

Activities: Putting green, arts and crafts room, shuffleboard courts, woodworking shop, sewing and weaving room, chapel services, library, meeting rooms, meditation room, billiards room, exercise room, croquet.

Availability: Two-bedroom apartments have six-month to one-year waiting list. A fully refundable deposit of $1,000 per person places you on waiting list. Immediate placement for some units. Assisted Living has a three- to six-month waiting list.

Health services and rates: Physical, occupational, and recreational therapy. Dentist and podiatrist available on-site.

- 50 Assisted Living units

	Entrance fee	*Daily fee*
Single	$32,000–48,000	$51–64.75
Double	$42,000–58,000	$67–80.75

Daily rental $63 per person.

- 120-Bed health center

Residents	$72/day
Nonresidents	$91/day

For convalescent care, residents pay $8/day for the first 15 days; $57.50/day for 16–90 days. During the 90-day period, a continuous evaluation will be made to determine whether permanent health care is necessary. If permanent care is required, the 90-day period of nominal charge will not apply.

"Presbyterian Retirement Communities, the owner and manager of Westminster Towers, is a church-related, not-for-profit corporation dedicated and committed to providing Continuing Care services for the elderly, both healthy and frail, by creating and administering excellent residential and health care facilities."

MARRIOTT STRATFORD COURT

3830 Tampa Road
Palm Harbor, FL 34684
(813) 787-1500 or (800) 772-2622
Diane Truppi, sales manager

Type of community: Continuing Care, modified contract

This six-story apartment-style building faces Tarpon Outlet Canal and offers full water views. This full-service Independent Living retirement community offers a continuum of care including Assisted Living and Skilled Nursing. Located on 20 acres with trees and lawns, Stratford Court is close to hospitals and shopping. It is a ten-minute drive from Honeymoon Island State Park, which has beaches, a picnic area, wildlife walk, and ferry service to nearby Caladesi Island.

Financial plan: Monthly rental. $500 interest-bearing refundable deposit.

Ownership and management: Owned and managed by Marriott Senior Living Services, a wholly owned subsidiary of Marriott Corporation. Marriott owns and manages 13 retirement communities in Arizona, California, Florida, Illinois, Indiana, Maryland, New Jersey, Pennsylvania, Texas, and Virginia. Opened in January 1992.

Minimum age: 62 years (if couple, spouse may be younger).

Population: 233 residents; 58% women, 42% men, 65% couples.

Number of units: 219 apartments; 40 Assisted Living suites, 60 nursing beds.

Dining plan: 30 meals a month, plus continental breakfast, included in the monthly fee. Private dining room. Cocktail lounge.

Services: *Included in the monthly fee:* Weekly housekeeping, scheduled transportation, on-site parking, individual secured storage.

At additional cost: Beauty/barbershop, convenience store/gift shop, postal services, limo service, companion service, valet parking.

Activities: Activity center, exercise room, creative arts center, game room, card room, billiards, multipurpose room, pool, spa.

Availability: Limited.

Health services and rates: Agreement with local hospital for health screenings and education at no additional cost.

- 40 Assisted Living suites
  Private room with bath/dressing area $51–73/day
- 60-Bed Skilled Nursing facility
  Semiprivate $95/day
  Private $120/day

INDEPENDENT LIVING HOUSING

Type/size of apartment	*Monthly fee*
Studio, 399 sq. ft.	$1,135
1-Bedroom, 459–610 sq. ft.	$1,235–1,590
1-Bedroom/den, 680 sq. ft.	$1,450–1,675
2-Bedroom, 890–1,039 sq. ft.	$1,720–2,295
2-Bedroom/den, 1,079 sq. ft.	$2,300–2,450

**For double occupancy add $395 to the monthly fee. All utilities included except telephone. Fully equipped kitchens, individually controlled heating and air-conditioning, wall-to-wall carpeting, window treatments, 24-hour emergency call system, cable TV hookup. Washer/dryer hookups in most residences.*

"Although Stratford Court respects the individual's need for privacy, residents will enjoy all the qualitative benefits of living in and contributing to a caring community, fostering life of the mind with a sense of purpose. Excellent service is more than just a business philosophy, it's been a Marriott family tradition for over 60 years. And all that we've learned as a leader in the service and hospitality industry is applied to satisfy the needs of older adults living in our retirement communities."

ST. MARK VILLAGE

2655 Nebraska Avenue
Palm Harbor, FL 34684
(813) 785-2576
Doug Fresh, vice president, marketing service director

Type of community: Nonprofit Continuing Care, modified contract

Accreditation: Continuing Care Accreditation Commission

Ideally located on 11 acres in a thriving suburban neighborhood on the west coast of Florida, St. Mark Village is a complex of Independent Living apartments with courtyards and gardens. It is close to supermarkets, drugstores, and banks. Five levels of care are offered including Assisted Living and Skilled Nursing as well as an Alzheimer's center with Assisted Living and Skilled Nursing services.

Financial plan: Entrance fee plus monthly fee. Deposit of 10% of entrance fee due upon application. Refund policy provides a "trial period" of four years. If resident leaves during that time, the entrance fee will be refunded less a 4% processing fee and less 2% per month or fraction of month the resident lived at the Village. To be placed on a waiting list, a deposit of $1,000 is required for a studio or one-bedroom, and $1,500 is required for a two-bedroom.

Ownership and management: Sponsored by St. Mark Lutheran Church, Dunedin, Florida. Managed by St. Mark Village, Inc. Board of directors made up of local Christian business and professional persons who meet regularly to review the operation and determine policy. Opened in 1980.

Minimum age: 62 years.

Population: 550 residents; 65% women, 35% men, 30% couples.

Number of units: 324 Independent Living apartments; 100 Assisted Living apartments, 60 Skilled Nursing beds, 51 Alzheimer's beds (31 Assisted Living; 20 Skilled Nursing).

Dining plan: One meal per day included in the monthly fee. Private dining room.

INDEPENDENT LIVING HOUSING

Type of apartment	*Entrance fee**	*Monthly fee*
Studio	$32,500	$680
1-Bedroom	$48,500–51,500	$875*
2-Bedroom	$67,500–67,500	$1,155*
Deluxe 2-bedroom	$73,500–77,500	$1,310*

**For double occupancy add $3,000 to the entrance fee; $260 to the monthly fee. All utilities included. Fully equipped, all-electric kitchen, individually controlled heating and air-conditioning, wall-to-wall carpeting, draperies, screened balconies, 24-hour emergency call system.*

Services: *Included in the monthly fee:* Weekly maid service, laundry facilities, assigned parking, scheduled transportation.

At additional cost: Beauty/barbershop, ice cream parlor, guest accommodations.

Activities: Outdoor swimming pool, whirlpool spa, exercise programs, shuffleboard courts, crafts/hobby room, woodworking shop, men's den with billiards tables, group trips.

Availability: Units available. Priority waiting list.

Health services and rates: Residents receive 15% discount in Assisted Living and 30 free days per year in nursing center, 10% discount thereafter. Physical and rehabilitative therapy available.

- 100 Assisted Living apartments (34 apartments on campus, 66 apartments one mile from campus)
  Studio $1,500/month
  1-Bedroom $1,910–2,135/month
- 60-Bed Skilled Nursing center
  Semiprivate $84/day
  Private $100/day
- 51-Bed Alzheimer's unit provides the special care needed by those who suffer from various stages of Alzheimer's disease and related disorders. Available for admission to residents and members of the local community. 31 beds have Assisted Living services; 20 have Skilled Nursing services.
  Alzheimer's Unit

	Monthly fee	*Daily fee*
Semiprivate	$1,850	$90
Private	$2,200	$105

"St. Mark Village is dedicated to providing superior housing, health care, and related service to the elderly. Its mission is to provide the highest quality of life possible to its residents by maintaining a living environment that meets the needs of the body, mind, and spirit. This is accomplished through excellence in leadership, management, innovation, and research."

AZALEA TRACE

10100 Hillview Road
Pensacola, FL 32514
(904) 478-5200
Betty A. Herring, director of marketing

Type of community: Not-for-profit Continuing Care, all-inclusive contract

Located on more than 55 landscaped acres on one of the highest points of land in the area, Azalea Trace offers Independent Living apartments in six-story and three-story buildings, in addition to single-story garden apartments. Health care center is separate from apartments. Campus has nature trails, a small pond, and is filled with azaleas and towering pines. Picnic and cookout area for residents' use. The community is

INDEPENDENT LIVING HOUSING

Type/size of unit	*Entrance fee 1/2**	*Monthly fee**
Studio, 412–560 sq. ft.	$41,700–51,400/62,500–78,500	$843–920
1-Bedroom, 612–1,024 sq. ft.	$65,500–106,700/104,800–170,700	$946–998
2-Bedroom, 925–1,372 sq. ft.	$98,000–149,100/156,800–238,600	$1,014–1,160

**For double occupancy add $7,500 to the entrance fee for traditional plan; $10,000 to the entrance fee for return-of-capital plan; and approximately $500 to the monthly fee. Studios and 1-bedrooms available for monthly rental ($1,520–1,810). Wall-to-wall carpeting, electric kitchen, private terrace or balcony, 24-hour emergency call system, cable TV (optional), individually controlled heating and air-conditioning.*

adjacent to the campus of the University of West Florida. Pensacola Gulf Coast, Escambia Bay, medical facilities, shopping malls, Pensacola Junior College, and the Pensacola Naval Air Station are all nearby. The community is located one hour from Mobile, Alabama, four hours from New Orleans and six hours from metropolitan Atlanta.

Financial plan: Entrance fee plus monthly fee or monthly rental (for one-bedroom and master studio units only). Two plans for entrance fee: **1)** Traditional plan: refund less 2% per month of residency. **2)** Return-of-capital plan: up to 90% refund of entrance fee.

Ownership and management: A subsidiary of Baptist Health Care, Inc., a not-for-profit health care system that operates four acute care hospitals, Skilled Nursing facilities, home health, mobile diagnostic, and other health care services throughout Northwest Florida and South Alabama. Opened in 1981.

Minimum age: 62 years.

Population: 360 to 370 residents; 68% women, 32% men, 44% couples.

Number of units: 284 Independent Living apartments; 106-bed health center.

Dining plan: One meal per day in formal dining room included in the monthly fee. Private dining room available. Dietary department. Special diets and tray service available.

Services: *Included in the monthly fee:* Scheduled transportation, weekly housekeeping and flat-linen services, washers and dryers for personal use, parking.

At additional cost: Beauty/barbershop, group tours, laundry and dry cleaning pick-up and delivery service, valet service, individualized taxi service.

Activities: Full-time activities director. Indoor swimming pool and hot tub, library, arts and crafts studio, card games, bingo, community lounges, greenhouse, private gardens, exercise room, auditorium, woodworking shop, game room, sewing room, greenhouse, chapel, nature walks, lectures, facilities for crafts and hobby activities.

Health services and rates: Recuperative care and unlimited long-term care on-site included in monthly fee. Only extra charge is for two additional meals per day.

- Assistance-in-living available in resident's apartment
  First five days at no extra cost. After five days, the rate is $1.75 per 15 minutes of assistance.
- 106-Bed health care center

"Only minutes away from the beach, Azalea Trace is a spacious community with active residents. People come from all parts of the country and all walks of life to enjoy Azalea Trace's beautiful campus and surroundings."

COVENANT VILLAGE OF FLORIDA

9201 West Broward Boulevard
Plantation, FL 33324
(305) 472-2860
Glen Schultz, director of marketing

Type of community: Not-for-profit Continuing Care, modified contract

Accreditation: Continuing Care Accreditation Commission

Surrounded on two sides by a 77-acre park in Plantation, Covenant Village features lake and garden views. One-, two-, three-, and five-story Mediterranean-style (white stucco with red-tiled roofs) apartments house Independent Living. Assisted Living and Skilled Nursing are connected to apartments by covered walkways. Native palms and flowers line walkways and lawns on the 20-acre campus. Golf courses and parks are nearby as are shopping facilities and churches. The community is 12 miles from the sand beaches of the Atlantic Ocean. Proximity to Fort Lauderdale affords

INDEPENDENT LIVING HOUSING

Type/size of apartment	*Entrance fee**	*Monthly fee**
Studio, 488–532 sq. ft.	$41,500	$755
1-Bedroom, 689–766 sq. ft.	$55,000	$920
2-Bedroom, 1,009–1,076 sq. ft.	$75,500	$1,035

**For double occupancy add $5,500 to the entrance fee and $315 to the monthly fee. All utilities except telephone included. Complete electric kitchen, wall-to-wall carpeting, draperies, individually controlled heating and air-conditioning, kitchen pantry, 24-hour emergency call system, screened balcony/patio.*

exposure to wide variety of cultural, educational, and recreational facilities.

Financial plan: Entrance fee plus monthly fee. Entrance fee has a prorated refund if resident withdraws within 50 months. $1,350 deposit required with application of which $1,000 is refundable.

Ownership and management: Owned/managed by the Evangelical Covenant Church/Covenant Retirement Communities, owner/manager of 12 retirement communities in California, Connecticut, Florida, Illinois, Minnesota, and Washington. Covenant Retirement Communities was founded in 1886. Opened in 1977.

Minimum age: 62 years. *Note:* Covenant Village asks that residents have respect for the Christian faith.

Population: 440 residents; 74% women, 26% men, 28% couples.

Number of units: 300 Independent Living apartments; 43 Assisted Living units, 60-bed Skilled Nursing facility.

Dining plan: One meal each day (dinner Monday–Saturday, lunch on Sundays and holidays) is included in the monthly fee. Breakfast and lunch are available at a modest charge. If resident is away for more than seven consecutive days, there is a reduction in the monthly fee, which reflects the meal savings.

Services: *Included in the monthly fee:* Housekeeping, flat-linen service, scheduled transportation, parking, laundry facilities.

At additional cost: Guest accommodations, beauty/barbershop, gift shop.

Activities: Heated swimming pool, whirlpool, shuffleboard courts, woodworking, crafts, ceramics, library, gardening areas for flowers, billiards and Ping-Pong, exercise classes, hike and bike paths, adjacent 77-acre city park, cultural events in nearby Miami and Fort Lauderdale, shopping excursions, chapel.

Availability: Waiting list.

Health services and rates: Residents' care agreement provides 60 days of Skilled Nursing care in the health care center at no increase in the resident's monthly fee except for additional meals and for services/supplies not normally provided in the residency agreement.

- 43-Room Assisted Living center
  Private $69/day
- 60-Bed Skilled Nursing facility
  Semiprivate $113/day
  Private $162/day

"The mission of Covenant Retirement Communities is to provide a balance, through facilities and programs, between security and independence for the resident, assisting in the achievement of the resident's maximum physical, mental, emotional, and spiritual capabilities and enjoyment. Prospective residents are invited to come to Plantation and spend two or three days at the Village at no cost."

JOHN KNOX VILLAGE OF POMPANO BEACH

651 S.W. 6th Street
Pompano Beach, FL 33060
(305) 782-1300
Bob Milanovich, director of marketing

Type of community: Nonprofit Continuing Care, all-inclusive contract

Accreditation: Continuing Care Accreditation Commission

Located on a 55-acre tropical paradise with two lakes and a recognized rare bird habitat, the Village's Independent Living apartments are located in 16-story and ten-story high-rise buildings, a three-story mid-rise building, and villas. Assisted Living apartments and the health center are housed separately. The Village is conveniently located within 35 miles of three international airports and two seaports and is serviced by the city transit system. It is located 1/2 mile from Cypress Shopping Center, eight miles from malls, and three miles from beaches.

Financial plan: Entrance fee plus monthly fee. If a resident should leave within the first four years of occupancy, there is a partial refund of the entrance fee. Should the resident pass away during the first year, 50% of the entrance fee will be refunded.

Ownership and management: John Knox Village of Florida, Inc. Opened in 1967.

Minimum age: 65 years.

Population: 940 residents; 68% women, 32% men, 25% couples. (The greatest percentage of residents come from the Chicago area.)

Number of units: 640 Independent Living apartments; 60 Assisted Care apartments, 177-bed Skilled Nursing facility.

INDEPENDENT LIVING HOUSING

Village Towers	*Entrance fee*	*Monthly fee**
Studio, 562 sq. ft.	$47,900	$802.75
1-Bedroom, 790 sq. ft.	$59.500–66,900	$877.25
2-Bedroom, 1,147 sq. ft.	$96,900	$921.75
Cassels Tower/Eastlake		
Efficiency, 375–390 sq. ft.	$35,900	$712.75
Studio, 535 sq. ft.	$45,900	$802.75
1-Bedroom, 750–780 sq. ft.	$65,900–66,900	$877.75
1-Bedroom, 950 sq. ft.	$77,900	$890.75
2-Bedroom, 1,113–1,170 sq. ft.	$96,900	$921.75
Garden Villa apartments		
1-Bedroom, 700 sq. ft.	$59,900	$877.75
1-Bedroom, 860 sq. ft.	$70,900	$890.75
2-Bedroom, 1,008–1,400 sq. ft.	$79,900–111,900	$921.75–972.75

**For double occupancy add approximately $400 to the monthly fee. All utilities except telephone included. Complete kitchens, washer/dryer, individually controlled heating and air-conditioning, 24-hour emergency call system, wall-to-wall carpeting. Most apartments have patios or balconies.*

Dining plan: 15 meals per month are included in the monthly fee. Residents may choose a more comprehensive meal program for additional charge. Private dining room and catering services available.

Services: *Included in the monthly fee:* Biweekly housekeeping, weekly flat-linen service, medical claims filing, 24-hour transportation within the Village, scheduled transportation to town, homemaker service for daily chores and personal care, parking.

At additional cost: Ice-cream shop, gift shop, beauty/barbershop, purified water machines.

Activities: Heated swimming pool, whirlpool, shuffleboard courts and horseshoe area, billiards tables, bingo, chapel, planned social activities, five libraries.

Availability: Waiting list depends on type of apartment. Priority wait list.

Health services and rates: Professional nursing care provided 24 hours a day. If residents move into Assisted Living or health center, they continue to pay their monthly fee, plus $453 per month for the additional meals. Physicians' fees (internist, opthalmologist, dentist offices on-site), therapy services, medical supplies for special nursing care, diet supplements, walkers, etc., are additional.

- 60 Assisted Living units
- 177-Bed Skilled Nursing facility (semiprivate and private rooms)

"John Knox Village has a great feeling of community spirit and our residents are known for their friendliness. We offer relaxed, south Florida living in beautiful, botanical surroundings. Our life care provides a planned, secure future, unencumbered by the worries so many of today's older citizens face."

BAY VILLAGE

8400 Vamo Road
Sarasota, FL 34231
(813) 966-5611
Ted A. Benjamin, director of marketing

Type of community: Not-for-profit Continuing Care, modified contract

Accreditation: Continuing Care Accreditation Commission

Built on 15 acres of quiet countryside in the midst of magnificent pines, Bay Village offers breathtaking views of surrounding country, Sarasota Bay, and the Gulf of Mexico. Gardens and other landscaping have been planned for a natural appearance. A 12-story modern apartment building with three connected wings houses Independent Living residences. Nursing facilities are on-site; two large hospitals are approximately seven miles from Bay Village.

Financial plan: Entrance fee plus monthly fee. The entrance fee is refundable on a prorated basis. $1,500 deposit with application, of which $1,400 is refundable.

Ownership and management: Founded by Pine Shores Presbyterian Church. Opened in 1975.

INDEPENDENT LIVING HOUSING

Type/size of apartment	*Entrance fee single/double*	*Monthly fee single/double*
Studio, 459 sq. ft.	$46,500/56,700	$359/398
1-Bedroom, 689 sq. ft.	$76,400/102,600	$565/633
2-Bedroom, 1,148 sq. ft.	$124,100/153,500	$857–878/919–941

All utilities except telephone included in the monthly fee. Wall-to-wall carpeting, full kitchen, draperies of resident's choice, 24-hour emergency call system.

Minimum age: 65 years; must submit Pastor's report as a character reference or meet with minister of Pine Shores Church. It is not necessary to be Presbyterian.

Population: 430 residents; 75% women, 25% men, 20% couples.

Number of units: 324 Independent Living apartments; 107-bed health care center.

Dining plan: No meals included in the monthly fee. Three meals per day offered. Basic plan, one meal per day: $245 per person per month.

Services: *Included in the monthly fee:* Parking, scheduled transportation.

At additional cost: Beauty/barbershop, guest accommodations, deli, gift shop, housekeeping services.

Activities: Lectures, films, choral get-togethers, vespers, billiards and cards, hobbies and crafts, library, large heated swimming pool, therapy pool, shuffleboard courts.

Availability: Waiting list of one year or longer, depending upon accommodation desired.

Health services and rates: There is no extra charge for short-term convalescent care except for meals, special services, and medications. Cost of personal laundry, medicines, and therapy treatments ordered by physician additional. Health center rooms accommodate two, three, or four patients. Visiting dentist and podiatrist.

- 107-Bed nursing facility $1,185/month

"At Bay Village, all accommodations as well as health care facilities and activities are under one roof, making it a very convenient and efficient place to live. We guarantee 24-hour immediate health care assistance to all our residents. We also have one of the largest libraries of any retirement communities, holding over 6,000 volumes. Last year Bay Village received one of the highest ratings among retirement communities in America."

PLYMOUTH HARBOR, INC.

700 John Ringling Boulevard
Sarasota, FL 34236-1589
(813) 361-7514
John W. Ames, associate executive director

Type of community: Not-for-profit Continuing Care, modified contract

Plymouth Harbor is centrally located on 15 waterside acres of spectacular Coon Key between the mainland of Sarasota and St. Armand's Key. Plymouth Harbor consists of a 25-floor tower in addition to East, West, and North Garden apartments, which house Independent Living apartments, Assisted Living, and Skilled Nursing. Beautiful walking paths follow the water's edge.

Financial plan: Entrance fee plus monthly fee. Application fee $500–1,500, depending upon size of apartment.

Ownership and management: Plymouth Harbor, Inc. Affiliated with the United Church of Christ. Volunteer board of 14 trustees composed of local business persons and professionals. Opened in 1966.

Minimum age: 65 years.

Population: 340 residents; 73% women, 27% men, 44% couples.

Number of units: 246 Independent Living apartments; 10 Assisted Living apartments, 60-bed health care center.

Dining plan: Evening meal included in the monthly fee for studio and efficiency residents only. Residents of one- and two-bedrooms must purchase 15 dinner tickets each month for $146.25. Private dining room and catering services available for private parties.

INDEPENDENT LIVING HOUSING

Tower apartments	*Entrance fee*	*Monthly fee**
Studio, 450 sq. ft.	$37,500	$907.50
Efficiency, 491 sq. ft.	$47,500	$1,007.50
1-Bedroom, 651–980 sq. ft.	$85,000–115,000	$950–1,350
2-Bedroom, 1,082–2,225 sq. ft.	$130,000–275,000	$1,650–2,750
East and West Garden apartments		
Studio, 593 sq. ft.	$42,000	$1,007.50
Efficiency, 600 sq. ft.	$52,500	$1,057.50
1-Bedroom, 819–1,148 sq. ft.	$95,000–135,000	$1,025–1,550
2-Bedroom, 1,399–1,700 sq. ft.	$170,000–180,000	$1,750–2,125
North Garden apartments		
1-Bedroom, 877–928 sq. ft.	$110,000–115,000	$1,300
2-Bedroom, 1,281–1,489 sq. ft.	$160,000–170,000	$1,750–1,825

**For double occupancy add $100 to the monthly fee. All utilities and cable TV included. Kitchen appliances, carpeting, basic draperies, choice of paint colors, 24-hour emergency call system. All garden apartments have glassed-in balconies.*

Services: *Included in the monthly fee:* Weekly housekeeping and flat-linen service, open parking areas, scheduled transportation.

At additional cost: Beauty/barbershop, gift shop, newspaper delivery to door, laundry facilities, carport, garage parking, guest accommodations.

Activities: Library, two swimming pools and spa, hobby room, exercise room, gardening, crafts, woodworking, billiards, shuffleboard courts, movies, bridge, lectures, singing and dancing groups, travelogues.

Availability: Extensive waiting list. More than two-year wait for one-bedroom and five-year wait for two-bedroom.

Health services and rates: Residents receive 30 free days of nursing care in the health center (two extra meals a day are the only charges).

- 10 Assisted Living apartments
- 60-Bed health care center

Semiprivate	$104.70/day plus two extra meals
Private (24 rooms)	$139.70/day plus two extra meals

"We have a unique location and great credibility in the community. Every three floors is a 'colony,' and each one has a director and associate director as part of our active residents' association. Plymouth Harbor has a 26-year history of excellence with a strong financial position and is debt-free."

LAKE SEMINOLE SQUARE

8333 Seminole Boulevard
Seminole, FL 34642
(813) 391-0500, ext. 237
Dee Reynolds, marketing department

Type of community: Continuing Care, modified contract

This six-story condominium complex is located on 17 acres on Lake Seminole. Landscaped grounds with gardens feature more than 200 varieties of roses.

Fishing and boating on lake, bird estuary, picnic area, and indoor and outdoor walking track are offered. Constructed in five wings with all residences, health care, and activities under one roof, Lake Seminole Square is close to beaches, shopping, and community center.

Financial plan: Purchase fee plus monthly fee. Minimum of 50% refund of purchase fee after two years.

Ownership and management: Owned by Freedom Group located in Bradenton, Florida, owner of five retirement communities in Florida, Michigan, and Arizona. Opened in March 1990.

Minimum age: 62 years.

Population: 382 residents; 71% women, 29% men, 47% couples.

Number of units: 306 Independent Living apartments; 34 Assisted Living units, Skilled Nursing available across the street at Freedom Square, sister community.

Dining plan: Three plans: **1)** Prices listed include 365 meals per year. **2)** Reduction of monthly fee, payment of $4 per meal eaten. **3)** One meal per day with daily credit if off campus for more than seven consecutive days. Two private dining rooms, five large dining rooms.

Services: *Included in the monthly fee:* Weekly housekeeping and flat-linen services, scheduled transportation.

At additional cost: Beauty/barbershop, bank, valet, guest accommodations.

Activities: Full activities program. Planned out-of-town trips, climate-controlled indoor walking track and exercise room, library, indoor heated pool and spa, activities at local performing arts centers, shuffleboard, putting green, horseshoes.

Availability: Waiting list. For one-bedroom, two to six months; for two-bedroom, one to two years.

Health services and rates: Staff of companions will provide additional services (shopping, laundry, care, companionship) to Independent Living residents as requested on hourly rate. Residents retain use of their apartments and pay a daily rate during the first 360 days in Assisted Living or Skilled Nursing; there after, residents' apartments are turned over and they receive a 15% discount on daily rates. Speech, physical, occupational, audiology, and restorative therapies.

- 34 Assisted Living beds $1,925–2,800/month
- 240 Skilled Nursing beds: 120 beds at Seminole and 120 beds at Freedom Square (sister community, across street)
  Semiprivate $110/day
  Private $145/day
- 46-Bed Alzheimer's/limited-memory unit
  Semiprivate $120/day
  Private $145/day

INDEPENDENT LIVING HOUSING

Type/size of apartment	*Purchase fee**	*Monthly fee**
1-Bedroom, 776 sq. ft.	$69,500	$1,155
1-Bedroom/porch, 880/908 sq. ft.	$79,000/83,000	$1,250
Deluxe 1-bedroom, 1,075 sq. ft.	$100,000	$1,400
1-Bedroom/den, 1,336/1464 sq. ft.	$130,000/140,000	$1,500/1,650
2-Bedroom/den, 1,528 sq. ft.	$135,000–200,000	$1,750

**For double occupancy add $5,000 to the purchase fee and $550 to the monthly fee. All utilities except telephone included. Fully equipped kitchen, draperies, 24-hour emergency call system, wall-to-wall carpeting, wallpapered rooms, individually controlled heating and air-conditioning.*

"Lake Seminole Square is a successful debt-free community where residents come first. We have a number of quality assurance programs such as monthly surveys, suggestion box, and department service guarantees. These programs ensure residents get the best possible service. We will get it right, or residents won't pay for it. Seminole is competitive with Pinellas County nursing centers for prices and fees for services."

WESTMINSTER OAKS

4449 Meandering Way
Tallahassee, FL 32308
(904) 878-1136
Gayle Pease, marketing representative

Type of community: Not-for-profit Continuing Care, modified contract

Accreditation: Continuing Care Accreditation Commission

Located on a spacious 96-acre tract in Tallahassee, surrounded by oak trees and azalea gardens, Westminster Oaks is a five-story brick Independent Living apartment complex that also offers duplexes, Assisted Living, and Skilled Nursing facilities. Nearby universities, Florida A&M and Florida State University, offer sports and cultural programs.

Financial plan: Entrance fee plus monthly fee or monthly rental. Two entrance fee plans: **1)** Traditional (refund is prorated should resident leave within four years). **2)** Guaranteed refund (choice of 50% or 90% of entrance fee is refunded). Resident must be 82 years or younger to choose the guaranteed refund. Fully refundable $1,000 per person deposit is required to establish priority for apartment.

Ownership and management: Presbyterian Retirement Communities, Inc., owner and manager of four other communities in Florida: Westminster Asbury, Bradenton; Westminster Towers, Orlando; Winter Park Towers, Winter Park. Opened in 1982.

INDEPENDENT LIVING HOUSING

Oaks South apartments	*Entrance fee 1*	*Entrance fee 2—50%**	*Monthly fee*
Studio, 425 sq. ft.	$36,000–39,000	$50,400–54,600	$704
1-Bedroom, 630 sq. ft.	$56,000–61,300	$78,400–85,820	$947–1,288
2-Bedroom, 1,065 sq. ft.	$82,000	$114,800	$1,531
Chason Garden			
1-Bedroom, 728 sq. ft.	$57,000–62,300	$79,800–87,220	$987–1,173
2-Bedroom, 1,144 sq. ft.	$87,220	$116,200	$1,572
The Village			
2-Bedroom, 1,560 sq. ft.	$98,500+	$167,450+	$460
3-Bedroom, 1,774 sq. ft.	$98,500+	$167,450+	$460

**90% refund entrance fees are higher than 50% plan. Monthly rentals range from $1,064 to $2,402. For double occupancy in studios or 1-bedrooms add $10,000 to the traditional entrance fee and $14,000 to the 50% guaranteed refund entrance fee. No charge for second person in 2-bedroom or The Village. For double occupancy add $265 to the monthly fee for studio and 1-bedroom; $120 to the monthly fee for 2-bedroom.*

All utilities except telephone included. Fully equipped electric kitchen, individually controlled heating and air-conditioning, 24-hour emergency call system. Village residents have electronic garage door openers and must pay fair portion of real estate taxes.

Minimum age: 62 years.

Population: 330 residents; 75% women, 25% men, 35% couples.

Number of units: 165 Independent Living apartments and 32 duplexes; 60 Assisted Living apartments, 60 Skilled Nursing beds.

Dining plan: One meal per day included in the monthly fee. Additional meals available at cost. Two private dining rooms.

Services: *Included in the monthly fee:* Biweekly housekeeping, parking, scheduled transportation.

At additional cost: Beauty/barbershop, country store, thrift shop.

Activities: Library, spa, arts and crafts, shuffleboard, sewing/needlework/weaving room, painting studio, pottery room, woodworking shop.

Availability: Priority waiting list.

Health services and rates: Entrance fee residents with three-meal/day contract receive 15 days free for a period not exceeding 90 days. Residents who have one- or two-meal/day contract pay cost of additional meals for first 15 days. Rental residents receive five days of free convalescent care per year in health center. Application may be made directly to Assisted Living (two plans: entrance fee plus daily fee or daily fee only). Patients with Alzheimer's and related memory problems are accepted.

- 60 Assisted Living apartments

	Entrance fee	*Daily fee*
Single, 221 sq. ft.	$32,000	$51–67.50
Suite, 442 sq. ft.	$48,000	$69.50–86

For double occupancy add $10,000 to the entrance fee. Daily fee only available for single: $63/day.

- 60-Bed Skilled Nursing facility

16–90 days*	$58.50/day
Resident permanent care, semiprivate, after 90 days	$73.50/day

**During the first 90 days a continuous review of status will be made to determine whether permanent health care is necessary. If it is determined that the resident requires permanent health care, the 90-day convalescent care charges do not apply.*

"The board and administration of Presbyterian Retirement Communities are committed to respecting the dignity, rights, self-respect, and independence of the senior individual."

THE CANTERBURY TOWER

3501 Bayshore Boulevard
Tampa, FL 33629
(813) 837-1083
Leslie Coughlin-Lea, marketing coordinator

Type of community: Nonprofit Continuing Care, modified contract

Located in the beautiful Bayshore historic district with old Southern homes, oaks, and palm trees, this 14-story apartment building is situated on the west coast of Florida overlooking Hillsborough Bay. A courtyard on lobby level contains a butterfly garden and a Canterbury rose garden. All residences have bay views. Tampa is home to a major league football team, a soc-cer team, theater, symphony, ballet, universities, art museums, and medical schools. Florida's west coast beaches are nearby.

Financial plan: Entrance fee plus monthly fee.

Ownership and management: Owned by Canterbury Tower, Inc. Managed by board of directors of Canterbury Tower. Opened in 1977.

Minimum age: 62 years.

Population: 150 residents; 66% women, 34% men, 20% couples.

Number of units: 125 Independent Living apartments; 40-bed Skilled Nursing facility.

INDEPENDENT LIVING HOUSING

Type/size of unit	*Entrance fee*	*Monthly fee**
Studio, 505 sq. ft.	$39,270	$749
1-Bedroom, 808 sq. ft.	$63,410	$996
2-Bedroom, 1,071–1,402 sq. ft.	$85,470–95,461	$1,241

**For double occupancy add $599 to the monthly fee. All utilities included except long-distance telephone. Fully equipped kitchens, 24-hour emergency call system, balcony, wall-to-wall carpeting, cable TV access, individually controlled heating and air-conditioning.*

Dining plan: One meal per day included in the monthly fee. Private dining room available. Special diets and tray service.

Services: *Included in the monthly fee:* Housekeeping, flat-linen service, transportation to medical appointments, scheduled transportation.

At additional cost: Beauty/barbershop, guest accommodations.

Activities: Social director. Heated swimming pool, exercise room, library, game room, arts and crafts room, meeting rooms, fitness center, billiards room, card room, chapel services, Wedgewood Room available for private dining and parties.

Availability: Waiting list for larger apartments. Fully refundable 10% deposit secures place on waiting list.

Health services and rates: Assisted Living services are offered in resident's apartment at no additional charge. Health center offers long- and short-term care. Activities program, social service program, rehabilitation care, patient care programming conferences, and large sundeck for resident's use. Physical and occupational therapy available.

- 40-Bed Skilled Nursing facility
  Semiprivate $105/day
  Private $125/day

"Canterbury Tower is the only retirement living community where Assisted Living is provided in the resident's apartment at no extra cost. We seek to provide, on a nonprofit basis, well-designed surroundings at the lowest possible cost so that residents may continue living in comfort, peace, and contentment."

Luana and Bob, 71 and 74 years

The Tamalpais, Greenbrae, California

"You have to move in before you think you are ready."

Luana and Bob put their names on a waiting list at a life care community near their alma mater nine and one-half years ago, long before Bob thought he was ready. "It reminded me of our college campus and brought me back to my college days," says Luana.

When they realized they were ready, Luana says it was like an epiphany, like choosing the person you're going to marry. "You make the decision and roll with it. You can't wait to move into a retirement community until you're ready," she cautions. "If you wait too long you aren't able to make the decisions that are necessary." Luana prepared for the move over time by slowly giving things away. First the top shelves were emptied; then the bottom. And she made it a practice to discourage gifts, other than edible ones.

"I sort of believe in cooperating with the inevitable," explains Bob, a retired consulting engineer. "The time had come. I was a little tired of maintenance at the house and was even ready to give up gardening. Incidentally, The Tamalpais gave us some very helpful financial recommendations, including setting up a Unitrust which, in all our research, we didn't know anything about and which will help to protect our estate."

"There are trade-offs," says Luana. "I thought I would miss stepping out onto my patio, but we've discovered that the camaraderie in the high-rise is exhilarating. This place sparkles, and we love exploring our new surroundings. We like living here more than we ever imagined we would."

Luana and Bob's advice: Don't wait too long to move.

VILLAGE ON THE ISLE

950 Tamiami Trail South
Venice, FL 34285
(813) 484-9753
John Spittal, executive director

Type of community: Nonprofit Continuing Care, modified contract

The community consists of four residential complexes (Matthew and Trinity Halls for Independent Living, Mark Manor for Assisted Living and personal care, and Luke Haven for Skilled Nursing). Multilevel buildings up to six stories are located on a 15-acre campus on the island of Venice. The community is convenient to shopping, dining, and cultural areas and one mile from the Gulf of Mexico.

Financial plan: Entrance fee plus monthly fee. Three plans: **1)** Refund less initial 4% plus 2% per month of residency. **2)** 50% refund. **3)** 90% refund. Monthly rental program available for Assisted Living and personal care units.

Ownership and management: Owned by bond holders. Managed by local board of trustees. Opened in 1982.

Minimum age: 62 years.

Population: 367 residents; 59% women, 41% men, 44% couples.

Number of units: 234 Independent Living apartments; 103 Assisted Living units, 60-bed health center.

Dining plan: One meal per day included in the monthly fee. The Garden Room is available for private parties.

INDEPENDENT LIVING HOUSING

Type/size of unit	*Entrance fee 1/2**	*Monthly fee**
Studio, 414 sq. ft.	$39,500/52,500	$816
1-Bedroom, 552–852 sq. ft.	$49,500–71,500/66,000–86,500	$983–1,305
2-Bedroom, 828–1,148 sq. ft.	$66,000–79,200/89,000–105,000	$1,283–1,500

**Plan 3 (90% refund) also available for higher entrance fee. For double occupancy add $243 to the monthly fee. All utilities except telephone included. Balconies or patios, 24-hour emergency call system, fully equipped kitchens, wall-to-wall carpeting, individually controlled heating and air-conditioning, cable TV (optional).*

Services: *Included in the monthly fee:* Biweekly housekeeping, transportation within the Venice area, open parking.

At additional cost: Flat-linen service, beauty/barbershop, covered parking, guest accommodations, country store.

Activities: Full-time activities director. Nondenominational chapel, swimming pool, spa with therapy jets, library, exercise room, shuffleboard courts, whirlpool, game room, billiards room, arts and crafts center, gardening area, musical programs, classes on various topics, exercise classes, cultural events, dress-up days, woodworking shop.

Availability: Current availability.

Health services and rates: Physical and occupational therapy available. Personal care offers more services than Assisted Living.

- 103 Assisted Living units

	Entrance fee 2	*Monthly fee**
Apartments	$31,000–59,000	$1,199–1,787

**For double occupancy add between $450 and $650 to the monthly fee. Monthly rental available for $1,516–2,204.*

	Entrance fee 2	*Monthly fee**
• Personal care	$31,000–59,000	$1,552–2,254

**For double occupancy add between $580 and $890 to the monthly fee and rent. Monthly rental available for $2,001.*

- 59-Bed health center

Semiprivate	$89/day
Private	$116/day

"Village on the Isle's family of residents enjoys an active, independent lifestyle in a beautiful, friendly environment. Housekeeping and delicious meals are included as is transportation; health care services are available on our 15-acre campus, located one mile from the Gulf of Mexico Beach."

INDIAN RIVER ESTATES–EAST/WEST

2250 Indian Creek Boulevard West/7730 Indian Oaks Drive
Vero Beach, FL 32966
(407) 569-3200
Phillip Martinello, marketing representative

Type of community: Nonprofit Continuing Care, all-inclusive contract

East and West Estates, along with a 60-bed health center and 48-bed Assisted Living unit, are located on a 100-acre campus in the middle of an orange grove and separated by a small lake. The West campus is made up of four three-story apartment buildings and a central facility. The East campus has five three-story apartment buildings and a central facility surrounded by a lake. Twenty villas are also part of the East campus. Covered walkways connect all buildings. Grass courtyards and tree-lined walks are located throughout the campus. The Center for the Arts and Riverside Theater are close by; the beach is ten miles away, and the Orlando area is 1¼ hours away. The average temperature in Vero Beach is 82 degrees. Indian River citrus is world renowned. Vero Beach serves as the winter home for the Los Angeles Dodgers.

Financial plan: Entrance fee plus monthly fee.

Ownership and management: Owned and managed by Adult Communities Total Services, Inc.(ACTS), developer of 15 communities throughout Pennsylvania, Florida, and North Carolina with more than 18 years of experience. West Estates opened in 1990; East Estates opened in 1986.

Minimum age: 60 years.

INDEPENDENT LIVING HOUSING

Type/size of apartment	*Entrance fee*	*Monthly fee single/double*
Studio, 787 sq. ft.	$82,000–85,000	$858/N/A
1-Bedroom, 745 sq. ft.	$93,000–96,000	$896/$1,543
2-Bedroom, 1,069 sq. ft.	$118,000–121,000	$1,049/$1,668
3-Bedroom, 1,387–1,495 sq. ft.	$148,000–160,000	$1,174/1,797
Villas		
2-Bedroom, 1,750 sq. ft.	$168,000	$1,703 (2 people)
3-Bedroom, 1,952 sq. ft.	$178,000	$1,805 (2 people)

For Indian Village East, Entrance fees are $2,000 lower; monthly fees remain the same. All utilities except telephone included. Emergency call system, fully equipped kitchens, individually controlled heating and air-conditioning, wall-to-wall carpeting, cable TV, pets allowed.

Population: East, 557 residents; West, 162 residents; 60% women, 40% men, 60% couples.

Number of units: Independent Living: East, 354; West, 234; 48 Assisted Living, 60-bed health center.

Dining plan: Two meals per day included in the monthly fee. Private dining room and catering.

Services: *Included in the monthly fee:* Open parking, laundry room, flat-linen service, transportation, housekeeping.

At additional cost: Covered parking, beauty/barbershop.

Activities: Full-time activity director. Swimming pool, tennis court, films, concerts, lectures, parties, day trips, tours, arts and crafts, billiards, exercise classes, woodworking shop, whirlpool, theater-style auditorium, library, fishing, croquet, shuffleboard, biking, gardening.

Availability: Waiting list for villas. Apartments available immediately.

Health services and rates: Unlimited health care and Assisted Living included in resident's monthly fee.

- 48 Assisted Living suites
- 60-Bed health center

"The employees of Indian River Estates strive daily to render unto our residents the highest levels of service and quality possible. Our employees always regard our residents with the utmost respect while endeavoring to accommodate and enhance their dignity and quality of life."

GEORGIA

CANTERBURY COURT

3750 Peachtree Road, NE
Atlanta, GA 30319
(404) 261-6611
Bob Noble, director of marketing

Type of community: Nonprofit Continuing Care, modified contract

Canterbury Court is housed in an elegant mid-rise building lined with balconies located in the heart of Atlanta's beautiful Buckhead, a vibrant residential community. Located on three acres of maintained woodlands and gardens with winding, paved footpaths, a greenhouse and a conservatory, the community is in vicinity of shopping, fine dining, and cultural activities and adjacent to a major bus line. Independent Living, Assisted Living, and Intermediate Nursing are available.

Financial plan: Entrance fee plus monthly fee. Two plans: **1)** Nonrefundable entrance fee. **2)** Entrance fee is refundable less 1% per month and a 4% processing fee for the first 16 months of residency, remaining at 80% thereafter.

Ownership and management: Sponsored by Saint Luke's Episcopal Church and All Saints Episcopal Church. Opened in 1966; expansion of a new wing in 1991.

Minimum age: 62 years (individuals must move in before their 85th birthday).

Population: 132 residents; 79% women, 21% men, 14% couples.

Number of units: 130 Independent Living apartments; 16 Assisted Living units, 31 Intermediate and Skilled Nursing beds.

Dining plan: Three meals per day included in the monthly fee. If the resident desires two meals a day, $90 is deducted from the monthly fee. Apartment room service is available at additional cost. Garden solarium or private dining room is available for private parties.

Services: *Included in the monthly fee:* Weekly maid and flat-linen service, laundry rooms on each floor, shuttle transportation to malls and special events,

INDEPENDENT LIVING HOUSING

Type/size of apartment	*Entrance fee 1/2**	*Monthly fee**
Efficiency, 355–500 sq. ft.	$30,000–42,000/51,000–73,000	$975–1,178
1-Bedroom, 660–725 sq. ft.	$49,500–63,500/84,000–110,000	$1,418–1,659
2-Bedroom, 1,000–2,190 sq. ft.	$72,500–115,500/125,000–195,000	$1,808–2,889

**For double occupancy add $10,000 to the nonrefundable entrance fee ($17,000 to the refundable entrance fee) and $500 to the monthly fee. All utilities except telephone included. Wall-to-wall carpeting, individually controlled heating and air-conditioning, 24-hour emergency call system, sheer draperies. Most apartments have balconies and either kitchenettes or fully equipped kitchens.*

24-hour porter and parcel delivery service to apartments.

At additional cost: Beauty/barbershop, convenience store, private banking service, reserved parking spaces, guest accommodations.

Activities: Woodworking shop, arts and crafts, gardening, library, exercise facility.

Availability: Apartments are available.

Health services and rates: Residents receive 15 free days per year in the health care center after which residents requiring temporary nursing care pay the daily fee listed. Staffed by registered nurse director, licensed nurses, and nursing assistants. Includes nutrition education, dispensing med-ication, checking blood pressure, and arranging transportation to personal physicians if desired. Residents who move in to the health care center or Assisted Living on a permanent basis pay the monthly fees listed below.

- 16 Assisted Living apartments
  - Studio $1,335/month
  - 1-Bedroom $1,830–2,348/month
  - 1-Bedroom alcove $1,570/month
- 31 Intermediate and Skilled Nursing beds
  - Semiprivate $1,447/month
  - Private $1,663/month

Residents may receive short-term nursing care for $23.50 per day.

"For more than 25 years, the people at Canterbury Court have formed a truly close-knit community. Our pleasant, open atmosphere springs from shared interests and a sincere concern for others."

CLAIRMONT PLACE

2100 Clairmont Lake Road
Atlanta, GA 30033
(404) 633-2555
Robert Raines, sales and marketing associate

Type of community: Independent Living and Personal Care

This seven-story building is located on 23 wooded acres with an eight-acre lake and walking paths. Independent Living and personal care are on-site. Located in a quiet neighborhood, Clairmont Place is minutes from shopping, restaurants, universities, and medical facilities.

Financial plan: Purchase price plus monthly fee (a combination of use and service fee and condominium association fee) or monthly rental (owners may rent their condominiums).

Ownership and management: Owned by Mutual of New York. Managed by Grace Management, Inc., operator of eight retirement communities across the United States. Opened in 1990.

INDEPENDENT LIVING HOUSING

Type of condominium	*Purchase price*	*Monthly fee**
Alcove, 470 sq. ft.	$62,500	$498.25
1-Bedroom, 690 sq. ft.	$92,800	$548.89
1-Bedroom/sunroom, 814 sq. ft.	$100,000	$573.29
1-Bedroom/sunroom/deluxe, 875 sq. ft.	$110,000	$586.43
2-Bedroom, 993 sq. ft.	$116,000	$622.07
2-Bedroom/sunroom, 1,116 sq. ft.	$130,000	$645.41

**For double occupancy add $332.99 to the monthly fee. Utilities not included. Wall-to-wall carpeting, individually controlled heating and air-conditioning. All have terraces except 1-bedroom and 2-bedroom/sunroom.*

Minimum age: 55 years.

Population: 217 residents; 78% women, 22% men, 36% couples.

Number of units: 190 Independent Living condominiums; 22 personal care apartments.

Dining plan: 30 meals a month with choice of lunch or dinner included in the monthly fee. Private dining room.

Services: *Included in the monthly fee:* Scheduled transportation, parking, biweekly maid service, weekly flat-linen service, cable TV connections, one-year free maintenance of major appliances.

At additional cost: Beauty/barbershop, seamstress, legal and accounting consultant, conveniently located laundry room.

Activities: Exercise programs, crafts, cards, bingo, Bible study, chapel, walking paths, volunteer opportunities, local excursions, continual educational opportunities, lectures/seminars (in-house and out in the community), plays, concerts, and symphonies.

Availability: Resale and rentals available.

Health services and rates: Podiatrist, masseuse, wellness program, hearing specialist, pharmacist available. Residents may be admitted directly to the personal care facility after a personal assessment.

- Respite care (short-term, temporary care) is offered to residents and those in the surrounding community for $77/day
- 22 Personal care apartments $1,770/month

"Clairmont is a lot of things, but most of all it is peace of mind. Our homeowners are independent-minded seniors who no longer want the burden of large homes and yards. They prefer a lifestyle of unencumbered freedom, comfort, and convenience."

LENBROOK SQUARE

3747 Peachtree Road, NE
Atlanta, GA 30319
(404) 233-3000
Ruth Proctor, marketing director

Type of community: Nonprofit Continuing Care, all-inclusive contract

Accreditation: Continuing Care Accreditation Commission

This 17-story high-rise building located in the Buckhead area on historic Peachtree Road offers Independent Living, Assisted Living, and Intermediate and Skilled Nursing care. The campus includes a gazebo, secured strolling area, and a greenhouse. The surrounding Buckhead area is a combination of affluent residential neighborhoods, upscale shopping malls, and thriving business community. The neighborhood provides limitless shopping opportunities, entertainment, and cultural activities.

Financial plan: Entrance fee plus monthly fee. Entrance fee is fully refundable.

Ownership and management: Not-for-profit corporation, Lenbrook Square Foundation, Inc., managed by a board of directors. Developed by Lenbrook properties. Opened in 1983.

Minimum age: 62 years.

Population: 309 residents; 77% women, 23% men, 13% couples.

Number of units: 270 Independent Living apartments; 60-bed health care center.

Dining plan: No meals included in the monthly fee. Three meals served daily. Residents are required to have at least 25 meals per month, midday or evening (breakfast, $4.20; lunch, $5.25; dinner, $9). Charge for these meals and additional meals are added to monthly fee. Tray service and special diets, when

INDEPENDENT LIVING HOUSING

Type/size of apartment	*Entrance fee**	*Monthly fee**
Studio, 344 sq. ft.	$37,800	$702
1-Bedroom, 676–769 sq. ft.	$88,200–107,750	$1,254–1,327
2-Bedroom, 912–1,260 sq. ft.	$116,500–193,200	$1,462–2,354
3-Bedroom, 1,457–1,588 sq. ft.	$183,750–216,050	$2,352–2,716

**For double occupancy, except for 3-bedroom units, add $5,250 to the entrance fee and $368 to the monthly fee. All utilities except telephone included. Individually controlled heating and air-conditioning, wall-to-wall carpeting, fully equipped kitchen, cable TV hookup, 24-hour emergency call system, private balconies.*

approved by administration for medical reasons. Private dining room and in-house catering for special occasions. Taproom.

Services: *Included in the monthly fee:* Scheduled transportation, weekly flat-linen service and housekeeping, covered parking.

At additional cost: Beauty/barbershop, sundry store, laundry facilities, pharmacy delivery, bank, post office, laundry and dry cleaning pick-up, guest accommodations.

Activities: Arts and crafts, shuffleboard, horseshoes, putting green, cards, billiards, exercise classes and equipment, Jacuzzi, bingo, game nights, dances, movies, study groups, ceramics, monthly bridge parties, birthday celebrations, quarterly wine-and-cheese parties to welcome new residents, gardening, in-house entertainment, outings to the theater, concerts, restaurants.

Availability: Short waiting list.

Health services and rates: Residents are guaranteed nursing care in the health care center at a monthly fee no greater than that of the least expensive one-bedroom apartment. There are additional charges for additional meals, medical supplies, therapies, physicians. Podiatry and dentistry available.

- Assisted Living services are available to residents in their own apartments for a daily fee according to service rendered
- 60-Bed Intermediate and Skilled Nursing facility

"Lenbrook's philosophy is to establish an environment that ensures a high quality of life and human dignity for all residents. Lenbrook Square's greatest assets are our residents."

SAINT ANNE'S TERRACE, INC.

3100 Northside Parkway, N.W.
Atlanta, GA 30327
(404) 238-9200
Lucia McGowin, marketing director

Type of community: Not-for-profit Independent Living and Assisted Living

Located in a quiet residential neighborhood in beautiful northwest Atlanta within easy access of Interstate 75, the low-rise four-story building surrounds courtyard gardens. The community features three solariums, two outdoor patios, and easy access to West Paces Ferry Hospital, physicians' offices, shopping centers, and major banks.

Financial plan: Monthly fee.

Ownership and management: Saint Anne's Episcopal Church. Opened in 1987.

Minimum age: 62 years.

INDEPENDENT LIVING HOUSING

Type/size of apartment	*Monthly fee**
1-Bedroom, 520–810 sq. ft.	$1,248–1,766
2-Bedroom, 885–1,080 sq. ft.	$1,810–2,198

**For double occupancy add $300 to the monthly fee. All utilities except telephone and cable TV included. Individually controlled heating and air-conditioning, wall-to-wall carpeting, fully equipped kitchen, 24-hour emergency call system. Small pets allowed.*

Population: 104 residents; 86% women, 14% men, 11% couples.

Number of units: 97 Independent Living apartments.

Dining plan: Four-course dinner each day included in the monthly fee. Private dining room.

Services: *Included in the monthly fee:* Weekly housekeeping and flat-linen service, laundry services, scheduled transportation.

At additional cost: Beauty/barbershop with manicurist, pharmacy delivery services, guest accommodations, convenience store.

Activities: Game/crafts room, library, exercise room, woodworking shop, reading group, gardening group, walking paths, evening theater, day trips, sewing group, bridge, watercolor classes, lectures, musical events.

Availability: Priority waiting list.

Health services and rates: Wellness clinic. Once a week nurse checks blood pressure. Home health services provide nurses' aids in residents' apartments as needed for additional charge.

- Assisted Living services are provided by independent agency
- Saint Anne's will assist residents in finding long-term care if required

"Our goal is to provide the best quality retirement lifestyle in one of Atlanta's quiet, established, residential neighborhoods."

WESLEY WOODS

1841 Clifton Road, N.E.
Atlanta, GA 30329
(404) 728-6205
Mark Strong, marketing director

Type of community: Nonprofit Continuing Care, modified contract

The Towers, a 13-story high-rise of Independent Living apartments is located on 18 wooded acres that offer walking trails along Peachtree Creek. Situated on a campus setting in Atlanta's Druid Hills, Wesley Woods has Intermediate and Skilled Nursing as well as access to acute hospital care. The community offers the region's first comprehensive geriatric assessment program and is close to Emory University, shopping at Lenox Square, and downtown Atlanta.

Financial plan: Monthly rental fee. Deposit equal to one month's rent required. Lease may be canceled with 30 days notice.

Ownership and management: Wesley Homes, Inc. Opened in 1965.

Minimum age: 62 years.

Population: 210 Independent Living residents; 10 to15 couples.

Number of units: 202 Independent Living Apartments; 270 Intermediate Nursing beds, 100-bed Skilled Nursing facility, 100-bed geriatric hospital.

INDEPENDENT LIVING HOUSING

Type/size of unit	*Monthly fee*
Studio, 283 sq. ft.	$465
1-Bedroom, 646 sq. ft.	$567
2-Bedroom, 671 sq. ft.	$633

All utilities except telephone included. Individually controlled heating and air-conditioning, kitchenette, carpeting, draperies, 24-hour emergency call system.

Dining plan: Breakfast is included in the monthly fee. Lunch is an additional $221/month; dinner, $238/month; lunch and dinner, $430/month.

Services: *Included in the monthly fee:* Weekly housekeeping and flat-linen services, transportation, laundry facilities.

At additional cost: Beauty/barbershop.

Activities: Exercise, field trips, speakers, outings, programs organized by Emory students, music therapist.

Availability: No waiting list.

Health services and rates: Team-specialist approach to diagnosis and treatment. Neuropsychiatry service, Parkinson's Disease clinic, psychiatry services (depression), Alzheimer's care. Geriatric affiliate of the Robert W. Woodruff Health Science Center of Emory University, which serves as teaching/research center for the Southeast. Memory assessment clinic is a specialized neuropsychiatry clinic designed to assess memory loss and to provide treatment and ongoing care to patients. Physical, occupational, and speech therapy at additional cost, as are physicians' services.

- 270-Bed Intermediate Nursing

	Regular nursing	*Alzheimer's care*
Semiprivate	$1,753/month	$1945/month
Private	$1,950/month	$2,142/month

- 171-Bed Skilled Nursing facility $80–124/day
- 100-Bed geriatric hospital (warm, homelike comfort)

Rates and payment vary according to medical need and type of insurance.

"Wesley Woods Geriatric Hospital introduces a new concept in medical care for the elderly. The medical problems of aging require a distinctly different point of view. Conditions of aging are frequently characterized by multiple interrelated problems. A team approach addresses these multiple issues from an interdisciplinary perspective. Geriatricians provide outpatient services to older people and their families who need to be reassured about health status, as well as for those who need special attention for more immediate medical problems."

SAVANNAH COMMONS

1 Peachtree Drive
Savannah, GA 31419
(912) 927-0500 or (800) 382-1578
Carol C. Ratliff, retirement counselor

Type of community: Independent and Assisted Living

Four-story modern apartment complex is located on 11 acres. Outdoor patio, gardens, lighted walking paths, and park benches are offered. The community is located near St. Joseph's Hospital and Savannah Mall. Nearby Armstrong College provides many cultural and educational opportunities.

Financial plan: Monthly rental fee.

INDEPENDENT LIVING HOUSING

Type/size of apartment	*Monthly rental fee**
1-Bedroom, 600 sq. ft.	$1,125
2-Bedroom, 800 sq. ft.	$1,350

**For double occupancy add $350 to the monthly fee. All utilities except telephone included. Kitchen, walls-to-wall carpeting, miniblinds, individual heating and air-conditioning, 24-hour emergency call system.*

Ownership and management: Owner, Richard Bradfield; managed by Retirement Corporation of America, headquartered in Atlanta. Opened in 1987.

Minimum age: 62 years.

Population: 112 residents; 81% women, 19% men, 5% couples.

Number of units: 132 Independent Living apartments; 18 Assisted Living units.

Dining plan: Dinner plus continental breakfast daily included in the monthly fee. Optional lunch provided. A dining room meal credit is provided if resident is absent for seven consecutive days or longer. Tray service to apartments, when approved. Private dining room. Cocktail lounge.

Services: *Included in the monthly fee:* Weekly housekeeping and flat-linen services, scheduled transportation, self-service laundry facilities.

At additional cost: Beauty/barbershop.

Activities: Arts and crafts studio for pottery, ceramics, sewing and hobby clubs, billiards, card room for bridge clubs, poker, chess, exercise room, individual private whirlpools, outdoor gardening areas, nature trails, Bible study.

Availability: Limited.

Health services and rates: Savannah Commons assists residents in finding medical specialists. Blood pressure monitoring. Periodic health education seminars. Assisted Living offered under Independent Plus Program.

- 18 Assisted Living 1-bedroom apartments; monthly fees start at $1,725/month

"For many years our residents have worked to provide financial security for themselves and their families. Now is their time. Savannah Commons is designed for our residents' pleasure, comfort, and security. Most, if not all, of their present expenses are contained in the monthly fee."

SAVANNAH SQUARE RETIREMENT COMMUNITY

1 Savannah Square Drive
Savannah, GA 31406
(912) 927-7550
Michelle Ryan, director of marketing

Type of community: Continuing Care, modified contract

Three squares and one building are set on 15 acres in the suburbs of Savannah. The design complements the historic squares and architecture of old Savannah. Walled garden provides privacy and security. One-story cottage apartments and two-story apartment buildings house Independent Living, Assisted Living, and personal care residences and a health care center.

Financial plan: Monthly fee.

Ownership and management: Privately owned by Alexis Tarumianz, owner and manager of Mountain Creek Manor, Chattanooga, Tennessee, and Walden Oaks, San Antonio, Texas. Opened in 1987.

INDEPENDENT LIVING HOUSING

Cottage apartments	*Monthly fee**
1-Bedroom, 793 sq. ft.	$1,425
2-Bedroom, 1,106 sq. ft.	$1,685
2-Bedroom deluxe, 1,586 sq. ft.	$2,050
Riceland Hall	
1-Bedroom, 780 sq. ft.	$1,575
2-Bedroom, 936 sq. ft.	$1,750

**For double occupancy add $290 to the monthly fee. All utilities except long-distance telephone included. Wall-to-wall carpeting, miniblinds, 24-hour emergency call system, private patio or balcony, washer/dryer hookups, basic kitchen appliances.*

Minimum age: 60 years.

Population: 150 residents.

Number of units: 98 Independent Living apartments; 16 Assisted Living apartments, four personal care cottages, 40 Skilled Nursing beds.

Dining plan: The evening meal is included in the monthly fee. Private dining room for residents' use. Square Café is open for breakfast and lunch. Lounge with bar.

Services: *Included in the monthly fee:* Weekly maid and flat-linen service, chauffeured transportation.

At additional cost: Beauty/barbershop, café.

Activities: Exercise, bridge, weekly coffees, Mystery Ride, happy hour at 5 p.m., bingo, arts and crafts, Jacuzzi, library, book review, Bible study, monthly program with live entertainment.

Availability: Limited.

Health services and rates: Independent Living residents receive 15 free days in the health care center. Physical, occupational, and speech therapy are available.

- 16 Assisted Living apartments
  1-Bedroom, 780 sq. ft. $2,225/month
  2-Bedroom, 936 sq. ft. $2,350/month

  **For double occupancy add $290 to the monthly fee. Care services for second person may be added as needed at additional charge.*

- 4 Personal care cottages
  1-Bedroom, 793 sq. ft. $2,225/month
  2-Bedroom, 1,106 sq. ft. $2,250/month
- 40 Skilled Nursing beds
  Semiprivate $71/day
  Private $91/day

"Savannah Square has all the comforts of home without all the hassles. In fact, we take care of almost everything, so that residents can remain active and independent. Our trained personnel are available as needed. Our residents never have to worry about getting locked into a living situation that lacks flexibility because they know we can meet their changing needs."

ILLINOIS

MARRIOTT CHURCH CREEK

1250 West Central Road
Arlington Heights, IL 60005
(708) 506-3200
Gina Gajewski, marketing manager

Type of community: Continuing Care, modified contract

This community is housed in a four-story modern, red brick apartment-style building with two duck ponds nearby. Central common area is a beautiful four-story garden atrium with skylights and ample room for entertaining visitors. This area features a piano bar area, dance floor, and player piano. Independent Living apartments with adjacent health center and Assisted Living suites are available. The community is conveniently located 25 miles northwest of Chicago near Northwest Community Hospital, shopping malls, banks, theaters, and restaurants.

Financial plan: Monthly rental. To reserve an apartment a $2,500 security deposit (fully refundable and interest bearing) and one month's rent in advance is required.

Ownership and management: Owned and managed by Marriott Senior Living Services, a wholly owned subsidiary of Marriott Corporation. Marriott owns and manages retirement communities in Arizona, California, Florida, Illinois, Indiana, Maryland, New Jersey, Pennsylvania, Texas, and Virginia. Opened in 1987.

Minimum age: 65 years (if couple, spouse may be younger).

Population: 267 residents; 80% women, 20% men, 8% couples.

Number of units: 243 Independent Living apartments; 50 Assisted Living Suites, 120 Intermediate and Skilled Nursing beds.

Dining plan: Two meals per day included in the monthly fee. Third meal available for an additional $150 per month. Private dining room.

Services: *Included in the monthly fee:* Weekly housekeeping and flat-linen service, regularly scheduled

INDEPENDENT LIVING HOUSING

Type/size of apartment	*Monthly fee**
Studio, 480 sq. ft.	$1,395–1,475
1-Bedroom, 576 sq. ft.	$1,585–1,730
2-Bedroom, 810 sq. ft.	$2,300–2,390

**For double occupancy add $370 to the monthly fee. All utilities except telephone and cable TV included. Wall-to-wall carpeting, large closets, full-length sheer curtains, fully equipped kitchens, individually controlled heating and air-conditioning, 24-hour emergency call system, cable TV hookup.*

transportation, parking, Charter Club (discount services/products from local merchants).

At additional cost: Great Lakes cruises, beauty/barbershop, guest accommodations, conveniently located laundry rooms, gift shop/convenience store, banking services, assistance with checkbook balancing and filling out medical and financial forms, personal assistance.

Activities: Exercise room (low-impact armchair exercises), library with large-print books, travelogue series, board and card games, billiards, current events discussions, concerts, Bible study, social hours, walking club (Happy Hoofers), big-screen TV with VCR, piano bar, arts and crafts room.

Availability: Waiting list for studios and two-bedrooms.

Health services and rates: Wellness clinics. Physical, occupational, and speech therapy plus podiatrist, hearing specialist, pharmacist, and dentist. Individual and family counseling available for additional fee.

- 50 Assisted Living suites

Semiprivate	$81/day
Private	$126/day

- 120-Bed Nursing facility

	Intermediate Nursing	*Skilled Nursing*
Semiprivate	$91/day	$102/day
Private	$137/day	$144/day

"Residents enjoy all the qualitative benefits of living in and contributing to a caring community, fostering life of the mind with a sense of purpose. Excellent service is more than just a business philosophy, it's been a Marriott family tradition for over 60 years. And all that we've learned as a leader in the service and hospitality industry is applied to satisfy the needs of older adults living in our retirement communities."

THE MOORINGS

811 East Central Road
Arlington Heights, IL 60005
(708) 956-4304
sales office

Type of community: Not-for-profit Continuing Care, modified contract

Situated on 45 acres of beautifully landscaped grounds, conveniently located in Arlington Heights, a suburb of Chicago, the site includes a national landmark round barn, Independent Living apartments and villas, and a full-service health center.

Financial Plan: Entrance fee plus monthly fee. Two plans: **1)** Founder's fee program. Partial refund during the first 24 months of residency. **2)** Endowment fee program. 80 percent refund.

Ownership and management: Owned and operated by the Lutheran General HealthSystem. Opened in 1988.

Minimum age: 62 years.

Population: 340 residents; 70% women, 30% men, 20% couples.

Number of units: 294 Independent Living residences; 68 Assisted Living units, 120-bed health center.

Dining Plan: A continental breakfast plus daily choice of lunch or dinner is included in the monthly fee. Additional meals are available on an à la carte basis. The menu is reviewed by a registered dietitian. Private dining room and party rooms.

Services: *Included in the monthly fee:* Weekly housekeeping and flat-linen services, scheduled

INDEPENDENT LIVING HOUSING

Type of apartment	*Entrance fee 1**	*Monthly fee*
1-Bedroom, 530–685 sq. ft.	$51,000–80,000	$1,208–1,345
2-Bedroom, 947–1078 sq. ft.	$102,000–107,000	$1,538
Villa		
2-Bedroom, 1,276 sq. ft.	$136,000–151,000	$1,671

**Plan 2 entrance fees range from $81,000–260,000; plan 2 monthly fees are the same. For double occupancy add $10,600 to the entrance fee, approximately $800 to the monthly fee. All utilities included. Fully equipped kitchen, individually controlled heating and air conditioning, wall-to-wall carpeting and window treatments, 24-hour emergency call system, cable TV hookup. Largest 1-bedroom has patio or balcony. Villas have attached garage, patio, fireplace, washer and dryer.*

transportation, heated underground parking, laundry facilities, personal storage area.

At additional cost: Beauty salon, convenience store, guest suites.

Activities: Indoor heated swimming pools; walking, jogging and bicycle paths; fitness programs; exercise center with whirlpool, water aerobics; game and card rooms, bridge, billiards room, woodworking shop, fine arts studio, music room, library, meditation area, religious study, garden club, weekly movies, travelogues, cultural and recreational outings, volunteer programs.

Availability: Short waiting list for apartments; limited number of villas available.

Health services and rates: Residents receive 90 days of health care included in their monthly fee. Residency includes application to the long-term care insurance program. Blood pressure monitoring, outpatient services, and health education programs.

- 68 Assisted Living units
  - Semiprivate $64–69/day
  - Private $76–80/day
  - Suite $104–127/day
- 120 Skilled Nursing beds $130–175/day

"The mission of The Moorings of Arlington Heights is to serve older adults by providing alternatives that will enrich their quality of life, preserve their individual dignity, and encourage maximum independence. At The Moorings, we realize that service is more than giving: it is also receiving."

THE HOLMSTAD

700 West Fabyan Parkway
Batavia, IL 60510
(708) 879-4100
Susan Shearer, director of marketing

Type of community: Not-for-profit Continuing Care, modified contract

Accreditation: Continuing Care Accreditation Commission

Located on 38 scenic acres in the Fox Valley, The Holmstad provides a tranquil setting that is about an hour away from the many cultural, entertainment, and shopping opportunities in Chicago. Residents enjoy the privacy of their individually decorated apartments or fourplex homes, as well as the use of a variety of graciously appointed community areas. Assisted Living and Skilled Nursing are on campus.

Financial plan: Entrance fee plus monthly fee. $1,350 application fee, $1,000 of which is refundable.

Ownership and management: Owned/managed by the Evangelical Covenant Church/Covenant Retirement Communities, which owns/manages retirement communities in California, Connecticut, Florida, Illinois, Minnesota, and Washington. Covenant Retirement Communities was founded in 1886. Opened in 1976.

Minimum age: 62 years.

Population: 414 residents; 70% women, 30% men.

Number of units: 326 Independent Living apartments and 44 fourplex homes; 30 Sheltered Care rooms, 121-bed Skilled Nursing facility.

Dining plan: One meal is included in the monthly fee. Lunch and dinner are served daily. Optional continental breakfast. Private dining room available by reservation. Delivered meals available.

Services: *Included in the monthly fee:* Biweekly housekeeping, weekly flat-linen service, scheduled bus service, laundry facilities.

At additional cost: Beauty/barbershop, gift shop, minimart, automatic bank teller, guest accommodations, additional housekeeping, financial facilitators, other transportation.

Activities: Pastoral care. Interest groups, exercise programs, crafts, cards and games, woodworking shop, library, gardening, Bible study, chapel service, music groups and programs, residents' association, shopping trips and many off-campus activities (sporting events, museums, zoos, galleries, concerts, lectures, city tours).

Availability: Limited. Please call for current information.

Health services and rates: Residential health clinic staffed daily by registered nurse who provides consultative services, resident health monitoring, wellness programs. Scheduled services of general and specialist physicians and services. Rehabilitation therapies available.

- 30 Sheltered Care singles $78.30/day
- 121 Skilled Nursing beds $122.10/day

"The mission of the Holmstad is to serve as an extension of the Evangelical Covenant Church by providing excellence in personalized care through a continuum of services from Independent Living through health care needs. The Holmstad is committed to serving people of all denominations through a balance of services, programs, and facilities designed to enhance opportunities for dignity, security, and discovery of maximum potential. Prospective residents are invited to spend a complimentary three-day visit at The Holmstad."

INDEPENDENT LIVING HOUSING

Type/size of unit	*Entrance fee single/double*	*Monthly fee single/double*
Studio, 450 sq. ft.	$48,000	$660
1-Bedroom, 610 sq. ft.	$66,000/72,600	$800/1,128
2-Bedroom, 875 sq. ft.	$90,500/99,500	$1,045/1,373
Fourplex home		
1-Bedroom, 825 sq. ft.	$81,750/89,925	$745/863
2-Bedroom, 1,100 sq. ft.	$101,700/111,870	$994/1,112

All utilities except telephone included in the monthly fee. Fully equipped kitchen, wall-to-wall carpeting, drapes, wallpaper in kitchen/bath, individually controlled heating and air-conditioning, 24-hour emergency call system.

Mary Alice and Max, 73 and 75 years

Epworth Villa, Tulsa, Oklahoma

"What really motivated us is that Max and I had to make decisions for three of our relatives—my mother, Max's mother, and my aunt—when they became ill."

"We went through full-time care in the home for my mother, but it was so difficult to keep and oversee help 24 hours a day. Then there was the move to the nursing home," explains Mary Alice, "which meant going through all her belongings and selling the house. We had to handle everything, and we don't want our children to have to do that for us. Who knows how long we'll live, or what our condition will be. Moving into a Continuing Care retirement community with an all-inclusive contract brings great peace of mind."

Mary Alice moved her aunt into Epworth Villa six years ago after investigating alternatives. "We like this plan where you buy in, and there are no additional fees, except two additional meals, should Assisted Living or Skilled Nursing be required. And, if one of us becomes ill and ends up in Skilled Nursing, the other one can stay in the apartment. Visiting is easy because everything is under one roof."

Mary Alice and Max looked at communities near their daughters in Colorado and their son in Dallas, but found the prices in Oklahoma to be less expensive, and they were already familiar with Epworth Villa because of Mary Alice's aunt. Also, both Mary Alice and Max grew up in Oklahoma and have many relatives in the area.

"There's a lot of emotion," says Mary Alice, "when you start to sort through your things. I don't know how one can get so emotional over a dish that one's mother used at Thanksgiving, but. . . . We gave things of value to our children, and we enjoy seeing our things in their homes. We haven't found moving in to be a difficult adjustment."

A decorator at Epworth Villa helps people move in. She advised Mary Alice and Max on what pieces of furniture to bring with them. As it turned out, the moving truck beat them to their new home; because the decorator had a floor plan, she was able to supervise the unpacking, and every piece of furniture was in the right place waiting for them.

"Our son is a corporate benefits specialist," says Max, "and at first he thought it was just crazy for us to give up our home. He thought taking out an insurance policy would be an alternative, but none of us could find one for any amount of money that really protects you for an indefinite amount of time." Their middle daughter is an activities therapist and has seen firsthand what happens when families have to make decisions on behalf of parents. Once their oldest daughter visited Epworth Villa, she agreed the move was a good idea.

"Our children never have to worry about having to put us into some kind of facility and going through all the accompanying anguish," continues Max, echoing Mary Alice's thoughts. "Neither will they have to worry about having to come up with the money for Skilled Nursing care or, for that matter, will we. Many people say, as long as we have money we should keep our independence and not move into a retirement community. However, we know any number of people who have stayed in their own homes, but when the time comes cannot get dependable care in their home, no matter how much money they have. Most illnesses wind up killing the caregiver as well as the patient, which I think is less likely to happen to us at Epworth Villa because of all the support systems. The other thing to remember, of course, is that you're not locked up here. You can enjoy independent living in a nice apartment, and everything from fine dining to a beautiful swimming pool, without an attic full of stuff, and take off any time and never have a worry."

And, this summer as they have done for the last 15 years, Max, a former television news anchor, and Mary Alice will spend the season in the Colorado Rockies, where Mary Alice taught sewing as an art.

Advice from Max: "Don't wait until it's too late. Most Continuing Care communities require that you be able to live independently in order to be admitted."

WESTMINSTER VILLAGE, INC.

2025 East Lincoln Street
Bloomington, IL 61701
(309) 663-6474
Jean A. Daily, director of marketing

Type of community: Nonprofit Continuing Care, modified contract

Located on 48 acres, the Village is composed of three-story buildings and a social center with facilities for dining and recreation. Brick and stucco uniform buildings are surrounded by trees, open green areas, a gazebo, and walkways. Enclosed walkways join the buildings to the central complex. More cottages and landscaping is planned. The community is close to Illinois State University and Illinois Wesleyan University, which afford endless opportunities for personally fulfilling and creative activities.

Financial plan: Entrance fee plus monthly fee or monthly rental. Three entrance fee plans: **1)** Single installment life occupancy plan. **2)** Three installment life occupancy plan. **3)** Return-on-equity life occupancy plan. *Note:* Only Plan 3 is refundable.

Ownership and management: Owned and managed by Westminster Village, Inc. Opened in 1979.

Minimum age: 62 years.

Population: 330 residents; 63% women, 37% men, 40 couples.

Number of units: 241 Independent Living apartments; 45 Assisted Living units, 78-bed health center.

Dining plan: One meal per day included in the monthly fee.

Services: *Included in the monthly fee:* Twice monthly housekeeping, weekly flat-linen service, scheduled transportation, parking.

At additional cost: Beauty/barbershop, branch bank, pharmacy with sundry shop, guest accommodations.

Activities: Residence service director. Arts and crafts, bingo, shopping, cultural and educational trips, monthly birthday parties, exercise group, quilting, Scrabble, card groups, shuffleboard, billiards table, entertainment, library, vespers. Residents can attend all theater productions and concerts at Illinois Wesleyan and Illinois State University.

Availability: Waiting list, six months to one year.

Health services and rates: Outpatient physical therapy, podiatrist, dental service, laboratory ser-vice, prescription service. Hospitality suites are

INDEPENDENT LIVING HOUSING

Type/size of apartment	*Entrance fee 1/2/3**	*Monthly fee single/double*
Studio, 439 sq. ft.	$24,000/25,100/32,800	$742
1-Bedroom, 523 sq. ft.	$28,200/29,150/38,700	$770/1,110
2-Bedroom, 765 sq. ft.	$42,300/44,216/57,600	$826/1,181
2-Bedroom, 860 sq. ft.	$47,000/49,151/64,200	$851/1,222
2-Bedroom, 1,046 sq. ft.	$56,300/58,916/77,200	$897/1,279

**For double occupancy add $2,000 to the entrance fee for all plans. Monthly rental fees range from $896 for studio to $1,768 for largest 2-bedroom, with approximately $335 for double occupancy, plus $2,000 security deposit.*

All utilities except telephone included. Fully equipped kitchen, carpeting, draperies, 24-hour emergency call system, individually controlled heating and air-conditioning.

available for short-term stays (up to eight weeks) for residents not requiring intensive nursing—ideal for post-hospital recuperation or temporary stays while family is away.

- 45 Assisted Living units

Efficiency/resident	$904/month
2-Bed unit/nonresident	$1,940/month

- 78-Bed health center

	Intermediate Nursing	*Skilled Nursing*
Semiprivate	$66/day	$79/day
Private	$102/day	$114/day

Note: *Nonresidents pay approximately $10/day more than residents (if space available).*

"Westminster Village is a friendly, warm community that our residents find informal, comfortable, and clean."

THE HALLMARK

2960 North Lake Shore Drive
Chicago, IL 60657
(312) 880-2960
Mary Pat Scoltock, marketing director

Type of community: Independent Living with Continuum of Care

This 37-story apartment building overlooks Lake Michigan and offers spectacular views of Lincoln Park and the Chicago skyline. Located on Chicago's famous Gold Coast, the building is faced outside in red- and blue-glazed brick, with marble and bird's-eye maple paneling in the public rooms and landscaped outdoor deck. The Hallmark is minutes from downtown Chicago's Magnificent Mile.

Financial plan: Monthly rental fee. $2,500 fully refundable deposit.

Ownership and management: Owned by The Prime Group, Inc. Opened in 1990.

Minimum age: 62 years.

Population: 340 residents; 74% women, 26% men, 17% couples.

Number of units: 344 Independent Living apartments

Dining plan: Continental breakfast daily and choice of 15 meals included in the monthly fee. Private dining room and catering services.

Services: *Included in the monthly fee:* Housekeeping and flat-linen services, scheduled transportation, Golden Care long-term insurance.

At additional cost: Guest accommodations, additional housekeeping, bank, beauty/barbershop,

INDEPENDENT LIVING HOUSING

Type/size of apartment	*Monthly fee**
Studio, 510 sq. ft.	$1,400–1,475
1-Bedroom, 630–711 sq. ft.	$1,500–1,810
1-Bedroom/den, 780–960 sq. ft.	$2,050–2,495
2-Bedroom, 1,016–1,096 sq. ft.	$2,620–2,795
3-Bedroom (custom), 1,650 sq. ft.	$3,805–3,810

**For double occupancy add $400 to the monthly fee. All utilities except telephone included. Fully equipped kitchens, wall-to-wall carpeting, individually controlled heating and air-conditioning, 24-hour emergency call system, cable TV outlet.*

convenience store, pharmacy and dry cleaning pick-up and delivery, attached parking.

Activities: Full social, educational and fitness programs. Chorus, bingo, lectures, art classes, gourmet diner's club, book review club, movies, day trips, lectures.

Availability: Limited.

Health services and rates: All residents are covered by Golden Care long-term insurance, underwritten by Lloyd's of London. Satellite office of Saint Joseph Hospital's Center for Healthy Aging on-site offers routine health screenings, physician and home health care referrals, care management services. Saint Joseph Hospital next door.

- "Personally Yours" in-home Assisted Living program

"The Hallmark is located on Lake Shore Drive in Chicago. The skyline, Lake Michigan, Lincoln Park, and downtown Chicago are at your doorstep. The Hallmark offers the full reward of retirement for one affordable monthly fee. No ownership, endowment, or long-term financial commitment is involved."

OAK CREST DEKALB AREA RETIREMENT CENTER

2944 Greenwood Acres Drive
DeKalb, IL 60115
(815) 756-8461
Liz Hoppenworth, human resources

Type of community: Not-for-profit Continuing Care, modified contract

This modern three-story Y-shaped facility is located on a 31-acre campus adjacent to Kishwaukee Community Hospital, YMCA, and Kishwaukee Country Club and golf course. Campus includes Independent Living duplexes and apartments, personal care apartments, and a 60-bed health center. The grounds feature Japanese gardens, walking paths, and duck ponds. Nearby Northern Illinois University offers educational and cultural opportunities.

Financial plan: Entrance fee plus monthly fee. Entrance fee is refundable, prorated over five years. Good Samaritan Fund assists residents should they outlive their financial resources.

Ownership and management: The DeKalb Area Retirement Center, is a not-for-profit corporation, affiliated with the Northern Illinois Annual

INDEPENDENT LIVING HOUSING

Type/size of apartment	*Entrance fee*	*Monthly fee single/double**
Studio, 300 sq. ft.	$17,000	$990
Studio/kitchenette, 300 sq. ft.	$18,000	$990
1-Bedroom, 500–700 sq. ft.	$28,000–43,500	$1,264–1,681/1,554–2,067
1-Bedroom/balcony, 600+ sq. ft.	$36,000	$1,430/1,902
2-Bedroom, 800–900 sq. ft.	$45,000–51,000	$1,796–2,389/1,977–2,630
2-Bedroom/balcony, 900+ sq. ft.	$53,000	$2,027/2,724
Duplex, 1,150 sq. ft.	$135,000	$533/586

**Monthly fee includes meal plan; residents may choose 1, 2, or 3 meals, which alters the monthly fee. All utilities except telephone included. All apartments have wall-to-wall carpeting, draperies, individually controlled heating and air-conditioning, 24-hour emergency call system.*

Conference of the United Methodist Church. Operates under the sole discretion of the ecumenical board of directors. Opened in 1980.

Minimum age: 62 years. Although the community is affiliated with the Methodists, it is committed to serving all people.

Population: 183 residents; 82% women, 18% men, 13% couples.

Number of units: 80 Independent Living apartments and 14 duplexes; 28 personal care apartments, 60-bed health center.

Dining plan: Three different plans: one, two, or three meals a day can be included in the monthly fee. Special diets can be accommodated. Private dining room.

Services: *Included in the monthly fee:* Weekly housekeeping and flat-linen services, outdoor parking, storage locker, counseling, washers and dryers in every wing.

At additional cost: Beauty/barbershop, guest accommodations, garage.

Activities: Woodworking shop, crafts and hobby rooms, billiards table, shuffleboard, outdoor walking area, Little Theater, library, garden plots, public balcony and sundeck, therapy and exercise room.

Availability: Limited.

Health services and rates:

- 28 Personal care apartments with 24-hour attendants

Studio	$1,595/month
1-Bedroom	$2,082–2,769/month
2-Bedroom	$2,646–3,519/month

- 60-Bed health care center. For Independent Living residents, there is no charge for first five days each calendar year in health center. The next 85 days are billed at half the resident's fee. At 90 days, the daily rate is billed at the regular resident's rate.

Semiprivate	$82/daily for residents
	$96/daily for nonresidents
Private	$140/daily for residents

"Independence is a basic value of older adults and one that the DeKalb Area Retirement Center places high in its priorities. When people desire retirement living, we have a community for them that guarantees their future at the highest possible level of independence and security. Our goal is to provide a continuum of care for older adults."

FAIRVIEW VILLAGE

250 Village Drive
Downers Grove, IL 60516
(708) 769-6000
Dee Hunt, marketing director

Type of community: Nonprofit Continuing Care, all-inclusive contract

Situated on 40 acres in suburban Downer's Grove, 25 miles from downtown Chicago, Fairview Village's landscaped, parklike grounds surround country townhouses, English garden homes, and a five-story apartment building all occupied by Independent Living residents. Sheltered Care and Intermediate and Skilled Nursing care are also offered.

Financial plan: Entrance fee plus monthly fee. 100% of entrance fee is refundable.

Ownership and management: Owned and managed by Fairview Ministries, Inc. Fairview Baptist Home opened in 1972; Fairview Village opened in 1991.

Minimum age: 55 years.

Population: 600 residents; 71% women, 29% men, 30% couples.

Number of units: 28 country townhouses and 28 English Garden homes for Independent Living; 218 congregate living Village apartments, 66 Sheltered Care beds, 126 Intermediate Nursing beds, 40 Skilled Nursing beds.

Dining plan: Various meal options available. Private dining room. Special dietary needs will be met.

Services: *Included in the monthly fee:* Scheduled transportation, weekly housekeeping and flat-linen services, counseling services, assistance with insurance forms.

At additional cost: Beauty/barbershop.

Activities: Bus trips, frequent meals at area restaurants, volunteer opportunities, continuing education opportunities, men's discussion groups, ceramics and sewing classes, exercise classes, concerts, baking, chapel, prayer meetings.

Availability: Waiting list for Independent Living. Limited availability for Village apartments.

Health services and rates: Three levels of care are offered for Sheltered Care and Intermediate and Skilled Nursing. Fees for these services for Independent Living residents are covered by the monthly fee. Medications and medical supplies are billed in addition to the monthly fee. Intravenous therapy, ventilation therapy, isolation techniques provided. Nonresidents may be admitted when space is available.

- 66 Sheltered Care apartments

	Nonresident monthly fee
Single, 300 sq. ft.	$2,367
2-Room (single), 600 sq. ft.	$3,299
2-Room (double), 600 sq. ft.	$4,122

- 126 Intermediate Care beds

Semiprivate	$3,402
Private	$4,354

- 40 Skilled Nursing beds

	Nonresident monthly fee
Semiprivate	$3,661
Private	$4,982

"Fairview Village desires to create a quality of life that is dignified and reflective of your personal preferences. One of our greatest assets is our campus setting on 40 acres with our own nine-acre park, ponds and gardens."

INDEPENDENT LIVING HOUSING

Country townhouses	*Entrance fee**	*Monthly fee*
2–3-Bedroom, 1,250–1,600 sq. ft.	$185,000–205,000	$500
English garden homes		
2-Bedroom, 1,150 sq. ft.	$162,000–182,000	$550/650
Village apartments		
Studio, 600 sq. ft.	$80,000	$900
1-Bedroom, 636–887 sq. ft.	$120,000	$900/1,100
2-Bedroom, 887–1,344 sq. ft.	$170,000	$1,450

**For double occupancy add $10,000 to the entrance fee; $450 to the monthly fee. All utilities except telephone are included for apartment residents. Townhouse/home residents are charged separately for utilities. Apartments, townhouses, and homes have wall-to-wall carpeting, 24-hour emergency call system, individually controlled heating and air-conditioning, full kitchen. Attached garages available for townhouses and homes. Townhouses have fireplaces.*

KING HOME

1555 Oak Avenue
Evanston, IL 60201
(708) 864-5460
Candace McGuire, director of admissions

Type of community: Nonprofit Continuing Care, all-inclusive contract

Accreditation: Continuing Care Accreditation Commission

This classic club-like environment located on a shady, tree-lined street is within walking distance of downtown Evanston. Gentleman's lifestyle is enhanced by daily maid service, morning paper, beautifully prepared meals, and game room complete with billiards table and big-screen TV.

Financial plan: Monthly fee only.

Ownership and management: One of six communities in Evanston operated by Presbyterian Homes, a private nonprofit organization, governed by a board of directors. Founded in 1911, merged with Presbyterian Homes in 1985.

Minimum age: 60 years.

Population: 76 (men only).

Number of units: 56 Independent Living/sheltered care; 20 Intermediate Care beds.

Dining plan: Three meals per day included in the monthly fee. Private Dining room and catering.

Services: *Included in the monthly fee:* Housekeeping five days a week, weekly flat-linen service, scheduled transportation, reserved parking, personal laundry, dry cleaning, *Chicago Tribune* subscription, barber.

At additional cost: Guest accommodations.

Activities: Golf outings, exercise class, music appreciation, discussion groups, bridge, movies, holiday parties. Excursions to ball games, theater, concerts, local landmarks and museums, events at Northwestern University.

Availability: No waiting list.

Health services and rates: Long-term nursing care covered in residents' monthly fee and available at King Home's health care center. Full-time medical director—a board-certified internist with a subspecialty in geriatric medicine. Interdisciplinary team of staff physicians, nursing staff, occupational, physical, and speech therapists, dietitians, social workers, pharmacist, 20 physician specialists. McGaw Care Center on Presbyterian Homes main campus contains Hansen Clinic, a full-service outpatient clinic for residents. It provides laboratory testing, X rays, diagnostic examinations, annual dental for residents. 24-hour on-call physician and nurse. Professional counseling and social services. Complete pharmacy located within Hansen Clinic. Sheltered Care available at King Home.

"King Home was founded in 1911 as a place where honorable men could retire at a reasonable expense. Today's residents enjoy comfortable suites and the attentions of a gracious staff that strives to enhance each man's independence and significance."

INDEPENDENT LIVING HOUSING

Type of apartment	*Monthly fee only*
1-Bedroom suite	$1,800–1,850

All utilities except telephone included in the monthly fee. Carpeting, 24-hour emergency call system, individually controlled heating and air-conditioning. Each suite has bedroom, bathroom, and living room.

TEN TWENTY GROVE

1020 Grove Street
Evanston, IL 60201
(708) 570-3422
Holly Halliday, director of admissions

Type of community: Nonprofit Continuing Care, choice of modified or all-inclusive contract

Accreditation: Continuing Care Accreditation Commission

Ten Twenty Grove offers a sophisticated blend of urban amenities and suburban grace. The modern nine-story apartment building is located on a quiet, residential street near downtown Evanston—vintage North Shore suburb of Chicago. It is within walking distance to Evanston's lakefront parks and beaches. Many apartments have gorgeous views of Lake Michigan or the downtown Chicago skyline.

Financial plan: Entrance fee plus monthly fee. Two plans: both include health services, prescriptions medicines, rehabilitative therapies. **1)** Includes all future nursing care. **2)** Prepays for 180 days of nursing care per person, after which care is available at 90% of the daily community rate.

Ownership and management: One of six communities in Evanston operated by Presbyterian Homes, a private nonprofit organization, governed by a board of directors. Opened in 1991.

Minimum age: 60 years.

Population: 85 residents.

Number of units: 46 Independent Living apartments; 35 Assisted Living units, 210-bed nursing facility.

Dining plan: No meal plan included, although occasional meals may be taken at King Home dining room across the street. Private dining room and catering available at King Home.

Services: *Included in the monthly fee:* Weekly housekeeping, transportation, laundry facilities.

At additional cost: Underground parking.

Activities: Residents may participate in activities with Westminster Place and King Home campus residents. Outings to ball games, the opera, theater, concerts, local landmarks, museums, and events at Northwestern University.

Availability: Waiting list for larger units.

Health services and rates: Residents on Plan 1 receive unlimited health care included in their monthly fee. Residents on Plan 2 receive 180 free days per person, after which they pay 90% of the daily rate. 24-hour nurse and infirmary available across the street at King Home. Assisted Living at Wilson Sidwell Apartments and Skilled Nursing at McGaw Care Center (see Westminster Place).

"Ten Twenty Grove provides a unique retirement option for independent, active adults who don't want to make a major lifestyle change but want the security that comes from knowing that comprehensive health care services are available to them. Residents can relax and enjoy today knowing that they have planned well in advance for their future needs."

INDEPENDENT LIVING HOUSING

Type of apartment	*Entrance fee 1/2*	*Monthly fee*
1-Bedroom	$65,000/35,000	$1,250
2-Bedroom	$99,500/49,500	$1,450
2-Bedroom, 2-bath	$110,500/60,000	$1,650

All utilities except telephone and cable TV included in monthly fee. Fully equipped eat-in kitchen, 24-hour emergency call system, individually controlled heating and air-conditioning. Apartments may be customized.

WESTMINSTER PLACE

3200 Grant Street
Evanston, IL 60201
(708) 570-3422
Sharon Petersen, director of residential admissions

Type of community: Nonprofit Continuing Care, choice of modified or all-inclusive contract

Accreditation: Continuing Care Accreditation Commission

Situated in a quiet, family neighborhood of beautiful homes and mature trees, Westminster Place's 40-acre grounds feature winding walkways lined with old-fashioned lampposts, lush lawns, fountains, and abundant gardens. The community is made up of four distinct neighborhoods and Independent Living options—One Calvin Circle, One Arbor Lane, Knox and Calvin Circle cottages, and Trinity Court townhouses. Westminster Place is composed of low-rise apartment buildings and cozy brick townhouses and cottages. All units are single story. Beautiful public areas include a stately library, elegant dining room, and outdoor garden atrium. The chapel carillon rings out seasonal music at noon and dusk. Shopping, theaters, restaurants, lakefront, and Northwestern University are a few minutes' drive away.

Financial plan: Entrance fee plus monthly fee. Two plans: **1)** All future nursing home care is included. **2)** Prepays for 180 days of nursing care per person, after which care is available at 90% of daily community rate. Entrance fee is approximately half of Plan 1 and monthly fee is slightly less than Plan 1.

Ownership and management: One of six communities in Evanston operated by Presbyterian Homes, a private nonprofit organization, governed by a board of directors. (Westminster Place, Geneva Place, Ten Twenty Grove, King Homes [men only], Wilson/Sidwell Assisted Living Apartments, McGaw Care Center.) Opened in 1961.

Minimum age: 65 years.

Population: 350 residents; 80% women, 20% men, 30% couples.

Number of units: 250 Independent Living apartments, townhouses, and cottages; 35 Assisted Living units; 210-bed nursing facility (99 Intermediate, 111 Skilled).

Dining plan: Three meals available at additional charge per person per month: one meal, $225; two meals, $360; three meals, $450. Meal plans can be altered. Private dining room and catering.

Services: *Included in the monthly fee:* Weekly flat-linen service, scheduled transportation, laundry facilities. Apartments receive weekly housekeeping; cottages and townhouses, twice monthly.

At additional cost: Beauty/barber shop, decorating services, gift shop, guest accommodations.

INDEPENDENT LIVING HOUSING

Type/size of unit	*Entrance fee 1/2*	*Monthly fee 1/2*
Studio, 384 sq. ft.	$47,500/25,000	$1,620/1,150
1-Bedroom, 581–768 sq. ft.	$74,500–82,500/39,500–52,000	$1,565–2,160/1,500–1,615
2-Bedroom, 742–1,344 sq. ft.	$100,000–201,000/53,000–106,500	$1,710–2,335/1,750–1,870
3-Bedroom, 1,728 sq. ft.	$241,000/128,500	$3,005/2,535

All utilities except long-distance telephone included in the monthly fee. Fully equipped kitchen, 24-hour emergency call system, individually controlled heating and air-conditioning. All cottages and townhouses and One Arbor Lane apartments have washers/dryers and dishwashers. Cottages, townhouses, first floor apartments have patios. 18 floor plans.

Activities: Activities director. Weaving, knitting, sewing, woodworking, painting or ceramics, exercise class, Bible or literary discussion groups, bridge, movies, holiday parties. Outings to ball games, the opera, theater, concerts, local landmarks, museums, and events at Northwestern University.

Availability: Waiting list for larger units. May take smaller unit while waiting for desired unit.

Health services and rates: Full-time medical director works with interdisciplinary staff of three other board-certified physicians, nursing staff, occupational, physical, and speech therapists, dietitians, social workers, pharmacists, and 20 consultant physician specialists. Full-service outpatient clinic for residents provides laboratory testing, X rays, diagnostic examinations, annual dental, hearing, and eye examinations and follow-up care. 24-hour on-call physician and nurse. Professional counseling and social services. Complete pharmacy. Specially designed unit for people with memory impairments such as Alzheimer's.

- 35 Assisted Living apartments

	Entrance fee 2	*Monthly fee*	*Monthly fee only*
Studio	$25,000	$1,725	$1,890
1-Bedroom	$39,500	$2,055	$2,260
2-Bedroom	$53,00	$2,290	$2,520

- 210-Bed nursing facility

	Intermediate Nursing	*Skilled Nursing*
Semiprivate	N/A	$147.50/ day
Private	$160.50–170.50/ day	$170.50/ day

"Westminster Place's most distinctive features are its comprehensive medical services and its people. Residents are a very social, well-established group mostly of retired community and business leaders. Some still maintain their positions on boards or university faculties. They enjoy the quiet, Christian atmosphere of Westminster Place and the respectful care of its dedicated staff."

THE DEVONSHIRE

1700 Robin Lane
Lisle, IL 60532
(708) 963-1600
RoseAnn Urban, director of marketing

Type of community: Independent and Assisted Living

The Devonshire has 324 apartments in a five-story building on 15 acres of landscaped grounds. The property adjoins the Lisle Park district and offers a two-mile paved walking path, trees, pond, and flowers. The town of Lisle, population of 21,000, is 1/2 mile away.

Financial plan: Monthly rental fee. Refundable $2,500 deposit.

Ownership and management: Privately owned. Opened in March 1990.

Minimum age: 62 years.

Population: 357 residents; 79% women, 21% men, 21% couples.

Number of units: 305 Independent Living units; 19 Assisted Living units.

Dining plan: Two plans: Plan 1 includes 30 dining certificates, plus breakfast (included in monthly fee listed above). Plan 2 includes 20 dining certificates, plus breakfast. Private dining room and catering available.

Services: *Included in the monthly fee:* Weekly housekeeping and flat-linen services (Plan 1) or bimonthly housekeeping (Plan 2), scheduled transportation, use of laundry rooms,

At additional cost: Beauty/barbershop, guest suites, bank, ice-cream parlor.

INDEPENDENT LIVING HOUSING

Type/size of apartment	*Monthly rental fee**
Studios, 438–480 sq. ft.	$1,285–1,425
1-Bedroom, 600–612 sq. ft.	$1,695–1,800
2-Bedroom, 854 sq. ft.	$2,390

**For double occupancy add $470 to the monthly rental fee. All utilities except telephone included. Fully equipped kitchen, wall-to-wall carpeting, 24-hour emergency call system, individually controlled heating and air-conditioning.*

Activities: Trips to concerts and plays, college courses, painting, ceramics, book discussion groups, current events, cards, movies, entertainment/social hours, theme dinners, excursions.

Availability: Limited.

Health services and rates: Royal Treatment Program: Attendants are available from 7 a.m. to 10 p.m. to assist residents in daily activities.

- 18 Assisted Living units (fee determined by service needed)
  1-Bedroom $2,500–3,000/month

"The Devonshire offers residents the flexibility to be as active or as private as they want to be on a daily basis, with a sense of security that services are available to meet their changing needs."

COVENANT VILLAGE OF NORTHBROOK

2625 Techny Road
Northbrook, IL 60062
(708) 480-6380
Nancy Baughman, marketing director

Type of community: Not-for-profit Continuing Care, modified contract

Accreditation: Continuing Care Accreditation Commission

Five one-story and three two-story apartment buildings, and 48 cottages house Assisted Living and Skilled Nursing facilities, located on a 55-acre campus. Large outdoor recreation area and small lagoon surrounded by overhanging trees and flower gardens provide areas for outdoor enjoyment. A central building serves as the center of activity for the community and houses the beauty/barbershop, spacious dining room, gift shop, creative arts center, woodworking shop, minimart, and auditorium/multipurpose fellowship center. Private garden terrace room is available for residents' use. YMCA and Northbrook Covenant Church are adjacent to campus; Chicago's cosmopolitan center is just minutes away.

Financial plan: Entrance fee plus monthly fee. Entrance fee amortizes at 2% per month of residency.

Ownership and management: Owned by the Evangelical Covenant Church. Operated by Covenant Retirement Communities, which operates 12 retirement communities in six states: California, Washington, Minnesota, Illinois, Connecticut, and Florida. Opened in 1965.

Minimum age: 62 years.

Population: 500+ residents; 70% women, 30% men, 23% couples.

Number of units: 304 Independent Living apartments and 48 cottages; 50 Assisted Living units, 100-bed health center.

Dining plan: Two meals per day (lunch and dinner) included in the monthly fee. Lunch is optional. Private dining room available.

INDEPENDENT LIVING HOUSING

Type/size of unit	*Entrance fee**	*Monthly fee single/double*
Studio, 440–550 sq. ft.	$47,900	$890/N/A
1-Bedroom, 625–650 sq. ft.	$62,000–65,000	$1,052/1,552
2-Bedroom, 672–900 sq. ft.	$82,000–89,900	$1,160/1,685
Custom apartments	Prices available upon request	
Cottages (varying floor-plans)	Prices available upon request	

**For double occupancy add 10% to the entrance fee. All utilities except telephone included. Patio or balcony, wall-to-wall carpeting, 24-hour emergency call system, fully equipped kitchens, individually controlled heating and air-conditioning, satellite TV.*

Services: *Included in the monthly fee:* Parking, flat-linen service, weekly transportation to shopping, free use of washers and dryers. Free membership to north suburban YMCA with swimming pool, indoor walking/jogging track, and other activities.

At additional cost: Private housekeeping, garages, beauty/barbershop, transportation to doctor appointments, guest accommodations.

Activities: Activities director. Creative arts center, woodworking, auditorium/multipurpose fellowship center, weekly chapel services, classes, seminars, Bible study, library, gardening areas, shuffleboard, bowling green, gardening.

Availability: Waiting list varies according to accommodations chosen.

Health services and rates: Emergency and consultative nursing service available. Wellness program. Physical, occupational, and speech therapy.

- 50 Assisted Living apartments
  Studio $82.50/day
- 100-Bed Skilled Nursing facility
  Semiprivate $116.50
  Private $204.88

"Located on 55 beautifully landscaped acres in the suburb of Northbrook, Covenant Village provides easy access to the recreational and cultural resources of the Chicago area. Covenant Village is an accredited Continuing Care community, one of only five facilities in the state that have achieved national accreditation by the Continuing Care Accreditation Commission. This distinction assures consumers that Covenant Village meets and exceeds the highest standards of the industry. Owned by the Evangelical Covenant Church, Covenant Village of Northbrook and the 11 other not-for-profit Covenant retirement communities reflect a 100-year tradition of caring and financial stability."

FRIENDSHIP MANOR

1209 21st Avenue
Rock Island, IL 61201
(309) 786-9667
Penny Harrington, marketing representative

Type of community: Nonprofit Continuing Care, choice of modified or all-inclusive contract

Nestled in a ten-acre, tree-lined residential section of Rock Island, this three-story apartment complex offers Independent Living and Assisted Living apartments, a Skilled Nursing facility, and a chapel all connected by enclosed walkways. Friendship Manor is close to the airport, hotels, shopping centers, and other services.

Financial plan: Entrance fee plus monthly fee or monthly rental. Two entrance fee plans: **1)** Endowment plan: no additional charges for use of the health center. **2)** 90% refundable plan: residents receive ten free days in the health center and then pay the private pay rate minus a 10% discount. The refund is made when the apartment is resold. With the rental plan, residents pay the private pay rate at the health center at all times. A $750 deposit is fully applicable to entrance endowment ($100 is non-refundable processing fee). For those on the rental plan, the security deposit ranges from $2,000 to $4,000 depending upon size of apartment. Tree of Life Endowment assists residents who run out of funds.

Ownership and management: Owned and managed by the International Order of King's Daughters and Sons, Illinois Branch, a nondenominational, non-profit organization. Opened in 1979.

Minimum age: 62 years.

Population: 228 residents; 75% women, 25% men, 20% couples.

Number of units: 221 Independent Living apartments; 34 Assisted Living units, 63 Skilled Nursing beds.

Dining plan: Meals are optional. Noon and evening meals available for $5 each. Private dining room. Tray service.

Services: *Included in the monthly fee:* Biweekly housecleaning, scheduled transportation, flat-linen service, parking, complimentary supply of stationery upon move-in, storage facilities.

At additional cost: Beauty/barbershop, gift shop, banking, washers and dryers, local newspaper delivery, copy machine, notary public, dry cleaning pick-up, postage/package mailing service.

Activities: Crafts studio, hobby/woodworking shop, exercise/game room, library; planned social, cultural, recreational, and spiritual activities; talking books program, big-screen TV-VCR, monthly birthday dinners, style shows.

Availability: Waiting list and future's list. Periodically apartments are available for immediate occupancy.

Health services and rates: Residents who have paid endowment entrance fee pay no additional charges to use the health center. Residents who selected the 90% refundable entrance fee receive ten free days in the health center, after which they pay the rate below minus a 10% discount.

- 34-Bed Assisted Living area
  For monthly rental residents and nonresidents $60/day
- 63-Bed Skilled Nursing facility
  For monthly rental residents and nonresidents $82/day

"Friendship Manor provides a continuum of care with Christian values that has encouraged a sense of community among all residents. Our residents have a strong residents' association that encourages good communication between residents, staff, and the board of trustees. The facility also has a strong Tree of Life Endowment Program. The development committee is chaired by a resident and several residents sit on the committee. The implementation of this development program and endowment was initiated by the commitment of residents to provide benevolent assistance to others."

INDEPENDENT LIVING HOUSING

Type/size of apartment	*Entrance fee 1*	*Monthly fee**	*Monthly rental**
Studio, 405 sq. ft.	$35,640	$657	$665
1-Bedroom, 636 sq. ft.	$63,500	$797	$995
Deluxe 1-bedroom, 810 sq. ft.	$75,500	$797	$995
2-Bedroom, 867 sq. ft.	$79,900	$968	$1,175

**For double occupancy add $400 to the monthly fee. All utilities except telephone included. Wall-to-wall carpeting, individually controlled heating and air-conditioning, cable TV, 24-hour emergency call system.*

CLARK-LINDSEY VILLAGE

101 West Windsor Road
Urbana, IL 61801
(217) 344-2144
Laurie Melchi, residency councellor

Type of community: Nonprofit Continuing Care, modified contract

Located on 30 parklike acres, Clark-Lindsey Village is bordered on the south and east by the 130-acre Meadowbrook Park. Rich farmland close by lends a country atmosphere, while urban advantages are just around the corner. The Independent Living center, health center, and Assisted Living units are housed in connected one- and two-story red brick buildings. The University of Illinois and Parkland Community College offer residents concerts, theater, sports events, and a wide range of courses.

Financial plan: Entrance fee plus monthly fee. A one-time membership fee that is due at the time of application: $1,500 per person.

Ownership and management: Clark-Lindsey Village, Inc. An administrator is under the guidance of a ten-member volunteer board of directors made up of local citizens with specialized knowledge and talents to offer the community. Opened in 1978.

Minimum age: 62 years (if couple, spouse must be at least 55).

Population: 300 residents; 66% women, 34% men, 25% couples. Residents come from varying backgrounds and professions.

Number of units: 154 Independent Living apartments; 25 Assisted Living units, 76 Intermediate and Skilled Nursing facility, 15-bed Alzheimer's unit.

Dining plan: Main meal each day is included in the monthly fee. Additional meals are optional at nominal fee. Private dining room. Special diets are available upon the request of personal physician.

Services: *Included in the monthly fee:* Housekeeping every two weeks, weekly flat-linen service, scheduled transportation, parking.

At additional cost: Convenience store, beauty/barbershop, banking services, private garages, personal laundry facilities.

Activities: Woodworking shop, arts and crafts shop, billiards, Ping-Pong tables, personal garden areas, shuffleboard, croquet, music areas, exercise equipment and classes, literary, music and card groups, lectures, volunteer projects, putting contests.

Availability: Waiting list. Three to six months for one-bedroom; two years for two-bedroom.

INDEPENDENT LIVING HOUSING

Type/size of apartment	*Entrance fee*	*Monthly fee single/double*
Studio, 482 sq. ft.	$26,000	$710/NA
1-Bedroom, 536 sq. ft.	$36,000	$795/1,130
2-Bedroom, 787–875 sq. ft.	$49,000–54,000	$930/975–1,280/1,325
Corner, 950 sq. ft.	$61,000	$1,055/1,405
Deluxe, 1,072–1,269 sq. ft.	$75,000–87,000	$1,180/1,410–1,530/1,760

All utilities except telephone and cable TV included in the monthly fee. Full kitchen with major appliances, wall-to-wall carpeting, individually controlled heating and air-conditioning, 24-hour emergency call system.

Health services and rates: Staffed by experienced nurses and guided by an on-staff director and a hospital-physician advisory board composed of local physicians. Residents of five years or more receive discounted rates for health center.

- 25 Assisted Living units

Resident	$86/day
Nonresident	$96/day

- 76 Nursing beds; 15 Alzheimer's beds

	Intermediate	*Skilled*
Resident	$77/day	$95/day
Nonresident	$87/day	$105/day

Prices are for semiprivate rooms. For private, add $22/day for Intermediate, $27/day for Skilled.

"Clark-Lindsey Village was one of the first communities of its kind and has operated continuously since 1978. Its history is one of an established, populated, functioning, financially sound community."

INDIANA

MEADOWOOD

2455 Tamarack Trail
Bloomington, IN 47408
(812) 336-7060
Jane E. Sefton, marketing director

Type of community: Continuing Care, modified contract

Garden homes and mid-rise apartments are located on 30 rolling acres bordered by a wooded forest preserve and covered scenic walking paths. Meadowood is closely associated with Indiana University and its nationally known school of music in addition to theater, university classes and programs, and sports. Griffy Lake, state parks, and Lake Monroe are all nearby. Indianapolis International Airport is 50 miles away.

Financial plan: Monthly rental fee. Deposit of $1,000 holds apartment or garden home for 30 days, at which time a one-year renewable lease is signed. The $1,000 deposit is a one-time fee that will be returned upon completion of one year of occupancy and expiration of the lease, provided there are no damages or breakages.

Ownership and management: OFC Corporation. Opened in 1982.

Minimum age: 55 years.

Population: 250 residents; 72% women, 28% men, 25% couples.

Number of units: 92 garden homes, 92 mid-rise apartments for Independent Living; 22 Assisted Living units, 25 Skilled Nursing units, 15 comprehensive nursing beds.

Dining plan: Thirty to 31 meals included in the monthly fee. Private dining room. Additional meals available at cost.

INDEPENDENT LIVING HOUSING

Type/size of apartment	*Monthly fee single/double**
Studio, 360 sq. ft.	$729
1-Bedroom, 538–607 sq. ft.	$952–1,093/1,202–1,343
2-Bedroom, 826–887 sq. ft.	$1,250–1,317/1,500–1,567
3-Bedroom, 1,253 sq. ft.	$1,676/1,926
Garden homes	
1-Bedroom, 573–642 sq. ft.	$925–1,059/1,175–1,309
2-Bedroom, 822–934 sq. ft.	$1,211–1,289/1,461–1,539
3-Bedroom, 1,263 sq. ft.	$1,597/1,847

**Water, sewage, trash pickup included in the monthly fee. Fully equipped kitchen. Homes have option of garage or carport, patios that can be screened, glassed, or open. Washer/dryer and dishwashers available for rent.*

Services: *Included in the monthly fee:* Scheduled transportation, monthly housekeeping.

At additional cost: Beauty/barbershop, bank.

Activities: Films, golf outings, university classes, concerts, theater, sporting events, greenhouse/gardens, bus tours, travelogues, croquet, Meadowood Singers, mall walking, bookmobile, bridge, exercise, swimming at the YMCA, lectures.

Availability: Waiting list.

Health services and rates: Allied health staff and director of nursing, along with Bloomington Hospital, offers screening/diagnostic services at discounted fees or at no cost. Complete rehabilitative services, including physical, occupational, respiratory, speech, and hearing therapy. Wellness program.

- 22 Assisted Living units $81/day
- 25 Skilled Nursing beds
  Semiprivate $102/day
  Private $154/day

"Meadowood is closely associated with Indiana University, providing many cultural opportunities for residents. Rand-McNally and the publishers of *Money* selected Bloomington, Indiana, as one of America's top ten cities for retirement living."

FOUR SEASONS RETIREMENT CENTER

1901 Taylor Road
Columbus, IN 47203
(812) 372-8481
Mildred E. Doty, admissions counselor

Type of community: Not-for-profit Continuing Care, modified contract

Accreditation: Continuing Care Accreditation Commission

The community consists of 13 residential wings and an 84-bed health center located on 25 landscaped acres near the east side of Columbus. All wings are single-level design and interconnected with lounges, all under one roof. The brick and steel buildings were designed by Norman Fletcher, Architects Collaborative of Boston. The large A-frame chapel reaches high above the complex. The grounds have been newly landscaped with trees and walking trails. The community is close to several shopping centers, Clifty Creek Center, Fair Oaks Mall, Columbus Center, Eastbrook Plaza, golf courses, restaurants, banks, and other businesses. Two major medical facilities, groceries, and a large hospital are less then a mile away.

Financial plan: Entrance fee plus monthly fee or monthly rental. Entrance fee refundable less amortization rate over a period of 48 months. $250 nonrefundable application fee.

Ownership and management: Owned and operated by Baptist Homes of Indiana, Inc., which also operates Hoosier Village, Indianapolis, and The Towne House, Fort Wayne. Opened in 1967.

INDEPENDENT LIVING HOUSING

Type/size of unit	*Entrance fee**	*Monthly fee**	*Monthly rental*
Studio, 240–336 sq. ft.	$24,000–47,000	$980	$1,475
1-Bedroom, 490–826 sq. ft.	$33,000–58,000	$950–1,005	$1,500–2,010
2-Bedroom, 826–1,060 sq. ft.	$68,000–84,500	$1070–1,195	$1,780–2,125

**For double occupancy add $3,000 to the entrance fee; $255 to the monthly fee. All utilities except telephone included. Fully equipped kitchens, wall-to-wall carpeting, patios, 24-hour emergency call system, cable TV, individually controlled heating and air-conditioning.*

Minimum age: 65 years.

Population: 175 residents; 70% women, 30% men, 20% couples.

Number of units: 95 Independent Living apartments; 84-bed health center.

Dining plan: One meal per day included in the monthly fee. Special diets available.

Services: *Included in the monthly fee:* Biweekly housekeeping, weekly flat-linen service, some transportation.

At additional cost: Personal laundry service, beauty/barbershop, transportation, garages, guest accommodations.

Activities: Full-time activity director. Trips to symphony in Indianapolis, shopping excursions, luncheons out to local and nearby restaurants, day and overnight trips, grocery and pharmacy shopping weekly, library and bookmobile, chapel, many varied programs and demonstrations, birthday party with entertainment monthly, active residents' council, involvement in special marketing events planned quarterly, watercolor painting, organized and spontaneous bridge, canasta and euchre games, Trivial Pursuit weekly.

Availability: Three-month to three-year waiting list.

Health services and rates: Residents receive 60 days free in the health center. Respiratory, physical, occupational, and speech therapy. Some assistance to residents offered in apartments. Pharmacist consultant.

- 84-Bed health center

	Entrance fee resident	*Monthly rental resident*
Semiprivate	$86/day	$99/day
Private	$99/day	N/A

Private suites under construction.

"The privacy and security of the Four Seasons' estate-like complex is complemented by the accessibility of its location near major highways. The exceptional quality of life can be seen throughout the community. Residents love everything being on one floor with an outside door and patio, and they appreciate the interconnecting hallways where they can walk with ease."

CONCORD VILLAGE

6723 South Anthony Boulevard
Fort Wayne, IN 46816
(219) 447-1591
Susan Wolpert, manager

Type of community: Not-for-profit Continuing Care, modified contract

Concord Village is housed in low-rise brick buildings located on a 43-acre campus. Heated corridors connect Concord Village, the chapel, and the Lutheran Home (Assisted Living and Intermediate Nursing). Vegetable and flower gardens are on the grounds. Shopping centers and restaurants are within close proximity. Public transportation stops at the main entrance.

Financial plan: Advance deposit plus monthly fee. Nonrefundable $250 application fee required. Each month a certain amount ($100–250) of the gross monthly rental is deducted from the advance deposit. Remainder of the advance deposit will be returned to the resident upon departure.

Ownership and management: Owned and managed by Lutheran Homes, Inc., affiliated with Lutheran Congregation in Northeast Indiana. Opened in 1978.

Minimum age: 55 years.

Population: 207 residents.

Number of units: 178 apartments; 88 Assisted Living units, 240 Intermediate Nursing beds.

INDEPENDENT LIVING HOUSING

Type/size of apartment	*Advance deposit**	*Monthly fee**
1-Room, 355 sq. ft.	N/A	$415
2-Room, 670 sq. ft.	$39,750	$400
1-Bedroom, 670–905 sq. ft.	$39,750–53,750	$400–465
2-Bedroom, 950–1,541 sq. ft.	$55,750–99,750	$485–730

**All utilities except telephone included. Individually controlled heating, wall-to-wall carpeting, draperies, 24-hour emergency call system. 1- and 2-room mini-apartments have 2-burner stove, refrigerator, garbage disposal. 1- and 2-bedroom apartments have fully equipped kitchen and air-conditioning.*

Dining plan: No meals included in the monthly fee. Noon meal available for additional cost ($4 per meal).

Services: *Included in the monthly fee:* Laundry facilities. Residents of mini-apartments may purchase a full residential service program, which includes weekly housekeeping, routine doctor calls,shampoo/hair set every other week, three meals per day for $18.65 per day.

At additional cost: Beauty/barbershop, maid service, guest accommodations, parking, newspaper delivery, additional storage.

Activities: Ceramics, needlework, billiards, bowling, card parties, trips to cultural and area events, bingo, picnics, theater performances, crafts, progressive dice, Bible study, diner's club, shopping expeditions, exercise, movies, concerts, choir, gardens.

Availability: Units available. Priority waiting list.

Health services and rates: Lutheran Home provides Assisted Living and three levels of Intermediate Nursing. Concord Village residents receive priority. If the resident's advance deposit balance is higher than the deposit required for admission to the health center, the difference will be refunded to the resident. Dentist, podiatrist, ophthalmologist, physical therapy available. Day care also available. Free monthly blood pressure checks. Direct admission to Lutheran Home requires a nonrefundable application fee of $250 plus a choice of two plans: advance deposit plus daily fee or daily fee only.

- 88 Assisted Living Units
  75 Singles, 5 doubles, two 2-room suites

With advance deposit fee*	$48.50/day
With daily fee only	$54.50/day

- 240 Intermediate Nursing beds

	*With advance deposit**	*Daily fee only*
Limited care	$61.50–67.50	$67.50–73.50
Comprehensive Care I	$70.50–76.75	$76.75–82.75
Comprehensive Care II	$79.25–85.25	$85.25–95.75

**Advance deposit fee: $12,000.*

"Lutheran Homes, Inc., is determined to accommodate God's people with a resourceful living experience."

THE TOWNE HOUSE

2209 St. Joe Center Road
Fort Wayne, IN 46825
(219) 483-3116
Evelyn Ross, admissions counselor

Type of community: Not-for-profit Continuing Care, modified contract

Accreditation: Continuing Care Accreditation Commission

This four-story apartment building is located on a wooded 20-acre campus that includes Krause Memorial Park and offers a half mile of paved walkways. Located on Fort Wayne's northeast side, The Towne House offers Independent Living, Assisted Living and a health care center on campus. The community is adjacent to Concordia Seminary; Riviera, Washington Square, and Northcrest Shopping Centers as well as three area hospitals are all nearby. Glenbrook Mall, the largest in the area, is 1 1/2 miles away.

Financial plan: Entrance fee plus monthly fee or monthly rental. Entrance fee is refundable less a monthly percentage amortization over 48 months. $250 application fee.

Ownership and management: Owned and managed by Baptist Homes of Indiana, Inc., which operates two other communities in Indiana: Four Seasons and Hoosier Village. Opened in 1965.

Minimum age: 65 years.

Population: 125 residents; 80% women, 20% men, 15 couples.

Number of units: 125 Independent Living apartments; 99 Assisted Living units, 84-bed health center.

Dining plan: Choice of one, two, or three meals per day. Private dining room available. Special diets accommodated.

Services: *Included in the monthly fee:* Weekly housecleaning, flat-linen service, parking, scheduled transportation.

At additional cost: Beauty/barbershop, personal laundry, carports, transportation, guest accommodations.

Activities: Full-time program director. Movies, concerts, lectures, theater, various outings and tours, ice-cream socials, seminars, picnics, exercise classes, bingo, group walks, bridge, chapel, Bible study, local excursions to the Fort Wayne Philharmonic, the Civic Theater, and the Art Museum, book reviews, continuing education courses, choir, woodworking shop, library, garden club, exercise classes.

Availability: No waiting list at present.

Health services and rates: Medicare-approved health center provides short- and long-term care. Pet therapy, respite care, and family involvement programs offered. Activities director and recreational activities scheduled in health center. The first 60 days of health care for entrance-fee residents is included in their monthly fee. After 60-day period, resident must pay both apartment monthly fee and health center fee unless apartment is vacated (then health center charge only). Therapies available, including music therapy. Daily delivery by pharmacy, audiology screening. Access to three area hospitals.

• 99 Assisted Living units	*Monthly fee**	*Monthly rent**
Studio, 315 sq.ft.	$1,210	$1,700
1-Bedroom, 420–616 sq. ft.	$1,255–1,270	$1,890–2,060
• 84-Bed health center		
Semiprivate	$78/day	$83/day
Private	$95/day	$100/day
Deluxe private	$115/day	$120/day

**Nonresident entrance fees from $22,000 to $35,000. For double occupancy add $3,000 to the entrance fee; $425 to the monthly fee and rent.*

"The mission of The Towne House Retirement Community is to enhance the quality of life for older adults within a secure environment that supports their needs, values, interests, and independence while encouraging personal and spiritual development. The Towne House has earned national accreditation from the Continuing Care Accreditation Commission. This designation assures you that our community is financially sound, offers a complete range of services, and provides a superior lifestyle for residents."

INDEPENDENT LIVING HOUSING

Type/size of unit	*Entrance fee**	*Monthly fee**
Deluxe Yorktown, 630 sq. ft.	$41,000	$955
1-Bedroom, 616 sq. ft.	$44,000–58,000	$965
2-Bedroom, 880–1,232 sq. ft.	$60,000–82,000	$1,060–1,170

**For double occupancy add $3,000 to the entrance fee; approximately $225 to the monthly fee. All utilities except telephone included. Wall-to-wall carpeting, individually controlled heating and air-conditioning, fully equipped kitchens or kitchenettes, 24-hour emergency call system.*

WESLEY MANOR

1555 North Main Street
Frankfort, IN 46041
(317) 659-1811
Wayne McElfresh/Beulah Roustio, marketing
Charles Hefley, vice president of administration

Type of community: Continuing Care, modified contract

Wesley Manor is situated on 53 rolling acres just north of Frankfort. Independent Living residents may select from duplexes, fourplexes, sixplexes, and single-family homes in the Wesley Manor Village. In addition, one-, two-, and three-room apartments are available in the Manor building. The grounds contain an extensive apple orchard, a recently renovated greenhouse, areas for garden plots, beautiful rose gardens, and plenty of airy walkways. Assisted Living and health care center are on campus. Two holes of the Frankfort Golf Course are situated on the Wesley Manor property, allowing residents to play the course at no cost. Located halfway between Lafayette and Indianapolis, the community has easy assess to Chicago. Downtown Frankfort is within easy walking distance. Shopping, theater, Indianapolis Symphony, Purdue University, and various athletic events are nearby.

Financial plan: Entrance fee plus monthly fee. 5% deposit of entrance fee holds unit for 60 days.

Ownership and management: Owned and operated by Wesley Manor, Inc. Opened in 1961.

Minimum age: 60 years.

Population: 366 residents; 70% women, 30% men, 35% couples.

Number of units: 186 Independent Living apartments, 12 sixplexes, 4 fourplexes, 22 duplexes, 36 ranch-style homes; two floors of Assisted Living units in the 80-bed health center.

Dining plan: Three meals per day included in the monthly fee for apartment residents. Other residents are welcome to use dining room for small charge. Private dining rooms available.

Services: *Included in the monthly fee:* Housekeeping, laundry service (for apartment residents), regularly scheduled transportation, washers and dryers. Village residents receive lawn care, snow removal, trash pick-up.

At additional cost: Garages and carports, beauty/barbershop.

Activities: Heated indoor swimming pool, water aerobics classes, well-stocked library, year-round greenhouse, recreation room, bowling alley, ceramics studio, crafts room, photography studio, social center, woodworking shop, art studio, private garden plots, 18-hole golf course, Bible study, worship services, bridge, community tennis courts, needlework and quilting classes, archives, numerous excursions.

Availability: No waiting list at present.

INDEPENDENT LIVING HOUSING

Type/size of apartment	*Entrance fee*	*Monthly fee single/double*
Studio, 405–418 sq. ft.	$15,000–25,000	$1,021/1,766
1-Bedroom, 688–822 sq. ft.	$39,500–49,500	$1,302/2,047
2-Bedroom, 1,088 sq. ft.	$59,500	$1,584/2,329
Village homes		
Sixplex, 1,000 sq. ft.	$30,000	$200/200
Fourplex, 2,000 sq. ft.	$52,000	$200/200
Duplex and single homes	Appraised value	$200/200

All utilities except telephone included for apartments. Cable TV hookup, 24-hour emergency call system, wall-to-wall carpeting, kitchenettes. Village homes have garages.

Health services and rates: Residents can stay at Wesley Manor for 120 days for recuperation from illness or surgery, during the winter months, or just to see if Wesley Manor is the right place for them. This program ("Temporary Loving Care") is offered year-round and entitles visitor to three meals/day, housekeeping, and all in-house activities. Physical therapy center, complete dental and medical unit. If Independent Living residents move into Assisted Living or Skilled Nursing, they pay the monthly fee listed below. Nonresidents pay an entrance fee.

- Assisted Living (2 floors)

	Entrance fee	*Monthly fee**
Studio	$29,500	$1,409
1-Bedroom	$49,500	$1,691

**For double occupancy with only one person requiring care add $745 to the monthly fee; when both persons require care, add $1,130 to the monthly fee.*

- 80 Skilled Nursing beds

	Entrance fee	*Daily fee*
Semiprivate	$20,000	$77
Private	$20,000	$115.50

- Temporary Loving Care

Residential	$41
Assisted Living	$68
Comprehensive health care	$82.50–129

"Wesley Manor is a uniquely special retirement community, offering a wide variety of amenities in an atmosphere of comfort, security, and care. The motto of Wesley Manor is, 'A wonderful place to call home.' "

GREENCROFT

1721 Greencroft Boulevard, Box 819
Goshen, IN 46526-0819
(219) 537-4000
Gene E. Yoder, president

Type of community: Not-for-profit Continuing Care, modified contract

Accreditation: Continuing Care Accreditation Commission

Greencroft's main campus is located on 167 acres; a second facility is located in the neighboring town of Elkhart. Independent Living residences include the condominium-style units of two, three, four, and six apartments arranged in quiet cul-de-sacs throughout the Goshen campus, one- and two-bedroom apartment homes and a nine-story apartment building in downtown Elkhart (previously the historic Hotel Elkhart). Assisted Living apartments and health care facilities offering Intermediate and Skilled Nursing are on campus. A senior center on the Goshen campus provides educational, health and wellness, recreational programs and volunteer and travel opportunities to Greencroft residents and seniors from the surrounding community.

Financial plan: Entrance fee plus monthly fee or monthly rental. Two entrance fee plans: **1)** Life lease payment and monthly fee for Court apartments and Manor IV homes. A portion of the life lease is invested into a fund deposit account, which is later refunded to the resident when the apartment is vacated. The fund deposit amount varies according to your age or that of the younger spouse at the time of the apartment purchase. **2)** Market refund plan. When the resident's apartment is reoccupied, an 80% refund of the apartment's market value is made (as set by the Greencroft Board, based on current market factors). *Note:* Two federally subsidized apartment buildings with apartment homes are available for rent (based on the resident's ability to pay).

Ownership and management: Sponsored by Mennonite Health Services, sponsor of six other continuing care retirement communities in Arizona, Illinois, Kansas, Michigan, and Ohio. Opened in 1967.

Minimum age: 55 years.

Population: 1,050 residents; 75% women, 25% men, 30% couples.

Number of units: 687 Independent Living apartments; 87 Assisted Living apartments, 240-bed health care facility.

Dining plan: Independent Living residents have the option of paying for one meal a day. Private dining room and catering services available.

Services: *Included in the monthly fee:* Shuttle transportation within Greencroft community.

At additional cost: Beauty/barbershop, banking, off-campus transportation, laundry facilities (in apartment buildings).

INDEPENDENT LIVING HOUSING

Court apartments	*Entrance fee 1*	*Monthly fee**	
1-Bedroom, 570–800 sq. ft.	$35,350–48,000	$299–358	
2-Bedroom, 690–1,240 sq. ft.	$41,400–88,300	$321–424	
Manor IV homes			*Monthly rental*
1-Bedroom, 560 sq. ft.	$41,500	$336	$390
2-Bedroom/2-bath 840 sq. ft.	$63,500	$406	$582
2-Bedroom/den, 840 sq. ft.	$63,800	$390	$585

**All utilities except telephone and cable TV included in the monthly fee. Complete kitchens, individually controlled heating and air-conditioning, choice of wallpaper, carpeting, floor coverings. Carports or garages for Court residents.*

The Tower apartments/Elkhart, IN			
Studio, 310–490 sq. ft.	$16,500–31,000	$232–328	$165–280
1-Bedroom, 370–800 sq. ft.	$20,500–51,000	$270–413	$200–445
2-Bedroom, 900 sq. ft.	$59,900	$498	$500

**All utilities except telephone included in the monthly fee. Fully equipped kitchen, wall-to-wall carpeting, sheer draperies, 24-hour emergency call system.*

Activities: Exercise programs, excursions, health spa, woodworking, crafts, special events, concerts, lectures, croquet, library, horseshoes, singing groups, bridge, pinochle, pool, photography club, organ recitals, walking groups, performing arts group, gardening, classes (computers, investing, driving), movies, bingo.

Availability: Waiting list.

Health services and rates: Periodic clinics are available to monitor blood pressure, nutrition, foot care, other preventive services. Physical and speech therapy, dietary services, social services, and pastoral care are available. Personal assistance program provides residents with assistance in their apartments. Parkinson's, Alzheimer's, and grief support groups are available.

- 86 Assisted Living studio apartments (Central Manor)

Single	$1,007–1,053/month
Double occupancy	$1,438–1,484/month

- 240-Bed nursing facility

	Intermediate Nursing	*Skilled Nursing*
Semiprivate	$89/day	$119–143/day
Private	$110–115/day	$143/day

"At Greencroft, we're dedicated to providing quality lifestyle alternatives that meet our residents' changing needs. Residents enjoy a wealth of exciting social, cultural, and recreational programs, comfortable living facilities, beautifully landscaped grounds, and a caring, friendly staff that is available when they need assistance. A senior center is located on campus adjacent to the Goshen College campus."

GREENWOOD VILLAGE SOUTH

295 Village Lane
Greenwood, IN 46143
(317) 881-2591
Brenda Thompson, marketing director

Type of community: Not-for-profit Continuing Care, modified contract

Two apartment buildings (Independent Living at The Arms and Assisted Living at The Manor), individual cottages, and a 95-bed health center are located on a 58-acre suburban campus that offers two ponds and one mile of walking paths. The community is close to many shopping areas, professional services, recreational facilities, and social and cultural activities as well as Community South, Johnson County, and St. Francis hospitals. The Towers is a separate HUD-subsidized Independent Living facility that is also part of Greenwood Village South.

Financial plan: Entrance fee plus monthly fee. Monthly rent for The Towers.

Ownership and management: Owned by local not-for-profit organization with board of directors made up of area professionals. Managed by the Life Care Services Corporation, which manages over 50 retirement communities in the United States. Opened in 1962.

Minimum age: 62 years.

Population: 500 residents; 75% women, 25% men, 20% couples.

Number of units: 169 Independent Living apartments,174 HUD-subsidized apartments, and 58 cottages, 60 Assisted Living suites, 95-bed nursing facility.

Dining plan: Three meals per day are included in the monthly fee for apartments. Private dining room and special diets available.

Services: *Included in the monthly fee:* For apartments: housecleaning, flat-linen service, scheduled transportation, laundry facilities.

At additional cost: Beauty/barbershop, bank, sundries shop, individual limousine service.

INDEPENDENT LIVING HOUSING

Type/size of unit	*Entrance fee single/double**	*Monthly fee single/double**
Studio, 325–367 sq. ft.	$19,300–19,900/ N/A	$908–912
Alcove, 402 sq. ft.	$21,000/23,900	$934
1-Bedroom, 486–734 sq. ft.	$36,900–46,958/39,600–49,396	$979–1,583
2-Bedroom, 811 sq. ft.	$55,862/59,042	$1,073/1,605
Cottage, 1,300–2,500 sq. ft.	$76,426–89,900	$255–434

**All utilities except telephone included for apartments. Individually controlled heating and air-conditioning, 24-hour emergency call system, wall-to-wall carpeting, kitchenettes. Cottages have fully equipped kitchens and utilities are not included.*

Activities: Full-time social director. Cookouts, parties, croquet, shuffleboard, fitness room, exercise classes, card room with full kitchen, book reviews, arts and crafts, chapel, Bible study, woodworking shop, greenhouses, various local outings to areas of interest, billiards room, library, painting, movies, ice-cream socials, bingo, residents' council.

Availability: Up to two year waiting list, depending upon unit size. $1,000 deposit required.

Health services and rates: Health center with medical director. Hydrotherapy available. Medical clinic, physician office visits three days weekly.

- 60 Assisted Living units

	*Entrance fee**	*Monthly fee**
Studio	$22,200	$1,219

**For double occupancy add $3,400 to the entrance fee, $604 to the monthly fee.*

- 95 Intermediate and Skilled Nursing beds

	Residents	*Nonresidents*
Intermediate	$74/day	$83/day
Skilled		
Semiprivate	$82/day	$92/day
Private	$108/day	$120/day

"Greenwood Village South is the south side's premier retirement community. It is the only community offering the full Continuum of Care ranging from Independent Living to Assisted Living and Intermediate and Skilled Nursing care."

THE FORUM AT THE CROSSING

8505 Woodfield Crossing Boulevard
Indianapolis, IN 46240
(317) 257-7406
Kristie Campbell, leasing counselor

Type of community: Continuing Care, modified contract

Located on ten acres, the three-story brick building houses Independent Living, Ambassador suites, Assisted Living, and Skilled Nursing. Grounds feature an outdoor patio, fountain, benches, and walkways. The community is located two minutes away from major shopping centers and 20 minutes from downtown Indianapolis.

Financial plan: Monthly rental plan.

Ownership and management: Managed by The Forum Group, Inc.,owner/manager of 27 retirement communities in the United States. The Forum

INDEPENDENT LIVING HOUSING

Type/size of apartment	*Monthly rental fee**
1-Bedroom, 587–788 sq. ft.	$1,475–2,020
2-Bedroom, 884–1,385 sq. ft.	$2,030–3,560

**For double occupancy add $375 to the monthly fee. All utilities except telephone included. Wall-to-wall carpeting, fully equipped all-electric kitchen, cable TV, individual temperature control, 24-hour emergency call system.*

Group has been developing and managing the highest quality retirement communities for over 25 years. Opened in 1986.

Minimum age: 62 years.

Population: 190 residents; 80% women, 20% men, 7% couples.

Number of units: 99 Independent Living apartments; 18 Ambassador service apartments, 14 Assisted Living suites, 60 nursing beds.

Dining plan: One meal per day included in the monthly fee. Private parties can be accommodated in special section of dining room or multipurpose room.

Services: *Included in the monthly fee:* Weekly housekeeping and flat-linen services, scheduled transportation, lighted parking.

At additional cost: Beauty/barbershop, gift shop, garages, guest accommodations.

Activities: Bridge and other games, movies, trips (symphony, theater, shopping), travelogues, exercise class, library, chapel, greenhouse/garden plots, crafts room, monthly theme parties.

Availability: Limited.

Health services and rates: Residents receive 15 credit days per year in the health care center, up to a lifetime maximum of 45 days. Ambassador services, including supervision of medication and assistance with daily life and chores, are available in apartments at additional cost. Physical, occupational, and speech therapy available on-site.

- 14 Assisted Living units

Suite	$92/day

- 60-Bed health center

	Intermediate Nursing	*Skilled Nursing*
Semiprivate	$96/day	$107/day
Private	$124/day	$139/day

"The Forum is the only community in Indianapolis that has five different levels of service, all under one roof."

HOOSIER VILLAGE

5300 West 96th Street
Indianapolis, IN 42628
(317) 873-3349
Amy Snyder, admission counselor

Type of community: Not-for-profit Continuing Care, modified contract

Accreditation: Continuing Care Accreditation Commission

Hoosier Village is nestled in the northwest corner of Indianapolis on 150 acres of beautiful grounds covered with pines and native hardwoods. It is a natural retreat that combines the comfort and pace of country living with the opportunities and amenities of the city nearby. Walking trails on the tailored lawn lead to several private fishing ponds. Although the Hoosier Village campus is a natural setting, it is not isolated. Nearby are many stores, restaurants, a hospital, and theaters to which transportation is provided. A variety of single-level floor plans including homes, doubles, and

INDEPENDENT LIVING HOUSING

*Residence apartments**	*Entrance fee*	*Monthly fee*	*Monthly rental*
Studio, 300 sq. ft.	$25,000	$975	$1,530
1-Bedroom, 450–675 sq. ft.	$33,000–45,000	$1,085–1,200	$2,035–2,150
2-Bedroom/patio, 840 sq. ft.	$52,000	$1,345	$2,445
Duplex			
2-Bedroom double, 1,178 sq. ft.	$50,000	$515	$1,435
Homes			
2-Bedroom, 1,900+ sq. ft.	$65,000	$570	N/A
*Deercrest apartments***			
1-Bedroom, 672 sq. ft.	$50,000	$650	$1,405
2-Bedroom, 948–1,007 sq. ft.	$61,000–66,000	$750	$1,575–1,655
2-Bedroom/den, 1,221 sq. ft.	$78,000	$850	$1,855

**For double occupancy in Residence apartments add $3,000 to the entrance fee and $210 to the monthly fee; add $250 to the monthly rental fee. **For double residence in Deercrest apartments add $3,000 to the entrance fee and $120 to the monthly fee and the monthly rental fee. All utilities except telephone included. Wall-to-wall carpeting, 24-hour emergency call system, draperies, carpeting, individualy controlled heating and air-conditiong. Two-bedroom double has private garage, courtyard, full kitchen. Deerfield apartments have spacious patio, full kitchen, private entrance.* Note: *home residents pay electric.*

apartments are available for Independent Living. The Residence Building contains Assisted Living units. On-site health center offers short- and long-term nursing care.

Financial plan: Entrance fee plus monthly fee or monthly rental fee. Prorated 48-month refund on entrance fees. $250 application fee.

Ownership and management: Baptist Homes of Indiana, Inc., owner and manager of The Townhouse, Fort Wayne, and Four Seasons, Columbus. Opened in 1952.

Minimum age: 65 years.

Population: 185 residents; 75% women, 25% men, 20% couples.

Number of units: 26 Independent Living apartments (26 additional under construction), 14 duplexes, and 10 homes; 68-bed health center.

Dining plan: One meal per day included in the monthly fee for those in Residence apartments. Meal purchase plans available for Deercrest, duplex and home residents (one meal, $130; two meals, $260; three meals, $350 per person). Private dining room available.

Services: *Included in the monthly fee:* Housekeeping and flat-linen services for Residence apartments, parking.

At additional cost: Gift emporium, branch banking, beauty/barbershop, post office, limousine service, shopping service, carports.

Activities: Public lounges, activity rooms, exercise room, library, chapel. Nearby colleges offer fine arts presentations, as well as excursions to area theaters, libraries, museums, symphony concerts, and operatic performances.

Availability: Waiting list.

Health services and rates: Entrance fee residents receive 60 days of free health care and a reduced rate thereafter. Residents on the monthly rental fee plan must pay both apartment and health center costs if they enter the health center and want to keep their apartment. Registered nurses and visiting or on-call physician available 24 hours each day. Services available for additional fee include diagnostic laboratory, X ray, dental, physical/occupational/speech therapy, podiatry. Respite care for short stays.

- Assisted Living services offered in Residence Building in addition to monthly fee $270
- 70-Bed nursing facility*
  Entrance fee/monthly rental residents
  Semiprivate $87/97/day
  Private $97/117/day

**Rooms may be decorated with residents' furnishings and personal possessions.*

"Hoosier Village is the only Continuing Care retirement community in the Indianapolis area to have earned accreditation by the National Continuing Care Accreditation Commission. This designation is an endorsement of Hoosier Village's fiscal responsibility, complete range of services, and superior quality of lifestyle. Hoosier Village is also licensed by the Indiana State Department of Health for both residential living and comprehensive nursing care."

MARQUETTE MANOR

8140 Township Line Road
Indianapolis, IN 46260
(317) 875-9700
Pam Anderson, marketing director

Type of community: Not-for-profit Continuing Care, modified contract

Independent Living apartments are housed in a brick building that also contains a bank, beauty/barbershop, gift shop, women's dress shop, library and chapel, on a 46-acre campus in a suburban setting. Forty-eight cottages surround the main building, which makes an ideal walking area. A 78-bed health center is on-site. The community is located close to Castleton Square, Lafayette Square, and Glendale shopping centers, professional services, recreational facilities, churches, social and country clubs, and St. Vincent's and Humana hospitals.

Financial plan: Entrance fee plus monthly fee. Two plans: **1)** Endowment plan: prorates 90% of refund over 48 months. **2)** Return of capital plan: refunds 90% of entrance fee.

INDEPENDENT LIVING HOUSING

Type of unit	*Entrance fee 1/2*	*Monthly fee**
Efficiency	$26,650–29,210/46,100–50,530	$765
Studio	$33,450–38,420/57,870–66,470	$765–778
1-Bedroom	$43,400–53,340/75,080–92,280	$795
2-Bedroom	$65,770–90,630/113,780–156,790	$842–1,365

**For double occupancy add $406 to the monthly fee. All utilities except telephone included. Fully equipped kitchen, individually controlled heating and air-conditioning, 24-hour emergency call system, wall-to-wall carpeting, balcony (optional), cable TV service.*

Ownership and management: Owned by a local not-for-profit corporation. Retirement Living, Inc. Managed by Life Care Services Corporation, which has been instrumental in the planning, development, or management of more than 50 retirement communities throughout the United States. Opened in 1981.

Minimum age: 62 years.

Population: 324 residents; 75% women, 25 % men, 14% couples.

Number of units: 247 Independent Living apartments and 48 cottages; 78-bed health center.

Dining plan: One meal per day included in the monthly fee. Special diets available through registered dietitian at no charge. Meal delivery service. Private dining room.

Services: *Included in the monthly fee:* Biweekly housekeeping, weekly flat-linen service, scheduled transportation, lighted off-street parking.

At additional cost: Carports and garages, beauty/barbershop, valet services, laundry facilities, guest accommodation.

Activities: Full-time social director. Activities range from bingo to cruises. Meeting rooms, arts and crafts facilities, library, black-and-white photo lab, chapel, woodworking, painting, volunteering, billiards, meeting room, game room, gardening, ceramics, Claypool Dress shop (a women's dress shop).

Availability: Waiting list for all 2-bedrooms: 2-bedroom, six months; larger 2-bedroom, one year; cottages, one year.

Health services and rates: Health center attached to the Manor provides Intermediate and Skilled Nursing. Physical, occupational and speech therapy services available. Pharmaceutical services. Assistance in living available for extra fee.

- 50 Assisted Living units $50–80/day
- 78-Bed nursing facility
  Semiprivate $90/day
  Private $155/day

Note: *For those entering health center directly, a deposit of 30 times the daily rate is required.*

"The Marquette Manor Foundation, Inc., is a separate, volunteer, not-for-profit foundation that acts as an impartial and confidential body to review applications for hardship support. The first objective of the foundation is to provide assistance to residents who may need financial aid to remain in the Manor. Our prospects are primarily obtained by resident referrals."

WESTMINSTER VILLAGE

1120 Davis Avenue
Terre Haute, IN 47802
(812) 232-7533
Anthony Mundell, executive director

Type of community: Not-for-profit Continuing Care, modified contract

Westminster Village is housed in a seven-story brick apartment complex located on 55 acres south of Terre Haute. The grounds feature walking and bicycling paths, a fishing pond, and a gazebo. The neighborhood offers excellent shopping, medical facilities, banking, entertainment, and an adjacent golf course.

Financial plan: Entrance fee plus monthly fee. Three plans: **1)** Endowment: entrance fee is amortized at a rate of 2% per month. **2)** Return of Capital: a higher entrance fee, which is 75% refundable. **3)** Amortized endowment: 10% of the entrance fee is required as down payment. The balance can be paid over a 120-month period at 9% interest rate.

Ownership and management: Owned by Westminster Village of Terre Haute, Inc., a

INDEPENDENT LIVING HOUSING

Type/size of unit	*Entrance fee 1/3**	*Entrance fee 2**	*Monthly fee**
Studio, 420 sq. ft	$29,950	$41,500	$569
1-Bedroom, 490 sq. ft.	$35,700–37,800	$49,900–52,500	$614
2-Bedroom, 700–1,100 sq. ft.	$53,550–68,000	$75,100–96,600	$663–777

Note: *Monthly fee for Plan 3 ranges from $341 to $784 higher than the monthly fees listed above. *For double occupancy add $289 to the monthly fee. All utilities except telephone included. Fully equipped kitchen, wall-to-wall carpeting, sheer draperies, individually controlled heating and air-conditioning, 24-hour emergency call system.*

not-for-profit organization whose board of directors is comprised of professionals from the Terre Haute community. Managed by Life Care Services Corporation of Des Moines, Iowa. LCS has more than 30 years of experience in the development and management of over 50 retirement communities in the United States. Opened in 1981.

Minimum age: 55 years.

Population: 250 residents; 76% women, 24% men, 20% couples.

Number of units: 244 Independent Living apartments; 38 Assisted Living apartments, 78-bed nursing facility.

Dining plan: One meal per day is included in the monthly fee. Additional meals available at cost. Special diets can be accommodated. Tray service.

Services: *Included in the monthly fee:* Biweekly apartment cleaning, weekly flat-linen service, scheduled transportation.

At additional cost: Beauty/barbershop, sundry shop, carports.

Activities: Gardening, shuffleboard, painting, ceramics, woodworking shop, motor coach trips, country fair, concerts, card games, arts and crafts center, library.

Availability: Limited.

Health services and rates: Health center with emergency, recuperative, and long-term care, and therapy services. Residents on Plan 1 or Plan 2 receive 15 free days of health care per year.

- 38 Assisted Living apartments

Studio	$1,630/month
1-Bedroom	$1,665/month
2-Bedroom	$1,770–1,800/month

**For double occupancy add $375 to monthly fee.*

- 78-Bed health center

	Intermediate Nursing	*Skilled Nursing*
Semiprivate	$81/day	$90/day
Private	$101/day	$110/day

"Westminster Village has an ideal location; it is adjacent to a golf course, near the largest shopping center between Terre Haute and St. Louis, and close to a large regional airport."

PINES VILLAGE

3303 Pines Village Circle
Valparaiso, IN 46383
(219) 465-1591
Jackie Holmes, retirement counselor

Type of community: Not-for-profit Continuing Care, modified contract

This two-story brick apartment complex on a 14-acre campus features a small pond, flower and vegetable

INDEPENDENT LIVING HOUSING

Type/size of unit	*Entrance fee 1/2**	*Monthly fee 1/2**
Efficiency, 420 sq. ft.	$35,250–37,100/1,765–1,855	$631–646/984–1,016.50
1-Bedroom, 504–630 sq. ft.	$45,580–49,290/2,280–2,465	$658–679/1,114–1,172
2-Bedroom, 735–861 sq. ft.	$61,850–66,780/3,095–3,340	$755–785/1,374–1,453

*Note: *Entrance fee rates lower and monthly fees rise in proportion to entering age of resident. For double occupancy add $231 to the monthly fee. All utilities except telephone included. Fully equipped kitchens, 24-hour emergency call system, individually controlled heating and air-conditioning, wall-to-wall carpeting, cable TV.*

gardens, walks, and a general parklike atmosphere. Independent Living, Assisted Living, and health care center are on-site. Major shopping mall is a few hundred feet away, and a university is close by in Valparaiso. The community offers easy access to miles of beaches along the shores of Lake Michigan. Indiana Dunes National Lakeshore State Park, many county and city parks, vineyards, orchards, barns and livestock zoos, museums, and historical homes are all nearby. Chicago and South Bend are one hour away.

Financial plan: Entrance fee plus monthly fee. Two plans: **1)** Standard entrance fee plus monthly fee. Includes lifetime nursing care benefits of 1.5% of entrance fee, paid directly to Skilled Nursing when resident moves into the health center. Refund of entrance fee, less 10%, declines over 60 months. **2)** Lower entrance fee plus higher monthly fee. Under Plan 2, qualified residents may convert to Plan 1 after three months.

Ownership and management: Owned and operated by Indiana Retirement Communities, Inc., a not-for-profit organization with a local board of directors. Opened in 1983.

Minimum age: 60 years.

Population: 119 residents; 75% women, 25% men, 10% couples.

Number of units: 111 Independent Living apartments; 40 Assisted Living suites, 190-bed health center.

Dining plan: One meal per day included in the monthly fee. Private dining room and tray service available.

Services: *Included in the monthly fee:* Open parking, housekeeping, flat-linen service, scheduled transportation, personal laundry facilities, guest rooms.

At additional cost: Garages, beauty/barbershop.

Activities: Social director. Library area, hobby/crafts room, woodworking shop, multipurpose room, card shop, gardening, shopping trips, dinners out, theater, lunches, trips to other cities.

Availability: Six-month waiting list. $250 places future resident on preferred waiting list.

Health services and rates: Residents on Plan 1 receive lifetime nursing-care benefits of 1.5% of the entrance fee they paid. This amount (ranging from $249 to $945) is payable monthly directly to Whispering Pines Health Care Center once the resident moves in. Intermediate, Skilled, and hospice care and 350-bed Porter Memorial Hospital are on campus. All levels of therapy are offered.

- 40 Assisted Living apartments
  Efficiency/1-Bedroom $1,740–1,940/month
- 190-Bed health center

	Intermediate Nursing	*Skilled Nursing*
Semiprivate	$75/day	$90/day
Private	$85/day	$100/day

"Pines Village's mission is to strive to keep the spirit of life alive."

IOWA

GREEN HILLS

2200 Hamilton Drive
Ames, IA 50010
(515) 296-5000 or (800) 336-8883
Elin Herrman, marketing director

Type of community: Equity-ownership Continuing Care, modified contract

Green Hills is located on 30 acres at the southwest corner of Highway 30 and Elwood Drive and bordered by a wooded area. The community is comprised of Independent Living apartments in an eight-story tower, brick townhomes with attached garages, and a health center. Residences have expansive views of the rolling countryside and the nearby Iowa State University campus.

Financial plan: Purchase fee plus monthly fee.

Ownership and management: Owned by the residents and the not-for-profit University Retirement Corporation, a subsidiary of the Achievement Foundation of the Iowa State Alumni Association. Green Hills is managed by the Life Care Services Corporation of Des Moines, Iowa, developer and manager of over 50 retirement communities in the United States. Opened in 1986.

Minimum age: 55 years.

Population: 162 residents; 67% women, 23% men, 35% couples.

Number of units: 60 Independent Living apartments and 40 townhomes; 40-bed health care center.

INDEPENDENT LIVING HOUSING

Type/size of apartment	*Purchase fee*	*Monthly fee*
1-Bedroom, 600–720 sq. ft.	$85,000–95,000	$380–450
2-Bedroom, 910–1,110 sq. ft.	$105,000–125,000	$560–700
3-Bedroom, 1,400 sq. ft.	$150,000	$841–887
Townhomes		
1-Bedroom, 920–1,130 sq. ft.	$125,000	$328–402
2-Bedroom, 1,180–1,350 sq. ft.	$135,000–187,000	$460–525

All utilities included except long-distance telephone and electricity. Individually controlled heating and air-conditioning, fully equipped kitchen, high-quality appliances, 24-hour emergency call system. Some town homes have lofts, some have basements; all have patios.

Dining plan: No meals included in the monthly fee. Lunch is served daily, and dinner is served two evenings per week for additional fee.

Services: *Included in the monthly fee:* Bimonthly housekeeping, flat-linen service, all exterior and some interior maintenance, scheduled transportation.

At additional cost: Beauty/barbershop.

Activities: Woodworking, arts and crafts, gardening, library, exercise classes, music program, discussion groups, scheduled shopping trips and outings, easy access to Iowa State University events, theater, concerts, sports, lectures, and classes.

Availability: Limited.

Health services and rates: Independent Living residents receive three free days per year in the health care center plus 12% discount from the regular daily rate charged to nonresidents. A medical director is on call 24 hours a day.

- 40-Bed health care center (residential care and Intermediate Nursing)

Semiprivate	\$80/day
Private	\$93/day
Private suite	\$105/day

"At Green Hills, residents own their own Continuing Care retirement condominium or townhome. They hold the title; so if they elect to mortgage, they can take the tax write-offs. Residents are also building equity and either they or their estate can benefit from the sale."

HERITAGE HOUSE

1200 Brookridge Circle
Atlantic, IA 50022
(712) 243-1850
Dennis Crouse, administrator

Type of community: Continuing Care, modified contract

Set on 17 landscaped acres, Heritage House is composed of a seven-story main building that contains one- and two-room Independent Living units, a health center, and a "Helpful Living" floor. The two-story brick Brookridge Apartments are attached to the main building by a covered corridor and contain one- and two-bedroom Independent Living apartments. Each floor has its own visiting lounge and kitchenette. The complex features beautiful views of surrounding grounds and the city of Atlantic. Independent Living, Assisted Living, and Skilled Nursing are available. The local YMCA is one block away; nearby are the Community Arts Council and an 18-hole golf course. Atlantic is less than an hour's drive from Omaha/Council Bluffs and less than $1^1/_2$ hours from Des Moines.

Financial plan: Entrance fee plus monthly fee or monthly fee only. Two entrance fee plans: **1)** Refundable entrance fee: 90% refund within the first 90 days, thereafter refund is reduced by 1% per month with total amortization over $7^3/_4$ years. **2)** Nonrefundable entrance fee: lower entrance fee and no refund.

Ownership and management: Wesley Retirement Services, Inc., which owns and manages four retirement communities in Iowa. All communities are related to the Iowa Conference of the United Methodist Church. Opened in 1963.

Minimum age: 60 years.

Population: 150 residents; 73% women, 27% men, 10% couples.

Number of units: 31 Independent Living apartments, plus 45 one- and two-room living units; 15 Assisted Living rooms, 46-bed Skilled Nursing facility.

Dining plan: Three meals per day included in the monthly fee for main building one and two rooms without kitchenette. Choice of one, two, or three meals for two rooms with kitchen and apartments. Private dining room.

INDEPENDENT LIVING HOUSING

Main building apartments	*Entrance fee 1/2*	*Monthly fee*	*Monthly fee only*
1-Room, 275 sq. ft.	$16,500/13,500	$764	$989
1-Room, large 350 sq. ft.	$20,000/17,250	$764	$1,038
2-Room, 535 sq. ft.	$31,000/23,250	$1,120	$1,545
2-Room/kitchen, 550 sq. ft.	$34,500/26,000	$913*	$1,388*
Apartments			
1-Bedroom, 763 sq. ft.	$41,325/N/A	$464*	$1,014*
2-Bedroom, 915 sq. ft.	$50,075/N/A	$500*	N/A

Note: *Prices listed are for single occupancy. Double occupancy is available for additional cost. *Based on one meal per day (1- and 2-room not asterisked have three meals per day included in the monthly fee). All utilities are included in the monthly fee. Individually controlled heating and air-conditioning, 24-hour emergency call system. Apartments have fully equipped kitchens.*

Services: *Included in the monthly fee:* Scheduled transportation, weekly or biweekly housekeeping depending on plan selected.

At additional cost: Gift shop, laundry facilities, covered parking.

Activities: Arts and crafts, day trips, shuffleboard, bingo, exercise program, coffee hour, card and game room, movies, men's pool, horseshoes, picnics.

Availability: Waiting list.

Health services and rates: Residents who are on Plan 1 are allowed 10 free days of health center care annually and a total of 90 days lifetime. Plan 2 residents are allowed five free days of health care annually, up to 45 days maximum in a lifetime. Physical therapy is available at additional cost.

- 15-Bed Assisted Living floor
  - 1-Room $982/month
  - 2-Room $1,322/month
- 46-Bed Skilled Nursing facility $55/day

"Our goal is to provide services to older adults in a Christian, caring way to enhance their physical, social, spiritual, and emotional health and to promote optimum independence and an active lifestyle. We have a solid, stable, caring group of employees and volunteers that share this goal. The friendly, small-town atmosphere of Atlantic, Iowa, is part of what makes Heritage House such a wonderful place to live and enjoy life."

THE WESTERN HOME

420 East 11th Street
Cedar Falls, IA 50613
(319) 277-2141
Avis Handorf, director of admissions

Type of community: Nonprofit Continuing Care, modified contract

The Western Home, which is made up of four 4-story brick buildings surrounded by trees and lawns, offers Independent Living, residential care, and Intermediate Nursing. Across the street is a community park with a nine-hole golf course. The community is located five blocks from downtown Cedar Falls.

Financial plan: Entrance fee of $2,000 for one person or $3,500 per couple. 50% percent of the fee is refundable if the resident voluntarily leaves the facility within 90 days.

INDEPENDENT LIVING HOUSING

Type of room	*Monthly fee single/double*
1-Room	$850–1,044/1,448–1,484
Suites	$1,145/1,400

All utilities except telephone included. All rooms have draperies, wall-to-wall carpeting, 24-hour emergency call system, cable TV. Air conditioner and room refrigerator each additional $50 annually.

Ownership and management: Nonprofit agency with heritage in the Evangelical United Brethren and the United Methodist Church. Opened in 1912.

Minimum age: 60 years.

Population: 331 residents; 80% women, 20% men, 10% couples.

Number of units: 221 Independent Living apartments; 34 Residential Care rooms, 127 Intermediate Nursing beds.

Dining plan: Three meals per day included in the monthly fee. Tray service available for additional fee. Kitchenettes located throughout buildings.

Services: *Included in the monthly fee:* Weekly housekeeping and laundry, open parking.

At additional cost: Bed making, garage rental, guest accommodations.

Activities: Gardening plots, annual carnival with auction, annual crafts and baked goods bazaar, ice-cream socials, concerts, celebrations for Mother's and Father's days, birthday parties, men's and women's breakfasts, movies, plays, day trips, exercise classes, sing-alongs, games, reading groups, coffee and discussion sessions, religious study groups.

Availability: Varies with level of care.

Health services and rates: Medication is monitored at no additional charge.

- 34 Residential Care rooms (assistance with bath, shampoo, dressing)
  Semiprivate $1,122–1,358/month
  Private $1,268–1,667/month
- 100-Bed Intermediate Nursing facility
  Semiprivate $78–83/day
  Private $82–87/day
- 20 Skilled Nursing beds
  Semiprivate and private $95/day
- Respite care available on temporary basis (up to 30 days) $75/day

"The Western Home staff members are committed to providing a comfortable, friendly retirement home and health care services as needed for people physically and emotionally able to live independently. An important part of life at The Western Home are the activities, and the major goal of the activity department staff is to keep residents active at the highest level possible in all dimensions of life: physical, psychological, social, and spiritual."

THE METH-WICK COMMUNITY, INC.

1224 13th Street, N.W.
Cedar Rapids, IA 52405
(319) 365-9171
Martha Allbee, director of sales

Type of community: Not-for-profit Continuing Care, modified contract

Accreditation: Continuing Care Accreditation Commission

INDEPENDENT LIVING HOUSING

Greenwood Terrace apartments	*Entrance fee 1*	*Monthly fee single/double*
Efficiency, 530 sq. ft.	$53,110–63,750	$308/369
1-Bedroom, 742 sq. ft.	$80,591–82,947	$369/443
2-Bedroom, 1,060 sq. ft.	$101,988–106,984	$432/518
3-Bedroom, 1,272 sq. ft.	$114,031–117,391	$493/591

**No utilities except water included in the monthly fee. Fully equipped kitchen, washer/dryer, individually controlled heating and air-conditioning, 24-hour emergency call system, porches.*

The Manor apartments	*Entrance fee 1/2**	*Monthly fee single/double*
Studio, 300 sq. ft.	$39,950/23,000	$496
Jumbo studio, 345 sq. ft.	$44,490/26,400	$565/666
1-Bedroom, 600 sq. ft.	$62,950/40,000	$879/948
1-Bedroom, 740 sq. ft.	$72,500/46,100	$879/948

All utilities except long-distance telephone included. Studios do not have kitchens; 1-bedroom suites have optional kitchenette; 1-bedroom has full kitchen. Garages with automatic door openers are optional.

Brendelwood duplex townhomes	*Entrance fee 1**	*Monthly fee single/double**
2-Bedroom, 1,250 sq. ft.	$135,880–141,880	$249/299
2-Bedroom, 1,515 sq. ft.	$154,730–160,730	$275/325

No utilities included. Optional features: gas fireplace, enclosed patio or deck, shutters.

Situated high on a hilltop on 60 rolling, landscaped acres, this community offers four-story apartment buildings and duplex townhomes and a variety of Independent Living options. The city of Cedar Rapids offers many cultural and entertainment possibilities as well as golf courses, the Cedar River, and more than 70 parks for fishing and boating. Kirkwood Community College and two fully accredited four-year colleges offer continuing education opportunities.

Financial plan: Entrance fee plus monthly fee. Two plans: **1)** Entrance fee is refundable minus 10% to 28% depending upon the length of residency. **2)** Nonrefundable entrance fee option for Manor residents. $500 application fee.

Ownership and management: Not-for-profit corporation with 18-member volunteer board of trustees. Affiliated with the United Methodist Church. Opened in 1961.

Minimum age: 62 years (spouse must be 55 years).

Population: 262 residents; 75% women, 25% men, 25% couples.

Number of units: 140 Independent Living apartments and 12 townhouses; 22 Assisted Living rooms, 65 nursing beds.

Dining plan: Greenwood/Brendelwood: No meals included in the monthly fee, but may be purchased. Manor: Studio residents are required to select two- or three-meals/day plan ($337 or $431 added to monthly fee). Manor residents in apartments with kitchen facilities may select the one-meal/day plan at $243/month additional. Catering available.

Services: *Included in the monthly fee:* Annual housecleaning for Greenwood/Brendelwood residents; weekly housekeeping and flat-linen services, scheduled transportation for Manor residents.

At additional cost: Personal laundry service, housekeeping for Greenwood and Brendelwood; beauty/barbershop, gift shop, post office, guest accommodations.

Activities: Exercise room and classes, van trips for entertainment/shopping, arts and crafts, flower/vegetable garden beds, game room with billiards table, shuffleboard courts, Bible study, library.

Availability: Waiting list for Manor one-bedroom and Greenwood one- and two-bedrooms.

Health services and rates: Weekly doctor clinic with medical director. All residents receive five free days per year in health center. Manor residents are entitled to 18 trips to and from medical appointments per year. Therapy and rehabilitative services. Community care services provided in resident's apartment (medication assistance, companion, etc.), charged by the hour.

- 22 Assisted Living rooms — $19/day added to monthly fee
- Respite care (short-term stays) — $49/day
- 65-Bed licensed nursing facility

Semiprivate	$72/day
Private	$81/day
Private plus	$88/day
Private deluxe	$97/day

"Because Meth-Wick is a fee-for-service Continuing Care community, residents only pay for the services they use. At Meth-Wick, we know that everyone's different. Some people want to cook their own meals, while others appreciate the convenience of having someone else tackle the cooking chores. We've created various 'bundles' of services that residents can choose from so that they can tailor their choices to their individual lifestyle."

CALVIN MANOR

4210 Hickman Road
Des Moines, IA 50310
(515) 277-6141
Richard J. Shaffer, executive director

Type of community: Nonprofit Continuing Care, modified contract

Calvin Manor is housed in a three-story apartment building set on four acres of landscaped grounds in a residential area of northwest Des Moines. Independent Living, Assisted Living, and nursing care are on-site. The community offers easy access to downtown Des Moines, local transportation, Des Moines Municipal Airport, Civic Center, Veterans' Auditorium, Des Moines Art Center, Science Center and Botanical Center, Iowa Historical Society, churches, parks, and municipal golf course. Beaverdale neighborhood shopping complex is only a few blocks to the north. Drake University, which has a performing arts center, Olmstead Center for lectures, and a fieldhouse and stadium for sports events, are nearby.

Financial plan: Entrance fee plus monthly fee. Refund of entrance fee less initial 20% and 1% per month of residency.

Ownership and management: Operated as an agency of the Synod of Lakes and Prairies, Presbyterian Church. Opened in 1965.

Minimum age: 60 years.

Population: 119 residents; 85% women, 15% men, 5% couples.

Number of units: 110 Independent Living apartments; 18 Assisted Living units, 59-bed health center.

Dining plan: Three meals per day included in the monthly fee. Tray service and special diets available.

Services: *Included in the monthly fee:* Weekly housekeeping, personal and flat-linen service, free use of small laundry rooms on each floor, off-street

INDEPENDENT LIVING HOUSING

Type/size of unit	*Entrance fee*	*Monthly fee**
Studio, 281–350 sq. ft.	$16,500–20,000	$747–833
Alcove, 400–485 sq. ft.	$23,500–28,500	$917–1,047
1-Bedroom, 500–680 sq. ft.	$30,000–39,000	$1,073–1,308

**For double occupancy add $310 to the monthly fee. All utilities except telephone included. Individually controlled heating and air-conditioning, small picture window, 24-hour emergency call system. Kitchenettes are located at several points throughout the building for residents' use.*

parking, use of washer and dryer, scheduled transportation.

At additional cost: Bed making, escort services, garages, beauty/barbershop, guest rooms.

Activities: Activity director. Trips, one or two events almost every day for education and enjoyment, hobby and recreation rooms, library, residents' council, weekly worship services, Bible study, woodworking, weaving, gardening.

Availability: Two-month waiting list for apartments.

Health services and rates: Residents receive ten free days per year in health care center, if ordered by physician. Intermediate Nursing offered. Physical therapy center; various therapies offered. Home health care available. Social worker on-site.

- 18 Assisted Living $47/day
- 59-Bed health care center
  Semiprivate $71/day

"A quality assurance coordinator ensures that the goals of resident care are consistent, achievable, and optimal and meet with residents' satisfaction. The quality assurance program coordinates research and development, identifies opportunities as well as problems, and addresses consumer expectations and technical performance within Calvin Manor."

HEATHER MANOR

600 East Fifth Street
Des Moines, IA 50316
(515) 243-6195
Evelyn Gore, marketing director

Type of community: Nonprofit Continuing Care, all-inclusive contract

Offering spectacular views of the river, this twin-towered 12-story contemporary apartment complex is located on 4.5 acres across the river from Des Moines's downtown business district and the Capitol and offers beautifully appointed public rooms and a panoramic view of the Des Moines skyline from the dining room. Independent Living, Assisted Living services, and a nursing facility are available. The community is minutes from the city's famed Art Center, Veterans' Auditorium, legitimate theater, dinner theater, civic center, botanical center, extensive downtown climate-controlled skywalk system, and the state Capitol.

Financial plan: Entrance fee plus monthly fee. Deposit equals 10% of entrance fee and ensures reservation for 90 days.

Ownership and management: Owned by the Iowa State Education Association and managed by Life Care Services, which manages 50 communities in the U.S. Opened in 1970.

Minimum age: 62 years (if couple, spouse may be younger).

Population: 110 residents; 83% women, 17% men, 6% couples. Because Heather Manor is sponsored

INDEPENDENT LIVING HOUSING

Type/size of apartment	*Entrance fee*	*Monthly fee single/double*
Studio, 367 sq. ft.	$30,000	$944
1-Bedroom, 521 sq. ft.	$47,500	$1,028/1,603
Custom 1-bedroom, 582 sq. ft.	$52,500	1,037/1,629
Deluxe 1-bedroom, 735 sq. ft.	$67,500	$1,059/1,655
Custom 2-bedroom, 812 sq. ft.	$79,500	$1,344/2,066

All utilities except telephone included. Basic cable TV, individually controlled heating and air-conditioning, fully equipped kitchens, 24-hour emergency call system.

by the ISEA, some persons have incorrectly assumed that only retired teachers are accepted. In fact, residents represent all vocations and come from all parts of the United States.

Number of units: 112 Independent Living apartments; 44 Skilled Nursing beds.

Dining plan: Choice of one meal per day included in the monthly fee. Special diet and room tray service is available. Private party rooms.

Services: *Included in the monthly fee:* Twice daily shopping trips, thrice weekly grocery store trips, biweekly trips to two major shopping malls, doctor and dental appointments by private limousine, biweekly housekeeping, weekly flat-linen service, personal laundry facilities.

At additional cost: Beauty/barbershop, guest accommodations, carports.

Activities: Television lounge, library, terrace-level recreation rooms, bridge, afternoon teas, morning coffees, lectures, films, birthday and anniversary celebrations, hobbies, games and crafts, piano, organ, outside social, travel, recreational and educational trips.

Availability: Three of the six floor plans have waiting lists.

Health services and rates: All fees for health services, with the exception of doctors, discount prescriptions through dispensary, and podiatrist, are covered under resident's entrance fee and monthly fee. Physical therapy is also available. There is an extra charge for a private room.

- Assisted Living services available in resident's apartment — $10/hour for regular services, $22/hour for all services
- 44-Bed nursing facility Nonresidents — $85/day

"For 22 years, Heather Manor's philosophy has been to provide residents with a beautiful private home without any of the cares of home ownership and with all the amenities expected in fine hotels and condominiums. The community also provides a full range of activities so that residents can be as active as they wish and maintain physical and mental health as long as possible. This philosophy seems to be proven by the fact that more than one-fourth of the new residents became interested through a present resident."

FRIENDSHIP HAVEN

South Kenyon Road
Fort Dodge, IA 50501
(515) 573-2121
Michael Libbie, director of development

Type of community: Not-for-profit Continuing Care, modified contract

Located on 40 acres atop a bluff overlooking the city of Fort Dodge, Friendship Haven is bordered on the south

INDEPENDENT LIVING HOUSING

Type/size of cottage	*Entrance fee*	*Monthly fee**
1-Bedroom, 800–1,000 sq. ft.	$35,000	$375
2-Bedroom, 1,200–1,600 sq. ft.	$40,000–55,000	$385
3-Bedroom, 1,350 sq. ft.	$50,000	$425

**For double occupancy add $130 to the monthly fee. All utilities except telephone included. Fully equipped kitchen, wall-to-wall carpeting, draperies, 24-hour emergency call system, individually controlled heating and air-conditioning.*

by Highway 20 and on the north by a large wooded area where deer are often seen. Friendship Haven is the largest private retirement complex in Iowa. Townhouses and two four-story brick apartment buildings contain Independent Living. Assisted Living and nursing facility are on-site.

Financial plan: Entrance fee plus monthly fee.

Ownership and management: Related by faith to the United Methodist Church. Opened in 1950.

Minimum age: 62 years.

Population: 615 residents.

Number of units: 44 Independent Living cottages; 294 Assisted Living apartments, 241-bed nursing facility; 44-bed Alzheimer's unit.

Dining plan: Three meals a day included in the monthly fee.

Services: *Included in the monthly fee:* Weekly housekeeping and flat-linen services, scheduled transportation, parking.

At additional cost: Beauty/barbershop, guest accommodations.

Activities: Activities director. Library, trips, concerts, civic events, bingo, movies, games, writing classes, nearby community college offering continuing education classes, chapel.

Availability: Waiting list for townhouses 10 to 12 years; Assisted Living six months to two years.

Health services and rates: Independent Living residents receive a $3 per day credit in the health center. Full program of professional services offered. Adjacent to hospital and medical center. Physical therapy department with pool and spa. Alzheimer's disease and related disorders unit.

- 294 Assisted Living units
  - Double $1,370/month
  - Single $685/month
- 241 Nursing beds
  - 4-Bed room $45/day
  - Semiprivate $48–56/day
  - Private $51–59/day
- 44-Bed Alzheimer's unit
  $66–81/day

"Friendship Haven has been involved in retirement living for more than 40 years. Our family environment means that caring is a way of life. Our facilities, services, and professional staff are prepared to help solve the problems that concern you most."

HALCYON HOUSE

1015 South Iowa Avenue
Washington, IA 52353
(319) 653-7264
John Nye, administrator

Type of community: Nonprofit Continuing Care, modified contract

Halcyon House is a campus-style complex of three- and four-story modern brick apartment buildings and a health center linked by covered walkways and

INDEPENDENT LIVING HOUSING

Type/size of apartment	*Entrance fee 1/2*	*Monthly fee**	*Monthly fee only**
Studio, 400 sq. ft.	$19,000/22,670	$522	$638
1-Bedroom, 800 sq. ft.	$33,000/37,050	$771	$701/747
2-Bedroom, 1,200 sq. ft.	$49,000/53,850	$1,080	$979/1,018

**Prices listed have one meal included in the monthly fee. All utilities except telephone included. Cable TV, wall-to-wall carpeting, 24-hour emergency call system. Additional monthly charge for property taxes (studio, $11; 1-bedroom, $32; 2-bedroom, $53).*

surrounded by lawns, trees, and resident gardens. Independent Living, Assisted Living, and Skilled Nursing are available. Located at the edge of Washington in a residential neighborhood, the community is within a block of Washington County Hospital.

Financial plan: Entrance fee plus monthly fee or monthly fee only. Two entrance fee plans: **1)** Nonrefundable entrance fee. **2)** Refundable entrance fee is amortized over 7¾ years, during which period there is a refund available. A Good Samaritan Fund exists to assist those whose funds become depleted.

Ownership and management: Owned and managed by Wesley Retirement Services, Inc., and South Iowa Methodist Homes, Inc., which owns and manages four other communities in Iowa. Affiliated with the Iowa Conference of the United Methodist Church. Opened in 1959.

Minimum age: 55 years.

Population: 150 residents.

Number of units: 90 Independent Living apartments; 14 Assisted Living rooms, 29-bed health center.

Dining plan: Choice of no meals or one meal included in the monthly fee. Additional meals available. All meals are served family style. Special diets with doctor's orders.

Services: *Included in the monthly fee:* Weekly or bimonthly housekeeping, depending on plan selected, community minibus for shopping trips, reserved parking, personal laundry facilities.

At additional cost: Beauty/barbershop, guest accommodations.

Activities: Television lounge, library, recreation rooms, bridge clubs, afternoon teas, morning coffees, lectures, films, birthday and anniversary celebrations, hobbies, games, arts and crafts, piano, organ, church services, gardening.

Availability: Waiting list.

Health services and rates: There has been a moratorium on guest (nonresident) admissions for several years because the health center has been filled with residents. Physical therapy and whirlpool baths available at additional cost.

- 14 Assisted Living units*

Single room	$1,818/month	$210/day
2-Room suite	$1,573–2,241/month	$230/day

**Applications may be made directly to Assisted Living with residents receiving priority.*

- 29-Bed Intermediate Nursing facility

Double	$58.25/day
Single	$65.50/day

"Deciding how to spend your retirement years is a major step. Unfortunately, too many people postpone this decision until they are no longer sufficiently independent to enjoy the benefits that a retirement community has to offer—or the one of their choice has a long waiting list. It is important to plan so you can direct your own future. In a continuing care retirement community, you never again have to leave home. Halcyon House is a place for those who plan ahead and come to enjoy the full benefits of the community."

FRIENDSHIP VILLAGE

600 Park Lane
Waterloo, IA 50702
(319) 291-8100
Velda Phillips, administrator

Type of community: Not-for-profit Continuing Care, all-inclusive contract

Friendship Village consists of a three-story apartment building of brick and wood construction, a health center, and separate garden apartments all on a 25-acre parklike campus. Residential structures are nestled into the landscape that features trees, gardens, a lake, and three courtyards. The community is ten miles from the University of Northern Iowa. The Waterloo–Cedar Falls community provides opportunities for various arts and cultural activities. City parks, public golf courses, three area hospitals, Waterloo Municipal Airport, and Crossroads Shopping Center are all nearby. The community is close to Interstate 380 and U.S. Highway 20 and a half block from Covenant Medical Center. Many physician and dental offices are located in the surrounding residential neighborhood.

Financial plan: Entrance fee plus monthly fee. Two plans: **1)** Nonrefundable. **2)** Estate refund. With estate refund, entrance fee is higher and refunded less 1% per month of residency or 11% of entrance fee, whichever is greater.

Ownership and management: Owned by local interfaith evangelical, not-for-profit corporation, Friends of Faith Retirement Home, Inc. Managed by local, not-for-profit interfaith board of directors. Opened in 1968.

Minimum age: 62 years.

Population: 360 residents; 75% women, 25% men, 17% couples.

Number of units: 295 Independent Living apartments; 67-bed health center.

Dining plan: Three meals per day included in the monthly fee for studios; one meal per day for all other units. Special diets, tray service, and private dining room available.

INDEPENDENT LIVING HOUSING

Type/size of unit	*Entrance fee 1/2*	*Monthly fee**
Studio, 287 sq. ft.	$24,000/35,750	$825
Alcove, 480 sq. ft.	$37,500–43,000/51,000–58,750	$805
1-Bedroom, 576 sq. ft.	$49,500–57,000/66,250–76,500	$830
2-Bedroom, 864 sq. ft.	$62,000–71,500/81,500–93,750	$855
Garden apartment, 750 sq. ft.	$69,000/86,750/91,750–117,250	$880

Custom apartments also available. Prices upon request.
**For double occupancy in studio add $495 to the monthly fee; all others add $380 to the monthly fee. All utilities included. Fully equipped kitchen (except in efficiencies), individually controlled heating and air-conditioning, 24-hour emergency call system, wall-to-wall carpeting, cable TV.*

Services: *Included in the monthly fee:* Housecleaning, flat-linen service, scheduled transportation, parking.

At additional cost: Beauty/barbershop, guest accommodations.

Activities: Three full-time social directors. Meeting rooms, activities and crafts areas, party facilities, library, woodworking shops, game room, walking paths, tours, lectures, musical programs, films, holiday and birthday festivities, exercise rooms, vespers, billiards, bridge tournaments, shuffleboard, picnics, symphony and theater outings, chorus, men's fellowship group, women's luncheon organization, theater party, volunteering, bingo, baking, music classes, sing-alongs, resident councils, support groups, family council.

Availability: 150 persons on waiting list at present. Length of wait depends on size and availability of unit desired.

Health services and rates: Unlimited nursing care in semiprivate room included in the resident's monthly fee. If resident desires private room, the difference between semiprivate and private room ($5) must be paid by resident. Therapy services available at additional charge. Companion placement service available through Friendship Village social work department at additional cost.

- 67-Bed health center

"Friendship Village is a life care retirement community offering a comfortable, secure living environment with long-term nursing care provided as part of the package. The 67-bed health center is Medicare-certified and therefore qualified to provide a skilled level of care. Health center nurses respond to emergency calls from the apartments, and staff is also available to assist with non-emergency needs, wellness, and teaching. The campus is attractive with ample well-landscaped grounds and attractively appointed common areas. Residents are encouraged to maintain an independent lifestyle via support services available."

KANSAS

SALINA PRESBYTERIAN MANOR

2601 East Crawford
Salina, KS 67401
(913) 825-1366
Rosella Riblett, director of marketing

Type of community: Not-for-profit Continuing Care, modified contract

Salina Presbyterian Manor is located on 40 acres, 11 of which are landscaped. A six-story building houses one- and two-bedroom Independent Living apartments; efficiencies and deluxe one-bedroom units are located in the two-story connecting wing. Duplexes are arranged in a cul-de-sac close to the main facility. Two hospitals, several facilities providing mental health services and counseling, and more than 60 physicians are all within the locale of the community. Nine modern shopping centers, many restaurants and nightclubs, four movie theaters, the Salina Bicentennial Center, civic orchestra, community theater, art center, museum, chorale, Municipal Concert Band, four local colleges, and 50 churches are all in and around Salina. Recreational opportunities in the area include YMCA, YWCA, three golf courses, two bowling alleys, seven swimming pools, eight tennis court areas, and numerous parks. Municipal golf course and new Airport Park with senior citizens exercise area are located directly across from the Manor.

INDEPENDENT LIVING HOUSING

Type/size of apartment	*Entrance fee 1/2*	*Monthly fee*	*Monthly rent**
Efficiency, 400 sq. ft.	$24,400/32,500	$557	$881
1-Bedroom, 550 sq. ft.	$35,000/46,700	$591	$1,063
Deluxe 1-bedroom, 800 sq. ft.	$48,800/65,100	$703	$1,356
2-Bedroom, 750 sq. ft.	$46,700/62,300	$664	$1,283
Deluxe 2-bedroom, 1,250 sq. ft.	$74,250/99,000	$788	$1,772

**For double occupancy add $197 to the monthly fee. All utilities except telephone and cable TV included. Wall-to-wall carpeting, kitchenette or kitchen, individually controlled heating and air-conditioning, cable TV (optional), 24-hour emergency call system.*

Type/size of duplex	*Entrance fee 1/2*	*Monthly fee*	*Monthly rent*
1-Car garage, 1,292 sq. ft.	$77,500/103,300	$565	$1,245
2-Car garage, 1,415 sq. ft.	$84,000/112,000	$593	$1,347

Fully equipped kitchens, garages, walk-in closet, utility room with washer and dryer, central heating and air-conditioning, cable TV (optional), wall-to-wall carpeting, 24-hour emergency call system, rear patios with privacy fence and individual garden plot.

Financial plan: Entrance fee plus monthly fee or monthly rental. Two entrance fee plans: **1)** Life use fee, 80% of which is amortized over a ten-year period; 20% is nonrefundable. **2)** Estate preservation fee, 75% of which is refundable regardless of length of stay; 25% is nonrefundable. Resident may choose to pay an entrance fee at time of occupancy, which reduces the monthly fee by $47 for resident's entire tenure at the community.

Ownership and management: Owned and operated by Presbyterian Manors of Mid-America, Inc. Opened in 1980.

Minimum age: 65 years.

Population: 160 residents; 75% women, 25% men, 5% couples.

Number of units: 64 Independent Living apartments and 10 duplexes; 18 Assisted Living units, 60-bed health center.

Dining plan: One meal per day is included in the monthly fee for apartment residents. Meals optional for duplex residents. Tray service available at extra cost. Dietary department on site. Selective menus permit individual preference options.

Services: *Included in the monthly fee:* Free use of laundry facilities located on each floor, scheduled transportation, off-street parking.

At additional cost: Beauty/barbershop, covered parking, housekeeping and laundry, transportation to professional appointments.

Activities: Two full-time activity directors. Library and reading room, chapel and multipurpose room, recreational areas, lounge areas, gardening, residents' council, exercise groups, card games, Trivial Pursuit, bingo, crafts, book reviews, slide presentations, talks, discussion groups, monthly potluck supper, Bible study, dining out, concerts, theater outings, occasional day trips, exercise equipment, walking paths, shuffleboard, croquet, horseshoes, golf (directly across the street).

Availability: Short waiting list for the apartment and duplex units. $500 nonrefundable application processing fee required for the waiting list.

Health services and rates: Residents receive 12 days each year of health care at no extra charge. Licensed nurses, restorative aides, certified medication aides, and certified nursing assistants are available at all times. Restorative services include physical, occupational, speech, and audiology therapists who develop individual plans for residents. Recreational therapy, Assisted Living services, home health agency (offering health care in the home during short-term illness) all available.

- 18 Assisted Living units*
  Efficiency $1,813/month
- 60-Bed health center*
  Semiprivate $66.55/day for residents
  Private $88.55/day for residents

**Direct admission entrance fee to Assisted Living and health center is $5,000.*

"The residents of Salina Presbyterian Manor have made both a personal and financial commitment to the Manor. The management, in turn, has made a commitment to the residents to operate the facility in a fiscally sound manner. The Manor is an ecumenical retirement community and welcomes persons of all faiths. Living in a community of persons with shared interests and concerns as well as the security of a protective environment makes this life-style most appealing. The city of Salina has a healthy, four-season climate contributing to longer life expectancy than the national average. Currently, 26.1% of the Salina population is over 50 years of age."

EMPORIA PRESBYTERIAN MANOR

2300 Industrial Road
Emporia, KS 66801
(316) 343-2613
Cathy Harding, marketing representative

Type of community: Not-for-profit Continuing Care, modified contract

Emporia Presbyterian Manor is composed of six duplex villa units and three four-story apartment buildings plus a 60-bed health center. The 17-acre campus is beautifully landscaped with a small pond and vegetable, fruit, and flower gardens. Emporia has a population of 28,000.

Financial plan: Entrance fee plus monthly fee or monthly rental. Two entrance fee plans: **1)** Life use fee: 20% nonrefundable; 80% amortizes over period of ten years. **2)** Estate preservation plan: 25% is nonrefundable; the remaining 75% is returned to resident or resident's estate upon withdrawal. A nonrefundable $500 processing fee is required for entrance to the residential and health care areas.

Ownership and management: Owned and operated by Presbyterian Manors of Mid-America, Inc., owners and operators of 18 retirement communities located in Kansas and Missouri. Opened in 1985.

Minimum age: 65 years (or disabled).

Population: 131 residents; 88% women, 12% men, 5% couples.

Number of units: 6 duplex villa units and 69 apartments in Independent Living; 60-bed health center.

Dining plan: One meal per day included in the monthly fee (for apartments only). Special diets available. Tray service offered at extra charge. Private dining room available.

Services: *Included in the monthly fee:* Scheduled transportation, once-a-month housekeeping, parking, laundry facilities.

At additional cost: Weekly or daily housekeeping services, beauty/barbershop, covered parking, laundry service.

Activities: Library, classes, bingo, manicures, zoo trips, "stamps-on-wheels," exercise class, crafts club, church service videos. Off-campus activities include the Learning Connection (classes and scheduled activities and additional fee paid by the Manor).

Availability: Waiting list varies according to accommodations chosen.

Health services and rates: Residents receive 12 days free of charge in health center (not including

INDEPENDENT LIVING HOUSING

Type/size of unit	*Entrance fee 1/2*	*Monthly fee**
Studio, 379 sq. ft.	$25,000/33,300	$521
1-Bedroom, 574 sq. ft.	$35,000/46,700	$565
2-Bedroom, 779–902 sq. ft.	$52,000–65,000/ 69,300–86,700	$616–639
Villas		
2-Bedroom, 1,300 sq. ft.	$63,500/84,700	$408

Note: *Monthly rental also available at the following prices: studio, $924; 1-bedroom, $1,120; 2-bedroom $1,540–1,820; 2-bedroom villa, $1,439. *For double occupancy add $358 to the monthly fee or monthly rent. Apartments have 24-hour emergency call system, individually controlled heating and air-conditioning, fully equipped kitchen, wall-to-wall carpeting, balcony or patio, walk-in closets (except in studios), cable TV (optional).*

supplies, physician fees, or prescriptions). Home health department offers basic health care, extended health care by a registered nurse, and outpatient physical therapy. Home health services available at extra cost are: registered nurse supervisory visit, registered nurse assessment, tray delivery, medicine setup, injections, home health aide, clinical visits, whirlpool, special transportation, and lab work.

• 60-Bed health center

	Intermediate Nursing	*Skilled Nursing*
Semiprivate	$65/day	$75/day
Private	$79/day	$88/day

"Emporia Presbyterian Manor's philosophy is based on the tradition of caring."

WESLEY TOWERS

700 Monterey Place
Hutchinson, KS 67502
(316) 663-9175
Sonja Albers, admissions director

Type of community: Not-for-profit Continuing Care, modified contract

This community is made up of the three-wing, five-story Wesley Towers, two-story Wesley Manor, one-level Asbury Apartments, and Wesley and Aldersgate Drive duplexes in addition to an Assisted Living center and a health center, all located on a 75-acre campus. The apartments, Assisted Living center, and health center are connected by enclosed walkways. The grounds feature a private park and arboretum, indoor walking trails, and two garden plots. Nearby are Alco Plaza and Northgate Shopping Centers, Kansas State Fairgrounds, Hutchinson Community College, YMCA, Kansas Cosmosphere and Space Center, sports arena, leisure art center, convention hall auditorium, Carey Park and golf course, Prairie Dunes Club and golf course, Highlands Club and golf course, and Hutchinson's Municipal Airport, as well as various area churches.

Financial plan: Entrance fee plus monthly fee. $500 deposit upon application, refundable if decision to live at Wesley Towers is withdrawn. Duplexes offer 85% refund of value of unit upon vacating.

Ownership and management: Sponsored by the Kansas West Conference of the United Methodist Church. Managed by 24-member board representing the community and the Kansas West Conference of the United Methodist Church. Opened in 1969.

INDEPENDENT LIVING HOUSING

Type/size of apartment	*Entrance fee*	*Monthly fee*
Congregate living		
1-Room, 280–352 sq. ft.	$2,500	$799–979
2-Room, 476–632 sq. ft.	$2,500	$1,183–1,483
3-Room, 690–840 sq. ft.	$2,500	$1,563–1,810
4-Room, 970 sq. ft.	$2,500	$1,971
Independent Living		
2-Room, 575–700 sq. ft.	$2,500	$790–942
Patio homes, 1,055 sq. ft.	$78,000	$160+*
Duplexes, 1,150–1,550 sq. ft.	$85,000–120,000	$240+*

**For monthly fee for homes/duplexes add 1/360 of 85% of the value of the unit to the basic fee each month. Apartments have lighted carport, cable TV, patio or balcony, 24-hour emergency call system, wall-to-wall carpeting, fully equipped kitchens. Duplexes/patio homes have private garages.*

Minimum age: None.

Population: 330 residents; 75% women, 25% men.

Number of units: 137 Independent Living apartments, 42 duplexes, 4 patio homes; 60-bed Assisted Living center, 70-bed health center.

Dining plan: One meal per day included in the monthly fee for congregate living units. Meals for those in Independent Living or extra meals are optional. Special diets accommodated.

Services: *Included in the monthly fee:* Services for Independent Living: lawn care, snow removal, transportation to doctors' appointments.

At additional cost: Beauty/barbershop, housekeeping and laundry, guest accommodations.

Activities: Library, exercise room/therapeutic pool, woodworking shop, swimming pool, chapel, crafts room, carpentry shop, meeting rooms, welcoming parties for new residents, exercise classes, games, art classes, craft bazaars, lectures, concerts, movies, picnic outings, trips to restaurants, plays and museums, residents' council, choir.

Availability: Waiting list varies according to size of unit.

Health services and rates: Licensed Intermediate and long-term nursing care facility on site. Physical, occupational, and speech therapies; audiology, dentistry, and dietary service available. Temporary admission to health center or Assisted Living available at substantially reduced rates.

- 60-Bed Assisted Living center
  - Double $64.75–71.25/day
  - Single $72.75–79.25/day
- 70-Bed health center
  - Semiprivate $73.75–79.25/day
  - Private $87.25–93.25/day

"Wesley Towers is located on a 75-acre campus with 330 residents and 190 employees. The community continues to grow with the building of duplexes and modifications being made to the health care wing to accommodate individuals with dementia."

NEWTON PRESBYTERIAN MANOR

1200 East Seventh Street
Newton, KS 67114
(316) 283-5400
Mary Jane Fitts, marketing director

Type of community: Not-for-profit Continuing Care, modified contract

The main apartment building houses Independent Living garden apartments, Assisted Living units, and health care center; the separate three-story Broadway apartment building and 11 individual cottages are also located on the 30-acre campus. All buildings are brick and situated on beautifully landscaped grounds.

Financial plan: Entrance fee plus monthly fee or monthly rent. Two entrance fee plans: **1)** Life use fee: Refundable less 20% at occupancy and 10% per year thereafter. **2)** Estate plan fee: 75% refundable at any time.

Ownership and management: Owned by Presbyterian Manors, Inc., which owns 14 other manor communities throughout Kansas and Missouri. Managed by Presbyterian Manors of Mid-America, Inc. Opened in 1948.

Minimum age: 65 years.

Population: 175 residents; 76% women, 24% men, 10% couples.

Number of units: 47 Independent Living apartments and 11 cottages; 55 Assisted Living units, 40-bed health center, 20-unit special care section.

Dining plan: Meals are optional.

Services: *Included in the monthly fee:* Laundromat.

At additional cost: Beauty/barbershop, housekeeping service, scheduled transportation.

Activities: Residents' council, exercise classes, spiritual life program, bus trips, community outings, arts and crafts, horticulture, music programs.

Availability: Limited. $3,000 entrance fee required for the waiting list. Fee is refundable, less $500.

Health services and rates: Residents receive 12 days per year free health care in health center. Physical and occupational therapists, audiologist, and psychologist available. Music and horticultural therapists on-site. Specially designed special care unit, opened in 1986, has a secured area allowing freedom of movement and an enclosed courtyard to encourage walking for those with Alzheimer's and related disorders.

- Respite care $46.65/day
- 55 Assisted Living units
  Private room $1,352–1,394/month
  Single $1,892/month
  Double $1,350 per person
- 40-Bed health center; 20-unit special care section
  Semiprivate $82/day
  Private $94/day

"The Manor is proud of its 45-year history of providing quality care in a Christian environment. The 30-acre campus creates a wonderful home for our residents. The Apple-a-Day preschool on site allows residents involvement in intergenerational programs."

INDEPENDENT LIVING HOUSING

Garden apartments	*Entrance fee 1/2**	*Monthly fee**	*Monthly rent**
Studio, 470 sq. ft.	N/A	N/A	$764
1-Bedroom, 664 sq. ft.	$32,000/42,700	$473	$941
2-Bedroom, 712 sq. ft.	$42,000–45,000/ 56,000–60,000	$546	$1,140
Broadway apartments			
1-Bedroom, 445 sq. ft.	$21,500–28,000/ 28,700–37,300	$388–407	$649–770
2-Bedroom, 1,050 sq. ft.	$41,000/54,700	$425	$965
Cottage	Variable	$194	$952
Duplex	Variable	$194	$789

**All utilities except telephone included. Wall-to-wall carpeting, 24-hour emergency call system, fully equipped kitchens, cable TV, laundry facilities. Balconies in Broadway apartments.*

Ruth, 82 years

Sherwood Oaks, Cranberry Township, Pennsylvania

"I have a limited income and wanted to find a community I could afford and still have money to travel and see my children, who are in Cleveland, Chicago, and Michigan."

Ruth moved into Sherwood Oaks nine years ago at the behest of her brother-in-law and sister, who live in Pittsburgh and thought it would be the perfect place for her to retire. She grew up in the Pittsburgh area, returned to vacation every summer, and had friends and family in the area. In fact, she knew some of the people (local residents) who had helped start Sherwood Oaks and were living in the community.

But Ruth said it wasn't until 1986, when she was lying in her apartment in Chicago with a broken leg, that she knew it was time to move. She looked at a few communities in the Chicago area but she had grown tired of the cornfields and telegraph poles of Illinois and missed the hills of Pittsburgh. "I had my application in and had paid an application fee," says Ruth, "and there was only one studio apartment available, which I took immediately."

As a retired program director in Special Education in Illinois, Ruth has a limited income from her pension, Social Security (hers and from her husband, who died 30 years ago), and modest investments. She was very concerned about finding a place that would allow her to live within her means. "I have a limited income and wanted to find a community I could afford and still have money to travel and see my children, who are in Cleveland, Chicago, and Michigan."

Continuing Care with an all-inclusive contract was the perfect answer for Ruth because all services, including unlimited health care, are covered by her monthly fee, meaning there are no surprises. "The only things besides the monthly fee that I pay for are my long-distance telephone calls; everything else is included. Because Sherwood Oaks is Continuing Care with an all-inclusive contract, each resident receives an income tax deduction, because we are paying for future medical care. Many of us, myself in particular, have other deductions as well."

At Sherwood Oaks Ruth finds herself surrounded by many old friends, several of whom she went to grade school with in Pittsburgh.

Ruth's advice: "Personally, I don't think you need to follow your children. Many people do, but to me, my kids deserve to have their own lives; they should not be sitting around worrying about their mother. My children, to this day, are very thankful that I am here. They know I'm taken care of."

THE FORUM AT OVERLAND PARK

3501 West 95th Street
Overland Park, KS 66206
(913) 648-4500
Tamara Galliher, leasing counselor

Type of community: Continuing Care, choice of modified or all-inclusive contract

The three-story brick-and-frame traditional-style structure is designed to blend with the local architecture and to create a feeling of residential elegance both inside and out. Carefully selected furnishings grace the common areas. Independent Living apartments plus Assisted Living and a nursing facility are offered. Located in an established neighborhood, The Forum offers convenient access to several nearby shopping centers.

INDEPENDENT LIVING HOUSING

Type/size of apartment	*Entrance fee*	*Monthly fee**	*Monthly rental fee**
1-Bedroom, 650–800 sq. ft.	$49,500	$950	$1,970
2-Bedroom, 903–1,300 sq. ft.	$69,500–109,500	$1,350–1,650	$2,595

**For double occupancy add $450 to the monthly fee. All utilities except telephone included. Fully equipped all-electric kitchen, wall-to-wall carpeting, individually controlled heating and air-conditioning, 24-hour emergency call system.*

Financial plan: Entrance fee plus monthly fee or monthly rental fee. The entrance fee is amortized over 50 months at a rate of 2% per month.

Ownership and management: The Forum Group, Inc., which has 25 years of experience in managing retirement communities with 27 communities in the United States. Opened in 1989.

Minimum age: 62 years.

Population: 129 residents; 74% women, 26% men, 19% couples.

Number of units: 117 Independent Living apartments; 30 Assisted Living units, 60-bed nursing facility.

Dining plan: 30 meals per month are included in the monthly fee.

Services: *Included in the monthly fee:* Weekly housekeeping and flat-linen services, scheduled transportation, laundry facilities.

At additional cost: Beauty/barbershop.

Activities: Full-time program director. Exercise classes, arts and crafts, Bible study, bingo, movies, outings to local and popular landmarks, guest lectures, classes and meetings, folk dances, billiards room, greenhouse, library.

Availability: Limited.

Health services and rates: Residents who pay an entrance fee plus monthly fee receive unlimited care at the health care center. Rental residents pay per rates listed below.

- 30 Assisted Living units — $1,350–2,500/month
- 60-Bed nursing facility
  Semiprivate — $79/day
  Private — $106/day

"The Forum at Overland Park is Kansas City's premier full-service retirement community providing a convenient and worry-free lifestyle in a distinctive setting. An abundance of services and amenities and the availability of on-site health care provide our residents with all the ingredients for a healthy and secure lifestyle."

ALDERSGATE VILLAGE

7220 S.W. Asbury Drive
Topeka, KS 66614-4718
(913) 478-9440
Betty J. Edson, director of marketing

Type of community: Continuing Care, modified contract

Located on 237 acres that feature a hard-surface nature trail, three fishing ponds, open spaces, and landscaped areas, the modern two-story apartment complex houses apartments for Independent Living. Assisted Living, nursing care, and an Alzheimer's unit are located in a separate building. Single-story cottages, duplexes, triplexes, and fourplexes are also available. Aldersgate Village is located five minutes from

Westridge Mall and north of the Lake Sherwood area; a golf course is within a half mile. A fire station is on the grounds; church and an elementary school are located just west of campus. Child care for employees and local residents was added recently.

Financial plan: Three plans: **1)** Entrance fee plus monthly fee. **2)** Advance payment plan plus monthly fee with amortized refund over the first ten years. **3)** Build and occupancy plan: the resident provides funds to pay the cost of building cottage for which resident receives lifetime use.

Ownership and management: Owned and managed by the United Methodist Homes, Inc. Opened in 1979.

Minimum age: 55 years (average age at admission is 77).

Population: 310 residents; 37% couples, 12% singles, 51% widowed. Residents come from 30 states. 42 different occupations are represented as well as 11 religious denominations.

Number of units: 102 Independent Living apartments and 69 cottages and duplex, triplex, and fourplex units; 32 Assisted Living suites, 60 Skilled Nursing beds.

Dining plan: Optional. Residents may purchase meal tickets at 10% discount. Private dining room.

Services: *Included in the monthly fee:* Use of public parlors for private gatherings, bimonthly housekeeping, weekly flat-linen service, maintenance inside and outside.

At additional cost: Beauty/barbershop, guest accommodations, sundry shop.

Activities: Fully equipped woodworking shop, ceramics, drawing, painting, all kinds of sewing, weaving looms, three ponds stocked with fish, nature trail, exercise classes/equipment, day trips, week trips, chaplain and social work service, very active residents' council, volunteer opportunities, gardening, billards tables, recreation room, big-screen TV-VCR.

Availability: One-bedroom apartments available; one- to two-year waiting list for others.

INDEPENDENT LIVING HOUSING

Type/size of apartment	*Entrance fee*	*Monthly fee**	*Advance pay*	*Monthly fee**
Efficiency, 541 sq. ft.	$5,000	$892	$33,300	$528
1-Bedroom, 674 sq. ft.	$5,000	$1,096	$52,000	$663
Alcove 1-bedroom, 817 sq. ft.	$5,000	$1,232	$61,400	$726
2-Bedroom, 894 sq. ft.	$5,000	$1,638	$68,000	$815
2-Bedroom, 959 sq. ft.	$5,000	$1,714	$70,000	$853
Duplex, triplex, fourplex				
1-Bedroom, 811 sq. ft.	$5,000	$1,013	$46,800	$628
2-Bedroom, 1,091 sq. ft.	$5,000	$1,299	$68,000	$748
Cottages				
2-Bedroom, 1,113 sq. ft.	$5,000	$1,299	$70,000	$748

**For double occupancy add $212–233 to the monthly fee. All utilities except telephone included for apartments. Full kitchens, carpeting, draperies, cable TV, optional carports, 24-hour emergency call system. Cottages/plexes have garage.*

Health services and rates: Health center has enclosed patio, library, and chapel. Outpatient clinic services include lab services, podiatrist, audiologist, dentist, physician, nurse assessments. Physical, occupational, speech, and massage therapies provided at additional cost. Home health service provided by Village nurse. Respite care (30 days or less) provided if space available.

- 60 Assisted Living rooms
  Single or double (300 sq. ft.) $1,497–1,979/month
  2-Room suite (528 sq. ft.) $3,652/month (for two persons only)
- 60-Bed Skilled Nursing facility
  Semiprivate $73.25–82.25/day
  Private $88–97/day

"The mission of the United Methodist Homes, Inc., is to create and maintain a viable, comprehensive continuum of care for older adults that ensures their right to respect and dignity as members of the human community; to provide programs and services that enable older adults to achieve optimum participation in meeting their social, emotional, spiritual, and physical needs; to be an advocate for programs and services that protect the rights and enhance the quality of care available to older adults."

BREWSTER PLACE

1205 West 29th Street
Topeka, KS 66611
(913) 267-1666
Maggie Rader, marketing director

Type of community: Nonprofit Continuing Care

Accredited: Continuing Care Accreditation Commission

Four Independent Living complexes are clustered on a beautifully landscaped 15-acre campus featuring tree-lined sidewalks, manicured lawns, a gazebo, and gardens. Apartments and duplex cottages with attached garages are available. The newest residence building features penthouse apartments in a three-story luxury building. Home health services, respite care, and Skilled Nursing services available. Topeka offers fine dining, theater, golf, museums, dance. Easy access to Topeka by car or bus service. A large shopping center, including a supermarket, bank, service station, barbershop, package store, clothing store, and dry cleaners is less than two blocks away.

Financial plan: Entrance fee plus monthly fee. Entrance fee is amortized over a period of years based on the age of the resident upon entry into the community.

Ownership and management: The Congregational Home. Managed by a board of directors consisting of leading public-spirited men and women, businessmen, and clergy. Opened in 1964.

Minimum age: 62 years.

INDEPENDENT LIVING HOUSING

Type/size of apartment	*Entrance fee*	*Monthly fee**
Studio, 350–450 sq. ft.	$32,600	$442
1-Bedroom, 650 sq. ft.	$39,100	$477
2-Bedroom, 1,200 sq. ft.	$67,000	$724
Cottages, 1,400 sq. ft.	$70,000–90,000	$1,080

**For double occupancy add $125 to the monthly fee. All utilities except telephone included. Carpeting, curtains, modern fully equipped kitchens, individually controlled heating and air-conditioning, 24-hour emergency call system. Many apartments have balconies. Cottages have private patios, carports or garages. Pets are welcome.*

Population: 360 residents; 75% women, 25% men, 15% couples.

Number of units: 257 Independent Living apartments and 22 cottages: 77-bed health center.

Dining plan: Three meals per day paid à la carte. Special diets are available when ordered by a physician. Catering service.

Services: *Included in the monthly fee:* Biweekly housekeeping, laundry rooms, carports (when available).

At additional cost: Beauty/barbershop, private housecleaning/chores, discounts on cruises and trips.

Activities: Fully equipped exercise room and exercise classes, sauna and whirlpool, woodworking shop, library, chapel with weekly nondenominational services, chaplain services.

Availability: Waiting lists range from a few months to several years, depending on the type of unit.

Health services and rates: Residents are entitled to 14 free days per year (noncumulative) of health care; those who have conditions that qualify for Medicare coverage are eligible for 100 days of Skilled Nursing care after a three-day hospital stay. Professional registered nurses are on duty 24-hours per day. A part-time medical director, psychiatric consultant, dentist, podiatrist, and physical therapist complement the full-time staff. A home health program is available to residents in their home or in designated areas throughout the campus. Services include blood pressure checks and assistance with daily living. A nominal fee is charged for most home health services.

- 77-Bed health care center

Semiprivate		$73/day
Private		$130/day

- Skilled Nursing

Semiprivate	$1,745/month	$64/day
Private	$2,563/month	$85/day

"Brewster Place from the day of its inception has been committed to excellence. We continue this philosophy and we are the only Continuing Care retirement community in the state of Kansas that is nationally certified by the Continuing Care Accreditation Commission."

LARKSFIELD PLACE

7373 East 29th Street North
Wichita, KS 67226-3405
(316) 636-1000
Sharon Dillon, marketing director

Type of community: Not-for-profit Continuing Care, all-inclusive contract

This Independent Living apartment complex with three wings of two-, three-, and four-story residences is located on a 50-acre campus that offers fishing lakes, garden plots, outdoor patios, and beautiful views of Wichita. The complex features Mediterranean stucco-and-brick construction with beautiful balcony flower boxes and patio border gardens. Two lakes are populated with fish and waterfowl. A health center is adjacent to the complex; shopping, churches, bowling lanes, and golf courses are just blocks away.

Financial plan: Entrance fee plus monthly fee. $20,000 of entrance fee serves as Continuing Care fee, which is nonrefundable. Remainder of the entrance fee is 100% refundable when resident leaves community for any reason and the apartment is reoccupied.

Ownership and management: Owned and operated by Wesley Retirement Communities, Inc., a not-for-profit Wichita organization. Opened in 1988.

Minimum age: 55 years.

Population: 180 residents; 67% women, 33% men, 33% couples.

Number of units: 150 Independent Living apartments; 74-bed health center.

INDEPENDENT LIVING HOUSING

Type/size of unit	*Entrance fee**	*Monthly fee**
1-Bedroom, 480–750 sq. ft.	$61,500–124,500	$1,150–1,725
2-Bedroom, 911–1,500 sq. ft.	$103,500–175,700	$1,655–2,545
3-Bedroom, 1,680 sq. ft.	$174,300	$2,855

**For double occupancy add $20,000 to the entrance fee, $460 to the monthly fee. All utilities, except telephone, included. Fully equipped kitchens, wall-to-wall carpeting, (some have patios or balconies), 24-hour emergency call system, cable-ready.*

Dining plan: 30 meals per month included in the monthly fee. Restaurant-style menu dining. Private dining room available. Special diets accommodated.

Services: *Included in the monthly fee:* Biweekly housekeeping, flat-linen service, scheduled transportation, laundry facilities.

At additional cost: Beauty/barbershop, garages and carports.

Activities: Full-time activities staff. Swimming pool, arts and crafts, billiards, card games, land or water exercises, fishing, games, gardening, life enrichment seminars, bingo, woodworking, volunteer work, Bible study, ice-cream socials, movies, Jacuzzi, library, indoor and outdoor walking courses, exercise room, residents' council, all-purpose auditorium; planned social, cultural, recreational, and spiritual activities.

Availability: Waiting list for two-bedroom apartments.

Health services and rates: Fees for licensed health center offering Intermediate and Skilled Care (including Alzheimer's) are covered by $20,000 of the resident's original entrance fee. Lifetime health care does not include physician visits and fees, hospitalization, drug/alcohol abuse, mental illness, two additional daily meals, medication, special therapy or special equipment. Medical director on-site. Assisted Living facility in planning stages.

- 74-Bed health center

"The philosophy of Larksfield Place is for every person to live the highest quality of life possible, no matter at what stage of aging they are. Larksfield Place has a moving assistance program, which provides help in planning, packing, and carrying out your move to the community. The first eight hours are at no charge; each additional hour offered at a nominal fee."

WICHITA PRESBYTERIAN MANOR

4700 West 13th Street
Wichita, KS 67212
(316) 942-7456
Sydney Thornbrugh, director of administrative services

Type of community: Not-for-profit Continuing Care, modified contract

Ground-level apartment buildings are located on a 13-acre parklike campus in a suburban setting near shopping areas and interstate highway. Each unit has an outside entrance with patio. The grounds feature sidewalks and lighted walking areas. Duplex, cottage, and congregate living are offered for Independent Living residents; Assisted Living and a health care center are on-site.

Financial plan: Entrance fee plus monthly fee or monthly rental. Every resident pays a $5,000 entrance fee. Two entrance fee plans: **1)** Life use fee: refund of entrance fee upon withdrawal, less initial 20% and 10% per year of remaining balance thereafter. **2)** Estate preservation plan: 75% of entrance fee is refundable at any time upon withdrawal. (Those choosing the monthly rental option must pay a one-time entrance fee of $5,000.)

Ownership and management: Owned by Presbyterian Manors, Inc. Operated by Presbyterian Manors of Mid-America, Inc., owners and operators of 16 facilities located in Kansas and Missouri. Presbyterian Manors is one of the oldest and largest not-for-profit Continuing Care organizations in the Midwest. Opened in 1970.

Minimum age: 65 years.

Population: 204 residents; 82% women, 18% men, 23% couples.

Number of units: 98 Independent Living apartments; 30 Assisted Living units, 60-bed health center.

Dining plan: Meals for Independent Living residents are optional. Special diets and tray service available.

Services: *Included in the monthly fee:* Laundry facilities, parking, scheduled transportation.

At additional cost: Beauty/barbershop, housekeeping and laundry service.

Activities: Library, chapel, variety of special events, slide shows, shopping trips, movies, exercise programs.

Availability: Waiting list for direct admission to health care center and apartments. One year for one-bedroom apartments; longer for two-bedroom apartments.

Health services and rates: Residents receive 12 days per year of nursing care at no additional cost except physicians' fees and prescriptions. Staff at F. G. Holl Health Care Center are experts in the fields of nursing, nutrition, social services, rehabilitation, and pastoral care. Medical director on-site. Home health care includes: registered nurse visits, transportation for medical appointments, assistance with bathing, dressing, walking, etc., rehabilitative therapy, meal delivery when ill. Entrance fee option for health center: Residents admitted directly to the health care center may choose to pay a $500 application fee plus ongoing charge of $4/day rather than the $5,000 entrance fee.

- 30 Assisted Living units

	Monthly fee single/double
Private room (176–180 sq. ft.)	$1,530/1,750
Private 2-room suite	$2,660/2,965

- 60-Bed health center

Semiprivate	$67/day
Private	$77/day
Larger private	$120/day

INDEPENDENT LIVING HOUSING

Type/size of unit	*Entrance fee 1/2**	*Monthly fee**
1-Bedroom, 531–662 sq. ft.	$39,500/53,300	$275–440
2-Bedroom, 800–810 sq. ft.	$49,500/66,000	$300–470
Duplex, 1,200 sq. ft.	$72,500–79,500/96,700–105,900	$225–265

Monthly rent also available; add approximately $1,000 to the monthly fees listed above. All utilities except telephone and cable TV included (duplex fee does not include utilities). Wall-to-wall carpeting, 24-hour emergency call system, individually controlled heating and air-conditioning, fully equipped kitchen, cable TV, patios.

"Wichita Presbyterian Manor provides active retirement living and a lifestyle to enjoy. As a not-for-profit Continuing Care community, Wichita Presbyterian Manor provides a continuum of lifestyle options, including Independent and congregate living, Assisted Living with home health services, and nursing care. Our beautifully landscaped 13-acre campus features simplexes and duplexes as well as apartments, suites, and individual rooms within our main Manor building. All living accommodations are on one level. Our apartments feature individually accessed patios and outside entrances. We take pride in the quality and flexibility of our staff—professionals dedicated to serving you."

KENTUCKY

THE LAFAYETTE AT COUNTRY PLACE

690 Mason Headley Road
Lexington, KY 40504
(606) 259-1331
Shirl Flint, marketing director

Type of community: Continuing Care, modified contract

This five-story traditional brick structure was designed to blend with the local architecture and create a feeling of elegance both inside and out. Walking paths and summer flower beds surround the campus. Carefully selected furnishings grace the common areas. Independent Living apartments and a health care center are on-site. The community offers easy access to Keeneland airport, Lexington Opera House, University of Kentucky, shopping, and medical services.

Financial plan: Monthly rental fee.

Ownership and management: Locally owned and managed by The Forum Group, Inc., which owns and manages 27 retirement communities in the United States and has more than 25 years experience in the retirement living industry. Opened in 1985.

Minimum age: 60 years.

Population: 206 residents; 75% women, 25% men, 10% couples.

Number of units: 100 Independent Living apartments; 111-bed health care center.

Dining plan: One meal per day and continental breakfast included in the monthly rental fee. Private dining room available.

Services: *Included in the monthly fee:* Weekly housekeeping, flat-linen service, laundry facilities on each floor, scheduled transportation, Forum Ambassador service.

At additional cost: Transportation with Fayette County, beauty/barbershop, overnight guest room, personal laundry.

Activities: Full-time program director. Water exercises and swimming pool, movies, lectures, exercise classes, travel tours, scheduled transportation to cultural and sporting events, library, arts and crafts, bridge, happy hours, game room.

INDEPENDENT LIVING HOUSING

Type/size of apartment	*Monthly rental fee**
1-Bedroom, 650–690 sq. ft.	$1,425–1,500
2-Bedroom, 850–900 sq. ft.	$1,700–1,750

**For double occupancy add $250 to the monthly rental fee. All utilities except telephone and cable TV included. Fully equipped electric kitchen, wall-to-wall carpeting, individually controlled heating and air-conditioning, 24-hour emergency call system, balcony or bay window.*

Availability: Limited. Waiting list depends on floor plan.

Health services and rates: Residents receive ten free days per year in the health care center, up to a lifetime total of 30 days. Medical director, list of attending physicians and therapists always available. Activities program promotes self-esteem, psychological well-being, and physical rehabilitation. Physical, occupational, and speech therapies are available.

- Ambassador services (Assisted Living) in residents' apartments
  Level 1 add $450 to monthly fee
  Level 2 add $600 to monthly fee
- 111-Bed Skilled Nursing facility
  Semiprivate $89–132/day
  Private $105–160/day

"The Lafayette at Country Place is the only retirement community in Lexington to offer an attached, Skilled Nursing health care center, 24-hour doorman/security, Ambassador program (Assisted Living), and a tax credit. The staff is dedicated to meeting the needs of all Independent Living residents as well as any health care concerns that may arise."

THE FORUM AT BROOKSIDE

200 Brookside Drive
Louisville, KY 40243
(502) 244-6318
Suzanne S. Phillips, director of marketing

Type of community: Continuing Care, modified contract

Located on a 38-acre campus, The Forum at Brookside offers Independent Living apartments and villas, a 60-bed health center, a picnic area, and nature trail. Four mid-rise apartment buildings adjoining the clubhouse feature automatic doors and elevators. Five one-level floor plans are available for airy, spacious villas. Resident-inspired landscaping has received top county honors. Nearby the Kentucky Center for the Arts offers orchestra, ballet, and theater performances. The community offers easy access to two major malls, grocery stores, medical buildings, and parks.

Financial plan: Entrance fee plus monthly fee or montly rental. Two plans: **1)** Traditional: nonrefundable entrance fee. **2)** Estate plan: 100% refundable entrance fee.

Ownership and management: Owned and managed by The Forum Group, Inc., which has more than 25 years experience in retirement communities and 27 facilities across the country. Opened in 1984.

Minimum age: 62 years.

Population: 192 residents; 65% women, 35% men, 16% couples.

Number of units: 117 Independent Living apartments and 99 villas; 20 Assisted Living units, 40-bed health center.

INDEPENDENT LIVING HOUSING

Type/size of unit	*Entrance fee 1/2*	*Monthly fee**	*Monthly rental**
1-Bedroom, 594 sq. ft.	$37,000–80,000	$1,150	$1,775
2-Bedroom, 877 sq. ft.	$56,000–119,000	$1,350	$2,375
2-Bedroom villa, 1,258 sq. ft.	$58,000–123,000	$1,475	$2,550

**For double occupancy add $494 to the monthly fee, $374 to the monthly rental. All utilities except telephone included. Wall-to-wall carpeting, individually controlled heating and air-conditioning, satellite TV, 24-hour emergency call system, walk-in closets, fully equipped kitchens, patio or balcony. Villas come with or without a carport.*

Dining plan: 30 meals per month included in the monthly fee. Private dining room available. Executive chef and pastry chef.

Services: *Included in the monthly fee:* Biweekly housekeeping and flat-linen services, scheduled and personal reserved transportation.

At additional cost: Beauty/barbershop, guest villas available by reservation.

Activities: Full-time program director. Full-size heated indoor swimming pool, exercise room and classes, nature trail, shuffleboard court, adult education classes, chapel, bridge, library, Bible study, book reviews, card games, social hours, book-mobile, game nights, various outings, movies, guest lectures, crafts room, multipurpose room, woodworking shop, numerous one-day and overnight trips.

Availability: Some floor plans have short waiting lists.

Health services and rates: Residents who have paid entrance fee receive six months of nursing care credit. Rental plan residents receive 15 days per year; 60 days total credit care at health center. Physical, occupational, and speech therapies on-site as well as 24-hour on-call pharmacy services.

- 20 Assisted Living units
  Semiprivate $68/day
  Private $91/day
- 40-Bed health center
  Semiprivate $113/day
  Private $138/day

"The Forum at Brookside is Louisville's premier, full-service retirement community providing a convenient and worry-free lifestyle in a distinctive setting. Newly redecorated, with an abundance of services and amenities, The Forum also provides on-site health care. Within the active resident association, a hospitality committee greets and assists new move-ins from out-of-state or the local area. Superb staff tends to every need."

TREYTON OAK TOWERS

211 West Oak Street
Louisville, KY 40203
(502) 589-3211
Lisa Brown, marketing director

Type of community: Not-for-profit Continuing Care, modified contract

Located in historic Old Louisville, this 12-story apartment complex includes a greenhouse and garden courtyard with reflecting pool and shaded benches. Independent Living and Assisted Living residences and a health center are available. The community is close to Victorian mansions in historic Old Louisville, the Louisville Ballet, symphony orchestra, Actors Theater, and the University of Louisville.

Financial plan: Entrance fee plus monthly fee. Three plans: **1)** Traditional: entrance fee amortizes at rate of 3% per month of residency. **2)** Return of capital: 90% refund of entrance fee, regardless of length of stay. **3)** Monthly installment: resident pays an initial deposit on the apartment, then a monthly fee along with a percentage of the entrance fee for a period of ten years.

INDEPENDENT LIVING HOUSING

Type/size of apartment	*Entrance fee*	*Monthly fee**
1-Bedroom, 564 sq. ft.	$39,400	$914
2-Bedroom, 846 sq. ft.	$67,800	$1,216
2-Bedroom /den, 1,368 sq. ft.	$111,200	$1,529

**For double occupancy add $126 to the monthly fee. All utilities except telephone and cable TV included. Fully equipped kitchen, 24-hour emergency call system, wall-to-wall carpeting, individually controlled heating and air-conditioning.*

Ownership and management: Owned by a local not-for-profit corporation with members of its board of directors selected from the immediate area. Managed by Life Care Services of Des Moines, Iowa, who have developed and managed over 50 continuing care communities across the United States. Opened in 1984.

Minimum age: 62 years.

Population: 273 residents; 70% women, 30% men, 30% couples.

Number of units: 207 Independent Living apartments; 16 Assisted Living units, 60-bed health care center.

Dining plan: One meal per day included in the monthly fee. Private dining room available. Food service director/chef on site. Special diets and tray service available.

Services: *Included in the monthly fee:* Twice-monthly housekeeping, weekly flat-linen service, open parking, scheduled transportation.

At additional cost: Beauty/barbershop, covered parking, guest accommodations.

Activities: Full-time activities director. Exercise class, fully equipped exercise gym, coffee hours, library, greenhouse and garden courtyard, card games, sing-alongs, Ping-Pong/billiards room, game room, regularly scheduled outings to various cultural events in the area (as well as malls, sporting events, movies, museums, and historic sites), video-equipped Kentucky Room, Oak Room Auditorium, whirlpool, bus tours, overnights and extended travel throughout the United States, fitness spa, bridge.

Availability: No waiting list at present.

Health services and rates: Health center offers emergency, recuperative, and long-term care. Thirty days of Skilled Nursing health care is included in the monthly fee. After a 30-day period, residents receive a 20% discount off the published health care center rates. Medical director on call 24 hours a day. Personal care center with private dining room, social events lounge, and an activities room. Assistance with medication, personal care, and meals is provided under the supervision of a licensed LPN director. Physical, speech, occupational, and respiratory therapies are available.

- 16 Assisted Living units
  - 1-Bedroom $2,086/month
  - 2-Bedroom $2,494/month
- 60-Bed health center
  - Semiprivate $83/day
  - Private $99/day

"As our residents proudly attest, life at Treyton Oak Towers is anything but retiring. Here, residents are part of a thriving, bustling community—a vital community of active individuals enjoying a world of opportunities and stimulating challenges. Our residents' lifestyle is as full as they want it to be, enhanced by elegant surroundings, fine dining, diverse activities, entertainment, travel, education, and gracious amenities. Treyton Oaks offers residency programs designed to protect both our residents' health and their financial independence."

WESTMINSTER TERRACE/ROSE ANNA HUGHES PRESBYTERIAN HOME

2116 Buechel Bank Road
Louisville, KY 40218
(502) 499-9383
Joyce Snipp, admissions coordinator

Type of community: Nonprofit Continuing Care, modified contract

Westminster Terrace is located on a ten-acre campus, which is a bird sanctuary, in a suburban neighborhood in southeast Louisville. A four-story modern, brick apartment building houses Independent Living. The

INDEPENDENT LIVING HOUSING

Type/size of apartment	*Entrance fee*	*Monthly fee**	*Monthly rental**
Studio, 309–335 sq. ft.	$20,000–21,000	$870–890	$1,105–1,125
1-Bedroom, 509–670 sq. ft.	$25,000–30,000	$1,380–1,430	$1,715–1,775
2-Bedroom	$50,000	$1,890	N/A

**For double occupancy add $285 to the monthly fee or monthly rent. All utilities except telephone included in the monthly fee. Wall-to-wall carpeting, individual thermostats, 24-hour emergency call system. Many have full kitchens; some have balconies.*

Rose Anna Hughes building contains Assisted Living apartments and has a large atrium that features a 12-sided skylight in the dining room. Adjacent to Rose Anna Hughes is a health center connected by hallway to Independent Living. Nearby are Bashford Manor Mall and Showcase Cinemas.

Financial plan: Entrance fee plus monthly fee or monthly rental. Residents who choose the entrance fee plan pay a smaller monthly fee and receive a discount in the health center.

Ownership and management: Presbyterian Homes and Services of Kentucky, Inc. Rose Anna Hughes Presbyterian Home opened in 1947. Westminster Terrace opened in 1966.

Minimum age: 65 years.

Population: 105 residents; 80% women, 20% men, 10% couples.

Number of units: 75 Independent Living apartments; 32 Assisted Living apartments (all wheelchair accessible), 30 unit personal care wing, 112-bed nursing facility.

Dining plan: Three meals per day included in the monthly fee. Tray service available during illness.

Services: *Included in the monthly fee:* Scheduled transportation, weekly housekeeping and flat-linen services, parking, laundromat.

At additional cost: Sundries store, beauty/barbershop.

Activities: Full-time director. Exercise classes, arts and crafts, musical events, movies, holiday celebrations and religious programs, Bible study, frequent outings (theaters, museums, restaurants, sites of interest, shops), garden plots, big-screen TV, pet therapy, bridge, volunteering.

Availability: Limited availability, depending on type of apartment.

Health services and rates: Social workers, nursing staff, chaplains, dietitians. Physical, occupational, and speech therapies available.

- 32 Assisted Living studio and 1-bedroom apartments*
  $960–1,440/monthly fee or
  $1,200–1,800/monthly rental

* *Nonresident entrance fee: $21,500–30,000.*

- 30 Personal care units
  Small semiprivate $51.50/day
  Large semiprivate $56/day
  Private $67/day
- 112-Bed nursing facility
  Intermediate, semiprivate $84.75/day
  Skilled, semiprivate $98.00/day

"Westminster has five levels of care, which enables a resident to move in and, when needed, easily relocate to another area as more care is required."

LOUISIANA

ST. JAMES PLACE

333 Lee Drive
Baton Rouge, LA 70808-9960
(504) 769-1407
Charles Brady, retirement counselor

Type of community: Nonprofit Continuing Care, all-inclusive contract

Nestled on a quiet and picturesque 40-acre site, a three-story brick structure and 20 garden homes of southern colonial architectural design house Independent Living residents. A 60-bed health center is on campus. Beautifully maintained grounds include nature trails and walkways, a fishing lake and picnic areas, swimming pool, carefully tended lawns, a registered live oak, a camellia garden and bountiful azaleas, wisteria, and yellow jasmine. The community offers easy access to churches, hospitals, shopping areas, and entertainment centers. The surrounding neighborhood is principally residential and located one mile south of Louisiana State University, which provides additional entertainment and cultural interest.

Financial plan: Entrance fee plus monthly fee. A deposit equal to 10% of the entrance fee is paid at the time application is submitted for residency.

Ownership and management: St. James Place of Baton Rouge, Inc., not-for-profit; managed by a board of directors that serves gratuitously. Opened in 1983.

Minimum age: 62 years.

Population: 235 residents; 80% women, 20% men, 20% couples.

Number of units: 188 Independent Living apartments; 60-bed health center.

Dining plan: One meal a day is included in the monthly fee, with option to purchase others. Three meals are served daily.

Services: *Included in the monthly fee:* Scheduled transportation, regular housekeeping, weekly flat-linen service.

INDEPENDENT LIVING HOUSING

Type/size of apartment	*Entrance fee**	*Monthly fee**
Studio, 401 sq. ft.	$49,850	$747
1-Bedroom, 619 sq. ft.	$67,550–92,900	$867–1,014
2-Bedroom, 872–1,008 sq. ft.	$97,600–124,750	$1,025–1,214
Suite, 1,020–1,583 sq. ft.	$116,750–179,950	$1,267–1,650

**For double occupancy add $6,600 to the entrance the fee, $458 to the monthly fee. All utilities except telephone included. Individually controlled heating and air-conditioning, 24-hour emergency call system, fully equipped kitchen. Most apartment have a patio or balcony. Eleven different floor plans.*

At additional cost: Beauty/barbershop, grocery store, ice-cream parlor.

Activities: Fitness center with swimming pool and Jacuzzi. Exercise classes both in and out of the water. Arts and crafts room, shuffleboard court, woodworking shop, bus tours, seminars on health and finance, movies.

Availability: Limited. Waiting list for some apartments.

Health services and rates: Residents receive unlimited nursing care at no additional charge except the cost of two additional meals. There is a weekly nurses clinic where residents can have their blood pressure checked. Free flu shots; other health maintenance services.

- 60-Bed health center

"St. James believes that its residents should be encouraged and supported to learn and gain new knowledge, to act for increased self-fulfillment, to enjoy life to the fullest, and to contribute to the betterment of the St. James Place community and to the community at large. St. James Place is known for its delicious southern cuisine and for being a warm and friendly community with an efficient and courteous staff."

MARYLAND

GINGER COVE

4000 River Crescent Drive
Annapolis, MD 21401
(410) 266-7300
Betty Ann Bunnemeyer, director of marketing

Type of community: Nonprofit Continuing Care, all-inclusive contract

Located just south of Annapolis on 30 wooded acres, Ginger Cove is situated on Gingerville Creek, which flows into the South River and on into the Chesapeake Bay. The community is made up of red brick–and-wood traditional-style Independent Living housing, interconnected on the first level. Assisted Living services and nursing facilities are on-site. The grounds feature beautiful waterfront views. Walking paths stretch around the perimeter of the property and down to the water where gazebos overlook the creek. The United States Naval Academy and historic houses are nearby in Annapolis. Crabbing by the pier is a popular pastime among residents.

Financial plan: Entrance fee plus monthly fee. Entrance fee is 90% refundable.

Ownership and management: Managed by the Life Care Services Corporation of Des Moines, Iowa, which is responsible for the development of more than 50 communities across the United States. Opened in 1988.

Minimum age: 60 years.

Population: 320 residents; 73% women, 27% men, 41% couples.

Number of units: 243 Independent Living apartments; 43-bed health care center.

Dining plan: One meal of resident's choice each day included in the monthly fee. Additional meals are available at cost.

Services: *Included in monthly fee:* Weekly housekeeping and flat-linen services, personal laundry facilities, regularly scheduled transportation.

At additional cost: Ice-cream parlor, beauty/barbershop, cocktail lounge, sundries shop, bank.

INDEPENDENT LIVING HOUSING

Type/size of unit	*Entrance fee**	*Monthly fee**
1-Bedroom, 740–890 sq. ft.	$123,000–165,000	$1,318–1,450
2-Bedroom, 1,040–1,190 sq. ft.	$175,000–222,000	$1,582–1,714
2-Bedroom/den, 1,340 sq. ft.	$235,000–249,000	$1,845

**For double occupancy add $11,000 to the entrance fee, $791 to the monthly fee. All utilities except telephone included. Fully equipped kitchens, enclosed sunrooms, 24-hour emergency call system.*

Activities: Full-time resident services director. Arts and crafts studio, library, billiards room, chapel/ auditorium, woodworking shop, garden plots, indoor pool, saunas, whirlpool, exercise area, pier for crabbing and fishing.

Availability: A one-year waiting list for the largest apartments. Some apartments are available for immediate occupancy.

Health services and rates: Unlimited nursing care is included in the monthly fee. Medical director on call 24 hours a day. One hour of Assisted Living services per day in resident's apartment for the first 90 days needed is included in resident's monthly fee, after which resident receive 1/2 hour of services each day for an unlimited number of days.

- 43-Bed health care center

"Ginger Cove enjoys the advantages of a pastoral waterfront setting just 4 1/2 miles from the center of Annapolis, with its historic buildings, quaint shops, and restaurants. Residents also enjoy easy access to cultural events in both Baltimore and Washington, D.C. Croquet is a popular sport with more than 60 residents participating; Ginger Cove plays annual matches with both the United States Naval Academy and St. John's College."

EDENWALD

800 Southerly Road
Baltimore, MD 21286-8403
(410) 339-6000
Anita E. Martin, director of marketing

Type of community: Not-for-profit Continuing Care, all-inclusive contract

Edenwald is a luxurious 18-story high-rise complex that houses 241 Independent Living apartments offering six distinctive floor plans. The adjoining health care center offers Assisted Living in the Domiciliary for persons who no longer want the responsibility of an apartment and need the availability of nursing attention and guidance. Located in Towson, Maryland, on 4 1/2 acres of beautifully landscaped grounds between Goucher College and Towson Town Center, one of the largest shopping malls on the East Coast, the facility is within fifteen minutes of downtown Baltimore and fifty minutes of Washington, D.C.

Financial plan: Entrance fee plus monthly fee. Refund is based on voluntary leaving of the community: 90% refund less 1% for each month of residency. No refund after 7 1/2 years.

Ownership and management: Owned by the General German Aged People's Home of Baltimore. Managed by board of directors comprised of 20 of Baltimore's key leaders in business, law, medicine, nursing, education, and finance. Opened in 1985.

Minimum age: 62 years.

INDEPENDENT LIVING HOUSING

Type/size of unit	*Entrance fee**	*Monthly fee**
Studio, 485–530 sq. ft.	$59,000–64,500	$1,175
1-Bedroom, 620–765 sq. ft.	$90,500–115,000	$1,410–1,564
2-Bedroom, 975 sq. ft.	$140,500	$1,801
Penthouse, 1,275 sq. ft.	$187,500	$2,192

**For double occupancy add $15,000 to the entrance fee, $627 to the monthly fee. All utilities except telephone included. Fully equipped kitchens, balconies, 24-hour emergency call system, wall-to-wall carpeting, cable TV (optional), individually controlled heating and air-conditioning.*

Population: 400 residents; 70% women, 30% men, 10% couples.

Number of units: 241 Independent Living apartments; 48 Assisted Living units, 67-bed health center.

Dining plan: One meal per day included in the monthly fee in formal dining room or informal cafeteria. Private dining room available for special functions. Tray service as authorized.

Services: *Included in the monthly fee:* Biweekly housekeeping and flat-linen services, scheduled transportation.

At additional cost: Underground parking, beauty/barbershop, guest accommodations, gift shop and general store (operated by residents' association).

Activities: Full-time activities director and community center. Conversation areas, painting, weaving, lectures, religious services, exercise programs, library, wood shop. Various planned trips to Washington, D.C., New York City, local theater, concerts, ballet, and other cultural activities.

Availability: Less than one-year wait for smaller units, up to two years for larger ones. $1,200 deposit for waiting list, $1,000 of which is refundable.

Health services and rates: Unlimited health care is included in the monthly fee. Residents are assessed for breakfast and lunch while in the health center. Medical, dental, and physical and occupational therapy services available. Activity program for those in nursing care. Assisted Living offered in the Domiciliary. Nonresidents may enter Assisted Living directly.

- 48 Assisted Living studios

Nonresident entrance fee	$44,000
Nonresident monthly fee	$1,329

- 67-Bed nursing center

"Edenwald is committed to maintaining a homelike atmosphere in the delivery of its services and to helping those it serves live their lives with joy, dignity, comfort, and security and thereby achieve a life of significance."

ROLAND PARK PLACE

830 West 40th Street
Baltimore, MD 21211
(410) 243-5800
George Lerkner, director of marketing

Type of community: Not-for-profit Continuing Care, all-inclusive contract

Accreditation: Continuing Care Accreditation Commission

Roland Park Place is located on a seven-acre pastoral campus, originally the site of the Greenway estate, home of one of Baltimore's first settlers. Three 17th-century Victorian gothic cottages remain under protection of the historical society and house Independent Living residents. Three wings of the main building open onto a beautiful courtyard filled with oak trees, flower gardens, walking paths, and a gazebo. Independent Living apartments in the modern seven-story building have views of the courtyard on one side and the Key Bridge, Inner Harbor, and downtown Baltimore on the other. The community also offers Assisted Living and a health care center. Johns Hopkins University and the Baltimore Museum of Art are located a few minutes away.

Financial plan: Entrance fee plus monthly fee. Entrance fee is refundable less 4% occupancy charge and 1.6% per month service charge. No refunds are made after 60 months of residency. $1,000 refundable deposit for single occupancy; $1,500 for double occupancy.

Ownership and management: Not-for-profit corporation, sponsored by the First English Evangelical Lutheran Church, the board of directors of the Lutheran Hospital of Maryland, and the Lutheran Home and Hospital Association. Opened in 1984.

INDEPENDENT LIVING HOUSING

Type/size of apartment	*Entrance fee*	*Monthly fee**
1-Bedroom, 574–864 sq. ft.	$84,500–141,500	$1,603–2,262
2-Bedroom, 864–1,152 sq. ft.	$140,300–194,500	$2,262–3,206

**For double occupancy add $539 to the monthly fee. All utilities except telephone included. Draperies, wall-to-wall carpeting, fully equipped kitchen, individually controlled heating and air-conditioning, 24-hour emergency call system.*

Minimum age: 65 years for apartments; 62 years for cottages.

Population: 320 residents; 80% women, 20% men, 5% couples.

Number of units: 238 Independent Living apartments; 10 Assisted Living units, 48-bed health center (Intermediate and Skilled Nursing).

Dining plan: One meal per day is included in the monthly fee. Three meals per day are served and available at a nominal sum to residents and guests.

Services: *Included in the monthly fee:* Scheduled transportation for medical appointments, biweekly apartment cleaning, weekly flat-linen service, parking space/valet parking.

At additional cost: Beauty/barbershop, sundry shop, commercial bank branch.

Activities: Fitness center equipped with a hot tub, sauna, and various types of exercise equipment, arts and crafts, library, cultural and educational enrichment programs.

Availability: Waiting list: one-bedroom apartments usually available within six months; two-bedroom apartments have a somewhat longer wait.

Health services and rates: Unlimited nursing services are included in resident's entrance and monthly fees. Physician on call 24 hours. Assisted Living care offered in resident's apartment. Therapists are available on an as-needed basis, and costs may be reimbursable by the resident's insurance program.

- 10 Assisted Living units
- 48 Comprehensive nursing-care beds

"Many people who have worked hard all their lives and planned for their retirement have chosen Roland Park Place. A typical resident wants to be free from the loneliness that can come from living alone, free from the fear of an accident or health problem that may need prompt and appropriate attention, and free from the rigors of maintaining his or her own home. Carefree retirement allows residents to enjoy a secure and fulfilling life."

CHARLESTOWN

715 Maiden Choice Lane
Catonsville, MD 21228
(410) 247-3400
Michael Erickson, marketing

Type of community: Not-for-profit Continuing Care, modified contract

Charlestown is located on a 110-acre hilltop campus that features manicured courtyards, beautiful woods, and dramatic vistas of the Baltimore skyline and the Francis Scott Key Bridge. Formerly St. Charles College and Seminary, Charlestown is bounded by private fenced-in woods on three sides and offers a 2½-acre pond, wooded nature trails, and a Skyline Walk that surrounds a large grassy field that presents a grand view of Baltimore. Fourteen Independent Living apartment buildings, three community centers, a health center, and Assisted Living are connected by enclosed, air-conditioned and heated walkways. The community offers a pharmacy counter, lounge with big-screen TV,

INDEPENDENT LIVING HOUSING

Type/size of unit	*Entrance fee*	*Monthly fee**
Efficiency, 456 sq. ft.	$45,000–52,000	$647–705
Studio, 541 sq. ft.	$58,000–72,000	$708–776
1-Bedroom, 694 sq. ft.	$81,000–114,000	$793–940
2-Bedroom, 954 sq. ft.	$97,000–210,000	$934–1,115
St. Charles units, 960–1,700 sq. ft.**	$135,000–264,000	$968–1,195

**For double occupancy add $345 to the monthly fee. Ground-floor residences with patios require an additional $7,000 deposit. All utilities except telephone included. Individually controlled heating and air-conditioning, 24-hour emergency call system, walk-in closets, cable TV, fully equipped kitchen, some patios or balconies, wall-to-wall carpeting. The St. Charles units have personal laundry room with washer and dryer and all-glass sunrooms. Pets are allowed. **Sizes of individual units available upon request.*

laundry room, library, crafts room, and medical center. Our Lady of the Angels Chapel, a work of marble and mosaic artistry, is on-site. Charlestown is located minutes away from the Baltimore Beltway and ten minutes from Harborplace and downtown Baltimore with its many cultural attractions, including the Lyric Opera House, the Morris Mechanic Theater, and the Meyerhoff Symphony Hall. BWI Airport is 12 minutes away.

Financial plan: Entrance fee plus monthly fee. Entrance fee 100% refundable upon reoccupancy of vacated apartment.

Ownership and management: Owned by The Charlestown Retirement Community, Inc. Managed by their board of directors. Opened in 1983.

Minimum age: 62 years.

Population: 1,500 residents; 70% women, 30% men. In 1992, 92% of new residents were couples.

Number of units: 1,313 Independent Living apartments; 132 Assisted Living apartments, 122-bed health center.

Dining plan: One meal per day included in the monthly fee. Special diets and tray service available. Five dining rooms located in the community. Three private dining rooms available.

Services: *Included in the monthly fee:* Open parking, scheduled transportation.

At additional cost: Beauty/barbershop, reserved parking, housekeeping.

Activities: Chapel, concerts and musical performances in the chapel, all-season aquatics center, cultural events, exercise rooms, classrooms, college classes, woodwork shop, crafts room, TV and bridge clubs and lounge, 220-seat drama theater, library and reading room, music room, card and games room, City Lights Club, billiards room, gardening, Bible discussion groups, wooded nature trails, group trips, dance studio, Skyline Walk, closed-circuit TV broadcasts and TV studio, movies, guest speakers, Stitch 'n' Chat knitting club, current events discussion groups, ham radio club, writing groups.

Availability: Waiting list varies according to accommodation desired. $1,000 deposit for futures list gives a prospective resident higher priority. Members of the list qualify for admission to the Charlestown Care Center if temporary or long-term nursing care is needed at any time before becoming a Charlestown resident.

Health services and rates: On-site medical center managed by Johns Hopkins Health System offers four full-time physicians, a nurse practitioner, 24-hour in-house health care staff. Specialists with office hours include a podiatrist, ophthalmologist, orthopedic surgeon, dentist, and audiologist. Fully equipped on-site dental office with two chairs and X ray equipment. Home health care and physical therapy available. St. Agnes Hospital is less than two miles away. Paradise Pharmacy on site provides prompt pick-up and delivery of prescriptions and discounts on pharmaceuticals.

- 32 Assisted Living studios
  Nonresident entrance fee — *Monthly fee*
  $58,500–79,000 — $968–1,195
- 122-Bed health center
  Semiprivate — $103/day

"Charlestown is one of the largest communities in the U.S. offering care for life. It has its own voting precinct. Main Street, Charlestown Square, and Cross Creek Station serve as the centers of activity of Charlestown, offering convenience stores, coffee shops, a postal center, beauty salons, and two banks all within the community."

CLASSIC RESIDENCE BY HYATT

8100 Connecticut Avenue
Chevy Chase, MD 20815
(301) 907-8895
Leslie Groom, director of marketing

Type of community: Independent Living with Continuum of Care

Located just inside the Washington Beltway in a residential setting, the 17-story apartment building features spectacular views of the Bethesda skyline, the adjoining golf course, and eight landscaped acres. Independent Living and Assisted Living apartments are available; referral to nearby nursing facilities is provided. The community is convenient to all Washington, D.C., attractions.

Financial plan: Monthly fee. One month's rent is security deposit.

Ownership and management: Jointly developed and owned by Forest City Residential Development, Inc., of Cleveland, Ohio, and Classic Residence by Hyatt, an affiliate of the Hyatt Corporation. Managed by Hyatt, which also manages Classic Residences in California, Connecticut, New Jersey, Nevada, and Texas. Opened in 1990.

Minimum age: 55 years.

Population: 325 residents; 75% women, 25% men, 10% couples.

Number of units: 319 Independent Living apartments; 22 Assisted Living apartments.

Dining plan: Continental breakfast daily and 25 dinners included in the monthly fee. Classically Caring Cuisine offers meals low in sodium, fat, and cholesterol. Catering services.

INDEPENDENT LIVING HOUSING

Type/size of apartment	*Monthly fee**
1-Bedroom, 660–750 sq. ft.	$1,750–2,100
1-Bedroom/study, 890–960 sq. ft.	$2,300–2,500
1-Bedroom/den, 990–1,035 sq. ft.	$2,720–2,900
2-Bedroom/2-bath, 1,200 sq. ft.	$3,100–3,300

**For double occupancy add $450 to the monthly fee. All utilities except telephone included. Wall-to-wall carpeting, window treatments, spacious closets, washer/dryer, modern kitchen, large windows with views, individually controlled heating and air-conditioning, 24-hour emergency call system. Many apartments have balconies.*

Services: *Included in the monthly fee:* Weekly housekeeping and flat-linen services, full-time move-in coordinator, 24-hour concierge, scheduled transportation, lighted garage parking, additional storage, first year's electric bill. Classic Club membership: long-term care insurance underwritten by Lloyd's of London, complimentary overnight accommodations at Classic Residences, membership in airline club, exclusive travel opportunities.

At additional cost: Beauty/barbershop, dry-cleaning pick-up and delivery, guest accommodations, additional transportation, housekeeping/personal laundry services, prescription drug/grocery delivery service.

Activities: Personalized computer lifestyle profile provides full-time resident relations/programming staff with opportunity to individually tailor a variety of educational, cultural, social, and recreational programs to residents' interests. Classes, lectures, movies, concerts, dances, cultural outings. Indoor swimming pool with lifeguard, art studio, billiards room, card room, club room, well-stocked library, outdoor walking paths.

Availability: Waiting list for certain apartment styles.

Health services and rates: All residents are covered by long-term care insurance, underwritten by Lloyd's of London. Assisted Living is staffed by a director and certified nursing assistant. Furnished apartments are available for short-term recovery from temporary illness. Residents who relocate to Assisted Living remain eligible to receive long-term care insurance benefits. Classic Residence can arrange for immediate access to reputable nursing facilities nearby.

- 22 Assisted Living apartments

	*Monthly fee**
1-Bedroom, 660–750 sq. ft.	$2,800
1-Bedroom/study, 890–960 sq. ft.	$3,000
1-Bedroom/den, 990–1,035 sq. ft.	$3,300

**For double occupancy with one person needing care add $450 to the monthly fee; for both residents needing care add $750.*

"A distinguished leader in the hospitality industry for more than three decades, Hyatt has set the standard for high-quality accommodations and attentive service. Classic Residence has built upon Hyatt's expertise, bringing innovative cuisine, striking interior design, and personalized, supportive services to the senior living industry."

BROADMEAD

13801 York Road
Cockeysville, MD 21030
(410) 527-1900
Karolyn S. Huffman, director of admissions

Type of community: Not-for-profit Continuing Care, all-inclusive contract

Accreditation: Continuing Care Accreditation Commission

Broadmead has 242 Independent Living units arranged in 16 clusters on an historic 84-acre estate. Each apartment's front door opens out to a common landscaped courtyard, and all apartments are connected by a covered walkway system to the center. Additionally, 27 units in the central building are especially designed for those who find walking difficult. The campus has walking areas and a nature trail designed by residents; horse stables, riding trails, and hiking paths are throughout the countryside. Restaurants and shopping are nearby. The community is within two miles of Oregon Ridge State Park offering a nature center, dinner theater, and summer concerts (Baltimore Symphony). Broadmead is convenient to multiple quality hospitals and offers easy access to cultural, sporting, and entertainment events in Baltimore and the marinas.

INDEPENDENT LIVING HOUSING

Type/size of unit	*Entrance fee**	*Monthly fee**
Studio, 485 sq. ft.	$59,000	$1,393
1-Bedroom, 700–875 sq. ft.	$94,600–112,400	$1,671–2,507
2-Bedroom, 870–1,040 sq. ft.	$122,800–140,600	$1,950–2,785

**For double occupancy add $16,000 to the entrance fee, $836 to the monthly fee. All utilities included. Wall-to-wall carpeting, individually controlled heating and air-conditioning, 24-hour emergency call system, private patio, flower garden area around patio, fully equipped kitchen.*

Johns Hopkins University, Goucher College, Loyola College, and Towson State University as well as many historic sights and landmarks are all in the Baltimore area. Broadmead is located 30 to 40 minutes from Baltimore Washington International Airport and the Pennsylvania Station, and within a two-hour drive to Washington, D.C., Annapolis, and Philadelphia.

Financial plan: Entrance plus monthly fee. Refund of entrance fee less 6% for first month of residency and 2% for each month thereafter for a total of 48 months.

Ownership and management: Owned and managed by Friends Lifetime Care Center of Baltimore, Inc. Opened in 1979.

Minimum age: 65 years.

Population: 415 residents; 75% women, 25% men, 17% couples.

Number of units: 269 Independent Living residences; 16 Assisted Living units, 79-bed nursing facility.

Dining plan: Three meals per day included in the monthly fee. Two meals optional. Special diets, tray service included. Guesthouse with private dining and party facilities.

Services: *Included in the monthly fee:* Weekly housekeeping and flat-linen services, regularly scheduled transportation for shopping, laundry facilities.

At additional cost: Carports, laundry and cleaning pick-up, beauty/barbershop, UPS receiving/sending service, bank branch, guest house overnight stays.

Activities: Residents' council, auditorium, meeting rooms, libraries, outdoor and indoor recreational areas, ceramics, art, sewing, woodworking, photography, volunteering, gardening, indoor swimming pool and Jacuzzi, exercise studio.

Availability: Waiting list, availability depending on unit. Deposit of $1,150 ($1,750 for married couple) for priority list; $1,000 ($1,500 for married couple) is applied toward entrance fee once applicant is accepted.

Health services and rates: Broadmead Medical Services, Inc., runs on-site health services. Health care, Assisted Living, visits at Broadmead's clinic, referrals to outside specialists when necessary, transportation to specialists, prescription coverage, laboratory workups, physical and occupational therapies, and administration of health insurance claims are all included in the residents' monthly fee. Massage therapist, dentist, ophthalmologist, and podiatrist available at extra charge.

- 16 Assisted Living
- 79-Bed nursing facility

"The Quaker tradition speaks to Friends' values, which include a capacity for love, concern for one another, personal integrity, appreciation for the simple things of life, and a belief that there is that of God in each person. The purpose of Broadmead is to encourage the personal independence of older individuals through a warm and congenial environment that is both personally and intellectually stimulating and that offers the opportunity to pursue a productive and satisfying life."

WILLIAM HILL MANOR

501 Dutchman's Lane
Easton, MD 21601
(410) 822-8888 or (800) 432-0899
Sue Davis, admissions coordinator
Beth M. Weems, marketing director

Type of community: Continuing Care, modified contract

Located on spacious grounds within the town limits of Easton, William Hill Manor lies in the heart of Maryland's scenic Eastern shore. The area's colonial heritage is reflected in the Manor's period architecture. Independent Living residences are located in the three-story brick Georgian manor house as well as individual cottages that surround the community. The health care center and Assisted Living facility are adjacent to the manor house and are connected by walkways. The community is centrally located within an 80-mile radius of the major metropolitan areas of Washington, D.C., and Baltimore, as well as the shores of the Atlantic Ocean.

Financial plan: Entrance fee plus monthly fee. Purchase option with guaranteed buy-back for cottages.

Ownership and management: Private corporation. Largest stockholder is William Hill Manor president, Dr. David Hill. Managed by a board of directors. Opened in 1981.

Minimum age: 62 years.

Population: 245 residents; 71% women, 29% men.

Number of units: 63 Independent Living apartments and 55 cottages; 19 Assisted Living units, 76 comprehensive nursing beds.

INDEPENDENT LIVING HOUSING

Type/size of apartment	*Entrance fee single/double*	*Monthly fee single/double**
Single, 260 sq. ft.	$5,548	$1,387
Studio, 326 sq. ft.	$6,356	$1,589
1-Bedroom, 525 sq. ft.	$12,822/16,860	$2,137/2,810
Deluxe 1-bedroom, 652 sq. ft.	$13,536/17,574	$2,256/2,929
2-Bedroom, 756 sq. ft.	$14,406/18,444	$2,401/3,074

Cottages	*Purchase price*	*Entrance fee single/double*	*Monthly fee single/double*
1-Bedroom, 900 sq. ft.	$72,000	$4,500/5,500	$1,511/2,029
2-Bedroom, 1,176 sq. ft.	$98,000	$5,500/6,500	$1,739/2,303
2-Bedroom/den, 1,530 sq. ft.	$138,000	$6,000/7,000	$1,889/2,422

**All utilities except telephone included in the monthly fee. Individually controlled heating and air-conditioning, wall-to-wall carpeting, draperies, and 24-hour emergency call system.* Note: *Freestanding deluxe cottages up to 2,600 square feet are available at additional cost. All cottages sold with deed transfer and guaranteed buy-back agreement. Monthly fee includes utilities up to $150 per month. Wall-to-wall carpeting, full kitchen with appliances and washer/dryer, individually controlled heating and air-conditioning, 24-hour emergency call system.*

Dining plan: Three meals per day included in the apartment monthly fee; one meal per day included in the cottage monthly fee. Additional meals available. Catering. Private dining room.

Services: *Included in the monthly fee:* Scheduled transportation, flat-linen service, housekeeping supplies. For apartments: housekeeping services five days per week; cottages receive weekly housekeeping.

At additional cost: Beauty/barbershop, gift shop, private transportation, guest accommodations.

Activities: Full-time social director. Crafts sessions, game nights, exercise groups, theater and cultural outings, literature corner, current events classes, movies, music appreciation, painting classes, church services, dancing, shopping trips, in-house seminars, entertainment programs. Opportunities for involvement in Talbot County offerings such as Academy of the Arts, historical society, garden clubs, fishing, boating, hunting, golfing, YMCA.

Availability: 12-month waiting list.

Health services and rates: Medical director and director of nursing work closely with area physicians and Memorial Hospital in Easton (minutes from the Manor). Residents may use the services of their own physicians or those of the center's. In-house physical therapy. Specialist referrals for speech therapy, audiologist, podiatrist, oncologist, ophthalmologist, dermatologist.

- 19 Assisted Living units
  - Semiprivate $98/day
  - Minisuite $112/day
  - Deluxe suite $140/day
- 76-Bed nursing facility
  - Semiprivate $95–97/day
  - Private $115–185/day

"William Hill Manor is relatively small when compared to most communities. It promotes a family atmosphere between staff and residents in a country club setting. The mission of William Hill Manor is to provide quality service through a personal commitment to excellence, ensuring the ultimate in retirement living. A video overview of the community can be requested by calling the 800 number."

ASBURY METHODIST VILLAGE

201 Russell Avenue
Gaithersburg, MD 20877
(301) 216-4106
Lidia Pugh, marketing coordinator

Type of community: Not-for-profit Continuing Care, modified contract

Accreditation: Continuing Care Accreditation Commission

Asbury Methodist Village is located on a 130-acre campus bordering Historic Old Towne Gaithersburg. Four high-rise Independent Living brick apartment buildings are connected by covered glass walkways to apartment/community centers and dining rooms. The grounds feature a large pond and beautiful landscaping. Montgomery County Golf course is three miles away; Athletic Express racquetball and exercise club is across the street. Dulles, National, and Baltimore/Washington airports are all within 45 minutes.

Financial plan: Entrance fee plus monthly fee. Two plans: **1)** Standard entrance fee, amortized over the first 60 months of residency. **2)** 90% refundable entrance fee, 45% higher than standard entrance fee.

Ownership and management: Asbury Methodist Homes, Inc., a not-for-profit corporation related by tradition to the Baltimore Conference of the United Methodist Church but not legally or financially controlled by the conference. Eighteen-member board of trustees. Asbury was the first retirement community to receive an A rating on its tax-free bonds. Opened in 1926.

Minimum age: 65 years (if couple, spouse must be at least 60).

INDEPENDENT LIVING HOUSING

Type/size of apartment	*Entrance fee 1/2*	*Monthly fee**
Studio, 538 sq. ft.	$42,000/60,900	$742
1-Bedroom, 688 sq. ft.	$55,500/80,475	$873
2-Bedroom, 1,030 sq. ft.	$103,500/150,075	$1,173/1,471
2-Bedroom, 1,107 sq. ft.	$110,500/160,225	$1,239/1,537
3-Bedroom, 1,598 sq. ft.	$195,000/282,750	$1,561/1,862

**All utilities except telephone included in the monthly fee. Wall-to-wall carpeting, full kitchen, carpeting, individually controlled heating and air-conditioning, 24-hour emergency call system.*

Population: 1,400 residents; 66% women, 34% men, 34% couples.

Number of units: 577 Independent Living apartments (32 villas under construction); 196 Assisted Living suites, 285-bed Skilled Nursing center.

Dining plan: Dinner included in the monthly fee with option for lunch at additional cost.

Services: *Included in the monthly fee:* Scheduled transportation.

At additional cost: Laundry services.

Activities: Exercise classes, 100 garden plots, garden clubs, art studio, woodworking shops, computer room, photography room, indoor and outdoor swimming available nearby, square dancing, trips, theater, Keese School of Continuing Education classes.

Availability: Limited. Smaller apartments from eight months to one year.

Health services and rates: Outpatient services such as ophthalmology, dentistry, gynecology, podiatry, X ray, rehabilitative therapies, social services, volunteer services. Recuperative and respite care. United Methodists have priority for direct admission.

- 196 Assisted Living suites

	Entrance fee	*Monthly fee*
Single	$37,500	$1,682–1,868
Double	$47,500	$2,394–2,661

- 285-Bed nursing facility

Semiprivate	$124.70/day
Private	$134.30/day

"Asbury Methodist Village is a nonprofit, church-related Continuing Care retirement community that offers opportunities to all people for meaningful and creative living within an environment that provides the highest possible quality of life. Personal independence, intellectual stimulation, recreational and learning activities, a graceful and beautiful 130-acre campus, and a high quality of health care are all hallmarks of life at Asbury, whose strong financial reserves and healthy financial ratios continue to set standards in the retirement field."

GLEN MEADOWS

11630 Glen Arm Road
Glen Arm, MD 21057
(410) 592-5310
Frances Foltz and Meredith Snediker, marketing representatives

Type of community: Nonprofit Continuing Care, modified contract

The original stone building constructed in the late 1800s is sometimes referred to as the "castle on the hill." Situated on a 483-acre campus on a hill overlooking Glen Arm Valley, Glen Meadows offers

INDEPENDENT LIVING HOUSING

Type/size of apartment	*Entrance fee*	*Monthly fee**
Studio, 260–370 sq. ft.	$42,000–56,200	$820–870
1-Bedroom, 380–600 sq. ft.	$72,400–97,100	$1,000–1,060
1-Bedroom/den, 610–670 sq. ft.	$108,200	$1,090
Patio homes		
1-Bedroom, 672 sq. ft.	$112,900	$1,060
1-Bedroom/den, 768–784 sq. ft.	$119,600–120,020	$1,090–1,120
2-Bedroom, 896 sq. ft.	$125,800	$1,160
2-Bedroom/den, 1,024 sq. ft.	$163,100	$1,190

**For double occupancy add $370 to the monthly fee. All utilities except telephone included. Wall-to-wall carpeting, draperies, individually controlled heating and air-conditioning, modern kitchen appliances, 24-hour emergency call system, cable TV.*

patio homes and apartments for Independent Living residents. The main building houses apartments, health care center, library, fitness center, full-service bank, woodworking shop, beauty/barbershop, formal dining room, coffee shop, and chapel. The Great Hall features cathedral ceilings and stained-glass windows and is used for special activities, meetings, and entertainment. Newly renovated patio homes are connected to the main building by covered walkways. The campus features two large ponds stocked with fish, gardening areas, and 1½ miles of nature trails. Glen Meadows is located 12 minutes from downtown Towson and 20 minutes from Bel Air and Baltimore.

Financial plan: Entrance fee (100% refundable when apartment or patio home has been resold and reoccupied), plus a monthly fee. $150 application fee. Deposit: $1,000 or $1,500 (for one and two persons, respectively).

Ownership and management: Presbyterian Senior Services, Inc., manages the community as a joint effort by the Presbytery of Baltimore, in existence for over 200 years, and Presbyterian Homes, Inc., which presently operates 18 facilities in five states and has been in existence for 76 years. Opened in 1991.

Minimum age: 62 years.

Population: 200+ residents.

Number of units: 114 Independent Living patio homes and 101 apartments; 16 Assisted Living units, 30-bed health care center.

Dining plan: One meal daily included in the monthly fee. An elegant dining room. A skylit café for breakfast and lunch is available but not included in the meal plan.

Services: *Included in the monthly fee:* Weekly housekeeping, weekly flat-linen service, scheduled transportation, maintenance of major appliances.

At additional cost: Barber/beautyshop, country store, newspaper delivery, dry cleaning.

Activities: Trips to the theater, museums, malls, and grocery stores. Arts and crafts, woodworking, ceramics, exercise room with stationary bikes and treadmills, Bible study, lecture programs, cards, musical entertainment, and more.

Availability: Immediate availability.

Health services and rates: 30 days of nursing care provided to residents at no additional charge. Eligible residents participate in a two-year group, long-term care insurance plan. A physician is on call around the clock and on-site 1/2 day a week. Physical therapy, speech therapy, oxygen therapy, podiatry, laboratory, pharmacy, dental, and ophthalmology services available.

- 16 Assisted Living units
- 30-Bed health center
  Private room $103/day

"Tradition is part of Glen Meadows's heritage. A tradition that has continued for almost 100 years is the ringing of the bells. The School Sisters of Notre Dame used the bells to order the day, as we do now at noon and 6 p.m. The apartment building, which contains the bell tower and all the common facilities, was formerly the home of the sisters. The Great Hall was formerly the chapel. Glen Meadows's unique features include community size, views, and proximity to metropolitan areas, all in a beautiful country setting, in addition to the experience of an established nonprofit care provider."

COLLINGTON EPISCOPAL COMMUNITY

10450 Lottsford Road
Mitchellville, MD 20721
(301) 925-9610
Ann Hammond, admissions coordinator

Type of community: Nonprofit Continuing Care, all-inclusive contract

Nestled on 128 acres of rolling hills in Prince George's County, Collington combines a peaceful wooded setting with close proximity to shopping, cultural, and recreational opportunities. Covered walkways connect dwellings to all community buildings. Overlooking a serene six-acre lake, three-story garden apartments offer Independent Living as do individual cottages with patios, clustered in 11 distinct neighborhoods. The eastern boundary is a natural park owned by the state of Maryland.

Financial plan: Entrance fee plus monthly fee. Two plans: **1)** Entrance fee amortized at a rate of 2% per month for 25 months after which entrance fee remains 50% refundable. **2)** Entrance amortized at a rate of 2% per month for 50 months. Refundable deposit equal to 10% of entrance fee.

Ownership and management: Independent nonprofit corporation operated by Collington board of directors. Opened in 1988.

Minimum age: If under 65 years, there is a surcharge. Average age is 79.

Population: 400 residents; 70% women, 30% men, 33% couples.

Number of units: 120 Independent Living apartments and 180 cottages; 47 Assisted Living beds, 37-bed Skilled Nursing facility.

Dining plan: Three meals a day included in the monthly fee. Partial credit for missed meals. Private dining room and catering.

Services: *Included in the monthly fee:* Bimonthly housekeeping, weekly flat-linen service, scheduled transportation, self-service laundry centers.

At additional cost: Beauty/barbershop, coffee shop, country store, bank, transportation, guest accommodations.

Activities: Residents' association participates in developing stimulating activities program. Fitness center with equipped exercise room, 75-foot heated indoor pool, exercise programs, arts, meditation, music programs, game rooms, library, seminars.

Availability: Limited. Waiting list varies with size of accommodation.

Health services and rates: Unlimited health care included in resident's monthly fee. Dentists and podiatrists available. Rehabilitation therapists and nurses can provide care in resident's apartment or cottage. Employees in health center provide professional supervision or assistance on temporary or permanent care for no additional charge. Recreational and therapeutic activities designed to help residents lead active and satisfying lives.

- 47 Assisted Living units
- 37-Bed Skilled Nursing facility (semiprivate/private)

"Collington's greatest asset is its residents. They are a diverse and fascinating group with an amazing range of educational, vocational, and travel backgrounds and experience. Many of them are very active through the residents' association in creative arts, volunteer activities, and continued vocational interests."

BEDFORD COURT

3701 International Drive
Silver Spring, MD 20906
(301) 598-2900
Kimberly Gotard, retirement counselor

Type of community: Continuing Care, modified contract

Bedford Court is housed in a seven-story brick apartment building set on six acres with an adjoining three-story health care center. Located in a suburban, residential neighborhood, the community features a courtyard and walking area with duck pond. Post office and bank are nearby; complete shopping center is just steps away.

Financial plan: Entrance fee ($7,000), fully refundable with interest, plus monthly fee. Optional annuity plans, specifically designed for Marriott residents, available. Individual long-term care insurance policies available to cover nursing care. Fully refundable priority deposit of $1,000.

Ownership and management: Owned by Health and Rehabilitation Investment Trust. Managed by Marriott Senior Living Services, a wholly owned subsidiary of Marriott Corporation. Marriott manages 13 retirement communities in Arizona, California, Florida, Illinois, Indiana, Maryland, New Jersey, Texas, and Virginia. Opened in March 1992.

Minimum age: 60 years.

Population: 260 residents; 75% women, 25% men, 17% couples.

Number of units: 215 apartments; 76 Assisted Living units, 43 nursing beds.

Dining plan: Monthly fee includes 30 meals. Private dining room. Cocktail lounge.

Services: *Included in the monthly fee:* Scheduled transportation, weekly housekeeping, flat-linen service, on-site parking, secured storage area.

INDEPENDENT LIVING HOUSING

Type/size of apartment	*Entrance fee*	*Monthly fee**
1-Bedroom, 612 sq. ft.	$7,000	$1,790–2,390
Deluxe 1-bedroom, 630–792 sq. ft.	$7,000	$1,790–2,390
2-Bedroom, 900–960 sq. ft.	$7,000	$2,590–3,050
Deluxe 2-bedroom, 1,034–1,059 sq. ft.	$7,000	$3,190–3,290
Premier 2-bedroom/den, 1,224 sq. ft.	$7,000	$3,409–3,990

**For double occupancy add $415 to the monthly fee. All utilities except telephone and cable TV included. Balconies, full kitchens with pass-throughs, wall-to-wall carpeting, window treatments, individually controlled heating and air-conditioning, master TV antenna and cable wiring, 24-hour emergency call system.*

At additional cost: Beauty/barbershop, country store/gift shop, banking center.

Activities: Library/reading room, auditorium, game/card room, arts studio, health club and spa.

Availability: Waiting list for two-bedroom. Limited availability for other floor plans.

Health services and rates: Physical, occupational, and speech therapies available. Greater Washington, D.C., Rehabilitative Center is across the street.

- 76 Assisted Living suites

Private	$74–104/day (fee depends on level of care)

- 43-Bed nursing facility

Semiprivate	$132/day
Private	$153/day

"Residents enjoy all the qualitative benefits of living in and contributing to a caring community, fostering life of the mind with a sense of purpose. Excellent service is more than just a business philosophy, it's been a Marriott family tradition for over 60 years. And all that we've learned as a leader in the service and hospitality industry is applied to satisfy the needs of older adults living in our retirement communities."

Marilyn, 73 years

Smith Ranch, San Rafael, California

"My son thought I was a little late moving into a retirement community, but the truth is I wasn't ready to leave Winnetka and my friends."

In 1994, when she finally moved in to Smith Ranch, Marilyn was ready. "My daughter, who lives with her family nearby, was all for it, and my son, Rick, who is building a home in Napa, thought I was a little late moving in," she explains. "The truth is I wasn't ready to leave Winnetka and my friends. It's a traumatic move, with lots of decisions of what to take with you, packing and unpacking, and where to put things once you move in."

Marilyn looked at numerous communities in Illinois, Florida, and California before making her decision. "I finally decided that I wanted to be near my children and so chose Northern California. What spurred me on was that I was having trouble with my vision and my eye doctor in Florida said I had cataracts, which would require surgery at some point. I had seen Smith Ranch, stayed overnight several times, and felt very comfortable there."

Fortunately, the unit she wanted was available for sale (Smith Ranch is an equity community) and Marilyn moved in quickly. Her surgery was scheduled for two weeks after her arrival. She recovered in the nearby hospital used by Smith Ranch residents and then nurses attended to her in her villa as she required assistance.

"I've never liked high-rises," explains Marilyn, "so this setup is perfect for me. I love the grounds, which are beautifully planted and manicured. I like the ambiance—men have to wear jackets at dinner and over half of the residents are couples, which is nice. I do think a community like this is the answer for people who can afford it."

Her grandson's school is only fifteen minutes away, so Marilyn can pick him up after school if her daughter can't. She says she is happy to be close to her family, but misses her friends and neighbors. She says she sometimes wonders if family members have the time that friends and neighbors seem to. Recently, though, a friend and neighbor of hers from Ohio moved in to Smith Ranch, so now she has both family and friends nearby.

FAIRHAVEN

7200 Third Avenue
Sykesville, MD 21784
(410) 795-8800
Susan Matiasen, admissions director

Type of community: Nonprofit Continuing Care, all-inclusive contract

Accreditation: Continuing Care Accreditation Commission

Fairhaven is located on what was once a 300-acre farm owned by Frank and Viola Beasman. The gently rolling landscaped countryside features native wildflowers and gardens planted by residents. The grounds, designated as a bird sanctuary by the Maryland Ornithological Society, offer nearly 5,000 feet of walking trails. Buildings are designed to blend harmoniously with Fairhaven's sloping, spacious setting. Living facilities are connected by covered walkways to the Beasman Center, which houses all common areas. Assisted Living and a health care center are on-site. The grounds include a three-hole golf course, garden plots, and a putting green. Major golf courses and other forms of recreation are nearby. A county park nearby offers a lake for fishing.

Financial plan: Entrance fee plus monthly fee. Two plans: **1)** Entrance fee is refundable less 2% per month for the first 50 months of occupancy. **2)** 90% refundable entrance fee. $1,000 deposit; $1,500 deposit for couples.

Ownership and management: Sponsored by the Episcopal Ministries to the Aging, Inc., which is a nonprofit membership corporation separate and distinct from the Episcopal Diocese of Maryland. Opened in 1980.

Minimum age: 65 years.

Population: 429 residents; 70% women, 30% men, 25% couples.

Number of units: 278 Independent Living cottages and apartments; 28 congregate care apartments, 29 Assisted Living apartments, 99-bed health center.

INDEPENDENT LIVING HOUSING

Type/size of apartment	*Entrance fee 1**	*Monthly fee single/double**
Efficiency, 300 sq. ft.	$52,000	$1,370
Studio, 360 sq. ft.	$62,000	$1,400
Studio/alcove, 441 sq. ft.	$72,000	$1,490
1-Bedroom, 546 sq. ft.	$95,000–110,000	$1,645/2,735
1-Bedroom/den, 661 sq. ft.	$102,000–117,000	$1,850/2,940
2-Bedroom, 852 sq. ft.	$106,000–121,000	$1,885/2,885
Cottages		
1-Bedroom, 764 sq. ft.	$116,000	$2,055/3,145
1-Bedroom/den, 946 sq. ft.	$116,000–131,000	$1,875/2,965
2-Bedroom, 1,112 sq. ft.	$124,000–131,000	$2,070/3,160
2-Bedroom/den, 1,320 sq. ft.	$141,000–156,000	$2,250/3,340

*Note: *90% refundable entrance fees range from $85,800–321,750. For double occupancy add $15,000 to the entrance fee, $945 to the monthly fee. All utilities except telephone included. Draperies, wall-to-wall carpeting, individually controlled heating and air-conditioning, all-electric fully equipped kitchen, sound-proof construction, connections to a central satellite system, 24-hour emergency call system. Cottages and ground-level apartments have patios. Carports additional.*

Dining plan: Three meals a day are included in the monthly fee. Special diets are accommodated when prescribed by a physician.

Services: *Included in the monthly fee:* Scheduled transportation, weekly flat-linen and housecleaning services, parking, self-service laundry centers, storage space.

At additional cost: Beauty/barbershop, coffee and gift shop, bank, newspaper delivery, laundry and dry cleaning.

Activities: Indoor swimming/therapeutic pool with whirlpool and greenhouse, classes in crafts, musicals, gardening, library, outings to concerts, lectures and plays, trips to Washington and Baltimore, fall foliage tours, par-3 golf course, woodworking shop, religious services, and residents' council.

Availability: Waiting list of one to five years.

Health services and rates: Unlimited health care is covered by the entrance and monthly fees. Residents continue to pay the fee for the last unit occupied when they move into the health center. At least one staff physician visits the health center daily and other physicians are on call at all times. Registered nurses are always available and physical and recreational therapy are available as needed. Each room has a lovely view of the surrounding countryside. Long-term residents are encouraged to decorate the room as they please. On-site ambulatory care center provides acute, chronic, and emergency health care services including: primary care physicians, podiatry, ophthalmology, radiology, dermatology, audiology, gynecology, psychiatry, speech therapy, physical therapy, dental services including oral surgery and periodontics, and preoperative and postoperative surgery.

- 29 Assisted Living units
- 99-Bed health center

"The residents at Fairhaven are very active in the planning and execution of over 75 programs and activities. One of the most popular and well-attended classes here is the painting class in the art studio."

CARROLL LUTHERAN VILLAGE

205 St. Mark Way
Westminster, MD 21158
(410) 848-0090
Breta Marie Crumbacker, director of marketing

Type of community: Nonprofit Continuing Care, modified contract

Accreditation: Continuing Care Accreditation Commission

Carroll Lutheran Village is comprised of apartment buildings, separate cottages, and a health center located on a 90-acre partially wooded campus overlooking Wakefield Valley and a 27-hole golf course. The campus is rural yet close to town amenities. Westminster's population is over 10,000. Views of mountain range are available from apartments. Access available to nearby urban centers of Baltimore, Washington, D.C., Frederick, Hanover, and the historic community of Gettysburg, Pennsylvania.

Financial plan: Entrance fee plus monthly fee. Two plans: **1)** Entrance fee amortizes over eight years at 1% per month. **2)** Higher entrance fee and guaranteed 2/3 refund. 25% deposit of the entrance fee is due when the occupancy agreement is signed. All deposits fully refundable until date of occupancy.

Ownership and management: Owned by 28 participating Lutheran churches in the Westminster Conference of the Delaware-Maryland Synod, Evangelical Lutheran Church in America. Managed by Carroll Lutheran Village, Inc. Opened in 1980.

Minimum age: 60 years.

Population: 322 residents; 73% women, 27% men, 21% couples.

INDEPENDENT LIVING HOUSING

Type/size of apartment	*Entrance fee*	*Monthly fee**
Studio, 389 sq. ft.	$45,000	$398
1-Bedroom, 552–717 sq. ft.	$62,000–69,000	$476–520
2-Bedroom, 890–1,462 sq. ft.	$94,000–167,000	$635–839
Cottages		
1-Bedroom, 750 sq. ft.	$71,000–75,000	$188–208
2-Bedroom, 900–1,250 sq. ft.	$90,000–159,000	$188–208
Individual, 1,250–1,400 sq. ft.	$160,000–200,000	$188–208

**For double occupancy add $180 to the monthly fee for apartments, $20 to the monthly fee for cottages. All utilities included for apartments; cottages pay own utilities. Wall-to-wall carpeting, cable TV (optional), individually controlled heating and air-conditioning, fully equipped kitchen, patio or balcony, 24-hour emergency call system. Real estate taxes are invoiced separately once a year.*

Number of units: 209 Independent Living apartments and 48 cottages; 99-bed health center.

Dining plan: One meal per day, five days per week, included in the monthly fee for apartment residents. Fee-for-service cafeteria for lunch and weekend meals.

Services: *Included in the monthly fee:* Parking, scheduled transportation for shopping and medical appointments.

At additional cost: Laundry facilities, beauty/barbershop, housekeeping, guest accommodations.

Activities: Art classes, exercise classes, religious services, organized outings, shopping excursions, shuffleboard courts, crafts and hobby rooms, horseshoe court, music classes, outdoor exercise course, game rooms, golf course adjacent to property, fitness classes, community events, gardening, horseshoe pit, workshop, walking/exercise trail. An active residents' association with committees: religious life, workshop, quality of life, library, social. Residents are an integral part of the activity program.

Availability: Waiting list from six months to three years, depending on type of residence.

Health services and rates: Three levels of care: minimum, Intermediate, and Skilled. Therapy services offered. Assisted Living facility in planning stage. Prices reflect semiprivate rooms. For private room add $21/day.

- 99-Bed health center

Minimum care	$97/day
Intermediate	$108/day
Skilled	$122/day

"Carroll Lutheran Village is a Continuing Care retirement community dedicated to the ministry of caring in a Christian atmosphere, fostering quality life and services for the whole person. The Village is blessed with a large group of supporters known as the Friends of the Village. These caring volunteers organize crafts, hold fund-raisers, operate the gift shop, and provide the many little extras that make life special. You are welcome to become a part of this valuable organization."

HOMEWOOD AT WILLIAMSPORT

2750 Virginia Avenue
Williamsport, MD 21795
(301) 582-1472
Priya Kurtz, marketing director

Type of community: Nonprofit Continuing Care, modified contract

Situated on 26 acres of beautifully landscaped grounds amid a quiet residential community, Homewood at Williamsport offers traditional New England housing, walkways, and garden plots. The community center has restaurant, full-service banking, postal service, convenience store, and fitness center. Homewood is located in historic Washington County, Maryland, site of the Civil War battle of Antietam. Battlefield National Historic Park is approximately 15 miles away. Nearby are three other national parks, and Hagerstown offers the Maryland Symphony, the Washington County Museum of Fine Arts, and plenty of theater and shopping, including the Valley Mall. Baltimore and Washington, D.C., are one hour away.

Financial plan: Entrance fee plus monthly fee. Entrance fee depreciates for refund purposes over ten years. $2,500 deposit. There is an entrance fee surcharge of 1% per year for residents under the age of 70 years.

Ownership and management: Homewood Retirement Centers of the United Church of Christ, owner/manager of two other Continuing Care communities in Pennsylvania and one in Maryland. Nursing care opened in 1932; Retirement community opened in 1981.

Population: 450 residents; 70% women, 30% men, 25% couples.

Number of units: 126 Independent Living cottages and 114 apartments; 33 Assisted Living rooms, 110-bed Skilled Nursing facility (51 beds reserved for Alzheimer's patients).

Dining plan: There is a meal minimum of $40 per resident per month. Lunch is served every day and dinner is available on scheduled weeknights. Residents are billed monthly.

Services: *Included in the monthly fee:* On-campus transportation.

At additional cost: Beauty/barbershop, restaurant, bank, postal service, convenience store, housekeeping, chores and laundry service.

INDEPENDENT LIVING HOUSING

Type/size of apartment	*Entrance fee*	*Monthly fee**
Studio/alcove, 400 sq. ft.	$36,200	$345
1-Bedroom, 530–630 sq. ft.	$54,900–56,100	$345
2-Bedroom, 720–800 sq. ft.	$66,300	$345
Cottage		
1-Bedroom/den, 800 sq. ft.	$73,100	$345
2-Bedroom, 880 sq. ft.	$76,450	$345
2-Bedroom/den, 1,100 sq. ft.	$95,700	$345

**For double occupancy add $395 to the monthly fee. Residents are responsible for paying electricity, telephone, cable TV, and property taxes. Wall-to-wall carpeting, draperies, individually controlled heating and air-conditioning, fully equipped kitchens, 24-hour emergency call system. Cottages have washer/dryer.*

Activities: Exercise room, sauna, whirlpool, swimming pool, water exercise classes, cards, bingo, library, gardening, painting class, and organized excursions.

Availability: Limited.

Health services and rates: Health center offers respite care and Intermediate and Skilled Nursing, plus an Alzheimer's wing.

- 33 Assisted Living rooms
  $59/day, plus fee for services
- 110-Bed health care center
  Nursing care $94–99/day
  Alzheimer's special care $114–124/day

"Homewood offers a carefree retirement lifestyle with an unobtrusive safety net of services and security, at a price most can afford."

MASSACHUSETTS

APPLEWOOD AT AMHERST

1 Spencer Drive
Amherst, MA 01002-9921
(413) 253-9833
Eileen Vincent, director of marketing

Type of community: Not-for-profit Continuing Care, all-inclusive contract

Three-story contemporary colonial Independent Living apartment buildings are situated on ten acres of orchard land in Pioneer Valley. The community offers views of the majestic Holyoke Range and Pelham Hills and is a short distance from the college towns of Amherst (University of Massachusetts, Amherst, Hampshire), Northampton (Smith), and South Hadley (Holyoke), which offer classroom experience and diverse cultural programs. The beautifully landscaped site is threaded with nature trails and walkways. Assisted Living services are offered on campus; Skilled Nursing facility is off-premises. Opportunities abound for the outdoor enthusiast: golf, swimming, hiking, tennis, and wildlife and bird sanctuaries. Applewood offers easy access to the Massachusetts Turnpike and Interstate 91 and is 45 minutes from Bradley International Airport and the Berkshires.

Financial plan: Entrance fee plus monthly fee. Entrance fee is 90% refundable.

Ownership and management: Not-for-profit community conceived and developed by area residents who wanted to ensure security and comfort in their retirement years. Opened in 1992.

Minimum age: 62 years.

Population: 135 residents; 64% women, 36% men, 32% couples.

Number of units: 103 Independent Living apartments; Skilled Nursing is contracted out to nearby facility.

INDEPENDENT LIVING HOUSING

Type/size of apartment	*Entrance fee*	*Monthly fee**
Studio, 440 sq. ft.	$101,000	$855
1-Bedroom, 615 sq. ft.	$157,000 or $162,000	$1,087
2-Bedroom/1-bath, 834 sq. ft.	$187,000 or $192,000	$1,261
2-Bedroom/2-bath, 920–1,040 sq. ft.	$195,000–238,000	$1,365–1,667
2-Bedroom/den, 1,191–1,228 sq. ft.	$266,000–277,000	$1,899–1,957

**For double occupancy add $316 to the monthly fee. All utilities except telephone included . Fully appointed kitchens, balconies and patios, individually controlled heating and air-conditioning, 24-hour emergency call system, wall-to-wall carpeting, window coverings, washers/dryers.*

Dining plan: Choice of one main meal per day included in the monthly fee. Private dining room for parties and special occasions.

Services: *Included in the monthly fee:* Weekly housekeeping and flat-linen services, transportation.

At additional cost: Long-term care insurance, beauty/barbershop, daily housekeeping, individualized transportation, newspaper delivery, secretarial and notary services, guest suites, personal laundry service, full-service grocery store. Parking garage one-time charge of $8,500 (90% refundable).

Activities: Library, fitness center, audio-equipped meeting room, walking trails, learning, social, and recreational programs.

Availability: Limited.

Health services and rates: Routine care, screenings, flu shots, and first aid on-site. Variety of wellness programs and nutritional counseling. If residents want to participate in Continuing Care, they must have long-term care insurance; four different policies available up to full Continuing Care (in addition to entrance and monthly fees).

- Assisted Living services are available in resident's apartment.
- Skilled Nursing is contracted out to facility nearby.

"Applewood is Pioneer Valley's first full Continuing Care retirement community."

CARLETON-WILLARD VILLAGE

100 Old Billerica Road
Bedford, MA 01730
(800) 429-8669
Mary Jane Harvey, marketing director

Type of community: Nonprofit Continuing Care, modified contract

Accreditation: Continuing Care Accreditation Commission

Located on a 65-acre wooded campus, Carleton-Willard Village offers 91 clustered one-level townhouses, 43 terrace apartments in a three-story building, 25 additional apartments in a luxury three-story building constructed in 1993, Assisted Living suites, and a health center. Main Street, Carleton-Willard Village's shopping arcade, re-creates a 19th century New England town center and serves as center of the community. The community is convenient to nationally recognized medical facilities, local shopping, one of New England's largest malls, cultural entertainment, houses of worship, and the Boston area. Lexington, Lincoln, and historic Concord are also nearby.

Financial plan: Entrance fee plus monthly fee. Entrance fee amortizes at 1% per month of residency for period of 100 months.

Ownership and management: Owned and managed by Carleton-Willard Homes, Inc. Opened in 1982.

Minimum age: 65 years.

Population: 235 residents; 82% women, 18% men, 18% couples.

Number of units: 91 Independent Living townhouses and 68 apartments; 80 Assisted Living suites, 120-bed health center.

Dining plan: One meal per day included in the monthly fee for Independent apartments and townhouse residents.

Services: *Included in the monthly fee:* Housekeeping, flat-linen service, scheduled transportation, parking.

At additional cost: Beauty/barbershop, transportation to symphony, theaters, lectures, museums, and cultural events, guest accommodations.

INDEPENDENT LIVING HOUSING

Type/size of apartment	*Entrance fee**	*Monthly fee**
Studio, 395 sq. ft.	$60,000	$1,071
1-Bedroom, 612 sq. ft.	$75,000	$1,187
2-Bedroom, 758 sq. ft.	$110,000	$1,344
Townhouses		
1-Bedroom, 705–791 sq. ft.	$130,000	$1,310
2-Bedroom, 940–1,410 sq. ft.	$160,000	$1,471–1,897
2-Bedroom/study, 1,410 sq. ft.	$225,000	$1,987
Luxury apartments		
1-Bedroom, 725/810 sq. ft.	$180,000	$1,470
2-Bedroom, 1,020 sq. ft.	$215,000	$1,575
3-Bedroom/study, 1,525 sq. ft.	$250,000	$1,995

**For double occupancy add $5,000 to the entrance fee, $575 to the monthly fee. All utilities except telephone included. Wall-to-wall carpeting, 24-hour emergency call system, individually controlled heating and air-conditioning, fully equipped kitchens, patios or balconies, cable TV. Townhouses have sliding glass doors to rear grounds, some with patios or decks, some with fireplaces.*

Activities: Activities department, residents' activities committee, and residents' association. Gardening clubs, community newsletter, 300-seat auditorium for various events, billiards room, arts and crafts room, florist, library, exercise room, woodworking shop, lawn croquet court, putting green.

Availability: Waiting list. Deposits for waiting list: $1,375 for single, $1,875 for couple; $375 is nonrefundable.

Health services and rates: Health center offers diagnostic, therapeutic, preventive, rehabilitative, and support services. Residents receive 60 free days in health center. After 60 days resident pays 80% of current rate for health center. Physical and occupational therapy offered.

- 80 Assisted Living units

Private	$77/day
2-Room suite	$135/day

- 120-Bed health center

	Intermediate Nursing	*Skilled Nursing*
Semiprivate	$167/day	$177/day
Private	$179/day	$191/day

"Carleton-Willard Village was the first Continuing Care retirement community (CCRC) built in Massachusetts and remains the only CCRC in the state to be accredited by the Continuing Care Accreditation Commission. Carleton-Willard's extensive Learning in Retirement program brings noted lecturers from universities and cultural institutions in the greater Boston area to speak and lead seminars on-site. Our comprehensive wellness program, which includes exercise, nutrition, and proactive medical screening, has been an integral part of the Village since its inception."

THE VILLAGE AT DUXBURY

286 Kings Town Way
Duxbury, MA 02332
(617) 585-2334
Laura Wendrow, marketing director

Type of community: Continuing Care, modified contract

Nestled on 30 wooded acres on Massachusetts' South Shore, three-story buildings of traditional New England architecture house Independent Living and Assisted Living. A nursing facility is adjacent. The seashore town offers quaint shops, tennis, golf, swimming, boating, and fishing. The Village at Duxbury is located 40 minutes from Boston and 30 minutes from Cape Cod.

Financial plan: Cooperative, real estate ownership. Purchase price plus monthly fee.

Ownership and management: Welch Duxbury Development Corporation, an affiliate of the Welch Healthcare and Retirement Group, a local family-owned company in business for more than 40 years and in partnership with the FIDUX group, an affiliate of Fidelity Investments. Opened in Spring 1994.

Minimum age: 62 years.

Population: 100+.

Number of units: 128 Independent Living apartment homes; 40 Assisted Living units.

Dining plan: Meal plans are optional. Three meals available daily in café or restaurant. Private dining room is available for private entertaining.

Services: *Included in the monthly fee:* Flat-linen service, housekeeping, shuttle service.

At additional cost: Beauty/barbershop, convenience store, post office, banking service, guest suites.

Activities: Activities director. Woodworking shop, gardening, creative arts center, exercise activities, indoor pool, library, auditorium, walking trails, croquet.

Availability: 80% of the apartments have been presold.

Health services and rates: All residents have priority access to the nursing care at Bay Path Center, adjacent to The Village. Wellness programs are included in the monthly fee. Optional long-term care insurance policies are available.

- 40 Assisted Living apartments $3,200/month (no purchase or entrance fee)

"The Village is a cooperative, which offers the advantages of ownership without the obligation of maintenance. Owner residents have a voice in the management as voting members of the community; they elect a board of directors and receive tax benefits and potential appreciation of the cooperative investment."

INDEPENDENT LIVING HOUSING

Type/size of apartment	*Purchase price*	*Monthly fee**
1-Bedroom, 700–1,000 sq. ft.	From $139,500	From $980
2-Bedroom, 1,000–1,600 sq. ft.	From $204,500	From $1,260

**Real estate taxes and all utilities except telephone included. Individual temperature control, electric kitchen appliances including washer/dryer, wall-to-wall carpeting, and cable TV, 24-hour emergency call system. More than 10 floor plans of varying size and layout.*

WOODBRIAR

339 Gifford Street
Falmouth, MA 02540
(508) 540-1600
Elizabeth D. Phelps, administrator

Type of community: Independent Living, Assisted Living, and Alzheimer's care

Woodbriar is located on 22 quiet, wooded acres bordering Jones Pond, minutes from downtown Falmouth. A two-story brick building houses Independent and Assisted Living suites and special care units for Alzheimer's patients. Units overlook Jones Pond or extensive flower gardens. A nine-hole golf course constitutes a large portion of the grounds. Fine restaurants and shopping are within walking distance.

Financial plan: Monthly rental fee. No leases, but 30-day notice of intent to vacate in writing on the first of the month is required. First and last months' rent is payable prior to occupancy.

Ownership and management: Private corporation. Opened in 1976.

Minimum age: None.

Population: 100 residents; 73% women, 27% men, 2% couples.

Number of units: 79 Independent Living rooms; 22 Assisted Living rooms, 15-room special care unit.

Dining plan: Three meals per day included in the monthly fee. Meal credits for absences of two weeks or longer. Private parties can be arranged.

Services: *Included in the monthly fee:* Daily housekeeping, personal laundry facilities, chauffeured transportation, parking.

At additional cost: Beauty/barbershop, store, dry cleaning pick-up and delivery.

Activities: Card room, films, library, heated indoor swimming pool, day and overnight trips, nine-hole golf course, arts and crafts, exercise classes, guest speakers, cookouts in summer, beach trips, theater and shopping trips.

Availability: Short waiting list.

Health services and rates: Professional health monitoring services. Special care unit for Alzheimer's patients with residential supervision by registered nurse.

- 22 Assisted Living rooms
  Single $2,800/month
- 15-Room special care unit $3,100/month

"The Woodbriar is Cape Cod's first retirement community, established in 1976. It is a beautiful place to live fully with independence and grace, where activity is encouraged and privacy is respected."

INDEPENDENT LIVING HOUSING

Type of room	*Monthly fee**
Southern exposure, 400 sq. ft.	$1,860
Water or garden view with balcony, 400 sq. ft.	$1,990

**All utilities except telephone included in the monthly fee. Wall-to-wall carpeting, drapes, individually controlled heating and air-conditioning. Many suites have walk-out balconies, 24-hour emergency call system.*

LOOMIS HOUSE

298 Jarvis Avenue
Holyoke, MA 01040
(413) 538-7551
Cheryl Boman, admissions counselor

Type of community: Nonprofit Continuing Care, modified contract

Situated on five beautifully landscaped acres in the Connecticut River Valley, elegant brick buildings house Independent Living, Assisted Living, and Skilled Nursing care. Loomis House is surrounded by colleges and museums that provide a large cultural and educational source, from college theater, sports, and musical groups to classes. Springfield, which is a short drive away, offers symphony, a civic center, and Stage West.

Financial plan: Entrance fee plus monthly fee. Entrance fee is amortized at a rate of 1% per month of occupancy. Unamortized portion will be refunded if resident leaves before 100 months.

Ownership and management: Nonprofit corporation governed by board of directors.

Minimum age: 60 years.

Population: 72 residents; 80% women, 20% men, 10% couples.

Number of units: 56 Independent Living apartments; 10 Assisted Living units, 80-bed Skilled Nursing facility.

Dining plan: Dinner each day is included in the monthly fee. Breakfast and lunch available at additional cost. Private dining room and catering also available.

Services: *Included in the monthly fee:* Weekly housekeeping and flat-linen services, scheduled transportation.

At additional cost: Beauty/barbershop, gift shop, laundry facilities, guest accommodations.

Activities: Activities director. Woodworking shop, library, reading groups, seminars, lectures, active volunteer program, trips to symphony and local museums, arts and crafts, health and fitness, parties, happy hours, bridge games.

Availability: Three- to six-month waiting list.

Health services and rates: Full rehabilitative and restorative nursing program with high staffing levels.

- 10 Assisted Living rooms

	Nonresident entrance fee	*Monthly fee*
Single, 225 sq. ft.	$22,800	$1,680

- 80 Skilled Nursing beds

Semiprivate	$133/day
Private	$150/day

"The first Continuing Care retirement community in Massachusetts, Loomis House has more than 80 years of experience in nonprofit service to older persons. Loomis House has a strong sense of community and provides an opportunity to build and nurture new friendships in a setting where residents can receive the support services they need to remain independent for as long as possible."

INDEPENDENT LIVING HOUSING

Type/size of apartment	*Entrance fee*	*Monthly fee**
Studio, 270–368 sq. ft.	$26,600–35,300	$755–905
1-Bedroom, 425–638 sq. ft.	$49,500–57,800	$970–1,260
2-Bedroom, 746–875 sq. ft.	$66,900–76,100	$1,400–1,575

**For double occupancy add $360 to the monthly fee. All utilities except telephone included. Fully equipped kitchen, wall-to-wall carpeting, draperies, 24-hour emergency call system, individually controlled heating and air-conditioning.*

EVANSWOOD CENTER

18 Chipman Way
Kingston, MA 02364
(617) 585-4100
Joann Richards, admissions manager

Type of community: Nonprofit Continuing Care, modified contract

Located on more than 50 acres of wooded estate overlooking the shores of Silver Lake and Forge Pond, Evanswood Center offers Independent Living, Assisted Living, and Skilled Nursing on campus. Kingston is just north of where the Pilgrims landed and is steeped in history. The community is less than an hour by car from both Boston and Providence as well as Cape Cod.

Financial plan: Monthly rental fee. $150 application fee. Independent Living is subsidized by government. Residents pay 30% of monthly income.

Ownership and management: The Baptist Home of Massachusetts. Opened in 1973.

Minimum age: 62 years.

Population: 300 residents; 78% women, 22% men, 10% couples.

Number of units: 50 Independent Living apartments; 61 Assisted Living units, 164 Skilled Nursing beds.

Dining plan: Three meals per day included in the monthly fee.

Services: *Included in the monthly fee:* Weekly housekeeping and flat-linen services, scheduled transportation.

At additional cost: Beauty/barbershop, gift shop, laundry facilities.

Activities: Exercises, discussions, parties, weekly shopping trips, gardening, weekly worship service, bingo, Scrabble, movies, senior walkers, word games, picnics.

Availability: Waiting list for subsidized housing. Direct admission to Assisted Living and Skilled Nursing available.

Health services and rates: Health clinic. Adult day care program (8 a.m.–2:30 p.m.) available. Weekly Alzheimer's support group for family members and caretakers. Personal care assistance program provides variety of services available at additional cost as needed.

- 61 Assisted Living rooms
  Standard with 1/2 bath $1,710/month
  Corner with full bath $2,475/month*

  **Double occupancy available at $2,800/month.*

- 164-Bed health center*
  Semiprivate $176–189/day
  Private $198–210/day

  42 Beds are designated for Alzheimer's patients.

"Evanswood supports and assists women and men in living the latter years of their lives with purpose, dignity, and well-being."

INDEPENDENT LIVING HOUSING

Type/size of apartment	*Monthly fee single/double**
1-Bedroom, 528 sq. ft.	$200–240

**All utilities except telephone included in the monthly fee. Individually controlled heating and air-conditioning, 24-hour emergency call system, fully equipped kitchens on each floor, wall-to-wall carpeting, draperies.*

NORTH HILL

865 Central Avenue
Needham, MA 02192
(617) 444-9910
Nancy T. Leonard, marketing director

Type of community: Nonprofit Continuing Care, all-inclusive contract

Apartments and common areas are located in a graceful five-story building located on the crest of a hill. Sweeping views of the Boston skyline are available from the building. Several nature trails and gardens are located throughout the 55-acre campus. North Hills provides a health center adjacent to the main building and offers easy access to Boston.

Financial plan: Entrance fee plus monthly fee. Entrance fee is 90% refundable upon withdrawal from the community. Monthly fee remains the same whether resident is in the apartment or the health care center.

Ownership and management: Owned by Living Care Village of Massachusetts, Inc., a nonprofit corporation. Managed by Life Care Services of Des Moines, Iowa, manager of more than 50 Continuing Care projects throughout the United States. Opened in 1984.

Minimum age: 62 years.

Population: 376 residents; 79% women, 21% men, 51 couples.

Number of units: 339 Independent Living residences; 72-bed health center.

Dining plan: One meal per day included in the monthly fee. Three-meal-per-day plan available. Private dining room available.

Services: *Included in the monthly fee:* Housekeeping, flat-linen service, scheduled transportation.

At additional cost: Beauty/barbershop, guest accommodations.

Activities: Two social directors. Library, billiards room, card games, Olympic-size swimming pool with daily exercise classes, Jacuzzis, exercise room, woodworking and metalworking shop, arts and crafts studio, two greenhouses, gardening, putting green, several nature trails, concerts, plays, tours, lectures, meetings, movies, classes, regularly scheduled programs in the auditorium, two grand pianos for residents' use.

Availability: Short waiting list for some apartment styles.

Health services and rates: Unlimited health care and 12 hours of Assisted Living a year covered under the monthly fee. Resident continues to pay same monthly fee plus extra charge for additional meals while in health center. Health center is connected to main building by an enclosed walkway and offers preventive, emergency, and long-term recuperative care under the supervision of director of

INDEPENDENT LIVING HOUSING

Type/size of unit	*Entrance fee**	*Monthly fee**
Studio, 440 sq. ft.	$137,600–142,070	$1,129
1-Bedroom, 742 sq. ft.	$183,460–225,890	$1,240–1,352
2-Bedroom, 1,128 sq. ft.	$250,230–323,030	$1,463–1,637
3-Bedroom, 1,128 sq. ft.	$374,720–385,740	$1,703

**For double occupancy add $10,000 to the entrance fee, $880 to the monthly fee. All utilities included except long-distance telephone. Wall-to-wall carpeting, 24-hour emergency call system, fully equipped kitchens, individually controlled heating and air-conditioning, cable TV.*

nursing. Physician on call at all times. Many residents use their own physicians.

- 72-Bed health care center

"North Hill residents enjoy all the pleasures that life has to offer every day. Whether it be an afternoon at the symphony, a refreshing swim in our pool, a challenging game of bridge with neighbors, or a relaxing evening at home, you can live life to the fullest at North Hill. Health care is also an integral part of what North Hill has to offer with our excellent nursing facility right on the premises."

NEW POND VILLAGE

180 Main Street
Walpole, MA 02081
(508) 660-1555
Carol Ubertini, sales and marketing director

Type of community: Continuing Care, modified contract

Housed in a three-story, gray clapboard building, New Pond Village offers Independent Living apartments, an Assisted Living Center and a health center located on a 29-acre campus. The community offers a New England–style main street, village club, and an outdoor patio. Boston and its surrounding communities are 20 miles away.

Financial plan: Entrance fee plus monthly fee. Entrance fee is 90% refundable. A $10,000 initial insurance premium is included in the entrance fee and is not part of the refundable amount.

Ownership and management: Owned and operated by the Hillhaven Corporation, which has more than 40 years experience serving seniors. Hillhaven owns and/or operates 25 retirement communities across the United States. Opened in 1990.

Minimum age: 62 years.

Population: 200 residents; 80% women, 20% men, 38% couples.

Number of units: 148 Independent Living apartments; 32 Assisted Living units, 90-bed health center.

Dining plan: One meal per day included in the monthly fee. Flexible meal plans. Private dining room, special diets, and tray service available.

Services: *Included in the monthly fee:* Biweekly housekeeping, scheduled transportation, parking for residents and guests, monthly insurance premium.

At additional cost: Beauty/barbershop.

Activities: Painting, lecture series, whirlpool, library, billiards room, greenhouse/gardens, creative arts center, hobby shop, auditorium, health club, Jacuzzi, putting green, big-screen TV, walking club, fitness committee, wellness seminars, vacation exchange program.

INDEPENDENT LIVING HOUSING

Type/size of unit	*Entrance fee**	*Monthly fee**
1-Bedroom, 550–700 sq. ft.	$144,000–162,000	$1,244
2-Bedroom, 750–950 sq. ft.	$190,000–228,000	$1,686
3-Bedroom, 1,100 sq. ft.	$250,000	$2,134

**For double occupancy add $10,000 to the entrance fee, $477 to the monthly fee. All utilities except telephone included. Wall-to-wall carpeting, 24-hour emergency call system, individually controlled heating and air-conditioning, fully equipped kitchen, cable TV. Washers and dryers are located throughout the building.*

Availability: Immediate occupancy on some units.

Health services and rates: Health center offering Skilled Care and rehabilitation; 32-unit Assisted Living center (Aldridge House) on-site. Podiatrist, ophthalmologist, and licensed physical, occupational, recreational, and speech therapists available. Individualized therapeutic programs developed by a team of specialists. Wellness center offering nutritional counseling and equipment and programs for health maintenance, including a therapeutic Jacuzzi, scheduled exercise programs, plus regular screenings and clinics.

- 32 Assisted Living units

	Nonresident entrance fee	*Monthly fee*
1-Bedroom	$144,000	$2,201
2-Bedroom	$180,000	$2,576

**For double occupancy add $338 to the monthly fee; $25/day for up to 1 1/2 hours of personal care service.*

- 90-Bed health center

Semiprivate	$165–175/day
Private	$185–195/day

"Vacation Exchange Program: New Pond Village is part of the Hillhaven family, which owns and/ or operates 25 retirement communities across the United States. New Pond Village residents can vacation at any of our other communities for up to three weeks at a time. Other communities are located in Florida, Arizona, Colorado, and other states. New Pond Village Partners Program's one annual fee entitles nonresidents to numerous services, programs, and activities, including dining at New Pond Village, housekeeping sevices in your own home, personal emergency response, educational courses, and social activities."

THE WILLOWS

1 Lyman Street
Westborough, MA 01581
(508) 366-4730
Connie Driscoll, sales director

Type of community: Continuing Care, modified contract

Two four-story brick traditional Independent Living apartment buildings are connected to Assisted Living units and a health center. The Willows's common areas have been meticulously tailored to guarantee comfort and safety. The community is within walking distance of a 36-store shopping center, which includes a movie theater, and is close to fine restaurants. Boston is 30 minutes away.

Financial plan: Monthly fee. One-time fully refundable deposit and monthly fee.

Ownership and management: Privately owned by Dan and Dorothy Salmon, who have owned and managed retirement and health facilities in the area for more than 30 years. Opened in 1987.

Minimum age: 60 years (if couple, spouse may be younger).

INDEPENDENT LIVING HOUSING

Type/size of apartment	*Entrance fee**	*Monthly fee**
1-Bedroom, 725–740 sq. ft.	$110,000–145,000	$1,118
2-Bedroom, 950–1,150 sq. ft.	$156,000–250,000	$1,374

**For double occupancy add $7,500 to the entrance fee, $542 to the monthly fee. All utilities except telephone included. Washer and dryer, all-electric kitchen, individually controlled heating and air-conditioning, 24-hour emergency call system, decorator blinds, carpeting, wallpaper in kitchen and bath, balcony, patio, or bay window.*

Population: 220 residents; 75% women, 25% men, 10% couples.

Number of units: 172 Independent Living apartments; 30 Assisted Living units, 152 Skilled Nursing beds.

Dining plan: One meal per day included in monthly fee. Other meals available at additional cost. Private dining room.

Services: *Included in the monthly fee:* Weekly housekeeping and flat-linen service, local transportation.

At additional cost: Beauty/barbershop, general store, branch bank, coffee shop, snack bar.

Activities: Library, greenhouse, woodworking shop, arts and crafts room, sewing room, exercise facilities, sun terrace, bridge club, movies, visits by drama groups, walking club, trips to cultural events, discussion groups, community room with stage.

Availability: Waiting list.

Health services and rates: Visiting physicians and physical therapy available.

- 30 Assisted Living Units

	*Entrance fee**
Studio	$60,000–63,000
1-Bedroom	$123,500–143,000
2-Bedroom	$185,000

**Plus monthly fee of $2,899. For double occupancy add $1,449 to the monthly fee if second person requires Assisted Living or $542 for Independent Living residents.*

- 152 Skilled Nursing beds

Semiprivate	$162/day
Private	$200/day

"The Willows is an expression of uncompromising commitment to provide the best possible lifestyle for the active senior. Our philosophy is simple: this is your home. Our dedicated staff never loses sight of this. By nurturing the spirit of self-worth and independence of older persons, the coming years can be filled with dignity and peace of mind. The Willows's lifestyle offers unparalleled comfort, security, and freedom in a warm, friendly environment."

FOX HILL VILLAGE

10 Longwood Drive
Westwood, MA 02090
(617) 329-4433
John Van Londen, managing director

Type of community: Continuing Care, modified contract

Located on 83 landscaped, wooded acres covered with walking paths and trails, Fox Hill Village offers four wings of Independent Living cooperative apartments joined by a community center. Lawns, gardens, and woodlands make up the secluded campus grounds. Assisted Living and nursing care are on-site. The center of Westwood is minutes away; downtown Boston is less than 30 minutes away; and shopping at Chestnut Hill is nearby.

Financial plan: Purchase price plus monthly fee. Organized as a cooperative. Resident purchases share of stock. Resident receives 90% of resale value of unit.

Ownership and management: Developed by Massachusetts General Hospital and Brim of Massachusetts. Managed by Hillhaven Corporation, owner and/or manager of 25 retirement communities and over 300 nursing homes nationwide. Opened in 1990.

Minimum age: 62 years.

Population: 420 residents; 60% women, 40% women, 25% couples.

Number of units: 356 Independent Living apartments; 27 Assisted Living units, 70-bed health center.

INDEPENDENT LIVING HOUSING

Type/size of apartment	*Purchase price**	*Monthly fee**
1-Bedroom, 700–850 sq. ft.	$170,985–228,985	$1,321–1,440
2-Bedroom, 1,000–1,250 sq. ft.	$238,985–335,985	$1,645–1,763
Large 2-bedroom 1,450–1,500 sq. ft.	$341,985–386,985	$1,881
2-Bedroom Penthouse, 1,646–1,842 sq. ft.	$390,985–460,985	$2,706–2,359

**For double occupancy add $10,585 to the purchase price, $603 per month to the monthly fee. All utilities except telephone included. Wall-to-wall carpeting, 24-hour emergency call system, individually controlled heating and air-conditioning, patios or balconies, cable TV, fully equipped kitchens, washer and dryer.*

Dining plan: One meal per day (lunch or dinner) included in the monthly fee. Additional meals available. Private dining room available.

Services: *Included in the monthly fee:* Biweekly housekeeping, scheduled transportation.

At additional cost: Beauty/barbershop, underground parking, additional transportation, housekeeping, laundry service, guest suites, Village Pantry.

Activities: Art studio, crafts studio, card rooms, exercise room, spa, Jacuzzi, walking paths, greenhouse, conservatory, meeting rooms, 300-seat auditorium, game room, library, woodworking shop, croquet court, putting green, gardens, horseshoes.

Availability: Limited.

Health services and rates: Village health services team: nurse and social worker affiliated with Massachusetts General Hospital.

- 27 Assisted Living apartments*

	Insured/uninsured
1-Bedroom, 850 sq. ft.	$1,822/2,449/month
2-Bedroom, 1,000 sq. ft.	$2,217/2,844/month

**Nonresident purchase price: 1-bedroom $170,400–195,000, 2-bedroom $280,400–300,000.*

- 70-Bed health center

Semiprivate	$175/day
Private	$200–350/day

"Fox Hill Village is considered one of the premier full-service retirement communities in the Northeast. Located just 20 minutes from Boston, it offers its residents beauty and solitude along with the convenience of being minutes from the finest shops, theaters, and cultural centers. Fox Hill Village has been rated number one out of all the Hillhaven Corporation communities across the country in resident satisfaction for the past two years. Developed by Massachusetts General Hospital and the Hillhaven Corporation, Fox Hill Village offers the stability of ownership."

COUNTRY CLUB HEIGHTS

3 Rehabilitation Way
Woburn, MA 01801
(617) 935-4094
Catherine Gulman, marketing director

Type of community: Independent and Assisted Living

Housed in a seven-story apartment building on a grassy, wooded campus overlooking Woburn golf course, Country Club Heights is located 20 minutes from downtown Boston. Nearby are historic landmarks, nature walks, cultural events, New England Rehabilitation Hospital, Lahey Clinic, and Horn pond (a 101-acre recreational sight offering beaches, swimming, fishing, sailing, and miles of walking paths). Woburn Plaza and Burlington Mall are minutes away.

Financial plan: Monthly rent. $2,500 deposit. One-year lease.

Ownership and management: Owned and managed by Advantage Health Corporation, owner and manager of eight other retirement homes in Florida, Connecticut, and the New York area. Opened in 1979.

Minimum age: 62 years.

Population: 106 residents; 70% women, 30% men, 8% couples.

Number of units: 101 Independent Living apartments; 21 Assisted Living apartments.

Dining plan: Dinner each day included in the monthly fee. Lunch is optional.

Services: *Included in the monthly fee:* Weekly housecleaning and flat-linen services, scheduled transportation.

At additional cost: Beauty/barbershop.

Activities: Full-time activities director. Library, arts and crafts room, recreation area, activity room, card room, concerts, dining out, trips to Boston Symphony and theater, exercise classes.

Availability: Three- to six-month waiting list for some accommodations. Nonrefundable fee of $2,500 for waiting list, $500 of which is applied toward the first month's rent.

Health services and rates: Residents receive priority admission to New England Rehabilitation Hospital for nursing care. Assisted Living center on fourth and sixth floors of the apartment building. Morning and evening Assisted Care available in Independent Living apartments. Three options for Assisted Care (in addition to monthly fee).

- 21 Assisted Living apartments

24-Hour Assisted Care	$280/month
Morning care	$115/month
Morning and evening care	$215/month

"Our community living concept has been very successful for many reasons. There is no financial commitment necessary at Country Club Heights; it is strictly a rental community."

INDEPENDENT LIVING HOUSING

Type/size of unit	*Monthly rent**
Studio, 325 sq. ft.	$1,900
Alcove, 470 sq. ft.	$2,100
1-Bedroom, 590 sq. ft.	$2,300–2,500
2-Bedroom, 870 sq. ft.	$2,900

**For double occupancy add $250 to the monthly rent. All utilities except telephone included. Fully equipped kitchens, individually controlled heating and air-conditioning, wall-to-wall carpeting, 24-hour emergency call system, cable TV.*

MICHIGAN

GLACIER HILLS

1200 Earhart Road
Ann Harbor, MI 48105
(313) 663-5202
Jeannie Sager, administrator

Type of community: Nonprofit Continuing Care, modified contract

Glacier Hills is housed in a five-story contemporary apartment building located on 34 acres featuring walking trails and a pond. A solarium connects the nursing center to Independent Living. Local bus stops at front door, and the Ann Arbor Senior Taxi offers door-to-door transportation anywhere in Ann Arbor for $1.50. The University of Michigan provides residents with an educational atmosphere and access to cultural and sporting events.

Financial plan: Entrance fee plus monthly fee.

Ownership and management: Nonprofit corporation, managed by 17-member board of directors from the Ann Arbor community.

Minimum age: 62 years.

Population: 185 residents; 76% women, 24% men, 9% couples.

Number of units: 184 Independent Living apartments; 28 Assisted Living beds, 163-bed Skilled Nursing center.

Dining plan: One to three meals per day included in the monthly fee. Residents without kitchens have three meals a day in dining room, and those with kitchens are required to take a minimum of one meal a day in dining room.

Services: *Included in the monthly fee:* Biweekly housekeeping, weekly flat-linen services, personal laundry facilities, scheduled trips to shopping centers, doctors offices and hospitals, parking.

At additional cost: Beauty/barbershop, gift shop, grocery orders, personal shopping, personal laundry service, dry cleaning service, newspaper delivery, postal services, banking services.

INDEPENDENT LIVING HOUSING

Type/size of unit	*Entrance fee**	*Monthly fee**
Studio, 260–452 sq. ft.	$32,970–62,970	$937–1,231
1-Bedroom, 487–665 sq. ft.	$68,350–86,350	$1,302–1,566
2-Bedroom, 1,000 sq. ft.	$114,000	$1,814–2,099

**For double occupancy add $15,000 to the entrance fee, $299 to the monthly fee. Refundable entrance fees are $5,000–10,000 higher. All utilities except telephone included. Individually controlled heating and air-conditioning, wall-to-wall carpeting, kitchenettes in some apartments, 24-hour emergency call system.*

Activities: Personal garden areas, library, arts and crafts, sewing machines, exercise equipment, interdenominational worship services, residents' association, outings, card games, in-house movie channel, weekly lecture or concert series, holiday celebrations.

Availability: Studio apartments available. One- and two-bedroom apartments have nine-month to one-year waiting list.

Health services and rates: Residents receive 30 free days in nursing facility. After 30 days, they pay the resident daily rate. 24-Hour emergency nursing care, blood pressure and temperature checks at scheduled times. On-site dentistry and podiatry, occupational, physical, and speech therapy services.

- 28 Assisted Living apartments
  $695 in addition to the resident's monthly fee
- 163-Bed Skilled Nursing center
  Semiprivate $76/day residents
  $126/day nonresidents
  Private $116/day residents
  $166/day nonresidents

"Because of its location between the University of Michigan and Eastern Michigan University, Glacier Hills has become a teacher/learning community providing the most current developments in medical and geriatric care. This location also provides availability to some of the best medical technology in the world with the University of Michigan Hospital and St. Joseph Mercy Hospital within five miles of Glacier Hills."

PORTER HILLS

3600 East Fulton Street
Grand Rapids, MI 49546
(616) 949-4971
Marketing department

Type of community: Nonprofit Continuing Care, modified contract

Located on 35 acres adjacent to the country club and just outside the corporate limits of Grand Rapids, Porter Hills is 40 miles from Lake Michigan and five miles from Grand River. Beautifully landscaped grounds surround Independent Living apartments in three-story buildings. The grounds feature a pond with ducks, geese, and swans; a picnic area and a water fountain are also on campus. A chapel/meeting house is available on campus in addition to licensed child care.

Financial plan: Entrance fee plus monthly fee or monthly rental. Entrance fee is 50% refundable if residency is less than 5 1/2 years.

Ownership and management: Owned by Westminster Presbyterian Church. Operated by Porter Hills Presbyterian Village, Inc. Opened in 1970.

Minimum age: 62 years (if couple, spouse must be at least 55).

Population: 440 residents; 85% women, 15% men, 23% couples.

Number of units: 109 Independent Living apartments, 138 residential suites; 44 Assisted Living units, 101-bed Skilled Nursing facility.

INDEPENDENT LIVING HOUSING

Type/size of apartment	*Entrance fee*	*Monthly fee**	*Monthly rental fee**
2-Bedroom, 1,200 sq. ft.	$87,000	$350	$949
2-Bedroom, 1,400 sq. ft.	$133,000	$360	$1,810

**All utilities except telephone included in the monthly rental fee only. Fully equipped kitchen, individually controlled heating and air-conditioning, wall-to-wall carpeting, 24-hour emergency call system.*

Dining plan: Three meals per day included in the monthly rental fee only. No meals included for residents who have paid entrance fee; meals available at additional cost.

Services: *Included in the monthly fee:* Scheduled bus service, apartment maintenance.

At additional cost: Beauty/barbershop, convenience shop, café, guest accommodations.

Activities: Social director and five activity coordinators/therapists. Variety of social, recreational, intellectual, and spiritual programs. Bus trips, golf outings, Bible study, college courses, special luncheons, weekly bridge games, daily exercise classes, sing-alongs, spa, fitness trail, libraries, assembly rooms, woodworking shops, billiards room, chapel, solarium, book groups, arts and crafts, library, bell choir, mystery dinner theater, ticket arrangements and transportation to Grand Rapids Symphony, civic theater, and Broadway shows.

Availability: Waiting list three to five years for Independent Living.

Health services and rates: Personal care available through home health care agency in resident's Independent Living quarters. 24-hour skilled and basic care, physical therapy, registered dietitian. Dentist and podiatrist also available. Harmony Hall 16-suite wing for Alzheimer's/dementia residents.

- 44 Assisted Living units $1,651/month
- 101-Bed Skilled Nursing facility
  Semiprivate $110/day
  Private $140/day

"The purpose of Porter Hills is to maintain a gracious and secure home for elderly individuals and couples and to ensure that an appropriate array of supportive services are made available to them. Our role is to enable the residents to live as independently and as productively as their physical, mental, and emotional health permits."

VISTA GRANDE VILLA

2251 Springport Road
Jackson, MI 49202-1496
(517) 787-0222
Kristy I. Krueger, director of marketing

Type of community: Not-for-profit Continuing Care, all-inclusive contract

Vista Grande Villa offers Independent Living apartments in a four-story apartment building and a one-level health center. The community is located on a 20-acre campus that features green fields, flower gardens, and clusters of trees. Convenience store is located on-site. Assisted Living services and nursing services are available. Easy access to local churches and shopping areas is provided.

Financial plan: Entrance fee plus monthly fee. Entrance fee refundable less initial 10% and $1^1/_2$% per month of residency upon withdrawal. Return of capital plans also available.

Ownership and management: Nonprofit corporation managed by Life Care Services of Des Moines, Iowa, which also manages more than 50 other communities throughout the United States. Opened in 1972.

Minimum age: 62 years.

Population: 245 residents; 78% women, 22% men, 30% couples.

Number of units: 218 Independent Living apartments; 60-bed health center.

Dining plan: One meal per day included in the monthly fee. Special diets and tray service available. All foods are prepared under the supervision of a trained dietary supervisor and a consulting registered dietitian. Vacation discounts available after 14 days absence. Private dining room available.

INDEPENDENT LIVING HOUSING

Type/size of unit	*Entrance fee**	*Monthly fee**
Studio, 318 sq. ft.	$32,500	$707
Alcove, 389 sq. ft.	$45,000	$758
1-Bedroom, 520 sq. ft.	$57,000	$850
2-Bedroom, 736 sq. ft.	$79,000	$912

**For double occupancy add $10,000 to the entrance fee, $395 to the monthly fee. All utilities except telephone are included. Fully equipped kitchens, 24-hour emergency call system, wall-to-wall carpeting, individually controlled heating and air-conditioning, cable TV.*

Services: *Included in the monthly fee:* Twice monthly housekeeping, weekly flat-linen service, scheduled transportation, free laundry facilities, parking, seasonal cleaning every six months.

At additional cost: Beauty/barbershop, carports and garages, personal laundry service, guest accommodations.

Activities: Social/recreational director. Library, classes through Jackson Community College (painting, sewing, local history, music appreciation), travel slide shows, ethnic and holiday dinners, musical programs, lectures, repertory group appearances, day trips, weekly coffee hour, resident council, weekly chat and sew (weekly sewing session), singing, exercise classes, book reviews, movies, educational classes, billiards, woodworking, arts and crafts, local civic and cultural events, vespers, transportation to local churches, gardening, bridge, and shuffleboard tournaments.

Availability: Waiting may be necessary for certain units. Current occupancy information is available by phone.

Health services and rates: Residents receive unlimited health care at no additional cost, except for extra meals and miscellaneous expenses. Health care center offers preventive medical service, emergency care, and long-term care. Rehabilitation and physical therapy services are available. Pharmacy with registered pharmacist and convenience store with nonprescription drugs and groceries on-site. Staff at health center includes medical director, director of nursing, registered nurses, licensed practical nurses, certified nursing assistants, part-time physical therapist, and director of social services.

- Assisted Living units
  Nurse on duty to assist with various tasks in and out of resident's apartment. There is an extra fee depending on services needed.
- 60-Bed health care center

"At Vista Grande Villa, residents find a community of individual apartments in which everything is where they want it for effortless, comfortable living. Residents have privacy when they want to be alone. And when they want people around, they are there to share experiences and discover new interests."

FRIENDSHIP VILLAGE

1400 North Drake Road
Kalamazoo, MI 49006
(616)381-0560
Thea Travis, marketing director

Type of community: Nonprofit Continuing Care, all-inclusive contract

Five three-story apartment buildings are located on a 52-acre landscaped campus with a nature trail, walking path, and large vegetable and flower garden. Twenty acres of campus serve as a nature center. Independent Living residences and a health center are available. Friendship Village is located on Kalamazoo's west side near a residential neighborhood and close to many restaurants, specialty stores, shopping centers, and mall.

INDEPENDENT LIVING HOUSING

Type/size of unit	*Entrance fee 1/2**	*Monthly fee**
Studio, 300 sq. ft.	$28,800–31,900/45,967–50,915	$837
Alcove, 400 sq. ft.	$42,800–49,900/68,313–79,645	$886
1-Bedroom, 600 sq. ft.	$67,300–70,400/107,418–112,365	$999
2-Bedroom, 800 sq. ft.	$81,000–85,800/129,284–136,945	$1,097

**For double occupancy add $15,000 to the entrance fee for Plan 1, $23,941 to the entrance fee for Plan 2; $554 to the monthly fee. Plan 3 entrance fee is $30,000 (plus $7,500 for double occupancy); monthly fees range from $1,175 to $1,578. All utilities included. Cable TV, individually controlled heating and air-conditioning, wall-to-wall carpeting in living room and bedroom, fully equipped kitchens, 24-hour emergency call system.*

Financial plan: Entrance fee plus monthly fee. Three plans: **1)** Endowment: refundable less 1 1/2% for each month of residency up to 60 months. **2)** Return of capital: guaranteed 90% refund regardless of length of stay. Both plans provide same services. **3)** Modified: lower entrance fee with health center services on a fee-for-service basis. Financial assistance available if at some point after acceptance resident experiences financial difficulties.

Ownership and management: Operated by Lifecare, Inc., a nonprofit corporation whose board of directors is comprised of Kalamazoo area professionals. Managed by Life Care Services Corporation of Des Moines, Iowa, who have developed and managed more than 50 Continuing Care communities across the United States. Opened in 1975.

Minimum age: None.

Population: 300 residents; 85% women, 15% men, 10% couples.

Number of units: 246 Independent Living apartments; 57-bed health center.

Dining plan: Dinner each day included in the monthly fee. Breakfast and lunch optional. Private dining room available for special occasions. Room service available.

Services: *Included in the monthly fee:* Scheduled transportation, biweekly housekeeping, weekly flat-linen service, self-service washers and dryers, personal storage units.

At additional cost: Beauty/barbershop, garage, guest accommodations.

Activities: Full-time activities director. Game room, library, arts and crafts center, woodworking shop, large garden plot, chaplain services, a 20-acre nature preserve, exercise classes, college-accredited classes.

Availability: One-year waiting list for two-bedroom apartments. 10% deposit of entrance fee for preferred waiting list.

Health services and rates: Residents receive unlimited access to on-site health center with Skilled Nursing. Emergency nursing service available 24-hours a day. Health center provides short- and long-term care, recuperative care, and physical therapy department. Lifetime health care contractually guaranteed. Assisted Living and home health nursing provided in the apartment.

- 57-Bed health center

"Friendship Village offers three entrance fee options designed to fit the needs of our residents. Residents do not need to worry if our health center is full. If it is, we provide care in the apartment until a bed becomes available."

MINNESOTA

FRIENDSHIP VILLAGE

8100 Highwood Drive
Bloomington, MN 55438
(612) 831-7500
Richard F. Burke, sales director

Type of community: Not-for-profit Continuing Care, all-inclusive contract

Located minutes from downtown Minneapolis in a peaceful, pastoral setting, Friendship Village consists of two-story brick buildings connected by covered, heated walkways. The community also features a 66-bed health care center and a 39-bed Assisted Living facility. The landscaped grounds are dotted with park benches and walking paths. Friendship Village offers easy access to city attractions as well as the daily comforts of country-side living.

Financial plan: Entrance fee plus monthly fee. Two plans: **1)** Traditional: prorated portion of entrance fee is returnable should the residency agreement be voluntarily terminated within 100 months of occupancy. **2)** return of capital: should the residency agreement be canceled for any reason, up to 90% of the entrance fee is refunded. 10% of the entrance fee is paid with the application. Variation available: lower entrance fee and higher monthly fee.

Ownership and management: Life Care Retirement Communities/Life Care Services Corporation, planners, developers, and managers of more than 50 retirement communities in the U.S. Opened in 1979.

Minimum age: 62 years.

Population: 500 residents; 66% women, 34% men, 40% couples.

Number of units: 310 Independent Living apartments; 39-bed Assisted Living unit, 66-bed health center.

Dining plan: One meal per day included in monthly fee. Private dining room and party rooms.

Services: *Included in the monthly fee:* Weekly housekeeping and flat-linen services, scheduled transportation.

INDEPENDENT LIVING HOUSING

Type/size of apartment	*Entrance fee 1/2*	*Monthly fee**
Alcove, 436 sq. ft.	$52,750/75,250	$837
1-Bedroom, 577/648 sq. ft.	$69,000–71,500/98,750–102,500	$959
2-Bedroom, 871 sq. ft.	$99,000/142,500	$1,019
3-Bedroom, 1,440 sq. ft.	$123,000/177,000	$1,277

**For double occupancy add $469 to the monthly fee. All utilities except long-distance telephone included. Fully equipped kitchen, carpeting, linoleum, drapery rods, 24-hour emergency call system.*

At additional cost: Beauty/barbershop, on-site banking, garages, guest accommodations, banking.

Activities: Library, billiards, exercise area, woodworking shop, crafts room, shuffleboard, greenhouse and individual gardening spots, ceramics, Bible study, films, woodcarving, games, picnics, tours, lectures.

Availability: Units available. Priority waiting list.

Health services and rates: Emergency, recuperative, and long-term Skilled Nursing care is available on-site to all residents with no limit on usage. The only additional charge is for the two additional meals per day.

- 39 Assisted Living semiprivate and private rooms
  Nonresident daily fee $60+
- 66-Bed health care center

"Friendship Village is the only comprehensive life care retirement community in Minnesota, with an unmatched record of ten successful years of operation. A reputation for excellent service and management, a sound financial record, and three flexible entrance options are the features that distinguish Friendship Village from other retirement communities."

COVENANT MANOR

5800 St. Croix Avenue
Minneapolis, MN 55422
(612) 546-6125
Linda Lund, marketing representative

Type of community: Not-for-profit Continuing Care, modified contract

Accreditation: Continuing Care Accreditation Commission

This five-story brick apartment building is located on Bassett Creek Nature Preserve and walking trail. Independent Living, Assisted Living, and Skilled Nursing care are available on the same campus. Walking paths wind through manicured lawns and resident-managed flower and vegetable garden plots. Recreational gaming areas adjoin a gazebo, and park-style benches are abundant. Spring Gate Shopping Center is adjacent to the community, which offers easy access to the recreational and cultural resources of the Twin Cities.

Financial plan: Entrance fee plus monthly fee. Primary agreement provides a care benefit of 60 days of health care at no extra cost, followed by a 10% discount of the prevailing rates for nursing care or Assisted Living.

Ownership and management: Owned/managed by the Evangelical Covenant Church/Covenant Retirement Communities, which has been serving seniors since 1886 and is owner/manager of 12 retirement communities in California, Connecticut, Florida, Illinois, Minnesota, and Washington. A 13th community is planned in Colorado. Opened in 1980.

INDEPENDENT LIVING HOUSING

Type/size of unit	*Entrance fee**	*Monthly fee**
Alcove, 490 sq. ft.	$44,000	$795
1-Bedroom, 600–715 sq. ft.	$56,000–63,000	$945–985
2-Bedroom, 820–1,090 sq. ft.	$68,000–76,000	$1,060–1,165

**For double occupancy add 10% to the entrance fee, $425 to the monthly fee. All utilities except telephone included. Patio or balcony, 24-hour emergency call system, fully equipped kitchen, carpeting, drapes, individually controlled heating and air-conditioning.*

Minimum age: 62 years.

Population: 168 residents; 73% women, 27% men, 39% couples.

Number of units: 126 Independent Living apartments; 16 Assisted Living units, 119-bed health center.

Dining plan: One meal (evening meal, except Sunday at noon) per day included in the monthly fee. Dining room overlooks Bassett Creek Nature Preserve. Lunch is also available on monthly or daily plan.

Services: *Included in the monthly fee:* Biweekly housekeeping, weekly flat-linen service, local transportation, laundry facilities on each floor.

At additional cost: Beauty/barbershop, extra cleaning, indoor parking and outdoor garages, guest accommodations.

Activities: Activities director. Hobby and crafts room, woodworking shop, exercise room, auditorium/fellowship center, library, heated indoor swimming pool, whirlpool, variety of classes. Chapel services and Bible study are organized by the chaplain. Outdoor facilities include individual gardening areas, a gazebo, shuffleboard court.

Availability: One- to three-year waiting list for larger floor plans.

Health services and rates: Residents receive 60 days of health care at no extra cost. After the 60 days, residents receive a 10% discount on the prevailing rates for Assisted Living and Skilled Nursing.

- 16 Assisted Living rooms
  Studio $83/day
- 119 Skilled Nursing beds, including specialized unit for Alzheimer's patients.
  Semiprivate $109/day
  Private $124/day

"The mission of Covenant Retirement Communities is to serve as an extension of the Evangelical Covenant Church in ministering to the needs of seniors; to provide excellent and loving care through multiple levels of service; to provide a Christian environment enhancing each resident's awareness of his or her dignity, security, comfort, and peace of mind in harmony with Christ's model; to ensure that the service and facilities are maintained on a fiscally responsible basis; to provide a balance between security and independence for the resident that assists in the achievement of the resident's maximum physical, mental, emotional, and spiritual well-being. Covenant Manor is the first Continuing Care community in Minnesota to receive accreditation."

MISSOURI

CHATEAU GIRARDEAU

3120 Independence Street
Cape Girardeau, MO 63701
(314) 335-1281
Barbara Calvin, administrator

Type of community: Not-for-profit Continuing Care, modified contract

Accreditation: Continuing Care Accreditation Commission

A four-story residential building of traditional design contains Independent Living apartments and is connected by enclosed corridors to one-story buildings that house an Assisted Living center and a Skilled Nursing facility. Twenty-three individual residences in Chateau Estates, a new residential area connected to the main complex by paved drives and sidewalks, have just been completed with 11 more under construction. The community is located on 40 wooded acres and is convenient to shopping areas, hospitals, Southeast Missouri State University, doctors' offices, and banks.

Financial plan: Entrance fee plus monthly fee. Entrance fee is refundable on a prorated basis for the first two years of occupancy in apartments and first five years in Chateau Estates. Lifetime care guaranteed regardless of resident's ability to pay the fees in the future. $200 application deposit required for apartment waiting lists and $5,000 reservation deposit for a home in Chateau Estates.

Ownership and management: Cape Retirement Community, Inc., a local not-for-profit, nondenominational corporation with a 13-member board of directors. Opened in 1979; Assisted Living added in 1988 and Chateau Estates homes in 1993.

Minimum age: 62 years (if couple, spouse may be younger).

Population: 205 residents; 82% women, 18% men, 25% couples.

Number of units: 151 Independent Living apartments, 34 Chateau Estates homes; 32 Assisted Living units, 60 Skilled Nursing beds.

Dining plan: One meal per day included in apartment residents' monthly fee; other meals optional. All meals optional for Chateau Estates residents. Three dining rooms, including private dining room that can be reserved by residents.

Services: *Included in the monthly fee:* For apartments: bimonthly housekeeping, maintenance of appliances, weekly flat-linen service, parking. For Chateau Estates: bimonthly housekeeping, maintenance of residence and furnished appliances.

At additional cost: Beauty/barbershop, pharmacy/minimarket, self-service laundry facilities, guest accommodations, transportation.

Activities: Full activities program planned by staff and a committee of residents. Billiards room, woodworking shop, shuffleboard, croquet, trips to university programs, out-of-town trips on Chateau minibus, library, arts and crafts.

INDEPENDENT LIVING HOUSING

Type/size of apartment	*Entrance fee**	*Monthly fee single/double*
Studio, 256 sq. ft.	$20,900	$639
1-Bedroom, 525 sq. ft.	$38,775	$644/962
1-Bedroom/balcony, 525 sq. ft.	$40,500	$656/976
Expanded 1-bedroom, 587 sq. ft.	$45,775	$678/995
2-Bedroom, 953 sq. ft.	$58,990	$731/1,054
2-Bedroom/balcony, 953 sq. ft.	$61,200	$744/1,065
Chateau Estates homes		
2-Bedroom, 1,546 sq. ft.	$94,500	$375/395
2-Bedroom, 1,627 sq. ft.	$98,500	$390/410

**For double occupancy add $2,000 to the entrance fee. All utilities except telephone included for apartments. Carpeting, sheer curtains (only in apartments), fully equipped kitchen, individual temperature controls, 24-hour emergency call system.*

Availability: Short waiting list for apartments; houses immediate (being built as reserved).

Health services and rates: Physical, speech, and occupational therapies. Nursing assistance is available to Continuing Care residents in their apartments or homes on a 24-hour-a-day emergency basis. Supportive nursing care is available to these residents in their apartments or homes for short confinements. Blood pressure checks and other such services are always available through the Assisted Living center.

- 32 Assisted Living rooms
  Semiprivate $1,025/month
  Private $1,625/month

Residents are encouraged to bring their own furniture; furnished apartments available if desired. Couples may live together.

- 60 Skilled Nursing beds
  Semiprivate $64.50/day
  Private $79.50/day

"Chateau Girardeau offers a unique Continuing Care guarantee that assures its residents of lifelong services and care even though they may become unable to pay the applicable fees. Chateau Girardeau's accreditation is granted only to Continuing Care communities that meet rigorous standards of excellence; this accreditation certifies that Chateau Girardeau is true to its mission and has strong financial capabilities to meet present and future needs. It is the only Continuing Care retirement community of its type between St. Louis and Memphis."

FULTON PRESBYTERIAN MANOR

811 Center Street
Fulton, MO 65251
(314) 642-6646
Jane Mitchell, administrator

Type of community: Nonprofit Continuing Care, modified plan

The Manor is located in a pleasant residential neighborhood in a small town. Two-story traditionally designed buildings house Independent Living, Assisted Living, and Skilled Nursing. The site is fully landscaped and is within walking distance of businesses, shops, medical offices, and churches.

Financial plan: Monthly rental fee.

INDEPENDENT LIVING HOUSING

Type of apartment	*Monthly rental fee**
1-Bedroom	$950
2-Bedroom	$1,110

**All utilities except telephone included in the monthly fee. Wall-to-wall carpeting, cable TV, 24-hour emergency call system, fully equipped kitchens, individually controlled heating and air-conditioning.*

Ownership and management: Owned and operated by Presbyterian Manors of Mid-America, Inc., which also operates 15 other retirement communities throughout Missouri and Kansas and has more than 40 years of experience in the retirement industry. Opened in 1971.

Minimum age: 65 years.

Population: 81 residents; 79% women, 21% men, 3% couples.

Number of units: 78 Independent Living apartments; 41 Assisted Living suites, 36-bed health center.

Dining plan: No meals included in the monthly rental fee for Independent Living residents.

Services: *Included in the monthly fee:* None included for Independent Living residents.

At additional cost: Housekeeping and flat-linen services for Independent Living residents.

Activities: A full range of activities to meet any needs from spiritual and emotional to entertainment.

Availability: Waiting list.

Health services and rates: Independent Living residents receive 12 free days of health care after first year. During first year they receive one free day per month of residency and a credit of $45 per day for 18 additional days.

- 41 Assisted Living units
  - Private room $1,025–1,110/month
  - Suite $1,465–1,650/month
- 36-Bed health center
  - Semiprivate $65–69/day
  - Private room $78/day

"Presbyterian Manor's purpose is to provide persons 65 and older with accommodations and services especially designed to meet their physical, social, spiritual, and psychological needs and to contribute to their health and security with a sense of well-being and usefulness."

KINGSWOOD UNITED METHODIST MANOR

10000 Wornall Road
Kansas City, MO 64114
(816) 942-0994
Pam McNally, director of marketing

Type of community: Not-for-profit Continuing Care, modified contract

Located on 23 acres in a beautiful south Kansas City neighborhood, the community is convenient to shopping malls, entertainment, doctors, and many professional services. Independent Living residences with 23 floor plans are located in four 4-story buildings that join into central commons areas. The Medicare-certified health center is adjacent to the apartments and offers long- and short-term Skilled Nursing care and rehabilitative services.

Financial plan: Entrance fee plus monthly fee. Refundable life use fee returns 1% to residents to use each month as a credit against the monthly fee. After living at Kingswood for 100 months, residents

INDEPENDENT LIVING HOUSING

Type/size of apartment	*Entrance fee*	*Monthly fee**
Studio, 366 sq. ft.	$24,500	$901
1-Bedroom, 542–654 sq. ft.	$39,500–46,000	$1,197–1,366
1-Bedroom, 908 sq. ft.	$67,900	$2,119
2-Bedroom, 1,148–1,318 sq. ft.	$76,900–89,900	$1,996–2,333

**For double occupancy add $200 to the monthly fee. All utilities except telephone included. Fully equipped kitchen, individually controlled heating and air-conditioning, wall-to-wall carpeting, 24-hour emergency call system.*

will have collected 100% of the entrance fee and yet will continue to receive the same 1% credit each month. The refundable life use fee transfers should residents move permanently into the health center.

Ownership and management: Kingswood United Methodist Manor is a ministry of the United Methodist Church. Governed by a volunteer board of directors consisting of respected members of the Kansas City and Kingswood communities. Opened in 1982.

Minimum age: 65 years (if couple, spouse may be younger).

Population: 257 residents; 79% women, 21% men, 27% couples.

Number of units: 248 Independent Living apartments; 79 Skilled Nursing beds.

Dining plan: Main meal each day included in the monthly fee. Breakfast, lunch, and dinner are served daily. Two private dining rooms and catering available.

Services: *Included in the monthly fee:* Weekly flat-linen service, personal laundry facilities, scheduled transportation, bimonthly housekeeping.

At additional cost: Beauty/barbershop, convenience/gift shop, guest accommodations.

Activities: New Resident Koffee Klatch, Circle of Friends, Sew Easy, Arts Council Lunch Box Series, shopping trips, card night, Saturday night movies, trips to dinner theaters, musicals, the museum, the art gallery, sports events, the ballet and the symphony; holiday parties, Bible study, worship services, gardening, billiards, supports groups (for caregivers, the visually impaired, incontinence, breast cancer, Parkinson's disease).

Availability: Limited; priority waiting list.

Health services and rates: Clinic services include regular checkups and screenings, medication monitoring, night checks, dressing, bathing, ambulation, etc., plus homemaker assistance (simple meal preparation and housekeeping). Full-time social worker, assistance with filing medical claims, rehabilitative services, in-house physicians, doctors of podiatry, dentistry, audiology, ophthalmology/optometry, psychiatry/psychology available. Doctors of pharmacology review all prescription use and compatibility.

- 79-Bed nursing facility

Semiprivate	$82/day resident $92/day nonresident
Private	$151/day resident $151/day nonresident

"Kingswood Manor's mission is to provide residential and health care facilities, services, and opportunities for life enrichment for older adults in a Christian community. We are committed to making choices and opportunities available to residents every day."

JOHN KNOX VILLAGE

400 N.W. Murray Road
Lee's Summit, MO 64081
(800) 892-5669
Martha Fortner, sales manager

Type of community: Not-for-profit Continuing Care, modified contract

Accreditation: Continuing Care Accreditation Commission

Located on a 420-acre campus, 300 acres of which are developed and landscaped, John Knox Village has a fishing pond, a par-3 golf course, picnic areas, vegetable gardens, and a meadow with walking and jogging paths. The community offers four apartment complexes in addition to duplexes and houses. Kansas City attractions are located minutes away, from shopping malls to the Nelson Art Gallery, the Truman Sports Complex, and the American Royal Horse Show.

Financial plan: Entrance fee plus monthly fee or monthly rental. Four entrance fee plans: two all-inclusive and two modified. **1)** Platinum: health care at no additional cost for an unlimited time.* **2)** Gold: first 90 days of health care at no additional cost.* After the first 90 days, for an unlimited time period, resident pays only 50% of the room and care fees in the health center. **3)** Silver: identical to Platinum except the 50% discount on room and care fees is limited to 1,005 days. **4)** Bronze: first 30 days of health care at no additional cost; then resident pays only 50% of the room and care fees for the following 335 days. Monthly rental residents pay 100% of health care fees provided that there is space available in the health center.

**Resident always pays 100% for meals and ancillary items.*

Ownership and management: John Knox Village, Inc. Managed by an administrator under the guidance of a board of directors. Opened in 1970.

Minimum age: 60 years.

Population: 1944 residents; 77% women, 23% men, 15% couples.

Number of units: 1,600 Independent Living apartments, duplexes, and homes; 90 Assisted Living units, 430-bed nursing facility.

Dining plan: Three dining rooms. All meals are optional and may be charged to resident's account and billed monthly.

INDEPENDENT LIVING HOUSING

Type/size of apartments	*Entrance fee plans 1–4**	*Monthly fee plans 1–4**
Studio, 262–462 sq. ft.	$18,046–39,123	$359–614
1-Bedroom, 663–870 sq. ft.	$37,579–76,814	$615–1,027
2-Bedroom, 824–916 sq. ft.	$51.666–91,064	$808–1,267
Garden cottages		
576–816 sq. ft.	$28,691–78,573	$495–1,219
Duplexes/homes		
720–1,775 sq. ft.	$39,878–143,815	$717–1,364

**Prices are based on 100% refund the first year of residency and 0% thereafter. 50% and 100% refund options after year one are available at higher entrance fees. Monthly rental is also available. Prices upon request. All utilities except telephone are included. Fully equipped kitchen, 24-hour emergency call system, individually controlled heating and air-conditioning.*

Services: *Included in the monthly fee:* Weekly flat-linen and biweekly housekeeping services are provided to apartment residents, transportation within the campus and city limits of Lee's Summit.

At additional cost: Beauty/barbershops, gift shop, general stores, motel for guests on campus.

Activities: Bowling, billiards, ballroom and square dancing, two swimming pools, aqua dynamics, fishing, in the lake and golf on the par-3 golf course. Crafts classes, music groups, gardening, and many clubs and organizations. Outings and trips are scheduled each week to popular destinations.

Availability: Units adjacent to the golf course have a waiting list. Six new units of 1,775 square feet have been completed.

Health services and rates: 13 health center beds are designated for comprehensive rehabilitation; 36 beds for an Alzheimer's unit. Ambulance service with an average response time of two minutes is provided. Wheelchair escort service, nutrition counseling, wellness center. Adjacent to the village are Lee's Summit Hospital and Research Physicians Center, which offer professional services to residents. Health service rates are determined by the type of residency plan chosen. Basic costs for nonresidents are:

- 90-Room Assisted Living facility
  1-Bedroom $1,650/month single
  $2,475/month double
- 430-Bed health center
  Semiprivate $78/day
  $81.50/day Alzheimer's care
  Private $99/day
  $100/day Alzheimer's care

"The largest retirement community in America offers everything you may need in a self-contained community. John Knox Village has a very strong volunteer organization. Some residents help in the health center. The gift shops are operated by residents. A head start program for children with learning disabilities and local public schools are filled with resident volunteers from the Village. A preschool for employee's children and grandchildren called the Children's Village is on the campus."

ROLLA PRESBYTERIAN MANOR

1200 Homelife Plaza
Rolla, MO 65401
(314) 364-7336
Linda Hagler, administrator

Type of community: Not-for-profit Continuing Care, modified contract

Located in a pleasant, quiet residential setting with beautifully landscaped grounds and flower gardens, Rolla Presbyterian Manor offers Independent Living, resident care, and Skilled Nursing all on one level. The community is located across the street from a city park and within easy walking distance of businesses, shops, and medical offices.

Financial plan: Entrance fee plus monthly fee. Monthly rental. Two plans: **1)** Entrance fee plus life use fee. There is a one-time entrance fee of $4,500, payable upon acceptance of application. Life use fee is 80% refundable, with 10% nonrefundable each year. **2)** Estate preservation fee guarantees a 75% refund. A $500 processing fee is required with application. (In more than 40 years, no resident has ever been asked to leave due to lack of funds.)

Ownership and management: Presbyterian Manors, Inc., of Mid-America, a direct mission agency of the Synod of Mid-America of the Presbyterian Church, USA, owner and manager of 16 Presbyterian Manors in Kansas and Missouri. Opened in 1975.

INDEPENDENT LIVING HOUSING

Type/size of apartment	*Entrance fee 1/2*	*Monthly fee**
1-Bedroom, 750 sq. ft.	$40,000/30,000	$300
2-Bedroom, 1,000 sq. ft.	$46,700/35,000	$310

**Apartments can be rented by the month: 1-bedroom, $772; 2-bedroom, $877. Monthly fee is for single or double occupancy. All utilities except telephone included. Partially equipped kitchens, wall-to-wall-carpeting, 24-hour emergency call system.*

Minimum age: 65 years.

Population: 73 residents; 86% women, 14% men, 16% couples.

Number of units: 16 Independent Living apartments; 37 resident care rooms, 30 Skilled Nursing beds.

Dining plan: Meals available at an additional charge.

Services: *Included in monthly fee:* Housekeeping, scheduled transportation.

At additional cost: Beauty/barbershop.

Activities: Exercise, movies, special events, monthly international dinners.

Availability: Limited.

Health services and rates: Residents of Independent Living and residential care are entitled to 12 free days in the health care center each year. Dentist, podiatrist, physical, speech and occupational therapies, and audiology services available for additional cost. Residential care offers assistance with daily chores.

- 37 Residential care rooms
  - Private: $1,024–1,181/month resident; $1,174–1,331/month nonresident
  - 2-Room suite: $1,680/month resident; $1,830/month nonresident

  **For double occupancy add $370 to the resident monthly fee, $520 to the nonresident fee. Furniture is available.*

- 30-Bed nursing facility
  - Semiprivate: $67/day resident; $72/day nonresident
  - Private: $81/day resident; $81/day nonresident

"Rolla Presbyterian Manor is the only Continuing Care retirement community in the area. Rolla has a Good Samaritan Fund available for residents who can no longer afford to cover their own costs. The community provides a professional staff 24-hours a day and has a lower professional-to-resident ratio than other facilities in the area."

PARKSIDE MEADOWS

2150 Randolph Street
St. Charles, MO 63301
(314) 946-4966
Richard Ford, director of community relations

Type of community: Not-for-profit Continuing Care, modified contract

Located in historic St. Charles on a beautifully landscaped 13-acre campus adjacent to wooded Blanchette Park, the newly renovated facilities include Independent Living apartment complexes, Assisted Living, and Skilled Nursing. The community is 20 minutes from St. Louis International Airport and 30 minutes from the St. Louis Cardinals stadium, St. Louis Symphony Orchestra, Forest Park, art museum, zoo, and historic Union Station.

INDEPENDENT LIVING HOUSING

Type/size of apartment	*Entrance fee**	*Monthly fee**	*Monthly rental**
Efficiency, 380–400 sq. ft.	$38,500	$510	$854
1-Bedroom, 480–520 sq. ft.	$53,000–57,200	$585–610	$1,043–1,116
Deluxe 1-bedroom, 770–780 sq. ft.	$59,520	$620	$1,153
2-Bedroom, 725–800 sq. ft.	$65,500–72,800	$660–685	$1,290–1,363

**For double occupancy add $84–94 to the monthly fee and monthly rental. All utilities except telephone included. Fully equipped kitchen, wall-to-wall carpeting, sheer draperies, 24-hour emergency call system, cable TV, individually controlled heating and air-conditioning.*

Financial plan: Entrance fee plus monthly fee or monthly rental fee. Entrance fee is partially refundable, amortized over 16-year period at an average rate of 1/2% per month.

Ownership and management: Affiliated with the United Church of Christ and governed by a board of directors made up of 15 Christian men and women from various denominational backgrounds. Managed by CRSA, Inc., a professional management company in Memphis, Tennessee. Opened in 1977.

Minimum age: 62 years.

Population: 257 residents; 76% women, 24% men, 13% couples.

Number of units: 170 Independent Living units; 15 Assisted Living units, 60 Skilled Nursing beds.

Dining plan: Meals are optional and charged separately.

Services: *Included in the monthly fee:* Weekly housekeeping, scheduled transportation.

At additional cost: Beauty/barbershop.

Activities: Planned activities include trips to historic sites, cultural events, dining at area restaurants, shopping excursions, bingo, entertainment, various card and table games, quilting, barbeques, in-house movies, holiday get-togethers, birthday parties, educational seminars, exercise classes, big-screen TV, picnic and garden areas, tennis courts, horseshoes.

Availability: Waiting list from three months to two years.

Health services and rates: Rehabilitative services, including physical, occupational, and speech therapy, routine laboratory and diagnostic testing; ophthalmology, podiatry, dentistry, and other specialties available at additional cost. Home health services for apartment residents are available through home health agency that has an office on Parkside's campus.

- 15 Assisted Living units $68/day
- 60 Skilled Nursing beds
  Semiprivate $95/day
  Private $105/day

"Services are rendered to our residents by caring and professional staff members who are committed to Parkside's mission: to provide affordable apartment living and quality health care services for older adults who want to maintain an independent lifestyle within a community founded on Christian principles. Residents enjoy a gracious lifestyle in a warm and friendly community."

Betsy and Jack, 85 years

The McAuley, West Hartford, Connecticut (1988–1992)

Applewood, Amherst, Massachusetts (1992–)

"Location was the key—the geographical, topographical, cultural, social, and recreational environment . . . We also knew that health care services would be important down the road."

"We had originally hoped to come to Applewood," explains Jack. "We had heard about it through Mt.Holyoke—Betsy's alma mater—and it was in the planning stages. Unfortunately, construction was held up because of problems with the selected site. Meanwhile, we had sold our house in Old Saybrook, Connecticut, and had to move."

Betsy and Jack had done considerable research into retirement communities because their son, John, was on the board at Pennswood and had quietly recommended they begin looking. Pennswood had an eight-year waiting list, which was impractical. They looked in California, near their daughter, but felt their hearts were back East.

On the way home from visiting the Applewood office, Betsy and Jack stopped in to see The McAuley in West Hartford, which they had learned about from radio and newspaper advertisements. They met some old friends who had recently moved in and talked with the marketing person. They liked the community and thought it was a great location for them—The McAuley campus is contiguous with the St. Joseph College campus and hospital and there are numerous cultural activities in Hartford. They decided it would serve their urgent need.

"Location was the key," says Jack. "The geographical, topographical, cultural, social, and recreational environment. We were looking for a place with a big view, plus interesting things to do within the community as well as in the surrounding area. We also knew that health care services would be important down the road."

Betsy and Jack happily resided at The McAuley for four years. Then, during a visit to Mt. Holyoke in the fall of 1992, they saw the community—which had finally been built at a beautiful new site—and they fell in love with it. The location, the view, the apartments, the dining room, and the feeling of casualness that Applewood's small size promoted were all things they liked. Betsy and Jack returned to the McAuley and began to make arrangements, even though they had sworn they would never move again. Two-thirds of their entrance fee at the McAuley was refundable, and since Applewood's monthly fee was significantly less than they were paying at The McAuley, Jack calculated that if they lived at Applewood for five years the difference in the annual fees would almost offset the amount they would forfeit by moving. And, importantly, Applewood's entrance fee is 90% refundable (instead of 65%), which meant the move would have little impact on their estate.

They moved into Applewood in December 1992. According to Betsy, "It's not as difficult to move the second time." Betsy and Jack have found that because of the location (three colleges in the immediate area) many of the Applewood's residents have academic backgrounds—backgrounds they both share. Betsy is an enthusiastic member of the Activities Committee and is "learning in retirement." The openness of the campus allows Jack to happily cross-country ski right from his front door when not using the free season pass to a nearby downhill skiing facility provided him by his membership in the 70+ Ski Club. He is also an avid tennis player and, with Betsy, an ardent hiker.

"Our children were happy with our decision," says Betsy. "I think it was a relief to them. Wisely, they encouraged us, but didn't try to persuade us."

Advice from Betsy and Jack: Be sure to visit communities and talk to residents. Stay overnight, if possible. Spend time with the residents. Have a meal with residents—*not* with the marketing director. Look around the community carefully, because it's going to be your community, too. If you visit on a lovely day in the spring, think about what winter will be like, and vice versa. Also, examine the contract very carefully.

FRIENDSHIP VILLAGE OF SOUTH COUNTY

12503 Village Circle Drive
St. Louis, MO 63127
(314) 842-6840
Angela Wendell, marketing director

Type of community: Continuing Care, all-inclusive contract

Apartments are located in a four-story contemporary building, and private cottages also are available. Friendship Village is located on a 39-acre campus in Sunset Hills that features flower gardens, walkways, and a small fishing pond. Within a two-mile radius, everything is available including shopping centers, supermarkets, and St. Anthony's Hospital.

Financial plan: Entrance fee plus monthly fee. Two plans for entrance fee: **1)** Traditional entrance fees are refundable less 4% per month for two years. Traditional entrance fees are 54% less than the return of capital entrance fees. **2)** Return of capital entrance fees are 90% refundable.

Ownership and management: Life Care Services Corporation of Des Moines, Iowa. In existence since 1961, Life Care has developed more than 50 retirement communities and managed more than 40 throughout the United States. Managed by a board of directors. Opened in 1979.

Minimum age: 62 years.

Population: 480 to 500 residents; 70% women, 30% men, 15% couples.

Number of units: 181 Independent Living apartments and 40 cottages; 117-bed health care center.

Dining plan: One meal per day (resident's choice of breakfast, lunch, or dinner) is included in the monthly fee. Extra meals are $5.40 per meal or $130 per month. Special diets and tray service available.

Services: *Included in the monthly fee:* Biweekly housekeeping, flat-linen service, regularly scheduled transportation.

At additional cost: Beauty/barbershop, guest rooms, garage, rollaway beds, bank.

Activities: Social/recreational director. Exercise classes, social functions, arts and crafts, group tours, woodworking, clock repair, library, billiards, educational classes, movies, book reviews, sing-alongs, bookbinding, gardening, chaplain and nondenominational services, various volunteer opportunities.

Availability: Waiting list. Cottages, six months to one year; two-bedroom apartments, six months to one year.

INDEPENDENT LIVING HOUSING

Type of apartment	*Entrance fee/1*	*Entrance fee/2*	*Monthly fee**
Studio	$35,500	$52,260	$748
Alcove	$45,300	$70,290	$848
1-Bedroom	$70,700– 74,400	$116,060	$1,010–1,035
2-Bedroom	$100,500	$156,780	$1,136–1,231
Cottage	$117,400	$183,140	$1,298

**For double occupancy add $479 to the monthly fee for cottage or $500 to the monthly fee for apartments. All utilities included. Fully equipped kitchen, wall-to-wall carpeting, 24-hour emergency call system, individually controlled heating and air-conditioning, laundry facilities. Cottages have private garage space and laundry room.*

Health services and rates: Unlimited nursing care included in residents' monthly fee. 24-hour nursing available. Long-term nursing, physical therapy facilities, prescription drug administration, rehabilitative services. Assisted Living services are available to cottage and apartment residents on a short-term basis for an extra charge per service.

- 117-Bed Skilled Nursing facility
  Semiprivate $85/day
  Private $110/day

"Friendship Village offers Independent Living with the assurance of the unlimited use of our 117-bed Skilled Nursing facility. It's a new beginning with new friendships and the security of health care that's already paid for when needed."

GOOD SAMARITAN HOME

5200 South Broadway
St. Louis, MO 63111
(314) 352-2400
Laurie Schwartz, admissions coordinator

Type of community: Nonprofit Continuing Care, all-inclusive contract

Situated high on the bluffs of the Mississippi River with a commanding view of the bustling river traffic, the five-story brick building offers four levels of care: Independent Living, Assisted Living, Intermediate Nursing, and monitored resident care (dementia and Alzheimer's). Located ten minutes from downtown St. Louis and its wide array of restaurants and shopping, the Good Samaritan Home is close to historic Cherokee Street and the city's antiques row. German immigrants settled this neighborhood in the last century, and riverboat captains and prominent families built mansions along the bluffs lining the river. The community is located near highways and bus routes.

Financial plan: Entrance fee plus monthly fee. Entrance fee is refundable up to two years: first 90 days, 100% refundable; 90 days to one year, 75% refundable; second year, 50% refundable.

Ownership and management: Nonprofit corporation affiliated with the United Church of Christ. Governed by a 12-member board of trustees. Opened in 1958. The Good Samaritan Charitable Hospital was founded in 1854.

Minimum age: 60 years.

Population: 240 residents; 85% women, 15% men, 6% couples.

Number of units: 86 Independent Living rooms and apartments; 80 Assisted Living rooms and apartments, 82 Intermediate Nursing beds, 36 monitored care beds of which 26 are licensed for Intermediate care.

INDEPENDENT LIVING HOUSING

Type/size of unit	*Entrance fee single/double*	*Monthly fee single/double**
Single, 320 sq. ft.	$28,500	$749
Double, 425 sq. ft.	$28,500	$1,108
Apartment, 550 sq. ft.	$37,530/45,975	$997/1,198

**All utilities except telephone included. Wall-to-wall carpeting, individually controlled heating and air-conditioning, kitchenettes on each floor, 24-hour emergency call system. Furnished accommodations are available.*

Dining plan: Three meals per day are included in the monthly fee. Special diets are available when ordered by a physician.

Services: *Included in the monthly fee:* Weekly housekeeping and flat-linen services, personal laundry, regularly scheduled shopping trips.

At additional cost: Beauty/barbershop, mobile post office visits weekly.

Activities: Full-time activities director. Arts and crafts, music therapy, parties, bingo, trips to community events, library. A full-time chaplain offers worship services each Sunday in the chapel, Bible study, and vespers.

Availability: Limited availability.

Health services and rates: Biweekly doctor's hours, regularly scheduled dentist and podiatrist, registered physical therapist. Good Samaritan Home's physician, nursing care, prescription drugs prescribed by the Home's physician and dispensed by the Home's nursing staff all included in the monthly fee. If hospitalization is ordered by the Home's physician, it is provided at no extra charge. Monitored resident care is available for residents with Alzheimer's and related memory disorders.

- 80 Assisted Living units

	Nonresident entrance fee/monthly fee
Single	$28,500/1,181
Double	$50,175/2,066

- 32 Monitored resident units and 80 Intermediate Nursing units — $30,600/entrance fee $1,969/month

  A per diem rate is also offered for Assisted Living ($65/day), Intermediate or monitored care ($85/day), with a refundable deposit of one month's payment in advance.

"Founded more than 135 years ago as a charitable hospital, Good Samaritan Home has been providing residential care in the St. Louis community for close to 90 years. Quality, cost-effective, and compassionate care in a Christian setting has been the standard of this ministry from its beginning in 1856."

VILLAGE NORTH RETIREMENT COMMUNITY

11160 Village North Drive
St. Louis, MO 63136
(314) 355-8010
Arlinda Warren, director of marketing and sales

Type of community: Nonprofit Continuing Care, modified contract

Located on 44 acres in the quiet residential community of North St. Louis County, Village North offers Independent Living, Assisted Living, and Skilled Nursing. Buildings are connected by enclosed walkways and surrounded by manicured lawns and beautiful wooded land. The grounds feature a quiet fishing pond surrounded by picnic tables. Shopping, restaurants, banks, and churches are in the vicinity, and the Christian Hospital Northeast is around the corner. Regular outings are provided to the Fox Theater, the St. Louis Symphony, Queeny Park, and Busch Stadium, home of the St. Louis Cardinals. University of Missouri, St. Louis University, and Florissant Valley Community College are all in the area and offer a wide range of cultural and educational opportunities.

Financial plan: Monthly fee.

Ownership and management: Barne Jewish, Inc./Christian Health Services, a multihospital and nursing home ownership and management system. Opened in 1982.

Minimum age: 65 years.

Population: 240 residents; 84% women, 16% men, 9% couples.

INDEPENDENT LIVING HOUSING

Type/size of apartment	*Monthly fee**
Studio, 376 sq. ft.	$1,202
1-Bedroom, 582 sq. ft.	$1,561
2-Bedroom, 787 sq. ft.	$1,888

**For double occupancy add approximately $500 to the monthly fee. All utilities except telephone included. Individually controlled heating and air-conditioning, fully equipped all-electric kitchen, 24-hour emergency call system.*

Number of units: 213 Independent Living apartments; 60-bed health center.

Dining plan: One meal per day is included in the monthly fee. Tray service and special diets, when approved by administration for medical reasons.

Services: *Included in the monthly fee:* Scheduled transportation, personal laundry facilities, weekly flat-linen and housekeeping services.

At additional cost: Beauty/barbershop, mini-market, guest accommodations.

Activities: In-house entertainment, movies, bingo, arts and crafts, fishing, gardening, outings to local cultural and sporting events, regular theme parties, dancing classes, dinner club.

Availability: Limited. 96% occupied.

Health services and rates: Apartment residents receive 15 days of nursing care per year at no additional cost. Full rehabilitation center. Assisted Living services available to residents in their apartments.

- 60 Skilled Nursing beds

Semiprivate	$95/day
Private	$115/day

"Village North is geared toward the active senior who enjoys friendship, activity, and a strong sense of community. The facility's diversity allows people from all walks of life to immediately feel at home."

NEBRASKA

NORTHFIELD VILLA AND THE RESIDENCY

2550 21st Street
Gering, NE 69341
(308) 436-3101
Jack Musker, marketing director

Type of community: Nonprofit Continuing Care, all-inclusive contract

The Residency is housed in a two-story apartment complex on a 24-acre campus in Scotts Bluff, and Northfield Villa is located on a 22-acre campus in West Gering, facing the Scotts Bluff National Monument. The two communities are jointly run and are four miles apart. Salem Congregational Church is located next to The Residency.

Financial plan: Entrance fee plus monthly fee. Refund of entrance fee less 25% after first month, and 3% per month thereafter for period of 25 months. Deposit of 10% required.

Ownership and management: Owned and operated by Northfield Villa, Inc. Managed by a board of directors comprised of clergy and professional people. Northfield Villa opened in 1974; The Residency opened in 1992.

Minimum age: 62 years.

Population: 350 residents; 80% women, 20% men, 20% couples.

Number of units: 145 Independent Living apartments in Northfield Villa and 94 Independent Living residents in The Residency; 20-bed infirmary at The Residency, 49-bed health center at Northfield Villa.

INDEPENDENT LIVING HOUSING

Northfield Villa apartments	*Entrance fee*	*Monthly fee**
Studio, 450 sq. ft.	$36,950	$605
Studio-bedroom, 450 sq. ft.	$37,950	$605
1-Bedroom, 660 sq. ft.	$49,950	$618
2-Bedroom, 840 sq. ft.	$61,950	$708
The Residency		
1-Bedroom, 660–710 sq. ft.	$57,950–56,950	$668
2-Bedroom, 900–1,400 sq. ft.	$67,950–85,950	$668–914

**For double occupancy add $344.50 to the monthly fee. All utilities except telephone included. Fully equipped kitchens, wall-to-wall carpeting, individually controlled heating and air-conditioning, patio or balcony, cable TV, 24-hour emergency call system.*

Dining plan: One meal per day (dinner) included in the monthly fee.

Services: *Included in the monthly fee:* Scheduled transportation, biweekly maid service, flat-linen service, open parking.

At additional cost: Garage parking, beauty/barbershop.

Activities: Social director, Bible study, vespers, carpenter shop, library, gardening, exercise space, crafts room, various intellectual, spiritual, and physical activity programs.

Availability: Waiting list.

Health services and rates: Unlimited nursing care included in resident's monthly fee. Additional charge for two extra meals. Physician care and medical supplies for additional fee. Rehabilitation services available. Assisted Living provided.

- 20-Bed infirmary at The Residency
- 49-Bed health center at Northfield Villa

"Northfield Villa is the only life care community in Western Nebraska."

SKYLINE MANOR/VILLA

7300 Graceland Drive
Omaha, NE 68134
(402) 572-5750
Cindy Frieling, marketing director

Type of community: Nonprofit Continuing Care, all-inclusive contract

Located in a wooded area in northwest Omaha, Skyline Manor/Villa features beautifully landscaped grounds. The campus consists of six buildings, including a six-story high-rise. Omaha is the midwestern center for medical research and is home to many fine hospitals and health care services.

Financial plan: Entrance fee plus monthly fee. Entrance fee is refundable, declining over the first eight years.

Ownership and management: Owned by nonprofit corporation. Managed by Retirement Management Company, Lawrence, Kansas. Opened in 1969.

Minimum age: 62 years (spouse may be younger).

INDEPENDENT LIVING HOUSING

Manor apartments	*Entrance fee**	*Monthly fee**
Studio, 277 sq. ft.	$32,325	$589
1-Bedroom, 334 sq. ft.	$43,210–64,485	$652–765
1-Bedroom/den, 811 sq. ft.	$90,000	$1,116
Villa apartments		
Studio, 380 sq. ft.	$38,670	$609
1-Bedroom, 450–675 sq. ft.	$44,045–76,101	$632–872
Deluxe 1-bedroom, 706 sq. ft.	$80,085	$872
Comb., 900 sq. ft.	$95,075	$890

**For double occupancy there is a 25% addition to the entrance fee, approximately $325 to the monthly fee. All utilities except telephone included. Appliances, wall-to-wall carpeting, individually controlled heating and air-conditioning, 24-hour emergency call system.*

Population: 450 residents; 80% women, 20% men, 15% couples.

Number of units: 410 Independent Living apartments; 24 Assisted Living units, 100 nursing beds.

Dining plan: Lunch or dinner included in the monthly fee. Meals can be delivered to apartments. Private dining room.

Services: *Included in the monthly fee:* Scheduled transportation, semimonthly housekeeping.

At additional cost: Beauty/barbershop, guest accommodations.

Activities: Ceramics, two libraries, movies, sewing circles, billiards room, carpentry shop, garden plots, card games, movies, swimming, book reviews, exercise sessions, investment seminars, classes in creative writing, world geography, classic novels. Trips to ballet, theater, symphony, opera, restaurants. Weekly vespers, mass on Sundays and holy days. Adoptive school program with Adams School, intergenerational activities.

Availability: Some available, depending on apartment style.

Health services and rates: Unlimited health care included in resident's monthly fee. Residents continue to pay basic monthly fee should they move into Assisted Living or Skilled Nursing, the only additional charge being for extra meals. Nursing staff and physician on call 24 hours a day. Therapy services available.

- 24 Assisted Living rooms
- 40-Bed Intermediate Nursing facility
- 60-Bed Skilled Nursing facility

"We believe there are four reasons that contribute to longevity in a life care community: companionship, diet, medical care, and recreation. Our residents participate in the community; they are active in cultural, recreational and educational events. The energetic lifestyles of our residents show that they have not retired from living."

NEVADA

CLASSIC RESIDENCE BY HYATT

3201 Plumas Street
Reno, NV 89509
(702) 825-1105
Todd Kennerly, director of sales

Type of community: Independent Living with Continuum of Care

Located in a beautiful suburban setting in southwest Reno, adjacent to Washoe Golf Course and Club House, the two- and three-story buildings offer spectacular views of the Sierra Nevada Mountains. Independent Living residences and Assisted Living facility are provided. The community is convenient to shopping, hospitals, medical offices, and houses of worship.

Financial plan: Monthly fee. Nonrefundable deposit of $500. Fully refundable security deposit equal to one month's rent.

Ownership and management: Classic Residence by Hyatt, an affiliate of Hyatt Corporation, which owns and operates Classic Residences in Monterey, California; West Hartford, Connecticut; Chevy Chase, Maryland; Teaneck, New Jersey; Dallas, Texas. Opened in 1989.

Minimum age: 55 years.

Population: 160 residents; 63% women, 15% men, 22% couples.

Number of units: 124 Independent Living apartments; 24 Assisted Living apartments.

Dining plan: Continental breakfast daily with choice of lunch or dinner included in the monthly fee. Classically Caring Cuisine menu selections are low in sodium, fat, and cholesterol. Private dining room. Room service available for short-term illness.

Services: *Included in the monthly fee:* Weekly housekeeping and flat-linen services, covered parking, scheduled transportation, 24-hour concierge, move-in coordination. Classic Club membership: long-term insurance policy underwritten by Lloyd's of London, membership in airline club, exclusive travel

INDEPENDENT LIVING HOUSING

Type/size of apartment	*Monthly fee**
Studio, 436 sq. ft.	$1,450
1-Bedroom, 563 sq. ft.	$1,675
2-Bedroom, 1-bath, 731 sq. ft.	$2,085
2-Bedroom, 2-bath, 781 sq. ft.	$2,370

**For double occupancy add $325 to the monthly fee. All utilities except telephone included. Fully equipped kitchen, window treatments, wall-to-wall carpeting, patios or balconies, individually controlled heating and air-conditioning, cable TV, 24-hour emergency call system.*

opportunities, complimentary overnight accommodations at Classic Residences.

At additional cost: Additional housekeeping and flat-linen services, personal laundry service, on-site banking, beauty/barbershop.

Activities: Personalized computer lifestyle profile provides full-time resident relations/programming staff with opportunity to individually tailor a variety of educational, cultural, social, and recreational programs to residents' interests. Classes, lectures, movies, concerts, dances, cultural outings. Fitness center with Jacuzzi, art studio, well-stocked library, billiards room, club room.

Availability: Waiting list for certain apartment styles.

Health services and rates: All residents are covered by long-term care insurance underwritten by Lloyd's of London. Vision screening, monthly blood pressure check, hearing screening, arthritis support group available to all residents. Assisted Living residents who previously lived in Classic Residence remain eligible for long-term care insurance coverage. Assisted living is staffed 24-hours by licensed nurse on staff, trained attendants.

- 24 Assisted Living apartments

Studio, 436 sq. ft.	$2,150/month
1-Bedroom, 563 sq. ft.	$2,375/month
2-Bedroom, 731 sq. ft.	$2,785/month

**For double occupancy with one person needing care add $400 to the monthly fee. All Assisted Living apartments have complete kitchens and private baths.*

"A distinguished leader in the hospitality industry for more than three decades, Hyatt has set the standard for high-quality accommodations and attentive service. Classic Residence has built upon Hyatt's expertise, bringing innovative cuisine, striking interior design, and personalized, supportive services to the senior living industry."

NEW HAMPSHIRE

PLEASANT VIEW

227 Pleasant Street
Concord, NH 03301
(603) 225-3970
Bob Letridge, executive director

Type of community: Continuing Care, modified contract

Pleasant View is housed in a three-story fully restored Georgian-style apartment building with masonry walls and brick exterior constructed in 1927. The community is located on 47 parklike acres featuring open grassy fields, pathways for walking, surrounding woods, and views of the countryside. Spacious common areas are on each floor of the building. Independent Living, Assisted Living, and Skilled Nursing are on-site. The community is situated in a predominantly residential neighborhood that has experienced a recent growth of medical clinics. Concord Hospital is across the street; downtown Concord is one mile away.

Financial plan: Monthly rental. Month-to-month lease with one month's deposit.

Ownership and management: Owned and managed by the McKerley Health Care Centers, Inc., health care providers in the Concord area for more than 45 years. Opened in 1983.

Minimum age: 55 years.

Population: 70 residents; 82% women, 18% men, 9% couples.

Number of units: 72 Independent Living apartments; 180-bed health center.

Dining plan: One meal per day included in the monthly fee. Special diets, private dining room, and tray service available.

INDEPENDENT LIVING HOUSING

Type/size of unit	*Monthly rent**
Efficiency, 500 sq. ft.	$1,300
Studio, 600 sq. ft.	$1,350
1-Bedroom, 700–900 sq. ft.	$1,800
2-Bedroom, 1,000–1,100 sq. ft.	$2,100
Deluxe suites	
1-Bedroom	$2,100–2,500
2-Bedroom	$2,600–2,800/3,000–3,200

**For double occupancy add $450 to the monthly rent. All utilities except telephone and cable TV included. Kitchens, 24-hour emergency call system, individually controlled heating and air-conditioning, cable TV, wall-to-wall carpeting.*

Services: *Included in the monthly rent:* Weekly housekeeping and flat-linen services, scheduled transportation, use of personal laundry machines, individual parking.

At additional cost: Beauty/barbershop.

Activities: Full-time resident social director. Crafts and hobby studio, health club, library, theater, game room with billiards table, scheduled trips, heated swimming pool, films, speakers, cultural events, educational events, athletics, health club with Nautilus equipment, theater for concerts and lectures.

Availability: Some accommodations have waiting list.

Health services and rates: McKerley Homecare, on the garden level of Pleasant View, is under the direction of a registered nurse and offers Skilled Nursing, physical therapy, home health aide, companion and cleaning/homemaker services on-site. Concord Hospital is located across the street.

- Homecare (rates for Homecare vary according to services required)
- 180-Bed health care center

Semiprivate	$144/day
Private	$162–167/day
Suite	$177/day

"Pleasant View is backed by more than 45 years of experience in providing quality long-term care to the citizens of New Hampshire."

RIVERWOODS AT EXETER

7 RiverWoods Drive
Exeter, NH 03833
(603) 772-4700 or (800) 688-9663
Judy Lamoureux, associate director/
director of marketing

Type of community: Not-for-profit Continuing Care, all inclusive contract

Located on 83 wooded acres that feature walking trails, courtyards, and a river, RiverWoods's design emphasizes the residential character of the community. Seven different floor plans are available. The community is close to Phillips Exeter Academy, the University of New Hampshire, the White Mountains, Boston, and Portland, Maine.

Financial plan: Entrance fee plus monthly fee. Entrance fee is 90% refundable when residency is terminated. Application deposit of 35% of entrance fee required at time residence and care agreement is signed.

Ownership and management: Life Care Services of New Hampshire, a not-for-profit corporation. Opened in August 1994.

Minimum age: 62 years (if couple, spouse may be younger).

INDEPENDENT LIVING HOUSING

Type of apartment	*Entrance fee**	*Monthly fee**
Studio	$101,000	$995
1-Bedroom	$118,000–185,000	$1,15–1,935
1-Bedroom/den	$200,000	$1,940
2-Bedroom	$238,000–290,000	$2,100–2,415
2-Bedroom/den	$279,000	$2,415

**For double occupancy add $12,750 to the entrance fee, $525 to the monthly fee. All utilities except telephone and cable TV included. Fully equipped electric kitchen, individually controlled heating and air-conditioning, wall-to-wall carpeting, 24-hour emergency call system. Most apartments have either a solarium or a screened porch. Fifteen floor plans available.*

Population: 258 residents; 44% couples, 56% singles.

Number of units: Phase 1: 161 Independent Living units plus 20 Assisted Living apartments, 20 supported residential care units, and 20 Skilled Nursing beds. Phase 2: 39 Independent Living units.

Dining plan: The number of meals included in the monthly fee equals the number of days in the month. Tray service available to apartment. Private dining room, wet bar, and café.

Services: *Included in the monthly fee:* Flat-linen service, biweekly housekeeping service, scheduled transportation.

At additional cost: Café, beauty/barbershop, guest accommodations, gift shop.

Activities: Full-time activities director. Card rooms, indoor pool, art studio, woodworking shop, gardening, crafts room, exercise room, picnic area, walking trails, greenhouse, library, auditorium, lounges, health club, whirlpool.

Availability: Limited; some floor plans available.

Health services and rates: Residents receive unlimited health care at no additional cost to current monthly fee, except for the two additional meals. Direct entrance to health center on space-available basis requires nonrefundable entrance fee of $25,000.

- 20 Assisted Living units
- 20 Supported residential care units
- 20 Skilled Nursing beds

"Professionally planned and managed, this not-for-profit Continuing Care community is located in the culturally rich Seacoast region. One of the beauties of RiverWoods is that the community's growth has been shaped to preserve the traditional qualities of the historic town of Exeter."

KENDAL AT HANOVER

80 Lyme Road
Hanover, NH 03755-1218
(603) 643-8900
Jean G. Brophy, administrator

Type of community: Not-for-profit Continuing Care, all-inclusive contract

Located on a 64-acre site within the township of Hanover, Kendal at Hanover is just 2 1/2 miles north of the Dartmouth College Green. The partially wooded site is bordered on the west by the Connecticut River; across the river is a view of the hills of Vermont. Numerous cultural, academic, and recreational opportunities are available at Dartmouth. A golf course and the Storrs Pond recreational area are nearby. Hanover is a 2 1/2-hour drive from three major airports. Amtrak service is available to New York and Montreal. Local transportation is available. Independent Living apartments are housed in one-, two-, and three-story wood-frame buildings. Personal care and Skilled Nursing facility are available on campus.

Financial plan: Entrance fee plus monthly fee. Entrance fees are refundable over five years at 2% per month. $1,100 deposit places you on a priority waiting list. $100 nonrefundable registration fee ($150 for couples).

Ownership and management: The Kendal Corporation, a not-for-profit corporation governed by a board composed of members of the Religious Society of Friends (Quakers). The Kendall Corporation has communities in Pennsylvania, Ohio, and New York. Opened in 1991.

Minimum age: 65 years.

Population: 360 residents; 66% women, 34% men, 60 couples.

INDEPENDENT LIVING HOUSING

Type/size of apartment	*Entrance fee single/double*	*Monthly fee single/double**
Studio, 556–620 sq. ft.	$71,500	$1,415
1-Bedroom, 752 sq. ft.	$121,000/126,500	$1,740/2,510
1-Bedroom/den, 1,025–1,112 sq. ft.	$183,000/218,500	$2,125/2,755
2-Bedroom, 1,214 sq. ft.	$213,500/226,000	$2,190/2,955
2-Bedroom/den, 1,324–1,350 sq. ft.	$235,500/254,000	$2,510/3,280

**All utilities except telephone included in the monthly fee. Fully equipped kitchens, draperies, wall-to-wall carpeting, private patio or balcony, individually controlled heating and air-conditioning, 24-hour emergency call system.*

Number of units: 248 Independent Living units; 20 personal care rooms, 36-bed Skilled Nursing facility.

Dining plan: Three meals daily included in the monthly fee. Credits are available if fewer meals are taken. Private dining room.

Services: *Included in the monthly fee:* Weekly housekeeping and flat-linen services, covered parking, scheduled transportation.

At additional cost: Beauty/barbershop, branch bank, coffee shop, sundries/gift shop, group travel, guest accommodations.

Activities: Library, swimming pool, exercise and recreational facilities, films, lectures, study groups, play readings, musical events, community garden, trips to concerts and museums, outings for birdwatching, hiking, arts and crafts.

Availability: Limited, depending upon apartment style.

Health services and rates: Range of health services, including long-term care, is included in monthly fee. Residents who move permanently to the health center continue to pay the same monthly fee they have been paying in Independent Living or personal care unit. Direct admission to personal care unit may also be arranged if space is available. Physicians, nursing staff, social service staff, nutritionists, and specialists in recreational, physical, speech, and occupational therapies available on premises. All health care programs are focused on wellness and directed toward assisting each resident to maintain his or her highest level of self-care and independence. Dentistry and podiatry offered at additional fee.

- 20 Assisted Living rooms

	*Entrance fee**
1-Room with bath	$24,150
2-Room suite	$60,000

**Plus $3,110 monthly fee. These rates for nonresidents admitted directly to personal care.*

- 36 Skilled Nursing beds

"In establishing communities for older people, our mission is to provide conditions fostering independence, health, and security under which residents may realize their fullest potential. We are committed to excellence in all aspects of our operations as we seek to enhance the quality of life and to provide high-quality health care for each resident. Kendal operates within a framework of practices that arise from basic Quaker values. Of primary importance is our commitment to nurture a sense of community and to treat each resident with dignity and respect, as a valued individual, regardless of age or condition."

HILLCREST TERRACE

200 Alliance Way
Manchester, NH 03102
(603) 645-6500
Jacklyn Friedman, director

Type of community: Nonprofit Independent and Assisted Living

Located on 17 wooded acres that feature walking areas, Hillcrest Terrace is housed in a three-story building with five wings. The community is located six miles from nearest hospital.

Financial plan: Entrance fee plus monthly fee. Entrance fee is refundable, prorated monthly.

Ownership and management: Governed by the board of trustees under Optima Health. Managed by CRSA. Opened in October 1991.

Minimum age: 62 years.

Population: 175 residents; 70% women, 30% men, 43% couples.

Number of units: 143 Independent Living apartments; 70 Assisted Living units.

Dining plan: 25 meals per month included in the monthly fee. Tray service for health reasons. Private dining room.

Services: *Included in the monthly fee:* Biweekly housekeeping, scheduled transportation, parking.

At additional cost: Beauty/barbershop, covered parking, country store, flat-linen and laundry services, post office.

Activities: Activities director. Card and game rooms, crafts room, Jacuzzi, exercise facilities, special events, billiards, gardening, special trips, theater events.

Availability: Limited.

Health services and rates: Residents receive ten free days per year in Assisted Living. Optima Health (merger of two large hospitals) allows residents to plan for full continuum of care. Special speakers and seminars for healthy aging. Podiatrist available regularly for fee.

- 70 Assisted Living units $2,195–2,895/month

Add $384/month for additonal person with no assistance; add $658/month for additional person with assistance.

"The mission of Hillcrest Terrace is provide a high quality of health and residential care and services to the aging at affordable prices."

INDEPENDENT LIVING HOUSING

Type/size of apartment	*Entrance fee*	*Monthly fee**
Studio, 523–541 sq. ft.	$15,700–16,400	$1,365–1,420
1-Bedroom, 638–682 sq. ft.	$18,800–19,900	$1,620–1,780
2-Bedroom, 718–1,031 sq. ft.	$19,900–24,700	$1,780–2,205

**For double occupancy add $285 to the monthly fee. All utilities except telephone included. Fully equipped kitchen, wall-to-wall carpeting, draperies, 24-hour emergency call system, individually controlled heating and air-conditioning. $40 per month for garage; $45 per month for balcony.*

HUNT COMMUNITY

10 Allds Street
Nashua, NH 03060
(603) 882-6511
Elaine Ross, marketing director

Type of community: Not-for-profit Continuing Care, modified contract

This attractive continuing care retirement community is located on 16 partially wooded acres in downtown Nashua. The location provides shopping, banks, and entertainment all within walking distance. Two buildings providing 116 apartments for Independent Living are connected to the Wallace and Hunt Health Care Pavilions and the John M. Hunt Community Center.

Financial plan: Entrance fee plus monthly fee or monthly rental. Entrance fee amortizes at 2% per month of residency. Monthly fee only is adjusted to include the entrance fee spread out over the life of the resident.

Ownership and management: Nonprofit corporation organized under the laws of the state of New Hampshire. Volunteer board of directors. Licensed executive director. Opened in 1989.

Minimum age: 62 years.

Population: 180 residents; 70% women, 30% men, 25% couples.

Number of units: 116 Independent Living apartments; 12 Assisted Living units, 41-bed nursing facility.

Dining plan: One meal per day included in the monthly fee, to be taken in dining room or coffee shop. Residents may elect to receive credit in place of meal plan. Additional meals available.

Services: *Included in the monthly fee:* Biweekly housecleaning, transportation.

At additional cost: Beauty/barbershop, personal and flat-linen services, guest apartment.

Activities: Swimming, bowling, lectures, religious services, gardening, library, painting, bridge, fitness classes, crafts studio, woodworking shop, bingo, social hours, overnight trips, concerts, volunteer activities in the greater community.

Availability: $500 refundable fee for placement on waiting list.

Health services and rates: Residents receive 30 days per year free health care. Each resident's care is directed by his or her own physician. Some health care available in resident's apartment. Physical and occupational therapy at additional charge.

INDEPENDENT LIVING HOUSING

Type/size of unit	*Entrance fee**	*Monthly fee**	*Monthly rent**
Studio, 410 sq. ft.	$49,000	$1,087	$267
1-Bedroom, 640 sq. ft.	$70,000	$1,227	$2,681
2-Bedroom, 980 sq. ft.	$90,000	$1,969	$3,769

**For double occupancy in 1-bedroom apartments add $5,000 to the entrance fee, $400 to the monthly fee, $500 to the monthly rent. All utilities except telephone and electricity included. Wall-to-wall carpeting, 24-hour emergency call system, fully equipped kitchens, individually controlled heating and air-conditioning, cable TV, storage and parking.*

- 12-Bed Assisted Living facility (Wallace Pavilion)
  Private $90/day
- 41-Bed health center (Hunt Pavilion)
  Semiprivate $115/day
  Private $120/day

"Hunt Community offers a rich tradition of Independent Living in a warm and supportive environment. Residents take full advantage of opportunities available in the greater Nashua community as well as within the Hunt Community facilities. The campus provides for a tranquil lifestyle in an active urban setting."

NEW JERSEY

CADBURY

2150 Route 38
Cherry Hill, NJ 08002
(800) 422-3287
Betty Ann Van Isstendal

Type of community: Not-for-profit Continuing Care, all-inclusive contract

Accreditation: Continuing Care Accreditation Commission

Cadbury is located on 13 wooded, lakeside acres featuring walking paths and gardens. Everything at Cadbury is under one roof—Independent Living, Assisted Living, and Skilled Nursing facilities. Philadelphia is in close proximity. Shopping centers, theaters, and fine restaurants are only minutes away.

Financial plan: Entrance fee plus monthly fee. Refundable entrance fee. $250 per person application processing fee. Refundable $1,000 unit deposit.

Ownership and management: Sponsored by the Religious Society of Friends. Opened in 1977.

Minimum age: 65 years.

Population: 180 residents; 77% women, 23% men, 17% couples.

Number of units: 232 Independent Living apartments; 24 Assisted Living units, 120-bed Skilled Nursing facility.

Dining plan: Dinner each day included in the monthly fee in lakeview dining room or new coffee shop. Optional meal plans available. Private dining room.

Services: *Included in the monthly fee:* Weekly housekeeping and flat-linen services, scheduled transportation.

At additional cost: Beauty/barbershop, full-service branch bank.

Activities: Arts and crafts, library, picnics, billiards table, walking paths, heated indoor swimming pool, ceramics.

INDEPENDENT LIVING HOUSING

Type/size of apartment	*Entrance fee*	*Monthly fee single/double**
Studio, 371 sq. ft.	$40,000–569,000	$1,229/1,508
1-Bedroom suite, 743 sq. ft.	$90,000–112,500	$2,209/2,698
1-Bedroom/balcony, 750 sq. ft.	$102,000–107,000	$1,885/2,516
1-Bedroom/den/balcony, 995 sq. ft.	$120,000–123,000	$2,431/3,103

**All utilities included except telephone and cable TV. Individually controlled heating and air-conditioning, wall-to-wall carpeting, matching drapes, optional kitchenette, 24-hour emergency call system.*

Availability: Limited.

Health services and rates: Monthly fee covers health center fees. Fully equipped physical therapy room. Occupational and speech therapy programs included.

- 24 Assisted Living units
- 120-Bed Intermediate and Skilled Nursing facility (mostly semiprivate rooms)
  Semiprivate $153/day nonresident
  Private $198/day nonresident

"The enjoyment of a friendly community is one of the best reasons for entering a Continuing Care community. Cadbury offers Continuing Care retirement in the caring Quaker tradition. Situated on 13 acres in the midst of bustling Cherry Hill, we have the best of both worlds—the beauty of a country setting, with our lovely lake and lush foliage, and shopping malls, markets, library, and banks all within walking distance."

FRANCISCAN OAKS

19 Pocono Road
Denville, NJ 07834
(201) 586-6003
Jay Almquist, executive director

Type of community: Not-for-profit Continuing Care, all-inclusive contract

Located on a 13.9-acre site in historic Morris County adjacent to an acute care hospital, the community consists of Independent Living units in three four-story buildings, a community center, and a Skilled Nursing facility. Franciscan Oaks combines the advantages of small-town living with easy commuting to New York City, less than an hour away. The community is located 30 minutes from Newark Airport and only a few minutes from three major state and interstate highways.

Financial plan: Entrance fee plus monthly fee. Two plans: **1)** Entrance fee declines by 2% per month of residence in an Independent Living unit, 4% in Skilled Nursing unit. **2)** 50% refundable entrance fee. 10% deposit required upon execution of residence agreement. $250 nonrefundable application fee.

Ownership and management: Developed by St. Francis Life Care Corporation, a not-for-profit corporation affiliated with the Sisters of the Sorrowful Mother Health Care Ministry Corporation. Opened in June 1994.

Minimum age: 65 years (if couple, spouse may be younger).

Population: Anticipated number of residents is 250+.

INDEPENDENT LIVING HOUSING

Type/size of apartment	*Entrance fee 1/2**	*Monthly fee**
Studio	$70,000/86,250	$1,200
Efficiency, 530 sq. ft.	$95,000/115,000	$1,400
1-Bedroom/1-bath, 700 sq. ft.	$117,500–122,500/145,000–150,250	$1,625
1-Bedroom/2-bath, 792 sq. ft.	$132,500–145,000/160,000–175,000	$1,825
2-Bedroom, 947 sq. ft.	$168,500–172,500/175,000–200,000	$2,000
2-Bedroom/den, 1,060 sq. ft.	$189,500–214,500/207,500–250,250	$2,150–2,500

**For double occupancy add $10,000 to Plan 1 and $13,000 to Plan 2 entrance fee, plus $600 to the monthly fee. All utilities except telephone included. Fully equipped kitchen, laundry equipment, 24-hour emergency call system, individually controlled heating and air-conditioning, wall-to-wall carpeting.*

Number of units: 221 Independent Living residences; 60 Skilled Nursing beds.

Dining plan: One meal (lunch or dinner) each day is included in the monthly fee. Tray service is provided up to 14 days, if authorized by medical or executive director. Delivery charge applies after five days.

Services: *Included in the monthly fee:* Light weekly housekeeping, semiannual heavy cleaning, weekly flat-linen service, parking, scheduled transportation.

At additional cost: Beauty/barbershop, convenience store, covered parking, personal laundry, guest rooms.

Activities: Full-time activities director. Commons (community center) contains meeting and activity rooms, auditorium, swimming pool, fitness center, library.

Availability: Limited.

Health services and rates: Residents receive unlimited health care and continue to pay the same monthly fee if admitted permanently to Skilled Nursing care. This is also true if one member of a couple resides in the Skilled Nursing facility.

- 60 Skilled Nursing beds

"Franciscan Oaks has two advantages. It is operated by experienced health care providers who have made senior services one of their primary concentrations. It also is in a prime location, within easy reach of New York City, the New Jersey Shore, and the Poconos. For many older adults from the tri-state metropolitan area it provides a perfect retirement spot: country-style living close to family, friends, and city pleasures."

APPLEWOOD ESTATES

3 Applewood Drive
Freehold, NJ 07728
(908) 780-7370 or (800) 438-0888
Jack Titus, marketing director

Type of community: Nonprofit Continuing Care, all-inclusive contract

Centrally located on a beautiful 45-acre site in Freehold township, Applewood Estates is one hour from New York City and Atlantic City; 30 minutes from the Jersey Shore, and one hour and 15 minutes from Philadelphia.

Financial plan: Entrance fee plus monthly fee. 5% deposit required at time of application.

Ownership and management: Sponsored by CentraState Healthcare System. Opened in 1990.

Minimum age: 62 years.

INDEPENDENT LIVING HOUSING

Type/size of apartment	*Entrance fee**	*Monthly fee**
Studio, 436 sq. ft.	$59,500	$1,062
1-Bedroom, 639 sq. ft.	$102,730	$1,254
2-Bedroom, 894–1,046 sq. ft.	$140,580–163,300	$1,479–1,608
2-Bedroom, 1,175–1,278 sq. ft.	$183,850–205,480	$1,736–2,508

**For double occupancy add $6,450 to the entrance fee, $643 to the monthly fee. All utilities except telephone and cable TV included. Wall-to-wall carpeting, window treatments, individually controlled heating and air-conditioning, balcony or patio, all-electric kitchen, 24-hour emergency call system.*

Population: 290 residents; 75% women, 25% men, 30% couples.

Number of units: 240 Independent Living apartments; 30 Assisted Living units, 60-bed Skilled Nursing center.

Dining plan: Choice of one main meal (lunch or dinner) included in monthly fee. Tray service for approved medical reasons. Private dining room.

Services: *Included in the monthly fee:* Biweekly housekeeping, weekly flat-linen service, scheduled transportation, move-in coordination.

At additional cost: Beauty/barbershop, ice-cream shop, country store, banking services, guest accommodations.

Activities: Activities director. Crafts room, game room, woodworking shop, library, enclosed swimming pool, Jacuzzi, AquaDynamics, fitness center, gardening sites and greenhouse, needlecraft, bridge, poetry and singing clubs, ballroom dancing, bingo, billiards, film and lecture presentations in auditorium, daylong bus trips, men's club.

Availability: Limited availability for one-bedroom and studios.

Health services and rates: Unlimited nursing care is included in the monthly fee. Health clinic for routine medical treatment provided by on-staff registered nurse. Nurses' aide service available. Residents have access to many of the services offered at CentraState Medical Center, the first New Jersey hospital to be affiliated with a Continuing Care community.

- 30-Unit Assisted Living center
- 60-Bed Skilled Nursing center

"If you were to ask any Applewood resident what makes the community so special, the first answer would probably be the family-like feeling and sense of caring among residents and staff."

MEADOW LAKES

P.O. Box 70 Etra Road
Highstown, NJ 08520
(609) 426-6875
Barbara Heimstra, marketing representative

Type of community: Not-for-profit Continuing Care, all-inclusive contract

Accreditation: Continuing Care Accreditation Commission

One- and two-story apartment buildings connected by covered walkways that are heated in the winter and cooled during the summer are located on a 103-acre campus of woodlands and lakes. The grounds feature a nature preserve with trails and a fountain accenting center of the main courtyard. Schank's Pond runs through the middle of the community with an enclosed bridge connecting one side of the campus to the other and offering a view of the community's varied wildlife and graceful swans. The main lounge, auditorium, and dining room are at the heart of the community and connected to the health center. A 12-room guesthouse, which was the estate's original home, is located on the western side of the campus and offers eight bedrooms for residents' guests. The community is 11 miles from Princeton and in close proximity to New York City and Philadelphia.

Financial plan: Entrance fee plus monthly fee. Refundable entrance fee: 2% of the entrance fee is retained by the community for each month of occupancy for a maximum of 25 months, providing a refund of up to 50%. If resident is admitted to the health care center, the monthly rate will change to the standard monthly nursing rate and Meadow Lakes will deduct 3% per month of the balance of entrance fee. In all cases, the refund will be paid after a new resident has signed a residence-and-care agreement and paid an entrance fee for the living unit vacated.

INDEPENDENT LIVING HOUSING

Type/size of unit	*Entrance fee single/double*	*Monthly fee**
Studio	$50,000/ N/A	$1,550
2-Room	$90,500–112,500/102,500–124,500	$2,035–3,370
3-Room	133,500–165,000/145,000–177,500	$2,550–3,775
4-Room	$199,000/225,500	$2,985–4,080
Cottages	$262,000/275,000	$4,260–5,355

**All utilities except long-distance included. Wall-to-wall carpeting, 24-hour emergency call system, fully equipped kitchens, satellite TV access, patio or balcony, individually controlled heating and air-conditioning. Garden rooms available at selected locations.*

Ownership and management: Owned and operated by The Presbyterian Homes of New Jersey, Inc. Opened in 1965.

Minimum age: 62 years.

Population: 335 residents.

Number of units: 284 Independent Living residences and 4 cottages; 90-bed health center.

Dining plan: One meal per day included in the monthly fee. Lounges may be reserved for private parties and gatherings. Tray service available for small fee.

Services: *Included in the monthly fee:* Weekly housekeeping and flat-linen services, scheduled transportation, laundry facilities, assigned parking.

At additional cost: Beauty/barbershop, guest accommodations.

Activities: Sing-alongs, bumper pool, many lounges stocked with books and magazines, residents' forum, auditorium offering various cultural events, library, swimming pool, croquet courts, nature trails, putting green, shuffleboard courts, billiards, lawn bowling, fishing, tours, theater outings.

Availability: Waiting list depends on size of apartment desired.

Health services and rates: Clinic on-site. Health care services included in monthly fee are: staff physicians' services, complete annual physical, initial referral to medical specialists, inpatient nursing care, rehabilitation therapies, temporary nurse visits to apartment following discharge from health care center or hospital, social service counseling. Supplementary medical care is also available at Meadow Lakes for an additional charge. Staff physicians are on the premises during the day and on call at night.

- 90-Bed health care center
  Monthly nursing rate, in the event of a permanent move to health center, $2,255 per person

"The Presbyterian Homes of New Jersey, owner of Meadow Lakes, is a not-for-profit corporation providing a continuum of care that includes diverse programs and services to assist older adults of all faiths to live as independently as possible in a living environment of their choice."

MONROE VILLAGE

1 David Brainerd Drive
Jamesburg, NJ 08831
(908) 521-6400/ fax (908) 521-6540
Cindy Janssen, marketing director

Type of community: Not-for-profit Continuing Care, modified contract

This three-story apartment complex located on a 55-acre parklike campus features recreation areas and

INDEPENDENT LIVING HOUSING

Type/size of unit	*Entrance fee 1/2**	*Monthly fee**
Studio	$36,700/50,200	$1,175
1-Bedroom, 620–662 sq. ft.	$65,700–74,000/92,600–102,000	$1,524–1,716
2-Bedroom, 900–996 sq. ft.	$101,300–109,700/142,300–153,800	$1,906–2,224

**For double occupancy add $4,650 to the entrance fee, $440 to the monthly fee. All utilities except long-distance telephone included. Wall-to-wall carpeting, 24-hour emergency call system, fully equipped kitchen, cable TV, patio or deck, individually controlled heating and air-conditioning. Pets are allowed.*

a nature preserve with trails. Buildings are connected by covered walkways; the clubhouse serves as core of the community, housing the general services provided for the residents. Monroe Village is close to the Forsgate Country Club and Rossmoor, Concordia, Clearbrook, and Whittingham adult communities in Monroe Township, Middlesex County. The community offers easy access to Philadelphia, Princeton, and New York City and historic towns of central New Jersey.

Financial plan: Entrance fee plus monthly fee. Two plans: **1)** Traditional: smaller entrance fee with declining refund. Entrance fee is amortized at the rate of 2% per month from the date of occupancy for up to 50 months. **2)** Refundable entrance fee: should resident withdraw from the community, 10% of entrance fee will be retained. Up to 90% will be returned to resident when unit is resold. If resident is admitted permanently to the health center, Monroe Village will keep 2% per month of the balance and the resident's refund will depend on how long she or he stays in the health center.

Ownership and management: Owned and operated by The Presbyterian Homes of New Jersey, Inc., the sixth-largest not-for-profit Continuing Care provider in the nation. More than 2,000 people reside in 13 affiliated communities. Opened in 1988.

Minimum age: 65 years.

Population: 375 residents.

Number of units: 300 Independent Living residences; 60-bed nursing facility.

Dining plan: One meal per day included in the monthly fee. Four of the six lounges are available for private party catering.

Services: *Included in the monthly fee:* Housekeeping and flat-linen services, scheduled transportation, parking.

At additional cost: Beauty/barbershop, guest accommodations, banking facilities.

Activities: Activities director. Large auditorium, movies, concerts, church services, reading room, arts and crafts room, greenhouse, meeting rooms, lawn bowling, shuffleboard, horseshoes, putting green, tours, theater outings, recreation park, library.

Availability: Waiting list. Four months for a one-bedroom; 18 months for a two-bedroom.

Health services and rates: Health services included in the monthly fee: visits to Monroe staff physicians, annual physical examination, consultation with a medical specialist, rehabilitative nursing care and therapies at Monroe Village, temporary visits to resident's apartment after discharge from hospital or the health care center, emergency ambulance service, medical emergency calls, X-ray and laboratory services. Assisted Living services provided in resident's apartment.

- 60-Bed health center (Intermediate and Skilled Nursing)

Semiprivate	$147/day
Private	$159.50/day

"The Presbyterian Homes of New Jersey, owner of Monroe Village, offers more than 75 years of caring experience, stability, and history that is unsurpassed. Our philosophy promotes compassionate care, personal growth, and the dignity and respect of the individual."

HARROGATE

400 Locust Street
Lakewood, NJ 08701
(908) 905-7070
Don Johansen, administrator; Frank Monaco, associate administrator

Type of community: Not-for-profit Continuing Care, all-inclusive contract

This modern community is reminiscent of New England architecture of the past with its dormers, pitched roofs, lap siding, and shutters. Situated on a 40-acre wooded site that includes a 60-bed health center, the community has a commons area designed with all the amenities of a village main street and an imposing clock tower overlooking the community. A large flower garden decorates the main entrance and walking trails wind throughout the densely wooded acres. Ocean County's Atlantic shores are less than five miles away; New York City, Philadelphia, and Atlantic City are approximately 65 miles away.

Financial plan: Entrance fee plus monthly fee. Two plans: **1)** Traditional: 1% amortization per month of residency. **2)** Return-of-Capital plan: 90% refund of entrance fee regardless of length of stay.

Ownership and management: Developed and managed by Life Care Services of Des Moines, Iowa, which is involved in the development or management of more than 50 Continuing Care communities throughout the United States. Opened in 1988.

Minimum age: 62 years.

Population: 300+ residents; 75% women, 25% men, 20% couples.

Number of units: 289 Independent Living residences; 60-bed health center with 8 residential health care beds.

Dining plan: One meal per day included in the monthly fee. Professional chef, food service manager, and dietitian on-site. Private dining room available. Special diets and tray service available.

Services: *Included in the monthly fee:* Scheduled transportation, weekly housekeeping and flat-linen services.

At additional cost: Beauty/barbershop, valet parking, guest accommodations, garages available ($5,800–7,500).

INDEPENDENT LIVING HOUSING

Type/size of unit	*Entrance fee 1/2**	*Monthly fee**
Studio, 312 sq. ft.	$44,700/62,500	$1,146
Alcove, 459 sq. ft.	$61,500/79,900	$1,137
1-Bedroom, 592–741 sq. ft.	$75,000–90,100/97,000–116,000	$1,515–1,656
2-Bedroom, 894–1,152 sq. ft.	$114,200–146,000/146,200–188,000	$1,798–2,240

**For double occupancy add $5,000 to the entrance fee, $701 to the monthly fee. All utilities except telephone and cable TV included. Fully equipped kitchen, balcony or patio, 24-hour emergency call system, cable TV, individually controlled heating and air-conditioning, wall-to-wall carpeting.*

Activities: Full-time activities director. Indoor swimming pool, aqua exercise class, whirlpool, arts and crafts studio, bocce court, ceramics class, croquet, guest speakers, group trips, billiards room, library, card and game room, auditorium, indoor and outdoor lounges, shuffleboard, gardening areas, exercise room, sundeck, walking trails, party rooms.

Availability: Six-month waiting list.

Health services and rates: Independent Living residents continue to pay their monthly fee, with an extra charge for two additional meals should they move into the 60-bed Harrogate Health Care Center. Emergency health care and residential health care (8 beds) available. Physical, occupational, and speech therapies. Assisted Living services are billed hourly.

- Assisted Living services $16–24/hour
- 60-Bed health center

"Fewer than five miles from Ocean County's Atlantic shores, Harrogate is not unlike the quaint villages that have graced the coast for generations. Here, nature's beauty creates an oasis for the more than 300 people who have chosen to lead an active, independent life."

LEISURE PARK AT LAKEWOOD

1400 Route 70
Lakewood, NJ 08701
(908) 370-0444
Jill Lantz, director of sales and marketing

Type of community: Continuing Care, modified contract

Leisure Park's six-story brick modern apartment complex is set on 20 wooded acres. The community features landscaped grounds and a beautiful entrance foyer with skylights. A living room with a baby grand piano offers ample space for entertaining visitors, lectures, and concerts. Leisure Parks offers convenient access to Garden State Parkway; it is located 70 miles east of Philadelphia.

Financial plan: Monthly rental. $500 deposit.

Ownership and management: Owned by Leisure Care. Managed by Marriott Senior Living Services, a wholly owned subsidiary of Marriott Corporation. Marriott owns and manages 13 retirement communities in Arizona, California, Florida, Illinois, Indiana Maryland, Pennsylvania, Texas, and Virginia. Opened in 1987.

Minimum age: 62 years (if couple, spouse may be younger).

Population: 220 residents; 66% women, 34% men, 12% couples.

Number of units: 219 apartments; 42 Assisted Living rooms, 60 Skilled Nursing beds.

Dining plan: Two meals daily (breakfast and choice of lunch or dinner) included in the monthly fee. Private dining room.

INDEPENDENT LIVING HOUSING

Type/size of apartment	*Monthly fee**
Studio, 450–550 sq. ft.	$1,177–1,363
1-Bedroom, 591–648 sq. ft.	$1,988–2,028
2-Bedroom, 836 sq. ft.	$2,625–2,766

**For double occupancy add $350 to the monthly fee. All utilities except telephone included. Wall-to-wall carpeting, large closets, sheer draperies, fully equipped kitchens, individually controlled heating and air-conditioning, 24-hour emergency call system, master TV antenna.*

Services: *Included in the monthly fee:* Weekly housekeeping and flat-linen services, scheduled transportation, parking, secure storage areas.

At additional cost: Beauty/barbershop, gift shop/ general store, laundry rooms on each floor, guest accommodations, banking.

Activities: Exercise room, billiards table, dance floor, library, movies, walking club, travelogues, board and card games, Bible study, bowling, sing-alongs, spelling bees, nature walks.

Availability: Limited.

Health services and rates: Resident services available for additional fee: physical and speech therapy, travel companions (shopping, social events, medical appointments), wheelchair transport, morning/ evening personal care, medical supplies, medication reminders/blood pressure and pacemaker checks.

- 42 Assisted Living rooms

Semiprivate	$48/day
Private suite with bath	$71/day

- 60-Bed Skilled Nursing facility

Semiprivate	$128/day
Private	$147/day

"At Leisure Park, we believe that the satisfaction of our residents is the most important indicator that we are doing our job well. We have a comprehensive quality assurance program that continually evaluates our staff and practices. We regard our care practices to be exemplary and take pride in our staff of dedicated, trained professionals."

MEDFORD LEAS

Route 70
Medford, NJ 08055
(609) 654-3000 or (800) 331-4302 (except NJ)
Marianne Steely, director of admissions

Type of community: Not-for-profit Continuing Care, all-inclusive contract

Accreditation: Continuing Care Accreditation Commission

Located in the heart of New Jersey's unique Pinelands, Medford Leas is situated on a 160-acre arboretum and nature preserve. The grounds feature cultivated landscapes, courtyards, and private gardens. All resident contracts include full medical and nursing care. Two types of Independent Living are offered. Full-service units include meals, housekeeping, and transportation; partial-service units offer access to these services on a fee-for-service basis. Full-service units are connected with community and medical buildings by covered, enclosed walkways. Partial-service units include Woolman Commons (a satellite community in Mount Holly, New Jersey) and at the Medford campus: Rushmore, Woods Cottage, and the contemporary homes of Bridlington featuring one-, two-, and three-bedroom units clustered in groups of three. All residents have access to community activities and facilities. Medford Leas is two hours from New York City and only 18 miles east of Philadelphia.

Financial plan: Entrance fee plus monthly fee. Refundable deposit of $1,000 for a single; $1,500 for double and a nonrefundable $250 processing fee per person required with application.

Ownership and management: The Estaugh, a not-for-profit Quaker-related corporation founded by members of the Religious Society of Friends in 1914. Opened in 1971.

Minimum age: 62 years. Surcharge for residents under 65.

Population: 578 residents; 77% women, 23% men, 33% couples.

Number of units: 356 Independent Living units: 264 full-service apartments, 92 partial-service units (including 36 contemporary country homes); 50 Assisted Living apartments, 94-bed nursing facility.

INDEPENDENT LIVING HOUSING

Full-service apartments	*Entrance fee **	*Monthly fee**
Studio, 330–582 sq. ft.	$36,500–60,750	$1,399–1,469
1-Bedroom, 615–870 sq. ft.	$72,250–92,000	$1,666–1,737
1-Bedroom/den, 782–892 sq. ft.	$80,800–91,950	$1,691
2-Bedroom, 1,027–1,095 sq. ft.	$115,700	$2,223
2-Bedroom/den, 1,129–1,200 sq. ft.	$120,700–125,500	$2,248–2,264

**For double occupancy add approximately $20,000 to the entrance fee, between $700 and $1,000 to the monthly fee. All utilities included in the monthly fee. Fully equipped kitchen, 24-hour emergency call system. All apartments have patios. Real estate taxes (which are deductible from federal income tax) are payable quarterly and range from $455 to $3,572 annually (for both full-service and partial-service units).*

Partial-service apartments	*Entrance fee single/double*	*Monthly fee single/double**
Woolman Commons		
1-Bedroom, 769 sq. ft.	$73,650/90,650	$851/1,341
2-Bedroom/basement, 2,050 sq. ft.	$116,250/143,450	$1,138/1,646
2-Bedroom/Union Street, 1,159 sq. ft.	$120,200/144,300	$1,138/1,646
Rushmore		
1-Bedroom, 968 sq. ft.	$99,400/118,250	$924/1,432
2-Bedroom, 1,306 sq. ft.	$131,850/161,600	$1,264/1,721
3-Bedroom, 1,188 sq. ft.	$178,900/210,600	$1,328/1,902
Bridlington		
1-Bedroom, 1,075 sq. ft.	$131,350/157,800	$990/1,533
2-Bedroom, 1,525 sq. ft.	$170,450/201,950	$1,371/1,875
3-Bedroom, 1,830 sq. ft.	$185,450/216,950	$1,396/1,900
Woods Cottage (private house with two apartments)		
2-Bedroom, ground level, 983 sq. ft.	$140,750/172,500	$1,264/1,721
2-Bedroom, duplex, 1,305 sq. ft.	$135,750/166,400	$1,164/1,721

**All utilities except water and sewage are paid by resident. Fully equipped kitchens. Washer/dryer in Woolman Commons 2-bedroom units, Wood Cottages, Rushmore, and Bridlington units. Maintenance of buildings and common grounds handled by community.*

Dining plan: Three meals per day included in the monthly fee for full-service residents only. By special arrangement, credits on up to two of the three meals can be applied to the monthly fee. Coffee shop. Private dining rooms for entertaining and special occasions.

Services: *Included in the monthly fee:* Full-service residents receive weekly housekeeping and flat-linen services, transportation.

At additional cost: Beauty/barbershop, gift shop, thrift shop, guest accommodations and meals, laundry facilities, additional housekeeping.

Activities: Self-directed. Over 70 resident committees. Indoor swimming pool, greenhouse gardening, "farm" gardening, canoeing, organized exercise, nature walks and study, library, discussion groups, woodworking shop, trips, putting green, golf courses nearby, tennis courts, cultural pursuits, films, county bookmobile, music programs, shuffleboard, square and ballroom dancing, table games, birdwatching, bridge, travelogues, sewing and knitting, sports, singing, play reading, community volunteerism, newsletter, state-of-the-art auditorium.

Availability: Waiting list for all units. Waiting times vary depending upon type of unit.

Health services and rates: Monthly fees cover prescription drugs, Medicare deductibles, and co-insurance (except when away from community), transportation to medical appointments, unlimited temporary and long-term nursing care and Assisted Living. Services not covered are dentistry, dentures, refractions/corrective lenses, podiatry, hearing tests/aids, orthopedic appliances, psychiatric care, and treatment for drug/alcohol abuse. Full-time on-site medical director and part-time physician, both board certified in geriatric and internal medicine. Two geriatric nurse practitioners. More than 125 of the region's most respected specialists available for consultation as authorized by medical director, many of whom maintain offices in the outpatient medical center. On-site X ray, physical therapy, pharmacy, podiatry, ophthalmology, audiology, optician, dentistry, and low-vision center. 24-Hour emergency response to full-service residents.

- 50 Assisted Living apartments
- 94 Nursing beds

Semiprivate	$185/day nonresident
Private	$209/day nonresident

"At the heart of all that takes place in Medford Leas is the conviction that human beings bear a responsibility to care for one another. At Medford Leas, a fine balance is maintained. It is protection without pampering, care without coddling. It is an abiding sense of service combined with a recognition that what most adults desire is to live independently and to be relieved of anxiety about medical care. This is the time to pursue long-neglected interests and new ones. This is the time for talents to be developed and friends to be discovered. In keeping with Friends' belief, those who guide the community and those who call it home see themselves as contributing members of the wider community, helping each other, helping others."

Barbara, 88 years

Park Shore, Seattle, Washington

"A retirement community has been a good solution for me."

Although it's a terribly sad reason that led Barbara to become a resident at Park Shore, she admits that she is happy to have been a resident there for the past 20 years. "My husband had died and my son, Bob, was dying of cancer at 37," explained Barbara. "He was married and lived with his wife and two children in Seattle. I had come to Seattle to visit him when he was very ill and he said to me, 'Mom, I promised Dad that I would take care of you.' I talked about how nice I heard it was at Park Shore. Bob had had dinner there and seen it firsthand and we agreed it was a good place for me. Bob died shortly after this conversation and I applied to Park Shore and was accepted."

Her sister, who had been living alone, joined Barbara at Park Shore over 10 years ago and has moved into her own room in the Assisted Living wing. "It's nice to have her so near because it's easy for me to walk over and visit her." Barbara has a one-and-a-half room apartment with a complete bath, lots of cupboards, and space for a living area and a twin bed. Her lovely view encompasses the nearby park, lake, and mountains.

"I'm one of the few who's been at Park Shore this long," reports Barbara. "A retirement community has been a good solution for me."

THE EVERGREENS

309 Bridgeboro Road
Moorstown, NJ 08507-1499
(609) 273-0806
Pat Estis, director of marketing

Type of community: Not-for-profit Continuing Care, all-inclusive contract

Located on a wooded, 32-acre campus featuring azalea bushes, grassy fields, and flowers in a quiet residential neighborhood, The Evergreens includes a 100-bed health center, Independent Living, Assisted Living, spaces for gardening, a greenhouse, private barbecue patio, and many seating areas. Walking paths for residents' use are located in protected woodlands that surround The Evergreens. A stately red brick main building (built in the 1920s) serves as main lobby and reception area of the community. The surrounding neighborhood has many stately Victorian homes on tree-lined streets. Moorstown history dates back to the American Revolution and has many 19th-century homes and buildings. The community offers easy access to Philadelphia (10 miles), Atlantic City (50 miles), or New York City (80 miles).

Financial plan: Entrance fee plus monthly fee. Two plans: **1)** Traditional: entrance fee returned to resident less 2% per month of residency over the first 50 months (less 4% per month for each month spent in health center or personal care suite). **2)**90% refund: 90% of entrance fee returned to resident or resident's estate upon leaving The Evergreens regardless of length of stay. Monthly fees are the same for both the traditional and 90% refund plans.

Ownership and management: Owned by a not-for-profit corporation. Managed by board of trustees. Founded as an Episcopal corporation in 1919. (Moved to current location in 1949 as personal care facility; Continuing Care retirement community opened May 1994.)

Minimum age: 62 years.

Population: 300 to 350 residents anticipated.

Number of units: 212 Independent Living apartments; 40 Assisted Living, 60 Skilled Nursing beds.

Dining plan: One meal per day included in the monthly fee. Private dining room available.

Services: *Included in the monthly fee:* Weekly housekeeping, scheduled transportation, banking services available on-site, reserved parking.

At additional cost: Beauty/barbershop, flat-linen service, special transportation with personal assistance, room service, personal laundry and dry cleaning, covered parking, guest accommodations.

INDEPENDENT LIVING HOUSING

Type/size of unit	*Entrance fee 1/2**	*Monthly fee**
Studio, 510 sq. ft.	$57,500/89,000	$1,430
1-Bedroom, 625–991 sq. ft.	$81,900–114,500/126,750–177,250	$1,540–1,690
1-Bedroom, 1,038 sq. ft.	$134,900–143,000/208,125–221,540	$1,980–2,230
2-Bedroom, 1,038–1,282 sq. ft.	$156,740–183,150/242,950–283,880	$2,485–2,790
2-Bedroom/den, 1,480–1,735 sq. ft.	$204,260–225,460/316,600–349,460	$2,890–3,115

**For double occupancy with Plan 1 add $13,630 to the entrance fee, $550 to the monthly fee. For Plan 2 add $21,060 to the entrance fee, $550 to the monthly fee. All utilities except telephone included. Fully equipped kitchen, wall to wall carpeting, 24-hour emergency call system, washer and dryer, individually controlled heating and air-conditioning, private balcony or patio, cable TV.*

Activities: Coordinated activity and social programs. Gardening, greenhouse, woodworking shop, private barbecue patio, chapel, crafts and hobbies, billiards, card room, club room, game room, library, private health club with indoor swimming pool, book discussion groups, walking paths, croquet.

Availability: Waiting list for some units.

Health services and rates: Health care and personal care included in the monthly fee except additional meals. Medications up to $200 per month are covered. Private nursing-care rooms available at extra cost. The Evergreens has an on-site clinic that offers a variety of outpatient services, including regular blood pressure and cholesterol-level monitoring. During recuperation from an illness, daily assistance with bathing, dressing, grooming, and ambulation is provided.

- 40 Personal care beds
- 60-Bed health care center

"The Evergreens community center offers five dining rooms, a two-story glass atrium overlooking formal gardens, and a pond. There are state-of-the-art 24-hour emergency and security systems throughout the community."

CLASSIC RESIDENCE BY HYATT

655 Pomander Walk
Teaneck, NJ 07666
(201) 836-7474
Miriam Gross, sales director

Type of community: Independent Living with Continuum of Care

This five-story brick campus complex provides Independent Living and personal care apartments. The community features a lovely winter garden with glass roof and plants, library, and common rooms. Located in a wooded, residential neighborhood on 5 1/2 acres, the community is convenient to shopping malls, golf courses, tennis courts, schools, and places of worship and less than 30 minutes from downtown Manhattan.

Financial plan: $1,500 reservation fee plus monthly fee. Security deposit of one month's rent is held in an interest-bearing escrow account in resident's name.

Ownership and management: Jointly developed and owned by Forest City Residential Development, Inc., of Cleveland, Ohio, and Classic Residence by Hyatt, an affiliate of Hyatt Corporation. Managed by Classic Residence by Hyatt, which also owns/operates Classic Residences in Chevy Chase, Maryland; Reno, Nevada; Monterey, California; West Hartford, Connecticut; Dallas, Texas; Naples, Florida. Opened in 1989.

Minimum age: 55 years.

INDEPENDENT LIVING HOUSING

Type/size of apartment	*Monthly fee**
1-Bedroom, 632–880 sq. ft.	$2,650–2,800
1-Bedroom/deck, 669–861 sq. ft.	$2,950–3,200
2-Bedroom, 1-bath, 800–934 sq. ft.	$3,300–3,500
2-Bedroom, 2-bath, 902–1,407 sq. ft.	$3,400–4,200

**For double occupancy add $750 to the monthly fee. Special arrangements can be made for furnished apartments. All utilities except telephone and electricity included. Fully equipped kitchen, large windows, wall-to-wall carpeting with color-coordinated sheer window coverings, individually controlled heating and air-conditioning, 24-hour emergency call system. Many apartments have balconies.*

Population: 220 residents; 83% women, 17% men, 18% couples.

Number of units: 204 Independent Living apartments; 16 personal care apartments.

Dining plan: Continental breakfast and choice of lunch or dinner daily included in the monthly fee. Classically Caring Cuisine menu selections, low in sodium, fat, and cholesterol, are available at every meal. Private dining room and catering service. Room service available for short illness.

Services: *Included in the monthly fee:* 24-hour concierge, weekly housekeeping and flat-linen services, scheduled transportation, lighted parking, personal laundry machines in convenient locations on premises. Classic Club membership: long-term extended care insurance underwritten by Lloyd's of London, membership in airline club, complimentary overnight accommodations at other Classic residences, and exclusive travel opportunities.

At additional cost: Beauty/barbershop, guest accommodations, dry cleaning pick-up and delivery, additional housekeeping and personal laundry services.

Activities: Personalized computer lifestyle profile provides full-time resident relations/programming staff with opportunity to individually tailor variety of educational, cultural, social, and recreational programs to residents' interests. Classes, lectures, movies, concerts, dances, cultural outings. Arts and crafts studio, well-stocked library, clubroom, fitness center with Jacuzzi, outdoor walking paths.

Availability: Waiting list for certain apartment styles.

Health services and rates: Independent Living residents are covered by Golden Care long-term care insurance, underwritten by Lloyd's of London. Furnished apartment available for residents in need of short-term care. Residents who relocate to the personal care center from within Classic Residence remain eligible for long-term care insurance coverage.

- 16 Personal care apartments; staffed 24 hours/day with director and trained nursing assistants
  1-Bedroom, 632–680 sq. ft. $3,750–3,950/month*
  1-Bedroom/deck, 669–861 sq. ft. $3,850/month*

For double occupancy add $1,000 to the monthly fee.

"A distinguished leader in the hospitality industry for more than three decades, Hyatt has set the standard for high-quality accommodations and attentive service. Classic Residence has built upon Hyatt's expertise, bringing innovative cuisine, striking interior design, and personalized, supportive services to the senior living industry."

CRESTWOOD MANOR

P.O. Drawer B
Whiting, NJ 08759
(908) 849-4900 or (800) 526-1665
Mary McMullin, marketing director

Type of community: Not-for-profit Continuing Care, modified contract

Crestwood Manor is located on a 40-acre campus that includes a nature preserve, trails, and outdoor recreation areas. The focal point of the community is the clubhouse, which includes a restaurant, auditorium, game room, fitness center, beauty/barbershop, country store, and snack bar. The community consists of two-story, garden-style apartment buildings that have easy access to landscaped courtyards and parking. The town of Whiting is small and quaint and offers shopping and services. The community also offers easy access to the Jersey shore.

Financial plan: Entrance fee plus monthly fee. Refundable entrance fee: up to 90% of entrance fee will be refunded when apartment is resold. 10% of

INDEPENDENT LIVING HOUSING

Type/size of unit	*Entrance fee**	*Monthly fee**
Studio, 404 sq. ft.	$60,500	$1,030
1-Bedroom, 580–719 sq. ft.	$88,500–99,500	$1,318–1,581
2-Bedroom, 967 sq. ft.	$113,500	$1,890

**For double occupancy add $4,000 to the entrance fee, $515 to the monthly fee. All utilities except long-distance telephone included. Wall-to-wall carpeting, 24-hour emergency call system, fully equipped kitchen, cable TV, patio or balcony, self-service laundry on each floor of apartment building.*

entrance fee is retained by the Presbyterian Homes of New Jersey. When a resident is admitted permanently to the health center, Crestwood Manor will keep 2% per month of the 90%, and the refund will depend on the length of the resident's stay.

Ownership and management: Managed by Presbyterian Homes of New Jersey, Inc., whose other affiliates include Meadow Lakes in Highstown and Monroe Village in Jamesburg. Opened in 1990.

Minimum age: 62 years.

Population: 380 residents; 66% women, 34% men, 33% couples.

Number of units: 380 Independent Living residences; 60-bed health center.

Dining plan: One meal per day included in the monthly fee. Room service and catering of private parties available at additional cost.

Services: *Included in the monthly fee:* Weekly housekeeping and flat-linen services, scheduled heavy housekeeping, scheduled transportation, assigned parking area.

At additional cost: Beauty/barbershop, guest accommodations, concierge services.

Activities: Exercise room and classes, game room with billiards tables, religious services, library, meeting and activities rooms, greenhouse, thrift shop operated by residents, sing-alongs, trips to shopping malls and theaters, educational lectures, music programs, Bible study.

Availability: One-bedroom apartments are immediately available; short waiting list for studio and two-bedroom apartments.

Health services and rates: Medical services covered by the monthly fee include visits by Crestwood Manor staff physicians, annual physical examination, consultation with a medical specialist, rehabilitation nursing care and therapies, temporary nursing visits to resident's apartment following discharge from a hospital or the health center, meal tray service, emergency ambulance service, medical emergency calls.

Crestwood Manor does not currently have a separate Assisted Living unit, but personal care services (charged on a fee-for-service basis) are provided on an individual basis in resident's apartments. Should residents require temporary stay in health center, care is provided and apartment maintained at the regular monthly fee. Pending availability, direct admission to the health center is offered.

- 60-Bed health center $2,242/month

"The Presbyterian Homes of New Jersey, Inc., was founded in 1916 with the belief that each person's life is a gift from God and is meant to be lived with dignity and respect. The Presbyterian Homes today continues its mission of service to older adults based on this original belief. As New Jersey's largest provider of retirement housing and health care and the sixth-largest nonprofit provider in the nation, The Presbyterian Homes is an established leader in the field. More than 2,000 people reside in our 13 affiliated communities that we manage throughout the state. Residents feel secure knowing that in our 75-year history no individual has ever been asked to leave one of our communities because they have outlived their resources. Crestwood Manor residents participate in decisions that affect the community."

NEW MEXICO

LA VIDA LLENA

10501 Lagrima de Oro, N.E.
Albuquerque, NM 87111
(505) 293-4001 or (800) 922-1344
Arlene Samrock, marketing director

Type of community: Not-for-profit Continuing Care, modified contract

Located in a charming Southwestern setting, this community offers a three-story Independent Living apartment complex, separate townhouses, and a 60-bed health center all on a 21-acre campus in the foothills of the Sandia Mountains. The community features breathtaking vistas and easy access to golf courses, downhill and cross-country skiing, archaeological digs, and mountain resorts. The Sante Fe Opera, Indian pueblos, professional baseball, intercollegiate sports, horse racing, ten area museums, theaters, and world-class symphony orchestra are all nearby.

Financial plan: Entrance fee plus monthly fee. Two plans: **1)** 95% refund, less 1% per month for first 12 months of residency. **2)** 50% refundable. Move-out clause with amortization schedule for 4³/₄ years.

Ownership and management: Founded by St. John's Episcopal Cathedral, First Presbyterian Church, St. Paul's Lutheran Church and First United Methodist Church, all of downtown Albuquerque.

INDEPENDENT LIVING HOUSING

Type/size of apartment	*Entrance fee plan 1/2**	*Monthly fee plan 1/2**
Studio, 395 sq. ft.	$36,000/46,800	$945
1-Bedroom, 576 sq. ft.	$59,500/77,400	$1,108
2-Bedroom, 798–1,638 sq. ft.	$77,800–101,200/180,575–234,800	$1,315–2,159
Townhouses		
Ventura, 1,120 sq. ft.	$135,000/176,200	$1,764
Coronado, 1,215 sq. ft.	$159,300/207,100	$1,807
Eldorado, 1,412 sq. ft.	$185,300/241,000	$1,946
Alta Vista apartments (newly completed)		
1-Bedroom, 680 sq. ft.	$78,200/N/A	$1,017/N/A
2-Bedroom, 940–1,638 sq. ft.	$102,375–118,225/N/A	$1,331–1,537/N/A

**For double occupancy add $13,000 to the entrance fee, $626 to the monthly fee. All utilities except telephone and cable TV included. Fully equipped kitchens, 24-hour emergency call system, wall-to-wall carpeting. Townhouses have fully equipped kitchen, dishwasher, microwave, garbage disposal, washer/dryer, fireplace, skylights, fenced-in patio, entry planter at foyer, clerestory windows, whirlpool, outdoor barbecue grill. Pets are allowed in townhouses and on first floor of selected apartments.*

Managed by board of directors with representatives from each church. Opened in 1983.

Minimum age: 62 years.

Population: 286 residents; 79% women, 21% men, 24% couples.

Number of units: 297 Independent Living apartments and 22 townhouses; 33 Assisted Living suites, 60-bed health center.

Dining plan: One meal per day included in the monthly fee.

Services: *Included in the monthly fee:* Scheduled transportation to local areas, housekeeping and flat-linen services.

At additional cost: Beauty/barbershop, guest accommodations, bank.

Activities: Heated swimming pool, Jacuzzi whirlpool, ice-cream parlor, fitness center, chapel, games and activity rooms, library, woodworking, ceramics, weaving, bridge, H.O. gauge railroading, gardening, oil painting, festivals, concerts, exercise classes, fishing, movies, seminars.

Availability: Most units (except townhouses) currently available. $1,000 fee for waiting list is applicable toward entrance fee.

Health services and rates: Physical, inhalation, speech, and occupational therapies offered.

- 33 Assisted Living suites* $1,540/month

**Nonresident entrance fee: $61,504; for double occupancy add $31,000 to the entrance fee, $726 to the monthly fee.*

- 60-Bed health center

	Intermediate	Skilled
Semiprivate	$85/day	$405/day
Private	$110/day	$445/day

"The mission of La Vida Llena is to provide its residents with a lovely home, a wholesome family lifestyle, a protected environment, and a variety of activities tailored to enrich their golden years. This is achieved through the dedicated efforts of caring and professional staff who willingly place the needs and desires of the residents above every other consideration This results in a high level of stability, contentment, and satisfaction for the residents and their families."

THE MONTEBELLO

10500 Academy Boulevard
Albuquerque, NM 87111
(505) 294-9944
Pamela Bazant, director of marketing

Type of community: Continuing Care, modified contract

The Montebello offers elegant modern Scottsdale-type architecture, situated on an 11-acre campus near the foothills of the Sandia Mountains and overlooking Albuquerque. Located in a quiet residential neighborhood across the street from Albuquerque's premier country club community, The Montebello is one mile from shopping, restaurants, and banks, five miles from regional shopping centers, and 20 minutes from downtown Albuquerque. Independent Living, Assisted Living, Intermediate and Skilled Nursing are available.

Financial plan: Monthly rental fee.

Ownership and management: Managed by The Forum Group, Inc., owner and manager of 27 retirement communities in the United States, with more than 25 years of experience in retirement communities. Opened in 1987.

Minimum age: 60 years.

Population: 200 residents; 70% women, 30% men, 20% couples.

INDEPENDENT LIVING HOUSING

Type/size of apartment	*Monthly rental fee**
1-Bedroom, 691 sq. ft.	$1,500–1,900
1-Bedroom, 968 sq. ft.	$2,150
2-Bedroom, 1,027 sq. ft.	$2,000–2,300
2-Bedroom, 1,038 sq. ft.	$2,150–2,400
2-Bedroom, 1,402 sq. ft.	$2,900

**For double occupancy add $425 to the monthly rental fee. All utilities except telephone included. Wall-to-wall carpeting, walk-in closets, individual temperature control, fully equipped all-electric kitchen, 24-hour emergency call system, additional storage areas, patio or balcony. Pets allowed.*

Number of units: 114 Independent Living apartments; 15 Assisted Living suites, 56 Intermediate Nursing beds, and 4 Skilled Nursing beds.

Dining plan: Monthly rental fee includes one meal a day and continental breakfast. A private dining room is available for personal entertaining.

Services: *Included in the monthly fee:* Regularly scheduled transportation, weekly housekeeping and flat-linen services, self-service laundry facilities.

At additional cost: Beauty/barbershop.

Activities: Full-time recreational director. Guest lectures, movies, classes and meetings, swimming and exercise, travel tours, and weekly social hours. Library, arts and crafts room, billiards room, and exercise area.

Availability: No waiting list.

Health services and rates: Residents receive 15 days of free health care a year or a lifetime total of 60 days. A medical director, registered nurses, licensed practical nurses, nursing assistants, and registered dietitian on-site. Rehabilitation services including physical, occupational, and speech therapy.

- 15 Assisted Living suites $77/day
- 56 Intermediate Nursing beds
  Semiprivate $83/day
  Private $107/day
- 4 Skilled Nursing beds
  Semiprivate $150/day

"The Montebello offers flexible rental packages that do not require any entrance or endowment fee. Quality nursing care on-site is highly regarded by the medical community."

NEW YORK

Note: It was only in 1992 that the New York State Legislature passed a law allowing the prepayment of health care, making it possible for Continuing Care facilities to operate in the state. More facilities are in the planning stages.

ANDRUS RETIREMENT COMMUNITY

185 Old Broadway
Hastings-on-Hudson, NY 10706
(914) 478-3700
Maureen Carline, director of social services

Type of community: Nonprofit Independent Living with Continuum of Care

Located in the village of Hastings-on-Hudson, overlooking the Hudson River, 26 landscaped acres surround the seven-story residence that is furnished traditionally and accented by Andrus family antiques and works of art. Spacious lounges, an intimate writing room, a penthouse solarium, a library, and well-stocked pantries are accessible to all residents. Independent Living apartments, Assisted Living rooms, and Skilled Nursing facility are available. The community is 30 minutes from Manhattan.

Financial plan: Daily fee. No admissions fee. If and when a resident's money runs out, a mutually agreeable plan is made with Andrus. Residence at Andrus is secure, regardless of ability to pay, as long as the resident has not made misleading statements about his or her assets.

Ownership and management: Owned and operated by the nonprofit Surdna Foundation. Opened in 1953.

Minimum age: 65 years.

Population: 189 residents; 87% women, 13% men, 3% couples.

Number of units: 212 Independent Living rooms/suites; 13 Assisted Living rooms, 52-bed Skilled Nursing facility.

INDEPENDENT LIVING HOUSING

Type of room	*Daily fee single/double**
1-Room	$119/238
1-Room suite	$154/308
2-Room suite with bath	$162/322

**All utilities except long-distance telephone included in the daily fee. All apartments have individually controlled heating and air-conditioning, 24-hour emergency alert system. Furnished apartments available.*

Dining plan: Three meals/day included in daily fee.

Services: *Included in the daily fee:* Weekly housekeeping and laundry/flat-linen services; transportation to and from medical appointments, scheduled shopping trips and special events; parking.

At additional cost: Beauty/barbershop, postal and check-cashing services, gift shop.

Activities: Crafts, sewing, ceramics, woodworking shop, music, game rooms, paved garden paths, nature trail, shuffleboard courts, exercise, educational programs, concerts, special events, day trips, putting green.

Availability: Limited availability for private rooms. Waiting list for suites. Preference given to Westchester County residents.

Health services and rates: Included in the daily fee: services of attending physicians and 24-hour nursing personnel, all prescription and nonprescription medications ordered by Andrus doctors, all eyeglasses, dentures, hearing aids, orthopedic appliances, and special equipment, regular checkups. For temporary stays resident pays only the daily nursing fee.

- 13 Assisted Living rooms
  (rates depend upon services required)
- 52-Bed Skilled Nursing facility
  Private $162/day

"The founders of Andrus Retirement Community emphasized service to those of modest means and the poor. In keeping with this philosophy, ability to pay the stated charges is not a requirement for admission."

KENDAL AT ITHACA

2329 North Triphammer Road
Ithaca, NY 14850
(607) 257-4771 or (800) 253-6325
Karen Smith, director of admissions

Type of Community: Not-for-profit Continuing Care, all-inclusive contract

The community is set on a lovely, rolling 106-acre site above Cayuga Lake in the Finger Lakes region, one New York's finest recreational and cultural areas. Its main living room has a fireplace and a view of the western hills. Campus buildings are connected by a system of paths and covered walkways. About half of the land is undeveloped and provides safe and ample space for walking and jogging. Gardening space is available. Ongoing cultural and intellectual opportunities are provided by Cornell University and by Ithaca College and its music conservatory. Cayuga Lake, longest of the Finger Lakes, boasts more than 80 miles of shoreline with numerous coves for fishing and anchoring. Day trips

INDEPENDENT LIVING HOUSING

Type/size of unit	*Entrance fee single/double*	*Monthly fee single/double**
Studio, 570 sq. ft.	$77,500	$1,470
1-Bedroom, 761 sq. ft.	$128,500/145,500	$1,785/2,645
1-Bedroom/den, 1,000 sq. ft.	$195,000/212,000	$2,050/2,910
2-Bedroom, 1,100 sq. ft.	$209,000/226,000	$2,450/3,310
2-Bedroom/den, 1,350 sq. ft.	$245,000/262,000	$2,580/3,440

**All utilities except telephone and cable TV included in the monthly fee. Wall-to-wall carpeting, 24-hour emergency call system, fully equipped all-electric kitchen with seating for two, individually controlled heating and air-conditioning, covered porch or balcony, screen door on back door. Cathedral ceilings in cottages. Pets allowed.*

are offered to nearby lakes and wineries. Cross-country skiing, excellent lake and stream fishing, and a bird sanctuary are all close by, and four state parks are located within Tompkins County alone.

Financial Plan: Entrance fee and monthly fee. Under Revenue Ruling 76-481, a portion of every resident's entrance fee and monthly fee may be considered a medical expense for federal income tax purposes. Based on experience at other Kendal communities, it is estimated that 37% of the entrance fee can be counted as a one-time medical expense. In addition, 37% of the monthly fee can be counted each year as a medical expense. Contingency resources for fellow residents available through a residents' fund, which offers confidential assistance to those whose resources no longer meet their needs.

Ownership and management: The Kendal Corporation, a not-for-profit organization serving older people, owns and manages communities in Pennsylvania, New Hampshire, and Ohio. A majority of the directors are members of the Religious Society of Friends (Quakers). Opened in December 1995.

Minimum age: At least one spouse must be 65 (younger people are accepted on occasion).

Population: Residents come from eight states and one foreign country. Of those from New York State, 72% are from the greater Ithaca area.

Number of units: 210 Independent Living apartments and cluster cottages (five floor plans); 12 Assisted Living units, 36 Skilled Nursing beds.

Dining Plan: Choice of one meal per day included in the monthly fee. Choice of four dining rooms, restaurant-style and buffet-style. Café with inside and courtyard tables.

Services: *Included in monthly fee:* Biweekly housekeeping, weekly flat-linen service, annual heavy-duty cleaning (shampoo carpets, launder curtains), scheduled transportation.

At additional cost: Bank, gift shop, beauty/barbershop, small grocery store, guest accommodations.

Activities: Indoor swimming pool with lockers, fitness area. Auditorium with enhanced-hearing system, resident-directed library, activities area for individual and group hobbies. Gardening.

Availability: Limited.

Health services and rates: The initial entrance fee and ongoing monthly fees cover a comprehensive lifetime health care program featuring team-based case management. Routine health screenings, complete annual physical, prescription drugs (pharmacy on-site), transportation to medical appointments when referred and needed, home health care. Non-uniformed staff, low staff-to-resident ratio, restraint-free and individualized care based upon Quaker values and Kendal's more than 20 years of experience. On-site nurse practitioner and physician. On-site physical, occupational, and speech therapies, audiology, nutritional counseling, social and psychological counseling. Assistance with Medicare and other medical insurance billing. Day care center for preschool children. Intergenerational programming. Residents may bring their own furniture and favorite possessions for long stays.

- 12 Assisted Living units
- 36-Bed Skilled Nursing facility (all private)

"Kendal at Ithaca is New York's first Continuing Care retirement community. The rich and varied area around our community extends every opportunity to support residents' desires to live life to the fullest. The Kendal philosophy affirms that retirement and growing older can bring new opportunities for personal growth and development, even if emerging limitations necessitate a degree of dependency. Kendal's commitment is to ensure conditions that foster that realization of each person's full potential, respect individual privacy while nurturing a senses of community, and treat each person with dignity and respect regardless of age or condition."

MILLBROOK MEADOWS

560 Flint Road
Millbrook, NY 12545
(914) 677-8550 or (800) 433-6092
Mary Rhodes, marketing director

Type of community: Independent Living with Continuum of Care

Located in Millbrook, New York—almost equidistant (about 1½ hours by car) between New York City and the state capital of Albany—Millbrook Meadows lies in the magnificent Hudson Valley on a 450-acre estate and features two-story Independent Living apartments. The community is within an hour of the great music center, Tanglewood, as well as West Point, the Franklin Delano Roosevelt Library and Museum at Hyde Park, and college campuses.

Financial plan: Entrance fee plus monthly fee or monthly rental. 90% of the entrance fee is refundable to resident or resident's estate under the Return of Capital plan once the apartment home or cottage is reassigned (never more than 12 months).

Ownership and management: Owned by Millbrook Care Limited Partnership. Managed by Life Care Services Corporation, manager of more than 50 retirement communities across the country, with more than 30 years of experience. Opened in 1985.

Minimum age: 62 years.

Population: 120 residents; 66% women, 34% men, 33% couples.

Number of units: 136 Independent Living units.

Dining plan: Choice of lunch or dinner is included in the monthly fee. Tray service with diet modifications available. Additional meal available at a charge. Nutrition/special diet consultation available. Private dining room for personal entertaining.

Services: *Included in the monthly fee:* Housekeeping once every two weeks, weekly flat-linen service, open parking, free washer and dryer in common area, transportation for shopping, medical, and other professional appointments as well as on-campus and special activities.

At additional cost: Sundry/coffee shop, pub, beauty/barbershop, guest accommodations, carports.

Activities: Activities/social coordinator. Tennis court, outdoor pool, fitness center, nearby golf courses and riding stable, driving range, miles of nature trails, cross-country skiing, indoor and outdoor gardening. Lectures, movies, and live performances, group tours, and parties, library and book club, game,

INDEPENDENT LIVING HOUSING

Type/size of apartment	*Entrance fee/Monthly fee* *		*Monthly rent**
Studio, 423 sq. ft.	$57,000	$883	$1,933
1-Bedroom, 455–694 sq. ft.	$62,500–114,500	$1,033–1,388	$2,083–2,588
2-Bedroom, 893 sq. ft.	$121,000–190,000	$1,119–2,097	$2,419–4,097
Country cottages			
1-Bedroom, 581 sq. ft.	$92,000	$1,157	$2,207
1-Bedroom/study, 788–903 sq. ft.	$125,000–143,000	$1,344–1,507	$2,644–3,057
2-Bedroom, 1,276 sq. ft.	$169,000–182,000	$1,650–1,843	$3,400–3,843

**For double occupancy add $653 to the monthly fee. All utilities except telephone and electricity included. Full kitchen, wall-to-wall carpeting, individually controlled heating and air-conditioning, individual storage areas, 24-hour call monitoring system. Twenty floor plans available.*

crafts and woodworking rooms. 200-seat auditorium, lounges with fireplaces. Public and private art studios, art gallery, gymnasium.

Availability: Waiting list; some floor plans are available.

Health Services: Resident services director, a registered nurse, coordinates and orchestrates health care with Fishkill Health Related Center, Inc., Home Care Division, which provides part-time and full-time home nursing care for those requiring assistance with personal care, counseling, or housekeeping. The St. Francis Home Health Services (associated with St. Francis Hospital) provides programs of skilled, professional treatment and care.

"Millbrook Meadows is proud to provide the security of being completely debt-free. With no short- or long-term debt, our residents enjoy the peace of mind of a financially stable community."

THE GABLES AT BRIGHTON

2001 Clinton Avenue South
Rochester, NY 14618
(716) 461-1880
Craig Evans, executive director

Type of community: Independent Living with personal care services

Nestled in scenic suburban Brighton on a beautiful eight-acre site, the brick-and-stucco three-story gabled community features a bright, sunny lobby with cathedral ceiling and fireplace. Attractively appointed lounge areas are specially designed for group enjoyment. Independent Living with personal care services are available. The community is located ten minutes from downtown Rochester, the University of Rochester, and major shopping areas.

Financial plan: Monthly fee.

Ownership and management: Developed by AdvantageHEALTH in partnership with Aetna Life Insurance. AdvantageHEALTH operates seven retirement living facilities in Connecticut, Florida, Massachusetts, and New York as well as inpatient and outpatient rehabilitation hospitals. Opened in 1987.

Minimum age: 62 years.

Population: 130 residents; 25% men, 75% women, 10% couples.

Number of units: 103 Independent Living apartments.

Dining plan: Evening meal daily included in the monthly fee. Breakfast and lunch available at additional charge.

INDEPENDENT LIVING HOUSING

Type/size of apartment	*Monthly fee**
Studio, 600 sq. ft.	$1,350–1,750
1-Bedroom, 700 sq. ft.	$2,150–2,250
2-Bedroom, 900 sq. ft.	$2,750–3,000

**For double occupancy add $400 to the monthly fee. All utilities except telephone and cable TV included. Kitchens equipped with modern appliances; wall-to-wall carpeting and draperies, washer/dryer hookups, wiring for telephone and cable TV, individually controlled heating and air-conditioning, 24-hour emergency call system. Furnished apartments available for short-term leases (minimum of 60 days).*

Services: *Included in the monthly fee:* Weekly housekeeping and flat-linen services, scheduled transportation, ample parking.

At additional cost: Coin-operated laundromat, beauty/barbershop.

Activities: Full-time activities director. Card games, tournaments, trips, discussion groups, guest speakers, movies, concerts by students from Eastman School of Music, library, exercise area, shuffleboard, bingo, Trivial Pursuit, bocce, Bible study, arts and crafts classes.

Availability: Limited. Waiting list for some apartments.

Health services and rates: Personal care services and scheduled licensed nursing hours. Arrangements with local hospitals to assist residents in receiving emergency room care and hospitalization.

- Personal care services arranged by The Gables and contracted with a licensed home health care organization are available to residents in their apartments. This care includes three meals a day, assistance with activities of daily living, and certified home health aides supervised by a registered nurse.

"One of the valuable possessions that people have given us over the years is their trust—trust that we will provide what we say we will: a caring community, a competent staff and a safe, independent environment. We have worked hard to gain that trust and have worked even harder to keep it. Because we believe your financial independence in retirement is just as important as personal freedom, there is no initial investment required at any AdvantageHEALTH community."

June and Bud, 73 and 77 years

Morningside at Fullerton, Fullerton, California

"My number-one priority for moving was not physical security, but psychological security—knowing that June would be among friends if something happened to me."

June and Bud have lived in the town of Fullerton since 1948. "One of the reasons we decided to move into Morningside is that I basically retired from cooking after our 50th anniversary," explains June. "I had bypass surgery 10 years ago," says Bud,"and, although I am in good health, my number-one priority for moving was not physical security, but psychological security—knowing that June would be among friends if something happened to me. And, of course, the long-term potential of extended care interested both of us."

June and Bud also had extended-care insurance, which was extremely expensive and each year had more and more limitations. As a physician who followed health care reform carefully, Bud says he became convinced early that as long as insurance companies are involved in health care there will be no serious reform and that he and June couldn't wait to see if the government would offer any help.

When they decided to move into a retirement community June and Bud knew they didn't want to leave Fullerton. "We have a lot of friends here and are very active in our church," explains Bud. "We wouldn't have moved if we had had to leave the area." Fortunately for June and Bud, friends had investigated retirement communities and were convinced that Morningside was one of the best places they could find in California. "We liked the fact that Morningside was Continuing Care with an all-inclusive contract and that the only increased costs we would incur should we move into the extended care wing would be the two additional meals each day," comments Bud.

Bud says he also liked the fact that the community has a health and liaison advisory committee, some of whose members are residents, which meets monthly to monitor issues relating to Assisted Living and extended care.

According to June and Bud, preparation for the move itself was extremely difficult. They began the process 10 months before they intended to take up residence. "It's an extremely emotional thing," says Bud. "You have to have the psychological mind-set to give up the past and look at this move as a new chapter in your life. As hard as it was to do, we were pleased to be able to do it, to get rid of things ourselves. We thought of it as a gift of love to our daughter, so she wouldn't have to do it later. Too many people get stuck doing it for their relatives and it can be terribly traumatic. A friend of ours' mother died and it took him one full year before he could get around physically and emotionally to dealing with her house and possessions."

June and Bud enjoy the community and its activities. Bud says the activities director is outstanding. She received a federal grant in senior computer literacy and set up a laboratory with eight Macintosh computers, scanners, and color printers. "As a result," comments Bud, "an amazing number of people have become excited about computers and a learning center has been created." June and Bud recently took care of twin 13-year-old boys, children of friends, over a weekend. "We were afraid they might be bored," says Bud. "They said, 'Are you kidding? How could we be bored? There's golf, tennis, and swimming—this place is great!' "

June's advice: Investigate where you're going to move carefully from the financial standpoint. Remember, don't worry about being locked into a certain lifestyle; any place you live, you set your own. There are many activities to choose from.

Bud's advice: "If I were searching for a place, I would want very much to see that it was related to a major quality medical center nearby. Morningside is connected to St. Jude Hospital, less than a mile away, which has excellent physicians and wonderful rehabilitation services, which are used by Morningside."

THE OSBORN

101 Theall Road
Rye, NY 10580
(914) 967-4100
Ruth Bush, marketing director

Type of community: Not-for-profit Independent Living with Continuum of Care

Located near Long Island Sound in the historic city of Rye, the Georgian mansion of Miriam Osborn is set on 65 acres of beautifully landscaped grounds and gardens. The four-story mansion resembles a grand European hotel with verandas that have floor-to-ceiling windows and six lounges. A magnificent solarium, filled with huge pots of ferns and highlighted by bay windows, overlooks the sweeping lawns. Each room enjoys a unique view of the beautiful grounds. The community features four libraries, two gracious dining rooms, a 200-seat theater, an interdenominational chapel, and resident gardens. Independent Living and Skilled Nursing facility on campus.

Financial plan: Monthly and daily fees (billed monthly), depending upon type of housing. As a privately endowed nonprofit organization, the Osborn serves both the financially independent and those whose resources may not be sufficient to cover the actual cost of their stay.

Ownership and management: Not-for-profit corporation operated by a board of directors. Opened in 1908.

Minimum age: 65 years.

Population: 124 residents; 121 women, 3 men (until five years ago, The Osborn was a residence for women only).

INDEPENDENT LIVING HOUSING

Type of apartment	*Monthly fee**
Studio, 1/2 bath	$2,400
Studio, full bath	$2,600
Large studio	$3,000
1-Bedroom	$3,800
2-Bedroom	$4,300

**For double occupancy in apartments add $800 to the monthly fee. All utilities included except telephone. Carpeting, fully equipped kitchens or kitchenette, 24-hour emergency call system, individually controlled heating and air-conditioning.*

Type of room	*Daily fee*
Single room	$108–129
2-Room suites	$155
3-Room suites	$172

All rooms are carpeted and have 24-hour emergency call buttons. Kitchens on each floor. Furniture available if necessary.

Number of units: 120 Independent Living private rooms and two-room suites; Skilled Nursing facility.

Dining plan: Three meals a day included in the monthly and daily fees. Special teas, monthly specialty theme buffet suppers, dinner theater, and cocktail parties.

Services: *Included in the monthly fee:* Chauffeured trips, personal and flat-linen services, regular housekeeping.

At additional cost: Hairdresser, manicurists, seamstress, dry cleaning, Osborn Store, three resident-operated shops, guest accommodations.

Activities: Exercise classes, summer visits to Rye Beach, Rye Golf Club Pool, summer cookouts, classes with guest teachers, lecturers, and speakers, films, current events, classical music and opera, bridge and community games, arts and crafts studio, library, 200-person-capacity theater equipped with special audio devices for the hearing impaired, community volunteers, trips to restaurants and theater.

Availability: Limited. Waiting list for applicants who do not have sufficient resources to cover the cost of care. Applicants in this category will be considered for admission on a first-come-first-served basis as support funds from the Osborn endowment become available.

Health services and rates: Health services focus on disease prevention and restorative care. Comprehensive team approach to health care: geriatrician, geriatric nurse practitioner, gerontological nurses, social services, registered dietitian. Physical, occupational, and speech therapies at no charge. Ophthalmology, podiatry, and dental care available at extra charge.

- Personal care/Assisted Living services (24 hours a day)
  - Basic services $151/day
  - Enhanced $187/day
- Skilled Nursing facility
  - Semiprivate $206/day
  - Private $215/day

"There is a quality of life and sense of community at The Osborn combined with a remarkable setting that sets us apart from similar retirement centers. Residents and visitors are most impressed with the caring family of residents, staff, and volunteers that makes up The Osborn."

NORTH CAROLINA

BERMUDA VILLAGE

P.O. Box BVI
Advance, NC 27006
(910) 998-6535 or (800) 843-5433
Nancy H. Anders, director of marketing and sales

Type of community: Continuing Care, modified contract

Located on 50 acres within Bermuda Run Country Club and ten minutes west of Winston-Salem, this resort-like community offers elegant common rooms conveniently connected to the three-story apartment buildings by bright, climate-controlled walkways. Home ownership with a return of investment is offered for Independent Living condominium villas and apartments. Beautifully furnished lounges are located on each floor; the grounds feature outdoor terraces, a pond, and an enclosed swimming pool. Skilled Nursing facility was added in 1992. This area of North Carolina is ranked as the number-one place to live in America by Rand-McNally's Places Rated Almanac.

Financial plan: Purchase price plus monthly fee. Residents sell property themselves.

Ownership and management: Privately owned by Don G. Angel. Managed by Bermuda Village Retirement Community, Inc. Opened in 1984.

Minimum age: 55 years.

Population: 220 residents; approximately 65% couples. Residents from 23 states and many are retired key executives from top international corporations.

Number of units: 140 Independent Living condominiums and 97 villas; 6 Assisted Living beds, 16-bed Skilled Nursing facility.

Dining plan: $90 per month is charged per person for dining room privileges regardless of whether it is used. Additional meals available at cost (average, $8.95). Lakeside dining terrace. On the Rocks pub. Three private dining rooms. Meals delivered in case of illness.

Services: *Included in the monthly fee:* Full membership in Bermuda Run Country Club and use of all facilities (27-hole golf course, tennis complex, outdoor swimming pool), 24-hour emergency home repairs, valet parking, covered and uncovered parking, concierge, weekly housekeeping and flat-linen services.

At additional cost: Beauty/barbershop, village apothecary shop, transportation, covered parking.

Activities: Golf, tennis, indoor and outdoor swimming pools, whirlpool, walking courses, horseshoes, putting green, picnic areas, complete health spa, arts and crafts, art studio, billiards and Ping-Pong room, movies, woodworking, gardening, full social calendar of dinners, dance parties, and active clubs covering interests from bridge to investments.

Availability: Some units have waiting list.

Health services and rates: Residents are asked to contribute $5,000 to the health center in exchange for 65 days of any level of care at no charge. Satellite clinic operated by Bowman Gray School of Medicine (affiliated with Wake Forest University),

INDEPENDENT LIVING HOUSING

Type/size of apartment	*Purchase price*	*Monthly fee single/double*
1-Bedroom, 800 sq. ft.	From $129,500	$1,324–1,572
2-Bedroom, 1,250 sq. ft.	From $169,500	$1,843–2,091
2-Bedroom/study, 1,490 sq. ft.	From $199,500	$2,163–2,411
Villa		
2-Bedroom villa, 1,824–2,052 sq. ft.	From $262,500	$1,755–1,863
*New villas**		
1-Bedroom, 1,090 sq. ft.	From $175,000	$1,200–1,350
2-Bedroom, 1,250 sq. ft.	From $189,500	$1,200–1,350

**Under construction; to be purchased directly from developer.*

All utilities except telephone included for apartments. Apartments have nine-foot ceilings, sunrooms with miniblinds, oversized, lighted walk-in closets with carpeted shoe racks, wall-to-wall carpeting, draperies, wet bar (except 1-bedroom model), all-electric kitchen, individually controlled heating and air-conditioning, 24-hour emergency call system. Villas have all of the above plus 12-foot vaulted ceilings, choice of exterior styling, hardwood floors, ceiling fan in sunroom and master bedroom, disappearing stair to attic storage, 2-car garage with electronic doors, paved patios, screened trash areas. Villa owners pay own electricity.

one of the nation's outstanding medical research and gerontology centers. For recuperation from hospital stay or illness infirmary rooms are available. Staff will assist in the hiring of home help aides.

- Assisted Living facility
  2 apartments, 6 beds $75/day
- 16-Bed Skilled Nursing facility
  Private $120/day

"There's a spirit at Bermuda Village. For those who view retirement as a beginning Bermuda Village awaits with an exciting, active, and satisfying lifestyle, complemented by luxurious services, amenities, and a health care package designed to take care of you now and in the future."

DEERFIELD EPISCOPAL RETIREMENT COMMUNITY

1617 Hendersonville Road
Asheville, NC 28803
(704) 274-1531
Dick Weimann, executive director

Type of community: Nonprofit Continuing Care, modified contract

Located 12 minutes from Asheville, Deerfield is situated on 30 scenic acres and is convenient to a variety of shops and services. The community offers five areas of living: Independent Living houses, condos, studio apartments, and suites; domiciliary care rooms and Skilled Nursing care. The brick-and-wood-sided single-level buildings are surrounded by beautifully landscaped grounds, including a courtyard with a gazebo. Deerfield is convenient to the Blue Ridge Parkway, national and state parks, the Biltmore and Gardens, and golf and tennis clubs.

Financial plan: Monthly fee. Admissions fee of $5,000 ($7,500 per couple) payable upon admission, amortized over six months. Original investment for houses or condos is amortized over

INDEPENDENT LIVING HOUSING

Type of apartment	*Monthly fee*	
Studio	$1,555–1,605	
Suite (2-room)	$2,340–2,730	
Condos/homes	*Purchase price*	*Monthly fee*
2-Bedroom condos, 1,350–1,450 sq. ft.	$82,000–95,000	$462/unit
1–3-Bedroom homes, 900–2,200 sq. ft.	$60,000–160,000	$462/home

For apartments: all utilities except telephone included; wall-to-wall carpeting. For condos/homes: water, sewer, trash collection, groundskeeping included but not telephone or electricity.

a 90-month period with declining balance refunded if vacated during that period; 10% refunded after 90 months.

Ownership and management: Owned and operated by the Episcopal Diocese of Western North Carolina. Governed by board of directors. Opened in 1955.

Minimum age: 62 years.

Population: 125 residents; 75% women, 25% men, 10% couples.

Number of units: Independent living: 26 homes, 113 condos, 31 studios/suites; 8 domiciliary beds, 31 Skilled Nursing beds.

Dining plan: Three meals daily included in the monthly fee for studio/suite apartments. No meals included in the monthly fee for condos. Limited tray service available at additional charge. Private dining room.

Services: *Included in the monthly fee:* Scheduled transportation, parking, weekly maid service. Weekly flat-linen service included for studio/suite residents.

At additional cost: Laundry, beauty/barbershop, guest accommodations.

Activities: Exercise classes, social events, concert and symphony outings, movies, trips to local playhouses, Bible study, discussion groups, library service, guest speakers, Episcopal church services.

Availability: Limited, depending on floor plan.

Health services and rates: Residents receive up to 15 days at no charge per year in the Skilled Nursing facility.

- 8 Domiciliary care beds
  Private $2,995/month
- 31-Bed Skilled Nursing facility
  Semiprivate $2,980/month
  Private $3,890/month

"Asheville is the regional health care center for Western North Carolina. Specialists in almost any area of medicine can be found in the area. Deerfield is a small, intimate community located in the beautiful mountains of western North Carolina."

CAROL WOODS

750 Weaver Dairy Road
Chapel Hill, NC 27514
(919) 968-4511
Anita Magilou, marketing director

Type of community: Nonprofit Continuing Care, modified contract

Accreditation: Continuing Care Accreditation Commission

INDEPENDENT LIVING HOUSING

Garden apartments	*Occupancy fee single/double*	*Monthly fee single/double**
1-Bedroom, 678 sq. ft.	$72,500/78,000	$1,570/2,110
1-Bedroom/den, 801 sq. ft.	$91,200/95,700	$1,715/2,255
2-Bedroom, 957 sq. ft.	$104,300/107,600	$1,973/2,516
2-Bedroom/den, 1,078 sq. ft.	$120,500/124,000	$2,152/2,695
Deluxe 1-bedroom/den, 1,343 sq. ft	$141,300/148,100	$2,367/2,932
Deluxe 2-bedroom/den, 1,538 sq. ft.	$169,600/176,300	$2,479/3,045
Central apartments		
Studio, 447 sq. ft.	$43,300	$1,545
1-Bedroom, 611 sq. ft.	$65,900/69,500	$1,651/2,382
2-Bedroom, 635 sq. ft.	$67,500/73,900	$1,695/2,431
2-Bedroom, 850 sq. ft.	$98,100/100,800	$2,094/2,824

**All utilities except long-distance telephone and cable TV included in the monthly fee. Wall-to-wall carpeting, draperies or miniblinds, major appliances, 24-hour emergency call system, individually controlled heating and air-conditioning. All have doors opening onto private patios or balconies. Modifications to units may be made by residents at their own expense. Cottages have eat-in kitchen, den, utility room, deck, covered front porch. Optional cottage features include fireplace in den, carport, covered or screened porch, cabinets in den, additional closet space, patio in front.*

Located on 120 acres of rolling woodlands on the outskirts of Chapel Hill, the community's grounds are sprinkled with flowers and shrubs. The central apartments, dining room, aquatic center, and health center are all connected to the central complex by a series of enclosed walkways. Chapel Hill and central North Carolina are among the most popular retirement locations in the nation. Nearby universities—including University of North Carolina, Duke, and North Carolina State—combine with the state capital at Raleigh and the Research Triangle Park to attract a myriad of cultural and educational opportunities. The area is also known for advanced medical resources including Duke University Hospital, North Carolina Memorial Hospital, and Durham County General Hospital.

Note: *Carol Woods is undergoing a four-year expansion program including new garden units, a new health care facility, and extensions to the dining room. The present health center has recently been retrofitted for Assisted Living.*

Financial plan: Life occupancy fee plus monthly fee. Should a resident outlive what seemed to be adequate financial resources, community reserves are made available to provide assistance. Nonrefundable $100 application fee ($200 per couple).

Ownership and management: Nonprofit corporation. The governing body of the corporation is the board of directors. Residents are deeply involved in an advisory capacity and have a strong voice in management and administration through many committees. Opened in 1979.

Minimum age: 65 years (if couple, spouse must be at least 55).

Population: 379 residents; 71% women, 29% men, 18% couples.

Number of units: 280 Independent Living apartments; 30 sheltered living suites, 30-bed nursing facility.

Dining plan: One meal daily included in the monthly fee for garden apartments. Three meals included in the monthly fee for central apartments, although residents can request one or two and receive credit.

Additional meals optional at reduced cost. If residents miss a meal, they receive credit for another meal on that day.

Services: *Included in the monthly fee:* Weekly housekeeping and flat-linen services, annual heavy-duty cleaning, parking, van transportation.

At additional cost: Beauty/barbershop, Carol Woods Shop.

Activities: Golf, Ping-Pong, shuffleboard, pocket pool, exercise group, discussion groups. Regular meetings of foreign language, bird, book, bridge, painting, photo lab, sewing and crafts, weaving, and woodworking clubs; aquatic center with swimming pool and water aerobic classes. Resident committees.

Availability: Limited. Waiting list varies with apartment/cottage style and size.

Health services and rates: Residents receive up to 15 days inpatient care per year without additional daily charges. Unused days accumulate from year to year as a credit against future needs. In the event that specialized care is necessary, Carol Woods's health care benefits will, with limited exceptions, pay for hospitalization and medical specialists not covered by Medicare or supplemental insurance. Routine medical services provided by physician or geriatric nurse are available at no fee on a walk-in basis during clinic hours. Physical, speech, and occupational therapies provided by licensed therapists. Visiting specialists include an ophthalmologist and podiatrist. Dental screening provided. Limited laboratory services provided on premises.

- 30 Sheltered living units

	Resident	*Nonresident*
Semiprivate	$26.25/day	$108.25/day
Private	$39.75/day	$137.50/day

- 30-Bed Skilled Nursing facility

	Resident	*Nonresident*
Semiprivate	$38.75/day	$133/day
Private	$52.25/day	$160.50/day

"At Carol Woods, our commitment to a quality lifestyle is unsurpassed. Our clear status as a leader is reflected, in part, by the direct involvement of our administration in efforts to develop standards and regulations throughout the industry."

CAROLINA MEADOWS

100 Carolina Meadows
Chapel Hill, NC 27514-8505
(919) 942-4014 or (800) 458-6756
Teresa Tager, director of marketing

Type of community: Nonprofit Continuing Care, modified contract

Accreditation: Continuing Care Accreditation Commission

Carolina Meadows is located on 160 acres 3½ miles from the center of downtown Chapel Hill, the home of the University of North Carolina. Independent Living apartments and villas are brick with siding trim. The campus setting has numerous gardens and elaborate walking paths. Personal care and Skilled Nursing are on-site. University of North Carolina has a special, free program for persons over 65, enabling them to take up to eight hours of credit at no cost other than the $15 application fee. Near the community are major theater and sports events, music (jazz to symphony, outstanding church and choir programs). Duke University is in nearby Durham.

Financial plan: Entrance fee plus monthly fee and one-time nonrefundable Continuing Care reserve fee. Entrance fee is 100% refundable upon resale of unit. Residents are guaranteed a lifetime contract for continuing care. Nonrefundable $5,000 Continuing Care reserve fee ($7,500 for two persons) is used as reserve to strengthen the operation of the community. Thus no resident will be asked to leave simply on the basis of inability to pay. $300 nonrefundable application fee.

INDEPENDENT LIVING HOUSING

Type/size of apartment	*Entrance fee*	*Monthly fee single/double**
1-Bedroom, 717–790 sq. ft.	$74,700–82,800	$950/1,225
Deluxe 1-bedroom, 1,007 sq. ft.	$111,500	$950/1,225
2-Bedroom, 1,187 sq. ft.	$130,900	$950/1,225
Deluxe 2-bedroom, 1,302–1,312 sq. ft.	$144,600–145,800	$950/1,225
Superdeluxe 2-bedroom, 1,607 sq. ft.	$179,000	$950/1,225
Type of villa		
1-Bedroom, 1,444 sq. ft.	$148,500	$950/1,225
2-Bedroom, 1,766–1,830 sq. ft.	$182,500–194,500	$950/1,225
2-Bedroom/den, 1,848 sq. ft.	$197,500	$950/1,225

**All utilities except telephone included in the monthly fee. Fully equipped kitchens, 24-hour emergency call system, individually controlled heating and air-conditioning, hookup for washer/dryer. Pets permitted (small dogs under 20 pounds are permitted on first-floor apartments only and in all villas).*

Ownership and management: Nonprofit organization governed by nonpaid board of directors. Opened in 1983.

Minimum age: 50 years.

Population: 374 residents; 64% women, 36% men, 59% couples.

Number of units: 120 Independent Living villas and 240 apartments; 30 personal care beds, 20 Skilled Nursing beds.

Dining plan: $125 food allowance included in the monthly fee. Home meal delivery at additional charge. Lounge. Private dining room with expansion under construction.

Services: *Included in the monthly fee:* Scheduled transportation.

At additional cost: Guest accommodations, housekeeping, handyman services, beauty/barbershop.

Activities: Library, croquet court, gardening space, horseshoes, two bocce courts, two tennis courts, classrooms, exercise facilities, arts and crafts facilities, woodworking shop. Six holes of par golf (three more under construction). Enclosed swimming pool, greenhouse, Jacuzzi, new exercise room, auditorium under construction.

Availability: Apartments and villas are available.

Health services and rates: Residents are free to select their own physician or utilize the services of University of North Carolina Memorial Hospital's Department of Family Medicine or Duke University's medical facilities or others.

- 30 Personal care beds

Semiprivate	$68/day
Private	$78.50/day

- 20 Nursing beds

	Intermediate Nursing	*Skilled Nursing*
Semiprivate	$105/day	$120/day
Private	$115/day	$138/day

"Carolina Meadows is sensitive to pocketbook issues. To keep monthly service fees lower, an 'optionality' principal is used, meaning residents pay for only the services they select, including housekeeping and medical services."

SHARON TOWERS, THE PRESBYTERIAN HOME AT CHARLOTTE, INC.

5100 Sharon Road
Charlotte, NC 28210
(704) 553-1670
Linda Bennett, executive director

Type of community: Nonprofit Continuing Care, modified plan

Sharon Towers is tucked away in a heavily wooded, landscaped 23-acre site in southeast Charlotte. Four apartment floor plans are available in twin six-story buildings that offer dining, activities, and the health care center located under the same roof. Cottages and duplexes are also available. A nature trail winds through the woods with a gazebo along the way. Charlotte's premiere regional shopping center, the South Park Mall, is nearby.

Financial plan: Entrance fee plus monthly fee. A scholarship fund composed of charitable contributions and income from a trust fund with the Presbyterian Foundation is available for those residents in need of financial assistance.

Ownership and management: Governed by a not-for-profit corporation and the Presbytery of Charlotte. Members of the board of directors are elected by the presbytery. Opened in 1969.

Minimum age: 60 years.

Population: 292 residents; 90% women, 10% men, 5% couples.

Number of units: 202 Independent Living apartments; 20 private Assisted Living rooms, 96 Skilled Nursing beds.

Dining plan: Three meals a day are included in the monthly fee; however, residents with kitchen facilities may opt for a dinner and lunch meal plan.

Services: *Included in the monthly fee:* Weekly housekeeping and flat-linen services, scheduled transportation.

At additional cost: Beauty/barbershop, guest accommodations.

Activities: Recreational and crafts room, weekly art classes, shopping trips and outings to the mountains, concerts.

Availability: A limited number of single rooms and Assisted Living accommodations are available.

Health services and rates: Medical adviser, 24-hour registered nurse, and emergency assistance. An additional charge of $45 per day.

INDEPENDENT LIVING HOUSING

Type/size of unit	*Entrance fee*	*Monthly fee single/double**
Single, 273 sq. ft.	$28,500	$1,250
Large single, 300 sq. ft.	$30,500	$1,270
2-Room, 546 sq. ft.	$54,500	$1,480/2,500
2-Room/kitchenette	$56,500	$1,480/2,500
Duplex	$63,000	$1,480/2,635
Super duplex, 1,000–1,500 sq. ft.	$76,000	$1,480/2,635
Cottage	$89,000	$1,480/2,635

**All utilities except private telephone line included in the monthly fee. Individually controlled heating and air-conditioning, central antenna, some fully equipped small kitchens, wall-to-wall carpeting, 24-hour emergency call system.*

- 20 Assisted Living rooms $1,950/month
- 96-Bed Skilled Nursing facility
  Private $45/day
  (in addition to monthly fee)

"Sharon Towers is one of the community's oldest and most respected CCRCs. It is located on a lovely wooded site only a few blocks from South Park Mall. Entrance fees are reasonably priced, and Sharon Towers prides itself in its ability to provide quality care in a family-like environment."

THE PINES AT DAVIDSON

400 Avinger Lane, P.O. Box 118
Davidson, NC 28036
(704) 896-1100
Jim Irvin, marketing/development officer

Type of community: Nonprofit Continuing Care, modified contract

Designed with the architectural style and ambiance of a small village, The Pines is located on 47 wooded acres near Davidson College. The grounds offer abundant pine, cedar, and hardwood trees and meandering trails for relaxing walks. Routinely manicured grounds feature a variety of plants and trees under the supervision of a horticulturist. Apartments and clustered duplex cottages provide Independent Living residences. The community offers well-lighted, spacious common areas with wide corridors throughout. The Pines is within walking distance of downtown Davidson and an easy jaunt to Lake Norman, one of the South's largest freshwater lakes. Davidson College offers a wide variety of educational and cultural opportunities. Charlotte is 20 miles away and within an hour's drive or less are some of the most distinctive small towns and medium-size cities in the Carolinas.

Financial plan: Entrance fee plus monthly fee. Three plans: **1)** Standard entrance fee. **2)** 50% refundable entrance fee. **3)** 90% refundable entrance fee.

Ownership and management: Owned and managed by the nonprofit, church-affiliated Davidson Retirement Community, Inc. The board of directors is a volunteer board appointed by Davidson College Presbyterian Church session. An experienced management team works closely with the resident association. Opened in 1988.

Minimum age: 65 years (if couple, spouse must be at least 62).

Population: 300 residents; 65% women, 35% men, 25% couples.

INDEPENDENT LIVING HOUSING

Type/size of apartment	*Entrance fee 1**	*Monthly fee single/double**
Efficiency, 418 sq. ft.	$35,800	$1,071
Studio, 527 sq. ft.	$46,900	$1,124/1,726
1-Bedroom, 722 sq. ft.	$71,900	$1,272/2,007
2-Bedroom, 975 sq. ft.	$96,800	$1,405/2,208
1-Bedroom/den, 1,140 sq. ft.	$99,800	$1,449/2,252
Duplex cottage homes		
2-Bedroom, 1,565 sq. ft.	$109,500–128,000	$1,538/2,542

**50% and 90% refundable entrance fee plans are also offered. All utilities included. Wall-to-wall carpeting, miniblinds, private covered balconies or patios, 24-hour emergency call system, individual thermostat controls, large windows, fully equipped kitchens, pass-through from kitchen to dining area, high ceilings, spacious rooms.*

Number of units: 168 Independent Living apartments and 36 duplex cottages; 60-bed health care center.

Dining plan: One meal per day included in the monthly fee. Other meals available at additional charge. Private dining room and café. Catering. Limited tray service and special diets.

Services: *Included in the monthly fee:* Weekly housekeeping and flat-linen services, personal laundry facilities, parking, scheduled transportation.

At additional cost: Beauty/barbershop, bank, convenience store, snack bar, post office, gift shop, extra housekeeping services.

Activities: Activities director. Library, crafts facilities, woodworking, chapel, game rooms, theater, group tours. Residents can take advantage of membership privileges at River Run Country Club, a golf course community located just two miles away that offers an 18-hole golf course, dining facilities, tennis, swimming, stocked fishing ponds, and walking trails. Audit courses at nearby Davidson College; attend lectures, concerts, sporting events.

Availability: Because of The Pines's popularity, it has adopted a first-come-first-served policy on apartments and cottages. A future residency program is available.

Health services and rates: Residents are entitled to 14 noncumulative "exempt days" per calendar year in the health center, during which there is no increase in the monthly fee except for the costs of two additional meals per day and any ancillary health care costs. When the exempt days have been used, the resident pay 85% of the amount of the published per diem rate listed below. If care is short-term, the resident pays the health center rates while the apartment is reserved without charge. The health center, directed by a licensed physician and geriatrician, offers 24-hour, on-call assistance and an on-site clinic. Rehabilitative therapy programs. Home health care services.

- 60-Bed Assisted Living
  Private $78/day
- Intermediate Nursing
  Private $109/day
- Skilled Nursing
  Private $123/day

"Nearby Davidson College and River Run Golf and Country Club offer Pines residents an above-average menu of intellectual, cultural, and recreational programs without any initiation fees, annual dues, or minimum charges. Residents may audit courses at Davidson College without any registration fees. Because of these amenities, residents of The Pines are an active and attractive group of varied people."

THE FOREST AT DUKE

201 Pickett
Durham, NC 27705
(919) 490-8000
Nancy Williams, director of marketing

Type of community: Not-for-profit Continuing Care, all-inclusive contract

The Forest at Duke is situated on a 42-acre site that features walking trails, walled gardens, courtyards, and a pond. Apartments are designed around beautifully landscaped courtyards, a rose garden, and the wooded glen south of the pool and greenhouse. Cottages are situated in pairs to take advantage of the site's gentle elevation changes. Assisted Living and Skilled Nursing facility is in a wing of the main building. The community is ten minutes from Duke University and 25 minutes from Raleigh-Durham International Airport.

Financial plan: Entrance fee plus monthly fee. All entrance fees include a Continuing Care reserve of $8,000 per person plus a residence fee. Two refundable entrance fee plans: **1)** Amortized plan: 2% of residence fee accrues to the community each month (the refund decreases to 0% in 50 months). **2)** 50% refund plan: 2% of the residence fee accrues to the community each month for 25 months, after which

INDEPENDENT LIVING HOUSING

Type/size of apartment	*Entrance fee 1/2**	*Monthly fee**
Studio/bedroom, 553 sq. ft.	$72,220/100,080	$954
1-Bedroom, 717 sq. ft.	$90,280/125,120	$1,226
1-Bedroom/den, 914 sq. ft.	$105,920/146,800	$1,390
2-Bedroom, 1,144 sq. ft.	$130,000/180,160	$1,584
2-Bedroom/den, 1,243 sq. ft.	$142,040/196,820	$1,701
Cottages		
1-Bedroom/den, 1,207 sq. ft.	$142,040/196,820	$1,613
2-Bedroom, 1,445 sq. ft.	$156,480/216,860	$1,701
2-Bedroom/den, 1,662 sq. ft.	$170,940/246,880	$1,789

**For double occupancy add $18,060 to entrance fee Plan 1, $25,040 to entrance fee Plan 2, $546 to the monthly fee. All utilities except telephone included. All apartments have bay windows, porch or patio, fully electric kitchen, wall-to-wall carpeting, 24-hour emergency call system, individual thermostat control, cable TV outlets, washer/dryers. Cottages have dining rooms and carports attached by breezeway, hookup for washer/dryer.*

the refund remains at 50%. Application deposit: $300 processing fee and $1,000 refundable priority deposit.

Ownership and management: The Forest at Duke, Inc. Governed by board of directors composed of members of Duke University faculty and Duke University Medical Center, plus Durham residents. Opened in September 1992.

Minimum age: 65 years (if couple, spouse must be at least 62).

Population: 380 residents; 61% couples, 39% single. Residents come from 25 states, plus the District of Columbia. 38% are from Durham, 37% from outside North Carolina.

Number of units: 160 Independent Living apartments and 80 cottages; 30 Assisted Living units, 15 Intermediate Nursing beds, 15 Skilled Nursing beds.

Dining plan: Choice of one meal per day included in the monthly fee. Tray service is available when ordered by Forest physician. Private dining room. Dining terrace and café.

Services: *Included in the monthly fee:* Weekly housekeeping, medical claims filing, scheduled in-town transportation.

At additional cost: Bank, beauty/barbershop, guest accommodations, gift shop, convenience store.

Activities: Full-time activities director. Card room, billiards, indoor pool and whirlpool, art studio, woodworking shop, gardening, biking, exercise room, picnic area, walking trails, greenhouse, library, auditorium, community center.

Availability: Limited; priority waiting list. Those on waiting list retain a numbered position indefinitely. To join the waiting list a deposit totaling 15% of amortized entrance fee is required.

Health services and rates: Residents receive unlimited health care included in their monthly fee. Two extra meals daily at additional charge. For the first 10 days there is no charge for extra meals. For a married couple, the double occupancy monthly fee will continue in effect if one spouse moves permanently to the health center. A single resident who moves permanently to the health center pays 40% of daily fee instead of his or her monthly fee.

- 30 Assisted Living units, 15 of which may be specially used for individuals suffering from Alzheimer's disease and related dementia
- 15 Intermediate Care nursing beds
  Private $138/day nonresident
- 15 Skilled Nursing beds
  Private $138/day nonresident

"The Forest at Duke is a not-for-profit Continuing Care community that has been carefully planned by professionals using the industry's most reliable financial and actuarial assumptions. Equally important is our extensive involvement of prospective residents in the planning process. It is the intent of The Forest at Duke to develop a community that has no other mission than the provision of high-quality health and residential services to aging persons at affordable prices."

COVENANT VILLAGE, INC.

1351 Robinwood Road
Gastonia, NC 28054
(704) 867-2319
Martha Baker, director of special services

Type of community: Nonprofit Continuing Care, all-inclusive contract

Located on a 33-acre site in beautiful Gaston County, known for its 6,000 acres of lakes and streams, parks, museums, and festivals, Covenant Village's campus consists of one large brick building housing all resident apartments and the health center. The main building has a formal living/dining room with stone fireplace, card room, chapel, resident store, library, activity room, and individual parlors on each resident floor. Buildings have traditional architecture and furnishings with stone accents and porches. Cottages are traditional brick duplex units.

Financial plan: Entrance fee plus monthly fee. $1,000 application fee, which can be applied to entrance fee. Entrance fee is refundable, on a declining basis, during the first 25 months for apartment residents, 50 months for cottage residents.

Ownership and management: Owned and managed by Covenant Village, a private, nonprofit, church-affiliated corporation. Volunteer board of directors comprised of community leaders elected to represent nine local churches of five different denominations and the community at large. Opened in 1982.

Minimum age: 65 years.

Population: 225 residents; 83% women, 17% men, 30% couples.

INDEPENDENT LIVING HOUSING

Type/size of apartment	*Entrance fee*	*Monthly fee single/double**
Studio, 350 sq. ft.	$25,000–30,000	$1,115
1-Bedroom, 700 sq. ft.	$57,000	$1,286/2,250
2-Bedroom, 1,050 sq. ft.	$75,000	$2,550/2,550
Cottages		
2-Bedroom, 1,080 sq. ft.	$109,500	$1,113/1,756

**All utilities except telephone and cable TV included in the monthly fee for apartments. Cottage residents also pay for gas and electricity. Wall-to-wall carpeting, large closets, cable TV hookup, 24-hour emergency call system. Most apartments have balconies and kitchenettes.*

Number of units: 121 Independent Living apartments and 42 cottages; 38 Skilled Nursing beds.

Dining plan: Three meals a day included in the monthly fee for apartments. One meal per day included in the monthly fee for cottages.

Services: *Included in the monthly fee:* Weekly housekeeping and flat-linen services, scheduled transportation.

At additional cost: Beauty/barbershop, guest accommodations.

Activities: Exercise classes, games, entertainment, movies, musical programs, cultural, spiritual, and educational opportunities, trips, monthly socials.

Availability: Waiting list of two to eight years.

Health services and rates: For residents moving directly into the health center or those who move within the 90-day probationary period, the rate is $48.55 per day. Telephone, pharmacy, physician services, prosthetic devices, medical supplies, and any medical treatments or therapies not included in routine nursing care are additional.

- 38-Bed Skilled Nursing facility

Semiprivate	$1,115–1,457/month

**Additional charge for breakfast and lunch. Private rooms, when available, cost $34.50 per day in addition to the normal monthly fee.*

"Covenant Village's goal is to simply provide secure independent living for people who are active but want to be relieved of the burdens of maintaining a home, preparing meals, and worrying about what will happen as health needs may change."

CAROLINA VILLAGE

600 Carolina Village Road
Hendersonville, NC 28739
(704) 692-6275
Doley Bell, administrator

Type of community: Not-for-profit Continuing Care, all-inclusive contract

Carolina Village is located on a 52-acre site near the junction of Interstate 26 and U.S. 64. Five three-story connected buildings and single-level cottages are surrounded by fully landscaped grounds, nature trails, gardens, and walkways. The main living room has a fireplace, and there is a separate auditorium for meetings and events. Independent Living apartments and cottages, Assisted Living services, and nursing facility are on campus.

Financial plan: Entrance fee plus monthly fee. The entrance fee is refunded on a prorated basis should the resident leave the village.

Ownership and management: Owned and managed by a not-for-profit corporation. Volunteer board of directors. Opened in 1974.

Minimum age: 62 years.

Population: 365 residents; 75% women, 25% men, 30% couples.

Number of units: 212 Independent Living apartments and 57 cottages; 58 Skilled Nursing beds.

Dining plan: One meal a day is included in the monthly fee. Private dining room and catering services. Additional meals available for small charge. Tray service provided at the request of physician or director of nurses.

Services: *Included in the monthly fee:* Housekeeping, weekly flat-linen service, scheduled transportation, parking.

At additional cost: Card/snack shop, beauty/barbershop.

Activities: Gardening, variety of cultural and civic events, library, woodworking, dark room, arts and crafts room, travelogues, musicals in Village Hall.

INDEPENDENT LIVING HOUSING

Type/size of apartment	*Entrance fee single/double*	*Monthly fee single/double**
Studio, 300 sq. ft.	$32,900	$666
Efficiency, 440 sq. ft.	$42,000/58,500	$736/1,223
1-Bedroom, 600 sq. ft.	$54,400/70,900	$828/1,293
1- or 2-Bedroom, 740 sq. ft.	$63,000/79,500	$923/1,339
2-Bedroom, 900 sq. ft.	$73,400/89,900	$992/1,407
2-Bedroom, 1,040 sq. ft.	$81,900/98,400	$1,022/1,439
2-Bedroom, 1,200 sq. ft.	$108,900/112,400	$1,059/1,474
*Cottages***		
2-Bedroom, 945 sq. ft.	$66,400/78,900	$1,042/1,469
2-Bedroom, 1,092 sq. ft.	$75,400/87,900	$1,074/1,509
2-Bedroom, 1,260 sq. ft.	$85,400/97,900	$1,122/1,549
2-Bedroom/garden, 1,486 sq. ft.	$128,200/144,700	$1,268/1,691

**All utilities except telephone included. Electric kitchens, 24-hour emergency call system, wall-to-wall carpeting, individually controlled heating and air-conditioning. **An additional charge of $3,000 for winterized patios.*

Availability: Waiting list of two to ten years, depending on floor plan.

Health services and rates: Residents receive unlimited use of the health center 24 hours a day at no extra charge. Assisted Living services offered in residents' apartments. Residents who move in to the health care center permanently continue to pay the same monthly fee, plus additional charges for prescriptions, two extra meals a day, and special therapy.

- 58-Bed Skilled Nursing facility

"Carolina Village came into being because of the efforts of local citizens who felt the need for a retirement village where residents could live healthier, happier, and longer lives among pleasant surroundings, free from worry as to any future dependency."

THE PRESBYTERIAN HOME OF HIGH POINT

201 Greensboro Road, Box 500
High Point, NC 27260
(910) 883-9111
Anne Ripple, marketing director

Type of community: Not-for-profit Continuing Care, modified contract

Accreditation: Continuing Care Accreditation Commission.

The Presbyterian Home's 18 1/2-acre campus consists of one six-story apartment building and several three-story buildings that house Independent Living, Assisted Living, and Skilled Nursing units. Apartments, cottages, and duplexes feature a variety of one- and two-bedroom floor plans. The community is located less than a half-day's drive to either the mountains or the seashore and ten minutes from the regional airport. The area is rich in art museums, medical facilities, colleges and universities. Seven hospitals are located in the High Point/Greensboro/Winston-Salem area, which has one of the highest concentrations of health care facilities and medical professionals in the southeastern United States.

Financial plan: Entrance fee plus monthly fee. $200 application fee.

INDEPENDENT LIVING HOUSING

Apartments and cottages	*Entrance fee*	*Monthly fee**
Efficiency	$31,900	$1,000
1-Bedroom	$44,000–57,500	$1,075–1,150
2-Bedroom	$52,900–79,500	$1,250–1,325
Duplex	$75,500–85,500	$1,300–1,450
Cottage	$56,000–132,900	$1,150–1,525

**For double occupancy add $595 to the monthly fee. All utilities except telephone included. Wall-to-wall carpeting, draperies, 24-hour emergency call system. Twelve different floor plans.*

Ownership and management: Founded by the Synod of North Carolina of the Presbyterian Church (USA) under the parent organization The Presbyterian Homes, Inc. Opened in 1952.

Minimum age: 62 years for application; 65 for admittance.

Population: 300 residents; 84% women, 16% men, 8% couples.

Number of units: 120 Independent Living apartments; 69 Assisted Living units, 84-bed health care center.

Dining plan: Three meals per day included in the monthly fee. Private dining room.

Services: *Included in monthly fee:* Weekly housekeeping, laundry, dry cleaning, scheduled transportation.

At additional cost: Beauty/barbershop, guest accommodations.

Activities: Community college classes, creative writing, crafts, theater excursions, exercise classes, billiards, library, two overnight trips (two to three days). Swimming pool under construction.

Availability: Waiting list.

Health services and rates: Residents receive 30 "grace days" in the nursing unit per year at no additional charge. After the grace days, the resident pays 80% of the per diem rate for nursing accommodations. Physicians, medical/surgical specialists and practitioners, hospital costs, and all drugs and special treatments that cannot be provided by the health care facility are charged additionally. Assistance with filling in insurance forms.

- Residential care
  Single $1,495/month
  Double $1,650/month
- 69 Assisted Living units
  Resident $1,650/month
  Nonresident $1,890/month
- 10 Intermediate Nursing beds
  Private $92/day
- 74 Skilled Nursing beds
  Private $102/day

"The Presbyterian Home is one of only a few accredited communities in North Carolina. If a resident moves into the nursing facility, he or she continues to pay the same monthly fee."

GRACE RIDGE

500 Lenoir Road
Morganton, NC 28655
(704) 433-0061 or (800) 331-6941 in N.C.
Mary Anne Riggs, director of marketing

Type of community: Nonprofit Continuing Care, choice of modified or all-inclusive contract

Situated at the foot of the Blue Ridge Mountains, Grace Ridge is surrounded by numerous state parks, mountain retreats and resorts, and three golf courses. The 26-acre wooded sight contains a five-story building with breathtaking panoramic views. The community is an hour's drive from Asheville and Charlotte. Morganton is a lovely small city with many cultural attractions, including a community college, three museums, historical sights, and a 1,000-seat auditorium. Grace Ridge offers Independent Living residences and a health care center with domiciliary care and Intermediate and Skilled Nursing.

Financial plan: Entrance fee plus monthly fee. Four plans: **1)** The Continuing Care plan has the higher entrance fee but allows the prevailing monthly fee to apply to stays in the health care center. The Continuing Care entrance fee is fully amortized after 12 months. **2)** The standard plan has a lower entrance fee and the prevailing monthly fee does not apply to stays in the health care center. Health care center rates for the standard plan are equal to 80% of the private per diem charges in the health care center. The standard entrance fee is amortized at a rate of 4% per month up to 25 months. **3** and **4)** 50% and 90% refund options are available with both plans 1 and 2. An initial $1,000 deposit is required.

Ownership and management: Sponsored by Grace LifeCare, Inc., a subsidiary corporation controlled by Grace Hospitals, Inc.

Minimum age: 65 years (if couple, spouse must be at least 62).

Population: 180 residents; 69% women, 31% men, 9% couples.

Number of units: 114 Independent Living apartments and 20 cottages; 20 Assisted Living units, 8 Intermediate and 7 Skilled Nursing beds.

Dining plan: Three meals per day are available but only one daily meal is included in the monthly fee. Tray service is available if approved by the health care center. Private dining room and catering.

Services: *Included in the monthly fee:* Weekly housekeeping and flat-linen services, scheduled heavy cleaning, scheduled transportation.

INDEPENDENT LIVING HOUSING

Type of apartment	*Entrance fee 1/2**	*Monthly fee**
Studio	$22,500/29,500	$637
1-Bedroom	$39,500/51,500	$896
1-Bedroom	$44,500/57,500	$896
2-Bedroom	$59,500/76,500	$1,139
2-Bedroom	$75,000/95,500	$1,267
2-Bedroom	$85,000/95,500	$1,267
2-Bedroom cottage	N/A/116,750	$1,155

**For double occupancy add $5,000 to the entrance fee, $289 to the monthly fee. Double occupancy in cottages does not affect entrance fee but raises monthly fee by $387. All utilities except telephone and cable TV included. Fully equipped kitchen, carpeting, draperies, patio or balcony, 24-hour emergency call system, individually controlled heating and air-conditioning.*

At additional cost: Beauty/barbershop, guest accommodations, postal services, photocopies, dry cleaning.

Activities: Arts and crafts room, game room, exercise program, billards room, library, chapel, lounge and outdoor terrace, vegetable and flower gardens, planned group tours and travel opportunities, TV lounge, trips to concerts, theater productions, ballet.

Availability: Limited. Future residency program offers priority waiting list plus privileges, including meals, catering services, and social, recreational, cultural, and spiritual activities.

Health services and rates: Residents on Plan 1 receive unlimited health care services and the only additional cost to the monthly fee is the cost of two additional meals per day. Residents on Plan 2 pay 80% of private per diem for the level of care received. Therapy area, dispensary, nutrition, and health information programs. Physical and occupational therapies, limited pharmacy and laboratory tests are available at additional cost. Each resident is required to designate a licensed physician as his or her personal physician and is responsible for the cost of these services.

- 20 Assisted Living suites $66/day
- 8 Intermediate Nursing beds $89/day
- 7 Skilled Nursing beds $89/ day

"As a wholly owned subsidiary of Grace Hospital, Grace Ridge is debt-free, which allows both the entrance and monthly fees to be kept lower. Our great location offers a mild climate and an outstanding view of the Blue Ridge Mountains as well as close proximity to larger cities and resort areas."

ABERNETHY CENTER

102 Leonard Avenue
Newton, NC 28658
(704) 464-8260
Donald P. Flick, executive director

Type of community: Continuing Care, modified contract

Located on a 120 rolling acres just outside of Newton, the community consists of modern brick-and-steel buildings. The grounds offer beautiful landscaping with woods and gardens. The health center has a new wing. The campus is only 40 miles from Charlotte and ten miles from Hickory, where outstanding medical, cultural, educational, and shopping activities are available.

Financial plan: Entrance fee plus monthly fee. Entrance fee decreases from 100% and after five years remains at 55%.

Ownership and management: Owned and operated by United Church Retirement Homes, Inc., affiliated with the Southern Conference of the United Church of Christ. Opened in 1971

Minimum age: 62 years.

Population: 350 residents; 85% women, 15% men, 30% couples.

Number of units: 78 Independent Living apartments; 40 Assisted Living units, 174 Skilled Nursing beds.

Dining plan: None included in the monthly fee. Meals available at extra charge. Private dining space.

Services: *Included in the monthly fee:* Weekly housekeeping and flat-linen services, scheduled transportation, parking.

At additional cost: Beauty/barbershop, gift shop, guest accommodations.

Activities: Activities director. Game room, darkroom, complete workshop, television room, swimming pool, trips, library.

INDEPENDENT LIVING HOUSING

Type/size of apartment	*Entrance fee*	*Monthly fee single/double**
1-Bedroom, 875 sq. ft.	$47,250–53,000	$255/320
2-Bedroom, 1,150 sq. ft.	$49,750–63,500	$280/345
Duplex, 1,200 sq. ft.	$68,250–115,000	$295/360
Cottage, 1,500 sq. ft.	$82,000–110,500	$330/395

**Custom-designed units also available. All utilities except telephone included in the monthly fee. Fully equipped kitchen, carpeting, 24-hour emergency call system, individually controlled heating and air-conditioning.*

Availability: Waiting list. Six months to one year for Independent and Assisted Living.

Health services and rates: Residents are allowed 12 free health center days plus 12 nurse visits per year.

- 40 Assisted Living units $67/day
- 174 Intermediate and Skilled Nursing beds
  - Semiprivate $103/day
  - Private $122/day

"Abernethy Center offers a full Continuum of Care and a variety of à la carte options to suit residents' needs. Our refund policy for entrance fees is designed for middle-income people."

QUAIL HAVEN VILLAGE

200 Blake Boulevard
Pinehurst, NC 28374
(910) 295-2294
Susan McKenzie, marketing director

Type of community: Nonprofit Independent and Assisted Living

Located on 18 acres in south Pinehurst, Quail Haven Village offers a resort atmosphere. Situated within walking distance of the post office, banks, and golf courses, 27 one-story traditionally designed buildings make up the campus featuring a brick clubhouse in the center. Sports, including golf, tennis, and horseback riding, are available nearby. Excellent medical facilities are in the area.

Financial plan: Monthly rental fee.

Ownership and management: Owned by Morgan Keegan, Inc., Memphis. Managed by CRSA of Memphis. Opened in 1986.

Minimum age: No requirements.

Population: 126 residents; 80% women, 20% men, 10% couples.

Number of units: 97 Independent Living residences; 60 Assisted Living units.

Dining plan: One meal per day included in the monthly rental fee; others available at cost. Catering services available. Two community buildings will accommodate up to 50 for private sit-down dinner.

Services: *Included in the monthly fee:* Weekly housekeeping, scheduled transportation.

At additional cost: Barber/beautyshop, guest accommodations.

Activities: Two full-time activities directors. Card room, billiards, gardening, exercise room, walking trail, library, and living room.

INDEPENDENT LIVING HOUSING

Type/size of apartment	*Monthly rental fee*
1-Bedroom, 520–590 sq. ft.	$999–1,469
2-Bedroom, 690–781 sq. ft.	$1,299–1,809
2-Bedroom/2-bath, 1,210 sq. ft.	$2,199–2,399

For double occupancy add $200 to the monthly rental fee. All utilities except telephone included. Fully equipped kitchen, individually controlled heating and air-conditioning, wall-to-wall carpeting, 24-hour emergency call system. Seven floor plans available.

Availability: Some units available; waiting list for larger apartments.

Health services and rates: Residents receive six days free per year in domiciliary care unit. Medical director on campus. Will assist in locating residents in Skilled Nursing facility if necessary.

- 60 Assisted Living beds $58/day

"Special features of Quail Haven include a wonderful, caring staff, its nonprofit status, and 18 acres of beautifully sculptured grounds."

ARBOR ACRES, THE TRIAD UNITED METHODIST HOME, INC.

1240 Arbor Road
Winston-Salem, NC 27104-1197
(910) 724-7921
Dixie L. Clark, director of admissions

Type of community: Not-for-profit Continuing Care, all-inclusive contract

Accreditation: Continuing Care Accreditation Commission

Independent Living maisonettes and cottage units are spaced throughout 70 acres of gentle rolling hills. Studio apartments and dining room are in three wings, which surround a small lake with fountain. Walkways are enclosed. The community is located five minutes from downtown Winston-Salem and Lake Forest and the Coliseum, three minutes from Little Theater, four hours from the beach, and two hours from the mountains. Arbor Acres offers easy access to multiple shopping centers, theater, community service organizations, recreational parks, and major hospitals.

Financial plan: Entrance fee plus monthly fee. Entrance fee is refundable less $2,500 ($5,000 if two persons enter under one residency agreement) and less 2% a month for the first 50 months of residency. Members of the United Methodist Church are eligible to apply for financial assistance.

Ownership and management: Established as a ministry of the Western North Carolina Conference of the United Methodist Church. Board of directors composed of 37 members of the church. Opened in 1980.

Minimum age: 65 years (if couple, spouse must be at least 60).

Population: 400 residents. Majority of residents are Methodists from North Carolina; however, more than eight denominations from across the United States are represented.

Number of units: 76 Independent Living studios, 8 courtyard apartments, 76 maisonettes, 15 cottages; 29-bed Assisted Living facility, 125-bed Intermediate and Skilled Nursing center.

Dining plan: Three meals are included in the monthly fee for residential wings. Meals are optional for courtyard apartments, maisonettes, and cottages.

INDEPENDENT LIVING HOUSING

Residential apartments	*Entrance fee*	*Monthly fee single/double**
Studio, 359 sq. ft.	$22,000	$1,156/1,741
Efficiency, 359 sq. ft.	$22,000	$1,166/1,751
Courtyard apartments		
1-Bedroom, 560 sq. ft.	$32,000	$1,267/1,817
2-Bedroom, 800 sq. ft.	$45,000	$1,298/1,848
Maisonettes		
1-Bedroom, 800 sq. ft.	$53,000	$1,307/1,847
2-Bedroom, 800 sq. ft.	$75,000–112,000	$1,317/1,857
Cottages		
1,800–2,000 sq. ft.	$114,000/161,000	$1,355/1,899

**All utilities except telephone are included in the monthly fee. All apartments have wall-to-wall carpeting and full kitchens. Maisonettes and cottages have washer/dryers and individually controlled heating and air-conditioning.*

Services: *Included in the monthly fee:* Weekly housekeeping, minor personal appliance repair, parking space, flat-linen service, daily telephone check by staff, limited storage space.

At additional cost: Washer/dryer on each floor of apartment wings.

Activities: Gardening, painting, crafts, ceramics, woodworking, music, drama, billiards, bowling, shuffleboard, golf, croquet, swimming and swimnastics. Board game nights, travelogues, exercise programs, men's club meetings, day trips, birdwatching, art exhibits, diners' club, walking program, birthday parties, films. Many opportunities for worship, prayer, and Bible study.

Availability: Waiting list. Studios and nursing care units are most frequently available.

Health services and rates: Preventive health care through special consultations and seminars. Residents receive limited number of complimentary days of infirmary care for temporary minor ailments.

- 29-Bed Assisted Living unit
  Semiprivate $1,924/month*
  Private $2,150/month*

**Nonresident entrance fee: $22,000.*

- 125-Bed Intermediate and Skilled Nursing facility; includes 22-bed Alzheimer's unit
  Semiprivate $112/day*
  Private $125/day*

**Nonresident entrance fee: $2,500.*

"The Triad United Methodist Home is accredited by the Continuing Care Accreditation Commission of the American Association of Homes for the Aging. Essentially the industry's 'Good Housekeeping seal of approval,' accreditation is awarded to communities that have a clearly defined mission and that conform to rigorous CCAC standards. Arbor Acres has also been granted EAGLE (Educational Assessment Guidelines Leading Toward Excellence) designation by the United Methodist Association of Health and Welfare Ministries. Like CCAC accreditation, EAGLE recognizes and promotes the exemplary programming, including spiritual programming, that The Triad Home offers its residents. We believe healthy life is one that is fulfilled spiritually, physically, and socially. All residents are encouraged to achieve their full potential for health."

OHIO

ROCKYNOL RETIREMENT COMMUNITY

1150 West Market Street
Akron, OH 44313
(216) 867-2150
Terry Trivino, director of marketing

Type of community: Not-for-profit Continuing Care, modified contract

Accreditation: Continuing Care Accreditation Commission

The twin Rockynol Towers and a four-story brick Rockynol apartment building are located on 12 park-like acres in a well-established residential area. Scenic walkways surround Independent Living apartments, Assisted Living units, and health care center. A pond, stone bridge, and mature trees are on the property. Some of the many cultural, educational, and medical facilities within a three mile radius are Sand Run Park, Art Institute, YWCA and YMCA, City Hospital, General Hospital, Goodpark Golf, Quaker Square, Fairlawn country club, civic theater, main library, University of Akron, and various synagogues and churches.

Financial plan: Entrance fee plus monthly fee or monthly rental. If within the first 50 months of occupancy a resident terminates residency at Rockynol, the resident will receive a refund prorated to the nearest month. Entrance fee refunded less initial 10% and 2% per month of residency. Security deposit of one month's rent required for rental program.

INDEPENDENT LIVING HOUSING

Towers unit	*Entrance fee**	*Monthly fee**	*Monthly rental**
Studio, 294 sq. ft.	$28,000	$1,129	$1,599
1-Bedroom, 588 sq. ft.	$52,000	$1,575	$2,525
2-Bedroom, 882 sq. ft.	$74,000	$2,675	$3,999

**For double occupancy add $8,000 to the entrance fee, $482 to the monthly fee; $493 for 1-bedroom and $379 for 2-bedroom to the monthly rental.*

Rockynol apartments			
1-Bedroom, 575–653 sq. ft.	N/A	N/A	$1,323–1,486
2-Bedroom, 856–970 sq. ft.	N/A	N/A	$1,809–2,002
3-Bedroom, 1,325 sq. ft.	N/A	N/A	$2,454

**For double occupancy add $364 to the monthly rent. All utilities except telephone are included. All units have 24-hour emergency call system, cable TV, wall-to-wall carpeting, individually controlled heating and air-conditioning, fully equipped kitchen, cable TV. Some Rockynol apartments have balconies.*

Ownership and management: Owned and managed by Ohio Presbyterian Retirement Services, owner and operator of seven other communities across the state. One resident representative serves on the OPRS board of trustees with full voice and voting privileges. Opened in 1966.

Minimum age: 60 years.

Population: 271 residents; 78% women, 22% men, 19% couples.

Number of units: 79 Independent Living apartments; 64 Assisted Living units and 72 Skilled Nursing beds.

Dining plan: 25 meals per month included in the monthly rent for Rockynol apartments. Three meals per day included in the monthly fee for the Towers. Private dining room available.

Services: *Included in the monthly fee:* Weekly maid and laundry services (Towers only), free laundry facilities, scheduled transportation.

At additional cost: Garages, beauty/barbershop, guest accommodations.

Activities: Activities director. Library, art gallery, game and exercise room, Bible study, religious services, volunteering, breakfast club, antiques program, holiday concerts, bridge, sing-alongs, crafts, travelogues, bingo.

Availability: Waiting list.

Health services and rates: Residents receive seven free days of nursing care per year. Nursing home insurance program provides assistance with paying for extended stays in the health center. After 90 days, the insurance will cover $49/day of health care costs for as long as resident is in the health care center. The premium ($125/month for one person, $200/month for two) is included in the monthly rent for Rockynol apartment residents. Physical, occupational, and speech therapies and psychological services available. Respite care is available for $89 per day.

- 64 Assisted Living units

	Monthly fee	*Monthly rental*
Studio*	$1,679	$2,199
1-Bedroom*	$2,140	$3,120

**Nonresident entrance fee: $28,000 for studio, $52,000 for 1-bedroom. For 1-bedroom double occupancy add $8,000 to the entrance fee; $979 to the monthly fee; $1,014 to monthly rental.*

- 72-Bed health care center

	Resident	*Nonresident*
Semiprivate	$129/day	$115/day
Family semiprivate	$155/day	$141/day
Private	$155/day	$141/day

"Rockynol is distinguished by its longevity in the community. Services have been expanded as the needs of its senior population changes. Rockynol's health care philosophy reflects its mission and purposes. Residents are encouraged to achieve the highest level of wellness of which they are capable. Employees are trained to promote and enable the independence of each resident in a holistic, loving, comforting, and supportive manner."

CANTON REGENCY

4515 22nd Street, N.W.
Canton, OH 44708
(216) 477-7664
Christine K. Paul, admissions director

Type of community: Continuing Care, modified contract

This three-story community is built in a H-shape and offers an enclosed three-story garden atrium in the center. Canton Regency is close to Belden Village and other shopping centers, restaurants, theaters, and hospitals. Three levels of care are offered on-site: Assisted Living, Intermediate and Skilled Nursing.

Financial plan: Monthly rental. $450 fully refundable security deposit.

INDEPENDENT LIVING HOUSING

Type/size of apartment	*Monthly rental fee**
Studio, 396 sq. ft.	$987–1,097
1-Bedroom, 484 sq. ft.	$1,097–1,318
2-Bedroom, 748 sq. ft.	$1,759–1,869

**For double occupancy add $375 to the monthly fee. All utilities except telephone and cable TV included. Kitchenette, wall-to-wall carpeting, individually controlled heating and air-conditioning, 24-hour emergency call system.*

Ownership and management: Capital Realty. Opened in 1977.

Minimum age: 65 years (if couple, spouse must be at least 65).

Population: 232 residents; 80% women, 20% men, 12% couples.

Number of units: 148 Independent Living apartments; 32 Assisted Living apartments, 50 Intermediate and Skilled Nursing beds.

Dining plan: Breakfast and choice of lunch or dinner daily included in the monthly fee. Private dining room. Room service available for additional fee.

Services: *Included in the monthly fee:* Weekly housekeeping, flat-linen services, secure storage areas, scheduled transportation.

At additional cost: Beauty/barbershop, gift shop, guest accommodations, laundry rooms, pharmacy, dry cleaning, checkbook balancing, companion service arrangement, telephone reminders, mobile post office.

Activities: Exercise room/sauna, billiards table, dance floor, big-screen TV-VCR, library, movies, walking club (Happy Hoofers), travelogues, board and card games, Bible study, bowling, sing-alongs, spelling bees, nature walks.

Availability: Waiting list.

Health services and rates: Assistance with medication setups and reminders, laboratory services, individual and family counseling, physician, and podiatry clinics available for additional fee. Physical, occupational, whirlpool, and speech therapies available.

- 32-Room Assisted Living facility
  Private suite/bath $47/day
- 50-Bed nursing facility

	Intermediate Nursing	*Skilled Nursing*
Semiprivate	$75/day	$97/day
Private	$87/day	$85/day

"Coupling health care with the joy of living, Canton Regency offers a unique concept in care—a commitment to health and rehabilitation in a setting where personal strengths are encouraged."

LLANFAIR

1701 Llanfair Avenue
Cincinnati, OH 45224
(513) 681-4230
Sharon Menke, sales director

Type of community: Not-for-profit Continuing Care, modified contract

Accreditation: Continuing Care Accreditation Commission

Located in an urban parklike setting in the College Hill area of Cincinnati, Llanfair is situated on a 14-acre campus of trees, flower gardens, and walking paths. Independent Living, Assisted Living, and Skilled Nursing are available on campus. The community is centrally located within walking distance of shops and services, libraries, entertainment, excursions, and medical clinic and offers direct-route Queen City Metro service.

Financial plan: Entrance fee plus monthly fee. Non-refundable $100 application fee. Entrance fee is refundable on a prorated basis.

Ownership and management: Ohio Presbyterian Retirement Services, owner and manager of seven other communities across the state. Opened in 1956.

Minimum age: 60 years.

Population: 300 residents; 79% women, 21% men, 30% couples. About 62% of the residents are Presbyterian; residents of all backgrounds and faiths are welcome.

Number of units: 137 Independent Living apartments: 112 one- and two-bedroom apartments, 5 private 1 1/2 story homes, private rooms, 5 suites; 53 Assisted Living units, 75-bed health care center.

Dining plan: Three meals per day included in the monthly fee for Terrace residents. Evening meal for Larchwood/Belwood residents. Meal plans can be tailored.

Services: *Included in the monthly fee:* Terrace: Weekly housekeeping and laundry services. Larchwood/Belwood/cottages: Biweekly housekeeping and flat-linen services. Scheduled transportation is available for all residents.

At additional cost: Beauty/barbershop, sweet shop, minimarket, limited banking and postal services.

Activities: Musical performances, physical fitness, overnight outings, day excursions, picnics, festivals, billiards/card room, arts and crafts, gardening, walking trail with exercise stations, sundecks, library.

Availability: Waiting list depends upon type of accommodation.

Health services and rates: Seven days of Skilled or Intermediate Nursing care each year at no additional charge (except for personal care recipients). Llanfair

INDEPENDENT LIVING HOUSING

Terrace apartments	*Entrance fee**	*Monthly fee**
1-Room, 299 sq. ft.	$15,000	$1,065
Studio, 375 sq. ft.	$23,000	$1,300
1-Bedroom, 604 sq. ft.	$42,000	$1,556/1,981
2-Room suite, 600 sq. ft.	$33,000	$1,556/1,981
Large studio, 379 sq. ft.	$37,000	$1,556/1,981
Larchwood/Belwood		
1-Bedroom, 552 sq. ft.	$50,000–62,000	$702–1,127
1-Bedroom/patio, 552 sq. ft.	$55,000–65,000	$726–1,151
2-Bedroom, 852–1,073 sq. ft.	$74,000	$626–703
Cottage	$80,000	$605–682

**For Terrace apartments entrance fee is optional with higher monthly fee. All utilities except telephone included. Terrace: wall-to-wall carpeting, drapes, individually controlled heating and air-conditioning, 24-hour emergency call system. Largest suites have kitchenettes. Furnishings can be provided. Larchwood/Belwood: wall-to-wall carpeting, individually controlled heating and air-conditioning, fully equipped kitchen, 24-hour emergency call system. Pets are allowed in cottages only.*

Care (personal and health-related services in the resident's apartment) available with 24-hour staff. Additional charges depend on services required. Dentist, podiatrist, physical and occupational therapy offered. Supportive care unit for residents with Alzheimer's disease and related disorders. Nursing home insurance available at group rates. Nonresidents have choice of entrance fee and lower monthly/daily fees or no entrance fee and monthly/daily fees that are higher.

- 53 Assisted Living units

	Entrance fee	*Monthly fee*
1-Room	$8,200–12,000	$1,616
Studio	$20,000	$2,010–3,288
2-Room suite	$27,000	$1,876

- 75-Bed health care center with Intermediate and Skilled Nursing care

	*Daily fee**	*Daily fee only*
Semiprivate	$125	$136
Private	$143–153	$154-165

**Nonresident entrance fee: $8,200*

"For more than three decades Llanfair has been devoted to the physical, mental and, spiritual well-being of older adults. Llanfair offers a vital and enriching lifestyle with a community of interesting, friendly people from residents to staff and volunteers. Our campus center provides a place for social, educational, and cultural gatherings where you can experience the best of life at Llanfair."

MAPLE KNOLL VILLAGE

11100 Springfield Pike
Cincinnati, OH 45246
(513) 782-2717
Pat Reddish/Jeannie Paulini, retirement counselors

Type of community: Nonprofit Continuing Care, modified contract

Accreditation: Continuing Care Accreditation Commission

Maple Knoll Village is located on 54 wooded acres in greater Cincinnati. The grounds feature a duck pond, gazebo, walking trails, and gardens throughout. Single-level, cluster cottages as well as mid-rise and high-rise buildings for apartments and health center are available. Winter garden atrium, shops, bank, library, beauty/barbershop, and auditorium are all on the village's main street. Springdale Mall, Glendale Village Square, Tri-County Shopping Mall, Northgate and Forest Fair malls, several area churches and hospitals, public library, recreation, sports, and cultural activities are all located nearby.

Financial plan: Entrance fee plus monthly fee or monthly rental. Those paying an entrance fee (refundable life-use fee) pay a reduced monthly fee equal to the standard monthly fee minus 1% per month of the entrance fee paid. A resident may increase the entrance fee payment, which will result in an even greater reduction of the monthly fee. The range established is between $49,500 and $80,000. Refund of entrance fee amortizes over period of 8.3 years and in no case will exceed 90%.

Ownership and management: Owned and operated by Southwestern Ohio Seniors' Services, Inc. Opened in 1977.

Minimum age: 60 years.

Population: 552 residents; 90% women, 10% men, 18% couples.

Number of units: 77 Independent Living cottages (80 new cottages under construction) and 116 congregate apartments, 150 subsidized apartments; (60 Assisted Living apartments under construction), 174-bed health care center.

Dining plan: Congregate apartments include two meals per day in the monthly fee; Independent cottages include one meal per day in monthly fee. (Some cottages have optional meal plans.)

INDEPENDENT LIVING HOUSING

Type/size of apartment	*Entrance fee*	*Monthly fee**	*Monthly rent*
1-Bedroom, 540 sq. ft.	$19,000–20,600	$1,252–1,401	$1,442–1,607
2-Bedroom, 900 sq. ft.	$36,500–37,100	$1,534–1,636	$1,899–2,007
Cottages			
1-Bedroom, 825 sq. ft.	$22,500	$1,383	$1,298
2-Bedroom, 1,355–1,540 sq. ft.	$26,500–49,500	$1,685	$1,575–1,723
**2-Bedroom, 1,500–1,760 sq. ft.	$80,000–115,000	$1,800–2,200	N/A

**For double occupancy add $250–316 to the monthly fee. Apartments have 24-hour emergency call system, fully equipped kitchens, wall-to-wall carpeting, individually controlled heating and air-conditioning. Some cottages have washer/dryer, others have centrally located laundry facilities. **Eighty English manor–style cottages are under construction on 12 wooded acres in northeast section of Maple Knoll Village. Clustered in groups of two, four, and six homes, and single-level cottages with attached garages. Some have 9 1/2-foot ceilings, others vaulted ceilings. Five floor plans available. 80% of entrance fee is refundable.*

Services: *Included in the monthly fee:* Scheduled transportation, weekly housekeeping and flat-linen services.

At additional cost: Garages, beauty/barbershop, guest apartments.

Activities: Interdenominational chapel, ceramics, crafts workshops, carpentry workshops, recreational trips, game room, club room, library, movies, plays, weaving, exercises.

Availability: Waiting list for some accommodations.

Health services and rates: Residents receive 30 days per year free health care. Health care center offers ophthalmology, audiology, physical therapy, podiatry, dermatology, dentistry, otolaryngology, and general practice. Nationally recognized Alzheimer's care unit. 60-apartment Assisted Living facility plus health and wellness center, with indoor swimming pool, exercise rooms, and whirlpool spa, under construction.

- 174-Bed health care center
  - Semiprivate $127/day
  - Private $158–173/day

"Maple Knoll Village has a history of outstanding service to older adults for more than 145 years. For the past three years, we have been named as one of the top Continuing Care retirement communities in the nation by *New Choices* magazine. The Maple Knoll Center for Older Adults is a multipurpose senior center that provides services and activities for the neighboring six communities. The Center, located across the street from Maple Knoll Village, also serves the homebound through a meals-on-wheels program and offers counseling and referral services. Maple Knoll Child Center is a Montessori preschool for children three to six years of age, providing a place where older and younger persons can come together. A comprehensive program for the elderly goes beyond the provision of services within its own community and attempts to affect changes within society that lead toward a fuller life for all older people. We believe old age should not limit or change a person's right to experience life to its fullest through self-determination."

MARJORIE P. LEE

3550 Shaw Avenue
Cincinnati, OH 45208
(513) 871-2090
Ruth Weaver, director of admissions and marketing

Type of community: Nonprofit Continuing Care, modified contract

Located in the heart of Cincinnati's Hyde Park on a tree-lined residential street, this community offers Independent Living residences and Assisted Living and Skilled Nursing facilities located in a six-floor brick building. Each level of living has a courtyard with fountain. Residents take pride in their flower and vegetable gardens. The community is 1½ blocks from shopping, public library, banks, and restaurants in one of Cincinnati's most prestigious suburbs.

Financial plan: Entrance fee plus monthly fee or monthly fee only. Entrance fee plan offers refund provision based upon 100 months, annual health service benefit of $1,500 (shared by couples and not cumulative), and lower monthly fee due to an entrance fee credit determined by your age at time of entry. Monthly fee payment plan entitles resident to annual health service benefit of $500 (shared by couples and not cumulative). Paying the entrance fee entitles resident to credit based on age at entrance—66–70, .8%; 71–75, .9%; and 76+, 1.0%—to be deducted from monthly fee.

Ownership and management: Episcopal Retirement Homes, Inc., affiliated with Episcopal Diocese of Southern Ohio, owner and manager of communities in Cincinnati, Columbus, and Dayton. Opened in 1963.

Minimum age: 65 years.

Population: 223 residents; 80% women, 20% men, 14% couples.

Number of units: 117 Independent Living apartments; 16 Assisted Living suites, 60 Skilled Nursing beds.

Dining plan: Three meals per day included in the monthly fee. Continental breakfast room service. Private dining room and party room.

Services: *Included in the monthly fee:* Scheduled transportation, weekly housekeeping and flat-linen services.

At additional cost: Beauty/barbershop, branch bank, convenience store, guest accommodations, heated

INDEPENDENT LIVING HOUSING

Type/size of apartment	*Entrance fee**	*Monthly fee**
Studio, 400 sq. ft.	$16,000	$997
Deluxe studio, 400 sq. ft.	$22,100	$1,403
Alcove, 600 sq. ft.	$33,000	$1,694
1-Bedroom, 750 sq. ft.	$40,000	$1,935
Deluxe 1-bedroom, 800 sq. ft.	$42,000	$2,178
2-Bedroom, 950 sq. ft.	$58,000	$2,419
Deluxe 2-bedroom, 1,150 sq. ft.	$70,200	$2,963

**For double occupancy add $3,000 for studio, alcove, and 1-bedroom and $5,000 for 2-bedroom to the entrance fee; $600 to the monthly fee. All utilities except telephone included. Individually controlled heating and air-conditioning, 24-hour emergency call system, fully equipped kitchen, wall-to-wall carpeting.*

underground garage, grocery delivery, personal transportation, additional housekeeping and maintenance.

Activities: Lectures, travelogues, bridge, parties, movies on wide screen, exercise room and classes, van trips, concerts, activity center with crafts tools and supplies, gardening, library, music room, shuffleboard, billiards.

Availability: Limited.

Health services and rates: Two staff physicians hold office hours on-site twice weekly at no extra charge. Specialists in ophthalmology, otolaryngology, podiatry, and psychiatry and dental and physical therapy services available at additional cost. Home services from Enriched Living available on a fee-for-service basis.

- 16 Assisted Living units

	Care 1/ month	*Care 2/ month*
Studio, 250 sq. ft.	$1,770	$1,992
Studio, 300 sq. ft.	$2,076	$2,298
Studio, 350 sq. ft.	$2,321	$2,543
Deluxe studio, 450 sq. ft.	$2,687*	$2,909*

**For double occupancy add $580 to the monthly fee.*

- 60 Skilled Nursing beds

Semiprivate	$108/day
Private	$124/day
Deluxe private	$150/day

"Marjorie P. Lee's continuum of care facility is all under one roof, allowing easy 24-hour access to every level of care for people visiting a spouse or friend. We have six floors with lots of ancillary space for residents to use as an extension of their apartments."

FIRST COMMUNITY VILLAGE

1800 Riverside Drive
Columbus, OH 43212
(614) 486-9511
Rick Davis, vice president of marketing

Type of community: Nonprofit Continuing Care, modified contract

Accreditation: Continuing Care Accreditation Commission

Overlooking the scenic Scioto River Valley on 34 acres, First Community Village has tree-shaded lawns and rolling landscaped grounds. The community is located in suburban Arlington, less than ten minutes from downtown Columbus. A variety of ground-level floor plans exist within Independent Living. On-site Assisted Living facility is available as well as a Skilled Nursing facility.

Financial plan: Entrance fee plus monthly fee or monthly rental. Entrance fee is 100% refundable during first year and on declining basis for three more years. Monthly rental option available in some apartments.

Ownership and management: First Community Church. Opened in 1963.

Minimum age: 65 years for residents paying entrance fee; 55 for rental residents.

Population: 420 residents; 75% women, 25% men, 15% couples.

Number of units: 150 Independent Living apartments; 110 Assisted Living units, 175 Skilled Nursing beds.

Dining plan: No meals included in the monthly fees (except single North Garden) listed. Two meals available for an additional $305 per month; three meals for $490. Residents may change food service arrangements the first day of every month.

Services: *Included in the monthly fee:* Weekly housekeeping and flat-linen services, scheduled transportation, parking.

INDEPENDENT LIVING HOUSING

Terrace apartments	*Entrance fee**	*Monthly fee**	*Monthly rental*
Studio, 369 sq. ft.	$26,500	$795	$864
1-Bedroom, 505 sq. ft.	$53,500	$975	$1,328
Custom suite, 738 sq. ft.	$82,500	$1,226	N/A
North Garden			
Single, 250 sq. ft.	$20,500	$1,100	$533
1-Bedroom, 500 sq. ft.	$53,500	$1,204	$1,500
2-Bedroom, 1,000 sq. ft.	$93,000	$2,021	N/A
South Garden			
1-Bedroom, 500 sq. ft.	$53,500	$1,204	$1,620
2-Bedroom, 1,000 sq. ft.	$93,000	$2,021	$2,303

**For double occupancy add $6,000 to the entrance fee, approximately $350 to the monthly fee. All utilities except telephone and cable TV included. All apartments have carpeting, 24-hour emergency call system, full kitchens (except North Garden singles). Some Terrace apartments have deck or patio, washer/dryer. North Garden apartments also have draperies.*

At additional cost: Beauty/barbershop, bank, guest accommodations, store.

Activities: Arts and crafts, concerts, games, exercise classes, excursions, library, lectures.

Availability: Limited.

Health services and rates: Physical therapy, pharmacy services, social services, laboratory, X ray facilities available. If resident requires temporary recovery period while retaining an apartment, there is no additional charge except for meals and/or nursing. When long-term care is required, residents who have paid an entrance fee pay half of the Skilled Nursing daily fee. Rental residents do not receive discount, but are given priority admittance. Village finance department will assist with filling out and filing medical forms.

- 110 Assisted Living units
  Single $1,746/month
  Double $3,002/month
- 175-Bed Skilled Nursing facility
  Semiprivate $112/day
  Private $137/day

"First Community Village is a church-affiliated retirement community. One of the nation's first four to be accredited by the Continuing Care Accreditation Commission. Admission is open to all. We emphasize growth of body, mind, and soul through a thorough schedule of activities along with a close proximity to learning institutions such as Ohio State University."

THE FORUM AT KNIGHTSBRIDGE

4590 Knightsbridge Boulevard
Columbus, OH 43214
(614) 451-6793
Lynn Gentry, leasing counselor

Type of community: Continuing Care, modified contract

Three-story traditional brick-and-stucco buildings house Independent Living aprtments surrounding a community center that looks out on a picturesque wooded area. Located on the outskirts of Upper Arlington, one of the finest suburbs of Columbus, numerous cultural and shopping possibilities are available.

INDEPENDENT LIVING HOUSING

Type/size of apartment	*Monthly rental fee**
1-Bedroom, 585–679 sq. ft.	$1,675–2,095
2-Bedroom, 864–1,135 sq. ft.	$2,410–3,565
2-Bedroom/den, 1,205 sq. ft.	$3,985

**For double occupancy add $425 to the monthly fee. All utilities except telephone are included. Wall-to-wall carpeting, draperies, 24-hour emergency call system, fully equipped, all-electric kitchen, individually controlled heating and air-conditioning. Bay window, patio, or balcony.*

Financial plan: Monthly rental plan.

Ownership and management: The Forum Group, Inc., owner and manager of 27 retirement communities in the United States. Opened in 1989.

Minimum age: 62 years.

Population: 130 residents; 70% women, 30% men, 7% couples

Number of units: 120 Independent Living apartments; 60 ambassador suites (Assisted Living), 60 Intermediate and Skilled Nursing beds.

Dining plan: Resident's choice of one main meal plus continental breakfast per day included in the monthly fee.

Services: *Included in the monthly fee:* Weekly housekeeping and flat-linen services, self-service laundry facilities.

At additional cost: Beauty/barbershop, gift shop, garages/carports, ice-cream parlor/country store.

Activities: Library, billiards and game room, guest lectures, movies, classes, exercise classes, travel tours, transportation to special cultural and sporting events.

Availability: Limited.

Health services and rates: Residents receive 15 days per year of free health care in the health center or a lifetime total of 60 days. Long-term care insurance is available for those who qualify.

- 60 Ambassador suites (Assisted Living)* $1,595–3,195/month

  **Five floor plans available, all with kitchenette and private bath. Some suites are furnished.*

- 60-Bed nursing facility
  Semiprivate $103/day
  Private $132/day

"The Forum is a full-service, luxury rental retirement community designed to provide a pleasant and worry-free atmosphere. We are a community committed to consistent, quality services; resident satisfaction is our number one goal. All residences plus community center and three levels of health care are conveniently located under one roof."

FRIENDSHIP VILLAGE

5800 Forest Hills Boulevard
Columbus, OH 43231
(614) 890-8282
Claire Zwilling, director of marketing

Type of community: Not-for-profit Continuing Care, all-inclusive contract

Located in a beautiful suburban setting on 25 scenic acres, Friendship Village offers landscaped grounds that feature walkways and park benches. Unique design of the community maximizes natural light to enhance

INDEPENDENT LIVING HOUSING

Type/size of apartment	*Entrance fee*	*Monthly fee**
Studio, 287 sq. ft.	$29,500	$827
Alcove, 476 sq. ft.	$47,400	$887
1-Bedroom, 574 sq. ft.	$69,900	$947
2-Bedroom, 789 sq. ft.	$86,300–90,900	$1,122–1,185
2-Bedroom/garden, 864 sq. ft.	$96,100	$1,185
2-Bedroom/special, 1,004 sq. ft.	$110,800	$1,185

Note: *Return of Capital plan entrance fees (Plan 2) range from $48,675–182,820. Monthly fees are the same as entrance fee Plan 1. *For double occupancy (except studio) add $531 to the monthly fee. All utilities are included. Individually controlled heating and air-conditioning, humidifier, all-electric kitchen, carpeting, 24-hour emergency call system.*

all the common areas. The community contains Independent Living apartments and a health center and is within walking distance of shopping, banking, medical offices, and entertainment. Columbus is nearby.

Financial plan: Entrance fee plus monthly fee. Two plans: **1)** Traditional endowment plan in which a percentage of the entrance fee is refundable. **2)** Return of Capital plan, which returns up to 90% of the entrance fee to resident or resident's estate.

Ownership and management: Managed by Life Care Services Corporation of Des Moines, Iowa, planner, developer, and manager of more than 50 communities throughout the United States. Opened in 1978.

Minimum age: 62 years.

Population: 375 residents; 78% women, 12% men, 45 couples.

Number of units: 300 Independent Living apartments; 90-bed health center.

Dining plan: One meal per day included in the monthly fee. Additional meals available at extra charge. Special diet and tray service available. Private dining room.

Services: *Included in the monthly fee:* Biweekly housekeeping, weekly flat-linen service, scheduled transportation.

At additional cost: Beauty/barbershop, bank, village store.

Activities: Library, arts and crafts, woodworking shop, bridge tournaments, billards tables, exercise classes, outside excursions, personal gardening areas, lectures, films, recitals.

Availability: Priority waiting list.

Health services and rates: Residents receive unlimited health care. The only additional costs are for the two additional meals per day and ancillary charges for therapy services. Health center offers emergency care, long-term care, and therapy services.

- 90-Bed health center (semiprivate and private rooms)

"Continuing Care retirement is a concept that, more than any other alternative, permits residents to keep the very best of what they have attained without becoming dependent on others and assures them of the independence, dignity, and quality of life they've earned."

Mary and Sam, 78 and 79 years

Parkway Village, Little Rock, Arkansas

"If we should deteriorate to the point where we both need help, our children have growing families and have more than enough to take care of."

Sam retired 20 years ago. He and Mary moved into a condominium as a first step in their retirement. About eight years ago they began looking for a Continuing Care community. "We looked in Colorado, where our two children and four grandchildren live, Michigan, Tennessee, Pennsylvania, and Illinois," Mary and Sam explain. "One day we were looking through an army magazine when we saw an ad for Parkway Village. We have always liked Arkansas, so we went to take a look." Mary fell in love at first visit and Sam found that Parkway Village had all the facilities they desired. "We wanted to be near a big airport so we could travel easily and we also wanted to live in a cottage, not an apartment," he says.

Mary and Sam also wanted to move in while they were healthy and active so they could not only enjoy the community but make the decision to move for themselves. It was critical to them that they find a place where all of their needs could be met, a community that had all levels of care available as well as services they felt they would ultimately need. "For example, I think it's important to know that transportation will be available if and when we are no longer able to drive," comments Sam.

While some people gravitate to certain communities to be near their children, Mary and Sam felt it was of first and paramount importance to find a community that was self-contained and offered excellent medical care. "If we should deteriorate to the point where we both need help," says Mary, "our children have growing families and have more than enough to take care of. We felt that we're better off being taken care of by medical professionals."

Advice from Mary and Sam: Move in when you're young enough to get around and get acquainted. As long you can move, you can get around and make friends. "Unfortunately, we run into people who should be living here, but aren't," says Sam.

WESLEY GLEN RETIREMENT CENTER

5155 North High Street
Columbus, OH 43214-1592
(614) 888-7492
Jill Clegg, marketing director

Type of community: Nonprofit Continuing Care, modified contract

Located on 11 acres of rolling land, two eight-story modern towers contain Independent Living, Assisted Living, and Skilled Nursing accommodations. A third tower and 14 patio homes have been built and occupied recently. A woodsy ravine with a stream provides beautiful views and is ideal for walking, picnics, and gardening. The community is located south of Worthington and next door to one of Columbus's major shopping centers.

Financial plan: Entrance fee plus monthly fee or monthly fee only. $200 deposit with application.

Ownership and management: Methodist Retirement Center of Central Ohio. Opened in 1969.

Minimum age: 65 years.

Population: 275 residents; 79% women, 21% men, 22% couples.

INDEPENDENT LIVING HOUSING

Type/size of apartment	*Entrance fee**	*Monthly fee**	*Monthly fee only**
1-Room, 234–290 sq. ft.	$16,500–20,600	$654–695	$803–885
2-Room, 365–553 sq. ft.	$30,000–49,500	$879–1,085	$1,177–2,272
Patio Homes			
1-Bedroom, 968 sq. ft.	$89,000	$1,568	$2,270
2-Bedroom, 1,180 sq. ft.	$106,800	$1,818	$2,680

**For double occupancy add $12,700–14,600 to the entrance fee, $424 to the monthly fee. All utilities except telephone included. Individually controlled heating and air-conditioning, 24-hour emergency call system, wall-to-wall carpeting, draperies. Some 2-room apartments have kitchenettes.*

Number of units: 181 Independent Living apartments and 14 patio homes; 25 Assisted Living apartments,83-bed health care center, 20 special care beds.

Dining plan: Three meals per day are included in the monthly fee for apartment residents; one meal per day for patio home residents. Private dining room.

Services: *Included in the monthly fee:* Weekly housekeeping and flat-linen sevices, parking space.

At additional cost: Beauty/barbershop, gift shop, snack shop, scheduled transportation.

Activities: Library, arts and crafts, woodworking shop, gardening, birdwatching, book reviews, concerts.

Availability: Limited. Priority waiting list.

Health services and rates: Resident physician, podiatrist, and physical therapy facilities. A new Assisted Living and Alzheimer's facility has recently been completed and is operating to capacity.

- 25 Assisted Living apartments $65–85/day
- 83-Bed health care center with Intermediate and Skilled Nursing

	Resident	*Nonresident*
Semiprivate	$71/day	$109/day
Private	$80/day	N/A

"Wesley Glen is a community of good neighbors and gracious retirement living in a supportive Christian environment."

WESTMINSTER-THURBER RETIREMENT COMMUNITY

645-717 Neil Avenue
Columbus, OH 43215
(614) 228-8888
Joan Parks, director of marketing/admissions

Type of community: Not-for-profit Continuing Care, modified contract

Accreditation: Continuing Care Accreditation Commission

Surrounded by ten wooded acres located in the restored neighborhood of Victorian Village, Westminster-Thurber is five minutes from Ohio State University and downtown Columbus. The community consists of two high-rise buildings, complete with a rooftop swimming pool that looks out on the skyline of Ohio's capital city. Shopping and parks are within walking distance.

Financial plan: Entrance fee plus monthly fee or monthly fee only.

Ownership and management: Ohio Presbyterian Retirement Services, owner and manager of seven other retirement communities in Ohio. Opened in 1965.

Minimum age: 60 years.

INDEPENDENT LIVING HOUSING

Thurber Towers	*Entrance fee*	*Monthly fee**	*Monthly fee only**
Efficiency, 370 sq. ft.	$23,700	$529	N/A
1-Bedroom, 427–514 sq. ft.	$47,900–52,000	$585	$1,350–1,420
2-Bedroom, 630–860 sq. ft.	$60,300–75,000	$660	$1,625–1,860
Deluxe, 1,494 sq. ft.	$87,500 and up	$1,044	$2,555

**For double occupancy add $330 to the monthly fee. Telephone, electricity are billed directly to residents. Individually controlled heating and air-conditioning, wall-to-wall carpeting, window sheers and draperies, 24-hour emergency call system. Many apartments have balconies.*

Westminster	*Entrance fee*	*Monthly fee**	*Monthly fee only**
Studio, 365 sq. ft.	$23,500	$1,050	$1,435
1-Bedroom, 730 sq. ft.	$48,000	$1,440	$2,225
2-Bedroom, 1,095 sq. ft.	$70,000	$1,830	$3,015

**There is an additional fee for double occupancy, ranging from $225 to $340. All utilities except telephone included. Wall-to-wall carpeting, window draperies, 24-hour emergency call system, individually controlled thermostats.*

Population: 350 residents; 75% women, 25% men, 20% couples.

Number of units: 166 Independent Living apartments in Thurber Towers and 36 apartments in Westminster; 45 personal care apartments, 92-bed health care center.

Dining plan: Thurber Towers residents may purchase meals on an à la carte basis. Westminster residents have three meals per day included in the monthly fee.

Services: *Included in the monthly fee:* Laundry facilities on each floor of Thurber Towers.

At additional cost: Beauty/barbershop, dry cleaning, transportation, guest accommodations, scheduled housekeeping.

Activities: Rooftop swimming pool, library, exercise room, arts and crafts, woodworking shop, billiards room, gardening, planned excursions, symphony, residents' council.

Availability: Limited. Priority waiting list.

Health services and rates: Independent Living residents who have paid an entrance fee receive seven days per year of nursing care at no additional cost. Nursing home insurance is included in Thurber residents' monthly fee. Services offered at additional cost: physical, occupational, and speech therapies, podiatry, in-home health care, laboratory tests, pharmacy, and physicians' services.

- 45 Personal care apartments

	*Monthly fee**	*Monthly fee only*
Studio	$1,655	$2,050
2-Room	$2,175	$2,980

** Nonresident entrance fee: $23,500 for studio, $48,000 for 2-room. For 2-room double occupancy add $600 to the monthly fee. All utilities except telephone included plus three meals per day and housekeeping and flat-linen services.*

- 92-Bed health care center

	*Daily rate**	*Daily rate only*
Semiprivate	$104	$114

**Nonresident entrance fee: $23,500.*

"The greatest assets of Westminster-Thurber are our location, five minutes from the Ohio State University campus and from downtown Columbus; the fact that our residents pay only for services they need; our professional and caring staff; and our being part of an established retirement corporation, the Ohio Presbyterian Retirement Services."

TRINITY COMMUNITY

3218 Indian Ripple Road
Dayton, OH 45440
(513) 426-8481
Margery Jones, admissions/marketing director

Type of community: Nonprofit Continuing Care, modified contract

Located on 28 acres in a quiet country setting, Trinity's one- and three-story brick buildings house Independent Living apartments and cottages plus Assisted Living and Skilled Nursing. The community features a solarium, library, and chapel as well as lounge areas in every wing.

Financial plan: Entrance fee plus monthly fee (cottages); monthly or daily fee (apartments).

Ownership and management: United Church Homes. Opened in 1974.

Minimum age: None.

Population: 185 residents; 75% women, 25% men, 6% couples.

Number of units: 58 Independent Living apartments, 8 cottages; 43 Assisted Living apartments, 106 Skilled Nursing beds.

Dining plan: Three meals per day included in apartment resident's monthly fee. Cottage residents have one meal per day included in the monthly fee. Private dining room and catering available.

Services: *Included in the monthly fee:* Weekly housekeeping and flat-linen services, scheduled transportation.

At additional cost: Gift shop, beauty/barbershop.

Activities: Library, exercise classes, woodworking, billards tables, arts and crafts, walks, musical programs, bingo, painting classes, trips to the theater, sports and other community events.

INDEPENDENT LIVING HOUSING

Type/size of apartment	*Monthly fee single/double**
1-Room, 276 sq. ft.	$1,381.50/1,681.50
Double-room, 335 sq. ft.	$1,969.80/2,269.80
Efficiency, 450 sq. ft.	$2,097/2,397
1-Bedroom, 552 sq. ft.	$2,160.60/2,460.60
2-Bedroom, 776 sq. ft.	$2,319.60/2,619.60
*Cottages**	
2-Bedroom, 1,200 sq. ft.	$585/877.50

**Cottage residents pay $50,000 entrance fee. Daily fees for all accommodations except cottages range from $63 to $100. All utilities except telephone included. Individually controlled heating and air-conditioning, humidifier, fully equipped kitchen, 24-hour emergency call system. Cottages have garages with automatic door opener, washer/dryer.*

Availability: Units available. Priority waiting list.

Health services and rates:

- 43 Assisted Living apartments

	Daily fee single/double	*Monthly fee single/double*
Single room	$63.25/83	$1,915/2,490
Double room	$75/97.50	$2,250/2,925
1-Bedroom	$98.30/ 127.79	$2,949/ 3,833.70

- 106-Bed Skilled Nursing facility

Semiprivate	$103/day	$3,090/month
Private	$121/day	$3,630/month

"Trinity's location enables it to remain a quiet, friendly environment only minutes away from the activities of a growing metropolitan area. All units in Assisted Living and Independent Living have been renovated with new carpet, wallpaper, and paint. A new dining room, activities room, music room, and security system have recently been added."

OTTERBEIN LEBANON

585 North State Route 741
Lebanon, OH 45036
(513) 932-2020
Charles W. Peckham, Jr., administrator

Type of community: Not-for-profit Continuing Care, modified contract

Located on 1,475 acres of land in a rural setting, the community is 30 minutes from Dayton and Cincinnati and offers a variety of Independent Living units and four levels of health care including a unit for Alzheimer's care. An organized church is located on campus served by two full-time pastors. The rural setting features a private lake stocked for fishing, pavilion for picnics, nature trail, and access to nearby golf course.

Financial plan: Entrance fee plus monthly fee or monthly rental. Refundable entrance fee plus monthly fee required for Independent Living residents in one-, two-, and three-bedroom units with some exceptions based on age and financial status. 1% of entrance fee becomes a lifetime monthly credit regardless of area of residence. Pro rata refund available during first 100 months of residency. *Note:* Limited subsidy dollars are available to

INDEPENDENT LIVING HOUSING

Type/size of apartment	*Entrance fee*	*Monthly fee*
Studio, 400–600 sq. ft.	$9,400–38,800	$579–757
1-Bedroom, 600–775 sq. ft.	$14,600–52,200	$728–954
2-Bedroom, 775–1,100 sq. ft.	$19,000–73,100	$853–1,236
Cottages		
2-Bedroom, 1,105–1,500 sq. ft.	$19,000–91,300	$874–1,588
3-Bedroom, 1,456 sq. ft.	$100,900	$1,735
Congregate care		
Studio, 306–590 sq. ft.	$22,000–49,400	$550–940
1-Bedroom, 488–780 sq. ft.	$30,100–66,900	$652–1,152
2-Bedroom, 790 sq. ft.	$30,600–72,400	$1,221

All utilities except telephone included. 24-hour emergency call system. Thirty different floor plans available.

residents of Otterbein, members of the West Ohio Conference of the United Methodist Church, and persons residing in the West Ohio Conference area regardless of church affiliation.

Ownership and management: Owned by Otterbein Homes, affiliated with the West Ohio Conference of the United Methodist Church, owner of four other facilities. Opened in 1912.

Minimum age: 60 years (if couple, spouse must be at least 60); applications are accepted from persons age 55+.

Population: 730 residents. Residents come from across the United States and are not limited to Methodists.

Number of units: Independent Living: 37 cottages, 195 ranch-style duplexes, 89 congregate apartments; 118 Assisted Living units, 66 Intermediate Nursing beds, 132 Skilled Nursing beds, 40 Alzheimer's beds.

Dining plan: Main meal per day included in the monthly fee but may be deducted if not used.

Services: *Included in the monthly fee:* Scheduled transportation, apartment upkeep and repairs.

At additional cost: Country store, beauty/barbershop, full-service bank with lockboxes, post office, soda fountain, thrift shop, Shaker Cellar (used furniture and household goods).

Activities: Scheduled trips to theaters, symphony concerts, baseball games, museums, restaurants; extended two- to seven-day trips to area attractions. Gardening, greenhouses, photo darkroom, quilting, weaving, pottery, billiards, exercise programs, golf, movies, shuffleboard, organized table games, orchestra, men's and women's chorus, bell choirs, chime choirs, church choir, creative writing, painting and sketching, woodworking shop, travelogues, Bible study, arts and crafts, Adventures in Learning, residents' council. Volunteerism plays a prominent role in the community.

Availability: Waiting list. Independent Living averages one to eight years, depending on unit desired. Health care waiting time is two to 12 months, with the exception of Skilled Nursing, which may involve a longer wait.

Health services and rates: After the first 90 days of residency, resident receives a $750 credit per year toward admission to any of the four health care areas (visiting nurse, visiting aide service, home-delivered meals, and other nursing-related services). Long-term care insurance required of all Independent Living residents, except those over 80 years.

- 118 Assisted Living rooms (residents bring own furnishings)
  Semiprivate $54/day or $1,643/month
  Private $71/day or $2,160/month
- 66 Intermediate Nursing beds
  Semiprivate $80/day or $2,433/month
- 132-Bed Skilled Nursing unit
  Semiprivate $120/day or $3,650/month
- 40-Bed Alzheimer's care unit
  Semiprivate $113/day or $3,437/month

"Otterbein's Continuum of Care and availability of financial assistance attracts many applicants."

MOUNT PLEASANT VILLAGE

225 Britton Lane
Monroe, OH 45050
(513) 539-7760
Paul Frederick, marketing director

Type of community: Not-for-profit Continuing Care, modified contract

Accreditation: Continuing Care Accreditation Commission

One-story brick ranch-style cottages with landscaped lawns are located on 110 acres with a nature trail on-site. Seasonal gardens enhance the streets of the village. Mount Pleasant Place, a newly built three-story Georgian-style apartment residence, is on the west side

INDEPENDENT LIVING HOUSING

Type/size of apartment	*Entrance fee 1/2 **	*Monthly fee**
1-Bedroom, 650 sq. ft.	$45,000–47,000/67,500–70,500	$1,075
2-Bedroom, 945–970 sq. ft.	$60,000–62,000/90,000–93,000	$1,350
Cottage/homes		
2–3-Bedroom ranch	$80,000–100,000	$351/638

**For double occupancy add $5,000 to the entrance fee, $375 to the monthly fee. All utilities except telephone included. Individually controlled heating and air-conditioning, 24-hour emergency call system, cable TV. Apartments and homes have fully equipped kitchens. One pet allowed per apartment and cottage/home.*

of campus. The community offers easy access to Cincinnati and Dayton. A full range of health care services are on-site and available 24 hours a day.

Financial plan: Entrance fee plus monthly fee or monthly rent. Two plans: **1)** 50% refundable entrance fee. **2)** 90% refundable entrance fee. Entrance fee amortizes at 2% per month for 50 months in cottages.

Ownership and management: Owned and operated by Ohio Presbyterian Retirement Services, owner and operator of seven other communities in Ohio. Opened in 1953.

Minimum age: 60 years.

Population: 338 residents; 75% women, 25% men, 31% couples.

Number of units: 72 Independent Living apartments and 120 cottage/homes; 28 Assisted Living units, 99 Skilled Nursing beds, 12-bed special care/ Alzheimer's facility.

Dining plan: 25 meals per month included in the monthly fee for apartment residents. Private group dining available.

Services: *Included in the monthly fee:* Scheduled transportation. Housekeeping for Duplex Plus units. Room residents have weekly housekeeping and laundry services.

At additional cost: Housekeeping, beauty/ barbershop, transportation, guest accommodations.

Activities: Nature trail, bird sanctuary, shuffleboard courts, library, woodworking shop, arts and crafts program, exercise classes, Bible study, weekly chapel services, Mount Pleasant Singers, special programs, travel opportunities, Elderschool, seasonal activities, bus transportation to concerts and special outings, writers workshop, multipurpose activities building, billiards, volunteering.

Availability: Limited. $100 nonrefundable application fee places you on waiting list if application is accepted.

Health services and rates: 139-bed health center offers physical, speech, and occupational therapies and restorative nursing. Special care unit provides a sheltered environment for those with Alzheimer's disease and related disorders. Mount Pleasant's Elder Day Care Center provides structured daytime care in a comfortable homey setting for older adults with physical or memory problems.

- 10 Independent Living studios with services $1,035–1,310/month
- 28 Assisted Living private rooms

Monthly fees	*Monthly rent*
$1,640–2,000*	$1,936–2,296

**Nonresident entrance fee: $18,500.*

- 99-Bed nursing center
  Semiprivate $108.50/day*
  Private $121.50/day*
- 12-Bed special care unit for Alzheimer's patients
  Semiprivate $115/day*

**Non–entrance fee admissions pay an additional $12/day.*

"Mount Pleasant Retirement Village operates a Children's Village, a child development center located on the Village campus. In addition to providing excellent care for employees and other area children, the center gives Mount Pleasant residents a wonderful opportunity to interact with young children. The community was founded and operates on the Christian principle of concern for others. The Village is nondenominational and welcomes people of all religions and races. Our mission is to provide older adults with caring and quality services toward the enhancement of physical mental and spiritual well-being consistent with the Christian gospel."

KENDAL AT OBERLIN

P.O. Box 519
Oberlin, OH 44074
(216)775-0094
Barbara Thomas, administrator

Type of community: Nonprofit Continuing Care, all-inclusive contract

Kendal at Oberlin is situated on a 92-acre site containing woodlands, thickets, farmland, and ponds. Approximately 14 acres are designated wetlands. The community offers five apartment sizes in cottage clusters and/or apartments that have been designed to blend harmoniously with the natural setting and interact responsibly with the environment. Brick-and-clapboard siding is used throughout. Cottage clusters are arranged to give the feeling of neighborhoods; covered walkway system unobtrusively connects all buildings on campus. Assisted Living and Skilled Nursing facilities are available on campus. The rich cultural and academic life of Oberlin College and its conservatory of music is nearby. For a fee Oberlin College Athletic Club is available for use by Kendal at Oberlin residents. The community is located 35 miles from Cleveland and within walking distance of Oberlin's town center.

Financial plan: Entrance fee plus monthly fee. $1,100 deposit, $1,000 of which is fully refundable.

Ownership and management: The Kendal Corporation, a nonprofit corporation composed of members of the Religious Society of Friends, has communities in Pennsylvania, New Hampshire, and New York. Residents have strong participation in day-to-day operation. Opened in 1993.

Minimum age: 65 years.

Population: 225 residents; 68% women, 32% men.

Number of units: 192 Independent Living residences; 24 Assisted Living rooms.

Dining plan: One meal a day included in the monthly fee. Other meals available as desired for additional charge. Meal credits are available for extended periods of absence. Formal dining room and informal,

INDEPENDENT LIVING HOUSING

Type/size of apartment	*Entrance fee**	*Monthly fee**
Studio, 482 sq. ft.	$49,200	$1,367
1-Bedroom, 693 sq. ft.	$96,350	$1,564
1-Bedroom/den, 940 sq. ft.	$148,625	$1,955
2-Bedroom, 1,036 sq. ft.	$156,313	$2,206
2-Bedroom/den, 1,199 sq. ft.	$195,263	$2,569

**For double occupancy add $16,605 to the entrance fee, $865 to the monthly fee. All utilities except telephone included. Fully equipped kitchen, draperies, wall-to-wall carpeting, individually controlled heating and air-conditioning, 24-hour emergency call system, private balcony or terrace.*

cafeteria-style coffee shop. Meal tray delivery on physician's orders. Private dining room.

Services: *Included in the monthly fee:* Biweekly housekeeping, weekly flat-linen service, parking areas, scheduled transportation.

At additional cost: Beauty/barbershop, gift shop, branch bank, guest accommodations, grocery purchases in coffee shops, delivery of newspapers, covered parking.

Activities: 60 to 70 active resident committees. Gardening, films, discussion groups, play readings, concerts, art exhibitions, trips to local attractions, weaving, pottery, photography/darkroom, woodworking shop, exercise facilities, auditorium, library, study groups, bridge, birdwatching, volunteering. Oberlin College and Conservatory of Music offer extensive selection of concerts, lectures, classes, films, sports events, dramatic and dance attractions. For a fee, residents may use the college's athletic facilities.

Availability: Limited.

Health services and rates: Long-term care is included in the monthly fee. Team approach is used by physicians, nursing staff, and other professionals. Geriatric nurse practitioner and social services staff on-site. Physical, speech, occupational, and recreational therapies on-site. Insurance claim expert on premises handles residents' claim forms. Dentistry, eye care, podiatry services available at resident's expense.

The health center has a unique architectural design based on sensitivity to the comfort and needs of the older person. Rooms are grouped in neighborhood clusters around a Great Room, the nurse's station is a desk, and the nursing staff does not wear uniforms. Visiting is not restricted by established hours. Rooms are designed for single occupancy although some can accommodate two persons, if necessary. Health center residents are encouraged to bring their own furniture and surround themselves with their personal possessions.

- 24 Assisted Living rooms

"Through the concept of the Continuing Care retirement community, The Kendal Corporation seeks to provide a way of life for older people which counters ageism in our society and offers a better way to grow older. Our approach to Continuing Care is based on the philosophy that retirement and growing older can usher in new opportunities for growth and development, even if emerging limitations or infirmities necessitate a degree of dependency. The lifestyle offered in our communities seeks to make the later years independent, productive, and stimulating while providing security, assurance of quality health care, and relief from many of the burdens of day-to-day life in environments not designed for older people. Such a community contributes to life enrichment as residents have the opportunity to explore new experiences and new relaitonships and to cultivate lifelong concerns and interests."

DOROTHY LOVE RETIREMENT COMMUNITY

3003 West Cisco Road
Sidney, OH 45365
(513) 498-2391
Dan O'Connor, executive director

Type of community: Nonprofit Continuing Care, modified contract

Accreditation: Continuing Care Accreditation Commission

Set on 294 acres, the community features a three-story apartment building and ranch-style homes for Independent Living residences as well as Assisted Living units and a nursing center. On campus is a fishing pond, outdoor recreational areas, picnic shelter, small park, soon-to-be nature trails, multi-purpose activity center, and a health center. Dayton and Lima are a short drive away.

Financial plan: For apartments: monthly fee. Applicants place on deposit, at the time of submitting an application, the first month's rent plus an amount equal to one month's rent as a security deposit. This deposit is refunded at the end of the tenancy. Tenancy is defined as one year minimum. For ranch-style homes: entrance fee plus monthly fee.

Ownership and management: Ohio Presbyterian Retirement Services, owners/operators of seven other communities in Ohio. Opened in 1922.

Minimum age: 60 years.

Population: 250 residents: 82% women, 18% men, 23% couples.

Number of units: 72 Independent Living apartments and 39 ranch-style homes; 39 Assisted Living studio apartments, 96-bed Skilled Nursing facility.

Dining plan: Evening meal is included in the apartment monthly fee. Other meals available at additional charge. Arrangements can be made for private family dining.

Services: *Included in the monthly fee:* Twice-monthly housekeeping services, flat-linen service, scheduled transportation, nursing home insurance.

At additional cost: Beauty/barbershop, on-site banking, ice-cream parlor, gift shop, dry cleaning service, additional housekeeping, meal preparation, prescription pick-up, tax preparation, carpet cleaning, interior painting.

Activities: Library, three-wheel bicycles, card games, arts and crafts, woodworking, exercise classes, shuffleboard, billiards, walking trails, fishing pond, gardening, classes at nearby Edison State Community College, movies, slide shows, Dorothy Love Choir, Sunshine Band, music appreciation club, dining out trips, religious life programs, book clubs, active volunteer program (providing companionship, personal shopping, letter writing, reading).

Availability: Units available. Priority waiting list.

Health services and rates: Apartment and ranch-style home residents have priority access to health center. Rehabilitative services: physical, speech, and occupational therapies. Podiatrist, optometrist, audiologist. Home health care available on fee-for-service basis.

- 39 Assisted Living studio apartments

Studio	$1,988/month*

**Nonresident entrance fee: $21,200–24,000.*

- 96-Bed Skilled Nursing facility

Semiprivate	$96.75–113/day*
Private	$135.50–160.75/day*

**Nonresident entrance fee: $12,100 semiprivate, $24,100 private. Entrance fee is optional and partially refundable. Daily fee is lower with entrance fee.*

"Dorothy Love has been serving older adults from around the country since 1922 and has earned the approval of the Continuing Care Accreditation

INDEPENDENT LIVING HOUSING

Type/size of apartment	*Monthly fee**
1-Bedroom, 677–868 sq. ft.	$1,265–1,445
2-Bedroom, 1,023 sq. ft.	$1,685–1,735

**For double occupancy add $300 to the monthly fee. Garage rental is $45. All utilities except telephone and cable TV included. Fully equipped kitchen with appliances, individually controlled heating and air-conditioning, ample storage, 24-hour emergency call system.*

Ranch homes	*Entrance fee*	*Monthly fee*
Duplex, 1,300 sq. ft.	$45,000–100,000	$440
Single unit, 1,000 sq. ft.	$55,000–100,000	$480

Fully equipped all-electric kitchen, washer and dryer, attached garage with automatic opener, wall-to-wall carpeting, 24-hour emergency call system. Enclosed porches available on some homes.

Commission. Foremost among the many goals for the future are to continue being focused on the organization's mission (to provide older adults with caring and quality services toward the enhancement of physical, mental, and spiritual well-being consistent with the Christian gospel) and to continue the development of single-family homes."

WESTLAKE VILLAGE

28550 Westlake Village Drive
Westlake, OH 44145
(216) 892-4220
Susan Bartosch, director of marketing

Type of community: Independent and Assisted Living

Located on a 20-acre campus that offers walking trails, a courtyard, and ponds, the community features three-story Independent Living buildings and a two-story Assisted Living building. Cottages are situated in a neighborhood setting by a lake. Westlake Village is 10 minutes from major shopping and 20 minutes from Hopkins International Airport.

Financial plan: Monthly rental fee, plus $500 entrance fee.

Ownership and management: JMB Realty of Chicago, owners. Operations managed by Renaissance Group. Marketing managed by CRSA. Opened in 1989.

Minimum age: 50 years.

Population: 215 residents; 15% couples. Residents come from 20 states.

Number of units: 201 Independent Living apartments and 11 cottages; 56 Assisted Living units.

Dining plan: Continental breakfast and dinner daily included in the monthly rental fee. Private dining room and catering available.

Services: *Included in the monthly fee:* Weekly housekeeping, scheduled transportation.

At additional cost: Lunch in café, beauty/barbershop, personal laundry.

Activities: Full-time activities director. Billiards, greenhouse, whirlpool, exercise room, arts and crafts, gardening, library, pub, patio.

Availability: Limited.

Health services and rates: Physicians' appointments weekly.

- 56 Assisted Living units
  Alcove, efficiency $1,680/month
  1-Bedroom $2,010/month

  **Additional $360/month for administering medication.*

INDEPENDENT LIVING HOUSING

Type/size of apartment	*Entrance fee*	*Monthly rental fee**
1-Bedroom, 584–999 sq. ft.	$500	$1,260–1,870
2-Bedroom, 1,088 sq. ft.	$500	$1,980
Cottages		
2-Bedroom, 1,080 sq. ft.	$500	$1,500

**For double occupancy add $300 to the monthly fee. All utilities except telephone included. Fully equipped kitchen, individually controlled heating and air-conditioning, wall-to-wall carpeting, 24-hour emergency call system.*

- Respite care
  Residents $68/day
  Nonresidents $80/day

"Westlake Village is a carefully designed, state-of-the-art retirement facility. Equally important is our extensive involvement with prospective residents in decision making and moving in. Our goal is to make it easy and affordable for seniors to enjoy their independence and meet new friends."

BRECKENRIDGE VILLAGE

36500 Euclid Avenue
Willoughby, OH 44094
(216) 942-4342
Phyllis J. Shea, director of marketing

Type of community: Nonprofit Continuing Care, modified contract

Accreditation: Continuing Care Accreditation Commission

Located on 37 beautifully wooded acres in Willoughby, east of Cleveland, the community consists of both apartments and ranch-style homes. The homes are built in clusters of two to five, each with a common wall. Breckenridge has a conference room and a community room, and each floor has a lounge. Independent and Assisted Living, Intermediate and Skilled Nursing, and an Alzheimer's facility are available.

Financial plan: Entrance fee plus monthly fee for ranch-style homes or monthly fee only for apartments. A $200 per person nonrefundable application fee is required. Entrance fees may be paid on a prorated, partially refundable fee. A budget is prepared each year, and rate increases are based on increased costs reflected in this budget, which is reviewed by local council representatives, resident representatives, local/corporate management. The average increase has been between 4% and 5%.

INDEPENDENT LIVING HOUSING

Type/size of apartment	*Monthly fee only**
1-Bedroom, 615 sq. ft.	$1,290
2-Bedroom, 822 sq. ft.	$1,785–1,905
3-Bedroom, 925 sq. ft.	$2,100

**For double occupancy add $270 to the monthly fee. All utilities except telephone included. All-electric kitchen, 24-hour emergency call system, basic TV, individually controlled heating and air-conditioning, wall-to-wall carpeting. Washers/dryers can be installed in two- and three-bedroom apartments at additional cost.* Note: *One- and two-bedroom HUD rent subsidy apartments are available for individuals with an annual income of less than $23,000 per year or couples with annual income less than $27,000.*

Ranch homes	*Entrance fee**	*Monthly fee**
2-Bedroom, Phase 1 homes	$87,000	$365
2-Bedroom, Phase 2 homes	$90,000–116,000	$365
3-Bedroom, Phase 3 homes	$116,000	$365

**For double occupancy add $123 to the monthly fee. All utilities except telephone included plus maintenance, including appliances, lawn mowing, landscaping. Enclosed patio, fireplace, humidifier/electronic air cleaner, washer/dryer available at additional cost. All homes have garage, 2 full bathrooms, utility room, air-conditioning, wall-to-wall carpeting, 24-hour emergency call system.*

Ownership and management: Ohio Presbyterian Retirement Services, owner and manager of seven other communities in Ohio. Opened in 1913.

Minimum age: 60 years.

Population: 562 residents; 77% women, 23% men, 24% couples.

Number of units: 305 Independent Living apartments and 74 ranch-style homes; 17 Assisted Living units, 100-bed health care center, 17-bed Alzheimer's facility.

Dining plan: Dinner is included in the monthly fee. Private dining room.

Services: *Included in the monthly fee:* Biweekly housekeeping, laundry facilities, scheduled transportation, nursing home insurance.

At additional cost: Beauty/barbershop, gift shop, cafe, additional cleaning services, garage space for apartment dwellers.

Activities: Library, exercise room, arts and crafts, educational opportunities, field trips to theater productions, parks, and museums. Community outreach program.

Availability: Priority waiting list, six months to three years depending on type of unit.

Health services and rates: Physical, speech, and hearing therapies available as well as dental and podiatry services. Outreach services (companion aide and shopping services) available on a fee-for-service basis. Mandatory nursing home insurance (included in resident's monthly fee) pays a daily benefit of $49/day (more than $17,850 per year) if the resident spends more than 90 days in Intermediate or Skilled Nursing. Ranch home residents are allowed seven days of free nursing care per year. Home companion aides, case management and adult day care is offered to the community.

- 17 Assisted Living units $85/day
- 100-Bed health care center

Intermediate Nursing

	Entrance fee/ daily fee	*Daily fee only*
Semiprivate	$18,500/89	$105
Private	$22,000/120	$136

Skilled Nursing

	Entrance fee/ daily fee	*Daily fee only*
Semiprivate	$18,500/105	$121
Private	$22,000/146	$162

- 17 Alzheimer's beds $117/day

"Breckenridge Village's mission is to provide older adults with caring and quality services toward the enhancement of physical, mental, and spiritual well-being consistent with the Christian gospel."

OKLAHOMA

EPWORTH VILLA

14901 North Pennsylvania
Oklahoma City, OK 73134-6008
(405) 752-1200
Hank Sookne, director of marketing

Type of community: Not-for-profit Continuing Care, all-inclusive contract

Epworth Villa is located on a 30-acre site in northern Oklahoma City that features a fishing pond, one-hole golf course, residents' garden, gorgeous living room settings, atrium entryway with grand staircase, and six different public lounges. The complex is a Williamsburg design and consists of connecting three-story colonial apartment buildings and duplex cottages, as well as Assisted Living and Intermediate and Skilled Nursing. The community is centrally located within blocks of Quail Springs Mall, two miles from North Park Mall, and minutes from Mercy Memorial Hospital.

Financial plan: Entrance fee plus monthly fee. Two plans: **1)** Basic offers an annual health care benefit of $500. **2)** 75% Refundable: 75% refundable less 1% per month over the first 100 months and includes an annual health care benefit of $1,500 for enriched living services.

Ownership and management: Central Oklahoma United Methodist Retirement Facility, Inc., a corporation of the Central Oklahoma United Methodist Conference. Opened in 1990.

Minimum age: 62 years.

Population: 285 residents; 75% women, 25% men, 56 couples.

Number of units: 230 apartments and 5 garden duplexes; 30 Assisted Living units, 30 Intermediate Nursing beds, and 30 Skilled Nursing beds.

Dining plan: Choice of one meal per day included in the monthly fee. Additional meals available at a cost. Private dining room plus outdoor dining terrace. Special diets available when ordered by physician. Tray service provided for short periods when approved for medical reasons.

Services: *Included in the monthly fee:* Biweekly housekeeping, weekly flat-linen service, scheduled transportation, lighted parking areas.

At additional cost: Convenience store, ice-cream parlor, beauty/barbershop, guest accommodations.

Activities: Crafts room, game room, woodworking shop, billiards room, indoor heated pool, golf, fishing pond, various instructional classes, exercise/fitness center, putting green, walking trails, library, gardening areas, lectures, and outings to cultural events.

Availability: Limited.

Health services and rates: Independent Living residents are entitled to unlimited, on-site nursing care at no increase to their monthly fee except for a $6 daily charge for the other two meals served. On a limited basis, nonresidents may be admitted at the following rates:

- 30 Assisted Living units

Private, furnished	$1,765/month
Private, unfurnished	$1,675/month

INDEPENDENT LIVING

Type/size of apartment	*Entrance fee 1/2*	*Monthly fee*
Studio, 405 sq. ft.	$42,500/71,500	$794
Alcove, 486 sq. ft.	$50,000/84,000	$908
1-Bedroom, 648 sq. ft.	$65,500/110,000*	$1,078*
2-Bedroom, 816 sq. ft.	$81,500/137,000*	$1,248*
2-Bedroom, 918 sq. ft.	$108,000/153,000*	$1,362*
2-Bedroom, 1,080 sq. ft.	$106,500/181,500*	$1,476*
2-Bedroom duplex, 1,400 sq. ft.	$136,500/229,500*	$1,873*

**For double occupancy add $4,500 to Plan 1 entrance fee, $7,000 to Plan 2; $511 to the monthly fee. All utilities except telephone included. Wall-to-wall carpeting, full all-electric kitchen, 24-hour emergency call system, basic cable TV. Pets allowed within board restrictions.*

- 30 Intermediate Nursing beds
  - Semiprivate $70/day
  - Private $125/day
- 30 Skilled Nursing beds
  - Semiprivate $80/day
  - Private $135/day

"We are committed to Christian values as expressed in 'resident first' care, achievement of community, social fiscal integrity, and leadership for the future. We are Oklahoma City's only life care retirement community."

THE FOUNTAINS AT CANTERBURY

1414 N.W. 122nd Street
Oklahoma City, OK 73114
(405) 755-8952
Marylin Hilt, marketing director

Type of community: Continuing care, modified contract

Located on 59 landscaped acres, the community offers a cozy living room with fireplace and refreshment area, dining room overlooking the lake, solarium, and library/lounge area. The grounds feature walking paths, picnic areas, and gardens. Apartments and cottages are Independent Living residences. There is a worship chapel on campus. Assisted Living and Intermediate and Skilled Nursing (four levels) are available. The community is minutes from major medical centers, physicians' offices, and shopping centers in Oklahoma City.

Financial plan: Entrance fee plus monthly fee.

Ownership and management: The Fountains Affiliated Companies, owner of two other communities and manager of 12. Opened in 1985.

Minimum age: 62 years.

Population: 203 residents; 75% women, 25% men, 14% couples.

Number of units: 47 Independent Living apartments and 8 cottages; 60 Assisted Living apartments, 120-bed health care center.

Dining plan: One meal per day included in the monthly fee. Additional meals available at cost. Refreshment area. Private dining room.

Services: *Included in the monthly fee:* Light housekeeping, regularly scheduled transportation, parking.

At additional cost: Additional housekeeping and flat-linen services, beauty/barbershop, mailing services.

INDEPENDENT LIVING HOUSING

Type/size of apartment	*Entrance fee*	*Monthly fee*
1-Bedroom, 750 sq. ft.	$71,400	$1,251
2-Bedroom, 990–1,500 sq. ft.	$94,300–148,000	$1,489
Cottages		
1-Bedroom, 1,100 sq. ft.	$93,500	$780
2-Bedroom, 1,730 sq. ft.	$131,000	$1,251

All utilities except telephone included. Miniblinds, individually controlled heating and air-conditioning, washer/dryer hookup, fully equipped kitchens, 24-hour emergency call system. Cottages have attached garages.

Activities: Full-time activities director. Library, card room, worship services, Bible study, gardening, trips.

Availability: Several months waiting list.

Health services and rates: Staff of health care professionals work together in team approach with residents' physicians, families, therapists, and other specialists. Resident physician, registered nurse, and assistants on duty around the clock. Physical, exercise, occupational, speech, and other rehabilitative therapies are provided in extensive areas specially designed for these services. Whirlpool therapeutic tub in each wing. Routine medical checkups. On-site training with local schools and universities.

- 60 Assisted Living units
  Studio $1,756–1,968/month
  1-Bedroom $2,180–2,392/month

  **For double occupancy add $802 to the monthly fee. Furnished apartments available for short-term stays. Charges based on assistance required.*

- 120-Bed health care center
  Semiprivate $67–71/day
  Private $112–116 /day

"Compassion, courtesy, respect, and a sensitivity to the individual needs of each resident are among the special attitudes and commitments of the professional staff at Canterbury. Every resident and visitor at Canterbury is a guest, treated with gracious hospitality."

SPANISH COVE

1401 South Cornwell Drive
Yukon, OK 73099
(405) 354-1901
Jerry O'Hare, marketing director

Type of community: Nonprofit Continuing Care, all-inclusive contract

Twenty-four two-story Independent Living apartment buildings and a separate health center are located on 7¾ landscaped acres in a residential neighborhood. Small town with shopping centers, places of worship, and other amenities nearby. Attractions accessible to the community include Jewel Box Theater, Lyric Theater, state fair of Oklahoma, Ski Island Christmas Lights, and Broadway plays in Oklahoma City.

Financial plan: Entrance fee plus monthly fee. Four plans: **1)** No refund. **2)** Traditional: refund less 2% per month of residency or 22%, whichever is greater. **3)** Return of Capital (90%): 90% refund of entrance fee regardless of length of residency. **4)** Return of Capital plan (90-50%): from 1 year, 90% refund; 2 years, 80% refund; 3 years, 70% refund; 4 years, 60% refund; 5 years and thereafter, 50% refund. Refunds will be paid after the living unit is occupied and upon receipt of the new entrance fee.

INDEPENDENT LIVING HOUSING

Type/size of unit	*Entrance fee 1/2*	*Monthly fee**
Studio, 359 sq. ft.	$29,550/39,600	$713
1-Bedroom, 702 sq. ft.	$41,550–58,250/63,550–72,750	$779–918
2-Bedroom, 875 sq. ft.	$58,250–67,450/72,750–84,350	$918
3-Bedroom, 1,015 sq. ft.	$67,450/84,350	$987

Note: *Plan 3 entrance fees range from $66,132 to $140,864; Plan 4 begins at $56,034 for studio and $119,355 for 3-bedroom. *For double occupancy add $441 to monthly fee. All utilities except telephone and cable TV included. Wall-to-wall carpeting, 24-hour emergency call system, fully equipped kitchen, cable TV (optional), individually controlled heating and air-conditioning.*

Ownership and management: A nonprofit public trust governed by a seven-member board of trustees comprised of Spanish Cove residents, area professionals, and a representative from the Yukon city council. Opened in 1974.

Minimum age: None.

Population: 265 residents; 75% women, 25% men, 34% couples.

Number of units: 192 Independent Living apartments; 29-bed health center (22-bed expansion planned).

Dining plan: One meal per day included in the monthly fee. Special diets and tray service available. Private dining room available. Private dining room at no extra charge for family gatherings.

Services: *Included in the monthly fee:* Housekeeping, weekly flat-linen service, scheduled transportation (for shopping, doctor's visits, and airport), Notary Public services, tray service if ordered by the director of nursing services or the medical director.

At additional cost: Beauty/barbershop, personal laundry service, guest apartments.

Activities: Full-time activities director. Heated swimming pool, arts and crafts room, clubroom with billards table, book reviews, musical entertainment, special holiday events, parties, game night, bridge night, meeting rooms, gardening spots, exercise classes, library, chapel services, volunteering, visits to various theaters, trips to museums and towns near Oklahoma City.

Availability: 95% occupied. Waiting list is available and assures apartment of your choice. 10% deposit of entrance fee required for waiting list freezes the current entrance fee for a time limit of one year unless an extension is approved by the board. In the event of withdrawal from the list, the deposit is refunded less a service fee of $200.

Health services and rates: Lifetime health care at all levels included in resident's entrance fee. Only additional charges are for medications, physician charges, private attendants, lab services, dental care, ambulance service, rehabilitation services, extra meals, additional nursing supplies, personal laundry, oxygen, nutritional supplements, beauty/barbershop, and incidentals not included in the agreement. Health center is staffed 24 hours a day with registered nurses and licensed practical nurses and has a full-time activities director. Medical personnel include registered nurses, licensed practical nurses, certified medication aides, certified nurses aides, director, dietitian, medical records consultant, and social worker. Pharmacist and physical therapists are available on a consulting basis.

- Assisted Living is handled on as-needed basis in resident's apartment
- 29-Bed health care center, with 22 additional beds planned

"Spanish Cove is lifestyle and life care. Lifestyle includes no more worries about your roof, your furnace, or your appliances breaking down. No lawns to mow, no snow to shovel, no leaves to rake, or boxes to move. No utility bills to pay, no housekeeping to do—Spanish Cove even does the windows. Life care is provided to residents at no additional monthly service fee. Healthy living is enhanced by our home health or Assisted Living personnel who take care of our residents in their own apartments. Their mission is to assist each resident in achieving their highest possible level of physical, mental, and psychological independence. Spanish Cove uses a team approach including the resident and family members. We offer the security of a small town setting but with all the amenities of a big city just minutes away."

OREGON

CASCADE MANOR

65 West 30th Avenue
Eugene, OR 97405
(503) 342-5901
Ronald K. Minnice, marketing director

Type of community: Not-for-profit Continuing Care, modified contract

A multistory building housing Independent Living apartments and a 22-bed health center is located on five acres with views of surrounding gardens and ponds. The community features recently renovated common rooms and is located one block from major shopping. Eugene is a university community with population of 100,000+.

Financial plan: Entrance fee plus monthly fee. If residents move out of the Manor, the balance of the entrance fee will be refunded at less than 1% per month of the original payment.

Ownership and management: Presbyterian United Methodist and United Congregational. Opened in 1967.

Minimum age: 62 years.

Population: 110 residents; 76% women, 24% men, 40% couples.

Number of units: 89 Independent Living apartments; 22-bed health care center.

Dining plan: One meal per day included in the monthly fee. Private dining room and catering.

Services: *Included in the monthly fee:* Biweekly housekeeping and weekly flat-linen services.

At additional cost: Beauty/barbershop, post office, bank, scheduled transportation.

Activities: Library, concerts (piano and organ), gardening, guest speakers, local trips, vespers.

Availability: Waiting list.

Health services and rates: Residents receive five free days in the health center per year; $70 per day

INDEPENDENT LIVING HOUSING

Type/size of apartment	*Entrance fee*	*Monthly fee single/double**
Single, 428 sq. ft.	$34,500	$810
Semisuite, 642 sq. ft.	$51,500	$1,023/1,408
Double, 857 sq. ft.	$58,500	$1,235/1,620
Single semisuite, 1,070 sq. ft.	$85,750	$1,448/1,833

**All utilities included in monthly fee. Individually controlled heating, wall-to-wall carpeting, window sheers and draperies, 24-hour emergency call system.*

thereafter plus resident's monthly fee. If the resident moves permanently into the health center and gives up the apartment, the fee is $2,000 per month.

- 22-Bed health care center

"Cascade Manor is Eugene's only Continuing Care retirement community. Its residential location is an easy walk to post office, bank, and retail services."

ROGUE VALLEY MANOR

1200 Mira Mar
Medford, OR 97504
(503) 857-7214 or (800) 848-7868
admissions secretary

Type of community: Nonprofit Continuing Care, modified contract

Accreditation: Continuing Care Accreditation Commission

Situated on 200 acres atop Barneburg Hill, Rogue Valley Manor offers spectacular views of southern Oregon's forested and snowcapped mountains, blossoming pear orchards, and city lights of Medford. Located 27 miles north of the California border, the community consists of a ten-story modern apartment complex and two-story cottages. Assisted Living and Skilled Nursing are offered in a two-story modern medical services facility. Crater Lake National Park, California redwoods, the Oregon Coast, Mount Shasta, and other unspoiled places for which the Pacific Northwest are known are a short trip away.

Financial plan: Entrance fee plus monthly fee. Payment of nonrefundable $1,000 application fee.

Ownership and management: Rogue Valley Manor, a nonprofit corporation operated by a board of directors of civic-minded individuals from the area. It is sponsored by a noncontributing affiliation with the United Methodist Presbyterian (U.S.A.) and Episcopal churches. Opened in 1961.

Minimum age: 62 years (if couple, spouse must be at least 62).

Population: 594 residents. The majority of residents are from the West Coast.

Number of units: 220 apartments, 174 cottages (another 140 are under construction to surround a golf course being built); 35 Assisted Living apartments, 93 Skilled Nursing rooms.

INDEPENDENT LIVING HOUSING

Type/size of apartments	*Entrance fee*	*Monthly fee single/double*
Studio, 322–387 sq. ft.	$23,000–36,000	$790/1,505
1-Bedroom, 516–774 sq. ft.	$49,000–70,000	$880/1,555
2-Bedroom, 838–1,300 sq. ft.	$80,000–118,000	$1,185/1,560
Cottages		
Alcove, 580 sq. ft.	$53,000	$910/1,505
1-Bedroom, 790 sq. ft.	$81,000	$1,095/1,555
2-Bedroom, 1,168 or 1,243 sq. ft.	$101,000 or 108,000	$1,215/1,620
3-Bedroom, 1,556 sq. ft.	$152,000	$1435/1,815

All utilities except telephone included. Cottages pay own gas and electric. All-electric kitchen, miniblinds, individually controlled heating and air-conditioning, wall-to-wall carpeting, cable TV, 24-hour emergency call system. Note: *There is a separate monthly property tax, depending on apartment ($35.73 for studio to $172.64 for 3-bedroom). Pets that meet the criteria of the board of trustees are allowed in the cottages. Cottages have sunlit atrium and spacious deck.*

Dining plan: Three meals per day included in the monthly fee for apartment residents. For cottage residents one meal per day is included. Small dining rooms available for private parties.

Services: *Included in the monthly fee:* General housekeeping services, flat-linen service, scheduled transportation.

At additional cost: Beauty/barbershop, Manor Mart, convenience store, guest accommodations, parking in an indoor garage or carport.

Activities: Fitness center with pool and Jacuzzi. Swimming pool, shuffleboard, lawn bowl indoors and outdoors, wood- and metalworking, metal enameling, weaving, quilting, pottery, painting, garden plots, greenhouse, picnic areas. Library, chapel, vision and computer center. Bus trips to cultural and area events. Volunteer organizations (Retired Senior Volunteer Program, Foster Grandparent Program).

Availability: Limited. Priority waiting list.

Health services and rates: Medical clinic with complete physical therapy department as well as full-service dentist, audiologist, podiatrist, and pharmacists. Short-term daily convalescent care is available for residents recovering from a brief illness or surgery.

- 35 Assisted Living apartments

	Monthly fee single/double
Studio	$685/1,580
1-Bedroom	$1,020/1,630
1-Bedroom+	$1,110/1,630

- 93 Skilled Nursing rooms

Private	$1,400/month

"Rogue Valley Manor is the only Continuing Care retirement community in Oregon accredited by the Continuing Care Accreditation Commission of the American Association of Homes for the Aging. We offer a prospective resident visiting program for persons interested in visiting our facility from out of the area—two nights and three days for $25 per night for singles and $35 a night for couples. Three meals a day are included in this fee."

FRIENDSVIEW MANOR

1301 East Fulton Street
Newberg, OR 97132
(503) 538-3144
Sarah Barber, marketing director

Type of community: Nonprofit Continuing Care, modified contract

Friendsview Manor is situated on 16 beautifully landscaped acres featuring walking paths and a creek. The parklike grounds offer garden and barbecue space. A five-story modern apartment building houses Independent Living apartments and a health care center. Cottages and condominiums are also available for Independent Living. Golf courses and Champoeg State Park are nearby; Oregon's magnificent ocean beaches are 60 miles away; and the Cascade Mountain Range and Mt. Hood, 75 miles away.

Financial plan: Entrance fee plus monthly fee. If resident leaves prior to six months, the entrance fee minus 12% is refunded. After six months, entrance fee refunds are prorated (amortization is five years for apartments and nine years for condominiums). Nonrefundable $100 application fee.

Ownership and management: Sponsored by Friends Church of the Pacific Northwest (Quakers). Opened in 1961.

Minimum age: 65 years.

Population: 199 residents.

Number of units: 123 Independent Living apartments, 2 cottages, 2 duplexes, and 23 condominiums (fourplexes being built); 15-bed resident care facility, 37 Intermediate Nursing beds.

Dining plan: Three meals per day included in the monthly fee for apartment residents. Residents receive credit if more than 21 consecutive meals are missed. Private dining room. Tray service when ill.

INDEPENDENT LIVING HOUSING

Type/size of apartment	*Entrance fee*	*Monthly fee single/double*
Standard, 400 sq. ft.	*$27,000*	*$813/1,464*
Balcony/corner, 400 sq. ft.	$28,000–29,000	$813/1,464
2 Standards, 800 sq. ft.	$54,000	$1,626
Condominiums/cottages		
1-Bedroom, 625 sq. ft.	$40,000	$560/913
2-Bedroom, 1,008 sq. ft.	$56,000–60,000	$560/913
3-Bedroom, 1,311–1,480 sq. ft.	$65,000–70,000	$560/913

All utilities except long-distance telephone included for apartment residents; condominium residents pay utilities separately. 24-hour emergency call system. Condominiums and cottages have porches or covered patios.

Services: *Included in the monthly fee:* For apartment residents biweekly housekeeping and weekly flat-linen services, laundry facilities. Scheduled transportation for all residents.

At additional cost: Beauty/barbershop, carports, guest accommodations.

Activities: Exercise room, woodworking, sewing, billiards, shuffleboard, ceramics, oil painting, gardening, biking/walking trails, library, Bible study, trips, sing-alongs, continuing education and cultural/sporting events at George Fox College, volunteer committees.

Availability: Waiting list of four to six years.

Health services and rates: Residents receive 15 free days (per type of illness) in the health care center after which they pay a daily surcharge of $10 for resident care and $12 for Intermediate care in addition to their monthly fee. If resident moves into health care center long-term and gives up his or her Independent Living residence, the monthly fee is $746. Medications, physicians' visits are an additional expense. Consultations with dietitian, dentist, physical, speech, and occupational therapists; audiologist, podiatrist available at additional cost.

- 15-Bed resident care facility*
  Private, resident $746/month
  Private, nonresident $1,130/month
- 37 Intermediate Nursing beds
  Private $2,262/month

**Nonresidents are admitted on space-available basis with entrance fee of $1,000.*

"Friendsview Manor is a Christian community that operates as one large family offering lifetime care in a quiet setting. Our personalized staff of more than 100 employees care for our residents in the same loving way they would look after members of their own family."

CAPITAL MANOR

1955 Dallas Road, N.W., Suite 1200
Salem, OR 97304-4498
(503) 362-4101
Irene Burwig, admissions representative

Type of community: Nonprofit Continuing Care, all-inclusive contract

Nestled on 30 acres in the heart of the Williamette Valley, Capital Manor is beautifully landscaped with expansive lawns, rose and vegetable gardens, and nature trails. The community, composed of a ten-story apartment building, one-story villas built in clusters, and a separate health center, is located within the city limits of Salem, Oregon's capitol, and overlooks the Williamette River, offering views of the Coast Range and Cascade Mountains.

Financial plan: Entrance fee plus monthly fee. Residents may leave with a 60-day written notice of termination. During the first six months, the Manor will return the full entrance fee less the following: 15% of the apartment entrance fee or 25% of the villa entrance fee, monthly fee until apartment or villa is reoccupied (maximum charge is 90 days), and application fee, plus any unpaid charges. After six months and before the end of 50 months, the refund will be prorated.

Ownership and management: Capital Manor Corporation's board of directors. Board consists of Christian business people, civic-minded leaders living in the area who serve without pay. Executive director/administrator manages day-to-day operations. Opened in 1963.

Minimum age: 60 years (if couple, spouse may be younger).

Population: 461 residents (a good percentage men).

Number of units: 230 Independent Living apartments, 83 one-story villas; 58-bed health center.

Dining plan: Three meals per day included in apartment monthly fee. Villa residents have continental breakfast plus choice of lunch or dinner daily. Additional meals may be purchased.

Services: *Included in the monthly fee:* Weekly flat-linen service, biweekly housekeeping, scheduled transportation. Villa residents receive yard and building maintenance.

At additional cost: Beauty/barbershop, general store, gift shop, thrift shop, carport or garage space, guest accommodations.

Activities: Lap/swimming pool, spa, library, recreation rooms, hobby shops, exercise room, greenhouse and garden plots, putting green, concerts, movies, choral groups, chapel, wide range of classes, excursions.

Availability: Waiting list varies according to unit style.

Health services and rates: Doctor's clinic. Physical therapy, laboratory services offered. A fully equipped facility for short-term convalescent care for residents recovering from a brief illness or surgery. Long-term care for residents who are unable to maintain independence. Residents pay only $12 per day (subject to change) for health care. Manor physician assists in determining admission to the health care center.

- 58-Bed health care center

"Capital Manor is dedicated solely to providing a comfortable, caring, and carefree lifestyle for retired adults. We want each of our residents to feel at home and enjoy the highest level of health possible."

INDEPENDENT LIVING HOUSING

Type/size of apartments	*Entrance fee*	*Monthly fee**
1-Room, 338–415 sq. ft.	$24,800–28,650	$894–1,029
2-Room, 447–778 sq. ft.	$33,685–57,300	$1,143–1,657
Villas		
1-Bedroom, 702–795 sq. ft.	$57,330–60,060	$1,452–1,519
2-Bedroom, 1,068 sq. ft.	$79,170	$1,646
3-Bedroom, 1,341 sq. ft.	$90,635	$2,027

**For double occupancy in apartments add $200 to the monthly fee. Villas monthly fee is double occupancy; for single occupancy deduct $90 from the monthly fee. Apartments: All utilities except telephone included. Individually controlled electric heat, wall-to-wall carpeting, miniblinds, satellite dish television hookup, 24-hour emergency call system. Some apartments have small kitchenettes. Kitchens and laundry rooms on every floor for residents' use. Villas: Monthly utility allowance of $50 plus all of the above and full kitchen, washer/dryer, attached single garage, automatic garage door opener, outdoor deck. Options include central air-conditioning and cable TV. Villa residents may have pets.*

Camille, 90 years

Friendship Village, Minneapolis, Minnesota

"I don't know what I'd do without this place."

Camille has been a resident of Friendship Village for almost 20 years, since the community opened. A friend convinced her and her husband to sell their house and move."The first day our house was on the market, it sold," says Camille,"so we had to act quickly. My husband and I had looked at Friendship Village and liked it immediately." Camille's husband died ten years ago and Camille says,"I don't know what I'd do without this place."

For several years after Camille and Bill moved in they traveled extensively, visiting their son, who worked for the U.S. Department of State in the Soviet Union, as well as making trips to Germany, Norway, and California. "We loved to travel and used our apartment at Friendship Village as a home base," comments Camille.

Camille has loads of friends. She enjoys the variety of programs offered and participates in many community activities. She was chair of the book review group for years, arranging the monthly meetings and selecting the speakers, which she loved. She is still very involved with church and the services held at Friendship Village.

Recently, she fell in the bathtub and after struggling to reach the 24-hour emergency cord she pulled it to notify the health center that she needed help. Camille said someone came quickly and helped her up. Fortunately, she did not break any bones.

Her daughter Ann, who lives in Cincinnati, says she loves the security and peace of mind Friendship Village gives her. "It's so wonderful that there is someone always available to help my mother if she needs it. This certainly wouldn't be the case if she was still in her own home or living with me, so I'm very grateful."

PENNSYLVANIA

WESTMINSTER VILLAGE

803 North Wahneta Street
Allentown, PA 18103
(610) 464-6254
Lien Price, marketing director

Type of community: Nonprofit Continuing Care, modified contract

Accreditation: Continuing Care Accreditation Commission

Located in Lehigh Valley, Westminster Village offers a country atmosphere in an urban setting featuring all the conveniences of city life. A five-story apartment building houses Independent Living. Assisted Living, and Intermediate and Skilled Nursing are available. Shopping centers, libraries, theater, and community activities are minutes from Westminster Village. Nearby universities provide exceptional cultural and educational opportunities.

Financial plan: Entrance fee plus monthly fee. Entrance fee is refundable based on a 2% amortization per month for the first 50 months. $1,000 refundable application fee.

Ownership and management: Presbyterian Homes, Inc., owner and manager of 15 retirement communities and nursing homes in Delaware, Maryland, Ohio, and Pennsylvania. Opened in 1983.

Minimum age: 65 years.

Population: 82 residents; 76% women, 24% men, 21% couples.

INDEPENDENT LIVING HOUSING

Westminster House	*Entrance fee**	*Monthly fee single/double**
1-Bedroom, 600 sq. ft.	$55,100–57,350	$1,384/2,114
2-Bedroom, 760 sq. ft.	$78,900	$1,493/2,223
Deluxe 2-bedroom, 882 sq. ft.	$81,110	$1,533/2,263
Atrium apartment homes		
1-Bedroom, 576 sq. ft.	$59,500	$1,384/2,114
1-Bedroom/den, 691 sq. ft.	$68,700	$1,458/2,188
2-Bedroom, 864 sq. ft.	$85,400	$1,533/2,263
Deluxe 2-bedroom, 941 sq. ft.	$87,600	$1,583/2,313

**For double occupancy add $13,000 to the entrance fee. All utilities except telephone included. Wall-to-wall carpeting, custom interior decoration options, spacious balcony, individually controlled heating and air-conditioning, 24-hour emergency call system, fully equipped kitchen. Washer/dryer in Atrium apartments.*

Number of units: 68 Independent Living apartments; 111-bed nursing facility.

Dining plan: One meal per day included in the monthly fee. Catering services. Tray service if resident is ill. Special diets available.

Services: *Included in the monthly fee:* Housekeeping and flat-linen services, scheduled transportation, laundry facilities, outdoor reserved parking space.

At additional cost: Beauty/barbershop, gift shop.

Activities: Exercise room, trips (concerts, theater, restaurants, museums), cultural and educational opportunities, patio with gas grills for residents' use, spacious indoor recreation center, scheduled activities.

Availability: 1-bedrooms available; 18-month waiting list for 2-bedrooms.

Health services and rates: Health protection plan included in monthly fee. Physical and occupational therapy services available for apartment residents. Physician group practices on-site. Home health services available. Eldercare Program enables residents to live in their own apartments with the help of daytime care such as therapeutic recreation, physical and occupational therapies, medical support, administering of prescribed medications, two meals per day. Elder care program available for residents waiting for a long-term care bed and for Alzheimer's patients.

- 111 Intermediate and Skilled Nursing beds

Semiprivate (3-person room)	$115/day
Semiprivate (2-person room)	$122/day
Semiprivate (2-room deluxe)	$130/day
Private	$140/day

"By far the strongest link to the community is provided through the nearly 100 volunteers who contribute countless hours of service to Westminster health center residents. Through their gift of hours of service, volunteers and auxiliary members provide an extra dimension of caring that enhances the quality of life for all residents."

KIRKLAND VILLAGE

1 Kirkland Village Circle
Bethlehem, PA 18017
(610) 691-4500
Saundra C. Monk, marketing director

Type of community: Not-for-profit Continuing Care, all-inclusive contract

The three-story brick apartment complex with attached community center and health center is located on a 14-acre parklike campus in a suburban setting. Large courtyard is located in the center of complex and the grounds feature extensive landscaping, including flower and vegetable gardens. Independent Living, Assisted Living, Skilled Nursing, and special services for dementia-related illness are available. Cultural, educational, and shopping opportunities are nearby in Bethlehem, Easton, and Allentown. Muhlenberg and Cedar Crest colleges are located in Allentown; Moravian College and Lehigh University are in Bethlehem; Lafayette University is in Easton. Excellent medical facilities are nearby as well as spiritual services of all denominations.

Financial plan: Fees vary according to age at admission. Two residency investment plans: **1)** Estate preservation: a minimum of 70% refund of the apartment home investment after 18 months. **2)** Endowment plan: lower initial fee, which amortizes at 2% per month for 50 months with no refund thereafter. Residents may choose between two health service plans: the traditional health service plan provides unlimited Skilled Nursing and personal care, or the modified health service plan provides 14 days of Skilled Nursing or a commensurate amount of personal care with the unused days accumulating. Both plans provide unlimited wellness and emergency services within the apartment.

Ownership and management: Kirkland Village is a wholly owned subsidiary of Presbyterian Homes, Inc., a Pennsylvania-based nonprofit corporation.

INDEPENDENT LIVING HOUSING

Type/size of unit	*Entrance fee**	*Monthly fee**
1-Bedroom, 790 sq. ft.	$80,000+	$1,600
1-Bedroom/den, 924 sq. ft.	$90,000+	$1,700
2-Bedroom, 1,039 sq. ft.	$100,000+	$1,800
Deluxe 2-bedroom, 1,276 sq. ft.	$140,000+	$2,300

**For double occupancy add $650 to the monthly fee. All utilities except telephone included. Wall-to-wall carpeting, individually controlled heating and air-conditioning, private balcony or patio, fully equipped kitchen, washer and dryer, large walk-in closets, extra-high ceilings, 24-hour emergency call system, cable TV.*

Presbyterian Homes currently owns and operates 15 facilities in four states, providing care and services to more than 3,000 older adults. Opened in 1993.

Minimum age: 62 years.

Population: 200 residents; 70% women, 30% men, 7% couples.

Number of units: 93 Independent Living apartments; 38 Assisted Living suites, 60-bed nursing facility.

Dining plan: One meal per day included in the monthly fee. Formal dining room available for dinner or informal café available for breakfast, lunch, and dinner. Private dining room for special occasions. Meal delivery and special diets available at no extra cost when prescribed by medical director.

Services: *Included in the monthly fee:* Biweekly housekeeping, weekly flat-linen service, laundry, scheduled transportation, reserved parking spaces.

At additional cost: Beauty/barbershop, guest accommodations.

Activities: Walking/fitness trail, exercise room, gardening, crafts and hobby areas, scheduled activities and entertainment, men's and women's clubrooms, woodworking shop, ceramics studio, library, auditorium, and many cultural and educational opportunities.

Availability: No waiting list at present.

Health services and rates: Residents receive unlimited health care, including all meals, with no increase in monthly fee. Physical therapy department, pharmacy, and medical service area on-site. Assisted Living, all rehabilitation therapies, and home health services offered.

- 38 Assisted Living suites
- 60-Bed nursing facility

"Kirkland Village is the recipient of the Gold Seal Award for design by the Significant Seniors Housing Awards sponsored by the National Association of Home Builders. Our beautiful campus is located within minutes of the best hospitals, universities, theater, and other cultural activities."

NORMANDY FARMS ESTATES

1801 Morris Road
Blue Bell, PA 19422
(215) 699-8721
Patty Santiago, marketing director

Type of community: Nonprofit Continuing Care, all-inclusive contract

Elegantly styled after the famous rolling farms of Normandy, France, the community consists of 18 three-story brick buildings that house Independent Living apartments. Buildings are connected by enclosed walkways to the one-story Assisted Living residence and health center. The grounds feature walking paths, gardens, and extensive landscaping.

INDEPENDENT LIVING HOUSING

Type/size of apartment	*Entrance fee*	*Monthly fee single/double*
Studio, 390 sq. ft.	$59,000	$836
1-Bedroom, 558 sq. ft.	$91,000	$936/1,700
2-Bedroom, 822–913 sq. ft.	$111,000–121,500	$1,104/1,868
3-Bedroom, 1,169 sq. ft.	$130,500–140,500	$1,209/1,973

All utilities except telephone included. Wall-to-wall carpeting, large insulated windows, fully equipped kitchens, individually controlled heating and air-conditioning, 24-hour emergency call system (portable button), patios or balconies. Pets allowed.

Financial plan: Entrance fee plus monthly fee. $150 application fee. $1,000 deposit for apartment or placement on the waiting list. The deposit is credited toward the entrance fee.

Ownership and management: Owned by Adult Communities Total Services, Inc. (ACTS), and developed and managed by Total Care Systems, Inc. ACTS has more than 18 years of experience in Continuing Care and owns 15 retirement communities in Florida, North Carolina, and Pennsylvania. Opened in 1983.

Minimum age: 60 years.

Population: 530 residents; 70% women, 30% men, 20% couples.

Number of units: 350 Independent Living apartments; 27 Assisted Living apartments, 60-bed health center.

Dining plan: Breakfast and dinner each day included in the monthly fee. Private dining room for entertaining. Snack shop open daily and in the evening.

Services: *Included in the monthly fee:* Housekeeping, weekly flat-linen service, scheduled transportation, laundry facilities, parking.

At additional cost: Beauty/barbershop, banking services, gift shop, pharmacy, maid service, guest accommodations.

Activities: Billiards, woodworking shop, crafts room, card room, garden plots, library, theater-style auditorium, croquet, shuffleboard, garden plots, walking paths, biking.

Availability: Priority waiting list (three months to five years).

Health services and rates: Standard nursing care is covered by the monthly fee. Medical staff on duty 24 hours. Home health care is available.

- 27 Assisted Living units
- 60-Bed Skilled Nursing facility

"Normandy Farms provides an attractive lifestyle in an environment that provides a comprehensive plan of physical, social, and medical services. The full continuum of medical care is offered at no additional cost, which is what we call Continuing Care, with no fine print. Every ACTS community operates under a program of sound financial practices that offers each resident the finest possible services at the lowest cost."

BEAUMONT AT BRYN MAWR

601 North Ithan Avenue
Bryn Mawr, PA 19010
(610) 526-7000
Elena S. Brazer, director of marketing

Type of community: Nonprofit Continuing Care, all-inclusive contract

Situated on a 50-acre site in the heart of Philadelphia's Main Line, the community offers Independent Living

housed in two three-story buildings and private villas. The Austin Mansion, a beautifully restored Edwardian estate house built in 1912, has much of the original architecture and design still intact, including carved paneling and ornate frescoes and friezes. The estate house contains a clubroom, cocktail lounge, library, grand music room, and several intimate dining rooms and is adjacent to a multipurpose auditorium. The Beaumont is convenient to shopping, restaurants, places of entertainment, and historic sites along the Main Line as well as greater Philadelphia and Valley Forge. Bryn Mawr College, Rosemont College, and Villanova University are all within a mile. Churches and synagogues, 300-bed Bryn Mawr Hospital, and 475-bed Lankenau Hospital are also close by.

Financial plan: Purchase price plus monthly fee. Beaumont is a cooperative retirement community in which residents enjoy all the benefits and privileges of real estate ownership, including appreciation of value. Prices are determined by individual owners in conjunction with the board of directors. The community is debt-free.

Ownership and management: Owned by residents of the community and Beaumont Retirement Community, Inc., a nonprofit cooperative housing corporation. Managed by two boards of directors. Opened in 1988.

Minimum age: 60 years (if couple, spouse may be younger).

Population: 270 residents; 65% women, 35% men, 36% couples.

Number of units: 132 apartments and 68 private villas for Independent Living; 46-bed health center.

Dining plan: Flexible meal plan with 30 meals per person per month included in the monthly fee. Seven formal dining rooms and one private available. Special diets and tray service available. Licensed dietitian on-site.

Services: *Included in the monthly fee:* Weekly housekeeping and flat-linen services, scheduled transportation, garage parking.

At additional cost: Beauty/barbershop, personal transportation, guest suites, travel agency, gift shop.

Activities: Activities director. Indoor heated pool, whirlpool, exercise room, bridge clubs and tournaments, auditorium/multipurpose room, meeting rooms, fireplace lounge, music room, library, game room, walking trails, gardening areas, woodworking shop, outdoor activities, arts and crafts center, concerts, fashion shows, weekend trips, educational programs, movies, travelogues, seasonal parties, health club, crafts studio.

Availability: Five-year waiting list. $1,500 deposit, which is fully refundable or transferable toward the purchase of a unit at a later date, places you on the waiting list.

INDEPENDENT LIVING HOUSING

Type/size of apartment	*Monthly fee single/double**
1-Bedroom, 1,029–1,163 sq. ft.	$2,055/2,833
2-Bedroom, 1,298–2,346 sq. ft.	$2,254/3,032
Villas	
Walnut, 1,668 sq. ft	$2,574/3,353
Apple, 1,817 sq. ft.	$2,667/3,445
Chestnut, 1,970 sq. ft.	$2,787/3,565

**Purchase prices of units ranges from $200,000 to $400,000. All utilities except telephone and cable TV included in the monthly fee. Fully equipped kitchen, 24-hour emergency call system, wall-to-wall carpeting, washer and dryer, individually controlled geothermal heating and air-conditioning, balcony or patio. Each villa has a fireplace and a 1- or 2-car garage. Pets allowed.*

Health services and rates: Outpatient services, custodial, Intermediate and Skilled Nursing care, lab services and prescription service. Physical, occupational, and speech therapies available at additional cost. If necessary procedures or treatments are not available at the Bryn Mawr Hospital, other hospitals will be used. Beaumont covers costs not taken care of by Medicare and Blue Cross/Blue Shield 65 Special, providing the resident is under the care of or referred by a Beaumont physician.

Each resident is allowed up to six months residency in the health center at no additional cost unless the resident is permanently transferred by the resident review committee. Licensed Skilled Nursing, home care, Assisted Living, preventive health care, special diets, supplies, medications, and disposables included in the monthly fee. The resident is given the option to sell his or her apartment or villa. Once the unit is sold, he or she pays only the health center monthly fee. If unit is retained, resident pays both monthly fees. In the case of double occupancy of a home or apartment, the second person charge ceases when one person transfers permanently to the health center.

- 46-Bed health care center

"Beaumont at Bryn Mawr was conceived and developed as a nonprofit association to meet the need for a retirement facility of superior quality that would fulfill the health, social, and recreational needs of older persons who desire to adhere to the values and culture they previously enjoyed. To this end, Beaumont's objectives are to enable residents to live a meaningful, pleasant, rewarding, and dignified life in a friendly atmosphere; to satisfy the resident's need for independence and privacy through cooperative home ownership; to assure them of excellent health care and security; and to maintain among residents and staff a spirit of mutual concern to perpetuate the superior quality of life at Beaumont. Beaumont is the only resident-owned retirement community on Philadelphia's prestigious Main Line."

MENNO HAVEN VILLAGE

2075 Scotland Avenue
Chambersburg, PA 17201
(717) 263-8545
Karen Maclay, director of marketing

Type of community: Nonprofit Continuing Care, modified contract

Accreditation: Continuing Care Accreditation Commission

Organized and built by the Mennonite churches of Franklin County, Pennsylvania, Menno Haven Village offers five levels of care ranging from Independent Living to nursing care and including a unique adult day care program designed to meet the special needs of older adults with limited abilities. Situated on a 75-acre campus, Independent Living townhouses are located in one-story fourplex buildings clustered over the campus, separate from the health care and residential living facilities. Historic Chambersburg, population 22,000, is the county seat of Franklin County. The community is located near scenic Cumberland Valley, 45 miles southwest of Harrisburg, Pennsylvania, and 90 miles northwest of Washington, D.C., and Baltimore, Maryland; Chambersburg is easily accessible.

Financial plan: Entrance fee plus monthly fee.

Ownership and management: Nonprofit corporation managed by a board of directors. Opened in 1964.

Minimum age: 60 years for Independent Living, 64 years for Assisted Living. No age requirement in personal care or nursing.

Population: 328 Independent Living; 48 Assisted Living, 81 personal care, 171 nursing care.

Number of units: 232 Independent Living residences, 45 Assisted Living units, 79 personal care units, 173-bed nursing facility, 41-bed Alzheimer's facility.

Dining plan: No meals included for Independent Living. Residents do have option of utilizing the village inn or the coffee shop at their convenience.

Services: *Included in the monthly fee:* Scheduled transportation, personal laundry facilities, appliance maintenance.

At additional cost: Beauty/barbershop, coffee shop, restaurant, bank, gift shop, pharmacy, guest room, grocery store.

Activities: Slide shows, concerts, educational meetings, lectures, bus trips to community events, cards, exercise room, hobby center, shuffleboard, billiards, therapy pool, Jacuzzi, library, chapel service, Bible study, volunteer opportunities, resident choir.

Availability: Waiting list for Independent Living approximately three to five years, for Assisted Living approximately three years. Personal care wait is three to six months; no wait for nursing.

Health services and rates: Full range of health services. Services provided at an additional fee are dental, podiatry, physician, laboratory, X ray, occupational, speech, and physical therapies; pharmacy and emergency transportation. Adult day care program offered that allows the impaired older person to continue to live in the community while participating in a program of social, recreational, health, and rehabilitative activities. Designed to maintain or improve the level of functioning and provide an opportunity to reduce isolation and loneliness experienced by many homebound persons.

- 45 Assisted Living apartments

	Nonresident entrance fee	*Monthly fee single/double*
1-Bedroom	$35,000–47,400	$700/900

- 79 Personal care rooms

Nonresident entrance fee	*Daily fee single/double*
$500–2,000	$62/94

- 173-Bed nursing facility

	Intermediate Nursing	*Skilled Nursing*
Semiprivate (3 or 4 beds)	$79/day	$84/day
Semiprivate (2 beds)	$81/day	$86/day
Private	$91/day	$96/day

- 41-Bed Alzheimer's facility

Semiprivate (3 or 4 beds)	90/day
Semiprivate (2 beds)	$92/day
Private	$102/day

"A caring past—a promising future. This is the theme Menno Haven has selected to guide us in celebrating 30 years of Christian service to our residents. Menno Haven's mission includes providing resources for persons to enjoy a creative and fulfilling retirement, providing restorative and maintenance health services for aging or disabled persons, promoting good health practices in an atmosphere of concern for the whole person and providing spiritual resources that will help residents face all of life victoriously. The mission is reflected by employees and volunteers who express love for God through service to the residents, who demonstrate love that fosters dignity and self-respect in the residents, and who practice stewardship with honesty and integrity in carrying out their responsibilities."

INDEPENDENT LIVING HOUSING

Type of townhouse	*Entrance fee*	*Monthly fee*
1-Bedroom, 700–800 sq. ft.	$40,000–50,000	$175
2-Bedroom, 900–1,500 sq. ft.	$49,500–91,000	$175

All utilities except telephone included. Individually controlled heating and air-conditioning. Two entrances, inside/outside private storage, fully equipped kitchen with wood cabinets, coordinated carpeting and draperies, private porch/patio, washer and dryer, 24-hour emergency call system.

SHERWOOD OAKS

100 Norman Drive
Cranberry Township, PA 16046
(412) 776-8100
William A. Silbert, marketing director

Type of community: Not-for-profit Continuing Care, all-inclusive contract

Accreditation: Continuing Care Accreditation Commission

Sherwood Oaks is made up of one-story townhouses on an 84-acre wooded campus overlooking its own lake. Seven miles of covered walking paths are located throughout campus. The community features colonial-style architecture with shutters and brick-and-siding construction. The grounds include a large perennial garden, extensive vegetable gardens and fruit tree orchards, and a greenhouse. Sherwood Oaks is located 23 miles north of Pittsburgh, where Heinz Hall, Three Rivers Stadium, and the Benedum Center are located. Ross Park Mall is nearby. The community, which is located just off the Pennsylvania Turnpike at Interstate 79, offers easy access to University of Pittsburgh, Carnegie Mellon University, and their surrounding neighborhoods.

Financial plan: Entrance fee plus monthly fee. Two plans: **1)** Standard residence agreement: entrance fee refundable less initial 10% and 2% per month of residency. **2)** Estate protection plan: two refundable options are available: 90% refund of entrance fee regardless of length of residency or 100% refund available if resident remains for at least four years. 15% of entrance fee is due upon application.

Ownership and management: Owned and managed by Pittsburgh Lifetime Care Community, affiliated with the North Hills Passavant Health Corporation. Opened in 1982.

Minimum age: 62 years.

Population: 350 residents; 71% women, 29% men, 30% couples.

Number of units: 257 Independent Living townhouses; 37 Assisted Living units, 59-bed health care center.

Dining plan: One meal per day included in the monthly fee. Private dining room available for special occasions.

Services: *Included in the monthly fee:* Weekly housekeeping and flat-linen services, scheduled transportation.

At additional cost: Beauty/barbershop, coffee shop, guest house.

Activities: Indoor heated swimming pool and Jacuzzi, game rooms, library, hobby areas, greenhouse, gardening, card room, theater-style auditorium,

INDEPENDENT LIVING HOUSING

Type of Townhouse	*Entrance fee 1/2*	*Monthly fee**
Alcove, 579 sq. ft.	$65,000/97,500	$1,220
1-Bedroom, 904 sq. ft.	$81,000/121,500	$1,535
1-Bedroom/den, 904 sq. ft.	$93,500/140,250	$1,725
2-Bedroom, 1,118 sq. ft.	$93,500–120,300/140,950–180,450	$1,725–1,870
2-Bedroom/den, 1,118 sq. ft.	$129,300/193,950	$2,225
3-Bedroom, 1,495 sq. ft.	$165,000/247,500	$2,510

**For double occupancy add $710 to the monthly fee. All utilities included. Wall-to-wall carpeting, fully equipped kitchens, 24-hour emergency call system, patios, cable TV, individually controlled heating and air-conditioning. Pets allowed.*

woodworking shop, crafts rooms, music room, walking paths, Wimbledon croquet, bocce, shuffleboard, horseshoes, badminton court, practice putting green, seven miles of covered walkways.

Availability: Waiting list for some units.

Health services and rates: Residents receive unlimited nursing care, Assisted Living, and home health care at no extra charge. Health center affiliated with North Hills Passavant Hospital. Complete physical, speech, and occupational therapy programs available. Special wing with outdoor patio for dementia patients.

- 37 Assisted Living units
- 59-Bed health care center

"Sherwood Oaks was conceived of, designed, and developed by the senior adults who would eventually become its first residents. Their inherent understanding of their own needs and desires, as well as those of their peers, is reflected in the layout of the single-story townhouses (i.e., exceptionally large storage areas, spacious rooms, private patios) as well as the community center, which offers extraordinary recreation and crafts areas, excellent library with extensive periodicals section, the finest in facilities for the provision of occupational, physical, and speech therapies. With more than 60 different standing committees, the residents' association of Sherwood Oaks provides a stimulating and rewarding opportunity for continued involvement, growth, and personal fulfillment."

SPRINGHILL COMMUNITY

2323 Edinboro Road
Erie, PA 16509
(814) 868-5304
Carol Eller, marketing director

Type of community: Nonprofit Continuing Care, modified contract

Located on 36 wooded acres that feature walking trails, Springhill's five-story contemporary wood-and-brick building has a central commons area with two wings splitting into another two wings. A third wing branches off the main commons area to the Assisted Living wing. Forest View, the Skilled Nursing facility, is located on nine acres behind the Independent Living complex.

Financial plan: Entrance fee plus monthly fee. Entrance fee is 100% refundable. Required of all Independent Living residents is an additional $90 per month for Continuing Care insurance to cover 500 days of Assisted Living and another 500 days of Skilled care. $5,000 deposit for waiting list.

Ownership and management: Hamot Health Foundation. Independent and Assisted Living opened in 1990; Skilled Nursing opened in 1993.

Minimum age: 62 years (exceptions made).

Population: 195 residents; 75% women, 25% men, 35% couples.

Number of units: 129 Independent Living apartments; 34 Assisted Living units, 60-bed Skilled Nursing facility.

Dining plan: Continental breakfast plus daily meal credits included in the monthly fee. Private dining room and catering.

Services: *Included in the monthly fee:* Weekly housekeeping and flat-linen services, scheduled transportation.

At additional cost: Beauty/barbershop, guest accommodations.

Activities: Activities director. Golf, bowling, Springhill Choir, carpentry, billiards, poker, gardening, seminars, exercise, line dancing, art classes, civic projects, needlework, day/weekend trips, poets' corner.

Availability: Limited. Prospective members on waiting list have two rights of refusal before going to bottom of waiting list.

INDEPENDENT LIVING HOUSING

Type/size of apartment	*Entrance fee*	*Monthly fee**
1-Bedroom, 575/720 sq. ft.	$59,500/65,000	$1,365/1,420
1-Bedroom/den, 840 sq. ft.	$75,500	$1,535
2-Bedroom, 900 sq. ft.	$87,500	$1,755
2-Bedroom, 1,230 sq. ft.	$106,500	$1,975

**For double occupancy add $285 to the monthly fee. All utilities except telephone and cable TV included. Wall-to-wall carpeting, miniblinds, fully equipped kitchen, washer/dryer, 24-hour emergency call system, individually controlled heating and air-conditioning, patio or balcony.*

Health services and rates:

- 34 Assisted Living units*
  - Alcove $1,750/month
  - 1-Bedroom $1,935/month

**For second person without assistance, $740; with assistance, $1,085. Additional nursing care available for $60–180 per month.*

- 60 Skilled Nursing beds
  - Semiprivate $107/day
  - Private $138/day
  - Private/shower $144/day

"Springhill's sponsor, Hamot Health Foundation, has been a major institution in the Erie area for over 115 years. That relationship has enabled our residents to receive excellent care, enjoying a full Continuum of Care not only from Independent to Assisted Living to Skilled Nursing but returning from Skilled Nursing to Assisted or Independent Living. In addition, one unique characteristic of Springhill is the residents' interaction; the atmosphere of the social relationships is genuine."

FORT WASHINGTON ESTATES

1264 Fort Washington Avenue
Fort Washington, PA 19034
(215) 542-8787
Abby Layne, marketing representative

Type of community: Not-for-profit Continuing Care, all-inclusive contract

One-level brick exterior apartment complex and on-site health center are located on a 15-acre campus of green lawns surrounded by pines. Situated in a quiet suburban neighborhood, the community features walking paths throughout the grounds and enclosed walkways connecting the buildings. At the heart of the community is the activity center for recreation, arts and crafts, and dining. Banking and postal services are available on-site.

Financial plan: Entrance fee plus monthly fee.

Ownership and management: Owned by Adult Communities Total Services, Inc. (ACTS), a nonprofit organization that currently operates 15 communities in Florida, North Carolina, and Pennsylvania with more than 6,000 residents. Developed and managed by Total Care Systems, Inc. Opened in 1972.

Minimum age: None.

Population: 180 residents; 86% women, 14% men, 10% couples.

Number of units: 93 Independent Living apartments; 20 Assisted Living units, 60-bed health care center.

Dining plan: Two meals per day included in the monthly fee. Chef-prepared meals. Private dining room.

INDEPENDENT LIVING HOUSING

Type/size of unit	*Entrance fee**	*Monthly fee single/double**
Studio, 375 sq. ft.	$47,000	$896/ N/A
1-Bedroom, 530 sq. ft.	$75,000	$1,003/1,821
2-Bedroom, 810 sq. ft.	$101,000	$1,181/2,000

**For double occupancy add $5,000 to the entrance fee. All utilities except telephone included in the monthly fee. Fully equipped kitchen, individually controlled heating and air-conditioning, 24-hour emergency call system, laundry room on each floor, wall-to-wall carpeting, patio or balcony. Pets allowed.*

Services: *Included in the monthly fee:* Scheduled transportation, housekeeping, weekly flat-linen service, parking, free use of laundry room.

At additional cost: Maid service, beauty/barbershop.

Activities: Full-time activity director. Theater-style auditorium, library, billiards room, woodworking shop, activity/crafts room, fully equipped card room, garden plots, walking paths, biking, croquet, shuffleboard.

Availability: Waiting list varies according to accommodations desired. $1,000 deposit and $150 application fee for waiting list. Deposit is credited toward the entrance fee.

Health services and rates: Health care and Assisted Living included in residents' monthly fee. Medical staff on duty 24 hours daily. Staff includes resident nurse and full-time activity director. Regular doctor's and nurse's office hours. Home health care and physical and occupational therapies available.

- 20 Personal care units
- 60-Bed health care center

"Fort Washington Estates is a Continuing Care community where medical facilities are available for residents as needed at no additional cost."

WAVERLY HEIGHTS

1400 Waverly Road
Gladwyne, PA 19035
(610) 645-8600
Lynda Donovan, director of marketing

Type of community: Nonprofit Continuing Care, all-inclusive contract

The three-story brick apartment complex with stone Federal-style main building is located on a 54-acre campus that features trees, gardens, lawns, and spacious countryside views. Nature walks, community gardens, and individual garden areas are located throughout the campus. The community is located ten miles west of Philadelphia and within a few hours' drive of New York City and surrounding area.

Financial plan: Entrance fee plus monthly fee. Entrance fee returned to resident or estate upon withdrawal from the community when the vacated unit is resold to a new resident (refund will not exceed the original fee).

Ownership and management: Owned by Gladwyne-Waverly Associates and operated by Waverly Heights, Ltd., a nonprofit corporation. Independent board of trustees oversees the management of the community. Opened in 1986.

Minimum age: 60 years.

Population: 300 residents; 70% women, 30% men, 25% couples.

Number of units: 213 Independent Living apartments and 50 villas; 15 Assisted Living units, 60-bed nursing facility.

INDEPENDENT LIVING HOUSING

Type/size of unit	*Entrance fee**	*Monthly fee**
1-Bedroom, 716–1,020 sq. ft.	$124,835–212,695	$2,137–2,977
2-Bedroom, 1,100–1,310 sq. ft.	$212,695–284,750	$2,529–3,219
2-Bedroom villa, 1,450–1,578 sq. ft.	$284,750–319,755	$3,219–3,487

**For double occupancy add $15,655 to the entrance fee, $840 to the monthly fee. All utilities except telephone included. Cable TV, 24-hour emergency call system, wall-to-wall carpeting, individually controlled heating and air-conditioning, fully equipped kitchen, underground parking. Villas have garages with electric door openers and fireplaces.*

Dining plan: One meal per day included in the monthly fee. Private dining rooms available. Special diets and tray service available. Food preparation by a professional chef. Food credit for extended absences.

Services: *Included in the monthly fee:* Scheduled transportation, weekly housekeeping and flat-linen services, window washing, reserved garage and guest parking.

At additional cost: Laundry and dry cleaning services, guest accommodations.

Activities: Putting green, gardening, nature walks, residents' association, whirlpool, indoor swimming pool, arts and crafts room, Jacuzzi, exercise room, auditorium with stage, woodworking shop, library, pianos and organ, painting lessons, bridge, book reviews, book discussion groups, lecture and slide series, vocal performances, glee club, dramatic performances, weekly movies, fashion show, holiday bazaar, annual dog show, trips to cultural and special events (New York City).

Availability: Waiting list. Position on waiting list does not change in the event that prospective resident refuses an available unit.

Health services and rates: All medical care including Assisted Living and long-term nursing is fully covered for residents (with the exception of pre-existing health conditions and the use of non–Waverly Heights physicians). Muirfield Health Center offers 24-hour-a-day Skilled Nursing as well as recreational, occupational, physical, and speech therapies. Private rooms only.

- 15 Assisted Living units for nonresidents — $150/day
- 60-Bed health care center for nonresidents — $175/day

"Waverly Heights is distinguished by its elegant residential setting located on a beautifully landscaped former estate. Our full-service Continuing Care program includes comprehensive health care coverage (unlimited Skilled Nursing days, prescription drug coverage) and features a 100% recoverable entrance fee. Our lifestyle is resident driven, with 28 committees run by the men and women who live here. Committee activity ranges from cultural (art and music) to administrative (medical and building). In addition, five residents currently sit on the board of directors."

FOULKEWAYS

1120 Meetinghouse Road
Gwynedd, PA 19436
(215) 643-2200
Nancy B. Gold, director of admissions

Type of community: Not-for-profit Continuing Care, all-inclusive contract

Accreditation: Continuing Care Accreditation Commission

INDEPENDENT LIVING HOUSING

Type/size of unit	*Entrance fee single/double*	*Monthly fee*
Studio, 458 sq. ft.	$33,000/46,000	$1,383
1-Bedroom, 626–756 sq. ft.	$77,000/86,000	$1,660/2,766
1-Bedroom/den, 1,105 sq. ft.	$114,500/130,000	$2,420/3,172
2-Bedroom, 1,063 sq. ft.	$133,000/148,500	$2,420/3,172
Cottage, sq. ft. varies	$184,500/207,500	$3,112/3,803

All utilities included. Fully equipped kitchen, wall-to-wall carpeting, individually controlled heating and air-conditioning, patio or balcony, cable TV, window coverings, 24-hour emergency call system.

One- and two-story apartment complexes are located on a 94-acre wooded campus. Foulkeways includes a coffee shop, a large central area with a spacious lounge and art gallery, miles of paths winding through the woods, and a picnic grove on-site for residents' use. The community offers easy access to Philadelphia (20 miles) and New York (100 miles). Transportation by the Reading Railroad is available. Local shopping areas, theater, and orchestra are just a short trip away.

Financial plan: Entrance fee plus monthly fee. Entrance fee amortizes at 2% per month of residency.

Ownership and management: Managed by board of directors under the aegis of the Society of Friends (Quakers). Opened in 1967.

Minimum age: 65 years.

Population: 360 residents; 81% women, 19% men, 31% couples.

Number of units: 237 Independent Living apartments and 2 cottages; 32 Assisted Living units, 68-bed health care center.

Dining plan: Three meals per day included in the monthly fee. Private dining room available. Special diets and tray service available.

Services: *Included in the monthly fee:* Weekly housekeeping and flat-linen services, shopping trips, transportation to train station.

At additional cost: Beauty/barbershop, guest meals and accommodations.

Activities: Residents' association. Book reviews, arts and crafts, weaving, gardening and greenhouse, newsletter, music, theater, social issues, knitting, metalworking, woodworking, photography, billiards, volunteering, various shows in the auditorium, exercise classes, dancing, putting green, library, indoor game room, art gallery, natatorium housing an indoor swimming pool and therapy pool.

Availability: For smaller units, waiting list up to two years. Larger units have waiting list up to five years.

Health services and rates: Health care, Assisted Living, and extended care included in residents' monthly fee. Medical director on-site. Podiatry, dental work, and optometry at extra cost. Medical Center has two parlors, a beauty/barbershop, podiatrist clinic, occupational therapy room, physical therapy room and an outpatient clinic with examining rooms, dentist's office, and other support facilities.

- 32-Bed Assisted Living center
- 68-Bed Skilled Nursing facility

"The mission of Foulkeways at Gwynedd is to provide a community for elderly persons who want to maintain or improve their quality of life and their security within a framework of mutual caring and Quaker ideals."

PETER BECKER COMMUNITY

800 Maple Avenue
Harleysville, PA 19438
(215) 256-9501
Steve Cobb, admissions coordinator

Type of community: Nonprofit Continuing Care, modified contract

Located on a 54-acre campus, cottages are nestled in a wooded grove.

Financial plan: Entrance fee plus monthly fee.

Ownership and management: Owned and managed by nonprofit corporation. Opened in 1980.

Minimum age: 62 years for Independent Living; 65 years for health center.

Population: 300 residents.

Number of units: 144 Independent Living apartments and cottages; 40 Assisted Living units, 94 Intermediate and Skilled Nursing beds.

Dining plan: Three meals per day included in the monthly fee for studio rooms. One- and two-bedroom residents may contract for meals at additional cost (breakfast, $105; dinner, $144; supper, $119).

Services: *Included in the monthly fee:* Scheduled transportation, parking.

At additional cost: Beauty/barbershop, banking.

Activities: Exercise room, billiards, crafts room, woodworking shop, greenhouse, chapel, reading current events, spelling bees, shuffleboard, walking paths, bus trips to area attractions.

Availability: Waiting list.

Health services and rates: Admission can be made directly to both Assisted Living and Skilled Nursing for an entrance fee of $3,500/double or $5,000/single.

- 47 Assisted Living rooms
  - Semiprivate $64.50/day
  - Private $72.00–82.25/day
- 94-Bed nursing facility
  - Semiprivate $121.25/day
  - Private $137.75–145.50/day

"The goal of the founders of the Peter Becker Community has always been the establishment of a total Continuing Care community based on Christian principles that provides programs, care, housing, and preservation of dignity to any aging person."

INDEPENDENT LIVING HOUSING

Type/size of apartment	*Entrance fee*	*Monthly fee single/double**
Studio, 432 sq. ft.	$36,000	$506/544
1-Bedroom, 600–650 sq. ft.	$49,700	$545/583
2-Bedroom, 700–750 sq. ft.	$60,900	$605/643
Cottages		
Fourplex, 800–900 sq. ft.	$75,450	$533/571
Duplex, 1,300 sq. ft.	$108,500–122,500	$674/712–731/769

**All utilities included in the monthly fee. Full kitchens (except in studios), wall-to-wall carpeting, draperies, appliances. Some units have balconies or patios.*

THE QUADRANGLE

3300 Darby Road
Haverford, PA 19041-1095
(610) 642-3000
Renata Harrison, director of marketing

Type of community: Continuing Care, all-inclusive contract

Located on 74 wooded acres with brooks, ponds, and a number of specimen trees, the buildings were designed to complement the Linden House, an elegant English country manor house with lovely wood paneling, original moldings, and a number of woodburning fireplaces, that is the focal point of the community. Independent Living apartments and cottages, Assisted Living, and a Skilled Nursing facility are available. Some of the finest intellectual and cultural institutions in the country—Bryn Mawr, Haverford, Swarthmore, and Rosemont colleges and Villanova University—are only minutes away. Philadelphia is 30 minutes by train.

Financial plan: Entrance fee plus monthly fee. Three plans: **1)** 90% refundable entrance fee, higher entrance fee with a lower monthly fee. **2)** 90% refundable entrance fee, lower entrance fee with higher monthly fee. **3)** Nonrefundable entrance fee, lower entrance fee and the same monthly fee as Plan 1. Deposit: $1,000 single, $1,500 double.

Ownership and management: Owned and managed by Marriott Senior Living Services, a wholly owned subsidiary of Marriott Corporation. The Quadrangle board, the majority of whom are Quakers, plays an active role in admissions process, recommendation of key personnel, and many other aspects of the community. Marriott owns and operates 13 communities in Arizona, California, Florida, Illinois, Indiana, Maryland, New Jersey, Pennsylvania, Texas, and Virginia. Opened in 1989.

Minimum age: 65 years (if couple, spouse may be younger).

Population: 470 residents; 70% women, 30% men, 37% couples.

Number of units: 309 Independent Living garden-style apartments, 40 cottages; 36 Assisted Living rooms, 37 Skilled Nursing beds.

INDEPENDENT LIVING HOUSING

Type/size of apartment	*Entrance fee 1**	*Monthly fee 1**	*Entrance fee 2**	*Monthly fee 2**
1-Bedroom, 650 sq. ft.	$130,900	$1,508	$78,600	$1,932
1-Bedroom/den, 950 sq. ft.	$188,600	$1,859	$115,200	$2,512
2-Bedroom, 1,000 sq. ft.	$193,800	$2,042	$120,500	$2,768
Large 2-bedroom, 1,100 sq. ft.	$235,700	$2,338	$141,500	$3,166
Cottage				
1-Story cottage, 1,247 sq. ft.	$240,000	$2,528	$145,000	$3,257
2-Story cottage, 2,494 sq. ft.	$236,400	$2,903	$169,700	$3,712
Cottage/den, 1,452 sq. ft.	$253,500	$2,716	$163,400	$3,583
2-story cottage/den, 2,904 sq. ft.	$279,500	$3,092	$182,300	$4,048

**For double occupancy add $15,000 (nonrefundable) to the entrance fee, $613 to the monthly fee for apartments and $659 for cottages. Plan 3 has an entrance fee lower than Plan 1 ($92,000–213,000); the monthly fee is the same. All utilities except telephone included. Wall-to-wall carpeting, sheer curtains, individually controlled heating and air-conditioning, private balcony or terrace, 24-hour emergency call system. Cottages have two porches, electronic garage door opener, washer/dryers. Two-story cottages include a third bedroom and bath, a recreation room, and large unfinished storage area.*

Dining plan: One meal daily included in the monthly fee. Special diet if prescribed by medical director. Private dining room at Linden House and catering. Coffee shop. Full meal plan is available at an additional charge.

Services: *Included in the monthly fee:* Weekly housekeeping and flat-linen services, lighted parking areas, scheduled transportation, self-service washers and dryers, concierge services.

At additional cost: Gift shop, beauty/barbershop, convenience store, coffee shop, group travel arranged for special recreational occasions, bank branch office, covered parking, daily delivery of Philadelphia and New York newspapers, guest accommodations, laundry/dry cleaning pick-up and delivery.

Activities: Greenhouse, garden areas, putting green, six-hole golf course, tennis court, extensive library, arts and crafts room, painting and sculpture studio, woodworking shop, indoor swimming pool, hydrotherapy pool, exercise room, auditorium with stage.

Availability: Waiting list.

Health services and rates: Health services included in residents' entrance and monthly fees with the exception of nonprescription drugs, dentistry, and podiatry services, which are available at additional charge. Clinic, physical therapy, counseling, and social service staff.

- 36 Assisted Living apartments

	Nonresident
1-Room	$109/day
Deluxe 1-room	$156/day
1-Bedroom suite	$193–218/day

- 37 Skilled Nursing beds

	Nonresident
6 Semiprivate	$132/day
31 Private	$166/day

"Residents enjoy all the qualitative benefits of living in and contributing to a caring community, fostering life of the mind with a sense of purpose. Excellent service is more than just a business philosophy, it's been a Marriott family tradition for more than 60 years. And all that we've learned as a leader in the service and hospitality industry is applied to satisfy the needs of older adults living in our retirement communities."

KENDAL AT LONGWOOD/ CROSSLANDS/CONISTON/ CARTMEL

U.S. Route 1 and PA Route 52
Kennett Square, PA 19348
(610) 388-7001
Peg Cook, director of admissions

Type of community: Not-for-profit Continuing Care, all-inclusive contract

Accreditation: Continuing Care Accreditation Commission

Kendal at Longwood, Crosslands, Coniston, and Cartmel are related communities adjacent to each other and located in historic Chester County in southeastern Pennsylvania. They are designed to blend attractively into the local setting, amid spacious grounds. Kendal sits on 85 acres with Independent Living residences located in one-story buildings connected by covered walkways. Across a common boundary to the north, the 133-acre Crosslands contains Independent Living apartments in one- and two-story buildings built along a U-shaped ridge. Nearby Coniston and Cartmel communities offer Independent Living in homes that residents often choose as an intermediate step between living in their own homes and moving to Kendal/ Crosslands. Some of the many nearby attractions include Longwood Gardens, Winterthur, Delaware Art Museum, parks and nature preserves. Philadelphia and Wilmington are nearby.

Financial plan: Entrance fee plus monthly fee. Priority waiting list deposit of $1,100, plus $100 processing fee for Kendal and Crosslands. $1,000 Deposit, $500 application fee for Coniston and Cartmel.

Ownership and management: The Kendal Corporation, a nonprofit organization composed of members of the Religious Society of Friends. Other affiliated communities are located in Oberlin, Ohio; Hanover, New Hampshire; and Ithaca, New York. Kendal opened in 1973, Crosslands in 1977, Coniston in 1983, and Cartmel in 1989.

Minimum age: Kendal and Crosslands, 65 years; Coniston and Cartmel, 55 years.

Population: Kendal, 373; Crosslands, 394; Coniston, 32; Cartmel, 98.

Number of units: Kendal: 225 Independent Living apartments, 18 Assisted Living units, 86-bed nursing facility. Crosslands: 250 Independent Living apartments, 91-bed nursing facility. Coniston: 18 Independent Living units. Cartmel: 56 Independent Living units. Kendal and Crosslands each have separate health care centers.

Dining plan: Three meals per day are included in the monthly fee for Kendal and Crosslands residents (meal credits are available for meals not taken at the facility). Coffee shop. Private living rooms and dining rooms for special occasions. Coniston and Cartmel residents have no meals included.

Services: *Included in the monthly fee:* Kendal and Crosslands residents: scheduled transportation, weekly housekeeping and flat-linen services, lighted parking. Coniston and Cartmel residents: housekeeping.

At additional cost: Gift/sundries shop, branch banking, beauty/barbershop, guest accommodations, carports, daily newspaper delivery, laundry/dry cleaning pick-up and delivery service.

Activities: Play readings, concerts, lectures, films, art exhibitions, arts and crafts, photography, weaving, pottery, classes and study groups, indoor swimming pool at Crosslands, outdoor pool at Kendal, woodland walking paths, shuffleboard, putting green, croquet, tennis courts, health care center volunteers, gardening, newsletter publication, programs at nearby West Chester University and Pendle Hill (Quaker Study Center), excursions to Philadelphia and Washington, D.C., library, auditorium, 60 resident-sponsored committees.

Availability: Waiting list depending on type of unit desired. Coniston and Cartmel residents are provided priority access to Kendal and Crosslands on space-available basis and nursing care on fee-for-service basis.

INDEPENDENT LIVING HOUSING

Kendal and Crosslands apartments	*Entrance fee single/double*	*Monthly fee single/double*
Studio, 400 sq. ft.	$44,600	$1,390
Small 1-bedroom, 525 sq. ft.	$66,000/ 68,000	$1,515/2,490
1-Bedroom, 660 sq. ft.	$78,300/ 96,500	$1,530/2,770
1-Bedroom/study, 940 sq. ft.	$99,100/110,000	$1,805/2,835
1-Bedroom/den, 940 sq. ft.	$120,900/142,100	$1,940/2,980
2-Bedroom, 980–1,025 sq. ft.	$132,300/144,700	$2,430/3,040
Coniston and Cartmel units		
1-Bedroom/den/loft, 1,900–2,100 sq. ft.	$220,000 and up	$975
2-Bedroom/den, 1,800–1,900 sq. ft.	$220,000 and up	$975

All utilities except telephone included. Kendal and Crosslands apartments have wall-to-wall carpeting, draperies, individually controlled heating and air-conditioning, full kitchen or kitchenette, 24-hour emergency call system, terrace or balcony. Coniston and Cartmel units have fireplaces, deck/patio, 2-car garage, full kitchens, laundry room.

Health services and rates: Kendal and Crosslands residents receive lifetime health care, including Intermediate and Skilled Nursing at no additional cost. Hospital, medical, and surgical services, prescription medicines, physical, occupational, speech therapies, social service staff covered by entrance and monthly fees. Podiatry and dentistry available at additional cost. Coniston and Cartmel residents have priority access to health care services on a fee-for-service, space-available basis.

- 18 Assisted Living units
- 86-Bed nursing facility at Kendal, 91-Bed nursing facility at Crosslands

Single occupancy rooms, although two persons can be accommodated if necessary. Residents who are in the nursing facilities continue to pay the monthly fee for the apartment most recently occupied by that individual. Space permitting, Coniston and Cartmel residents as well as nonresidents may be admitted directly to the health center for temporary care for the following rates:

Intermediate care	$3,395/month or $112/day
Skilled care	$4,670/month or $154/day

"Kendal at Longwood and Crosslands offers a way of life that seeks to make the retirement years independent, productive, and stimulating. This is based on the assumption that growing older ushers in new opportunities for growth and development, even if emerging limitations at some point necessitate a degree of dependency."

BRITTANY POINTE ESTATES

1001 Valley Forge Road
Lansdale, PA 19446
(215) 855-3826
Gail Mohsenian, marketing representative

Type of community: Nonprofit Continuing Care, all-inclusive contract

Tucked away in Upper Gwynedd township, Brittany Pointe is designed to be an intimate, charming reflection of the region of France for which it is named. Landscaped lawns embrace graceful stone and brick residential buildings; rich farmlands frame the edge of the property, preserving the natural countryside that is so much a part of Brittany Pointe Estates. The interior features exquisite handmade French tiles that line the lobby, which overlooks a splashing fountain and reflecting pool. Not far from Philadelphia and close to a turnpike entrance, the community's three-story brick buildings are connected by covered walkways. Independent Living, Assisted Living, and Skilled Nursing are all on campus.

Financial plan: Entrance fee plus monthly fee. $150 application fee. $1,000 deposit, which is credited to entrance fee.

Ownership and management: Owned by Adult Communities Total Services, Inc. (ACTS), owner and manager of 15 retirement communities in Florida, North Carolina, and Pennsylvania. Opened in March 1994.

Minimum age: 60 years.

INDEPENDENT LIVING HOUSING

Type/size of apartment	*Entrance fee**	*Monthly fee single/double**
1-Bedroom, 776 sq. ft.	$108,000	$1,080/1,853
2-Bedroom, 1,094 sq. ft.	$140,000	$1,275/2,048
3-Bedroom, 1,413 sq. ft.	$162,000	$1,396/2,169

**For double occupancy add $5,000 to the entrance fee. All utilities except telephone included in the monthly fee. Fully equipped kitchens, individually controlled heating and air-conditioning, 24-hour emergency call system (portable button). Pets are allowed.*

Population: 147 residents; 61% women, 39% men.

Number of units: 99 Independent Living apartments (200 more planned); 45 Assisted Living apartments (in second phase of construction), 94 Skilled Nursing beds.

Dining plan: Breakfast and dinner daily included in the monthly fee. Private dining room for entertaining. Snack bar open daily and in the evening.

Services: *Included in the monthly fee:* Weekly flat-linen service, housekeeping, scheduled transportation, laundry facilities.

At additional cost: Beauty/barbershop, guest accommodation, postal and banking services.

Activities: Woodworking shop, activity/crafts room, fully equipped card room, billiards, theater-style auditorium, garden plots, walking paths, biking, croquet, shuffleboard.

Availability: Limited.

Health services and rates: Standard nursing costs are covered by monthly fee. Medical staff on duty 24 hours. Specialized health care services available, whirlpool baths.

- 45 Assisted Living units (in second phase of construction)
- 94-Bed Skilled Nursing facility

"Brittany Pointe Estates is the perfect community for those who have always longed for a home in the French countryside, yet want to be near enough to town to enjoy the sophisticated metropolitan pleasures."

LIMA ESTATES

411 Middleton Road
Lima, PA 19037
(610) 565-7020
Kathy Moran, marketing director

Type of community: Nonprofit Continuing Care, all-inclusive contract

Located on 54 acres in beautiful Delaware County, the 14-year-old campus has mature and well-maintained shrubs, plants, and trees on the grounds, including several large old beech trees. Two- and three-story traditional masonry buildings are connected by enclosed, heated walkways and centrally located elevators. Independent and Assisted Living and Skilled Nursing are offered. The community is 30 minutes from Philadelphia, a short trip to the historic Chadds Ford where Andrew Wyeth was born, and close to public transportation, churches, a mall, and colleges. The property is adjacent to Tyler Arboretum.

Financial plan: Entrance fee plus monthly fee. Entrance fee is refundable declining balance at 1% per month if resident moves out.

INDEPENDENT LIVING HOUSING

Type/size of unit	*Entrance fee*	*Monthly fee**
Studio, 375 sq. ft.	$59,000	$896
1-Bedroom, 549 sq. ft.	$93,000	$1,003
2-Bedroom, 795–810 sq. ft.	$118,000	$1,181
3-Bedroom, 1,130 sq. ft.	$139,000	$1,296

**For double occupancy add $819 to the monthly fee. All utilities except telephone included. Individually controlled heating and air-conditioning, wall-to-wall carpeting, draperies, fully equipped kitchens, patio or balcony adjoining each apartment, portable 24-hour emergency call system. Pets allowed.*

Ownership and management: Adult Communities Total Services, Inc.(ACTS), a nonprofit corporation that owns retirement and Continuing Care communities. Based in West Point, Pennsylvania, the company currently operates 15 communities in Florida, North Carolina, and Pennsylvania, with more than 6,000 residents. ACTS was established in 1971. Opened in 1979.

Minimum age: 60 years.

Population: 390 residents.

Number of units: 300 Independent Living apartments; 36 Assisted Living units, 60-bed nursing facility.

Dining plan: Breakfast and dinner are included in the monthly fee. Café. Private dining room for special occasions.

Services: *Included in the monthly fee:* Weekly flat-linen service, annual heavy housecleaning, transportation services, parking adjacent to apartments, washers and dryers available.

At additional cost: Beauty/barbershop, banking services, postal services, gift shop, housekeeping service.

Activities: Full-time activities director. Auditorium, library, billiards, woodworking shop, arts and crafts, cards, gardening, croquet, shuffleboard, day trips to theater, museums, and other attractions. Overnight and extended trips, cruises.

Availability: Waiting list, six months to five years.

Health services and rates: Full range of health care services included in the monthly fee. Residents continue to pay their regular monthly fee when they move into the health center. Physicians on-site, physical therapy, occupational therapy, podiatrist, home health care available in apartment.

- 36 Assisted Living units
- 60-Bed state-licensed Skilled Nursing facility

"Lima Estates as one of the 15 ACTS retirement communities has a history of financial stability and strength that goes back 22 years. As the leaders in Continuing Care, ACTS has learned what is important to our residents. There is a lot of caring, warmth, and friendliness in the community. Most of the staff have been here for more than five years and many have been here since the beginning. Lima Estates is not just a business—we are like a family. Our enclosed, heated walkways allow residents to move around the community without ever needing a coat or umbrella."

BETHANY VILLAGE

325 Wesley Drive
Mechanicsburg, PA 17055
(717) 766-0279
Steve McNaughton, sales marketing coordinator

Type of community: Nonprofit Continuing Care, modified contract

Located on 55 acres near the borough of Mechanicsburg, Bethany Village is a Continuing Care facility that features five creative living programs to provide appropriate levels of assistance for residents' personal needs: Independent Living cottages and court apartments, residential center apartments, personal care, and Skilled Nursing care. The living complex includes attractive lounges and an outdoor recreation area for residents' use.

Financial plan: Entrance fee plus daily fee (billed monthly based on number of days in month). Entrance fee amortizes at 10% per year for the first ten years. A full refund of entrance fee is guaranteed for any reason within seven days of signing the residency agreement.

Ownership and management: Owned and operated by Bethany Village Retirement Center, a subsidiary of United Methodist Homes for the Aging, Inc., owner of two retirement communities. Volunteer board of directors. Opened in 1964.

INDEPENDENT LIVING HOUSING

Type/size of apartment	*Entrance fee*	*Daily fee**
1-Bedroom, 700 sq. ft.	$58,000	$17–23
2-Bedroom, 1,062–1,464 sq. ft.	$79,000–95,000	$18–23.50
Cottages		
Various styles, 960–1,300 sq. ft.	$80,500–95,000	$16.75

**For double occupancy add $6 to the daily fee. Cable TV, 24-hour emergency call system, wall-to-wall carpeting, balcony or patio, individually controlled heating and air-conditioning, washer and dryer, fully equipped kitchen, carport or garage.*

Minimum age: 55 years for cottagers; 62 years for other levels (if couple, spouse must be at least 55).

Population: 400 residents with good mix of men and women, single, widowed, and couples.

Number of units: Independent Living: 95 single, unattached cottages/houses, 94 apartments; 27 residential living units, 56 Assisted Living units, 69-bed health care center.

Dining plan: Meal plans are optional for Independent Living residents ($5.50 per meal). Private dining room available.

Services: *Included in the monthly fee:* Scheduled and emergency transportation, parking.

At additional cost: Beauty/barbershop, pharmacy, gift shop, bank, mail room, guest accommodations.

Activities: Full-time activities director and activities center. Indoor recreation center, various trips to area cultural spots, pastoral services, residents' council, Bible study, gardening, exercise classes, slide/film presentations, fashion shows, Peach Festival, ice-cream socials, arts and crafts, card games, music hours, walking and reading programs, birthday parties, holiday celebrations, volunteering. Village Fair, held in the fall, and VENTURE learning for life series are activities that provide a unique opportunity for community interaction for the residents.

Availability: Four- to six-year waiting list for Independent Living. Six-month to two-year waiting list for residential living.

Health services and rates: Independent Living residents receive nursing care for $10 less than the prevailing daily rate during the first ten years of residence. Holistic health care center offers Intermediate and Skilled care provided by registered nurses and trained nursing assistants as ordered by each resident's personal physician. The following services are either at cost to the resident or covered by Medicare: medical evaluation, podiatry services, physical therapy, psychiatric consultation, laboratory services, contract pharmacy. Bethany Village also has contractual agreements with professionals in dentistry, ophthalmology, speech and occupational therapies, and a hearing consultant. A registered physical therapist is available five days a week.

- 27 Residential living rooms
  1-Bedroom $50.50/day*
  2-Bedroom $75/day*

  **Nonresident entrance fee: $42,000 for 1-bedroom, $54,000 for 2-bedroom.*

- 56 Assisted Living units
  Single 74/day
  1-Bedroom $115/day
- 69-Bed health care center
  Semiprivate $120/day
  Private $135/day

"At Bethany Village, the slogan 'An Adventure in Creative Living' exemplifies our philosophy of wellness and holistic health care for our aging population. Staff, administration, and residents work together to provide an exciting, vibrant community and, above all, a positive Christian atmosphere for all residents of the village."

MESSIAH VILLAGE

100 Mt. Allen Drive, P.O. Box 2015
Mechanicsburg, PA 17055-2015
(717) 697-4666
Linford Good, marketing director

Type of community: Nonprofit Continuing Care, modified contract

Accreditation: Continuing Care Accreditation Commission

Located on a 73-acre campus, the community's main building is encircled by duplex and quadraplex cottages and two three-story apartment buildings for Independent Living. It houses Sheltered Care, personal care, nursing care, and a special unit for persons with Alzheimer's disease. The campus features a creek, pond with picnic pavilion, wooded area with nature trails, and community garden plots. Messiah Village is ten miles from Harrisburg.

Financial plan: Entrance fee plus monthly fee. Entrance fee is always partially refundable. The fee is amortized at the rate of 3/4% per month for the first 100 months of occupancy. The unamortized portion (25% or greater) will be refunded within six months of the time the unit is vacated or upon resale of the unit, whichever comes first.

Ownership and management: Brethren in Christ Church. Opened in 1979.

Minimum age: 65 years.

Population: 680 residents; 75% women, 25% men, 20% couples.

Number of units: Independent Living: 129 apartments, 148 cottages; 100 Sheltered Care, 72 Intermediate Nursing beds, 120 Skilled Nursing beds, 50 Alzheimer's beds.

Dining plan: No meals included in the monthly fee. Meals may be purchased. There is a restaurant in the village.

Services: *Included in the monthly fee:* Scheduled transportation, parking.

At additional cost: Beauty/barbershop, bank, gift shop, restaurant, pharmacy, laundry facilities.

Activities: Swimming, bowling, shuffleboard, ceramics, crafts, excursions to shopping centers, restaurants, community events such as plays and musicals, Bible study, chapel, film, arts and crafts classes, picnics, and birthday parties.

Availability: Waiting list. Members of the Brethren in Christ Church may be granted admission priority.

Health services and rates: Home health services (companionship, housekeeping, transportation) available. Physical therapy.

- 100 Sheltered Care units

	Monthly	*Daily*
Single		
250–275 sq. ft.	$1,192–1,230	$39.75/41
Double		
377–492 sq. ft.	$2,325–2,400	$77.50/80

- 72 Intermediate Nursing beds

Single, 310 sq. ft.	$79/day

- 120 Skilled Nursing beds

Private	$100/day

- 50-Bed Alzheimer's care center

Semiprivate	$103/day
4-Bed room	$100/day

"Messiah Village offers a great location right by Harrisburg, a full Continuum of Care, and church affiliation."

INDEPENDENT LIVING HOUSING

Type/size of apartment	*Entrance fee*	*Monthly fee*
Studio, 456 sq. ft.	$44,000	$225
1-Bedroom, 624 sq. ft.	$61,500	$280
2-Bedroom, 960–1,120 sq. ft.	$94,500–129,000	$370–430
Cottages		
Fourplex, 700 sq. ft.	$57,000	$255
Duplex, 990–1,050 sq. ft.	$88,000	$295

Electric, telephone, and cable TV paid by resident. All apartments and cottages have carpeting, individually controlled heating and air-conditioning.

MARTINS RUN

11 Martins Run
Media, PA 19063
(215) 353-7660 or (800) 327-3875
Joan Sterrett, director of marketing/public relations

Type of community: Not-for-profit Continuing Care, all-inclusive contract

Accreditation: Continuing Care Accreditation Commission

Located on 22 landscaped acres 12 miles from Philadelphia, Martins Run offers everything under one roof including a large activity area attached to a three-wing Intermediate and Skilled Nursing facility. Eleven connecting two- and three-level apartment buildings house Independent Living apartments and Assisted Living. Beautiful outdoor views are available from apartments. Community and individual gardens and nature walks are located on the property.

Financial plan: Entrance fee plus monthly fee. Ninety-day trial period: if resident leaves community during that time, the entire entrance fee, less a small processing fee, is refundable. Should a resident leave after 90 days, 2% of the entrance fee will be absorbed into the community for each month of occupancy with the balance being refunded. Refundable application fee: $1,000.

Ownership and management: Independent, voluntary board of trustees made up of civic and business leaders, Martins Run residents, and relatives of residents oversee management, finances, and future planning of Martins Run. Opened in 1980.

Minimum age: 65 years.

Population: 220 to 230 residents; 75% women, 25% men; 29% couples; 98% of residents are Jewish.

Number of units: 197 Independent Living garden apartments; 20 Assisted Living studios, 20 Intermediate Nursing beds, 60-bed Skilled Nursing facility.

Dining plan: Dinner each day is included in the monthly fee. Breakfast and lunch available at additional cost ($30 per month for breakfast, $45 per month for lunch). Fine Kosher cuisine. Two seatings for dinner. Private rooms for entertaining and catering services available. Tray service when prescribed by Martins Run physician. Credits for meals and housekeeping will be given if a resident is away from the community for 30 days or longer.

Services: *Included in the monthly fee:* Weekly housekeeping and flat-linen services, transportation, parking, laundry facilities.

At additional cost: Beauty/barbershop, full-service bank, resident-operated commissary, daily

INDEPENDENT LIVING HOUSING

Type/size of apartment	*Entrance fee single/double*	*Monthly fee single/double*
Studio, 521 sq. ft.	$48,000	$1,250
1-Bedroom, 634 sq. ft.	$64,500/73,000	$1,330/2,190
2-Bedroom, 916 sq. ft.	$83,000/91,000	$1,845/2,640

All utilities except telephone included. Year-round climate control, 24-hour emergency call system, wall-to-wall carpeting, draperies and designer shades, fully equipped kitchens.

newspaper delivery, laundry/dry cleaning pick-up and delivery, notary public services.

Activities: 5,000 volume library, twice-weekly excursions to Philadelphia and to cultural events (museums, orchestra, ballet, theater, three nights a week in the summer to Mann Music Center), travelogues, lecture, musical performances, art and exercise classes, discussion groups, chapel, heated outdoor swimming pool, individual garden areas, card room, films, adjacent to municipal golf course.

Availability: Waiting list depends on size of apartment requested.

Health services and rates: The combination of the resident's entrance fee and monthly fee covers all medical care, from the outpatient clinic up to and including Skilled Nursing. If a resident moves permanently to the Skilled Nursing facility, the monthly fee paid is equal to that of a one-bedroom apartment.

- 20 Assisted Living private rooms with private bath
- 20-Bed Intermediate Nursing facility
- 60-Bed Skilled Nursing facility

"Historically, Martins Run was founded as the nation's first and only Jewish-oriented Continuing Care retirement community. We are now open to everyone and have been accredited by the Continuing Care Accreditation Commission."

RIDDLE VILLAGE

1048 West Baltimore Pike
Media, PA 19063
(610) 891-3777
Chuck Wininger, director of marketing

Type of community: Nonprofit Continuing Care, all-inclusive contract

Nestled on 40 acres in the heart of metropolitan Media, Riddle Village's charming Williamsburg architecture is surrounded by woodlands. Each residential building has five stories and is connected to others by enclosed walkways. Phase 2 building underway will consist of 50 additional Independent Living units. The community is convenient to shopping and cultural, educational, and recreational interests; the Philadelphia Airport is 15 minutes away.

Financial plan: Entrance fee plus monthly fee. Three plans: **1)** Entrance fee depreciates 1.5% per month for 67 months. **2)** Entrance fee is 25% more than Plan 1 and minimum refund is 50%. **3)** Entrance fee is 50% more than Plan 1 and minimum refund is 90%. $150 per person processing fee to reserve apartment along with 10% of Plan 1 entrance fee.

Ownership and management: Riddle Village Corporation. Cooperative Retirement Services of America, Inc. (CRSA). CRSA provides marketing, management, and financial consulting services to 32 senior housing developments in 15 states.

Minimum age: 62 years (if couple, spouse may be younger).

Population: 288 residents; 63% women, 37% men, 41% couples

INDEPENDENT LIVING HOUSING

Type of apartment	*Entrance fee 1**	*Monthly fee**
Studio	$79,400	$900
1-Bedroom	$105,400–119,400	$1,075–1,140
1-Bedroom	$131,400–145,400	$1,295–1,325
2-Bedroom	$169,400–184,400	$1,500–1,590
3-Bedroom	$258,800	$2,640

**For double occupancy add $9,500–10,450 to the entrance fee, $495 to the monthly fee. All utilities except telephone and cable included. Fully equipped kitchen, wall-to-wall carpeting, draperies, 24-hour emergency call system, washer/dryer, individually controlled heating and air-conditioning, balconies (except for studios).*

Number of units: 285 Independent Living units; 38 Assisted Living units, 60 Skilled Nursing beds.

Dining plan: Choice of one meal per day (buffet or sit-down) included in the monthly fee. Choice of two dining rooms. Two private dining rooms and tray service. Meal credit for residents absent seven days or longer.

Services: *Included in the monthly fee:* Weekly housekeeping and flat-linen services, scheduled transportation.

At additional cost: Beauty/barbershop, guest accommodations, bank, gift/convenience shop.

Activities: Full-time activities director. Enclosed swimming pool with Jacuzzi, adjacent fitness club and locker rooms, putting green, arts and crafts studio, auditorium/theater, game room.

Availability: Limited. Applications are being accepted for Phase 2 construction.

Health services and rates: Unlimited health care included in residents' monthly fee. State-of-the-art wellness center.

- 38 Assisted Living units
- 60 Skilled Nursing beds

"Riddle Village is a nonprofit Continuing Care community designed to provide retirement living in an atmosphere of peace and harmony to persons regardless of race, religious creed, color, sex, ancestry, or national origin. A carefully planned community, Riddle Village will provide residents with security and peace of mind."

MORAVIAN HALL SQUARE

175 West North Street
Nazareth, PA 18064-1432
(610) 746-1000
Phyllis S. Fisher, marketing

Type of community: Nonprofit Continuing Care, all-inclusive contract

Accreditation: Continuing Care Accreditation Commission

Situated on 14 landscaped acres in the historic town of Nazareth in close proximity to Bethlehem, Eastern, and Allentown, the community consists of two four-story Independent Living apartment buildings connected by sitting areas, a personal care center, and an Intermediate and Skilled Nursing facility. The grounds feature a garden court and outdoor patios with tables and umbrellas. Nazareth and the surrounding area offer an abundance of parks and activities. Delaware River National Recreation Area is 30 minutes away; the historic Delaware River is seven miles to the east. The YMCA is within walking distance.

INDEPENDENT LIVING HOUSING

Type/size of apartment	*Entrance fee**	*Monthly fee**
Studio, 292 sq. ft.	$59,900	$1,073
1-Bedroom, 500 sq. ft.	$75,900	$1,212
2-Bedroom, 692 sq. ft.	$89,900	$1,350

Note: *There are ten custom apartments. Fees are determined by size, options, and occupancy. *For double occupancy add $12,500 to the entrance fee, $500 to the monthly fee. All utilities except telephone included. Wall-to-wall carpeting, sheer draperies, pass-through window between kitchen and living room, all-electric kitchen, individually controlled heating and air-conditioning, cable TV, 24-hour emergency call system. For additional fee: dishwasher, microwave, washer/dryer. First floor apartments have cement patios with option of retractable awnings; 10 corner apartments have covered balconies.*

Financial plan: Entrance fee plus monthly fee. Guaranteed equity refund, a portion of the entrance fee is returned to the resident or the resident's estate when residency ends upon reoccupation of the apartment. $250 nonrefundable application fee. $1,000 deposit is applied to entrance fee.

Ownership and management: Eastern District of the Northern Province, Moravian Church in America. Opened in 1988.

Minimum age: 62 years (if couple, spouse may be younger).

Population: 250 residents; 78% women, 22% men, 15% couples.

Number of units: 118 Independent Living apartments; 34-room Assisted Living center, 61-bed nursing facility

Dining plan: Daily dinner is included in the monthly fee. Lunch is served; breakfast is available by tray service for additional charge.

Services: *Included in the monthly fee:* Housekeeping and flat-linen services, scheduled transportation, personal laundry facilities, parking.

At additional cost: Beauty/barbershop, personal transportation, guest accommodations, gift shop.

Activities: Full-time director. Exercise room, woodworking and crafts shop, library, photography lab, train collectors' room, lectures, billiards, shuffleboard, Bible study, trips, slide shows, walking club, investment club, garden plots, church services.

Availability: Prospective residents on waiting list may elect not to accept occupancy three times before the contract is considered broken. Individuals may place their names on more than one waiting list (there is a list for each type of accommodation) for a deposit of $1,000 per list.

Health services and rates: Independent Living residents continue to pay the same monthly fee if admitted to personal care or the nursing facility, with the additional charge for the two extra meals. Charges for medications, medical supplies, equipment, physicians services, therapy, and personal laundry will be in addition to the regular monthly fee. Individual care plan for each resident is established by an expert staff within first week of residency. Physical, occupational, and speech therapies available; optical repair services, laboratory, and X-ray services, social services. Admission may be made directly to Assisted Living or the nursing facility.

- 34-Room Assisted Living center
- 61-Bed semiprivate nursing facility

"Independence, new experiences and new friends, excellent meals served in pleasant surroundings, careful attention to residents' health needs—all this in a caring environment. The Moravian Church has a history of responding to the call of Scripture to respect and care for the aged—both by including the elderly in the life of local congregations and by establishing homes in which their lives are affirmed in relationship with God, self, and community."

THE BRETHREN HOME CROSS KEYS VILLAGE

2990 Carlisle Pike, P.O. Box 128
New Oxford, PA 17350
(717) 624-2161
Ilene M. Ruppert, admissions counselor

Type of community: Nonprofit Continuing Care, modified contract

Accreditation: Continuing Care Accreditation Commission

Nearly 300 Independent Living brick cottages and 12 apartments are located on a 200-acre wooded and landscaped campus that is curb- and step-free. The community offers 12 different styles of residences and more than three miles of paved walkways. The Pigeon Hills provide a scenic backdrop. Health care facilities and full-time bank are on campus. Philadelphia, Harrisburg, Baltimore, and Washington, D.C., are a short drive away. The community is conveniently located near shopping malls in Hanover, York, Lancaster, and Gettysburg; specialty shops, Corodus and Caledonia state parks, more than ten golf courses, six college campuses, three summer theaters, Harrisburg and York symphonies, historic Gettysburg, Gettysburg community concerts and Lancaster County and Orchard County are all nearby.

Financial plan: Entrance fee plus daily or monthly fee. Ten-year amortization of entrance fee. Refund provided under certain circumstances. $1,000 reservation fee for apartments and cottages is applied to entrance fee.

Ownership and management: Owned and managed by the Church of the Brethren. Opened in 1908.

Minimum age: 65 years.

Population: 800+ residents; 68% women, 32% men, 47% couples.

Number of units: 300 Independent Living cottages and 12 apartments; 111 Assisted Living units, 290-bed nursing facility

Dining plan: One meal per day included in the daily rate for apartments. Meals available to all residents on per-meal basis.

Services: *Included in the daily/monthly fee:* scheduled

INDEPENDENT LIVING HOUSING

Type/size of apartments	*Entrance fee*	*Daily fee*
1-Room, 350 sq. ft.	$20,000	$19.94–30.30
2-Room, 690 sq. ft	$33,000	$29.00–39.37

All utilities in apartment units included. Cable TV, kitchenettes, individually controlled heating and air-conditioning, wall-to-wall carpeting.

Cottage	*Entrance fee*	*Monthly fee**
Efficiency, 493 sq. ft.	$26,800	$175
1-Bedroom, 626–1,063 sq. ft.	$34,000–64,500	$181.50–202
2-Bedroom, 883–1,420 sq. ft.	$55,000–86,200	$193.50–218.25

**For double occupancy in cottages add $30 to the monthly fee. Fully equipped kitchen, washer and dryer, individually controlled heating and air-conditioning, wall-to-wall carpeting, cable TV. Modifications to cottages are available.*

transportation, parking, housekeeping for apartments, snow removal and lawn care for cottage units.

At additional cost: Beauty/barbershop, housekeeping for cottages, guest accommodations.

Activities: Interdenominational worship, crafts, hobbies, educational and cultural events, fine arts series, putting green, bocce court, fishing pond on campus, fully equipped workshop, garden plots, bus trips, weekly trips to shopping centers.

Availability: Waiting list from one to 2½ years depending on size of the cottage unit.

Health services and rates: $250 entrance fee for all admissions to the health center and Assisted Living. Physical, occupational, and speech therapies available. Staff physicians, regular podiatrist, access to off-campus dentist and ophthalmologist. Off-campus pharmacy offers next-day delivery. Health center has dementia wing housing 40 residents.

- 111 Assisted Living units

Single	$36.50–86/day
Double	$34–61/ day per person

- 290-Bed health center

	Intermediate Nursing	*Skilled Nursing*
Semiprivate	$83.50–86.50/day	$97.50–100.50/day
Private/ special care	$96.50–99.50/day	$110.50–113.50/day

"The Brethren Home is a nonprofit, nationally accredited Continuing Care retirement community located near historic Gettysburg and York among the scenic rolling hills of south-central Pennsylvania. The hands of many dedicated employees, volunteers, and residents work together to provide a comfortable, attractive, secure community for more than 800 maturing adults."

WHITE HORSE VILLAGE

535 Gradyville Road
Newton Square, PA 19073
(215) 358-3533
Cynthia J. Fischer, director of marketing

Type of community: Nonprofit Community Care, all-inclusive contract

Located in Delaware County horse country, White Horse Village is situated on an 83-acre parklike campus that is bounded by Ridley Creek State Park on the east and north. Independent Living is available in two two-story apartment buildings. The community is 25 minutes from historic Philadelphia and the Philadelphia Main Line. Neighboring communities include Newton Square, West Chester, Swarthmore, and Wallingford.

Financial plan: Entrance fee plus monthly fee. Two plans: **1)** Entrance fee amortizes at a rate of 2% percent of residency. **2)** Entrance fee is 90% refundable regardless of length of stay.

Ownership and management: Owned by White Horse Village, Inc., a nonprofit corporation. Short-term management contract with American Retirement Corporation of Memphis, Tennessee, which manages 17 communities in the United States.

Minimum age: 65 years (if couple, spouse may be younger).

Population: 421 residents; 65% women, 35% men, 54% couples.

Number of units: 102 Independent Living apartments, 88 garden apartments, 116 villa units; 39 Assisted Living units, 59 Skilled Nursing beds.

Dining Plan: One meal per day included in the monthly fee. Formal and informal dining locations

INDEPENDENT LIVING HOUSING

Type/size of apartment	*Entrance fee 1/2**	*Monthly fee**
Studio, 510 sq. ft.	$56,200/ 84,300	$1,179
1-Bedroom, 710 sq. ft.	$80,200/120,300	$1,445
1-Bedroom/den, 920 sq. ft.	$105,700/158,600	$1,707
2-Bedroom, 1,066 sq. ft.	$118,200/177,300	$1,779
Villa		
2-Bedroom, 1,328 sq. ft.	$149,000/223,600	$1,922

**For double occupancy add $7,900 to entrance fee for Plan 1; $12,000 to Plan 2; $670 to the monthly fee. All utilities except telephone included. Cable TV, fully equipped kitchen including dishwasher, washer and dryer, wall-to-wall carpeting, 24-hour emergency call system, individually controlled heating and air-conditioning.*

plus private dining room is available. Special diets available. Tray service offered when ordered by medical director.

Services: *Included in the monthly fee:* Weekly housekeeping and flat-linen services, transportation for medical appointments and shopping, reserved parking, transportation to meals.

At additional cost: Beauty/barbershop, group travel arranged for special social or sporting events and scenic excursions, branch banking.

Activities: More than 33 standing committees and 28 activities. Heated swimming pool with Jacuzzi, cocktail lounge, exercise center, library, conservatory, card room, billiards room, group travel program, clubhouse, auditorium, crafts rooms, recreation areas, shuffleboard, two fully equipped woodworking and metal shops, gift shop.

Availability: Waiting list varies according to unit desired. Completion of the priority list application form along with appropriate fee and preliminary medical and financial approval required for priority waiting list.

Health services and rates: Health care, excluding medication and selected services, is included in residents' entrance and monthly fees. Services not covered in health care fee include: drugs and pharmaceutical supplies, medical supplies, private duty nursing, physician visits, therapies, personal laundry, beauty/barbershop. Physical, occupational, and speech therapists as well as ophthalmology/optometry and audiological services available. White Horse Village has a cooperative contract with Bryn Mawr Hospital and Bryn Mawr Rehabilitation Center, which offers residents the therapies indicated above.

- 39 Assisted Living units
- 59 Skilled Nursing beds

"Our beautiful rural location sets us apart from many communities. Most of our apartments are single-story, garden-style units with lovely gardens. Our residents are vibrant and active people who consider White Horse Village their home."

PENNSWOOD VILLAGE

1382 Newtown Langhorne Road
Newtown, PA 18940
(215) 968-9110
Justine Richardson, admissions department

Type of community: Nonprofit Continuing Care, all-inclusive contract

Accreditation: Continuing Care Accreditation Commission

INDEPENDENT LIVING HOUSING

Type/size of apartment	*Entrance fee**	*Monthly fee**
Studio, 504 sq. ft.	$50,000	$1,402
1-Bedroom, 576–789 sq. ft.	$66,000–90,000	$1,683–1,963
1-Bedroom/den, 1,032 sq. ft.	$125,000	$2,244
2-Bedroom, 1,064 sq. ft.	$125,000	$2,244

**For double occupancy for all apartments except studio add $25,000 to the entrance fee, $841 to the monthly fee. All utilities except telephone included. Draperies, wall-to-wall carpeting, electric kitchens, individually controlled heating and air-conditioning, individual terrace or balcony, 24-hour emergency call system.*

This intergenerational Continuing Care community is situated on a 225-acre campus near Philadelphia and Princeton. The community is located across the field from the coeducational George School, a Quaker boarding school set on 225 acres. Newtown Friends, a Quaker elementary school is also nearby. Much interaction occurs between the community and both schools. The two-story buildings are connected by enclosed walkways. Independent Living apartments are offered as well as an Assisted Living unit and Skilled Nursing.

Financial plan: Entrance fee plus monthly fee. Entrance fee purchases Continuing Care contract. Three-month adjustment period during which residents are entitled to full refund of entrance fee should they depart. After adjustment period, residents are entitled to refund of entrance fee minus 3% of the principal amount for each month of occupancy. $1,000 refundable deposit per person or $1,500 for couple plus $200 processing fee per person or couple.

Ownership and management: 15-member board of directors includes three resident members who serve staggered three-year terms appointed by the board. Affiliated with the Religious Society of Friends (Quakers). Opened in 1980.

Minimum age: 65 years.

Population: 380 residents.

Number of units: 252 Independent Living apartments; 41 Assisted Living units, 45-bed Skilled Nursing facility.

Dining plan: Three meals a day included in the monthly fee. Credit is given if less than three meals a day are taken. Two dining rooms plus coffee shop open daily for all meals. American Heart Association Healthy Heart selections offered. Private dining room.

Services: *Included in the monthly fee:* Weekly housekeeping and flat-linen services, scheduled transportation.

At additional cost: Guest accommodations, gift shop, beauty/barbershop, carports.

Activities: Social, recreational, community programs. Arts and crafts including lapidary shop, woodworking shop, darkroom. Chamber music, singing groups, exercise/yoga, games, greenhouse, flower and vegetable garden plots. On the George School campus: nature trails, Olympic-size swimming pool, indoor and outdoor athletic events, movies, plays, lectures, concerts, tutoring.

Availability: Priority waiting list.

Health services and rates: Health care is included in residents' entrance and monthly fees. If residents are permanently transferred to Assisted Living or Skilled Nursing, they pay the monthly fee listed below. Dentist and podiatrist available.

- 41 Assisted Living units
  Single $1,683/month
- 45 Skilled Nursing beds
  Private $1,963/month

"Pennswood is not a typical leisure village. There is time for relaxation, but contemplative hours are likely to be balanced with a discussion of world affairs, a play or concert, or a hike along the Neshaminy Creek. Where others stress recreation, at Pennswood the emphasis is on re-creation. That hyphen is small but, we think, very important."

THE WOODS AT OXFORD MANOR

7 Locust Street
Oxford, PA 19363
(610) 932-2900
Diana Farrell, marketing counselor

Type of community: Nonprofit Continuing Care, modified contract

Accreditation: Continuing Care Accreditation Commission

Located on 14 acres, The Woods offers a landscaped, country environment. The centerpiece is the Mansion, a three-story brick structure housing the social space and dining facilities as well as five apartments. One- and two-bedroom cottages are designed to create an open, spacious atmosphere. The community is within driving distance of major metropolitan centers of West Chester, Lancaster, and Philadelphia and within walking distance of stores, banks, and post office of Oxford, a community of 4,000 located in scenic Southern Chester County.

Financial plan: Entrance fee plus monthly fee. Two plans: **1)** Declining refund plan entrance fee. If resident withdraws within the first 50 months of residence, resident receives a partial refund based on 2% amortization per month for the first 50 months. **2)** Slightly larger entrance fee and provides for a minimum of a 70% refund should you leave the village. Each resident pays a $6,000 community fee and a $12,000 health care trust fund upon entrance.

Ownership and management: Owned and managed by Presbyterian Homes, Inc., which owns and manages 16 other retirement communities in Pennsylvania, Maryland, Delaware, West Virginia, and Ohio. Opened in 1977.

Minimum age: 65 years.

Population: 190 residents; 68% women, 32% men, 56% couples.

Number of units: 5 Independent Living apartments and 31 cottages; 20 personal care rooms, 120 Skilled Nursing beds.

INDEPENDENT LIVING HOUSING

Type/size of apartment	*Entrance fee 1/2*	*Monthly fee**
1-Bedroom, 508–721 sq. ft.	$58,200–73,930/86,800–111,000	$1,480
2-Bedroom, 1,580 sq. ft.	$82,180/122,000	$1,775
Cottages		
1-Bedroom, 700 sq. ft.	$58,200/86,800	$1,480
2-Bedroom, 1,052 sq. ft.	$75,250/112,430	$1,775

**Estimated taxes are added to the monthly fee. For double occupancy add $545 to the 1-bedroom monthly fee, $525 to 2-bedroom fee. All utilities except telephone and cable TV included. Wall-to-wall carpeting, fully equipped kitchens, large closets, drapery rods, 24-hour emergency call system, individually controlled heating and air-conditioning. Cottages have laundry facilities and patio or porch.*

Dining plan: One meal per day included in the monthly fee. Tray service available. Private dining room.

Services: *Included in the monthly fee:* Weekly flat-linen service, twice monthly housekeeping, scheduled transportation.

At additional cost: Beauty/barbershop.

Activities: Outdoor recreation area, exercise room, trips to concerts, theaters, museums, cultural and educational opportunities, garden plots with flower beds.

Availability: Waiting list from two to five years.

Health services and rates: The health care trust fund allows Independent Living residents who need to be admitted to the health center to continue to pay their regular monthly fee rather than the per diem rate. There is no charge for prescription medication ordered by attending physician. Residents may apply for admission directly to the personal care or Skilled Nursing facility. Physical, speech, and occupational therapies and dental, podiatric, and audiological services are available. Residents enjoy the unexpected sound of children playing, which can be heard from Oxford Day Care Center, a program for preschool children, operated on the premises.

- 20 Personal care private rooms
  Single $68/day
- 120-Bed Skilled Nursing facility
  Semiprivate $121/day
  Private $132/day

"As a nonprofit Christian facility, Oxford Manor has incorporated empathy, loving care, and an absolute commitment to serve residents with the highest quality of care in every aspect of operation. Oxford Manor is unique because of the beauty of its country setting and the blending of the atmosphere of hospitality, for which the area is known, with innovative programming, growth and top-of-the-line service."

LEBANON VALLEY BRETHREN HOME

1200 Grubb Street
Palmyra, PA 17078
(717) 838-5406
Rev. Paul H. Boll, executive director

Type of community: Not-for-profit Continuing Care, modified contract

Located near beautiful Hershey and Lancaster in the famous Pennsylvania Dutch tourist area, Lebanon Valley Brethren Home is set on 100 acres, many of

INDEPENDENT LIVING HOUSING

Type of apartment	*Entrance fee*	*Monthly fee*
1-Bedroom	$39,900–51,000	$180–235
2-Bedroom	$52,900–73,500	$200–300
Cottages		
Studio	$24,375	$160
1-Bedroom	$31,200/42,500	$180/190
2-Bedroom	$44,000/57,300	$205/215
Duplex	$85,995/88,620	$245/270

All utilities except electricity included. Cable TV, 24-hour emergency call system, individual thermostat control.

which are still being farmed. Private, tree-lined streets and manicured lawns surround all Independent Living apartments and the health care center.

Financial plan: Entrance fee plus monthly fee. The entrance fee has a seven-year amortization schedule. For existing units entrance fee is paid in full upon signing the agreement. With new construction, 35% of the entrance fee is due upon signing the agreement, 35% when unit is under roof, and the final 30% when unit is completed. Fees are subject to change with 30 days' notice.

Ownership and management: Lebanon Valley Brethren Home. Opened in 1979.

Minimum age: 62 years.

Population: 392 residents.

Number of units: 157 Independent Living units; 38 personal care rooms, 40 residential care rooms, 58 Intermediate and 42 Skilled Nursing beds.

Dining plan: No meals included in the monthly fee for Independent Living. Meals available at extra cost. Therapeutic diets available.

Services: *Included in the monthly fee:* Housekeeping on scheduled basis, flat-linen service weekly.

At additional cost: Beauty/barbershop.

Activities: Library, reading room, therapeutic pool and exercise room, game room.

Availability: Varies according to type of unit.

Health services and rates: Two levels of Assisted Living available: residential and personal care. Physical, occupational, and speech therapies available at additional cost.

- 40 Residential rooms

	Monthly	*Daily*
Single	$3,000	$38
Double	$4,500	$57

- 38 Personal care units

Single	$3,000	$56
Double	$4,000	$90

- 100-Bed nursing facility

	Intermediate Nursing	*Skilled Nursing*
Semiprivate	$76.50/day	$87.50/day
Private	$89/day	$100/day

"Lebanon Valley offers opportunities for vibrant yet less stressful independent retirement living for the active elderly. We strive to alleviate distress and hardship for the elderly by providing support services in an environment designed for their care, while encouraging personal freedom and self-reliance."

CATHEDRAL VILLAGE

600 East Cathedral Road
Philadelphia, PA 19128
(215) 984-8622
Carole L. Owens, sales consultant

Type of community: Nonprofit Continuing Care, all-inclusive contract

Accreditation: Continuing Care Accreditation Commission

Situated on 40 acres in the suburban northwest corner of Philadelphia County adjacent to the historic community of Chestnut Hill, Cathedral Village is made up of apartments housed in ten garden-style buildings and townhouse units in two single-level buildings. All buildings are connected by covered, well-lit walkways to the main building (Houston Commons), outpatient and rehabilitation therapy departments, and to Bishop White Lodge, a 148-bed Skilled Nursing facility and Alzheimer's unit. A new health club with state-of-the-art exercise equipment and indoor swimming pool was recently added. The community features more than

INDEPENDENT LIVING HOUSING

Type/size of apartment	*Entrance fee single/double*	*Monthly fee single/double**
Studio, 382 sq. ft.	$41,500/N/A	$1,350/N/A
1½-Room, 544 sq. ft.	$56,000/N/A	$1,530/N/A
1-Bedroom, 710 sq. ft.	$80,000/90,000	$1,790/2,875
2-Bedroom, 1,032 sq. ft.	$125,000/140,000	$2,425/3,510
Townhouses		
2-Bedroom, 1,242 sq. ft.	$160,000/175,000	$2,810/3,900
Country apartments, 1,355 sq. ft.	$180,000/195,000	$2,930/4,015

**All utilities except telephone and cable TV included in the monthly fee. Balconies or patios, wall-to-wall carpeting, draperies, fully equipped kitchens (studios have kitchenettes), individually controlled heating and air-conditioning, 24-hour emergency call system, patio or balcony. Townhouses have patios and atriums.*

1½ miles of community roadways for walking or driving and is adjacent to a nature center with woods and trails for hiking and outdoor activities. Center City, filled with art, theater, and the history of Philadelphia, is 30 minutes away by car or public transportation.

Financial plan: Entrance fee plus monthly fee. The entrance fee is amortized at a rate of 2% per month.

Ownership and management: Cathedral Village Corporation is the sole owner. Cathedral Village is entirely self-managed in all areas of operation. Opened in 1979.

Minimum age: 65 years.

Population: 415 residents; 80% women, 20% men, 22% couples.

Number of units: 277 Independent Living apartments; 148-bed Skilled Nursing facility.

Dining plan: Three meals per day included in the monthly fee. A choice of menus is available at all meals. Dining facilities include an elegant formal dining room, a private dining room, and a new casual dining room, available 12 hours daily for breakfast, lunch, dinner, and take-out foods. Cathedral Village was the first retirement community of its size to assume complete responsibility for all dining services. The certified professional chef is a graduate of the Culinary Institute of America. Licensed dietitians on-site. Tray service available when recommended by the medical director.

Services: *Included in the monthly fee:* Weekly housecleaning and flat-linen services, transportation to shopping areas, hospitals for diagnostic studies, and specialists' offices, valet service to main meal if required.

At additional cost: Beauty/barbershop, laundry rooms located throughout the community, guest accommodations, personal transportation.

Activities: Residents' association. Trips to the Philadelphia Orchestra Series and to Center City theaters, guest lecturers, musical performances, slide shows and travelogues, volunteer work in and around the community, operation of the gift shop six days weekly and the library.

Availability: Waiting list depends on size, style, and location of apartment. Refusal of a unit does not change applicant's position on the waiting list.

Health services and rates: Unlimited health care included in residents' monthly fee. Primary physician care and surgical services, physicians available five days a week in outpatient department, on call 24 hours daily. Specialists, other physicians referred by staff physicians. Prescription medication written and/or approved by medical director. Community nurses available 24 hours a day for emergency care. Coordinator to arrange for appropriate companions (cost paid by resident). Physical, occupational, and speech rehabilitation therapies, podiatry. Semi-private hospital and/or Skilled Nursing facility accommodations (residents may request private room, paying the additional cost themselves).

- 148-Bed health care center

Direct entry to health center as available. Second floor of health center is a dedicated Alzheimer's unit. Environment is quiet and home-like.

"Cathedral Village is committed to promoting the highest quality of life for each resident. This is accomplished by encouraging the maximum independence, enhancement of dignity, financial security, personal choice, and optimum physical, psychological, and social well-being of each resident. Our approach to health care at all levels, from Independent Living to Skilled Nursing care, is based on each individual's unique response to aging and illness."

LOGAN SQUARE EAST

2 Franklin Town Boulevard
Philadelphia, PA 19103
(215) 563-1800, ex. 408
Peggy Brown, marketing director

Type of community: Nonprofit Continuing Care, all-inclusive contract

Located in downtown Philadelphia, this modern 24-story building and 128-bed health center are Center City's only Continuing Care retirement community. The community is close to Academy of Natural Sciences, Philadelphia Museum of Art, Fairmont Park, Rodin Museum, Pennsylvania Academy of Fine Arts, Cathedral of Saints Peter and Paul, Franklin Plaza Hotel and Convention Center, and Hahnemann Hospital. Shopping, professional offices, places of worship, theater, symphony, community college, and public library are all nearby.

Financial plan: Entrance fee plus monthly fee. Two plans: **1)** Declining refund: less 2% per month of residency. **2)** 90% Refund: 90% refund upon reoccupancy of the unit. $250 fee due upon application. 10% deposit of entrance fee due upon signing of residency agreement.

Ownership and management: Owned by Logan Square East, Inc. Opened in 1984.

Minimum age: 62 years.

Population: 500 residents; 70% women, 30% men, 10% couples.

Number of units: 322 Independent Living apartments; 128-bed health care center.

Dining plan: One meal per day included in the monthly fee. Special diets and tray service available. Private dining room available.

INDEPENDENT LIVING HOUSING

Type/size of apartment	*Entrance fee 1/2*	*Monthly fee**
Studio, 429–490 sq. ft.	$45,727–53,318/64,293–74,963	$1,369–1,506
1-Bedroom, 644–803 sq. ft.	$73,192–93,055/113,624–130,836	$1,887–2,076
2-Bedroom, 952–1,098 sq. ft.	$108,202–127,246/152,131–178,911	$2,136–2,579

**For double occupancy add $750 to the monthly fee. All utilities except telephone included in the monthly fee. Wall-to-wall carpeting, 24-hour emergency call system, fully equipped kitchens, individually controlled heating and air-conditioning.*

Services: *Included in the monthly fee:* Weekly housecleaning and flat-linen services, regularly scheduled transportation.

At additional cost: Dry cleaning, beauty/barbershop, guest accommodations.

Activities: Organized activities. Arts and crafts center, library, tours, lectures, movies, continuing adult education, exercise classes, dancing, walkers' club, bingo, shopping excursions, needlecraft.

Availability: Waiting list for some models and locations.

Health services and rates: Residents receive unlimited health care included in monthly fee with additional charges for extra meals. Physical and occupational therapy on-site. Medicare/Medicaid approved.

- Assisted Living services in resident's apartment $7.50 per 1/2 hour, $12/hour.
- 128-Bed health care center (nonresident fees)
  Semiprivate $124/day
  Private $151/day

"Logan Square East is the only full service retirement community in Center City Philadelphia offering a full range of health care services from Assisted Living to Skilled Nursing care."

THE PHILADELPHIA PROTESTANT HOME

6500 Tabor Road
Philadelphia, PA 19111
(215) 697-8000
Jamie R. McCloskey, director of admissions

Type of community: Nonprofit Continuing Care, modified contract

Accreditation: Continuing Care Accreditation Commission

Five interconnecting buildings are located on a 12-acre campus a half hour from downtown Philadelphia. The Home is adjacent to a residential area and has a parklike setting featuring walkways and benches. Parks and shopping centers are nearby and public transportation stops at the front door.

Financial plan: Two plans: **1)** Entrance fee, amortized over the first five years, plus monthly fee. **2)** Entrance fee, 90% refundable under term of occupancy, plus monthly fee (applicable to Independent Living apartments).

Ownership and management: Nonprofit organization supported by more than 40 congregations of different denominations. Management by volunteer board of directors. Opened in 1890.

Minimum age: 62 years.

Population: 500+ residents; 80% women, 20% men, 15% couples.

Number of units: 277 Independent Living apartments; 126 Assisted Living units, 106 Intermediate Nursing beds.

INDEPENDENT LIVING HOUSING

Independent Living units	*Entrance fee 1/2*	*Monthly fee**
Studio, 417 sq. ft.	$38,693–49,500/71,610–91,534	$383–474
1-Bedroom, 620 sq. ft.	$57,866–70,860/107,069–131,035	$472–558
2-Bedroom, 927 sq. ft.	$84,777–100,689/156,849–186,221	$544–617

**For double occupancy add approximately $40 to the monthly fee. All utilities except telephone included. Full kitchen, spacious living and dining areas, master antenna, 24-hour emergency call system.*

Dining plan: For residents of Independent Living, meals are available for $350 per month for three meals per day or $150 for dinner only. Meals can also be purchased individually.

Services: *Included in the monthly fee:* Scheduled transportation, parking.

At additional cost: Housekeeping, laundry, guest rooms, beauty/barbershop, commissary/gift shop.

Activities: Concerts, films, swimming pool, aquaaerobics, exercise classes, fine arts/crafts instruction, cooking classes, Bible study, off-campus trips to cultural entertainment, recreational, and shopping areas. Auditorium, games room, music room, arts and crafts, library, fitness center, bowling alleys, indoor swimming pool, greenhouse, outdoor gardens, and pavilion.

Availability: Five to eight years for Independent Living apartments. Immediate availability for Assisted Living.

Health services and rates: Applications may be made directly to Assisted Living.

- 126 Assisted Living units

*Monthly fee**	*Monthly fee only*
$1,135–2,000	$1,615–2,480

**Nonresident entrance fee: $22,119.*

- Short-term care $94/day
- 106-Bed Intermediate Nursing facility
  Semiprivate $3,284/month

"The Philadelphia Protestant Home, founded in 1889 and opened in 1890 to provide safe shelter and assistance for senior Philadelphians lacking adequate resources for self-care, now provides Independent Living, Assisted Living, and Intermediate Nursing care for adults aged 62 and older. More than 40 congregations work in cooperation with our Home to extend programs and services to all men and women of our wider communities; Christian ministry mission benevolence and charity are the foundation for our goal of providing accessible, affordable, high-quality Continuing Care for older adults."

ASBURY HEIGHTS

700 Bower Hill Road
Pittsburgh, PA 15243
(412) 571-5165
Lisa Powell, director of marketing

Type of community: Not-for-profit Continuing Care, modified contract

The community consists of 19 townhouses and seven interconnected apartment buildings located on 28 beautifully landscaped acres. Circular drives run through each living area of the community. Independent and Assisted Living and a health center are on site. Turn-of-the-century-style skylit mall centrally located within the community includes a beauty/barbershop, post office, ice-cream shop, and country

INDEPENDENT LIVING HOUSING

Type/size of unit	*Entrance fee*	*Monthly fee**
1-Bedroom, 527–844 sq. ft.	$94,045–149,439	$1,191–1,329
2-Bedroom, 801–1,084 sq. ft.	$135,731–177,304	$1,420–1,661
Garden apartments, 819 sq. ft.	$148,315	$1,473
Townhouses, 1,495–2,129 sq. ft.	$182,922–225,425	$1,229–1,441

**For double occupancy in 1- and 2-bedroom units add $229 to the monthly fee. All utilities except telephone included. Cable TV, 24-hour emergency call system, kitchenette, wall-to-wall carpeting, individually controlled heating and air-conditioning.*

store as well as benches and plants throughout. Dining room with panoramic view from top of Bower Hill Road. Asbury Heights is conveniently located close to public and private transportation.

Financial plan: Entrance fee plus monthly fee for Independent Living. Entrance fee is 90% refundable. Daily fee with no entrance fee for residential studio units.

Ownership and management: Owned and operated by the United Methodist Church. Opened in 1908.

Minimum age: 60 years.

Population: 300+ residents; 70% women, 30% men, 20% couples.

Number of units: 97 Independent Living apartments and 19 townhouses; 32 residential rooms, 58 Assisted Living units, 145-bed health care center.

Dining plan: One meal per day included in the monthly fee. Three meal per day option. Private dining rooms available. Dietary department able to meet any special dietary requirements. Seven days free tray service per year.

Services: *Included in the monthly fee:* Scheduled van transportation to and from local and nearby shopping malls, parking, weekly housekeeping and flat-linen services, complimentary TV, newspapers and magazines. Personal laundry facilities available on floors.

At additional cost: Personal laundry service, beauty/barbershop, guest accommodations.

Activities: Full-time activities director. Billiards, library, religious programs under direction of chaplain, sing-alongs, gardening, exercise, overnight outings, current events, book reviews.

Availability: 80 individuals on waiting list at present.

Health services and rates: Residents receive seven days of free care in nursing center (Skilled or Intermediate). Physician, podiatrist, pharmacy, rehabilitation services, dental and eye care, medications, nursing supplies, and X-ray services all at extra cost. Podiatrist, dentist, optician, and physical and vocational therapy specialists make regular visits to community to serve residents' medical needs. Occupational, physical, and speech therapies available. Weekly patient care conferences bring together each member of a patient's care team to summarize current health status, evaluate progress, and set new goals. Conferences combine input from patient's social worker, nurses, dietary specialist, volunteers, activities staff, and chaplain to continuously improve the quality of life for that patient.

- 32 Residential studios
  300–700 sq. ft. $77.50–100/day
- Residential rooms for
  respite care $42–76.25/day
- 58 Assisted Living rooms
  Single $47.50/day
  Double $63.50/day
  Single/bath $69/day
  Double/bath $117.50/day
- 145-Bed health care center
  Double $122.25/day per person
  Private room $143.75–178/day

"Asbury Heights is a not-for-profit Continuing Care retirement community affiliated with the United Methodist Church. We offer complete continuum of services on a fee-for-service basis to approximately 350 residents."

THE WESLEY VILLAGE

211 Roberts Road
Pittston, PA 18640
(717) 655-2891
Elaine Salus, director of admissions

Type of community: Nonprofit Continuing Care, modified contract

INDEPENDENT LIVING HOUSING

Type of unit	*Monthly rent**
Efficiency	$440
1-Bedroom	$650/675
2-Bedroom	$1,025

**For double occupancy add $35 to the monthly fee. All utilities are included. Individually controlled heating and air-conditioning, satellite TV, 24-hour emergency call system, wall-to-wall carpeting.*

Located on 57 acres of richly landscaped lawn and garden areas, The Wesley Village overlooks the Susquehanna River and Wyoming Valley. The community is comprised of three interconnecting contemporary buildings: Myers Manor Independent Living apartments (the Myers Art Exhibit is housed in the building), the Robert S. Anderson, M.D., Personal Care Facility, and the Partridge-Tippett Nursing Facility. Centrally located between Wilkes-Barre and Scranton, the community is near churches, banks, shopping areas, theaters, doctors' offices, and hospitals.

Financial plan: Monthly rental. Two security deposits, each equal to one month's rent, required.

Ownership and management: Sponsored by the United Methodist Home for the Aging of the Wyoming Conference. A board of directors made up of local business men and women and professionals. Opened in 1978.

Minimum age: 65 years.

Population: 350 residents.

Number of units: 116 Independent Living apartments; 20 Enriched Living apartments, 78-bed Assisted Living facility, 183-bed Skilled Nursing facility.

Dining plan: Independent Living residents are charged per meal: breakfast, $2.75/day; dinner, $6.50/day; supper, $4.25/day.

Services: *Included in the monthly fee:* Private parking, scheduled transportation, laundry facilities.

At additional cost: Laundry and housekeeping, gift shop, barber/beautyshop, coffee shop, convenience/snack shop, guest accommodations.

Activities: Craft classes, movies, parties, speakers and entertainment groups, seasonal outings, games, exercise, interest clubs.

Health services and rates: Full range of health care services. Enriched Living available for residents who live in Myers Manor Independent Living apartments but who need extra help with their daily routine. Provides a 24-hour staff that checks on residents regularly, assists them with meals, bathing, and medication. All Enriched Living apartments are furnished. Assisted Living unit provides 24-hour nursing supervision with personal hygiene, medication assistance, and social activities. Nursing facility staffed with registered nurses, licensed practical nurses, and nurses' aides, licensed speech and physical therapists, registered dietitians and social workers. Special program of activities designed for residents with Alzheimer's and other forms of aging disorders. Respite care provides short-term care up to one month.

- 20 Enriched Living apartments
  - Efficiency $1,350/month
  - 1-Bedroom $1,600/month
  - 2-Bedroom $2,000/month
- 78-Bed Assisted Living facility (2 levels of care)
  - Double $47–52/day
  - Private room $55–59/day
  - Single suite $88–92/day
  - Double occupancy $106–110/day
- 183-Bed nursing facility
  - Semiprivate $101–115/day
  - Private $107–121/day

"While Wesley Village is its own 'community,' we want to continue our residents' connection with the community where we reside. We encourage involvement of residents or staff in community activities—for example, making sleeping bags for the homeless, knitting hats, mittens, and scarves for children, making lap robes for residents, or answering phones for the local PBS station. We invite community groups to use our facility for meetings and programs. We pride ourselves on maintaining resident independence and continued contribution to our society."

RYDAL PARK

1515 On the Fairway
Rydal, PA 19046-1664
(215) 885-6800
Barbara Visconti, marketing director

Type of community: Continuing Care, all-inclusive contract

Accreditation: Continuing Care Accreditation Commission

Located in a quiet suburban environment on the 42-acre Rydal Estate, Rydal Park consists of five-story modern apartment buildings that house Independent Living. Assisted Living and a nursing facility are also on campus. Glass-enclosed walkways connect all buildings. The community features an indoor walking track, exercise room, outdoor garden plots, and putting green. Adjacent to Baederwood shopping centers, which contain theaters, restaurants, a supermarket, and shops, Rydal Park is less than a half hour from Philadelphia.

Financial plan: Entrance fee plus monthly fee. 90-day probationary period during which the entire entrance fee is refundable. A prorated refund is made upon a resident's withdrawal during the first 50 months. Processing fee ($250 for one person, $350 for two) and refundable $1,000 deposit required with application. Agreement provides that residents will not be asked to relinquish their residences should unforeseen financial reversals make it impossible to meet financial obligations.

Ownership and management: Philadelphia Presbytery Homes, Inc., established by the Presbytery of Philadelphia. Owner and manager of seven communities in Pennsylvania. Opened in 1974.

Minimum age: 65 years.

Population: 460 residents; 85% women, 15% men, 7% couples.

Number of units: 327 Independent Living apartments; 40 Assisted Living apartments, 120-bed Skilled Nursing facility.

Dining plan: Three meals per day included in the monthly fee. Private dining room.

INDEPENDENT LIVING HOUSING

Type/size of apartment	*Entrance fee**	*Monthly fee**
Studio, 260–316 sq. ft.	$32,400–41,100	$1,275–1,311
1-Bedroom, 525–640 sq. ft.	$62,500–84,200	$1,619–2,638
2-Bedroom, 760–813 sq. ft.	$98,700–109,700	$2,024–2,826
2-Bedroom, 1,347–1,483 sq. ft.	$175,000–224,200	$2,385–3,300

**For double occupancy depending upon size of apartment add between $11,000 and $20,000 to the entrance fee, between $720 and $1,000 to the monthly fee. All utilities included. Draperies, wall-to-wall carpeting, 24-hour emergency call system, individually controlled heating and air-conditioning. Full kitchens (except studios).*

Services: *Included in the monthly fee:* Scheduled transportation, parking, laundry facilities, regular housekeeping and flat-linen services.

At additional cost: Beauty/barbershop, Rydal shop, guest accommodations.

Activities: Billiards, shuffleboard, greenhouse, garden plots, library, chapel, auditorium, putting green, woodland trails, croquet, exercise room, excursions, cultural events.

Availability: Long waiting list for larger apartments (seven to ten years for two-bedroom); one to two years for one-bedroom. One to six months for a studio.

Health services and rates: Resident's monthly fee covers care in Rydal Park Medical Center, prescription medications, care of Rydal Park physicians, physical and occupational therapies. Should residents move into the medical center permanently, they continue to pay the same monthly fee they paid in Independent Living. Resident care department, pharmacy.

- 40 Assisted Living studios (nonresident fees)

*Entrance fee**	*Monthly fee single/double*
$45,100–46,400	$1,664/3,318

**For double occupancy add approximately $8,200.*

- 120-Bed Skilled Nursing facility

"Rydal Park's location is excellent—a wooded, suburban setting adjacent to shopping and recreation. Rydal Park's services are superb. Residents have the most comprehensive residence and care agreement to assure future health care in the finest setting. The financial stability of Philadelphia Presbytery Homes is recognized in the industry."

FOXDALE VILLAGE

500 East Marylyn Avenue
State College, PA 16801
(814) 238-3322 or (800) 253-4951
Margy Frysinger, admissions

Type of community: Not-for-profit Continuing Care, modified contract

Located on 19 acres in the geographical center of Pennsylvania near the campus of Penn State University, residential living residences, Assisted Living, and a health care center are arranged in a series of neighborhoods with views of state college's rolling hills. The area is rich in modern resources but has managed to retain the ambiance of country living. Daily direct flights to New York, Washington, D.C., and Philadelphia are available only minutes from town.

Financial plan: Entrance fee plus monthly fee. $1,000 refundable priority list deposit and a $200

INDEPENDENT LIVING HOUSING

Type/size of apartment	*Entrance fee**	*Monthly fee single/double**
Studio, 518 sq. ft.	$40,000	$1,223
1-Bedroom, 728 sq. ft.	$65,000	$1,349/1,990
1-Bedroom/den, 920 sq. ft.	$87,000	$1,475/2,116
2-Bedroom/bath, 924 sq. ft.	$84,000	$1,475/2,116
2-Bedroom/2-bath, 1,064 sq. ft.	$112,000	$1,606/2,247

**For double occupancy add $15,000 to the entrance fee except for 2-bedroom/2-bath, add $25,000 to the entrance fee. All utilities except telephone and electricity included in the monthly fee. Fully equipped kitchen, cable TV, carpeting, draperies, 24-hour emergency call system, individually controlled heating and air-conditioning, patio.*

nonrefundable registration fee. The entrance fee is amortized at a rate of 3% per month.

Ownership and management: Private, not-for-profit corporation, which is Quaker directed (majority of board of directors are Quakers).

Minimum age: 65 years (if couple, spouse must be at least 63).

Population: 230 residents; 140 women, 90 men.

Number of units: 148 residential apartments; 30 Assisted Living rooms, 32 private Skilled Nursing rooms.

Dining plan: Three meals a day included in the monthly fee. Credit is given if less than three meals per day are taken. At least one meal per day must be contracted. Dining room and coffee shop. Take-out meals are available from the coffee shop.

Services: *Included in the monthly fee:* Weekly housekeeping, transportation.

At additional cost: Gift shop, covered carports, beauty/barbershop, guest accommodations.

Activities: Strong residents' association, gardening club, book discussion group, weavers club, organized exercise, woodworkers club, film series, social issues forum, theater group, investors club, game room, computer room, extensive library, auditorium, crafts area. Residents may take classes at Penn State for no tuition on a space-available basis.

Availability: Limited.

Health services and rates: Outpatient office, pharmacy, physical therapy department, 24-hour emergency service.

- 30 Assisted Living units
  Private room, 160 sq. ft. $1,223/month
  Apartment, 320 sq. ft. $1,349/month
- 32 Skilled Nursing beds
  Single, 160 sq. ft. $1,223/month

"Foxdale is located in an area rich in modern resources but has managed to retain the ambiance of country living. A cost of living that is lower than most urban areas, the sense of security that grows out of small-town friendliness and neighborly concern and its varied physical beauty all combine to make Foxdale an ideal place to spend retirement years."

FRIENDSHIP VILLAGE OF SOUTH HILLS

1290 Boyce Road
Upper St. Clair, PA 15241
(412) 941-3100
Linda McCaig, sales manager

Type of community: Not-for-profit Continuing Care, all-inclusive contract

The four-story apartment complex is located on 63 parklike acres in a natural, suburban setting with gardens. Some apartments overlook nine-hole golf course that residents may use. The community is located within 15 miles of Pittsburgh, which offers many services, shopping districts, universities, professional sports centers, and cultural opportunities. South Hills Shopping Center is nearby. The community also offers easy access to Washington, D.C., and Philadelphia.

Financial plan: Entrance fee plus monthly fee. Two plans: **1)** Return of Capital plan: 90% return of entrance fee regardless of length of stay. **2)** Traditional entrance fee: refund less 2% per month of residency available for some studio and alcove apartments (limited number of traditional entrance fee plans available).

Ownership and management: Owned and operated by Life Care Retirement Communities, Inc. Managed by Life Care Services of Des Moines, Iowa, having more than 20 years of experience at more than 50 Continuing Care communities throughout the United States. Opened in 1984.

Minimum age: 62 years.

Population: 250 residents; 76% women, 24 % men, 14% couples.

Number of units: 291 Independent Living apartments; 60-bed health care center, 21-bed nursing section.

Dining plan: One meal per day included in the monthly fee with option of complete table service or buffet. Fine dining and dietitian services, special diets, and tray service available. Private dining room. Unused meal credits can be used for guest meals at no additional charge.

Services: *Included in the monthly fee:* Weekly housekeeping and flat-linen services, scheduled transportation for shopping, professional appointments, and worship services, personal laundry facilities available, outdoor parking.

At additional cost: Beauty/barbershop, garages, personal laundry, full-service bank and 24-hour automatic teller, convenience store.

Activities: Professional activities director. Chaplain and interdenominational chapel services. Billiards room, arts and crafts center, greenhouse, personal garden areas, woodworking shop, private card rooms, pub, 250-seat auditorium, exercise room and Jacuzzi, library, tours, lectures, films, holiday and birthday get-togethers, continuing adult education, exercise programs.

Availability: Waiting list varies according to accommodations.

Health services and rates: Residents receive unlimited use of health center and Assisted Living included in their monthly fee. Health center offers preventive, short-term and long-term recuperative care, including therapy services. A registered nurse supervises nursing care 24 hours a day and a physician is on call. Phase 3 construction will add special care unit tailored to patients with dementia, Alzheimer's, and related disorders.

- 60-Bed health care center
- 21-Bed special care unit

INDEPENDENT LIVING HOUSING

Type/size of apartments	*Entrance fee 1*	*Monthly fee**
Studio, 284 sq. ft.	$65,200	$947
Alcove, 420 sq. ft.	$86,200	$1,100
1-Bedroom, 552–696 sq. ft.	$116,300–141,300	$1,251–1,407
2-Bedroom, 840–984 sq. ft.	$168,200–197,100	$1,557–1,710
3-Bedroom, 1,200 sq. ft.	$242,200	$2,016
Phase 3 apartments		
1-Bedroom, 820 sq. ft.	$159,000	$1,472
2-Bedroom, 960–1,083 sq. ft.	$190,000–215,000	$1,720
2-Bedroom/den, 1,252 sq. ft.	$251,000	$1,928
3-Bedroom, 1,388–1,474 sq. ft.	$277,000–292,000	$2,116–2,190

**For double occupancy add $641 to the monthly fee. All utilities included. Cable TV, 24-hour emergency call system, individually controlled heating and air-conditioning, fully equipped kitchen, wall-to-wall carpeting.*

Bobbi and Pierre, 86 years

The Gables and Fowler Nursing Center, Guilford, Connecticut

"We had to make the decision for our parents; my father was getting forgetful. We knew we were in trouble."

The decision of where to move and when fell to Bobbi and Pierre's son, Peter, and daughter, Pat, when they felt Pierre was becoming senile and could no longer help Bobbi take care of their home on Cape Cod. At times Pierre would become forgetful and his behavior was erratic. It wasn't safe for him to drive anymore, something he didn't understand or appreciate, and it was a constant struggle for Bobbi to manage him.

All of these things worried Pat and Peter. One alternative was to find someone to come in and help, but at a certain point, Pat and Peter felt it would be too difficult for Bobbi to handle Pierre and care for the house. The only other sensible alternative was to move their parents to a retirement community. According to Pat, "Peter had gone through a search for his mother-in-law and was convinced a retirement community was the answer and felt we needed to make the move quickly so Bobbi and Pierre could be admitted as a couple."

"It wasn't so much a matter of where we wanted them to be," explains Peter, "it was a question of where they could get in. Cost was also a determining factor and we eliminated higher-priced communities with entrance fees." Pat and Peter wanted to find a community somewhere in the Northeast, convenient to their homes in New York City and Albany. One community Peter visited felt Pierre was not independent enough to be admitted. Another had a waiting list and recommended a new community, The Gables, which was being built near Guilford.

The Gables met several important criteria: they would accept Bobbi and Pierre, the facility was beautifully designed within a wooded setting and it was affordable. "We liked the fact that all The Gables required was a monthly rental with nothing up front," says Peter. "We weren't sure how long it would take to sell the house and therefore couldn't count on using that money. As it turned out, we weren't able to sell it for almost a year."

Pat and Peter also liked the fact that there was a full-time nurse on premises and good medical care in the area. Plus, The Gables had a relationship with the Fowler Nursing Center, an excellent nursing home located only ten minutes away. From search to move-in took approximately eight months. Pierre lived at The Gables for only a year, during which time he was diagnosed with Alzheimer's. The Gables helped arrange day care twice a week and finally two years ago Pierre moved to Fowler.

"The executive director at the time was very welcoming," says Pat. "My mother had said she would never move, but when Peter took her to visit The Gables she immediately liked the executive director, the country setting and the design, and—most importantly—she felt comfortable, so she agreed to move." Pat says it was very good for her parents to come in at the beginning. "There was a great sense of camaraderie among the residents, everyone was very warm and very welcoming; no cliques or social groups had formed. There was a sense of unity because it was one apartment building and the residents were all sharing the same space."

As it turned out, Bobbi and Pierre's apartment was on the same floor as the Assisted Living unit. Because the nurses were aware of Pierre's deteriorating condition they would often stop in to check on Bobbi and give her support. Pat says that when it was clear Pierre needed to be moved to the Fowler Nursing Center it was a pretty easy move. "Fowler is a fabulous place for my father. It's not institutional; it's an old house that's been enlarged and has the feeling of a home. Bobbi takes the bus to visit him twice a week and everybody at the nursing center knows her."

Pat's advice: When making your decision, imagine that you will eventually need health care. Investigate the Continuing Care options thoroughly so you won't have surprises or difficult decisions to make later. It's key to know how readily available this care is, how conveniently located it is (if it's off-campus), and the potential costs involved.

Peter's advice: Besides the obvious of moving in before it's too late, if you're making the decision for someone else, always keep in mind that person's style of living and routine and what kind of people they like to be around. This will help you find a place where they will feel comfortable.

WILLOW VALLEY MANOR, LAKES MANOR, MANOR NORTH

300 Willow Valley Lakes Drive
Willow Street, PA 17584-9491
(717)464-2787
Kimberly Miller, marketing director

Type of community: Nonprofit Continuing Care, all-inclusive contract

Accreditation: Continuing Care Accreditation Commission

Tucked away in the pastoral splendor of beautiful Willow Valley, the Manor and Lakes Manor have been developed by experts in the Continuing Care industry. This large, sprawling community has its own shopping mall, grocery, bank, pharmacy, and dry cleaners. The octagonal lobby and sweeping hallways are just two examples of the elegant design. Independent Living, Assisted Living, and Skilled Nursing care are offered. The community is located three miles from downtown Lancaster.

Financial plan: Entrance fee plus monthly fee. Guaranteed refund of 33% of entrance fee if resident moves after 71 months.

Ownership and management: Willow Valley Associates, a nonprofit corporation. Opened in 1984.

Minimum age: 60 years.

Population: 1,500 residents; 66% women, 34% men, 60% couples.

Number of units: 1,030 Independent Living residences; 100 Assisted Living units, 180-bed health care center.

Dining plan: Two meals per day included in the monthly fee except for mid-rises and villas. Private dining room.

Services: *Included in the monthly fee:* Weekly flat-linen service (except for mid-rises and villas), scheduled transportation, laundry facilities, twice yearly housecleaning.

INDEPENDENT LIVING HOUSING

Type/size of apartment	*Entrance fee**	*Monthly fee**
Studio, 430 sq. ft.	$55,900	$830
1-Bedroom, 625–660 sq. ft.	$89,400–91,900	$895–929
2-Bedroom, 905 sq. ft.	$110,900–115,400	$961–992
Deluxe 2-bedroom, 1,215 sq. ft.	$127,400–131,900	$1,044–1,057
Deluxe 2-bedroom/study, 1,453 sq. ft.	$131,900–151,900	$1,038–1,181

**For double occupancy add $508.50 to the monthly fee. All utilities except telephone included. Wall-to-wall carpeting, individually controlled central heating and air-conditioning, 24-hour emergency call system, all-electric kitchen, patio or balcony.*

At additional cost: Grocery, bank, pharmacy, dry cleaners.

Activities: Lectures, concerts, exercise classes, crafts, shopping excursions, parties. Modest annual fee covers swimming and golf.

Availability: Waiting list.

Health services and rates: Resident's monthly fee covers health care costs with the exception of outside physicians, therapists, and hospitalization. Occupational, speech, and physical therapies offered.

- 100 Assisted Living units
  Semiprivate $45–92/day
- 180-Bed Skilled Nursing facility
  Semiprivate $106/day
  Private $139/day

"Located in the rolling farmlands of beautiful Lancaster County, Willow Valley Manor, Lakes and Manor North provide a gracious retirement lifestyle to a regional population with residents hailing from 22 states and three countries. Our Continuing Care contract provides Assisted Living and Medicare-certified nursing care on-site at no additional charge."

MEADOWOOD

3205 Skippack Pike, P.O. Box 670
Worcester, PA 19490-0670
(610) 584-1000
Barbara Chierici, director of marketing

Type of community: Not-for-profit Continuing Care, all-inclusive contract

Located on 114 acres in a rural setting, 60 Independent Living units are housed in a two-story apartment building with remaining apartments clustered around greens in a campus setting. The community is surrounded by meadows, woods, gardens, and country vistas. All buildings are connected by covered walkways and interspersed with gardens. Walking paths are located throughout the wooded areas. The community is convenient to greater Philadelphia, shopping malls, and historical sites; it is approximately four miles from Skippack Village.

Financial plan: Entrance fee plus monthly fee. Two plans: **1)** 90% refundable: higher entrance fee, 90% refundable upon transference of residence to new resident. **2)** Declining refund: lower entrance fee, refundable less 2% per month of residency. Both options fully refundable within first 90 days of residency. 10% deposit of entrance fee and $100 processing fee reserves apartment.

Ownership and management: Meadowood is wholly self-governed and self-supported under its own board of directors. Opened in 1988.

Minimum age: 65 years.

Population: 305 residents; 67% women, 33% men, 39% couples.

Number of units: 256 Independent Living apartments; 51 Assisted Living units, 59-bed health care center.

INDEPENDENT LIVING HOUSING

Type/size of unit	*Entrance fee 1/2**	*Monthly fee**
1-Bedroom, 580–898 sq. ft.	$66,885–111,755/108,125–155,135	$1,465–1,668
2-Bedroom, 910–1,400 sq. ft.	$111,755–186,260/155,135–258,555	$1,938–2,901

**For double occupancy add $10,550 to Plan 2 entrance fee, $13,600 to Plan1 entrance fee, $844 to the monthly fee. All utilities except telephone included. Wall-to-wall carpeting, individually controlled heating and air-conditioning, fully equipped kitchens, washer and dryer, patios or balconies, 24-hour emergency call system.*

Dining plan: One meal per day included in the monthly fee.

Services: *Included in the monthly fee:* Weekly housekeeping and flat-linen services, scheduled transportation, open parking.

At additional cost: Beauty/barbershop, carports, additional transportation, guesthouse.

Activities: Residents' association. Library, community room, arts and crafts room, woodworking shop, gardening, entertainment programs, exercise equipment, social room, various seminars and trips.

Availability: Waiting list for some larger apartments. Future priority list: to reserve an apartment for sometime in the future, a $1,000 deposit and $100 processing fee per person is required. Deposit is refundable should move-in not take place, processing fee is not.

Health services and rates: Health care and Assisted Living, including prescription drugs and therapy, included in residents' entrance and monthly fees. Health center (Holly House) offers long- and short-term care connected to the Schultz Community Center. Resident Care Clinic for minor medical aid. Physical, occupational, and speech therapies offered. Podiatrist and dentist available on-site at additional cost. Direct entrance to Assisted Living on space-available basis. Nonresident fee listed below.

- 51-Unit Assisted Living section

Entrance fee	*Monthly fee*
$75,000–85,000	$1,905–2,150

- 59-Bed health care center

Semiprivate	$133/day
Private	$160/day

"Meadowood is a full Continuing Care community located on the rolling countryside of Montgomery County. The community won recognition as the best senior living facility in the 1989 annual design awards issue of *Restaurant/Hotel Design International* magazine."

PASSAVANT RETIREMENT AND HEALTH CENTER

401 South Main Street
Zelienople, PA 16063
(412) 452-5400
Joanne Kirkwood, director of resident relations

Type of community: Nonprofit Continuing Care, modified contract

The community is located on 42 acres in the historic town of Zelienople, which was once part of the 10,000-acre estate of entrepreneur Dettmar Friedrich Wilhelm Basse, who founded the original village in 1805 and named it in honor of his daughter, Zelie. Churches, banks, schools, and restaurants are within walking distance. The community is 45 minutes north of downtown Pittsburgh.

Financial plan: Entrance fee plus monthly fee. $75 nonrefundable application fee. $500 refundable deposit.

Ownership and management: Established by the Pittsburgh Synod of the Lutheran Church. A member of Lutheran Affiliated Services. Opened in 1905.

Minimum age: 65 years.

Population: 550 residents; 67% women, 33% men, 40% couples.

Number of units: 130 Independent Living cottages and 77 apartment units; 82 Assisted Living efficiency apartments, 166-bed Intermediate and Skilled Nursing facility.

Dining plan: Two meals provided weekly in the monthly fee. Additional meals available at cost. Tray service is available.

Services: *Included in the monthly fee:* Housekeeping twice monthly, van transportation.

INDEPENDENT LIVING HOUSING

Wittenberg Place apartments	*Entrance fee*	*Monthly fee**
1-Bedroom, 488–624 sq. ft.	$10,000–13,500	$905–1,235
2-Bedroom, 832 sq. ft.	$15,500	$1,395
Cottages		
Efficiency, 414 sq. ft.	$10,500	$955
1-Bedroom, 650 sq. ft.	$14,000–16,000	$1,285–1,450
2-Bedroom, 900–1,400 sq. ft.	$16,000–20,500	$1,460–1,875

**All utilities except telephone and cable TV included in the monthly fee. Wall-to-wall carpeting, fully equipped kitchens, window treatments, 24-hour emergency call system. Laundry hookups in every cottage with laundry facilities on each floor of the apartment building. Monthly fee for cottages includes property taxes. Cottage options: covered patio, central air-conditioning, humidifier, fireplace, attached 1-car garage.*

At additional cost: Beauty/barbershop, laundry services, housekeeping, major appliance repairs, nonlocal transportation, guest accommodations.

Activities: Arts and crafts classes, ceramic classes, exercise facilities, music classes, line dancing, bingo, discussion groups, movie matinees, bridge classes, scheduled trips, special entertainment, Bible study, Scripture and song, chapel. Nearby are nature trails and boating facilities, two golf courses, tennis courts, swimming pools, bowling alley, and places to fish, hunt, ice-skate, horseback ride, ski, and camp. Passavant residents operate a retirement learning center offering noncredit college courses in cooperation with Slippery Rock University. Active corps of volunteers helps with activities program, provides escort service, operates the gift shop, and makes friendly visits.

Availability: Waiting list (two months to one year).

Health services and rates: Three licensed physicians staff in-house clinic, make rounds five days a week and are on call 24 hours a day. Physical therapists, speech pathologists, and audiologists provide full range of rehabilitation services at additional cost. Visits by podiatrists, dentist, and psychiatrists. Respite (temporary) care is available. Every room in health center has lovely view of the campus and surrounding countryside.

- 82 Assisted Living units

	Entrance fee	*Monthly fee*
1-Room	$7,500	$1,300
2-Room	$12,500	$1,500

- 166 Nursing beds

	Intermediate Nursing	*Skilled Nursing*
Semiprivate	$81/day	$91/day
Private	$101/day	$111/day

"We affirm life as a gift from God and seek to provide services that create physical and spiritual well-being and bring to each individual the opportunity for significant relationships, meaningful activities, and security. Our residents find a caring atmosphere where the staff—as well as the other residents—are like family members and our friendliness and compassion are only exceeded by the high standards of care we offer."

SOUTH CAROLINA

MYRTLE BEACH MANOR

9201 North Kings Highway
Myrtle Beach, SC 29577
(803) 449-5283
Mary Lou Blackmon, executive director

Type of community: Continuing Care, modified contract

Located on six acres of South Carolina's loveliest seacoast, red brick, colonial-style apartments offer Independent Living and a Skilled Nursing facility. Myrtle Beach Manor is located 1½ miles north of the Myrtle Beach city limits.

Financial plan: Monthly rental fee.

Ownership and management: Managed by The Forum Group, Inc., which owns and manages 27 retirement communities in the United States and has more than 25 years of experience in the retirement living industry. Opened in 1969.

Minimum age: 60 years.

Population: 140 residents; 75% women, 25% men, 5% couples.

Number of units: 59 Independent Living apartments; 79-bed health care center, 17-bed Alzheimer's unit.

Dining plan: Three meals per day included in the monthly rental fee.

Services: *Included in the monthly fee:* Weekly housekeeping and flat-linen services, laundry facilities on each floor, scheduled transportation.

At additional cost: Transportation outside a five-mile radius of the community, beauty/barbershop, overnight guest room.

Activities: Full-time program director. Movies, lectures, exercise classes, travel tours, scheduled transportation to cultural and sports events, library, arts and crafts, bridge, happy hour.

Availability: Limited. Waiting list for some Independent Living apartments.

Health services and rates: Residents receive ten free days per year in the health care center, up to a lifetime total of 30 days. Medical director, list of attending physicians and therapists always available. Activities program in health care center promotes

INDEPENDENT LIVING HOUSING

Type/size of apartment	*Monthly rental fee**
Studio, 276–330 sq. ft.	$1,100–1,485
Efficiency, 500 sq. ft.	$1,675–1,786
1-Bedroom, 713 sq. ft.	$2,000

**For double occupancy add $350 to the monthly rental fee. All utilities except telephone and cable TV included. Wall-to-wall carpeting, individually controlled heating and air-conditioning, 24-hour emergency call system.*

self-esteem, psychological well-being, and physical rehabilitation. Physical, occupational, and speech therapies are available.

- 79-Bed Skilled Nursing center

Semiprivate	$75/day
Private	$83/day

- 17-Bed Alzheimer's unit

Semiprivate	$81/day
Private	$91/day

"Myrtle Beach Manor is a small retirement community that fosters more of a family-type atmosphere than most other communities. We offer the independent apartment lifestyle and if residents need nursing care they are provided with excellent service in our attached Skilled Nursing facility."

TENNESSEE

HERITAGE PLACE

2990 Hickory Hill Road
Memphis, TN 38115
(901) 794-8857
Jim Watson, manager

Type of community: Independent and Assisted Living

The community is located in the Hickory Hill neighborhood, near Apple Tree Shopping Center, convenient to churches, medical facilities, and entertainment. The two-story brick building with patios and balconies is surrounded by beautifully landscaped courtyards. A central building with six connecting wings houses Independent and Assisted Living.

Financial plan: Monthly fee. Security deposit of $1,000 required upon occupancy. This deposit is placed in an escrow interest-bearing account and refunded plus interest after the department is vacated, minus refurbishing costs. Residents do not sign leases.

Ownership and management: Holiday Retirement Corporation, owner and operator of 130 retirement facilities with some Assisted Living. Opened in 1983.

Minimum age: 55 years.

Population: 173 residents.

Number of units: 117 Independent Living apartments; 43 Assisted Living apartments.

Dining plan: Choice of lunch or dinner included in the monthly fee. Private dining room available for residents' use.

Services: *Included in the monthly fee:* Weekly housekeeping, scheduled transportation.

At additional cost: Beauty/barbershop, in-house banking services.

Activities: Planned social, educational, cultural, and recreational events. Fitness and exercise room, library, card and game rooms, arts and crafts, weekly worship and Bible study, garden plots.

INDEPENDENT LIVING HOUSING

Type/size of apartment	*Monthly fee single/double*
Studio, 510 sq. ft.	$1,055/1,405
1-Bedroom, 580 sq. ft.	$1,215/1,565
2-Bedroom, 960 sq. ft.	$1,405/1,755

All utilities except telephone included. Wall-to-wall carpeting, draperies, fully equipped kitchen, individually controlled heating and air-conditioning, 24-hour emergency call system. Bedroom apartments have patios or balconies.

Availability: Waiting list for two-bedroom apartments.

Health services and rates: Health programs provided by registered nurse. Short stays—by day, week, or month—available.

- 43 Assisted Living apartments

Studio	$1,755–2,105/month
1-Bedroom	$1,915–2,265/month
2-Bedroom	$2,105–2,455/month

"Heritage Place is unusual because it offers a choice of apartment size for Assisted Living. A short stay program offers a furnished apartment for those who want to come in for a day, week, or month to recuperate from surgery or to have a trial stay."

THE PARKVIEW

1914 Poplar Avenue
Memphis, TN 38104
(901) 725-4606
Beverly Wells, director of marketing

Type of community: Nonprofit Independent Living and Assisted Living

The community is housed in a ten-story luxury apartment building built in 1924. The lobby is elegantly designed with walnut paneling and the apartments are spacious. Located in midtown Memphis, The Parkview is close to Memphis's Brooks Museum of Art, the zoo, a nine-hole golf course, shopping and theater districts, medical centers, and several colleges: Rhodes College, Memphis State University, Christian Brothers College, and Memphis College of Art.

Financial plan: Monthly rental fee.

Ownership and management: Presbytery of Memphis. Opened in 1964.

Minimum age: 62 years.

Population: 121 residents. Some residents are still working part-time. Because of the large number of colleges in the neighborhood, The Parkview houses quite a few retired college professors.

Number of units: 106 Independent Living apartments; 15 Assisted Living apartments.

Dining plan: One meal per day of resident's choice included in the monthly fee for residents in apartments with kitchens. Other meal plans are available. Three meals are served daily.

Services: *Included in the monthly fee:* Weekly maid service, general cleaning, and flat-linen service, reserved parking, laundry facilities, and scheduled transportation.

At additional cost: Beauty/barbershop, guest accommodations.

INDEPENDENT LIVING HOUSING

Type/size of apartment	*Monthly rental fee**
Studio, 270–522 sq. ft.	$795–950
1-Bedroom, 598–974 sq. ft.	$1,025–1,395
2-Bedroom, 1,020–1,044 sq. ft.	$1,495–1,695
3-Bedroom, 1,415 sq. ft.	$1,995–2,395

**For double occupancy add $250 to the monthly rental fee. All utilities except telephone included. Wall-to-wall carpeting, miniblinds, 24-hour emergency call system.*

Activities: Full-time activities director organizes lectures, musical programs, Bible classes, and religious services. Bingo, bridge, exercise classes, outings to special events, library, gardening.

Availability: Independent Living has steady 97% occupancy rate; Assisted Living has 100% occupancy with waiting list.

Health services and rates: Nursing assistance available 24 hours a day.

- 15 Assisted Living apartments*

Small single	$1,495/month
Large single	$1,695/month

**For double occupancy add $350 without services, $700 with.*

"The Parkview is well known for superb service, an exceptionally caring staff, and marvelous food."

TEXAS

MESA SPRINGS

4149 Forrest Hill Road
Abilene, TX 79606
(915) 692-8080
Joyce Bond, executive director

Type of community: Not-for-profit Continuing Care, modified contract

Located on 112 prime acres near Wylie, one of the fastest-growing areas of West Texas, Mesa Springs offers residences designed with Texas-style architecture to blend with the countryside and the mountains of the Callahan Divide. Independent Living is offered in garden homes and apartments. The health care center has 60 Intermediate Nursing beds.

Financial plan: Entrance fee plus monthly fee. The entrance fee is fully refundable less $500 administrative fee when the unit is reoccupied.

Ownership and management: Hendrick Medical Development Corporation, owner and manager of Hendrick Medical Center. Opened in 1987.

Minimum age: 55 years.

Population: 29 residents; 50% women, 50% men, 50% couples.

Number of units: 22 Independent Living garden homes and 10 apartments; 60-bed health care center.

Dining plan: Lunch is included in the monthly fee. Extra meals available for additional fee.

Services: *Included in the monthly fee:* Weekly housekeeping and flat-linen services, self-service laundry facilities, covered parking, scheduled transportation.

INDEPENDENT LIVING HOUSING

Type/size of apartments	*Entrance fee*	*Monthly fee**
1-Bedroom, 717 sq. ft.	$17,950	$720
1-Bedroom/study, 862 sq. ft.	$21,950	$820
2-Bedroom, 1,006 sq. ft.	$23,450	$920
Garden homes		
1-Bedroom/study, 958 sq. ft.	$22,950	$925
2-Bedroom, 1,171 sq. ft.	$24,950	$1,025
2-Bedroom/study, 1,282 sq. ft.	$27,450	$1,280

**For double occupancy add $275 to the monthly fee. All utilities except telephone and electricity included for apartment residents. Garden home residents pay own utilities and have carports. Fully equipped kitchen, choice of carpeting and draperies, 24-hour emergency call system.*

At additional cost: Beauty/barbershop, guest accommodations.

Activities: Library, recreation rooms, exercise area, movies, trips to the Philharmonic and other cultural events, chapel, sing-alongs, Bible study, arts and crafts.

Availability: Units availabile. Priority waiting list.

Health services and rates: Intermediate Care offered at health care center including help with daily living activities and nursing care for those who are not in need of round-the-clock nursing care or supervision. Physical and occupational therapy, respiratory care, nutrition counseling provided at additional cost at Hendrick Medical Center. The entire network of Hendrick Medical Center services is available. Registered nurses on duty 24 hours.

- 60 Intermediate Nursing beds
  Semiprivate $1,999.50/month
  Private $2,635/month

"Our goal for residents is for them to live active, productive lives at Mesa Springs and to enjoy their normal at-home routine in a healthy, secure setting."

WESTMINSTER MANOR

4100 Jackson Avenue
Austin, TX 78731
(512) 454-4711
Mary Dunneback, marketing director

Type of community: Nonprofit Continuing Care, all-inclusive contract

A five-story apartment building and a 90-bed health center are located on a 5 1/3-acre urban campus featuring a large center courtyard, fountain, and gazebo. Smaller courtyards are located throughout the campus. Located in an old Austin neighborhood, Westminster Manor is convenient to all of Austin. Lake Austin, Medical Park Tower, and Seton Medical Center are nearby.

Financial plan: Entrance fee plus monthly fee. Two plans: **1)** Standard plan: refund of entrance fee less prorated amount per month of residency for a period of 50 months (no refund in the event of death). **2)** Return of Capital plan: up to 90% of entrance fee refunded regardless of when or why the resident terminates the residency agreement. A refundable deposit is also required upon payment of the entrance fee.

Ownership and management: Owned by Westminster Manor, Inc. Managed by Life Care Services Corporation of Des Moines, Iowa, responsible for the development of more than 50 communities across the country. Opened in 1967.

Minimum age: 62 years.

Population: 287 residents; 77% women, 23% men, 11% couples.

Number of units: 271 Independent Living apartments; 90-bed health care center.

INDEPENDENT LIVING HOUSING

Type/size of unit	*Entrance fee 1/2*	*Monthly fee**
Efficiency, 279–475 sq. ft.	$36,360–56,250/59,995–92,815	$873–1,043
1-Bedroom, 550–895 sq. ft.	$68,795–109,550/113,510–180,760	$1,068–1,533
2-Bedroom, 736–1,066 sq. ft.	$94,555–133,335/156,015–220,005	$1,239–2,020

**For double occupancy add $633 to the monthly fee. All utilities except telephone and cable TV included. Wall-to-wall carpeting, 24-hour emergency call system, balconies or patios. Some apartments have fully equipped kitchen.*

Dining plan: One meal per day included in the monthly fee. Special diets and tray service available at extra cost. Private dining room available.

Services: *Included in the monthly fee:* Scheduled transportation, weekly housekeeping, unsheltered parking for residents and their guests.

At additional cost: Beauty/barbershop, covered parking, additional housekeeping.

Activities: Movies, lounge area with grand piano and TV, library, 250-seat Harris Bell Hall for dances and events, exercise room, rooftop solarium, billiards, game room, chapel, special outings and excursions, choir, committees, lectures, classes, trips.

Availability: Waiting list for one- and two-bedroom units.

Health services and rates: Residents receive unlimited nursing care in the health center. Resident assumes responsibility for private physician fees and any medication or special treatment required. Some Assisted Living services not included in monthly fee.

- 90-Bed health care center

"Westminster Manor's mission is to 'invest in a caring manner.'"

CLASSIC RESIDENCE BY HYATT

5455 LaSierra Drive
Dallas, TX 75231
(214) 691-7612
Ruth Dodson, marketing representative

Type of community: Independent Living with long-term care insurance

This elegant ten-story building is located in the heart of the Dallas medical community. The 30,000 square foot lobby features a ten-story Winter garden atrium with a distinctive tile fountain, trees and flowers. Apartments feature atrium and/or city views. The community is within five miles of prestigious Park Cities and convenient to major shopping areas.

Financial plan: Monthly fee.

Ownership and management: Classic Residence by Hyatt, an affiliate of Hyatt Corporation, which owns and operates Classic Residences in California, Connecticut, Maryland, Nevada, and New Jersey. Opened in 1989.

INDEPENDENT LIVING HOUSING

Type/size of apartment	*Monthly fee**
1-Bedroom/study, 840 sq. ft.	$1,800–1,850
2-Bedroom, 1,065 sq. ft.	$1,655–1,930
2-Bedroom, 1,305 sq. ft.	$2,265
Penthouse floor	
1-Bedroom/study, 1,190 sq. ft.	$2,750
2-Bedroom/2-bath, 1,500 sq. ft.	$3,600

**For double occupancy add $450 to the monthly fee. All utilities except telephone included. Fully electric kitchen with dishwasher, disposal, microwave, full-size refrigerator with ice maker, range, pantry. Washer/dryer, wall-to-wall color-coordinated carpeting, miniblinds, individually controlled heating and air-conditioning, 24-hour emergency call system.*

Minimum age: 55 years.

Population: 170 residents; 60% women, 40% men, 45% couples.

Number of units: 147 Independent Living apartments.

Dining plan: Continental breakfast, plus choice of lunch or dinner included in the monthly fee. Classically Caring Cuisine menu selections low in sodium, fat, cholesterol available. Private dining room. Room service available for short-term illness.

Services: *Included in the monthly fee:* Weekly housekeeping and flat-linen services, 24-hour concierge, well-lighted covered parking with assigned spaces, scheduled transportation, move-in coordination service. Classic Club membership: long-term care insurance underwritten by Lloyd's of London, membership in airline club, complimentary overnight accommodations at each Classic Residence, exclusive travel opportunities.

At additional cost: Additional housekeeping, flat-linen and transportation services, beauty/barbershop, room service.

Activities: Personalized computer lifestyle profile provides full-time resident relations/programming staff with opportunity to individually tailor a variety of educational, cultural, social, and recreational programs to residents' interests. Classes, lectures, movies, concerts, dances, cultural outings. Art studio, well-stocked library, clubroom, fitness center with whirlpool, heated outdoor pool.

Availability: Waiting list for certain apartment styles.

Health services and rates: All residents are covered by long-term insurance, underwritten by Lloyd's of London. Emergency-response system automatically alerts 24-hour concierge.

"A distinguished leader in the hospitality industry for more than three decades, Hyatt has set the standard for high-quality accommodations and attentive service. Classic Residence has built upon Hyatt's expertise, bringing innovative cuisine, striking interior design, and personalized, supportive services to the senior living industry."

THE FORUM AT PARK LANE

7831 Park Lane
Dallas, TX 75225
(214) 369-9902
Louise Stokes, leasing counselor

Type of community: Continuing Care, modified contract

Located across from North Park Shopping Center, surrounded by the beautiful neighborhoods of the Park Cities, The Forum has been designed to blend harmoniously with the distinguished architecture of the area. Meticulous landscaping surrounds the community's five interconnected buildings, joined by spacious indoor concourses. Each building has a landscaped central courtyard. The community features gracious and elegantly decorated common areas and offers easy access to the North Central Expressway; all the excitement of Dallas is minutes away.

Financial plan: Monthly rental fee. $500 refundable application fee.

Ownership and management: The Forum Group, Inc., owner and manager of 27 communities across the United States, with more than 25 years of experience in retirement communities. Opened in 1990.

Minimum age: 60 years.

Population: 165 residents; 81% women, 19% men, 16% couples.

Number of units: 192 Independent Living apartments; 38 Assisted Living suites, 90 Skilled Nursing beds.

INDEPENDENT LIVING HOUSING

Type/size of apartment	*Monthly fee**
1-Bedroom, 651–934 sq. ft.	$1,700–2,600
2-Bedroom, 865–1,463 sq. ft.	$1,900–3,900

**For double occupancy add $400 to the monthly fee. All utilities except telephone included. All-electric kitchen, individually controlled heating and air-conditioning, plush carpeting, balcony/patio or bay window, walk-in closets, stackable washer/dryer, 24-hour emergency call system. Several apartments for pet owners available. Thirty-three floor plans available.*

Dining plan: Continental breakfast daily plus one meal daily included in the monthly fee. Private dining room.

Services: *Included in the monthly fee:* Weekly housekeeping and flat-linen services, scheduled transportation, storage locker, underground parking. Full-time move-in coordinator assists with all aspects of move.

At additional cost: Beauty/barbershop, guest accommodations, gift shop, country store, underground parking, on-site banking.

Activities: Indoor spa, exercise programs, library, billiards, greenhouse, arts and crafts room, trips to cultural and area events, travel tours, lectures, classes, sing-alongs, bridge, Bible study, mystery drive, men's poker, sewing circle.

Availability: Units available. Priority waiting list.

Health services and rates: Each resident receives 15 credit days a year in the health care center (a total of 60 days maximum). Wellness and exercise programs are offered. The health center is open to the public and Medicare certified.

- 38 Assisted Living suites
  - 1-Bedroom $2,100/month
  - 2-Bedroom $4,000/month
- 90-Bed Skilled Nursing facility
  - Semiprivate $86/day
  - Private $114/day

"To become America's leading retirement service provider is The Forum Group's main goal. This is our only business, not an adjunct to another business. And we have long-term, corporatewide commitment to quality and excellence."

GRACE PRESBYTERIAN VILLAGE

550 East Ann Arbor
Dallas, TX 75216
(214) 376-1701
Ray Miller, admissions counselor

Type of community: Nonprofit Continuing Care, modified contract

Accreditation: Continuing Care Accreditation Commission

Alice Creek divides the main complex, which contains traditional brick Independent Living apartments and conventional cottages from individual, freestanding cottages. Situated in a 20-acre heavily wooded setting, the community offers well-lighted walking paths throughout and patios with gas grills for residents' use. A 160-bed health center is on-site.

Financial plan: Monthly rent. Security deposit of one month's rent. Initial six-month lease, monthly thereafter.

Ownership and management: Owned, operated, and supported by Grace Presbytery of the Presbyterian Church, which appoints a voluntary board of directors. Opened in 1962.

Minimum age: None.

Population: 300 residents; 80% women, 20% men, 10% couples.

INDEPENDENT LIVING HOUSING

Type/size of apartment	*Monthly rent single/double**
1-Bedroom efficiency, 560 sq. ft.	$645/N/A
1-Bedroom, 590 sq. ft.	$720/770
2-Bedroom, 995 sq. ft.	$865/915
Deluxe 2-bedroom, 1,122 sq. ft.	$1,100/1,160

**All utilities included in the monthly rent. Fully equipped kitchen, 24-hour emergency call system, individually controlled heating and air-conditioning. Cottages have electric oven, washer and dryer hookup, carports, 24-hour emergency call system.*

Number of units: 311 Independent Living residences; 61 Assisted Living rooms, 160-bed health care center.

Dining plan: Three meals a day included in the monthly rent for apartment residents. Cottages offer an option of one, two, or three meals daily.

Services: *Included in the monthly fee:* Transportation to village planned events, personal and financial counseling, housekeeping for apartment residents.

At additional cost: Scheduled personal transportation, beauty/barbershop, guest cottages.

Activities: Exercise classes, arts and crafts, theater outings, museum trips, various speakers, shopping excursions, chapel services, political forums, picnics, bridge groups, volunteering in village activities and services.

Availability: Some accommodations have waiting list. $50 waiting list fee.

Health services and rates: Residents receive up to ten free days per year in the health center and 20% discount on health center charges if temporary stay exceeds ten days. Residents may use their own physicians or be under care of health center staff. Special care unit in conjunction with University of Texas Southwestern Medical Center for residents with Alzheimer's disease or related disorders. Health screening clinic provides minor medical services. The average length of service for medical and administrative staff is ten years.

- 61 Assisted Living units

Small room	$1,525–1,600/month
Large room	$2,125–2,745/month

- 160 Nursing beds

	Intermediate Nursing	*Skilled Nursing*
Semiprivate	$2,430	$2,890
Private	$2,685	$3,200
Extended care		$2,790/3,200

"Grace Presbyterian Village maintains a commitment to uncompromising quality in its programs and services."

RETIREMENT INN AT FOREST LANE

2920 Forest Lane
Dallas, TX 75234
(214) 241-4100
Judy Salmon, marketing coordinator

Type of community: Independent and Assisted Living

This modern three-story building is similar to a luxury suite hotel. The grounds feature gardens and walking paths. Shopping is nearby, and Dallas's best major medical facilities are just 20 minutes away.

INDEPENDENT LIVING HOUSING

Type of apartment	*Monthly fee**
Studio	$1,250
1-Bedroom	$1,565

**For double occupancy add $800 to the monthly fee. All utilities except telephone and cable TV included. Kitchenettes, thermostats, 24-hour emergency call system.*

Financial plan: Monthly fee.

Ownership and management: National Guest Homes, owner and manager of four other retirement communities in Texas and Tennessee. Opened in 1982.

Minimum age: None.

Population: 130 residents; 80% women, 20% men.

Number of units: 95 Independent Living apartments.

Dining plan: Three meals per day included in the monthly fee. Private dining room for residents.

Services: *Included in the monthly fee:* Weekly housekeeping and flat-linen services, scheduled transportation, parking, laundry rooms, complimentary guest meals and overnight guest accommodations (limited).

At additional cost: Beauty/barbershop.

Activities: Ceramics, game room with billiards table, bingo, exercise classes, films, spelling bees, scenic drives, community service projects.

Availability: Limited.

Health services and rates: Whirlpool baths. Guest Services, Inc., a home health company, provides Assisted Living services for residents in their apartments. If services beyond routine care are necessary, a schedule of additional costs can be provided.

- Assisted Living services $300/month

"Residents enjoy the comforts and securities of the Retirement Inn at Forest Lane plus they have assistance when they need it in order to maintain their independence."

DENTON GOOD SAMARITAN VILLAGE

2500 Hinkle Drive
Denton, TX 76201
(817) 383-2651
Rita Martin, director of resident services

Type of community: Nonprofit Continuing Care, modified plan

The community consists of a high-rise apartment building and brick duplexes and triplexes with access to public street. Intermediate and Skilled Nursing facility located on-site. The community is situated on 17 acres in a pleasant residential area featuring gardens, manicured lawns, and walking paths. Heated walkways link the community, which is within walking distance of a shopping center.

Financial plan: Entrance fee plus monthly fee or monthly rental fee only. $1,000 deposit for residents electing monthly rental fee only option.

Ownership and management: The Evangelical Lutheran Good Samaritan Society, a Christian charitable nonprofit corporation based in Sioux Falls, South Dakota. They own and operate 237 health care and retirement communities in 25 states. Opened in 1976.

INDEPENDENT LIVING HOUSING

Type/size of apartments	*Entrance fee*	*Monthly fee**	*Monthly fee only**
Studio, 290 sq. ft.	$5,500	$340	$440
Efficiency, 380 sq. ft.	$15,500	$580	$860
1-Bedroom, 520–700 sq. ft.	$20,000–30,000	$620–670	$1,000–1,150
2-Bedroom, 720–940 sq. ft.	$30,000–38,000	$680–720	$1,160–1,240
Duplex/Triplex			
Duplex, 1,366 sq. ft.	N/A	$960–1,010	
Triplex, 1,366 sq. ft.	N/A	$910–1,010	

**For double occupancy add $135 to the monthly fee. All utilities except telephone included. Individually controlled heating and air-conditioning, draperies, wall-to-wall carpeting, pleated shades, wallpaper, cable TV, 24-hour emergency call system. Some efficiencies, 1- and 2-bedrooms, duplexes, and triplexes have electric kitchens. Duplexes and triplexes have single-car garage with automatic door opener or carport.* Note: *Studios and some efficiencies do not have kitchens.*

Minimum age: 62 years (if couple, spouse may be younger).

Population: 248 residents; 59% women, 41% men, 33% couples.

Number of units: 108 Independent Living apartments, 30 duplexes/triplexes; 91 Intermediate and Skilled Nursing beds.

Dining plan: No meals included in the monthly fee. Three meals per day are served in the dining room and available at cost. Private dining room.

Services: *Included in the monthly fee:* Weekly housekeeping flat-linen services, bimonthly housekeeping, scheduled transportation.

At additional cost: Beauty/barbershop, washers/dryers on each floor, guest accommodations, resident store, additional housekeeping.

Activities: Library, arts and crafts, table games, exercise, garden plots, films, concerts, lectures, religious services, tours and trips.

Availability: Limited. Priority waiting list.

Health services and rates: Physical, occupational, speech, and audiology therapies available.

- 91 Intermediate and Skilled Nursing beds (five levels of care offered)

Semiprivate	$78–87/day
Private	$87–96/day

"The individualized care plan at Denton Good Samaritan Village emphasizes the development and care of the whole person, giving consideration to spiritual, social, emotional, and intellectual needs, as well as to the resident's physical well-being. It ensures that each resident receives the care and services most appropriate for his or her individual needs."

THE MONTEVISTA AT CORONADO

1575 Belvidere Street
El Paso, TX 79912
(915) 833-2229
Judy O'Connor, marketing director

Type of community: Continuing Care, modified contract

Nestled at the foot of scenic Franklin Mountain on 16 landscaped acres, The Montevista offers Independent Living and Assisted Living as well as Intermediate and

INDEPENDENT LIVING HOUSING

Type/size of apartment	*Monthly fee**
1-Bedroom, 667 sq. ft.	$1,660
1-Bedroom, 788 sq. ft.	$1,890
2-Bedroom, 908 sq. ft.	$2,220
2-Bedroom/den, 1,171 sq. ft.	$3,000

**For double occupancy add $360 to the monthly fee. All utilities except telephone included. All-electric kitchen, individually controlled heating and air-conditioning, plush carpeting, balcony or patio, walk-in closets, 24-hour emergency call system, basic cable TV. Pets welcome in selected apartments.*

Skilled Nursing. The community is housed in southwestern-style two-story cream stucco buildings with red-tiled roofs. The community offers mountain and valley views. The two-story lobby and lounge contain carefully selected furnishings. The community overlooks western El Paso and is near shopping malls, fine restaurants, and the Coronado Country Club.

Financial plan: Monthly rental fee.

Ownership and management: Managed by The Forum Group, Inc., owner and manger of 27 retirement communities throughout the United States. The Forum has more than 25 years of experience in retirement communities. Opened in 1987.

Minimum age: 60 years.

Population: 140 residents; 71% women, 29% men, 26 couples.

Number of units: 123 Independent Living apartments; 15 Assisted Living suites, 60 Intermediate Nursing beds, 60 Skilled Nursing beds.

Dining plan: Continental breakfast and 30 or 31 meals per month included in the monthly fee. Private dining room.

Services: *Included in the monthly fee:* Weekly housekeeping and flat-linen services, personal laundry facilities, scheduled transportation.

At additional cost: Covered parking, guest accommodations, beauty/barbershop.

Activities: Health and fitness classes, library, greenhouse, arts and crafts room, guest lectures, movies, music programs, trips to cultural and area events.

Availability: Units available. Priority waiting list.

Health services and rates: Excellent medical staff and state-of-the-art equipment. Both short- and long-term care Medicare and Medicaid certified. Daily therapies such as physical, speech, and occupational are available.

- 15 Assisted Living suites

Private	$68/day
Deluxe	$111/day

- 120 Nursing beds

	Intermediate Nursing	*Skilled Nursing*
Semiprivate	$75/day	$86/day
Private	$102/day	$108/day
Deluxe suite	$125/day	$165/day

"The Montevista is the only rental retirement community in El Paso with four levels of service in one distinctive building. To become America's leading operator of full-service retirement and health care communities is The Forum Group's main goal. This is our only business, not an adjunct to some other business. And, we have a long-term, corporatewide commitment to quality and excellence. We don't ever want anyone to downgrade their living standards to come live with us."

Ella, 81 years

Pennswood, Newtown Square, Pennsylvania

"I felt it was time to move in.
It's not the time for my kids to come running to me whenever anything goes wrong."

Ella had been on the waiting list at Pennswood for nine years. "We had very close friends who came in at the beginning and convinced my husband and me that we should sign up. We took a look and agreed, but it didn't work out because my husband wasn't well. When I decided to move in I had been at the top of the waiting list for a while. As an apartment would come up, the admissions office would call me and ask me if I was ready. There was never any pressure," explains Ella. "I was always told that the decision to move in was mine. Several times I said I wasn't ready and, after a discussion with the director of admissions, she agreed with me and I kept my spot on the waiting list."

In January of 1992 Ella broke her ankle and was operated on. Another operation was scheduled for January of 1993. "I felt it was time to move in. It's not the time for my kids to come running to me whenever anything goes wrong. I don't think they should be under that pressure to drop everything and come running. They have jobs and families. This, for me, was the most overwhelming argument for me to move into Pennswood."

Ella and her husband, who died in 1985, had an extensive art collection and lived in a large house. She knew she wouldn't be comfortable in three smallish rooms at Pennswood, so she hired an architect to work with her to create an environment that would work for her. The apartment was totally gutted. Three walls were left standing and the fireplace on the fourth wall was boarded up. Ella ended up with a big, open space with no doors and several sliding walls that she opens and closes between the living room, den, and bedroom as she likes. On these sliding walls (eight-by-eight foot panels) hangs much her art collection. She enlarged her patio and had it designed and landscaped, and took out the tubs in both bathrooms, turning one into a powder room and the second into a bathroom with a tiled walk-in shower. "Now I love the space and, in fact, many people come to see what I have done," Ella reports.

"When I arrived I was pleased to find such welcoming, friendly people. An amazing number are academics, some are writers, some have been deans at universities. There are a great number of people here who share similar educational backgrounds, which makes for wonderful conversations."

Ella has continued her work with the Philadelphia Art Museum, sails on a 28-foot sloop in the Chesapeake with her daughters in the summer, and travels. Her second book on Dutch tiles, *Dutch Floral Tiles in the Golden Age*, was published in Holland in December 1994.

BAYOU MANOR

4141 South Braewood
Houston, TX 77025
(713) 666-2651
René Parker, director of marketing

Located on 7½ well-manicured acres inside Loop 610 in the desirable southwest section of Houston, Bayou Manor offers spacious lawns and gardens. Independent Living apartments and a health care center are housed in seven-story modern buildings.

Type of community: Nonprofit Continuing Care, modified contract

Financial plan: Entrance fee plus monthly fee. Three plans: **1)** Moderate entrance fee, low monthly fee,

INDEPENDENT LIVING HOUSING

Type/size of apartment	*Entrance fee 1/2**	*Monthly fee**
Studio, 325–560 sq. ft.	$28,000–48,000/44,800–78,800	$835–1,100
1-Bedroom, 590–840 sq. ft.	$49,000–66,000/78,400–105,600	$1,130–1,410
2-Bedroom, 880–1,180 sq. ft.	$69,000–102,000/110,400–163,200	$1,470–1,820

**Plan 3 entrance fees, $5,600–13,800; monthly fees, $1,460–2,575 (available for apartments that are 900 sq. ft. or less). For double occupancy add $6,000 to the entrance fee for Plans 1 and 2, $1,200 for Plan 3. Add $465 to the monthly fee for all plans. All utilities except telephone included. Kitchen facilities, individually controlled heating and air-conditioning, choice of carpeting, custom lined draperies, 24-hour emergency call system.*

and an amortized entrance fee refund. **2)** Higher entrance fee and 100% refund after ten years. **3)** Low entrance fee, higher monthly fee. Entrance fee is 100% refundable after ten years. Refundable deposit of $1,000 is required for priority waiting list.

Ownership and management: Brazos Presybterian Homes, Inc., owner and manager of The Hallmark, Houston. Opened in 1963.

Minimum age: 65 years.

Population: 220 residents; 82% women, 18% men, 11% couples.

Number of units: 175 Independent Living apartments and 59 garden apartments; 60-bed health care center.

Dining plan: One meal per day included in the monthly fee. Additional meals available at cost.

Services: *Included in the monthly fee:* Weekly housekeeping, covered parking, scheduled transportation.

At additional cost: Beauty/barbershop, guest accommodations, gift shop, weekly banking.

Activities: Library, recreation rooms, gardening, crafts room, exercise classes, films, musical programs, shopping tours, lectures, trips to symphony, opera, ballet, and museums. Christian religious programs are scheduled on a regular basis.

Availability: Units available. Priority waiting list.

Health services and rates: Residents receive 30 free days for temporary stays per occurrence, noncumulative. Routine medical services available. Prominent Houston clinic is on 24-hour call for emergencies. Monthly fee covers medical and hospitalization costs *not* covered by Medicare (subject to certain exclusions).

- 60-Bed health care center*

Resident	$60/day
Nonresident	$90/day

**Permanent residence in health care center is $1,800/month.*

"The nonprofit status of Brazos Presbyterian Homes, Inc., assures that proceeds from previous endowments and revenue generated by current activities are returned to its facilities, giving them a financial stability that may not exist in an entrepreneurial operation of similar nature."

THE FORUM AT MEMORIAL WOODS

777 North Post Oak Road
Houston, TX 77024
(713) 956-0870
Mary Ann Lang, leasing counselor

Type of community: Continuing Care, modified plan

Located in Houston's exclusive River Oaks/Memorial district in a beautiful 18-story building, the community offers full-service Continuing Care. Nine distinctive floor plans are available; many have beautiful views

INDEPENDENT LIVING HOUSING

Type/size of apartment	*Monthly rental fee**
1-Bedroom, 520–948 sq. ft.	$1,450–2,700
2-Bedroom, 848–1,300 sq. ft.	$2,150–4,000

**For double occupancy add $400 to the monthly fee. All utilities except telephone included. Fully equipped kitchen, individually controlled heating and air-conditioning, wall-to-wall carpeting, walk-in closets, cable TV, 24-hour emergency call system.*

of the Galleria area. The gracious decor is reminiscent of the grand hotels featuring elegant foyers and numerous sitting areas. Assisted Living suites and Intermediate and Skilled Nursing care are under one roof.

Financial plan: Monthly rental.

Ownership and management: The Forum Group, Inc., owner and manager of 27 retirement communities in the United States, has been developing and managing retirement communities for more than 25 years. Opened in 1989.

Minimum age: 62 years.

Population: 272 residents; 78% women, 22% men, 17% couples.

Number of units: 209 Independent Living apartments; 36 Assisted Living suites, 132-bed health care center.

Dining plan: 30 meals per month and daily continental breakfast included in the monthly fee. Private dining room available.

Services: *Included in the monthly fee:* Weekly housekeeping, flat-linen, and light laundry services, scheduled transportation, concierge.

At additional cost: Personal laundry services, grocery, valet service, beauty/barbershop.

Activities: Library, crafts/activities room, billiards room, enclosed swimming pool and spa, aqua fitness, card games, bingo, bridge club, exercise classes, movies, musical performances, book-of-the-month club, trips to cultural entertainment in the area.

Availability: Waiting list for Assisted Living only.

Health services and rates: Independent Living residents receive 15 free days per year beginning on the 30th day of residency (lifetime total of 60 days). Physical, speech, and occupational therapies offered. Individual care programs are created by professional medical committee.

- 36 Assisted Living suites $60–130/day
- 132-Bed health care center

	Intermediate Nursing	*Skilled Nursing*
Semiprivate	$85/day	$100/day
Private	$120/day	$130/day

"The Forum is designed to provide a pleasant and worry-free atmosphere. We are a community committed to consistent, quality services; resident satisfaction is our number-one goal."

THE HALLMARK

4718 Hallmark Drive
Houston, TX 77056
(713) 622-6633
Jeny Knight, marketing director

Type of community: Nonprofit Continuing Care, modified contract

The Hallmark consists of two ten-story buildings containing one- and two-bedroom apartments, many with

views of the Houston Galleria and downtown Houston. The Hallmark has a licensed Assisted Living facility and a 42-bed health center. The grounds feature an outdoor garden and patio. The community is located within walking distance of the world-famous Galleria.

Financial plan: Entrance fee plus monthly fee. Three plans: **1)** Moderate entrance fee/low monthly fee and progressively reducing entrance fee refund. **2)** Allows for 60% of entrance fee to be refunded should resident leave for any reason. **3)** For one-bedroom only. Low entrance fee/high monthly fee with entrance fee fully refundable after ten years.

Ownership and management: Brazos Presbyterian Homes, Inc., which also owns and manages Bayou Manor in Houston and has been operating successfully in Houston for nearly 30 years. Opened in 1972.

Minimum age: 65 years.

Population: 136 residents; 83% women, 17% men, 20 couples.

Number of units: 141 Independent Living apartments; 4 Assisted Living beds, 42-bed health care center.

Dining plan: One meal per day included in the monthly fee. Add $125 per month for two meals per day or $200 for three meals per day. Private dining room.

Services: *Included in the monthly fee:* Weekly maid service, scheduled transportation, decorator service (eight hours) to assist with move.

At additional cost: Beauty/barbershop, guest accommodations, assigned parking.

Activities: Pool, library, exercise classes, activity room, billiards, trips to cultural and area events.

Availability: Priority waiting list for two-bedroom; one-bedroom available.

Health services and rates: Residents receive 30 free days of recuperative or postoperative care in the health care center (per occurrence; no annual limit). Long-term care is available at a preferred rate that covers medical and hospitalization costs not covered by Medicare. Prominent Houston medical clinic is on 24-hour call for emergencies. Routine medical services available in-house. Apartment nurse available for house calls. Nurse practitioner on-site. Dental, podiatry, physical therapy, and auditory services at extra cost. Assistance with filing insurance claims provided.

- 4 Assisted Living apartments at $2,000/month
- 42-Bed health care center
  Residents $67/day
  Nonresidents $100/day

"The Hallmark is a full-service licensed Continuing Care retirement community for those who are able to live independently but desire the availability of services and health care facilities on-site."

INDEPENDENT LIVING HOUSING

Type/size of apartment	*Entrance fee 1/2***	*Monthly fee***
1-Bedroom, 600–900 sq. ft.*	$46,000–66,000/78,200–113,100	$1,075–1,420
2-Bedroom, 1,170–1,400 sq. ft.	$101,500–116,000/172,600–197,200	$1,720–1,975
2-Bedroom, 1,620–1,800 sq. ft.	$140,000–154,500/238,000–262,700	$2,220–2,430

**Plan 3 for 1-bedroom only: entrance fees, $9,200–13,300; monthly fees, $1,950–2,460; for double occupancy add $1,400 to the entrance fee and $410 to the monthly fee. **For double occupancy add $7,000 to the entrance fee and $410 to the monthly fee. All utilities except telephone included. Kitchen facilities, individually controlled heating and air-conditioning, choice of carpeting, custom lined draperies, 24-hour emergency call system, satellite TV.*

MANOR PARK

2208 North Loop 250 West
Midland, TX 79707
(915) 689-9898 or (800) 523-9898
Chris Newman, community relations

Type of community: Nonprofit Continuing Care, modified contract

Situated on 40 acres in northwest Midland, Manor Park offers a variety of residences, including townhouses, garden homes, and apartments. The Mabee Health Care Center serves both the Trinity Towers and Manor Park communities. The community offers beautifully maintained grounds featuring an atrium, walking paths, and a garden area.

Financial plan: 100% refundable entrance fee plus monthly fee. $1,000 application fee to be applied to entrance fee. Several banks have indicated they will bridge-gap loans to persons moving to Manor Park.

Ownership and management: Midland Presbyter-ian Homes, Inc., operating since 1970. Debt-free corporation. Owner and manager of Trinity Towers, Midland, Texas. Opened in 1983.

Minimum age: 62 years.

Population: 214 residents.

Number of units: Independent Living: 73 townhouses, 27 garden homes, 30 apartments; 117 personal care rooms, 120-bed health care center.

Dining plan: Wallace apartment residents receive one meal per day in the monthly fee. For townhouse and garden home residents, meals are optional at $4 each.

Services: *Included in the monthly fee:* Weekly housekeeping and flat-linen services, scheduled transportation.

INDEPENDENT LIVING HOUSING

Wallace apartments	*Entrance fee*	*Monthly fee**
Studio, 516 sq. ft.	$34,250	$552
1-Bedroom, 693–882 sq. ft.	$44,500–68,000	$601–809
2-Bedroom, 1,078–1,197 sq. ft.	$82,000–93,500	$699–907
Townhouses		
1-Bedroom, 881 sq. ft.	$72,500	$436
2-Bedroom, 1,105/1,336 sq. ft.	$87,500/109,000	$532–569
3-Bedroom, 2,390 sq. ft.	$196,500	$661
Garden homes		
Efficiency, 516 sq. ft.	$35,750	$339
1-Bedroom, 693/882 sq. ft.	$48,750/69,250	$396–436
2-Bedroom, 1,078/1,197 sq. ft.	$82,500/94,500	$494–532
2-Bedroom (rental only)	$989–1,064	

**For double occupancy there is an additional charge ranging from $42–150. All-electric kitchens, individually controlled heating and air-conditioning, wall-to-wall carpeting, 24-hour emergency call system, cable TV hookup. Washers/dryers, double car garages, patios/garden areas included in townhouses. Pets allowed in selected apartments. Options for townhouses/garden homes include fireplace, garden window, extended breakfast nook.*

At additional cost: Beauty/barbershop, guest accommodations, gift shop, commissary, medical transportation.

Activities: Whirlpool, exercise equipment, library, game room, arts and crafts department, ceramics, gardening, walking path, chapel.

Availability: Limited.

Health services and rates: Residents receive eight free infirmary days per fiscal year in the Mabee Health Care Center, after which they pay $50 per day. Three levels of nursing available: personal care, Intermediate Nursing, and Skilled Nursing. Alzheimer's unit with adult day care facilities/program to be completed in August 1993.

- 117 Personal care rooms $937–2,063/month
- 120-Bed health care center (semiprivate, private, suite)
  Intermediate Nursing $1,374–2,753/month
  Skilled Nursing $1,479–2,920/month

"Manor Park is a retirement community that promotes an active and independent lifestyle. Making Manor Park unique are the modest monthly maintenance fees and the 100% refundable entrance fees."

TRINITY TOWERS

2800 West Illinois Avenue
Midland, TX 79701
(915) 694-1691 or (800) 523-9898
Chris Newman, community relations director

Type of community: Nonprofit Continuing Care, modified contract

Two beautiful, five-floor towers house residential and personal care and 40 adjacent apartments house Independent Living residents. Mabee Health Care Center offers personal, custodial, and nursing care at Manor Park. Trinity Towers is located near downtown Midland.

Financial plan: Monthly fee. $100 application fee to be applied to first month's rent. Security deposit of one month's rent is required upon entrance.

Ownership and management: Midland Presbyterian Homes, owner and manager of Manor Park, also in Midland. Skilled Nursing services for Trinity are located at Manor Park. Opened in 1970.

Minimum age: 62 years.

Population: 142 residents.

Number of units: 40 Independent Living apartments, 103 residential rooms; 117 personal care rooms, 1 respite care room, 120-bed health center all at Manor Park.

Dining plan: Meals are not included for apartment residents but are available at a charge. Tower residents have three meals a day included in the monthly fee.

Services: *Included in the monthly fee:* Weekly housekeeping and flat-linen services for Towers residents only, scheduled transportation, laundry facilities.

At additional cost: Beauty/barbershop, guest accommodations, gift shop/commissary, medical transportation.

Activities: Library, ceramics and crafts, community events, exercise class, special tours and trips, nondenominational religious services, game day, monthly birthday parties, special events.

Availability: Limited.

Health services and rates: Residents receive eight free infirmary days per fiscal year at on-site infirmary. There is a $35 per day charge for infirmary care after the eight free days. For personal care (patients

INDEPENDENT LIVING HOUSING

Type/size of apartment	*Monthly fee**
1-Bedroom, 752 sq. ft.	$536
2-Bedroom, 1,032 sq. ft.	$648
*Towers***	
1-Room	$943–965
Large suite	$1,312
First-floor suite	$1,378
Double room	$1,607–1,628

**Apartments residents: utilities not included. Kitchen facilities, 24-hour emergency call system, carpeting, draperies, individually controlled heating and air-conditioning. **Towers residents: for double occupancy add $300 to the monthly fee. All utilities included. Individually controlled heating and air-conditioning, 24-hour emergency call system, draperies, wall-to-wall carpeting.*

may be admitted directly as outside admissions), custodial care, and nursing, residents use Mabee Health Care Center, shared with Manor Park (see Manor Park for fees).

"Trinity Towers is a retirement community that has been meeting the needs of persons over age 62 for more than 21 years. During this time, growth has occurred to meet the changing needs of residents."

THE FORUM AT LINCOLN HEIGHTS

311 Nottingham West
San Antonio, TX 78209
(210) 824-2314
Lou Watson, leasing counselor

Type of community: Continuing Care, modified plan

Located on 15½ acres in the Alamo Heights residential section of San Antonio, two- and three-story brick garden-style buildings house spacious Independent Living apartments set in beautifully landscaped grounds. Carefully selected furnishings decorate the common areas. The Forum offers the ambiance of an established neighborhood along with convenient access to shopping and casual dining. Although it is within the city, the campus-like atmosphere is further enhanced by views of a nearby public golf course.

Financial plan: Monthly rental fee.

Ownership and management: The Forum Group, Inc., owner and manager of 27 retirement communities in the United States. Opened in 1989.

Minimum age: 55 years.

INDEPENDENT LIVING HOUSING

Type/size of apartment	*Monthly rental fee**
1-Bedroom, 598–733 sq. ft.	$1,450–2,295
2-Bedroom, 849–1,162 sq. ft.	$1,995–3,375

**For double occupancy add $325 to the monthly fee. All utilities except telephone included. Wall-to-wall carpeting, walk-in closets, fully equipped all-electric kitchen, individual temperature control, 24-hour emergency call system. Many apartments have bay window, patio, or balcony. Some feature a fireplace and washer/dryer.*

Population: 162 residents; 90% women, 10% men, 10% couples.

Number of units: 150 Independent Living apartments; 30 Assisted Living suites, 60-bed nursing center.

Dining plan: Continental breakfast and one main meal of resident's choice each day included in the monthly fee. Private dining room and catering available.

Services: *Included in the monthly fee:* Weekly housekeeping and flat-linen services, lighted parking, scheduled transportation, valet service.

At additional cost: Beauty/barbershop, Forum ambassador service, guest accommodations, covered parking, personal laundry.

Activities: Full-time program director. Heated outdoor swimming pool and spa, crafts room, library, card games, trips to cultural events, exercise programs, billiards room, Bible study.

Availability: Limited.

Health services and rates: Residents receive ten free days of nursing care per year or a lifetime total of 30 days. A medical director and list of attending physicians and therapists are always available, as is long-term care insurance.

- 30 Assisted Living units
  Suites (kitchenettes/private bath) $2,225–2,525/month
- 60-Bed nursing facility
  Semiprivate $74–88/day
  Private $99–105/day

"From the moment residents walk in the door at The Forum at Lincoln Heights they know they have found a lifestyle that meets their high personal standards. The dining atmosphere is one of casual elegance, where residents can enjoy delicious food in the company of friends and neighbors. An experienced, caring staff is there to serve, making residents feel at home in this old-fashioned San Antonio neighborhood."

THE TEMPLE MERIDIAN

4312 South 31st Street
Temple, TX 76502
(817) 771-1226
Karen Berry, director of occupancy development

Type of community: Continuing Care, modified contract

Two two-story apartment buildings with four wings and 56 cottages house Independent Living residences and Assisted Living units. A separate 24-hour health care center is attached to the main building, and a community center contains game rooms, meeting rooms, library, exercise room, billiards, ceramics room, and a spacious living room. The 21-acre campus is located in a residential neighborhood close to all services, including shopping, medical services, hospitals, and churches. A large, five-acre field of Texas native wildflowers brightens the site from early spring through fall. Spacious planting areas are located around cottages; private vegetable gardening spots and a large greenhouse are on-site. Walking paths wind throughout the campus, and a large fountain is located at the entrance.

Financial plan: Monthly fee.

Ownership and management: Owned and managed by LeGan, Inc., of Denver, Colorado, which owns and operates five other Meridians in Colorado. Opened in 1984.

Minimum age: 70 years.

Population: 250 residents; 80% women, 20% men, 29% couples.

Number of units: 115 Independent Living apartments and 56 cottages; 17 Assisted Living apartments, 60-bed health care center.

Dining plan: 180 meals per year included in the monthly fee. Special diets accommodated. Private

INDEPENDENT LIVING HOUSING

Type/size of unit	*Monthly fee**
Studio, 453 sq. ft.	$1,205
1-Bedroom, 540–734 sq. ft.	$1,265–1,560
2-Bedroom, 854 sq. ft.	$1,650
Cottages	
1-Bedroom, 1,003 sq. ft.	$1,599
2-Bedroom, 1,105–1,179 sq. ft.	$1,599–1,730

**For double occupancy add $250 to the monthly fee. All utilities except telephone and electricity included. Apartments have wall-to-wall carpeting, patio or balcony, individually controlled heating and air-conditioning, 24-hour emergency call system, walk-in closets, fully equipped kitchens.*

dining room available. Three meals per day included in Assisted Living.

Services: *Included in the monthly fee:* Private scheduled transportation service, maid service, weekly flat-linen service, outdoor parking, maintenance inside and outside cottages.

At additional cost: Carports, beauty/barbershop, guest accommodations.

Activities: Social director. Library, game room, multipurpose room, swimming pool, exercise room, arts and crafts room, greenhouse, shuffleboard court, woodworking shop, card and billiards room, calligraphy classes, films, concerts, diner outings, vespers, Bible study, bingo, aquasize in pool, health seminars, investment seminars.

Availability: Waiting list. $4,000 deposit for waiting list.

Health services and rates: Resident receives ten free health care days upon occupancy and accumulates one additional day per month, with a maximum of 30 days. Assisted Living special services available. The health center operates under Resident Centered Care, which emphasizes the personalized relationship between a resident and a specific staff member, who is that resident's primary caregiver.

- 17 Assisted Living units
  - 1-Bedroom $2,015–2,220/month
  - 2-Bedroom $2,345/month
- 60-Bed health center
  - Semiprivate $79/day
  - Private $123/day

"Temple Texas is a wonderful place to retire to because it combines access to the same quality of health care as a metropolitan city with the benefits of living in a small town. The best thing about living at Temple Meridian are the residents, our community setting and the continuum of care we offer, which allows us the flexibility to change with the needs of our residents."

ROLLING MEADOWS

3006 McNiel
Wichita Falls, TX 76309
(817) 691-7511
Esther Smith, marketing director

Type of community: Not-for-profit Continuing Care, modified contract

Situated on a 30-acre site, the community features lighted walkways that connect the rose garden and gazebo area with Independent Living cottages, constructed in groups of three and four. Three three-story Independent Living apartment buildings are connected by breezeways to a one-story health center. Shopping centers are located nearby.

Financial plan: Monthly rental fee. $500 security deposit.

Ownership and management: Wichita Falls Retirement Foundation. Opened in 1983.

Minimum age: 55 years and older.

Population: 250 residents; 76% women, 24% men, 22% couples.

Number of units: 92 Independent Living apartments and 56 cottages; 21 Assisted Living units, 84 Skilled Nursing beds.

Dining plan: One meal per day included in the monthly rental fee. Private dining room and catering available.

Services: *Included in the monthly fee:* Housekeeping twice monthly, scheduled transportation.

At additional cost: Beauty/barbershop, guest accommodations.

Activities: Two full-time activities directors, one for Independent Living residents and one for health care center. Full schedule of all types of activities.

Availability: Two-year waiting list or longer.

Health services and rates: Home health services and physical therapy available.

- 21 Assisted Living units
  $530 (plus resident's monthly rental fee)
- 84 Nursing beds

Semiprivate	$59.25/day
Private	$114.50/day

"Rolling Meadows is unique because it is the only retirement community with a full-care facility located within a 200-mile radius, halfway between Dallas/Forth Worth and Oklahoma City."

INDEPENDENT LIVING HOUSING

Type/size of apartment	*Monthly rental fee**
Studio, 490 sq. ft.	$1,180
1-Bedroom, 729 sq. ft.	$1,280
2-Bedroom, 852 sq. ft.	$1,380
Deluxe 2-bedroom, 975 sq. ft.	$1,480
Cottage	
1-Bedroom, 1,118 sq. ft.	$1,385
2-Bedroom, 1,247 sq. ft.	$1,485
Deluxe 2-bedroom, 1,336 sq. ft.	$1,535
3-Bedroom, 1,521 sq. ft.	$1,635

**For double occupancy add $250 to the monthly rental fee. All utilities except telephone included. Fully equipped kitchen, individually controlled heating and air-conditioning, wall-to-wall carpeting, 24-hour emergency call system.*

UTAH

THE CROSSLANDS

10970 South 700 East
Sandy, UT 84070
(801) 572-4456
John Weibel, marketing director

Type of community: Continuing Care, modified contract

Two- and three-story beige stucco Independent Living apartment buildings with balconies and patios are located in a quiet, secure neighborhood. Campus setting overlooks beautiful vistas of the Oquirrh and Wasatch mountains. A health center housing Skilled Nursing adjoins campus. The community is located 20 minutes from downtown Salt Lake City and is close to shopping, medical, cultural, and sports facilities.

Financial plan: Monthly fee. $200 deposit.

Ownership and management: Hillhaven Corporation, owner and manager of 22 retirement communities nationwide and 400 health care centers. Opened in 1986.

Minimum age: 55 years.

Population: 132 residents; 77% women, 23% men, 13 couples.

Number of units: 120 Independent Living apartments; 100-bed Skilled Nursing facility.

Dining plan: Three meals daily included in the monthly fee. Parlor may be reserved for private dinners and celebrations.

Services: *Included in the monthly fee:* Weekly housekeeping and flat-linen services, scheduled transportation, laundry facilities, parking.

INDEPENDENT LIVING HOUSING

Type/size of apartment	*Monthly fee**
Studio alcove, 460 sq. ft.	$1,150
1-Bedroom, 552 sq. ft.	$1,350
1-Bedroom/den, 749 sq. ft.	$1,585
2-Bedroom, 690 sq. ft.	$1,585
Suites, 897–1,109 sq. ft.	$1,685–2,100

**For double occupancy add $275 to the monthly fee. All utilities except telephone included. Individually controlled thermostats, scald-proof faucet in bathtub/shower, balcony or patio, wall-to-wall carpeting, miniblinds, full kitchen, 24-hour emergency call system. Small pets allowed.*

At additional cost: Personal laundry service, dry cleaning, beauty/barbershop, prescription delivery, gift shop/country store.

Activities: Library, gardening, bridge, billiards, aerobics, quilting, ceramics, chapel, movies, book reviews, trips to concerts, ballet, opera.

Availability: Limited.

Health services and rates: Wellness clinic. Independent Living residents receive priority entrance to the adjoining health center. Rehabilitation therapy is available, plus vacation care, adult day care or night care.

- 100-Bed Skilled Nursing facility

Semiprivate	$82–84/day
Private	$90/day

"All our services are offered on a convenient, monthly basis. Straight and simple. There are no surprises down the road. Residents know right up front what to expect and when to expect it. And that keeps money worries to a minimum. After all, retirement should be as worry-free as possible."

VERMONT

WAKE ROBIN

200 Wake Robin Drive
Shelburne, VT 05482
(802) 985-9400 or (800) 462-0856
Joyce Reddy-Bradbee, director of marketing

Type of community: Not-for-profit Continuing Care, all-inclusive contract

Wake Robin is situated on a 137-acre wooded site overlooking Lake Champlain and the Adirondack and Green Mountains. The community consists of Independent Living apartments and cluster cottages (with six freestanding cottages), Assisted Living, and Skilled Nursing. There are tennis courts on campus and hiking trails through the woods planned. The community is within walking distance of Shelburne Village, close to the town beach, and minutes from Burlington, which offers outstanding performing arts, a respected university, several colleges, a thriving business community, and splendid opportunities for shopping, dining, and recreation.

Financial plan: Entrance fee plus monthly fee. Two plans: **1)** Fully amortizing fee. The entrance fee decreases by 2 percent per month for 50 months (approximately 25% per year for four years). At the end of 50 months, there is no further refund. **2)** Partially amortizing fee. The resident pays a 20% higher entrance fee that amortizes at 2% per month for 25 months and will always receive at least a 50% refund. A portion (predicted range, 25–35%) of the entrance fee and monthly fee qualifies for a health care deduction on resident's federal income tax.

Ownership and management: Not-for-profit Wake Robin Corporation. Managed by a voluntary board of directors. Co-operative Retirement Services of America, Inc. (CRSA), which manages 30 communities in 16 states, provides oversight,

INDEPENDENT LIVING HOUSING

Type/size of apartment	*Entrance fee**	*Monthly fee**
1-Bedroom, 557–938 sq. ft.	$79,500–135,700	$1,208–1,643
1-Bedroom/den, 947–1064 sq. ft.	$136,500–163,700	$1,643–1,823
2-Bedroom/den, 1100–1344 sq. ft.	$172,600–220,300	$1,855–2,173
Cottage		
1-Bedroom/den, 984 sq. ft.	$175,700	$1,887
2-Bedroom/den, 1152–1344 sq. ft.	$202,800–244,000	$2,141–2,438

**For double occupancy add $17,860 to the entrance fee, $793 to the monthly fee. All utilities except telephone and cable TV included. Fully equipped kitchens, 24-hour emergency call system, wall-to-wall carpeting, patio or deck, individually controlled heating and air-conditioning, miniblinds, washer and dryer, storage space, assigned space in parking garage (apartment residents) or private enclosed garage (cottages). Pets allowed.*

auditing all systems and operations on a monthly basis. Opened in 1986.

Minimum age: 65 years (if couple, spouse must be at least 60); there is a monthly surcharge for residents 60–65.

Population: 190 residents (capacity 240); 67% women, 33% men, 40% couples.

Number of units: 114 Independent Living apartments (nine floor plans) and 61 cottage units (four floor plans); 30 Assisted Living units, 30-bed Skilled Nursing facility.

Dining Plan: One meal per day included in the monthly fee. Meal selection accommodates persons on special diets. Private dining room for personal entertaining. Coffee shop.

Services: *Included in the monthly fee:* Weekly light housekeeping, annual carpet cleaning, scheduled transportation, move-in assistance.

At additional cost: Beauty/barbershop, gift shop, and limited convenience store, branch office of the Merchants Bank, front door morning newspaper delivery, gift shop.

Activities: State-of-the-art fitness room, exercise classes, game room, library, cross-country ski trails, picnic benches, Shelburne Beach membership, tennis courts, greenhouse and outdoor garden plots, arts and crafts room, cultural and musical outings, book discussion group, woodworking shop, bridge, backgammon, a cappella group, nature study, sewing group. Within walking distance of the famous Shelburne Museum.

Availability: Limited availability. Priority depositor program. A fully refundable $1,250 deposit (of which $1,000 is fully refundable) gives prospective resident a priority status number that ensures the widest possible choice of residences. Over 350 individuals are priority depositors.

Health services and rates: Long term health care included in residents' monthly fee. If one member of a couple moves to the health center, the monthly fee remains the same as they are paying in Independent Living. If a single person moves to the health center permanently, the monthly fee is equivalent to the monthly fee the resident has been paying in Independent Living. Assistance with insurance claims. Periodic health screening checks, health education sessions, limited/temporary in-home assistance with some activities of daily living. Access to medical services, including scheduled office hours and emergency calls by physicians. Access to dental care, pharmacy, physical therapy, occupational therapy, speech therapy, and podiatry.

- 30 Assisted Living units
- 30-Bed Skilled Nursing facility (all private rooms)

"Wake Robin is Vermont's Continuing Care retirement community. The group of Vermonters who formed the founding committee saw a need for a Continuing Care community in the area. They chose the name Wake Robin (red trillium) because this early spring wildflower symbolizes the special beauty of Vermont at a time of year that suggests renewal and the vitality of a new community."

VIRGINIA

GOODWIN HOUSE

4800 Fillmore Avenue
Alexandria, VA 22311
(703) 578-1000
Carroll A. Oliver, senior vice president admissions/marketing

Type of community: Not-for-profit Continuing Care, all-inclusive contract

Accreditation: Continuing Care Accreditation Commission

This multistory brick building is located on a seven-acre site. The community features professionally landscaped grounds, resident gardens, walking paths, a roof deck and solarium. Goodwin House is located close to shopping, theater, and transportation and ten miles from Washington, D.C.

Financial plan: Entrance fee plus monthly fee. Three plans: **1)** Standard plan has entrance fee and monthly fee. **2)** Modified plan offers lower entrance fee and higher monthly fee. **3)** Refundable plan has a higher entrance fee and the standard monthly fee. This plan guarantees a 50% refund to the resident's estate. Fellowship Funds (confidential financial assistance) may be available to assist residents.

Ownership and management: Managed by the Goodwin House, Inc., board of trustees. Sponsored by the Episcopal Church Diocese of Virginia, also sponsor of Goodwin House West, Falls Church. Every resident is a member of the Goodwin House Association, which elects a residents' council of 11 members who meet monthly with administrators. Opened in 1967.

Minimum age: 65 years.

Population: 303 residents; 84% women, 16% men, 17% couples.

Number of units: 257 Independent Living units; 36 Assisted Living units, 60 Skilled Nursing beds.

INDEPENDENT LIVING HOUSING

Type/size of apartment	*Entrance fee 1/2/3*	*Monthly fee 1&3/2**
Small efficiency, 196 sq. ft.	$56,503/26,522/87,852	$1,275/1,741
Large efficiency, 238 sq. ft.	$68,184/31,827/105,972	$1,275/1,848
Bed alcove, 345 sq. ft.	$98,342/46,149/152,818	$1,335/2,158
Deluxe alcove, 360 sq. ft.	$100,726/47,210/156,632	$1,335/2,169
1-Bedroom (single), 400 sq. ft.	$107,401/50,923/166,884	$1,445/2,337
1-Bedroom (double), 400 sq. ft.	$120,037/56,228/186,552	$2,479/3,480

**Plans 1 and 3 have the same monthly fee (lower than Plan 2). All utilities except long-distance telephone included. Wall-to-wall carpeting, full kitchens with modern appliances, miniblinds, individually controlled heating and air-conditioning.*

Dining plan: Three meals a day are included in the monthly fee. Private dining room available.

Services: *Included in the monthly fee:* Weekly housekeeping and flat-linen services, resident parking area, scheduled transportation.

At additional cost: Beauty/barbershop, pharmacy, guest accommodations.

Activities: Resident services department administers a well-rounded program of fine arts, crafts, educational and social enrichment, and a volunteer program generated from church and community groups. Exercise programs, garden boxes.

Health services and rates: Emergency nursing supervision and long-term nursing care provided at no extra cost to the resident. When residents become permanent members of the Skilled Nursing or physical assistance unit, their apartments return to circulation for new residents. However, the residents continue to pay the same monthly fee. Transfer agreement with local hospital, scheduled physician outpatient services, recreational therapy available. Chaplain and social worker on-site. Medical claims department assists residents in submitting eligible claims to Medicare.

- 36-Bed Assisted Living unit
- 60-Bed Skilled Nursing facility

"Since 1967, the trustees and staff of Goodwin House have been committed to providing the greatest possible quality of life for every resident through a program of Independent Living, privacy, health care, support and security in a gracious atmosphere. With 25 years of experience in the life care field, the dedicated, caring staff provides this quality to all residents."

HERMITAGE IN NORTHERN VIRGINIA

5000 Fairbanks Avenue
Alexandria, VA 22311
(703) 820-2434
Jill Keel, director of marketing

Type of community: Nonprofit Continuing Care, modified contract

A mid-rise red brick building offers scenic views of the seven-acre wooded campus and downtown Washington, D.C., in the distance. Located in a quiet residential neighborhood, the community offers a licensed nursing facility for respite, recuperative, and long-term care and Assisted Living. Located ten minutes from Washington National Airport, the community offers easy access to doctors' offices, shopping, and downtown Washington.

Financial plan: Entrance fee plus monthly fee. Entrance fee is 90% refundable for the first month of residency; thereafter, less 3% per month (30 months).

INDEPENDENT LIVING HOUSING

Type/size of apartment	*Entrance fee single/double*	*Monthly fee single/double**
Studio, 320 sq. ft.	$62,000	$1,065
1-Bedroom, 480 sq. ft.	$95,500/110,500	$1,460/1,890
1-Bedroom, 640 sq. ft.	$100,000/118,000	$1,470–1,500/1,900–1,930
2-Bedroom, 960 sq. ft.	$112,500/131,000	$1,700/2,230

** All utilities except telephone are included in the monthly fee. Wall-to-wall carpeting, draperies, kitchenettes (except studios), 24-hour emergency call system, individually controlled heating and air-conditioning.*

Ownership and management: One of six communities owned by Virginia United Methodist Homes, Inc. Opened in 1962.

Minimum age: 65 years.

Population: 230 residents.

Number of units: 113 Independent Living apartments; 44 Assisted Living units, 101-bed Skilled Nursing facility.

Dining plan: Three meals per day are included in the monthly fee. Full-time dietitian.

Services: *Included in the monthly fee:* Weekly housekeeping and flat-linen services. Each floor is equipped with a washer/dryer, refrigerator, and oven. Scheduled transportation.

At additional cost: Beauty/barbershop, gift shop items, guest accommodations, personal laundry.

Activities: Arts and crafts classes, a variety of concerts and special programs in the auditorium, lectures and seminars by area professionals, indoor and outdoor gardening, cultural and social outings, exercise classes and equipment, library, and chapel.

Availability: Limited.

Health Services: Independent Living residents and Assisted Living residents are entitled to 30 free days of care per year after which time the daily cost will be prorated according to the reduced monthly fee below. Respite, recuperative, and long-term care. Registered nurses, certified nursing assistance, social worker, staff dietitian, chaplain, activities coordinator, speech, physical, and occupational therapists. Health and nutrition seminars. Alzheimer's support groups. Residents may also be admitted directly in to the health care center in which case there is an option of an entrance fee and monthly fee or daily rate.

- 44 Assisted Living units*

	Nonresident entrance fee	*Monthly fee single/double*
Studio	$62,000/N/A	$1,920/N/A
1-Bedroom	$95,500/110,000	$2,240/3,510

**Monthly lease with no entrance fee available from $2,150–2,510.*

- 103-Bed health care center*

Semiprivate	$2,450/month	$127/day
Private	$2,670/month	$137/day
Deluxe private	$2,870/month	$157/day

** Nonresident entrance fee $65,000.*

"Hermitage in Northern Virginia is northern Virginia's first full-service retirement community. As one of six communities joined by one nonprofit corporation, the result is increased financial efficiency, a broader base to exchange ideas, a stable management structure, and a strong commitment to residents."

THE WASHINGTON HOUSE

5100 Fillmore Avenue
Alexandria, VA 22311
(703) 379-9000
Colleen Ryan Mallon, director of marketing

Type of community: Nonprofit Continuing Care, modified contract

Located on one of the highest points in northern Virginia, this 12-story contemporary building offers panoramic views of northern Virginia and the Washington, D.C., skyline. Washington House offers Independent Living apartments, Assisted Living apartments and a 68-bed health care center.

Financial plan: Entrance fee plus monthly fee or monthly rental only. Three plans: **1)** 100% refundable entrance fee for the first year and 90% refundable thereafter. **2)** Entrance fee declines at a rate of 2% per month. After 50 months, there is no refund. **3)** Entrance fee is not refundable after the first 30 days of residence.

Ownership and management: The Arlington Hospital Foundation. Opened in 1972.

Minimum age: 62 years.

Population: 177 residents; 70% women, 30% men, 17% couples.

Number of units: 148 Independent Living apartments; 20 Assisted Living apartments, 68-bed health care center.

Dining plan: Continental breakfast and dinner are included in the monthly fee. A full breakfast may be purchased for $136 per person per month. Catering services offered in main dining room. Country café is open for lunch.

Services: *Included in the monthly fee:* Housekeeping twice a month.

At additional cost: Beauty/barbershop, country store, newspaper delivery, guest accommodations, dry cleaning, group trips and scheduled transportation, grocery delivery.

Activities: Group trips, exercise classes, outdoor gardening areas, woodworking shop, arts and crafts, ceramics, chapel, bridge groups, library, shuffleboard, bookmobile, ice-cream socials, sing-alongs, films, current events discussions.

Availability: No waiting list for most apartment types.

Health services and rates: Clinic services offered. Residents are free to select their own physicians. Residents may chose where to go for diagnostic services or major surgery from a number of excellent hospitals in the area. Registered nurses are available for consultation, administration of medicines, and other services. Physical, occupational, and speech therapies plus dental care, podiatry, ophthalmology, and audiology services offered on-site. Arlington Hospital is five minutes away.

- 20 Assisted Living apartments
  Studio $2,287–2,462/month
  1-Bedroom $2,652–2,714/month
  1-Bedroom, 2 people $5,305/month
- 68-Bed health care center
  Semiprivate $127/day
  Private $140/day

"Retirement offers the opportunity to experience a relaxing schedule, develop new friendships, and further current interests. The Washington House is a Continuing Care retirement community that provides these opportunities as well as carefree living, convenience, and security to its residents."

INDEPENDENT LIVING HOUSING

Type of apartment	*Entrance fee 1**	*Entrance fee 2**	*Monthly fee**
Studio	$82,000–95,000	$41,000–47,000	$1,066–1,094
1-Bedroom	$123,000–172,000	$61,000–80,000	$1,460–1,576
2-Bedroom	$200,000–229,000	$95,000–109,000	$1,835–2,576

Note: *Plan 3 entrance fee ranges from $2,000–5,000 less than Plan 2. Monthly rental only prices range from $1,660 to $3,379. *For double occupancy for Plan 1 add between $22,000 and $51,000 to the entrance fee 1, depending on size of unit. For Plan 2 add between $14,000 and $23,000 to entrance fee 2, and $537 to the monthly fee. All utilities except telephone included. Wall-to-wall carpeting, all-electric kitchenette, 24-hour emergency call system.*

THE JEFFERSON

900 North Taylor Street
Arlington, VA 22203
(703) 351-0011
Michael Boozell, sales manager

Type of community: Continuing Care, modified contract

Two-story modern twin tower condominium buildings are joined for the first four floors by lobby and walkways. The buildings face a landscaped park. The towers contain common areas, a health care center, Assisted Living suites, and Independent Living condominiums from 5th to 21st floors. The community is conveniently located for shopping, recreation, and easy access to Washington, DC's Metro transit system. Downtown Washington, the Kennedy Center, museums, and National Airport are just minutes away.

Financial plan: Purchase price of condominium plus monthly fee.

Ownership and management: Owned and managed by Marriott Senior Living Services, a wholly owned subsidiary of Marriott Corporation. Marriott owns and manages 13 retirement communities in Arizona, California, Florida, Illinois, Indiana, Maryland, Pennsylvania, Texas, and Virginia. Opened in 1992.

Minimum age: 62 years.

Population: 550 residents; 60% women, 40% men, 60% couples.

Number of units: 325 Independent Living apartments; 57 Assisted Living studios, 31 Skilled Nursing beds.

Dining plan: Thirty meals included in the monthly fee. Private dining room.

Services: *Included in the monthly fee:* Weekly housekeeping, scheduled transportation, secured storage areas.

At additional cost: Secured on-site covered parking, country store/gift shop, beauty/barbershop.

Activities: Full-time activities coordinator. Game room, activity center, exercise room with equipment, heated indoor swimming pool, library/reading room.

Availability: Waiting list.

Health services and rates: Wellness clinic. Physical, occupational, and speech therapies available. Dental care next door. Nurse may be sent to Independent Living residences on hourly basis.

- 57 Assisted Living studios (depending on size of room) $70–90/day
- 31-Bed Skilled Nursing facility
  Semiprivate $125/day
  Private $154/day

"Residents enjoy all the qualitative benefits of living in and contributing to a caring community, fostering life of the mind with a sense of purpose.

INDEPENDENT LIVING HOUSING

Type/size of apartment	*Purchase price*	*Monthly fee**
1-Bedroom, 675 sq. ft.	$123,700–150,800	$1,055
1-Bedroom/den, 800 sq. ft.	$153,900–227,300	$1,195
2-Bedroom, 1,000 sq. ft.	$212,300–289,100	$1,295
2-Bedroom/den, 1,350 sq. ft.	$318,900–362,500	$1,495

**For double occupancy add $425 to the monthly fee. All utilities except telephone and cable TV included. Full kitchens, washers/dryers, neutral wall-to-wall carpeting, window treatments, individually controlled heating and air-conditioning, 24-hour emergency call system. Floors 6–18 have balconies.*

Excellent service is more than just a business philosophy, it's been a Marriott family tradition for more than 60 years. And all that we've learned as a leader in the service and hospitality industry is applied to satisfy the needs of older adults living in our retirement communities."

THE COLONNADES

2600 Barracks Road
Charlottesville, VA 22901
(804) 971-1892
Kevin Suite, sales manager

Type of community: Continuing Care, modified contract

Built on 59 acres, The Colonnades consists of 180 apartments and 40 cottages and a central community center. The landscaped grounds provide residents with pleasant views. A walking trail and resident gardens have been added recently. The health care center is connected directly to the main building for easy accessibility. The community is located five minutes from downtown Charlottesville and the University of Virginia.

Financial plan: Entrance fee plus monthly fee or monthly fee only. Two 90% refundable plans: **1)** Standard plan has higher entrance fee and lower monthly fee. **2)** Modified plan has lower entrance fee and higher monthly fee.

Ownership and management: Owned and managed by Marriott. Sponsored by Foundations of the University of Virginia. Marriott owns and manages 13 retirement communities in Arizona, California, Florida, Illinois, Maryland, New York, Pennsylvania, and Virginia. Opened in 1991.

Minimum age: 62 years.

Population: 180 residents; 60% women, 40% men, 60% couples.

INDEPENDENT LIVING HOUSING

Type/size of apartment	*Entrance fee 1/Monthly fee**	*Entrance fee 2/Monthly fee**
1-Bedroom, 560 sq. ft.	$91,000–94,000/890	$45,500–47,000/1,220
Deluxe 1-bedroom, 620 sq. ft.	$102,000–109,000/920	$51,000–54,500/1,290
1-Bedroom/den, 772 sq. ft.	$121,500–129,000/1,010	$60,750–64,500/1,450
Deluxe 2-bedroom, 942 sq. ft.	$144,500–152,000/1,190	$72,250–76,000/1,710
2-Bedroom/den, 1,100 sq. ft.	$166,500–174,000/1,310	$83,250–87,000/1,900
2-Bedroom/den, 1,342 sq. ft.	$176,500–184,000/1,370	$88,250–92,000/2,000
Cottages		
2-Bedroom, 1,285 sq. ft.	$199,750–206,250/1,430	$99,875–103,125/2,110
2-Bedroom/den, 1,450 sq. ft.	$214,750–221,250/1,490	$107,375–110,625/2,260

Note: *Monthly fee only ranges from $1,240–3,150 plus $500 for double occupancy. *For double occupancy for Plan 1 add $6,000 to the entrance fee, $300 to the monthly fee; for Plan 2 add $4,000 to the entrance fee, $400 to the monthly fee. All utilities except telephone included. Balconies or patios, full kitchens (many with pass-throughs), washers/dryers, neutral wall-to-wall carpeting, window treatments, individually controlled heating and air-conditioning, 24-hour emergency call system, satellite cable TV.*

Number of units: 180 Independent Living apartments and 40 cottages; 44 Assisted Living units, 54 nursing beds.

Dining plan: 30 meals included in the monthly fee. Private dining room. Cocktail lounge.

Availability: Limited.

Services: *Included in the monthly fee:* Secured storage area, weekly housekeeping and flat-linen services, scheduled transportation, on-site parking. Because The Colonnades is cosponsored by the University of Virginia, residents have university privileges similar to staff and faculty.

At additional cost: Beauty/barbershop, banking center, country store/gift shop.

Activities: Activity center, creative arts center, card room, library/reading room, game room, woodworking shop, natural walking paths, health club with exercise equipment, heated indoor swimming pool and whirlpool, guest speakers, movies, book discussions, dances, and shows.

Health services and rates: Clinic operated by University of Virginia Health Services Foundation. Inpatient and outpatient therapies provided.

- 44 Assisted Living units

Studio*	$63/day
Suite	$112/day

**Furnished studios available.*

- 54-Bed nursing facility

Semiprivate	$89/day
Private	$120/day

"Our commitment is to strive to create attractive, comfortable, and secure residential communities that inspire pride and a sense of community. We will work to make our communities affordable and to provide quality health care in settings that emphasize the dignity and individuality of our residents. Most important, we listen to our residents and people planning for retirement because they are the best authorities on the quality and future directions of Marriott retirement communities."

THE VIRGINIAN

9229 Arlington Boulevard
Fairfax, VA 22031
(703) 385-0555
Monica Pietsch, admission director

Type of community: Nonprofit Continuing Care, choice of all-inclusive or modified contract

A contemporary five-story building with two lower walkout levels is situated in a residential neighborhood. The 32¾-acre campus is half wooded and half filled with flower and vegetable gardens. Shopping is available within a mile radius, and Washington, D.C., is 12 miles away. Licensed 100-bed health care center provides on a temporary or permanent basis Intermediate and Skilled Nursing on-site.

Financial plan: Entrance fee plus monthly fee or monthly fee only. The entrance fee may be refunded at 100% in the event the agreement is terminated during the first year less the cost of the health care center should these services be used during the first year. Commencing with the second year, the refund shall be an amount equal to the entrance fee less 1½% of the entrance fee for each month of occupancy minus health care center services used. Monthly fee only residents sign a one-year agreement.

Ownership and management: Governed by the Temple Foundation, Inc. Opened in 1980.

Minimum age: None.

Population: 307 residents; 78% women, 22% men.

Number of units: 300 Independent Living apartments; 100-bed health care center.

INDEPENDENT LIVING HOUSING

Type/size of unit	*Entrance fee**	*Monthly fee**	*Monthly fee only**
1-Bedroom, 600 sq. ft.	$82,500	$1,355–1,375	$1,828–1,967
2-Bedroom, 900 sq. ft.	$82,500	$1,725–1,805	$2,077–2,160
4-Room	$137,500	$2,329	

**For double occupancy (2-bedroom and 4-room apartment only) add $82,500 to the entrance fee, $500 to the monthly fee, approximately $675 to the monthly fee only. All utilities except telephone and cable TV included. Fully equipped all-electric kitchen. Individually controlled heating and air-conditioning, wall-to-wall carpeting, 24-hour emergency call system.*

Dining plan: Breakfast and dinner are included in the monthly fee. Lunch is available for a fee. Private dining room.

Services: *Included in the monthly fee:* Bimonthly housekeeping, self-service laundry center, regularly scheduled van service and bus for special outings.

At additional cost: Beauty/barbershop, convenience store, flat-linen service, guest accommodations, daily delivery of newspapers, grocery shopping service, dry cleaning service.

Activities: Organized classes: exercise, ballroom dancing, arts and ceramics, Bible reading. Bingo, bridge, canasta, movies, trips to the theater, shopping centers and museums, gardening, interdenominational services in community chapel, library.

Availability: Residences are available.

Health Services: Residents who pay an entrance fee receive unlimited days in health care center at no additional cost beyond the published monthly apartment fee for their present accommodation. Should the resident move into the health care center permanently, there is no additional charge beyond the published monthly apartment fee for a one-bedroom apartment. Residents who pay the monthly fee only pay the daily fees listed below. 24-hour registered nurse and nursing assistance. Two house physicians with weekly appointment schedules. Podiatrist, dentist, physical therapist, and ophthalmologist available on regularly scheduled basis. Free consultation with a licensed dietitian.

- Assisted Living Services in resident's apartment (rates available on request)
- 100-Bed health care facility
  Intermediate Nursing $119/day
  Skilled Nursing $129/day

"At The Virginian, you'll find the joy of independence, the company of fascinating people, the security of Continuing Care, and the dedication and commitment of a skilled staff that reflects the most important aspect of the community: it's a wonderful place to come home to."

GOODWIN HOUSE WEST

3440 South Jefferson Street
Falls Church, VA 20041
(703) 820-1488
Carroll A. Oliver, senior vice president admissions/marketing

Type of community: Not-for-profit Continuing Care, all-inclusive contract

The multistory brick building is located on an eight-acre professionally landscaped site that features resident gardens and walking paths. Independent Living, Assisted Living, and Skilled Nursing are available on premises. The community is located nine miles from Washington, D.C., and six miles from Alexandria and is close to shopping, theater, and transportation.

Financial plan: Entrance fee plus monthly fee.

INDEPENDENT LIVING HOUSING

Type/size of apartment	*Entrance fee single/double*	*Monthly fee single/double**
Studio, 367 sq. ft.	$70,787	$1,321
1-Bedroom, 590 sq. ft.	$101,124/137,079	$1,512/2,516
Deluxe 1-bedroom, 750 sq. ft.	$120,225/152,810	$1,573/2,579
2-Bedroom, 903 sq. ft.	$185,394	$2,011/3,017

** All utilities except long-distance telephone included in the monthly fee. All apartments have wall-to-wall carpeting, full kitchens with modern appliances, individually controlled heating and air-conditioning, 24-hour emergency medical alert call system, miniblinds.*

Ownership and management: Managed by the Goodwin House, Inc., board of trustees. Sponsored by the Episcopal Church Diocese of Virginia, also sponsor of Goodwin House, Alexandria. Every resident is a member of the Goodwin House Association, which elects a residents' council of 11 members who meet monthly with administrators. Opened in 1987.

Minimum age: 65 years.

Population: 318 residents; 64% women, 36% men, 20% couples.

Number of units: 264 Independent Living units; 60 Assisted Living units, 72-bed nursing facility.

Dining plan: Three meals a day included in the monthly fee. Private dining and party rooms available.

Services: *Included in the monthly fee:* Weekly housekeeping and flat-linen services, parking.

At additional cost: Beauty/barbershop, personal laundry equipment, pharmacy, guest accommodations.

Activities: Arts and crafts center, library and auditorium, billiards room, exercise programs, chapel, volunteer programs, educational and social enrichment programs.

Availability: Apartment available, depending on floor plan.

Health services and rates: Residents' monthly fee covers unlimited health care. Medical claims department assists residents by submitting eligible medical bills to Medicare. Chaplain and social worker on staff.

- 60-Bed Assisted Living unit
- 72-Bed Skilled Nursing facility

"Since 1967, the trustees and Goodwin House staff have been committed to providing the best possible quality of life for every resident through a program of Independent Living, privacy, health care support, and security in a gracious atmosphere. With 25 years of experience in the life care field, the dedicated, caring staff provides this quality to all residents."

THE FAIRFAX

9140 Belvoir Woods Parkway
Fort Belvoir, VA 22060-2703
(703) 799-1000
Nancy George, director of marketing

Type of community: Continuing Care, modified contract

The Fairfax was developed for the Army Retirement Residence Foundation, Potomac, and is open to retired officers of all U.S. uniformed services as well as members of the U.S. Foreign Service, U.S. Public Health Service, HOAA, and their spouses. Located in a beautiful country setting with an eight-acre lake, the community is close to Fort Belvoir Army Base and 20 minutes from the Washington, D.C., metropolitan area.

Financial plan: Entrance fee plus monthly fee. Two plans: **1)** Original plan, with higher entrance fee, lower monthly fee. **2)** Moderate plan, with lower entrance fee and higher monthly fee. All entrance fees 95% refundable. An interest-bearing, refundable deposit is required to reserve a unit.

Ownership and management: Owned and managed by Marriott Senior Living Services, a wholly owned subsidiary of Marriott Corporation. Developed under the sponsorship of the Army Retirement Residence Foundation, Potomac. Marriott owns and manages 13 retirement communities in Arizona, California, Florida, Illinois, Indiana, Maryland, New Jersey, Pennsylvania, Texas, and Virginia. Opened in 1989.

Minimum age: 55 years.

Population: 500 residents; 61% women, 39% men, 41% couples.

Number of units: 347 Independent Living apartments and 35 cottages; 45 Assisted Living suites, 60 nursing beds.

Dining plan: Choice of one main meal daily included in the monthly fee. Informal coffee shop, private dining room, and terrace.

Services: *Included in the monthly fee:* Weekly housekeeping, scheduled transportation, parking, concierge service.

At additional cost: Bank with safe-deposit boxes, network cash machine, country store, beauty/barbershop, gift shop, guest accommodations.

Activities: Heated indoor swimming pool, whirlpool, exercise area, jogging paths, bicycle trails, gardening areas, arts/crafts/woodworking shop, library, French club, happy hour, auditorium, library.

Availability: Waiting list for larger apartments and cottages.

Health services and rates: Speech, occupational and physical therapies, podiatry, dentistry, ophthalmology, audiology, respite care services offered. Wellness program.

- 50 Assisted Living suites
  - Unfurnished private $78/day
  - Furnished private $83/day
  - Suite $105/day
- 60-Bed nursing facility
  - Semiprivate $125/day
  - Private $145/day
  - Medicare certified $250/day

INDEPENDENT LIVING HOUSING

Type/size of apartment	*Entrance fee 1/Monthly fee**	*Entrance fee 2**
1-Bedroom, 605–887 sq. ft.	$101,100–151,800/1,344–1,410	$50,550–75,900
1-Bedroom/den, 816 sq. ft.	$133,900–188,900/1,475	$66,950–94,450
2-Bedroom, 890–1,189 sq. ft.	$156,300–271,800/1,431–1,617	$78,150–135,900
2-Bedroom/den, 1,402 sq. ft.	$274,300–324,900/1,814	$137,150–162,450
3-Bedroom, 1,500 sq. ft.	$288,600–348,700/1,886	$144,300–174,350
Cottages, 1,140–1,527 sq. ft.	$249,200–373,000/1,748–1,886	$124,600–186,500

Note: *Monthly fee for Plan 2 ranges from $1,730–2,954. *For double occupancy add $10,000 (nonrefundable Continuing Care fee) to the entrance fee, $588 to the monthly fee. All utilities except telephone included. Fully equipped kitchen, washer/dryer, 24-hour emergency call system, balcony or patio, individual heating and air-conditioning, master TV antenna, package shelf outside front door, storage locker.*

"Residents enjoy all the qualitative benefits of living in and contributing to a caring community, fostering life of the mind with a sense of purpose. Excellent service is more than just a business philosophy; it's been a Marriott family tradition for more than 60 years. And all that we've learned as a leader in the service and hospitality industry is applied to satisfy the needs of older adults living in our retirement communities."

Jean and Bob, 74 years

Waiting List, Presbyterian Home, Evanston, Illinois

"Being on the waiting list in the beginning was just fine with us. I don't think we were ready to make the move when we signed up."

Since Bob retired from Continental Bank in Chicago, he and Jean have been dividing their time between an apartment in Evanston and a condominium in Naples, Florida. Five years ago they joined the waiting list at Presbyterian Home so that Jean would have a place to move to if something happened to Bob. She loves the Evanston area, is a graduate of Northwestern University, and both she and Bob have many friends living at Presbyterian Home.

Before joining the waiting list, Bob asked to see information on Presbyterian Home's finances. Because of his financial expertise he felt qualified to examine the community's financial information on his own. He discovered, much to his satisfaction, that Presbyterian Home has a fine endowment. He particularly likes the fact that the community is continuing to expand, purchasing land and building deluxe and moderate income housing, as well as renovating. "The community is not just sitting still on their money. They are reinvesting and putting it to good use," according to Bob.

"Being on the waiting list in the beginning was just fine with us," he says. "I don't think we were ready to make the move when we signed up."

Last summer, however, due to a freak accident in which both Jean and Bob were hit by a car while crossing the street in Evanston, Jean ended up with a broken hip and fractured pelvis, injuries that landed her in the hospital for a week. "Luckily, because of our relationship with Presbyterian Home," explains Bob, "Jean was able to rehabilitate in the community infirmary. During her recovery an apartment came up but we were in no position to make a move, so we asked to remain on the waiting list." Jean and Bob are continuing to divide their time between Evanston and Florida, waiting for the right moment to move into Presbyterian Home.

Bob's advice: Carefully examine the financial conditions of a community before moving in. If you're not versed in finance, have your accountant examine the community's financials for you.

RAPPAHANNOCK WESTMINSTER-CANTERBURY

10 Lancaster Drive
Irvington, VA 22480
(804) 438-4000
Rebecca C. Davis, admissions/marketing associate

Type of community: Nonprofit Continuing Care, all-inclusive contract

Nestled between the Potomac and Rappahannock rivers and only minutes from the mouth of the Chesapeake Bay, this community is located on 113 wooded acres featuring a stocked lake, garden plots, and award-winning landscaping. The grounds are an official bird sanctuary and act as the site of the annual Virginia Rose Show. The community was designed to replicate the Northern Neck Farmhouse. Covered walkways connect 78 cottages to the Chesapeake Center, which has common rooms with fireplaces, an auditorium, library, beauty/barbershop, bank, elegant dining room, café, country store, and resident clinic. A temperate-controlled walkway leads from the center to 40 apartments in the three-story building overlooking Wood Duck Lake. Located in a resort area near several marinas and convenient to Richmond, Williamsburg, and Virginia Beach, the community provides its Independent Living residents a continuum of care at no additional cost.

Financial plan: Entrance fee plus monthly fee. Three plans with entrance fee refunds of up to 50%. The entrance fee recovery program provides residents the opportunity to have a full return of the entrance fee. The reservation fee is fully refundable for any reason before occupancy.

Ownership and management: Owned by Rappahannock Westminster-Canterbury. Managed by board of trustees comprised of area professionals. Affiliated with the Episcopal and Presbyterian churches. Opened in 1985.

Minimum age: 65 years.

Population: 135 residents; 71% women, 29% men, 47% couples.

Number of units: 118 Independent Living apartments; 18 Assisted Living units, 32 Intermediate and 10 Skilled Nursing beds.

Dining plan: One meal per day included in the monthly fee. Special diets available and arranged by the in-house dietitian. Private dining room available. Tray service at extra cost.

Services: *Included in the monthly fee:* Weekly housekeeping, lighted parking areas, transportation to local shops, delivered pharmaceutical items.

INDEPENDENT LIVING HOUSING

Type/size of apartments	*Entrance fee**	*Monthly fee**
Studio, 636 sq. ft.	$97,072	$1,304
1-Bedroom, 852 sq. ft.	$123,518	$1,720
2-Bedroom, 1,068–1,120 sq. ft.	$141,290–149,716	$1,911–2,012
Cottages		
Studio, 684 sq. ft.	$103,165	$1,481
1-Bedroom, 853 sq. ft.	$123,167	$1,740
2-Bedroom, 1,052–1,130 sq. ft.	$148,547–158,486	$2,005–2,157

**For double occupancy add $40,943 to the entrance fee, $706 to the monthly fee. All utilities except telephone included. Fully equipped all-electric kitchen, wall-to-wall carpeting, balcony or patio, individually controlled heating and air-conditioning, 24-hour emergency call system, cable TV. Cottages have private utility rooms. Some cottages have enclosed patios, which adds $25 to the monthly fee.*

At additional cost: Beauty/barbershop, scheduled trips and excursions, laundry and flat-linen services, guest rooms, bank, café.

Activities: Golf, groomed walking nature trails, Bible study, bridge, book discussions, fishing, exercise, bingo, lectures, movies, enclosed heated swimming pool, special excursions, library, crafts room, arts program, auditorium, activity areas, gardening plots, private eight-acre fishing lake, sundeck, gazebo, biking roads, woodland paths, bird sanctuary.

Availability: Waiting list.

Health services and rates: Assisted Living, Intermediate, and Skilled Nursing are provided at no additional cost to residents, except two extra meals daily, medical supplies, and prescription drugs. Resident selects own physician. Transfer to area hospitals can be arranged if necessary. Physical, occupational, and speech therapies and other special services available. Clinic offers blood pressure checks, hearing and eye care, EKGs, podiatry, pacemaker evaluations, hemoccult and glucose test, urinary tract screenings, flu shots and vaccinations. Temporary care in resident's cottage or apartment is available at extra cost. Rappahannock General Hospital is located within three miles of the community and allows for transfer should resident need acute care.

- 18 Assisted Living units
- 32 Intermediate Nursing beds
- 10-Bed Skilled Nursing facility

"Rappahannock Westminster-Canterbury, developed under guidelines established by the Episcopal and Presbyterian churches of Virginia, is dedicated to providing true life care for older adults as an expression of our Christian values and commitment. We believe that older individuals have a right to health and nursing care and to receive this care in an environment that diminishes worry and offers quality service as well as a happy, satisfying lifestyle. Rappahannock Westminster-Canterbury has a ministry to its residents to help them use their gifts fully, live their lives meaningfully, and make the very best of the years that God has given them."

WESTMINSTER-CANTERBURY

501 V.E.S. Road
Lynchburg, VA 24503
(804) 386-3500
Paula Jones, communications director

Type of community: Not-for-profit Continuing Care, choice of all-inclusive or modified contract

Accreditation: Continuing Care Accreditation Commission

Two seven-story residential buildings, connected by a spacious glass-walled bridge on the third-floor level, are located on 21-acre wooded campus. Fine arts center and symphony orchestra are available in Lynchburg. Randolph-Macon Women's College, Lynchburg College, Sweet Briar College, and Virginia Episcopal School offer many musical concerts, theatrical productions, sports activities, educational programs, and lectures. The Jessie Ball duPont Nature Trail is accessible from the community by a footbridge. Westminster Canterbury is located in the foothills of the Blue Ridge Mountains, close to Smith Mountain Lake.

Financial plan: Entrance fee plus monthly fee or monthly rental. Two plans for entrance fee refund and two options for health care: **1)** Basic refund plan: refund less 2% per month of residency for period of 50 months. **2)** Extended refund plan: 4% is retained for first four months, 1% per month of residency for remaining period of 96 months. Two options for health care: **1)** Unlimited health care in nursing center at no extra cost. **2)** Modified health care allows 365 days of free health care per lifetime and per diem rate (less 5%) thereafter. Resident has choice of either refund option and either health care option.

Ownership and management: Owned and managed by Westminster-Canterbury of Lynchburg, Inc.

Board of trustees composed equally of Presbyterians and Episcopalians who are prominent business and community leaders. Opened in 1980.

Minimum age: 65 years.

Population: 400 residents; 79% women, 21% men, 25% couples.

Number of units: 205 Independent Living apartments; 76 Assisted Living units, 105-bed health care center.

Dining plan: One meal per day included in the monthly fee. Private dining room available.

Services: *Included in the monthly fee:* Weekly housekeeping and flat-linen services, scheduled transportation, lighted parking lots.

At additional cost: Beauty/barbershop, guest rooms.

Activities: Chapel, crafts room, bridge groups, woodworking shop, billiards room, meeting and classrooms, gardening, bridge groups, horseshoes, shuffleboard, oil painting, watercoloring, ceramics, flower arranging, college continuing education courses, volunteering, swimming pool at the Presbyterian Home (adjacent to property), three golf courses in Lynchburg, library.

Availability: Waiting list depends on style of apartment desired. $1,000 deposit places you on waiting list.

Health services and rates: Resident has choice of two health plans under entrance fee option: unlimited health care offers unlimited number of days in the health center at no additional cost; modified health care offers 365 days of health care at no extra cost, after which resident pays regular rate less 5%. On-site resident clinic offers temporary care in apartments and other services. Physical, occupational, and speech therapies, podiatry and dental services.

- 76 Assisted Living units $68/day
- 105-Bed health care center

	Intermediate Nursing	*Skilled Nursing*
Semiprivate	$99/day	$104/day
Private	$114/day	$120/day

"Westminster-Canterbury is proud to be located in the heart of historic Virginia. It is convenient to many of the battlegrounds of both the Revolutionary and Civil wars and the breathtaking Blue Ridge Mountains. The Lynchburg area is home to numerous well-recognized educational and cultural institutions and is host to sports activities like the Tour Dupont Cyclist Race. The 21 acres that comprise the Westminster-Canterbury campus are beautifully landscaped and maintained for year-round beauty."

INDEPENDENT LIVING HOUSING

Type/size of apartment	*Entrance fee 1/2**	*Monthly fee**
Studio, 423–598 sq. ft.	$65,100–85,950/72,550–96,600	$1,509–1,706
1-Bedroom, 684–846 sq. ft.	$96,700–120,500/111,950–140,800	$1,840–2,034
2-Bedroom, 846–1,107 sq. ft.	$120,500–154,450/140,800–179,975	$1,344–1,501

**Prices listed are for unlimited health care plan. Modified health care Plan 2 entrance fees range from $33,450–122,775; monthly fees are the same for both health care plans. For double occupancy add $25,000 to the entrance fee for unlimited health care, $5,100 to the entrance fee for Plan 1 modified health care, $15,350 to the entrance fee for Plan 2 modified health care, and $395 to the monthly fee. All utilities except long-distance phone included. Fully equipped kitchen, individually controlled heating and air-conditioning, cable TV (optional), 24-hour emergency call system, wall-to-wall carpeting. Laundry rooms located on each floor of the apartment buildings.*

BRANDERMILL WOODS

14311 Brandermill Woods Trail
Midlothian, VA 23112
(804) 744-1173
Phyllis Musser, director of marketing

Type of community: Not-for-profit Continuing Care, modified contract

Single-level cluster homes grouped around cul-de-sacs and two three-story apartment buildings (Club Homes) are located on a 30-acre campus landscaped with trees and outdoor gardens. The Club Home apartment buildings are attached to the community clubhouse, which houses a lounge, billiards, meeting areas, crafts room, card and game room, exercise room with spa, dance floor, and restaurant. Within the surrounding Brandermill community are parks and recreation areas, boating facilities, a 1,700-acre lake, Brandermill Country Club, convenient shopping (Market Square Shopping Village), 15 miles of paved walking and biking trails, banks, medical offices, inn and conference center, and several restaurants. The community is close to Richmond and all its services and amenities.

Financial plan: Monthly rental. One month's rent for deposit. Residents commit to six- or 12-month rental.

Ownership and management: Owned by Senior Living Choices. Managed by Real Property Health Facilities Corporation. Opened in 1986.

Minimum age: 55 years.

Population: 137 residents; 57% couples.

Number of units: 197 Independent Living homes; 60 Assisted Living units, 60-bed health care center.

Dining plan: Meal plans are optional. Private dining room, special diets, and tray service available.

Services: *Included in the monthly fee:* Shuttle bus service within the community, transportation throughout the greater Brandermill community, all exterior building maintenance and reasonable interior maintenance.

At additional cost: Beauty/barbershop, housekeeping, flat-linen service, personal laundry, dry cleaning.

Activities: Activities coordinator. Meeting room, card areas, exercise room with spa, dance floor, activity rooms, various classes and cultural events, church services, billiards, movies, bowling, dinner club, shopping trips. Brandermill Country Club (membership optional) offers golf, five swimming pools, 22 tennis courts, a clubhouse, and pro shop.

INDEPENDENT LIVING HOUSING

Cluster homes	*Monthly rental**
2-Bedroom, 1,258 sq. ft.	$1,700–1,935
3-Bedroom, 1,461–1,488 sq. ft.	$2,190–2,305
Club Homes	
1-Bedroom, 890 sq. ft.	$1,615
2-Bedroom, 1,078–1,120 sq. ft.	$1,985

**For double occupancy add $150 to the monthly rental. All utilities except telephone included. Fully equipped kitchens, wall-to-wall carpeting, washer and dryer, 24-hour emergency call system, individually controlled heating and air-conditioning, cable TV. Cluster homes have patios and individual garages. Some Club Homes have sun rooms or porches. Pets are allowed but subject to certain regulations and restrictions.*

Availability: Waiting list for certain units.

Health services and rates: Residents receive ten free days per year in either Assisted Living or Skilled Nursing. Residents may maintain their home even if receiving health care for a lengthy period of time. Assistance with medications and monitoring blood pressure available. Therapies are available in health center.

- 60 Assisted Living units

Efficiency	$69/day
Studio	$71/day
1-Bedroom	$83/day

- 60-Bed health care center

	Intermediate Nursing	*Skilled Nursing*
Semiprivate	$94.50/day	$105/day
Private	$105/day	$115/day

"Brandermill Woods was chosen as the Best Planned Community in America. Brandermill offers multigenerational living with amenities especially designed for active retirement living. Our spacious, worry-free accommodations, the security of complete health care, a state-of-the-art security system, plus a three-star-rated restaurant make Brandermill Woods a unique community."

WARWICK FOREST

866 Denbigh Boulevard
Newport News, VA 23602
(804) 886-2000
Gloria Seitz, administrator

Type of community: Nonprofit Continuing Care, choice of all-inclusive or modified contract

The community is situated on a 13-acre campus in a residential neighborhood adjacent to the York County line and near the wooded watershed of Harwood Mill Reservoir. Independent Living apartments are located in a three-story building and single-story cottages, all connected to each other and to the health center by covered walkways. The community is located less than a half mile from an area hospital and several physicians' offices and less than a mile from churches, banking, and restaurants. Nearby Christopher Newport College in Newport News and the College of William and Mary in Williamsburg provide exceptional cultural and educational opportunities.

Financial plan: Entrance fee plus monthly fee or monthly rental only. Entrance fee is refundable less 2% per month over 50 months. Monthly rental fee

INDEPENDENT LIVING HOUSING

Type/size of apartment	*Entrance fee*	*Monthly fee*	*Monthly rental*
Alcove, 500 sq. ft.	$40,950/56,850	$780/1,250	$823/1,320
1-Bedroom, 672 sq. ft.	$55,650/72,450	$995/1,355	$1,051/1,431
Deluxe 1-bedroom, 778 sq. ft.	$61,750/79,500	$1,045/1,465	$1,103/1,547
2-Bedroom, 1-bath, 778 sq. ft.	$66,950/84,800	$1,095/1,465	$1,267/1,599
2-Bedroom, 2-bath, 850 sq. ft.	$69,600/87,000	$1,200/1,515	$1,314/1,663
Phase 2 cottages			
1-Bedroom, 767 sq. ft.	$61,750/79,500	$1,076/1,509	N/A
2-Bedroom, 1,150 sq. ft.	$76,760/95,700	$1,410/1,784	N/A

Every apartment floor plan except alcove is available in cottage residence as well as apartment. All utilities except telephone included in the monthly fee. Fully equipped kitchens, wall-to-wall carpeting, patio or balcony, individual heating and air-conditioning controls, 24-hour emergency call system. Washer/dryer in apartment and hookups in cottages.

with the option to convert to Continuing Care at any time. If resident decides to switch to Continuing Care, the cost difference between the monthly rental fee and the Continuing Care monthly fee can be credited against the entrance fee. The percentage that will be credited decreases 25% every six months over a two-year period.

Ownership and management: The Riverside Health System, the largest health care provider in eastern Virginia, in existence for 75 years. Owns and operates seven long-term care nursing homes, five acute care hospitals, and four wellness and fitness centers. Opened in 1988.

Minimum age: 65 years.

Population: 55 residents; 66% women, 33% male, 15% couples.

Number of units: 24 Independent Living apartments and 26 cottages; 385-bed health care center.

Dining plan: The evening meal is included in the monthly fee. Private dining room. Tray service available.

Services: *Included in the monthly fee:* Weekly housekeeping service and scheduled transportation.

At additional cost: Beauty/barbershop, guest accommodations.

Activities: Director of activities. Classes in creative writing, French, and calligraphy. Trips to museums, concerts, plays, speakers, and entertainers. Library, billiards room, creative arts room. Free membership at the Riverside Wellness and Fitness Center, including indoor track, Olympic-size swimming pool, exercise equipment, and so on.

Availability: Limited.

Health services and rates: All residents are guaranteed admission to health center and the first ten days of care at no charge. For residents who paid an entrance fee, any costs after this time that are not covered by Medicare or other insurance will be covered by residents' entrance fee. Should this credit become exhausted and a resident is not able to cover future care, the health center is certified as a Medicaid provider and can make applications to cover the cost of care. Monthly rental residents receive 10% off the normal per-day rates in the health center, which are listed below. HELP (Home Enhanced Living Program) is offered at $7.50/hour for Assisted Living. Health clinic staffed with a registered nurse.

- 385-Bed health care center

	Intermediate Nursing	*Skilled Nursing*
Semiprivate	$93.60/day	$117/day
Private	$101.70/day	$121.50/day

"Warwick Forest offers an active and healthy independent lifestyle in a caring community of friends and neighbors. Warwick Forest is large enough to provide all the services residents may need but small enough to give them the personal attention they deserve. Immediate access to professional health care, especially in emergencies, provides a feeling of security. The residential neighborhood atmosphere also offers all the conveniences residents are used to—shopping, libraries, theaters, and community activities are just minutes from the front door. Nearby colleges provide exceptional cultural and educational opportunities. Warwick Forest offers our residents the opportunity to enjoy their pastimes with a renewed spirit and a greater sense of security in an atmosphere in which their privacy is always respected."

THE HERMITAGE

1600 Westwood Avenue
Richmond, VA 23227
(804) 355-5721
Sara T. Cheely, director of admissions

Type of community: Continuing Care, modified contract

The Hermitage is a Georgian-style mansion located at the edge of Richmond's historic Ginter Park residential neighborhood. The central section of the building was formerly a private mansion built in 1911, with additions made in the 1950s. Surrounding the brick building are lawns, gardens, old trees, patios, and sidewalks. Important institutions in the neighborhood are Richmond Memorial Hospital, the Presbyterian School of Christian Education, and Union Theological Seminary.

Financial plan: Entrance fee plus monthly fee or monthly rental. Two plans: **1)** Entrance fee refunded on a prorated basis during first 30 months. **2)** Refundable entrance fee, regardless of length of stay. Persons 85 years and older are not eligible for Plan 2.

Ownership and management: Owned and managed by Virginia United Methodist Homes, Inc., which operates five other retirement communities. Opened in 1949.

Minimum age: 65 years.

Population: 350 residents; 88% women, 13% men, 3% couples.

Number of units: 140 Independent Living apartments; 50 Assisted Living units, 115-bed health care center.

Dining plan: Three meals per day included in the monthly fee.

Services: *Included in the monthly fee:* Weekly housekeeping, scheduled transportation, flat-linen service, washer/dryer on hall, assigned parking.

At additional cost: Beauty/barbershop.

Activities: Activities coordinator. Creative workshop, arts and crafts classes, library, chapel, Choristers, bingo, Bible study, movies, concerts, lectures, residents' council.

Availability: Current availability.

Health services and rates: 24-hour Intermediate Nursing. Staff of 108 registered nurses, licensed practical nurses, and certified nursing assistants. Medical director, social services coordinator, and physical and recreational therapy on-site. Short-term stays available in health center.

- 50 Assisted Living units*

Level 1	$1,486/month
Level 2	$1,835/month

**Nonresident entrance fee: $48,000*

- 115-Bed health center*

Semiprivate	$2,645/month	$97/day
Private	$2,906/month	$130/day

**Nonresident entrance fee: $24,000 for semiprivate, $48,000 for private.*

"The Hermitage is known for the individual attention available to its older population. The size is manageable. Resident and patient care teams of staff see that services are supplied as needed. Food is nutritious, tasty, and plentiful. The atmosphere is friendly and homelike. The spiritual life program is important."

INDEPENDENT LIVING HOUSING

Type/size of unit	*Entrance fee 1**	*Monthly fee**
Studio, 168 sq. ft.	$48,000	$1,128
2-Room single, 360 sq. ft.	$73,500	$1,647
2-Room double, 360 sq. ft.	$85,000	$1,128 (per person)
3-Room double, 528 sq. ft.	$104,000	$1,235 (per person)

**Entrance fees for Plan 2 are higher (studio 1 is $78,000) Also available for monthly rental ranging from $1,353–2,091. Utilities except telephone included. Carpeting, individually controlled heating and air-conditioning, 24-hour emergency call system, large window, bath, closet.*

LAKEWOOD MANOR

1900 Lauderdale Drive
Richmond, VA 23233
(804) 740-2900
Joan Pemberton, director of admissions

Type of community: Nonprofit Continuing Care, all-inclusive contract

Five contemporary, low-rise Independent Living contemporary apartment buildings and a community center are connected by covered walkways. The apartments and buildings are of brick-and-frame construction. Located on a 68-acre wooded campus in Richmond's suburban west end, Lakewood Manor is surrounded by walking trails and flower gardens. The community is convenient to shopping, churches, and professional services. Museums, theaters, and symphonies are nearby in Richmond.

Financial plan: Entrance fee plus monthly fee. Entrance fee refundable less 2% per month of residency.

Ownership and management: Owned and operated by Virginia Baptist Homes, Inc., which owns two other retirement communities in the area. Opened in 1977.

Minimum age: 65 years.

Population: 390 residents; 67% women, 33% men, 15% couples.

Number of units: 265 Independent Living apartments; 110-bed health care center.

Dining plan: One meal per day included in the monthly fee. Private dining room upon request. Tray service available.

Services: *Included in the monthly fee:* Biweekly housekeeping, scheduled transportation, parking, laundry facilities located on each floor of the apartment buildings.

At additional cost: Beauty/barbershop, newspaper delivery, guest accommodations, postal services, convenience store, full-service bank.

Activities: Library, activities room, exercise, walking paths, flower and vegetable gardening areas, billiards room, workshops, solarium lounge, woodworking shop, religious services, travelogues, arts and crafts areas. Museums, theaters, symphonies all in Richmond.

Availability: Six-month to two-year waiting list, depending on floor plan.

Health services and rates: Unlimited health care included in residents' entrance and monthly fees. Health center on-site offers emergency, recuperative, and long-term nursing care. Apartment residents have access to the staff physician. Clinical and pharmacy services available. Physical and rehabilitative therapies offered, as are special screenings and assistance with medications. If physicians determine that a resident requires long-term care, the apartment will be released. In the event the resident is able to live independently again, the first available apartment will be given to her or him.

- 110-Bed health care center

INDEPENDENT LIVING HOUSING

Type/size of unit	*Entrance fee single/double*	*Monthly fee single/double**
Studio, 472 sq. ft.	$52,000	$1,310
1-Bedroom, 472–822 sq. ft.	$52,500–77,800/97,500–109,300	$1,310–1,774/2,146–2,351
2-Bedroom, 874–937 sq. ft.	$86,600–90,600/122,000–127,600	$1,822/2,558

**All utilities except telephone included in the monthly fee. Fully equipped electric kitchens, individually controlled heating and air-conditioning, carpeting, cable TV, 24-hour emergency call system.*

"Lakewood Manor is a Christian life care community for all faiths, offering quality care provided by a thoughtful and friendly resident family and caring staff. Lakewood Manor residents have an active, interesting lifestyle yet continue to live independently in the privacy of their own apartments."

ST. MARY'S WOODS

1257 Mary Wood Lane
Richmond, VA 23339
(804) 741-8624
Nan Pascal, administrator

Type of community: Nonprofit Independent and Assisted Living

St. Mary's Woods is located in the west end of Richmond near the popular Gayton Crossing Shopping Center. It is a beautifully designed rustic modern exterior of brick and siding. The property is surrounded by a natural tree line and the campus is manicured by a full-time groundsman. Seasonal flowers are a priority that enhances the property. St. Mary's Woods is minutes from activities and shopping while being situated in a lovely, quiet residential neighborhood.

Financial plan: Month-to-month lease. $500 security deposit.

Ownership and management: Owned by the Catholic Diocese of Virginia and managed by Coordinated Services Management of Virginia. Opened in 1988.

Minimum age: 65 years.

Population: 124 residents; 80% women, 20% men, 6% couples.

Number of units: 58 Independent Living apartments; 60 Assisted Living units.

Dining plan: Dinner meal is included in the monthly fee. Lunch and breakfast are served daily. Licensed registered dietitian available for consultation. Private dining room.

Services: *Included in the monthly fee:* Weekly housekeeping and flat-linen services, van transportation on scheduled route.

At additional cost: Beauty/barbershop, personal laundry service, self-service laundry rooms.

Activities: Full-time recreational therapist. Community gardening plot, ceramics, arts and crafts, whirlpool facilities.

Availability: Short waiting list.

Health services and rates: On-site health clinic with a registered nurse.

- 60 Assisted Living units*
  Studio, 464 sq. ft. — $1,465/month
  1-Bedroom, 505–648 sq. ft. — $1,697–1,832/month

**For double occupancy add $530 to the monthly fee.*

INDEPENDENT LIVING HOUSING

Type/size of unit	*Monthly fee**
Studio, 464 sq. ft.	$1,125
1-Bedroom, 584–604 sq. ft.	$1,375–1,434
2-Bedroom, 741–761 sq. ft.	$1,859–2,001

**For double occupancy add $356 to the monthly fee. All utilities accept telephone included. All-electric kitchen, individually controlled heating and air-conditioning, 24-hour emergency call system, cable TV hookup. Five apartment floor plans, some with patios or bay windows.*

"St. Mary's Woods provides a gracious, caring environment, very conveniently located in the west end of Richmond close to all amenities. We are unique because of our month-to-month leasing option with no entrance fee."

WESTMINSTER-CANTERBURY

1600 Westbrook Avenue
Richmond, VA 23227
(804) 264-6256
Harry Baldwin, marketing director

Type of community: Nonprofit Continuing Care, all-inclusive contract

Accreditation: Continuing Care Accreditation Commission

The nine-story Independent Living building features a roof terrace that offers a panoramic view of the city. The community is located on a 25-acre landscaped campus on the northside of Richmond. Four of the community's gardens are featured in the Historical Garden Week tour. Westminster-Canterbury has an art gallery for the exhibit and sale of art by residents, a sidewalk café, and a men's lounge. The health center is adjacent to the main residence. Convenient shopping at Azalea Mall and downtown Richmond is available. The community is planning to open 19 larger garden apartments, a therapeutic swimming pool, and a coffee shop in 1995.

Financial plan: Entrance fee plus monthly fee. Two plans: **1)** Basic plan: refundable less 2% per month of residency. **2)** 80% refundable plan: 80% refund of entrance fee, regardless of length of stay.

Ownership and management: Founded by the Episcopal and Presbyterian Churches in Virginia. Opened in 1975.

Minimum age: 65 years.

Population: 680 residents; 70% women, 30% men, 30% couples (530 full-time employees).

Number of units: 344 Independent apartments; 90 Assisted Living apartments; 158-bed health care center.

Dining plan: Three meals per day included in the monthly fee. One-meal-per-day option available. Dietitian available. Private dining room and catering facilities.

Services: *Included in the monthly fee:* Housekeeping and flat-linen services, parking, scheduled transportation.

At additional cost: Beauty/barbershop, laundry rooms on each floor, concierge, valet.

Activities: Chapel, men's lounge with billards table, two auditoriums, 4,000-volume library, painting, pottery wheels and kilns, well-equipped woodworking shop, looms, nature trail, chipping range, areas for biking and strolling, individual garden plots,

INDEPENDENT LIVING HOUSING

Type/size of unit	*Entrance fee 1 single/double**	*Monthly fee single/double**
Studio, 380–522 sq. ft.	$69,200–76,200/N/A	$1,049–1,170/N/A
1-Bedroom, 571–760 sq. ft.	$79,000–90,200/114,500–130,800	$1,236–1,362/1,866–1,992
2-Bedroom, 810–951 sq. ft.	$93,800–110,800/136,100–160,700	$1,408–1,568/2,038–2,274
1-Bedroom, 1,044 sq. ft.	$113,000/163,800	$1,588/2,302

**Refundable entrance fee plan has higher entrance fee. All utilities included in the monthly fee. Fully equipped kitchenette, wall-to-wall carpeting, heat lamps, 24-hour emergency call system, cable TV.*

greenhouse, exercise room with whirlpool bath, scheduled exercise classes, nearby swimming pools and golf courses, card games, films, lectures, classes with local university students, residents' association, religious programs.

Availability: Waiting list varies from six months to seven years, depending upon apartment. $1,000 fully refundable application fee for waiting list.

Health services and rates: Residents receive unlimited health care included in monthly fee. Direct admission on space-available basis (fees listed below). Health center has two well-stocked libraries, an atrium with trees, and an enclosed courtyard with garden and fountain. Fully equipped and staffed in-house physical therapy department is provided to aid in rehabilitation (available at extra cost). Physicians visit regularly, and each resident receives a plan of care developed by a team of health care professionals. Registered pharmacist in community's own pharmacy. Pharmaceutical, ophthalmologic, and dental services available at extra cost. Home health care is available; adult day care and hospice care are offered for older people from the community as well as day care for children in the community.

- 90 Assisted Living units (nonresident fees)

*Entrance fee 1**	*Monthly fee*
$88,000–217,300	$1,511–3,541

**Refundable entrance fee plan available at higher entrance fee.*

- 133-Bed health care center

"'Treasure the art of living and hospitality' is the philosophy of Westminster-Canterbury. No resident is ever asked to leave for financial reasons. The community's Fellowship Fund, supported by contributions, is available to those who may need assistance in meeting the cost of living at Westminster-Canterbury."

ROANOKE UNITED METHODIST HOMES

1009 Old Country Club Road
Roanoke, VA 24017
(703) 344-6248
Gay Thompson, director of admissions

Type of community: Nonprofit Continuing Care, modified contract

A beautiful Georgian mansion built in 1916 and an English Tudor home converted into four one-bedroom apartments house Independent Living residences that are all on one level. 23 Independent Living apartments are located in a separate building. The community offers ten acres of landscaped grounds filled with 250 trees and a quarter of a mile of walking trails. Assisted Living and Skilled Nursing are on-site. The Blue Ridge Mountains can be seen in the distance on a clear day.

Financial plan: Entrance fee plus monthly fee.

Ownership and management: Virginia United Methodist Homes, Inc. Opened in 1964.

Minimum age: 65 years.

Population: 125 residents; 70% women, 30% men.

Number of units: 23 two-bedroom Independent Living apartments and 4 one-bedroom apartments; 32 Assisted Living units, 40-bed nursing facility

Dining plan: Independent Living monthly fee does not include meals. Meals can be purchased in the dining room.

Services: *Included in the monthly fee:* Weekly housekeeping and flat-linen services, scheduled transportation.

At additional cost: Beauty/barbershop, convenience store, guest rooms as available.

Activities: Full-time activities director. Bingo, movies, outings, theme dinner where residents come dressed in costume, vespers every Sunday by ministers of different denominations, flower and vegetable gardens available for resident gardeners, crafts and

INDEPENDENT LIVING HOUSING

Type/size of unit	*Entrance fee*	*Monthly fee**
1-Bedroom	$45,000	$340
2-Bedroom, 1,100 sq. ft.	$75,000	$440

**All utilities except telephone and electricity included in the monthly fee. Wall-to-wall carpeting, individually controlled heating and air-conditioning, 24-hour emergency call system.*

a library stocked with large-print books, current magazines, and daily newspapers.

Availability: Short waiting list.

Health services and rates: Independent Living residents receive the first 30 days per year of health care at no additional cost. If they remain in the health center for a longer time but not on permanent assignment, they pay the health care monthly fee and their Independent Living apartment is held for them. Residents may move directly into Assisted Living or the health center, in which case they are required to pay the entrance fee and monthly fee listed below.

- 32 Assisted Living units*
  Semiprivate $1,475/month
  Private $1,895/month
- 40-Bed nursing facility*
  Semiprivate $2,150/month

**Nonresident entrance fee: $42,500.*

"To get the most out of the surroundings at Roanoke United Methodist Home, all one really needs is a love of beauty. There's plenty of it here—from dogwoods that bloom every spring to the castlelike exterior of our main house. And in back of it all stand the softly misted peaks of the Blue Ridge Mountains. So whether our residents enjoy morning walks or reading the Sunday paper on our terrace, they always have a beautiful view right before their eyes."

WESTMINSTER-CANTERBURY IN VIRGINIA BEACH

3100 Shore Drive
Virginia Beach, VA 23451
(804) 496-1148 or (804) 496-1100
Sherry O'Shall, director of admissions

Type of community: Nonprofit Continuing Care, all-inclusive contract

The 14-story brick residential building is located on 16 acres of waterfront property overlooking Chesapeake Bay. Westminster-Canterbury's landscaping has won awards from the Virginia Beach Beautification Commission. The grounds feature many walking areas, especially right along the beach. Virginia Beach is renowned for its support of performing arts, offering an exciting array of activities and events year-round, including the Tall Ships of Harborfest, the Neptune Festival, the opera, ballet, and symphony. Historic Williamsburg and Jamestown are just an hour away. The community is a 20-minute drive from Norfolk International Airport.

Financial plan: Entrance fee plus monthly fee. Entrance fee is refundable less 2% per month up to 50 months. A portion of the entrance fee has been allowed by the IRS as a prepaid medical expense. A varying percentage of the monthly fee is tax-deductible yearly. $100 application processing fee. $1,000 fully refundable fee to be placed on the advanced reservation list.

Ownership and management: Founded by the Presbytery of Eastern Virginia of the Presbytery Church (USA) and the Episcopal Diocese of

Southern Virginia. A volunteer board of trustees composed of prominent business, religious, and community leaders directs the corporation. Opened in 1982.

Minimum age: 65 years.

Population: 410 residents; 79% women, 21% men, 16% couples. Several military facilities are located in the Virginia Beach area, which gives rise to a large number of residents of Westminster-Canterbury who have retired from the service.

Number of units: 335 Independent Living apartments; 36 Assisted Living suites, 75-bed nursing facility.

Dining plan: One meal per day of resident's choice included in monthly fee. Three meals are served daily.

Services: *Included in the monthly fee:* Weekly housekeeping and flat-linen services, laundry room on each floor, lighted parking area.

At additional cost: Beauty/barbershop, scheduled transportation, convenience store, dry cleaning pick-up/delivery, guest rooms and/or cot rentals, drugstore prescription delivery, daily newspaper delivery, shoe repair pick-up/delivery, valet parking.

Activities: Aquatic exercise classes in heated indoor swimming pool. Whirlpool and steam room. Exercise classes three times a week, vegetable and flower gardening, lectures, movies, bingo, bridge and shuffleboard, croquet court, dances, arts and crafts, including ceramics, weaving, china and tole painting, knitting, woodworking, and photography darkroom. A short drive to several golf courses. Weekly chapel services.

Availability: Studios are often available immediately; one-bedroom, one- to three-year waiting list; two-bedroom, three to five years.

Health services and rates: Residents receive unlimited care in health care, continuing to pay their monthly fee, plus the cost of two additional meals per day. All residents are required to have Medicare and a supplemental insurance that will cover Skilled Nursing should the need arise. Residents receive assistance with filing of health insurance forms. Regular health screenings are offered as well as exercise classes and physical therapy facilities.

- 36 Assisted Living studios
- 75-Bed health care center

"Westminster-Canterbury is unique in that it enjoys a waterfront location with a spectacular view of the Chesapeake Bay, which can be as bracing as it can be serene. A sense of family and friendliness prevails among the residents reflecting the caring nature of our staff. Residents are involved in the outside community as well as community projects; residents and staff often work alongside one another. A Fellowship Fund supported by contributions from residents, staff, and the community at large offers financial assistance in a range of special circumstances."

INDEPENDENT LIVING HOUSING

Type/size of apartment	*Entrance fee**	*Monthly fee**
Studio, 432–562 sq. ft.	$75,744–98,966	$927–1,072
1-Bedroom, 708–864 sq. ft.	$122,871–144,574	$1,239–1,425
2-Bedroom, 919–1,140 sq. ft.	$161,387–197,152	$1,479–1,727

**For double occupancy add $15,000 to the entrance fee, $410 to the monthly fee. All utilities except long-distance telephone are included. Individually controlled heating and air-conditioning, wall-to-wall carpeting, electric stove and refrigerator, miniblinds, 24-hour emergency call system.*

WILLIAMSBURG LANDING

5700 Williamsburg Landing Drive
Williamsburg, VA 23185
(804) 253-0303
E. Faye Burbage, director of marketing

Type of community: Not-for-profit Continuing Care, modified contract

Traditionally designed cluster homes, spacious manor apartments, residential buildings, and a health center are located on 84 acres of wooded Virginia countryside. The parklike campus features a rolling landscape, gazebos, park areas, winding pathways, and a peaceful vista overlooking calm waters. Landing Building is the focal point of the community, providing the main lounge and dining room, a bank, beauty/barbershop, pharmacy, convenience and gift shop, and Jacuzzi. The community has a swimming pool, tennis courts, garden plots, and wide verandas for residents' enjoyment. Colonial Williamsburg and the College of William and Mary are three miles away.

Financial plan: Entrance fee plus monthly fee. Entrance fee is 90% refundable after receipt of a replacement entrance fee from a new resident.

Ownership and management: Owned by Williamsburg Landing, Inc. Managed by American Retirement Corporation. Opened in 1985.

Minimum age: 64 years.

Population: 301 residents; 65% women, 35% men, 58% couples.

Number of units: 214 Independent Living apartments; 7 Assisted Living units, 37-bed health care center.

Dining plan: One meal per day included in the monthly fee. Private dining room, special diets, and tray service available

Services: *Included in the monthly fee:* Scheduled transportation, premiums for long-term care insurance, housekeeping, parking.

At additional cost: Beauty/barbershop, guest accommodations.

Activities: Activities committee. Swimming pool, tennis courts, gardening, concerts and tours, shopping

INDEPENDENT LIVING HOUSING

Type/size of apartment	*Entrance fee*	*Monthly fee**
1-Bedroom, 741–1,135 sq. ft.	$99,000–124,000	$1,555
2-Bedroom, 1,110–1,455 sq. ft.	$136,000–150,000	$1,591
Manor homes		
2-Bedroom, 1,268–1,298 sq. ft.	$145,000–146,000	$1,260
Cluster homes		
1-Bedroom, 1,310 sq. ft.	$164,000	$1,279
2-Bedroom, 1,287–1,302 sq. ft.	$176,000	$1,316
3-Bedroom, 1,915 sq. ft.	$205,000	$1,354

**For double occupancy add $494 to the monthly fee. All utilities except cable TV and telephone included for apartments (cluster home fees do not include utilities). All-electric kitchen, fireplaces (in cluster homes and select apartments), 24-hour emergency call system, wall-to-wall carpeting, individually controlled heating and air-conditioning.*

trips, exercise classes, educational events and classes through the College of William and Mary, aquasize pool, aquathenics pool, bridge, bingo, men's club, ice-cream socials, oil painting, Bible study, movies, various trips.

Availability: Waiting list varies. Information available upon request.

Health services and rates: Residents receive ten free days per year (noncumulative) in the health center at the semiprivate rate. Long-term care insurance program through Metropolitan Life insurance company is included in the monthly fee to cover the additional cost of personal and long-term care after 60 days. The health center is directed by a physician from the local community, in coordination with the executive director and the board of directors of Williamsburg Landing, and offers care for both long- and short-term stays. Physicians from several disciplines schedule appointments with residents in the pavilion. Rehabilitative services including whirlpool baths, pharmaceutical services, laboratory testing, medical and surgical supplies, and physical, speech, occupational, respiratory, and oxygen therapies. Direct admission to Assisted Living and health center on space-available basis.

- 7 Assisted Living units
  - Resident transfer $1,841/month
  - Direct admission $2,074/month
- 37-Bed health care center
  - Semiprivate $90/day
  - Private $115/day

"Williamsburg Landing enjoys a wonderful small college town atmosphere. Most of our residents are college educated and have had interesting and successful careers. They lead an active life, partaking in community events, taking advantage of educational opportunities at the College of William and Mary, and enjoying Colonial Williamsburg, both of which are nearby. We have a high percentage of resident couples."

SHENANDOAH VALLEY WESTMINSTER-CANTERBURY

300 Westminster-Canterbury Drive
Winchester, VA 22603
(703) 665-0156 or (800) 492-9463
Judy Smith, director of information/admissions

Type of community: Nonprofit Continuing Care, choice of all-inclusive or modified contracts

Situated on a 65-acre campus with a 14-acre restricted natural park, the community offers 2½ miles of walking trails, a vegetable garden, and a wildflower garden. The community is comprised of cottages, apartments, and an on-site health center. Administration and the health center are housed in two-story buildings. Independent Living apartments are in five-story buildings. The community is located only 65 miles west of Washington, D.C.

Financial plan: Entrance fee plus monthly fee. Two plans: **1)** Extensive Continuing Care ensures the residents access to the health center at no additional cost, except the price of two extra meals per day. **2)** Modified Continuing Care provides residents with 18 prepaid days of health care per year. Both plans offer a choice of three refund options: 100% refundable, 50% refundable or refundable on a prorated basis, amortized at a rate of 2% per month for 50 months.

Ownership and management: Westminster-Canterbury of Winchester. Opened in 1987.

Minimum age: 65 years (if couple, spouse must be at least 62).

Population: 163 residents from 23 states, England, China, Scotland, Manitoba, and Nova Scotia who have worked at a variety of occupations including education, business, law, and medicine.

INDEPENDENT LIVING HOUSING

Type/size of apartment	*Entrance fee 1/2**	*Monthly fee**
Studio, 485 sq. ft.	$53,000/39,000	$1,408
1-Bedroom, 709 sq. ft.	$89,000/66,000	$1,658
2-Bedroom, 910–1,195 sq. ft.	$112,300–136,000/87,550–102,000	$1,954–2,205
Cottages		
2-Bedroom, 1,380 sq. ft.	$153,000/123,000	$2,205

**For second person add $5,000 to the entrance fee for Plan 1, $3,750 to the entrance fee for Plan 2, and $809 to the monthly fee.* Note: *The entrance fees listed above are amortized at a rate of 2% per month for 50 months. 50% and 100% refund options are available. Entrance fees for these refundable options depend on the age of the resident at the time of moving in and on actuarial tables. All utilities in apartments except telephone included. In cottages, utilities are billed separately. Cottages have two bedrooms, two baths, living room, dining room, fully equipped kitchen, patio, carport, a laundry alcove with washer and dryer, four walk-in closets and storage. Apartments come with a full kitchen, wall-to-wall carpeting, and either a balcony or a patio. 24-hour emergency call systems in all residences.*

Number of units: 20 Independent Living cottages and 102 apartments; 40 Assisted Living units, 80-bed health care center.

Dining plan: One meal per day is included in the monthly fee. Casual dining in the café. Special diets if needed. Temporary tray service as approved by the health care staff. Additional meals can be purchased in the café for a nominal per-item fee. Private dining room.

Services: *Included in the monthly fee:* Weekly housekeeping, laundering, and flat-linen services, building and grounds maintenance, 24-hour security, scheduled transportation to shops and events.

At additional cost: Postal services and bank, beauty/barbershop, guest accommodations.

Activities: Arts and crafts room and programs, woodworking shop, vegetable and flower gardening, health and exercise programs, book review group, Bible study, oil painting, chess group, Great Decisions (a foreign policy discussion group).

Availability: Waiting list depends on size of accommodation. Longer wait for two-bedrooms and cottages. Future residency priority program ($1,000 fee) permits applicants to be placed on a future residency list, which entitles them to use of the dining room (at the guest meal rate) and the Commons. They have access to the health center on a space-available basis before assuming residency and are invited to participate in community activities. Future resident's fee is fully refundable at any time or it may be applied to the entrance fee at the time the future resident decides to move in.

Health services and rates: Nursing staff available 24 hours per day. On-site health clinic staffed by a r egistered nurse during business hours: consultations, outpatient examination, and treatments and prescribed therapies. Temporary home health care provided in resident's apartment or cottage when approved by the health center includes meals, medication, or medical treatment and routine temperature, pulse rate, and blood pressure checks. Hospital care for emergency medical treatment and specialized medical services is available at the local hospital, Winchester Medical Center, a state-of-the-art, regional 356-bed facility, a five minute drive from Shenandoah Valley Westminster-Canterbury.

- Catered Living

	Entrance fee	*Monthly fee*
Studio	$76,220	$1,956
1-Bedroom	$105,060	$2,190
2-Bedroom, 1-bath	$128,750	$2,425

- 40 Assisted Living units

Semiprivate	$82.15/day
Private	$100.00/day
Converted private	$140.36/day

- 80-Bed health care center

	Intermediate Nursing	*Skilled Nursing*
Semiprivate	$106.09/day	$117.24/day
Private	$114.73/day	$128.95/day

"The management supports and adheres to the Shenandoah Valley Westminster-Canterbury philosophy as outlined in our mission statement: that as a small community, we provide a friendly, caring family atmosphere for our residents. As a church-related community, we embrace all faiths, provide the utmost quality of care, while respecting the privacy and dignity of the residents. We encourage residents to use their gifts fully, live their lives richly, and to make the best of the years that God has given them."

Carmen and Albert, mid 80s

Waverly Heights, Philadelphia, Pennsylvania

"We knew our health wasn't going to improve with age."

"Our decision was simple," explains Carmen. "We had a home in Florida, but it was time for us to consider moving from Bald Peak, New Hampshire. We didn't need another big home."

Carmen and Albert began by looking at communities in Annapolis, Washington, and Florida and finally narrowed their selection process to the Philadelphia area because their son David, who is handicapped, lives nearby.

"We moved in four years ago," explains Carmen, "when we were in our early eighties. We have found it to be very advantageous to live here, particularly because we knew our health wasn't going to improve with age." Carmen says they like the lovely surroundings of Waverly Heights and specifically wanted a villa so they could have a little more privacy than they would have in an apartment. "We took a smaller villa first because that's all that was available," she says, "and about a year later moved into a larger one, which has a large living room that opens onto a lovely patio and garden, two large bedrooms including a master bedroom with greenhouse attached, two baths, a family room and dinette combination, plus more closet space and a two-car garage."

Carmen and Albert also like the fact there are no additional charges for nursing and medications should they be required. They still have their home in Florida and spend time there each year.

Carmen and Albert's advice: Don't wait too long to move; no one ever thinks they're ready.

WASHINGTON

JUDSON PARK

23600 Marine View Drive South
Des Moines, WA 98180
(206) 824-4000
Nancy Schmoll, retirement counselor

Type of community: Nonprofit Continuing Care, modified contract

Accreditation: Continuing Care Accreditation Commission

Independent Living apartments housed in a four-story U-shaped building and a 120-bed health center are located on seven acres of green lawns, wooded pathways, lush foliage, and flower gardens overlooking the waters of Puget Sound and the peaks of the Olympic Mountains. The community is located 30 minutes from downtown Seattle or Tacoma, 15 minutes from Sea-Tac Airport, and a half-mile walk to shops in Des Moines. Parks, library, banks, medical facilities, churches, Highline Community College, golf courses, tennis courts, indoor swimming pool, restaurants, marina, Southcenter Mall, and Sea-Tac Mall are all in the surrounding neighborhood.

Financial plan: Entrance fee plus monthly fee. Refund of entrance less 1.5% per month of residency.

Ownership and management: Owned and operated by American Baptist Homes of the West, owners of 17 communities. Managed by a board of trustees. Opened in 1963.

Minimum age: 62 years.

Population: 200 residents; 75% women, 25% men, 14% couples.

Number of units: 177 Independent Living apartments; 19 Assisted Living units, 120-bed off-site health care center.

Dining plan: Dinner meal included in the monthly fee. Breakfast and lunch optional at $100 and $140 respectively. Special diets available. Private dining room.

Services: *Included in the monthly fee:* Biweekly housekeeping, flat-linen service, scheduled shopping trips.

INDEPENDENT LIVING HOUSING

Type/size of unit	*Entrance fee**	*Monthly fee**
Studio, 371 sq. ft.	$22,100–26,980	$805
Studio, 433–534 sq. ft.	$33,655–43,090	$830–895
Studio, 557 sq. ft.	$39,805–43,090	$905
1-Bedroom, 680–908 sq. ft.	$63,970–79,500	$980–1,095

** For double occupancy add 10% to the entrance fee, $400 to the monthly fee. All utilities included. Cable TV, telephone, wall-to-wall carpeting, cooking facilities, refrigerator, food storage area, 24-hour emergency call system. Family dining rooms, kitchens with ovens, and laundry facilities on each floor.*

At additional cost: Beauty/barbershop, private transportation, guest accommodations, covered parking.

Activities: Activities director. Library, mobile library unit every other week, hobby rooms, woodworking shop, recreation room, billiards, shuffleboard, square dancing, exercise classes, whirlpool, prayer groups, Bible study, chapel, gardening, men's group.

Availability: Six-month to two-year waiting list. $250 fee for waiting list.

Health services and rates: Health center adjacent to retirement home. 24-hour Skilled Nursing. Health center staff includes registered nurses, licensed practical nurses, certified nursing assistants, registered dietitian, registered physical and occupational therapists, chaplain/social services coordinator, and physician/medical doctor. Portion of monthly fee pays for nursing home insurance.

- 19 Assisted Living units $1,745–2,300/month
- 120-Bed off-site health care center $112–126/month

"Judson Park is located on seven acres with stunning views of Puget Sound and the Olympic Mountains and has been serving the needs of the community for more than 30 years."

WESLEY HOMES

815 South 216th Street
Des Moines, WA 98198
(206) 824-5000
Jean Garner, director of marketing/admissions

Type of community: Not-for-profit Continuing Care, modified contract

Accreditation: Continuing Care Accreditation Commission

The 45-acre campus contains two-high rise apartment complexes (The Gardens and The Terrace), 67 cottages, and a health center. The campus grounds feature lawns, flower gardens, wooded paths, and picnic areas and are within one mile of Puget Sound's shoreline. Des Moines is a small community with shops and annual celebrations; several churches are located in the surrounding communities. Opportunities for community involvement are available. Olympic-size swimming pool and several golf courses are in the area. The community is close to Seattle with its glaciered mountains, tall trees, and beaches.

Financial plan: Entrance fee plus monthly fee. Two plans: **1)** Entrance fee paid in one lump sum. This is the only option available for applicants 85 years or older who must also pay a 10% surcharge on health care charges if and when care is required. **2)** Entrance fee paid in monthly installments, in addition to the monthly fee.

Ownership and management: Owned by an independent nonprofit corporation. Affiliated with the Pacific Northwest Conference of the United Methodist Church. Managed by a 21-member board of trustees. Opened in 1944.

Minimum age: Cottages, 62 to 80 years; apartments, 65 years.

Population: 623 residents; 72% women, 28% men, 38% couples.

Number of units: 311 Independent Living apartments and 67 cottages; 40 Assisted Living units, 140-bed nursing facility.

Dining plan: Two or three meals per day included in the monthly fee for apartment units. Cottage residents have option of choosing meal plan at extra charge. Registered dietitian on-site.

Services: *Included in the monthly fee:* Twice monthly housekeeping, weekly flat-linen service, scheduled transportation, open parking.

At additional cost: Covered parking, private transportation, beauty/barbershop, guest lodgings.

INDEPENDENT LIVING HOUSING

Type/size of apartment	*Entrance fee 1 single/double**	*Monthly fee**
Studio, 305 sq. ft.	$14,190–35,900/25,300–44,192	$975/1,496
Alcove, 504 sq. ft.	$28,770–75,600/51,290–93,130	$1,057–1,139/1,626–1,689
1-Bedroom, 606 sq. ft.	$32,870–8,8240/58,600–103,550	$1,238/1,779
2-Bedroom, 911 sq. ft.	$56,995–117,317/101,610–151,544	$1,501–1989
Cottages		
1–3-Bedroom, 1,200–1,300 sq. ft.	$80,000–150,000	$387–551

Note: *As entry age increases, entrance fee decreases for apartment units. Monthly entrance fee option/Plan 2 available for apartments only. The following fees for Plan 2 are in addition to the monthly fee listed above: studio, $200–259/316–400; alcove, $321–506 /509–803; double, $458–588/727–932. * For double occupancy add approximately $500 to the monthly fee. All utilities except telephone included. Cable TV, wall-to-wall carpeting, individually controlled heating and air-conditioning, 24-hour emergency call system in apartments. Only birds and fish allowed.*

Activities: Art groups, drama group, music group, game rooms, special purpose activity areas, shop space, weaving room, gardening, various religious services, golfing and swimming in area facilities. Proximity to Puget Sound and several parks makes it easy to enjoy fishing, boating, birdwatching, and nature walking.

Availability: Application fee ($450 for single person, $800 for couple) for waiting list. Waiting list varies according to size of accommodation chosen. Partial refund of fee if applicant chooses to remove name from list.

Health services and rates: Newly constructed 140-bed Skilled Nursing facility on campus has consolidated all health care in Wesley Homes health center. Within reach of hospitals and specialized medical facilities of the Pacific Northwest. Residents select their own physicians and are responsible for the payment of their medical expenses.

- 40 Assisted Living units
  Single room $49.10–65.45/day
- 140-Bed health care center
  Temporary resident $114.75/day
  Permanent resident $131.75/day

Wesley Homes celebrated its 50th anniversary in 1994.

PANORAMA CITY

150 Circle Drive
Lacey, WA 98503
(206) 456-0111
Howard Burton, admissions director

Type of community: Not-for-profit Continuing Care, modified contract

Accreditation: Continuing Care Accreditation Commission

More than 126 private homes and 200 garden court apartments as well as 212 multifamily units and three multilevel apartment complexes are located on 140 parklike acres bordered by Mt. Rainier, the Olympic Mountain range, and the southernmost tip of Puget

Sound. Independent Living and Skilled Nursing are on-site in addition to two banks, a travel agency, restaurant, pharmacy, and grocery store. Nearby are the State Capitol buildings, Washington Center for the Performing Arts, South Sound Shopping Center, St. Martin's College, Evergreen State College, South Puget Sound Community College, plus the hub of Olympia's medical services, including St. Peter's Hospital and many surrounding clinics. Four 18-hole golf courses and an international-class trapshooting range are within a 15-mile radius. The community is 30 miles from Tacoma, 60 miles from Seattle, and a two-hour drive from Portland, Oregon. Within one hour are Pacific Ocean beaches and Hood Canal. Victoria and Vancouver, B.C., are a half-day's journey away.

Financial plan: Security deposit plus monthly fee. Security deposit varies according to age of resident when entering the community and is refunded less 1 1/2% per month of residency. $2,000 deposit is the application fee required for registration. Security deposits decrease as entering age decreases.

Ownership and management: Self-owned and governed private nonprofit corporation. Opened in 1963.

Minimum age: 62 years.

Population: 1,200 residents; 60% women, 40% men, 33% couples.

Number of units: 850 Independent Living residences (apartments and private homes); 172 partial care units, 155-bed health center.

Dining plan: Meal programs are optional.

Services: *Included in the monthly fee:* Minibuses to shopping centers, churches, and activities off-campus, covered parking, washers/dryers.

At additional cost: Beauty/barbershop, bank, travel agency, grocery store, two banks, stock brokerage, pharmacy, guest accommodations, housekeeping, full-service restaurant AAA approved.

Activities: Full-time program director. Gardening, woodworking, lapidary, art studio, ceramics, weaving, handcraft shop, exercise rooms, billiards and card rooms, Bible study groups, art groups, shuffleboard, pitch-and-putt golf course, library and reading room, travel clubs, book review clubs, recreational groups, support groups, various clubs and organizations, happy hour, residents' council. Activities around the area including hunting, fishing, hiking, and golf. RV parking is available on six-acre fenced area.

Availability: Immediate occupancy in some units.

Health services and rates: Residents receive 30 days free care in the health center included in the monthly fee. Physical, massage, and speech therapies,

INDEPENDENT LIVING HOUSING

Type/size of apartments	*Security deposit**	*Monthly fee***
Studio, 364 sq. ft.	$38,000–46,000	$480–525
1-Bedroom, 700–730 sq. ft.	$51,000–87,000	$575–730
2-Bedroom, 950–1,000 sq. ft.	$76,000–124,000	$665–860
Garden court apartments		
1-Bedroom, 730–770 sq. ft.	$80,000–90,000	$680–730
2-Bedroom, 1,020–1,224 sq. ft.	$95,000–205,000	$720–930
Private homes, 1,473–1,746 sq. ft.	$140,000–280,000	$820–970

**Security deposits reflect entering age of 62–65. Fees decrease as entering age increases. For double occupancy add $50 to the monthly fee. All utilities included. Cable TV, patio or balcony, fully equipped kitchen, wall-to-wall carpeting, individually controlled heating, 24-hour emergency call system. Pets are allowed in the homes and garden apartments.*

mental health care, dental care, podiatry, dietary consultation, therapy bathing, laboratory services available. Patients remain under the care of their private physician. Home care is designed for residents who may require some or all of a variety of care services but want to enjoy an independent environment; available at an hourly rate.

Panorama medical program provides medical insurance to cover the cost of doctors, hospitals, and laboratories. There is also a group Skilled Nursing and custodial care insurance plan that can cover a portion of nursing-care fees for up to five years (rates available upon request). Memorial Clinic branch is now located at Panorama City; a doctor and dentist also have established private practices on-site.

- 172 Partial care units
  Studio and one-bedroom apartments (add $476 per person to the monthly fee currently being paid)
- 155-Bed health care center
  Semiprivate $105/day
  Private $175/day

"Celebrating its 30th anniversary, Panorama City is one of the oldest and largest Continuing Care communities in the country. Even though we have a large resident population with varied backgrounds, we are a tight-knit community. An advantage of Panorama City's size is the variety of housing options we offer."

COVENANT SHORES

9150 North Mercer Way
Mercer Island, WA 98040-3143
(206) 236-0600
Priscilla Miller, marketing director

Type of community: Not-for-profit Continuing Care, modified contract

Nine three-story apartment buildings (plus residential expansion plans) are located on a 12-acre wooded, waterfront campus on the north end of Mercer Island. The tranquil community is set among mature firs and surrounded by Lake Washington. Gardens and walkways are located throughout the grounds. Lakeside Fortuna Lodge serves as a center of activity for the community, housing the beauty/barbershop, library, and hobby, crafts, and game rooms. Each Independent Living apartment has easy access to the waterfront and the community's private 50-slip marina. Located minutes from Seattle's cosmopolitan center, the community offers Assisted Living apartments on premises and Skilled Nursing off-site.

Financial plan: Entrance fee plus monthly fee. Entrance fee amortizes at 2% per month of residency. $1,350 application fee. Apartment unit may be reserved for 90 days with a $5,000 deposit.

Ownership and management: Owned and managed by the Evangelical Covenant Church and Covenant Retirement Communities, owner and manager of 12 communities in California, Connecticut, Florida, Illinois, Minnesota, Washington. Covenant Retirement Communities was founded in 1886. Opened in 1978.

Minimum age: 62 years.

Population: 161 residents: 66% women, 34% men, 29% couples.

Number of units: 116 Independent Living apartments; 23 Assisted Living apartments.

Dining plan: One meal per day included in the monthly fee. Meal delivery in event of illness. Consultation for special dietary needs. Meal credits for missed meals.

Services: *Included in the monthly fee:* Partial housekeeping service, outside parking, local transportation, 25% discount for boat moorage at community's marina, outdoor parking, use of laundry facilities.

INDEPENDENT LIVING HOUSING

Type/size of unit	*Entrance fee**	*Monthly fee**
Studio, 462 sq. ft.	$47,000–50,000	$670
1-Bedroom, 630 sq. ft.	$81,000	$820
2-Bedroom, 940 sq. ft.	$101,000	$961

**For double occupancy add 10% to the entrance fee and $331 to the monthly fee. All utilities except telephone included. Fully equipped kitchen, 24-hour emergency call system, wall-to-wall carpeting, master antenna, cable TV (optional), balconies, individually controlled heating.*

At additional cost: Beauty/barbershop, personal housekeeping, indoor parking.

Activities: Full-time activity director. Shuffleboard, library, various classes, boating, hobby room, crafts room, game room, chapel services, religious seminars, Bible study, woodworking shop, gardening, walking paths, Jacuzzi, recreation rooms, trips.

Availability: Waiting list. Those on the waiting list are notified when a unit becomes available. If a unit is refused, your place on the waiting list remains the same. Application fee for waiting list is $1,350, which will either be applied toward the entrance fee upon acceptance of a unit or refunded less $350.

Health services and rates: Wellness clinic with registered nurse in charge. Podiatrist and hearing and vision screening available. 60 days of health care in semiprivate room in off-site health center included in entrance fee. After 60 days, Covenant Shores will pay 10% of health center rates for the resident's lifetime. Depending upon availability, admission may be made directly to Assisted Living. Residents of Covenant Shores who transfer to Assisted Living pay only the Assisted Living monthly fee.

- 23 Assisted Living studios*
  Studio, 300 sq. ft. $1,725/month

  **Nonresident entrance fee: $20,000.*
- Health center off-site

"The mission of Covenant Retirement Communities is to provide a balance, through facilities and programs, between security and independence for our residents. Our goal is to enable our residents to achieve their maximum physical, mental, emotional, and spiritual capabilities and enjoyment."

Note: Residents may transfer to another Covenant Retirement Community if they desire. All financial arrangements are based on the existing transfer policy.

BAYVIEW MANOR

11 West Aloha Street
Seattle, WA 98119
(206) 284-7330
Bill Heathman, admissions director

Type of community: Nonprofit Continuing Care, modified contract

This quiet community is located within a bustling neighborhood at the foot of Queen Anne Hill. The ten-story modern building that houses Independent Living apartments, Assisted Living units, and a health center offers sweeping views of Elliott Bay from each apartment. Conversation areas are located on each floor. The community is located within minutes of Seattle Center, museums, sports events, restaurants, and parks. Seattle Metro bus line is within a few steps.

Financial plan: Entrance fee plus monthly fee. Monthly rental plan is available for residents 85 years or under who reside in a studio.

Ownership and management: Affiliated with the First United Methodist Church of Seattle. Opened in 1961.

INDEPENDENT LIVING HOUSING

Type/size of apartment	*Entrance fee*	*Monthly fee single/double*
Studio, 324 sq. ft.	$32,405–38,250	$906
Alcove, 486 sq. ft.	$50,555–56,555	$1,093/1,517
1-Bedroom, 648 sq. ft.	$64,555–76,405	$1,267/1,689

Note: *Studio residents under 85 years of age may elect to pay only a monthly fee, which is $1,231. All utilities included. Kitchenettes, individually controlled heating and air-conditioning, wall-to-wall carpeting, draperies, 24-hour emergency call system. Balconies, cable TV.*

Minimum age: 62 years.

Population: 230 residents; 83% women, 17% men, 20% couples.

Number of units: 160 Independent Living apartments; 25 Assisted Living rooms, 50 Skilled Nursing beds.

Dining plan: Three meals per day included in the monthly fee. Private dining room and catering services available.

Services: *Included in monthly fee:* Housekeeping, flat-linen service, storage space.

At additional cost: Beauty/barbershop, guest accommodations, transportation, parking.

Activities: Bridge, billiards, gardening, hobby room, exercise, library, chapel, lectures, music groups, weekly chapel services, trips, special programs.

Availability: Waiting list up to six months.

Health services and rates: Independent Living residents receive three months in Assisted Living and 30 days in the nursing facility free of charge. Clinic services. Occupational therapy.

- 25 Assisted Living rooms $500/month
- 50 Skilled Nursing beds (private) $148/day

"We invite prospective residents to tour Bayview Manor, to have a complimentary lunch with us or spend the night in a guest room and see for themselves what comfort, security, and genuine caring can mean."

HORIZON HOUSE

900 University Street
Seattle, WA 98101
(206) 624-3700
Joan Carusel, director of marketing

Type of community: Nonprofit Continuing Care, modified contract

Independent Living apartment homes are located in high-rise and low-rise buildings located near the heart of downtown Seattle. A health center and Assisted Living apartments are on-site. Several outdoor garden and patio areas are available for residents' use. Mt. Baker and Mt. Rainier can be seen from Sky Lounge and many apartments. Located next to Freeway Park that features waterfalls and lush landscaping. Theaters, restaurants, public library, churches, stores, and the Seattle Art Museum are just a short walk away.

Financial plan: Entrance fee plus monthly fee. Entrance fee may be partially refundable less 1% per month of residency.

Ownership and management: Owned by Horizon House, Inc. Governed by a 17-member board of trustees, which includes five residents. Affiliated with the Washington North Idaho Conference of the United Church of Christ. Opened in 1961.

Minimum age: 65 years.

Population: 460+ residents; 77% women, 23% men, 37% couples.

INDEPENDENT LIVING HOUSING

Type/size of apartment	*Entrance fee**	*Monthly fee**
Studio, 320–420 sq. ft.	$17,050–42,750	$475
1-Bedroom, 560–780 sq. ft.	$56,000–110,000	$660
2-Bedroom, 800–936 sq. ft.	$86,400–158,750	$884
2-Bedroom/2-bath, 980–1,300 sq. ft.	$115,000–198,000	$1,051

**For double occupancy add $325 to the monthly fee. All utilities except telephone included. Fully equipped kitchens, wall-to-wall carpeting, drapes, 24-hour emergency call system, individually controlled heating.*

Number of units: 333 Independent Living apartments; 38 Assisted Living units, 56-bed health care center.

Dining plan: No meals included or required. Use of dining room is optional.

Services: *Included in the monthly fee:* Scheduled transportation.

At additional cost: Housekeeping, garage, beauty/barbershop.

Activities: Library, garden plots, chapel, rooms for private entertaining, Sky Lounge, physical fitness center, painting room, woodworking shop, sewing and weaving room, volunteering, bridge group, theater outings, study groups, one- to ten-day trips, movies, lectures, and evening programs.

Availability: Waiting list for all units. Studio and one-bedrooms under six months. Two-bedrooms, four to ten years.

Health services and rates: Residents receive up to 180 days of nursing care in health center at reduced rate. Fully equipped physical therapy department. Medical clinic, counseling services, podiatrist, dental clinic.

- 38 Assisted Living studios $57–85/day
- 56-Bed Skilled Nursing facility

Semiprivate	$16–71.50/day (first 180 days)
	$84.50–140/day (180 days+)
Private	$17–81.50/day (first 180 days)
	$94.50–150/day (180 days+)

"The Horizon House program and stimulating downtown location attract a dynamic clientele. The number of optional services, including elective meal service, promotes a completely independent lifestyle. Expansive health and wellness programs ensure that future Assisted Living and health care needs are provided for."

PARK SHORE

1630 43rd Avenue East
Seattle, WA 98112
(206) 329-0770
Doris Prucha, director of admissions/marketing

Type of community: Nonprofit Continuing Care, modified contract

This 15-story concrete building is located on the shores of Lake Washington. A sweeping panoramic view is available from the Top of the Park solarium and promenade deck on the 15th floor. Independent Living, Assisted Living, and Skilled Nursing accommodations are available. Residents and guests may arrive by water and use the private mooring. The community is located a few steps from the village of Madison Park where there is a beach, park, tennis courts, fine restaurants, shops, galleries, and banks.

Financial plan: Entrance fee plus monthly fee.

INDEPENDENT LIVING HOUSING

Type/size of unit	*Entrance fee*	*Monthly fee single/double*
1-Room, 445 sq. ft.	$33,000–38,000	$860/1,480
1½-Room, 630 sq. ft.	$61,000–69,000	$976/1,616
2-Bedroom, 875 sq. ft.	$89,000–138,000	$1,094/1,738
3-Bedroom, 1,320 sq. ft.	$145,000–198,000	1,333/1,983

All units have kitchenettes. Individually controlled heating and air-conditioning, draperies, carpeting, 24-hour emergency call system.

Ownership and management: Presbyterian Ministries, Inc., a nonprofit corporation sponsored by the Presbyterian Church (U.S.A.). Opened in 1963.

Minimum age: 62 years.

Population: 210 residents.

Number of units: 185 Independent Living units; 15 Assisted Living rooms, 34 Skilled Nursing beds.

Dining plan: Three meals a day are included in the monthly fee.

Services: *Included in the monthly fee:* Laundry facilities and solarium on each floor, weekly housekeeping and flat-linen services.

At additional cost: Beauty/barbershop, resident-run exchange shop.

Activities: Library, hobby and woodworking area, special programs that residents plan, including bridge parties, bingo parties, trips to symphony, ballet, museums, opera.

Availability: Waiting list of one to seven years, depending upon the type of apartment.

Health Services: Independent Living residents receive 20 free days of health care each year. Should the resident require continual care in the health care center, he or she may relinquish the apartment (there is no refund) and pay only the daily health center rates.

- 15 Assisted Living units $55/day
- 34 Skilled Nursing beds $100–$110/day

"Presbyterian Ministries, Inc., is a nonprofit corporation operating Continuing Care retirement facilities guided by the fundamental values of the Presbyterian Church (U.S.A.)."

THE NARROWS GLEN

8201 Sixth Avenue
Tacoma, WA 98406
(206) 564-4770
Nancy Studer, marketing director

Type of community: Independent and Assisted Living

This three-story Independent Living apartment complex and 15 units of Assisted Living are located on 27 acres of quiet wooded land in a residential neighborhood bordered by the Narrows Bridge on the west. The grounds include a rose garden, which has a tall rose tree in its center, and a wide pathway stemming from the main lounge and lined with lights. The community offers easy access to shopping, medical centers, and cultural, recreational, and civic resources. Titlow Park, Mt. Rainier, LaConner with its beautiful tulip fields, Seattle Center, and Puget Sound are all nearby.

Financial plan: Monthly rent and $250 deposit. Month-to-month or year lease.

Ownership and management: Owned and operated by The Hillhaven Corporation, which has more than 30 years of experience in serving seniors. Opened in 1987.

Minimum age: 55 years.

Population: 165 residents; 70% women, 30% men.

Number of units: 131 Independent Living apartments; 15 Assisted Living apartments.

Dining plan: One meal per day included in the monthly fee. Three meals per day are served. All food prepared on-site. Tray service and private dining room available.

Services: *Included in the monthly fee:* Weekly housekeeping and flat-linen services, scheduled transportation, parking space, free washers and dryers for personal use, participation in social, educational, and cultural programs.

At additional cost: Beauty/barbershop, covered parking, unscheduled transportation, additional housekeeping services.

Activities: Activities director. Shopping trips, parties, travelogues, card games, book reviews, dances, musical events, wellness programs, card room, billiards table, exercise equipment and classes, whirlpool/spa, library, gardening areas, movies, bingo, painting, creative writing, coffee hours, religious services.

Availability: Waiting list varies according to accommodations desired.

Health services and rates: Regular trips to local medical facilities are provided.

- 15 Assisted Living apartments*
  1-Bedroom,
  600–660 sq. ft.
  $1,975–2,275/month
  2-Bedroom,
  900–960 sq. ft.
  $2,375–2,675/month

**For double occupancy add $275 to the monthly fee.*

"Through special arrangements with other Hillhaven retirement communities throughout the United States, The Narrows Glen residents can reserve an apartment for a period of one to four weeks in another Hillhaven community while on vacation."

INDEPENDENT LIVING HOUSING

Type/size of unit	*Monthly fee**
1-Bedroom, 600–660 sq. ft.	$1,250–1,450
2-Bedroom, 900–960 sq. ft.	$1,600–1,850

** For double occupancy add $275 to the monthly fee. All utilities except telephone and cable TV included. Emergency call buttons, wall-to-wall carpeting, fully equipped kitchens, individually controlled heating, cable TV hookup, some units have private patio.*

WISCONSIN

ATTIC ANGEL

602 North Segoe Road
Madison, WI 53705
(608) 238-8282
Amy Dopke, business manager

Type of community: Nonprofit Continuing Care, modified contract

Accreditation: Continuing Care Accreditation Commission

This 12-story brick apartment tower is located four miles from Capitol Square and adjoins the Attic Angel Nursing Home. The complex overlooks the city parkway, campus gardens, and lawns. Shopping center, restaurants, theater, banks, post office, and medical offices are all nearby.

Financial plan: Entrance fee plus monthly fee. Entrance fee refundable less 4% per month, up to 25 months of residency.

Ownership and management: Owned and operated by the Attic Angel Association. Opened in 1975.

Minimum age: 62 years (current age range mid 70s to upper 90s).

Population: 72 residents; 88% women, 12% men, 8% couples.

Number of units: 68 Independent Living apartments (12 studios, 56 one-bedrooms); 64-bed nursing facility.

Dining plan: One meal per day included in the monthly fee. Private dining room available.

Services: *Included in the monthly fee:* Volunteer transportation (medical, weekly grocery shopping, and scheduled trips), biweekly housekeeping, storage/wardrobe locker.

At additional cost: Coin-operated laundry facilities, underground parking, beauty/barbershop, additional dietary services, specialized transportation, guest apartment.

Activities: Library, multipurpose room, crafts studio (weaving, ceramics, painting, quilting, etc.), greenhouse, rehab/exercise room, continuing education series, games, social functions, trips, musical programs, sing-alongs, bingo, big-screen TV, forums, support groups.

INDEPENDENT LIVING HOUSING

Type/size of apartment	*Entrance fee single/double*	*Monthly fee**
Studio, 400 sq. ft.	$16,000/N/A	$912
1-Bedroom, 580 sq. ft.	$23,700/27,700	$997*

**For double occupancy add $313 to the monthly fee. All utilities included. Fully equipped kitchenettes, wall-to-wall carpeting, individually controlled heating and air-conditioning, draperies, 24-hour emergency call system.*

Availability: Waiting list, two to five years. $1,000 deposit required to become part of waiting list.

Health services and rates: Residents receive five free nursing home care days per year. Physical, speech, and occupational therapies offered. 24-hour emergency services at no extra charge. Blood pressure and weight checks, professional health assessment and consultation regarding physical needs, filling medical dispensers and physician ordered treatments are provided by Tower health office nurse. Nursing facility has large living room, patios, gardens, two dining rooms, small lounges, aviary, and use of arts and crafts studio and greenhouse.

- 64-Bed nursing facility

Semiprivate	$97–120.50/day
Private/shared bath	$107–132.75/day
Private/private bath	$111.50–132.75/day

"Accredited by the Continuing Care Accreditation Commission, Attic Angel is a residential complex designed to ensure and prolong gracious independent retirement living, with the added security of health and nursing care. The Tower's size and our strong, personalized volunteer system permit uniquely individual attention to the needs and desires of residents."

MERITER RETIREMENT CENTER

110 South Henry Street
Madison, WI 53703
(608) 258-2500
Kathy Groth, director of housing operations

Type of community: Not-for-profit Continuing Care, modified contract

Accreditation: Continuing Care Accreditation Commission

Meriter Retirement Center, Methodist Health Center, Meriter Hospital, and Elderhouse (Assisted Living facility) are all within a few blocks of each other near the heart of downtown Madison. Courtyard and gardens are available for residents' use. Shops, farmers' markets, banks, library, civic center, university, and Capitol Square are all close by. Lake Mendota is located to the north and Lake Monona to the south.

Financial plan: Entrance fee plus monthly fee.

Ownership and management: Owned and operated by Meriter Retirement Services, Inc. Opened in 1975.

Minimum age: 62 years (if couple, spouse may be younger).

Population: 212 residents; 79% women, 21% men, 17% couples.

Number of units: 199 Independent Living apartments; 82 Assisted Living apartments, 120-bed nursing facility.

INDEPENDENT LIVING HOUSING

Type/size of apartment	*Entrance fee single/double*	*Monthly fee**
1-Bedroom, 500 sq. ft.	$13,500/15,200	$745–815
2-Bedroom, 750 sq. ft.	$21,500/24,000	$1,054–1,078
Deluxe 2-bedroom, 1,000 sq. ft.	$27,000	$1,428–1,560

**For double occupancy add $40 to the monthly fee. All utilities except telephone included. Fully equipped kitchens, wall-to-wall carpeting, drapes, individually controlled heating and air-conditioning, 24-hour emergency call system, cable TV hookup. Wallpaper optional for minimal fee.*

Dining plan: No meals included in the monthly fee. Evening meal offered weekdays; noon meal on weekends. Two options for dining plan: 30 meals per month ($170/month) or 15 meals per month ($100/month).

Services: *Included in the monthly fee:* Biweekly housekeeping, scheduled transportation.

At additional cost: Sheltered parking, coffee shop, self-service laundry facilities, hair care.

Activities: Cards, lecture series, classes, interdenominational church services, gardening, group outings to theater and restaurants, music programs, arts and crafts, travelogues, bingo, volunteer opportunities, residents' council.

Availability: Limited. One-bedroom apartments available. Two-year wait for two-bedroom.

Health services and rates: Access to weekday health office included in residents' monthly fee. Adult day care center offers daylong programs for $30/day. Podiatry services available at additional cost.

- 82 Assisted Living units

Studio	$1,134–1,460/month
1-Bedroom	$1,800–2,551/month

- 120-Bed health care center

	Intermediate Nursing	*Skilled Nursing*
Semiprivate	$105/day	$111/day
Private	$119/day	$127/day

"Meriter Retirement Services (MRS) exists to meet the retirement living needs and enhance the quality of life of all residents through the provision of personalized services. MRS is a member of a comprehensive health care system, Meriter Health Services."

OAKWOOD VILLAGE

6205 Mineral Point Road
Madison, WI 53705
(608) 231-3452
Donna Midthun, admissions coordinator

Type of community: Nonprofit Continuing Care, modified contract

Accreditation: Continuing Care Accreditation Commission

Set amidst 30 wooded acres, the campus includes a 15-story apartment building with a six-story gallery apartment wing; the Village Inn, a dining facility for Oakwood residents and their guests; and a 204-seat theater. Across from the main cluster of buildings are English Tudor cottages rented as apartments. Just beyond the cottages is Hebron Hall, Oakwood's Skilled Nursing facility, which offers Intermediate, Skilled, Skilled maximum, and Alzheimer's care. Three of the largest shopping centers in the city are in the immediate neighborhood. The community is located 20 minutes by bus from downtown Madison.

Financial plan: Entrance fee plus monthly fee. Entrance fee is refundable less 3% per month. A limited number of government-subsidized apartments are available to those who qualify for assistance.

Ownership and management: Oakwood Apartments Village, Inc., is a Wisconsin not-for-profit corporation operating in conjunction with Oakwood Lutheran Homes Association, Inc., with sponsorship from 37 Lutheran churches of southeastern Wisconsin. Nursing facility opened in 1948, Independent Living in 1976, Assisted Living in 1983.

Minimum age: 55 years.

Population: 445 residents; 75% women, 25% men, 16 couples.

Number of units: 211 apartments and 2 cottages for Independent Living; 60 Assisted Living units, 137-bed nursing facility.

Dining plan: The evening meal is available for an additional $150 per month. Rooms available for small group meals. Tray service at additional cost.

INDEPENDENT LIVING HOUSING

Type/size of unit	*Entrance fee*	*Monthly fee**
Studio, 430 sq. ft.	$9,500	$595
1-Bedroom, 517–588 sq. ft.	$12,500–13,000	$675–793
2-Bedroom, 660–735 sq. ft.	$18,000–22,500	$777–877
Deluxe, 947–1,034 sq. ft.	$24,500–26,500	$1,295–1,405
Cottage		
2-Bedroom	$14,000	$778

**All utilities except telephone included in the monthly fee. Wall-to-wall carpeting, draperies, kitchen or kitchenette, individual temperature control (air-conditioning can be installed for a small additional charge), 24-hour emergency call system.*

Services: *Included in the monthly fee:* Regularly scheduled transportation.

At additional cost: Coffee shop, gift shop, beauty/barbershop, Village store, coin-operated laundry washer/dryer, reserved parking stalls, garage parking, housekeeping.

Activities: Outings, musical programs, bowling, bingo, card games, arts and crafts, sing-alongs, weekly Bible study, an exercise room, exercise classes, hobby and crafts room, library, gardening, plays and music recitals in the Oakwood Theater, lectures, travelogues, and educational programs.

Health services and rates: Health clinic is open weekdays for checkups and consultation with a registered nurse. Full spectrum of nursing services and advanced rehabilitative therapies. Staffed with nurses, physical, speech, and occupational therapists, a pharmacist, social workers, and a chaplain. 24-hour emergency nursing service. Every resident of the nursing facility is assigned a primary nurse who develops an individualized care plan with supervisory physicians. A 16-bed Alzheimer's unit is on premises. Entrance can be made directly to Assisted Living. The entrance fee is partly refundable less 5% per month, amortized over 20 months.

- 60 Assisted Living units
  Private room, 300 sq. ft. $59/day

  **Nonresident entrance fee: $5,000.*

- 137-Bed nursing facility
  Semiprivate $101–125/day
  Private $111.50–136.50/day
  Larger room $113–169/day
- 16-Bed Alzheimer's unit $130–185/day

"The mission of Oakwood is to serve older or infirm persons in a loving, caring Christian community, responding to their physical, social, emotional, and spiritual needs; and to encourage a sense of independence, individuality, dignity, and worth throughout life. The Oakwood Foundation, which was incorporated in 1981, works to support the efforts of Oakwood Lutheran Homes and Oakwood Village apartments by seeking monetary and other gifts to more completely fulfill the mission of service to older and infirm persons."

MILWAUKEE CATHOLIC HOME

2462 North Prospect Avenue
Milwaukee, WI 53211-4462
(414) 224-9700
Maureen Wolff, director of marketing

Type of community: Nonprofit Continuing Care, modified contract

A six-story building located a short walk from scenic Lake Michigan houses Independent Living residences and a 56-bed Skilled Nursing facility. The

community features a beautiful, spacious chapel and is located ten minutes from downtown Milwaukee and its cultural and entertainment opportunities: Bradley Center, Performing Arts Center, Milwaukee Public Museum, the historic Pabst theater, and the new theater district. The Downer Avenue shopping district is three blocks away. The University of Wisconsin and La Farge Institute of Learning offer educational opportunities nearby. Also nearby are at least ten restaurants, two supermarkets, three movie theaters, three bakeries, fresh fish and meat markets, a drugstore, and the public library.

Financial plan: Entrance fee plus monthly fee or monthly fee only. Two 100% refundable entrance fee plans: **1)** Standard. **2)** Entrance fee less than that of Plan 1 but with higher monthly fee. Security deposit equal to one month's fee for residents on monthly fee only plan. Security deposit will be returned at the termination of the lease less the cost of refurbishing the apartment, if necessary.

Ownership and management: Nonprofit corporation. Board of directors made up of 10 to 15 area business professionals and community volunteers. Opened in 1913; new building in 1973.

Minimum age: 62 years.

Population: 190 residents; 85% female, 15% male, 4% couples.

Number of units: 140 Independent Living apartments; 56-bed Nursing facility.

Dining plan: Three meals per day included in the monthly fee. Residents may choose not to have breakfast and/or lunch: deduct $21 from the monthly fee for breakfast, $36 if you choose not to have lunch. Private dining room accommodates 25 people. Catering and tray service available.

Services: *Included in the monthly fee:* Biweekly housekeeping service, scheduled transportation.

At additional cost: Beauty/barbershop, convenience store, flat-linen service, guest rooms, chauffeur-driven stationwagon.

Activities: Full-time activities director. Recitals, lectures, Catholic service daily, Protestant services periodically, gardening, arts and crafts, men's breakfast, excursions to symphony, museum, zoo, County Stadium. Sing-alongs, choir, armchair travel club, library, bingo.

Availability: Approximately three-month waiting list for studio. Six-month to one-year waiting list for one-bedroom. One year waiting list for two-bedroom.

Health services and rates: Residents receive 30 days in the health center at no additional cost. Fully equipped dental clinic. Registered nurse on duty 24-hours a day. Medical director, physical, occupational, and speech therapists.

- 56-Bed Skilled Nursing facility

Semiprivate	$107.95–143.95/day
Private	$137.95–174.95/day

"Milwaukee Catholic Home is well known for its tasty food and variety of meal choices. Our hallways and community areas have just undergone major redecoration, making our home one of the

INDEPENDENT LIVING HOUSING

Type/size of unit	*Entrance fee 1**	*Monthly fee 1**	*Monthly fee only**
Studio, 294–375 sq. ft	$24,000–39,000	$754–884	$960–1,220
1-Bedroom, 620–828 sq. ft.	$63,200–88,000	$1,182–1,480	$1,724–2,180
2-Bedroom, 914–1,000 sq. ft.	$114,500	$1,593	$2,564

**For double occupancy add $288 to monthly fee. Plan 2 entrance fees range from $12,000–57,500, monthly fees from $857–2,070. All utilities except telephone included. Wall-to-wall carpeting, draperies, fully equipped kitchens or kitchenettes, individually controlled heating and air-conditioning, 24-hour emergency call system, cable TV.*

most charming retirement facilities in the state. We've just completed work on a beautifully decorated, stately library where residents can browse through books or borrow them. Our award-winning chapel is a beautiful, quiet place for worship or contemplation. The availability of our chaplain for daily services and counseling 40 hours a week is a plus. Because we listen to residents' needs and desires, we have been creating spacious, roomy apartments by combining smaller ones. We are located in a pleasant neighborhood close to many activities and services. Milwaukee is a bustling city that still maintains its hometown flavor. It offers many cultural and entertainment opportunities."

SAINT JOHN'S TOWER

1840 North Prospect Avenue
Milwaukee, WI 53202
(414) 291-4991
Lisa Luikonen, marketing coordinator

Type of community: Not-for-profit Continuing Care, all-inclusive contract

This modern ten-story, 173-apartment complex offers panoramic views of Lake Michigan. The community is located minutes away from Performing Arts Center, Bradley Center, Milwaukee theater district, libraries, museums, restaurants, and the University of Wisconsin-Milwaukee. St. John's health center adjoins the Tower.

Financial plan: Entrance fee plus monthly fee. 2% of entrance fee is required as deposit for priority waiting list. A portion of the entrance fee ($29,000 for one person, $59,000 for two) and the monthly fee ($280 for one, $420 for two) is allocated to the life care restricted fund. This represents a one-time federal tax deduction in the year paid.

Ownership and management: Saint John's Home of Milwaukee, a private, nonprofit corporation. Board of directors is made up of Episcopal laymen and clergy. The community is nonsectarian. Opened in 1979.

Minimum age: 65 years.

Population: 200 residents; 85% women, 15% men, 10% couples.

Number of units: 173 Independent Living apartments; 95-bed nursing facility.

Dining plan: No meals included in the monthly fee. Evening meal is $7 with certificate purchased in advance or at discounted price when purchased in quantity. Noon meal is $5 with certificate. Tray service is available.

Services: *Included in the monthly fee:* Laundry facilities on all floors, scheduled transportation.

At additional cost: Beauty/barbershop, grocery store, guest accommodations, parking, sidewalk cafe, postal services, check cashing, notary public.

Activities: Library, bookmobile, crafts, card room, lectures, art gallery, arts program, trips/tours, chapel, Bible study, workshops.

INDEPENDENT LIVING HOUSING

Type/size of apartment	*Entrance fee**	*Monthly fee**
Alcove/Studio, 400–475 sq. ft.	$38,600–45,900	$569–645
1-Bedroom, 600–1,075 sq. ft.	$57,900–104,000	$784–1,289
2-Bedroom, 875–1,475 sq. ft.	$84,500–152,300	$1,149–1,775

** For double occupancy add $10,000 to the entrance fee. All utilities except telephone included. All-electric kitchen, carpeting, draperies, storage lockers on lower level, 24-hour emergency call system.*

Availability: Units availability. Priority waiting list.

Health services and rates: Residents receive unlimited nursing included in their monthly fee. If residents move into the health center permanently, they continue to pay the monthly fee they have been paying in Independent Living.

- 95-Bed nursing center

	Nonresidents
Intermediate Nursing	$128/day
Skilled Nursing	$140 /day

"Residents find their lives at Saint John's are all that they want them to be and as bright as the sparkling waters of Lake Michigan. St. John's board of directors and a fine professional staff continue to explore new concepts to bring residents the best in retirement living."

THE VILLAGE AT MANOR PARK

3023 South 84th Street
Milwaukee, WI 53227-3798
(414) 541-2600
Gwen Bushyhead, marketing manager

Type of community: Continuing Care, modified contract

The community is located on a 20-acre parklike campus featuring a landscaped courtyard with waterfall, pond, many trees, a gazebo, and gardens. The Village at Manor Park consists of Independent Living apartments at Wesley Park, Assisted Living at Palmer House, and specialized care at Maplewood Center. The community is situated on the southwest side of Milwaukee with easy access to shopping centers, public transportation, and local hospitals in Milwaukee.

Financial plan: Entrance fee plus monthly fee.

Ownership and management: Owned and managed by Methodist Manor, Inc. Assisted Living opened in 1960, Independent Living opened in 1976.

Minimum age: 62 years (if couple, spouse may be younger).

Population: 225 residents; 78% women, 22% men, 25% couples.

Number of units: 221 Independent Living apartments (48 two-bedroom units under constructions, 1,114 to 1,296 sq. ft.); 134 Assisted Living units, 168-bed health center.

Dining plan: Meals optional for residents of Independent Living.

Services: *Included in the monthly fee:* Parking, free use of washers and dryers.

At additional cost: Beauty/barbershop, membership to Manor Park Senior Center for Wesley Park residents, indoor parking.

Activities: Leisure services department. Card games, shopping trips, vacations, senior center, hobby shop,

INDEPENDENT LIVING HOUSING

Type/size of apartment	*Entrance fee single/double*	*Monthly fee single/double**
Studio, 485 sq. ft.	$55,600/N/A	$571.50/N/A
1-Bedroom, 660 sq. ft.	$64,300/84,900	$688.50/926
2-Bedroom, 900 sq. ft.	$68,700/89,300	$884.50/1,130

** All utilities except telephone included in the monthly fee. Cable TV, fully equipped kitchens, 24-hour emergency call system, wall-to-wall carpeting, patio or balcony, Individually controlled heating and air-conditioning.*

ceramics center, greenhouse, woodworking shop, classes, musical events, library, game rooms.

Availability: Waiting list for two-bedrooms.

Health services and rates: Short- and long-term nursing, physical and occupational therapies, in-house radiology equipment and special care units for residents who require rehabilitation, intense nursing care and programming for Alzheimer's and related dementias. Medical Director on call 24 hours a day. Portion of entrance and monthly fees for Independent Living residents act as Continuing Care charges that pay for much of resident's health care should the need arise. Share Care, a respite care program for Independent Living residents, relieves families from the stress of giving around-the-clock care. Semi-independent and specialized care for stays of one to four weeks.

- 134 Assisted Living units*

Standard	$1,350–1,400/day
Large unit	$1,475/day
2-Room unit	$1,600–1,700/day

**Nonresident entrance fee: $6,000–9,500. For double occupancy add $370/month to monthly fee.*

- 168-Bed health care center

"What really distinguishes The Village at Manor Park is our interdisciplinary team approach and high level professional medical problem-solving on behalf of our residents, using expertise in nursing, rehabilitative therapies, social services, and pastoral care."

EVERGREEN MANOR RETIREMENT COMMUNITY

1130 North Westfield Street
P.O. Box 1720
Oshkosh, WI 54902-1720
(414) 233-2340
Allen C. Borgwardt, director of admissions

Type of community: Not-for-profit Continuing Care, modified contract

Located on a 36-acre suburban campus, Evergreen Retirement Community has three different types of Independent Living accommodations with all residents having assured access to Assisted Living and the health center. Evergreen Village has a cooperative residence, consisting of four buildings with eight one- or two-bedroom homes in each building and a sunlit verandah connecting all eight units. Evergreen Homes offers individual ranch-style, two-bedroom homes clustered in small neighborhoods. Evergreen Manor offers Congregate Living studio and one-bedroom apartments. Lake Winnebago, golf, and shopping is nearby.

Financial plan: Entrance fee plus monthly fee or monthly rental. Two plans: **1)** Purchase equity. 80–95% of market value is returned when Village home is resold. **2)** Evergreen Homes, Manor Apartments, and Terrace—fully refundable entrance fee if resident leaves within first 30 days. After 30 days, the entrance fee is prorated over five to ten years.

Ownership and management: Sponsored by the Wisconsin Conference of the United Methodist Church and affiliated with the Wisconsin State Chapter of the PEO Sisterhood and the Ladies Benevolent Society of Oshkosh. Managed by a voluntary board. Evergreen Village is a for-profit cooperative; the rest of Evergreen is not-for-profit. Evergreen Village opened in 1985, Evergreen ShareHaven in 1991.

Minimum age: 60 years (55 for Evergreen Village).

Population: 280 residents; 77% women, 23% men, 12% couples.

Number of units: Independent Living: 32 Evergreen Village homes, 24 two-bedroom ranch-style homes; 20 Assisted Living units, 108-bed health care center, 20 Alzheimer's beds.

Dining plan: Variety of meal plans offered for additional charge. Special diets available.

INDEPENDENT LIVING HOUSING

Village	*Entrance fee*	*Monthly fee*
1-Bedroom, 1,250 sq. ft.	$85,000–100,000	$562/654
2-Bedroom, 1,550 sq. ft.	$95,000–125,000	$562/659
Homes		
2-Bedroom, 983–1,300	$43,000–93,000	$420/534

** Gas heat, electricity, and telephone are not included. Evergreen Homes residents pay for cable TV. Village and a few homes have attached garages. Fully equipped kitchens, washer/dryers, 24-hour emergency call system.*

*Manor apartments**		
Studio, 268–319 sq. ft.	$11,000–15,000	$655/759
1-Bedroom, 536–612 sq. ft.	$26,000–36,000	$1,018–1,064/1,178–1,224

** All utilities except telephone included. Cable TV, 24-hour emergency call system, wall-to-wall carpeting; most include kitchenette or kitchen.*

Services: *Included in the monthly fee:* Weekly housekeeping, flat-linen service and laundry facilities for those in the Manor apartments.

At additional cost: Heated parking garage, beauty/barbershop, laundry and housecleaning in homes and Village.

Activities: Gardening, volunteering, woodworking, Bible study, exercise program, chapel, game room, greenhouse, residents' council, arts and crafts, shuffleboard, billiards table, weekly activities.

Availability: Waiting list. $1,000 deposit for waiting list for Evergreen Village and $500 for all other accommodations.

Health services and rates: Occupational, speech, and physical therapists on-site, billable to Medicare and/or insurance.

- 20 Assisted Living units*
  1-Room, 280 sq. ft. $1,229–1,788/month
  2-Room (double), 536 sq. ft. $2,458/month

  ** Nonresident entrance fees: $12,000/24,000. Includes approximately one-half hour of assistance daily.*

- 108-Bed health care center
  Semiprivate $92.50–107.50/day
  Private $104.50–119.50/day
- 20-Unit Alzheimer's facility
  Private $94/day

"While Evergreen Manor Retirement Community's doors are open to persons of any heritage or religious belief, we are a Christian, not-for-profit organization affiliated with the Wisconsin Conference of the United Methodist Church. This relationship was very important in Evergreen's development and continues to guide the values of the organization. A tangible expression of these values is the placement of the chapel in the center of the main building."

CEDAR RIDGE RETIREMENT CAMPUS

113 Cedar Ridge Drive
West Bend, WI 53095
(414) 276-4370
Steve Jaberg, executive director

Type of community: Not-for-profit Continuing Care, modified contract

Located on 50 acres, Cedar Ridge is nestled among rolling hills, wooded valleys, creeks, ponds, and wildlife on the west side of the city of West Bend. The Independent Living apartments and health center are housed in connecting three-story brick buildings.

Financial plan: Entrance fee plus monthly fee. Three plans: **1)** No refund. **2)** 50% refund. **3)** 95% refund.

Ownership and management: The Benevolent Corporation Cedar Campuses. Opened in 1986.

Minimum age: 62 years (55 with waiver from the board of directors).

Population: 430 residents; 65% women, 35% men, 40% couples.

Number of units: 312 Independent Living apartments; 415-bed health care center.

Dining plan: No meals included in the monthly fee. Meals available at additional cost.

Services: *Included in the monthly fee:* Monthly housekeeping.

At additional cost: Beauty salon/barbershop, dry cleaning service, convenience store, gift shop, pharmacy, guest accommodations, underground parking, transportation.

Activities: Swimming pool, whirlpool spa, 6,000-foot woodworking shop/lapidary area, greenhouse and potting room, music room, hobby room for model railroads and repair work, library, sewing room, gardening, billiards, Ping-Pong, darts, game rooms, shuffleboard, horseshoes, outdoor exercise course and classes, volunteer committees, chapel, and much more.

Availability: Waiting list.

Health services and rates: Outpatient health care services available to residents through Cedar Haven Rehabilitation Agency, which provides physical, occupational, and speech therapies. Dental suite and pharmacy on-site.

- 415-Bed health care center with Intermediate and Skilled Nursing
  Semiprivate $45.10/day

"Cedar Ridge Retirement Campus provides a safe, tranquil retreat where residents can have the freedom to live comfortably and independently while pursuing their own interests, being purposeful, and having opportunities for continued personal growth."

INDEPENDENT LIVING HOUSING

Type/size of apartment	*Entrance fee 1/2/3**	*Monthly fee**
1-Bedroom, 684 sq. ft.	$30,300/39,600/50,000	$363/413
2-Bedroom, 947 sq. ft.	$35,600/46,800/59,800	$425/475
2-Bedroom, 1,035 sq. ft.	$41,000/54,300/70,000	$482/532

**For double occupancy add $2,000 to the entrance fee. For third-floor apartments add $2,000–$4,000 to the entrance fee. All utilities except telephone included. Wall-to-wall carpeting, draperies, individually controlled heating and air-conditioning, 24-hour emergency call system.*

FAIRHAVEN

435 Starin Road
Whitewater, WI 53190
(414) 473-2140
Reverend David G. Yochum, administrator

Type of community: Nonprofit Continuing Care, modified contract

This four-story apartment complex contains a main lounge as well as nine small lounges, Fellowship Hall, and indoor garden. Fairhaven is centrally located in southeastern Wisconsin, within easy walking distance of Whitewater's library, university, stores, and churches. The community is an hour's drive from Milwaukee or Madison, two hours from Chicago.

Financial plan: Entrance fee plus monthly fee. $750 application fee.

Ownership and management: Fairhaven Corporation, affiliated with the Wisconsin Conference of the United Church of Christ. Opened in 1962.

Minimum age: 65 years.

Population: 265 residents; 75% women, 25% men, 18% couples.

Number of units: 160 Independent Living apartments; 84 Intermediate and Skilled Nursing beds.

Dining plan: No meals included in the monthly fee. Monthly charge for three meals per day is $350. Meals can be purchased individually.

Services: *Included in the monthly fee:* Flat-linen and heavy housekeeping services.

At additional cost: Beauty/barbershop, garages, scheduled transportation, guest accommodations.

Activities: Library, lectures, indoor and outdoor gardens, weaving, games and crafts, chorus, woodworking, trips and tours.

Availability: Limited. Priority waiting list.

Health services and rates: Health checks, personal care, medication administration available.

- 84-bed nursing facility $74–116/day

**Nonresidents add $4 per day. For double occupancy deduct $13 and double the daily fee.*

"Fairhaven is a visible ministry of God's love to older men and women. Its primary mission is to provide housing and health services that promote dignity and well-being along with spiritual, intellectual, cultural, and recreational vitality. Fairhaven is associated with the Wisconsin Conference of the United Church of Christ."

INDEPENDENT LIVING HOUSING

Type/size of apartment	*Entrance fee*	*Monthly fee*
Efficiency, 332 sq. ft.	$13,000–15,000	$384–401
Alcove, 493 sq. ft.,	$16,000–18,500	$446–492
1-Bedroom, 690 sq. ft.	$21,000–30,000	$574–754
2-Bedroom, 990 sq. ft.	$34,500–36,500	$858–871

All utilities except telephone included. Kitchenette, thermostat controls, extra storage space, 24-hour emergency call system.

Accredited Communities

An alphabetical listing of those communities accredited by the CCAC.

Communities That Provide Alzheimer's Care

These communities offer specialized Alzheimer's care. Other communities offer some amenities for those with Alzheimer's; this is noted in the directory entries for those communities.

Communities That Provide Respite Care

Aldersgate Village, Topeka, KS, 260
Asbury Heights, Pittsburgh, PA, 467
Asbury Methodist Village, Gaithersburg, MD, 284
Bixby Knolls Towers, Long Beach, CA, 61
Brewster Place, Topeka, KS, 262
Clairmont Place, Atlanta, GA, 198
Fairfax, The, Fort Belvoir, VA, 517
Homewood at Williamsport, Williamsport, MD, 293
Hoosier Village, Indianapolis, IN, 235
Marriott Villa Valencia, Laguna Hills, CA, 59
Newton Presbyterian Manor, Newton, KS, 257
Park Lane, The, A Classic Hyatt Residence, Monterey, CA, 70
Rancho Park Villa, San Dimas, CA, 88
Rockynol Retirement Community, Akron, OH, 395
Towne House, The, Fort Wayne, IN, 228
Trinity Towers, Midland, TX, 499
Village at Manor Park, The, Milwaukee, WI, 553
Wesley Village, The, Pittston, PA, 468
Western Home, The, Cedar Falls, IA, 243
Westlake Village, Westlake, OH, 416

Cost Comparison Worksheet

Monthly Cost Comparison: Retirement Community Monthly Fee vs. Current Housing Expenses

	Retirement community	*Private home/condo/apartment*
Monthly mortgage/rent	Included in the monthly fee	$__________
Maintenance/repairs	Included in the monthly fee	$__________
Utilities	Included in the monthly fee with some exceptions (telephone, cable TV)	$__________
Meals	1 to 3 meals included in the monthly fee	$__________
Transportation	Included in the monthly fee	$__________
Weekly housekeeping	Included in the monthly fee	$__________
Social events, outings	Included in the monthly fee	$__________
24-Hour security	Included in the monthly fee	$__________
Real estate taxes	Included in the monthly fee	$__________
Property insurance	Included in the monthly fee*	$__________
Lawn care	Included in the monthly fee	$__________
	Monthly fee: $__________	**Current monthly expenses: $__________**

**Not included where residents have purchased their apartment, condo, or cottage and have equity.*

Index